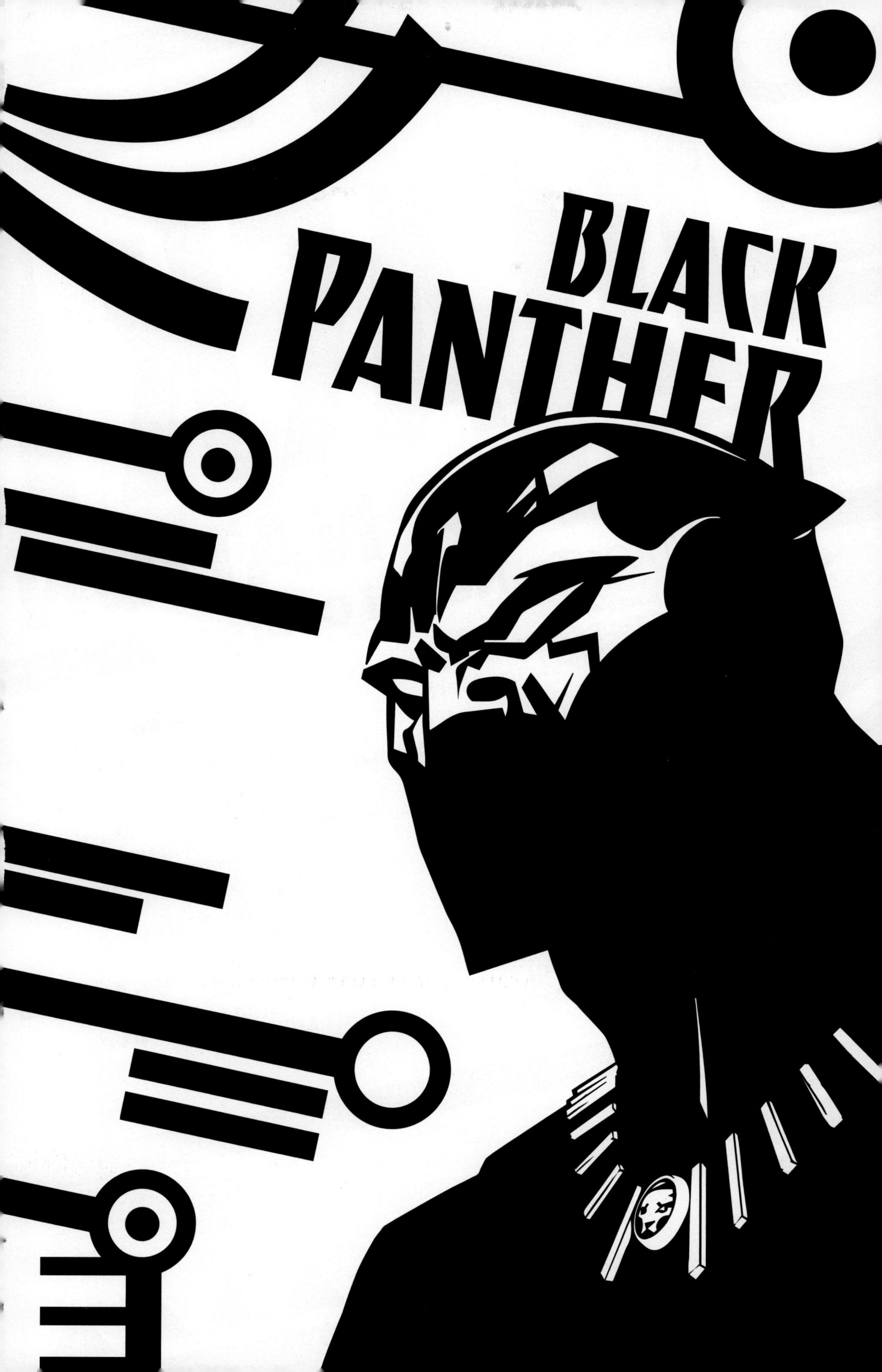
BLACK
PANTHER

# BLACK P

## VOL. 1

## A NATION

Writer/**Ta-Nehisi Coates**

**ISSUES #1-4**
Artist/**Brian Stelfreeze**
Color Artist/**Laura Martin**

**ISSUES #5-8**
Pencils/Layouts/**Chris Sprouse**
Inks/Finishes/**Karl Story**
with Walden Wong (#8)
Color Artist/**Laura Martin**

**ISSUE #9**
Artist/**Brian Stelfreeze**
Color Artist/**Laura Martin**

**ISSUE #10**
Layouts/**Chris Sprouse**
Finishes/**Karl Story**
Color Artist/**Laura Martin**

**ISSUE #11**
Layouts/**Chris Sprouse**
Finishes/**Goran Sudžuka,
Walden Wong, Karl Story &
Roberto Poggi**
Color Artists/**Laura Martin**
with Matt Milla, Larry Molinar,
Rachelle Rosenberg & Paul Mounts

**ISSUE #12**
Pencils/**Brian Stelfreeze &
Chris Sprouse**
Inks/**Brian Stelfreeze, Karl Story
& Scott Hanna**
Color Artists/**Laura Martin &
Matt Milla &**

**BLACK PANTHER VOL. 1: A NATION UNDER OUR FEET.** Contains material originally published in magazine form as BLACK PANTHER #1-12. First printing 2017. ISBN# 978-1-302-90415-9. Published by MARVEL WORLDWIDE, INC., a subsidiary of MARVEL ENTERTAINMENT, LLC. OFFICE OF PUBLICATION: 135 West 50th Street, New York, NY 10020. Copyright © 2017 MARVEL No similarity between any of the names, characters, persons, and/or institutions in this magazine with those of any living or dead person or institution is intended, and any such similarity which may exist is purely coincidental. **Printed in China.** DAN BUCKLEY, President, Marvel Entertainment; JOE QUESADA, Chief Creative Officer; TOM BREVOORT, SVP of Publishing; DAVID BOGART, SVP of Business Affairs & Operations, Publishing & Partnership; C.B. CEBULSKI, VP of Brand Management & Development, Asia; DAVID GABRIEL, SVP of Sales & Marketing, Publishing; JEFF YOUNGQUIST, VP of Production & Special Projects; DAN CARR, Executive Director of Publishing Technology; ALEX MORALES, Director of Publishing Operations; SUSAN CRESPI, Production Manager; STAN LEE, Chairman Emeritus. For information regarding advertising in Marvel Comics or on Marvel.com, please contact Vit DeBellis, Integrated Sales Manager, at vdebellis@marvel.com. For Marvel subscription inquiries, please call 888-511-5480. **Manufactured between 3/31/2017 and 6/12/2017 by R.R. DONNELLEY ASIA PRINTING SOLUTIONS, CHINA.**

10 9 8 7 6 5 4 3 2 1

# ANTHER
## UNDER OUR FEET

Letterer/**VC's Joe Sabino**
Logo Design/**Rian Hughes**
Cover Art/**Brian Stelfreeze**
**& Laura Martin**
Assistant Editor/**Chris Robinson**
Editor/**Wil Moss**
Executive Editor/**Tom Brevoort**

**BLACK PANTHER** CREATED
BY **STAN LEE** & **JACK KIRBY**

COLLECTION EDITOR/**JENNIFER GRÜNWALD**
ASSISTANT EDITOR/**CAITLIN O'CONNELL**
ASSOCIATE MANAGING EDITOR/**KATERI WOODY**
EDITOR, SPECIAL PROJECTS/**MARK D. BEAZLEY**
VP PRODUCTION & SPECIAL PROJECTS/**JEFF YOUNGQUIST**
SVP PRINT, SALES & MARKETING/**DAVID GABRIEL**
BOOK DESIGNERS/**JAY BOWEN & MANNY MEDEROS**

EDITOR IN CHIEF/**AXEL ALONSO**
CHIEF CREATIVE OFFICER/**JOE QUESADA**
PRESIDENT/**DAN BUCKLEY**
EXECUTIVE PRODUCER/**ALAN FINE**

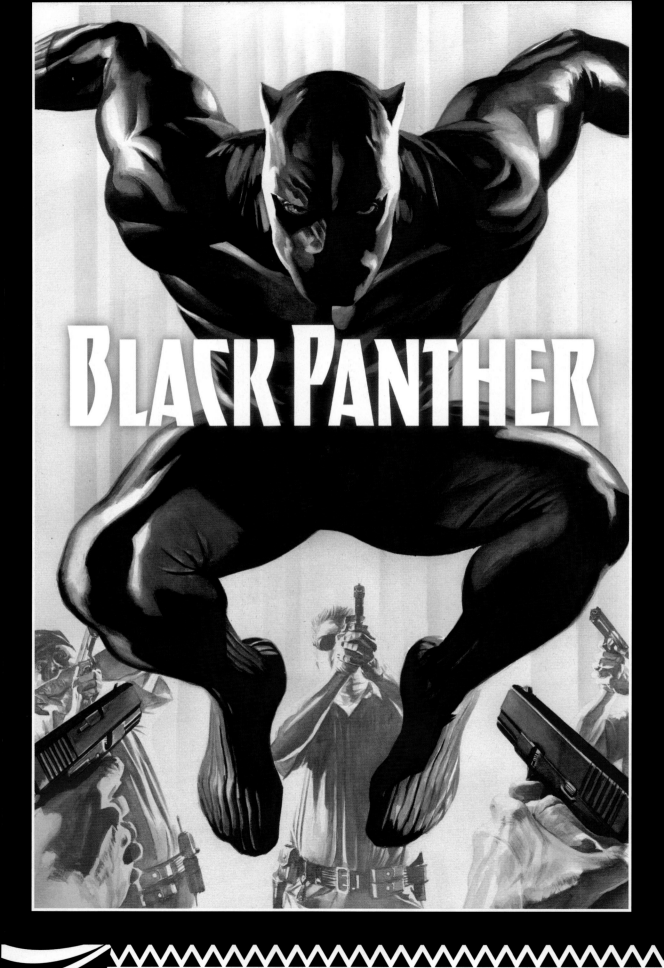

BLACK PANTHER

#1 VARIANT BY **ALEX ROSS**

# INTRODUCTION

## BY SETH MEYERS

Two things: I love Ta-Nehisi Coates, and I hate this. I don't hate this **comic**. I love it. I hate the pressure of having to write this introduction. Not only has Ta-Nehisi written one of the best books of recent years (*Between the World and Me*) and the best article about the Obama administration ("My President Was Black," *The Atlantic*), the man is a recipient of a MacArthur "Genius Grant" and he's a National Book Award winner. I think we can all agree this introduction would be better if he wrote it, but I guess it's not fair to ask him to do everything.

The first time Ta-Nehisi was a guest on *Late Night*, we talked about *Between the World and Me* and the very real, very difficult issues it addresses. (And as a side note, read that book. Then read that article. Then sit in a chair and stare at the wall and ask your brain why it can't think like that.) At the very end of the interview we discussed his just-announced Marvel gig to write *Black Panther*. He was excited. I was excited. I couldn't help but think, "Good for Ta-Nehisi! Finally he can take a break from reality and write some light, silly entertainment!" Silly me. The book you hold in your hands is entertaining as hell, but the real world lives in every panel. Don't read this book to escape the world we live in — read it to give you a better sense of the world we live in.

In Ta-Nehisi's hands, T'Challa is a leader, but he's not a perfect leader. He's a good man, but he doesn't always make good decisions. This is a book about wielding power. Not super-powers, but rather the power one wields over a people. Because in this book, punches and kicks don't knock over opponents, they knock over dominoes, and it's where they fall that matters most. It should come as no surprise to anyone who has read any of Ta-Nehisi's previous works that he is a writer who understands that every decision made has a consequence. And when you're a king, those consequences affect a nation.

That nation is, of course, Wakanda, and where Brian Stelfreeze, Chris Sprouse and Laura Martin bring it alive with their art, Ta-Nehisi brings it alive with his characters. T'Challa is the lead in this drama, but the supporting cast is as strong as you'll find in any comic. And refreshingly, many of them are women, all with their own nuances and motivations, none more memorable than Ayo and Aneka, former bodyguards turned renegade liberators. (I'm just saying, Ayo and Aneka should have their own book. What's that? They already do? *Black Panther: World of Wakanda*? Well, go buy that too!)

There are heroes and villains in this book, but they are all given such dimension that sometimes it's hard to tell the good from the bad. Sure, at first glance Tetu is the type of bad guy we've grown accustomed to in our comics, but when he's given an opportunity to express his point of view, it's harder to dismiss him as a mad man. And when T'Challa heads off in search of retribution after an attack and says of Wakanda, "We are terror itself," you start to doubt who exactly it is you're supposed to be rooting for. This is a book with far more hard questions than easy answers.

And if this all sounds heavy, I want to assure you there is also so much fun to be had. When Storm, Manifold, Misty Knight and Luke Cage arrive and Cage declares, "If you want to save a kingdom... call in THE CREW," I felt like I was staring at a page of a comic from my youth. Much has been written about how Coates used his childhood love of comics to inspire this book, and it's clear in moments like this.

Okay, that's enough of me. Why waste any more time reading the words of a non-genius, non-book-award-winner? Get to *Black Panther*. You won't be disappointed.

**EMMY AWARD WINNER SETH MEYERS IS THE HOST OF NBC'S** *LATE NIGHT WITH SETH MEYERS*. **PREVIOUSLY, HE WAS A CAST MEMBER AND HEAD WRITER ON** *SATURDAY NIGHT LIVE*, **ALSO SERVING AS ANCHOR FOR THE SHOW'S "WEEKEND UPDATE" SEGMENT.**

# BLACK PANTHER

**Tetu** and **Zenzi**, leaders of the insurgent group known as **The People**, have stoked the growing feelings of dissent among the citizens of Wakanda. They courted the assistance of former *Dora Milaje* **Ayo** and **Aneka**, now known as **The Midnight Angels**, to support their rebellion.

After Ayo and Aneka declined, Tetu turned to **Ezekiel Stane**, weaponeer and biotechnology expert, to raise the stakes of their war; repulsor-tech suicide bombers attacked a city square, killing many innocents and severely injuring Queen Mother **Ramonda**.

The situation now has King **T'Challa's** full attention, as he puts aside a very personal project: reviving his sister **Shuri** from living death. Unbeknownst to him, Shuri's mind travels the Djalia, a plane of Wakanda's collective past, present and future. She is guided by a griot spirit who has taken the visual form of Ramonda.

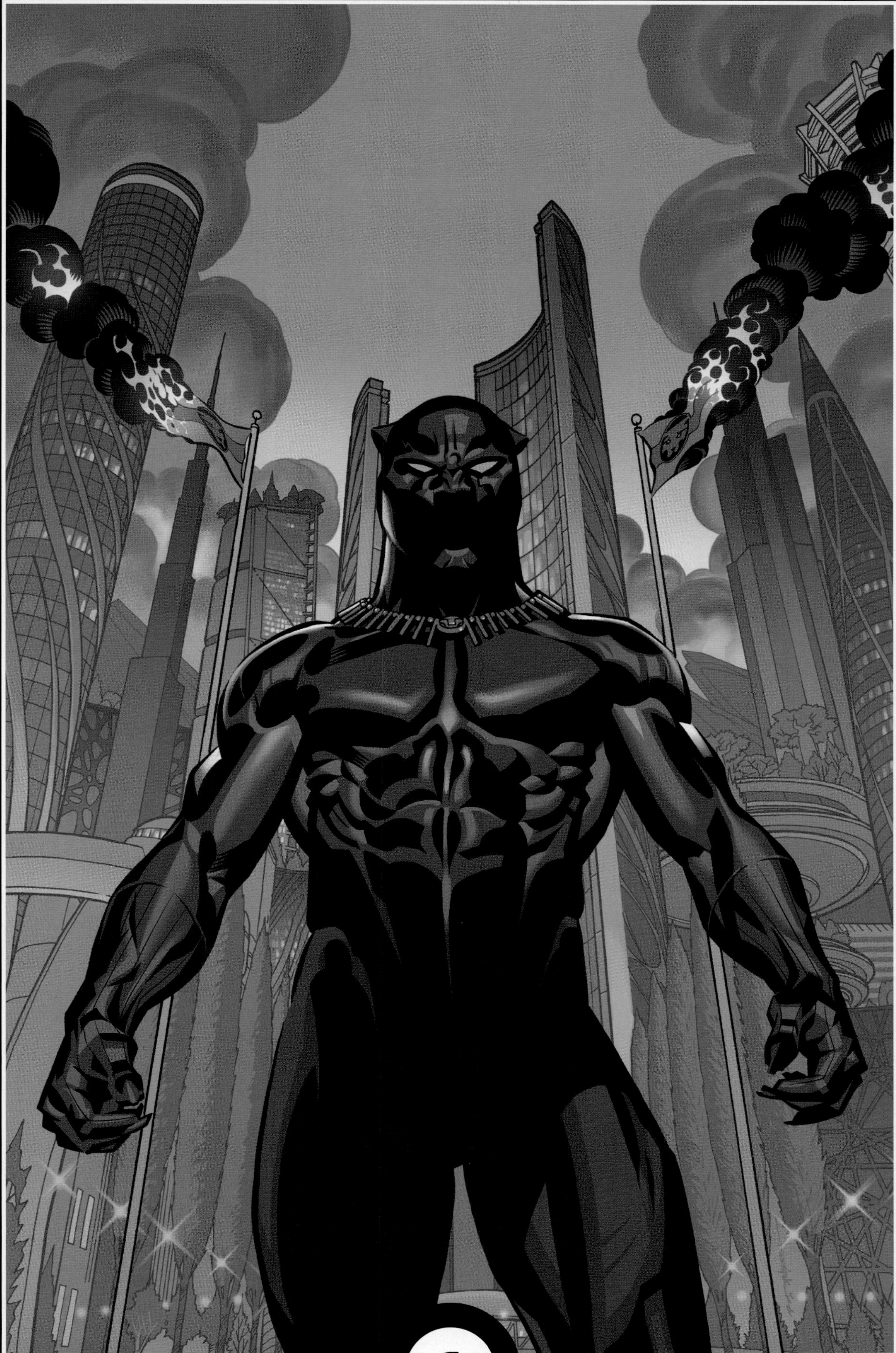

# 1

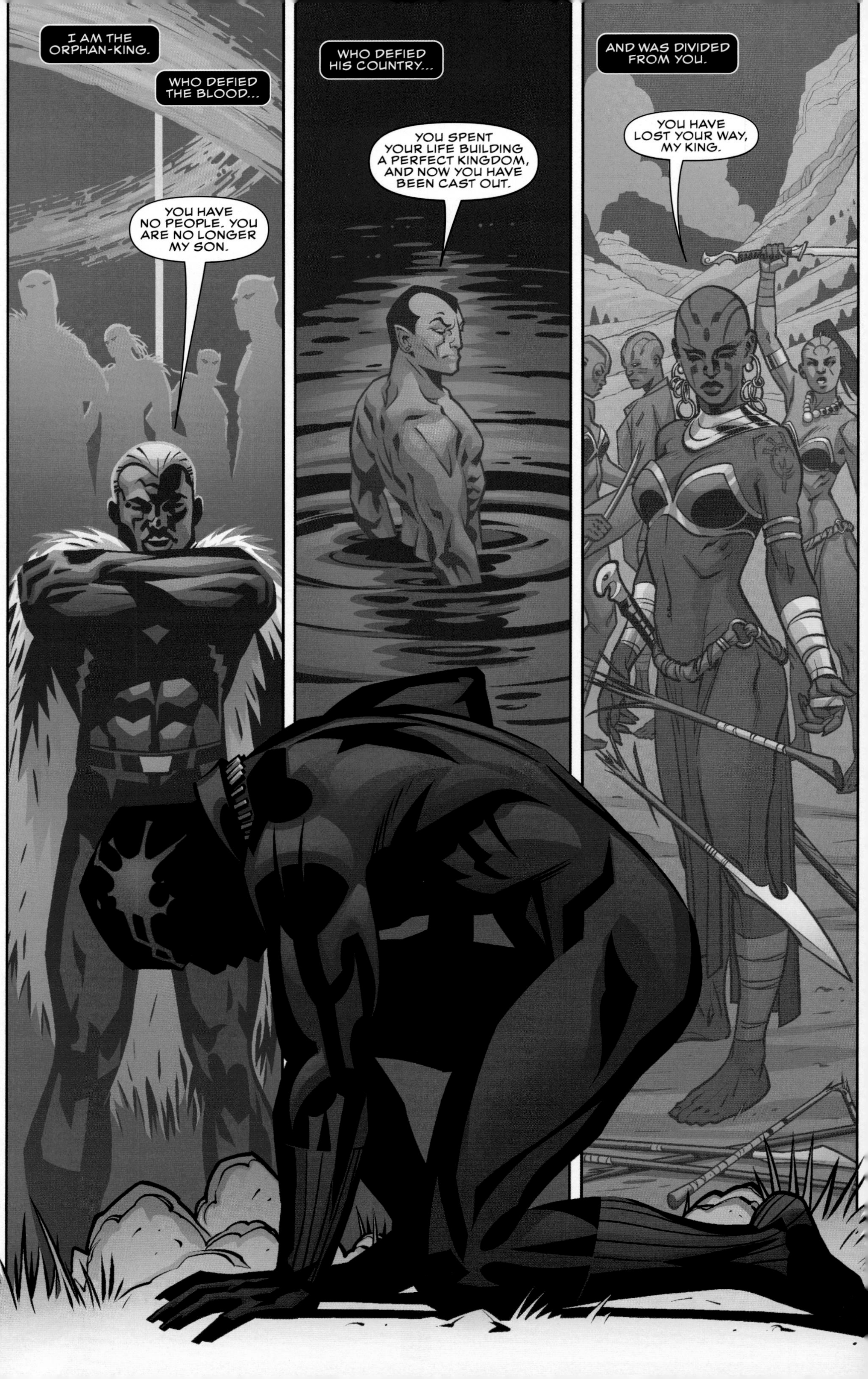
I AM THE ORPHAN-KING.
WHO DEFIED THE BLOOD...
YOU HAVE NO PEOPLE. YOU ARE NO LONGER MY SON.
WHO DEFIED HIS COUNTRY...
YOU SPENT YOUR LIFE BUILDING A PERFECT KINGDOM, AND NOW YOU HAVE BEEN CAST OUT.
AND WAS DIVIDED FROM YOU.
YOU HAVE LOST YOUR WAY, MY KING.

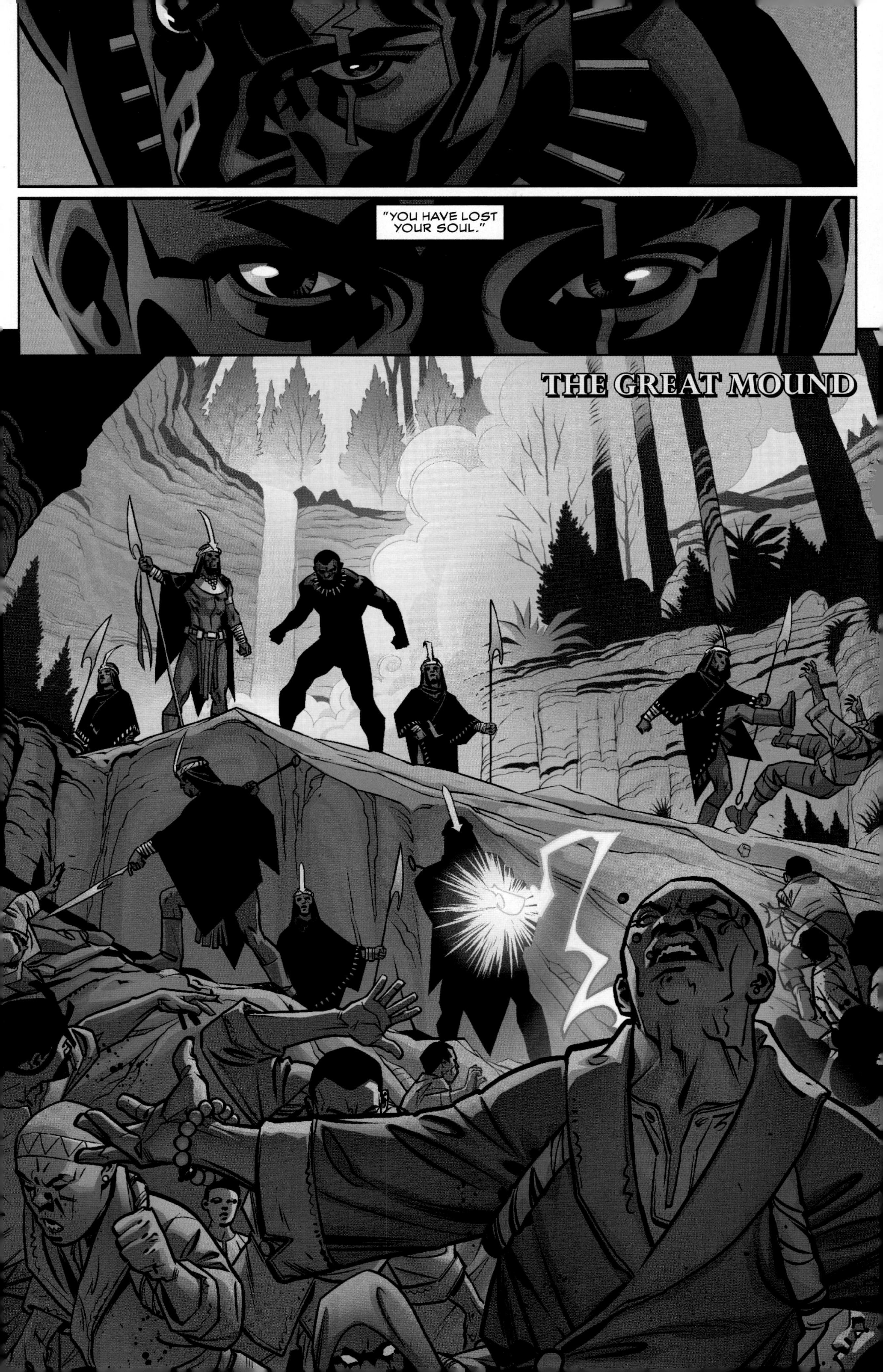
"YOU HAVE LOST YOUR SOUL."
THE GREAT MOUND

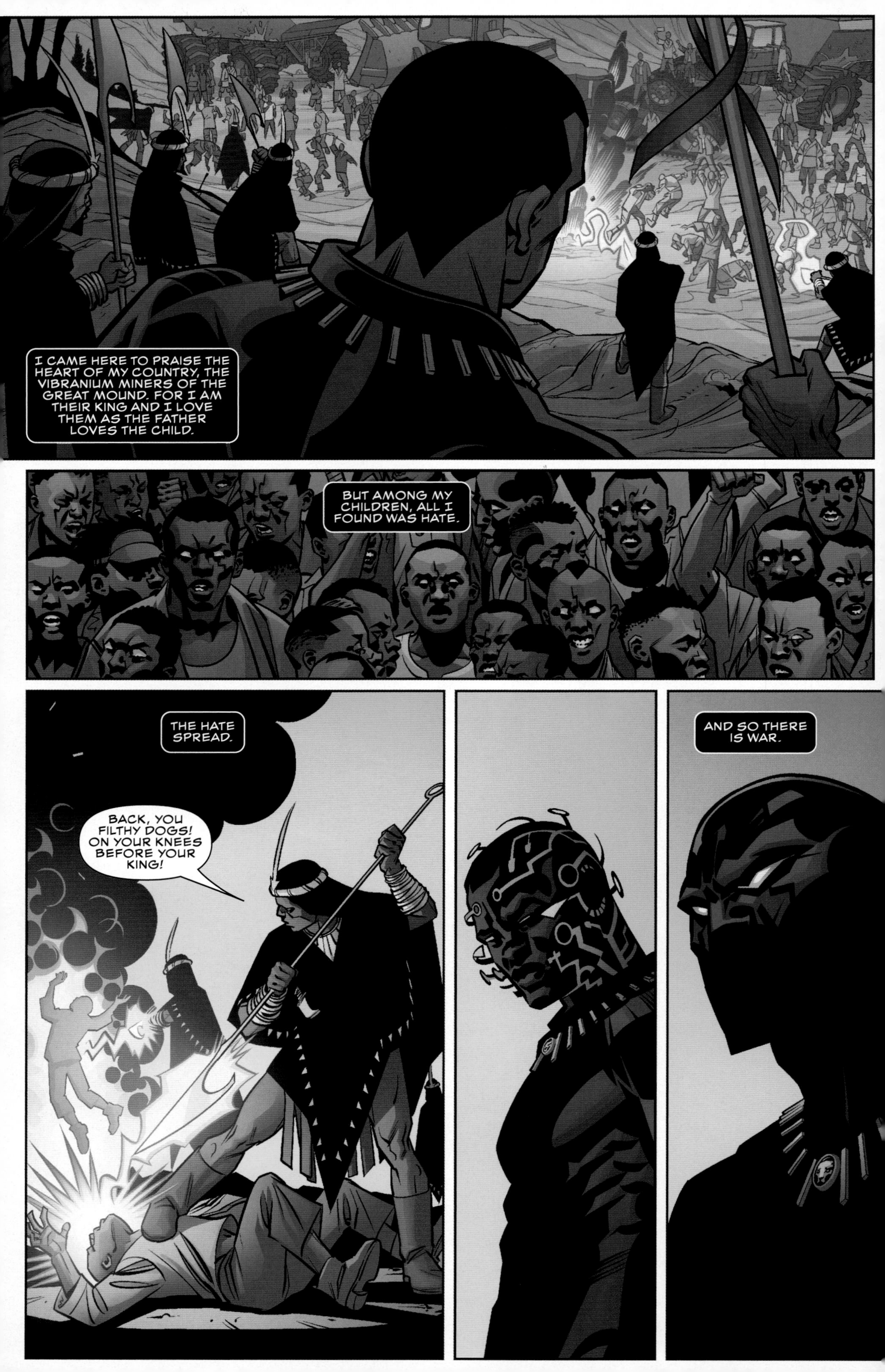
I CAME HERE TO PRAISE THE HEART OF MY COUNTRY, THE VIBRANIUM MINERS OF THE GREAT MOUND. FOR I AM THEIR KING AND I LOVE THEM AS THE FATHER LOVES THE CHILD.
BUT AMONG MY CHILDREN, ALL I FOUND WAS HATE.
THE HATE SPREAD.
BACK, YOU FILTHY DOGS! ON YOUR KNEES BEFORE YOUR KING!
AND SO THERE IS WAR.

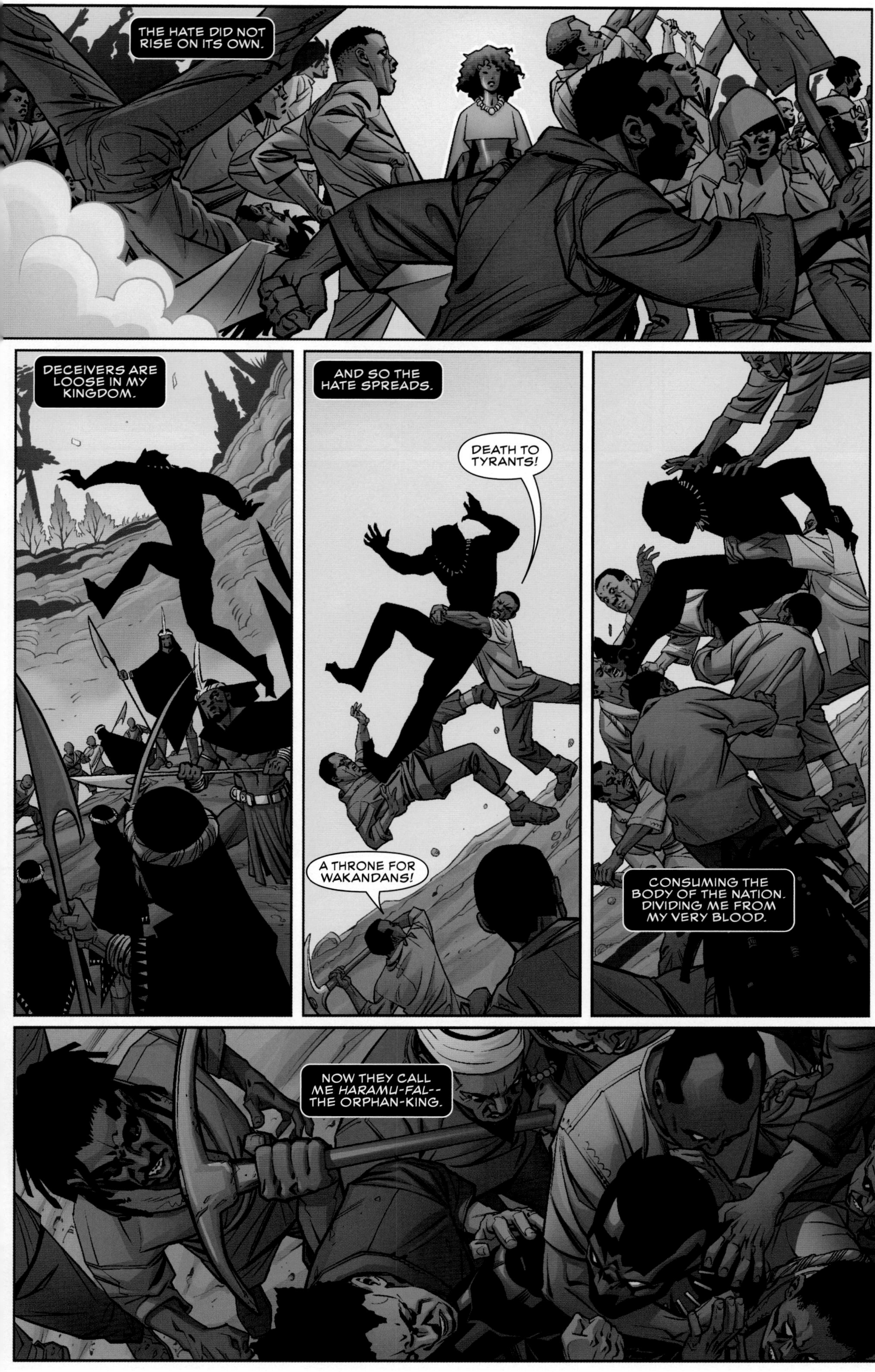
THE HATE DID NOT RISE ON ITS OWN.
DECEIVERS ARE LOOSE IN MY KINGDOM.
AND SO THE HATE SPREADS.
DEATH TO TYRANTS!
A THRONE FOR WAKANDANS!
CONSUMING THE BODY OF THE NATION. DIVIDING ME FROM MY VERY BLOOD.
NOW THEY CALL ME *HARAMU-FAL*-- THE ORPHAN-KING.

BUT I HAVE NOT FORGOTTEN MY NAME.

DAMISA-SARKI-- THE PANTHER.

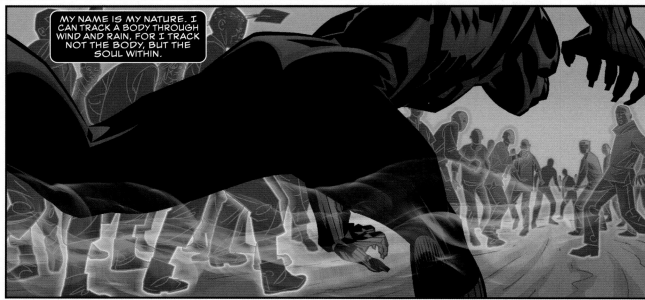

MY NAME IS MY NATURE. I CAN TRACK A BODY THROUGH WIND AND RAIN, FOR I TRACK NOT THE BODY, BUT THE SOUL WITHIN.

BUT THE DECEIVER'S SCENT HAS GONE STALE.

MY KING, WE MUST GO!

HER POWER FADES.

CALL THE SOLDIERS BACK, MY KING! WE MUST NOT MASSACRE OUR OWN PEOPLE!

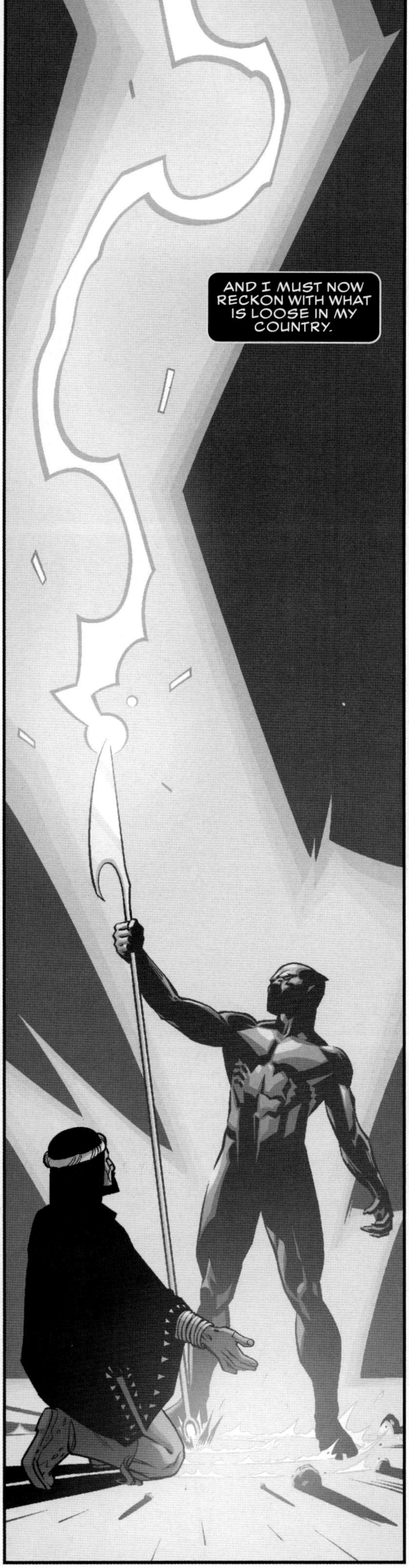
AND I MUST NOW RECKON WITH WHAT IS LOOSE IN MY COUNTRY.

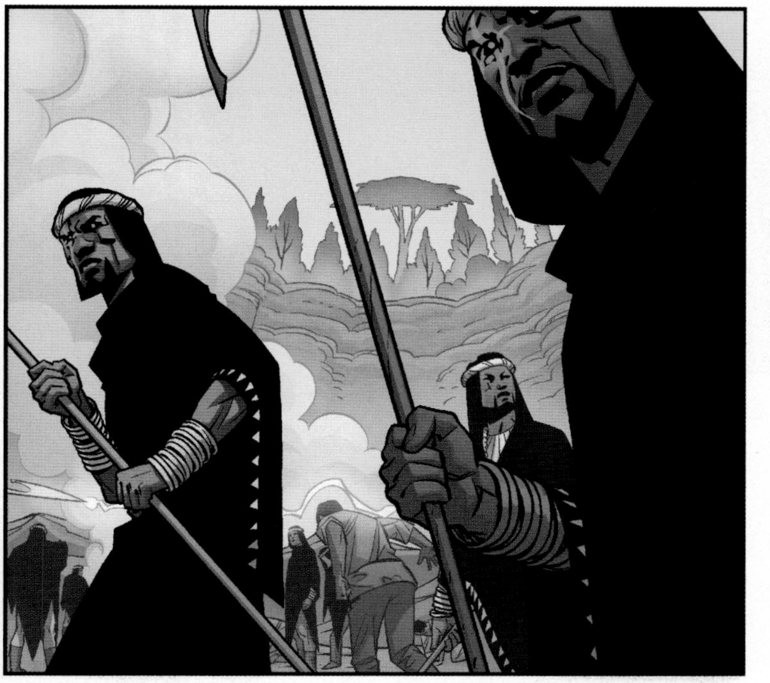

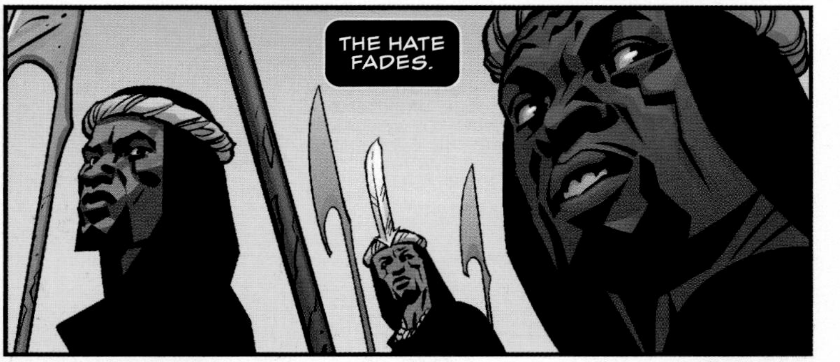
THE HATE FADES.

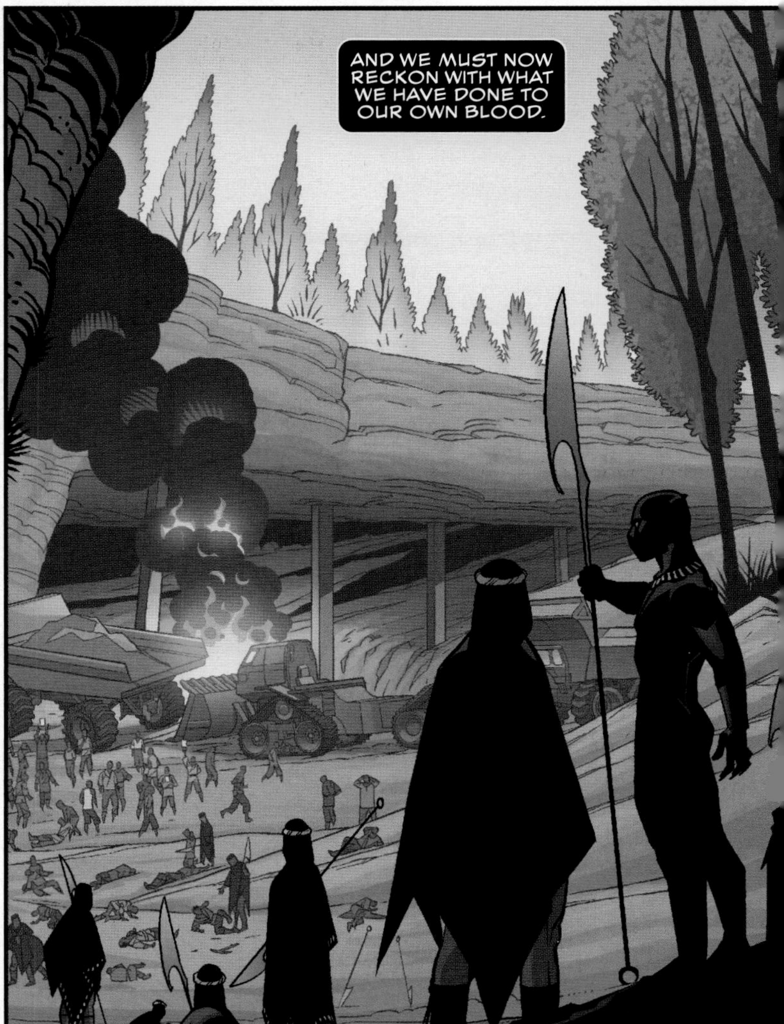
AND WE MUST NOW RECKON WITH WHAT WE HAVE DONE TO OUR OWN BLOOD.

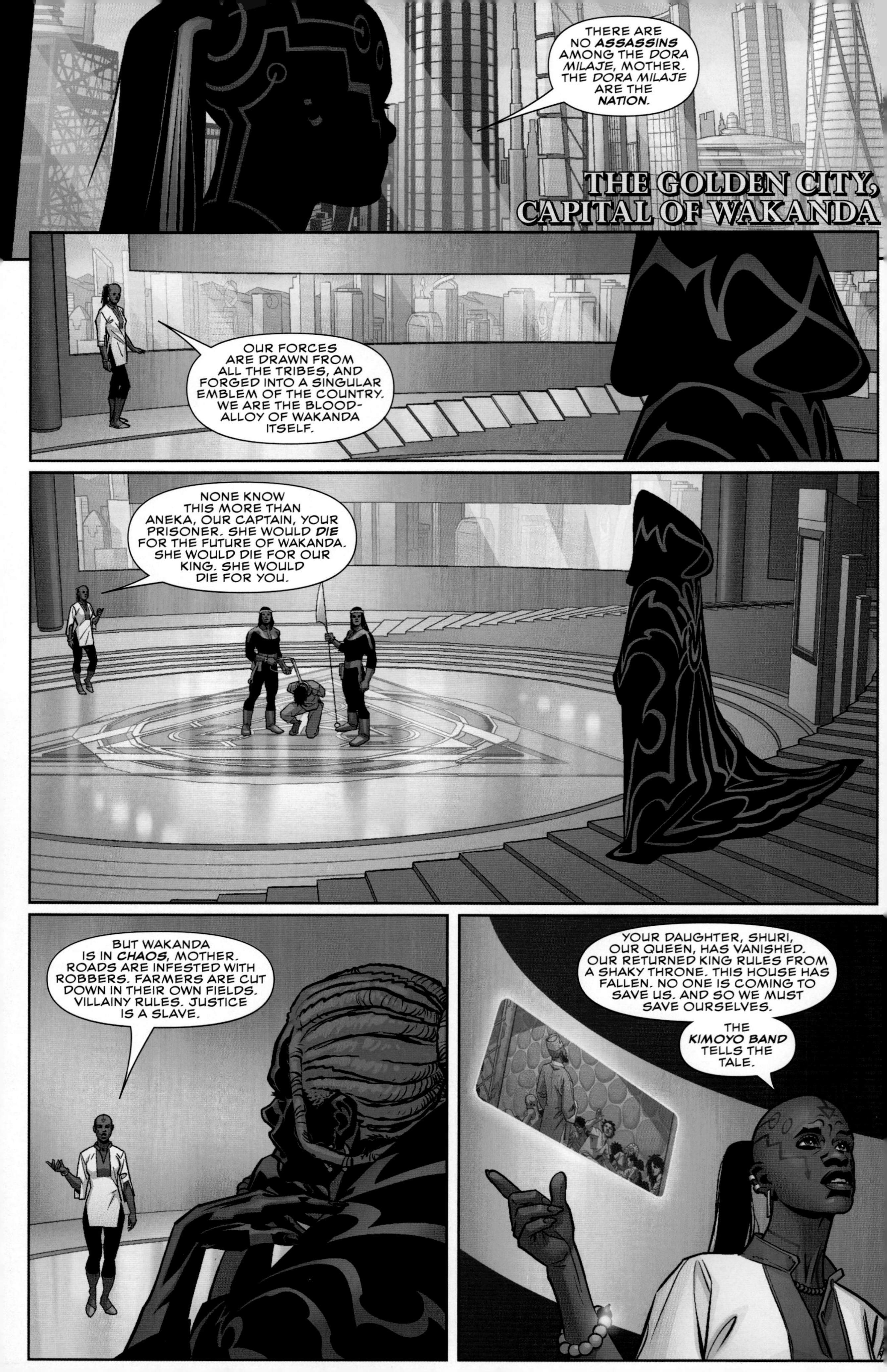
THERE ARE NO ASSASSINS AMONG THE DORA MILAJE, MOTHER. THE DORA MILAJE ARE THE NATION.
THE GOLDEN CITY, CAPITAL OF WAKANDA
OUR FORCES ARE DRAWN FROM ALL THE TRIBES, AND FORGED INTO A SINGULAR EMBLEM OF THE COUNTRY. WE ARE THE BLOOD-ALLOY OF WAKANDA ITSELF.
NONE KNOW THIS MORE THAN ANEKA, OUR CAPTAIN, YOUR PRISONER. SHE WOULD DIE FOR THE FUTURE OF WAKANDA. SHE WOULD DIE FOR OUR KING. SHE WOULD DIE FOR YOU.
BUT WAKANDA IS IN CHAOS, MOTHER. ROADS ARE INFESTED WITH ROBBERS. FARMERS ARE CUT DOWN IN THEIR OWN FIELDS. VILLAINY RULES. JUSTICE IS A SLAVE.
YOUR DAUGHTER, SHURI, OUR QUEEN, HAS VANISHED. OUR RETURNED KING RULES FROM A SHAKY THRONE. THIS HOUSE HAS FALLEN. NO ONE IS COMING TO SAVE US. AND SO WE MUST SAVE OURSELVES.
THE KIMOYO BAND TELLS THE TALE.

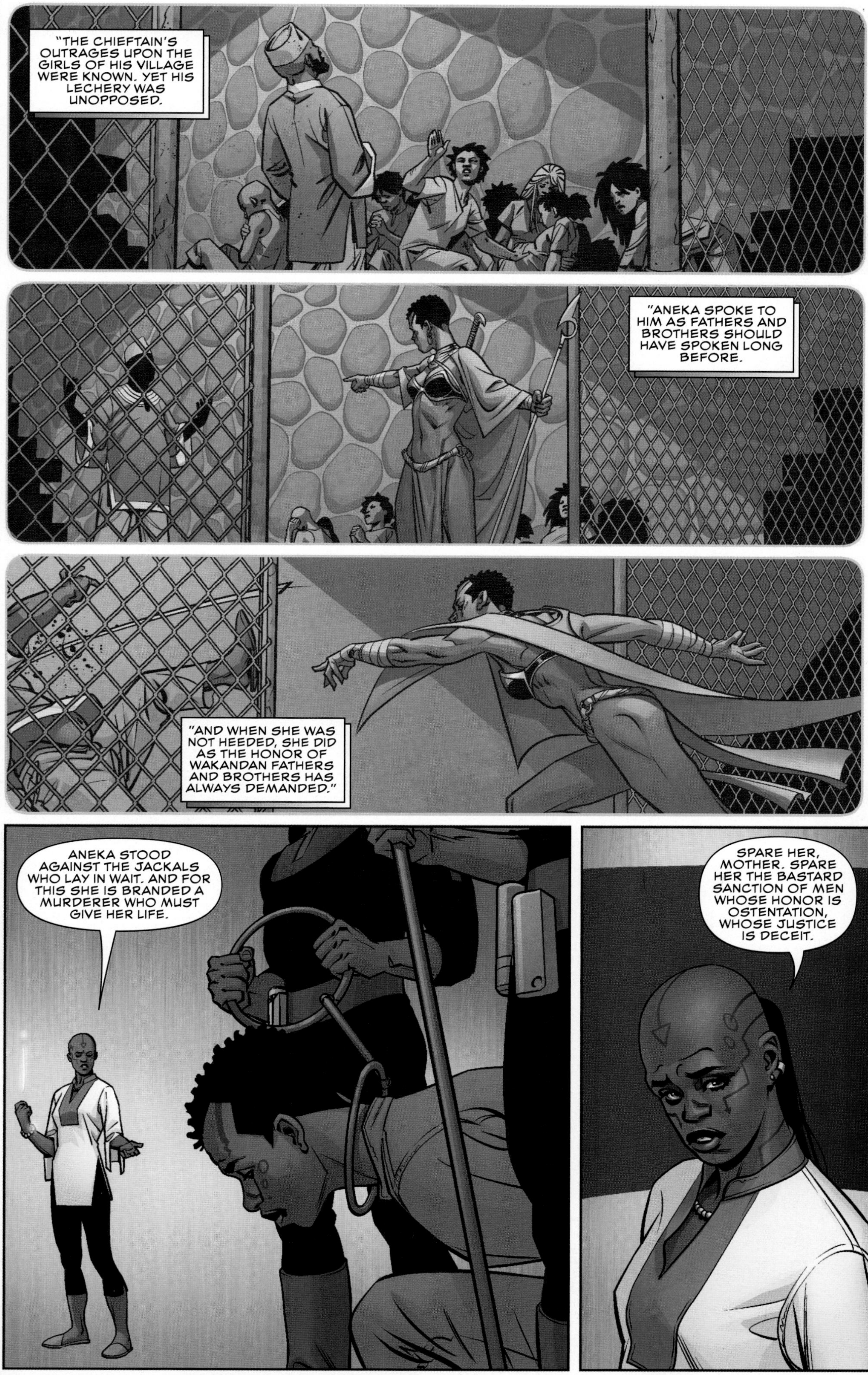
"THE CHIEFTAIN'S OUTRAGES UPON THE GIRLS OF HIS VILLAGE WERE KNOWN. YET HIS LECHERY WAS UNOPPOSED.
"ANEKA SPOKE TO HIM AS FATHERS AND BROTHERS SHOULD HAVE SPOKEN LONG BEFORE.
"AND WHEN SHE WAS NOT HEEDED, SHE DID AS THE HONOR OF WAKANDAN FATHERS AND BROTHERS HAS ALWAYS DEMANDED."
ANEKA STOOD AGAINST THE JACKALS WHO LAY IN WAIT. AND FOR THIS SHE IS BRANDED A MURDERER WHO MUST GIVE HER LIFE.
SPARE HER, MOTHER. SPARE HER THE BASTARD SANCTION OF MEN WHOSE HONOR IS OSTENTATION, WHOSE JUSTICE IS DECEIT.

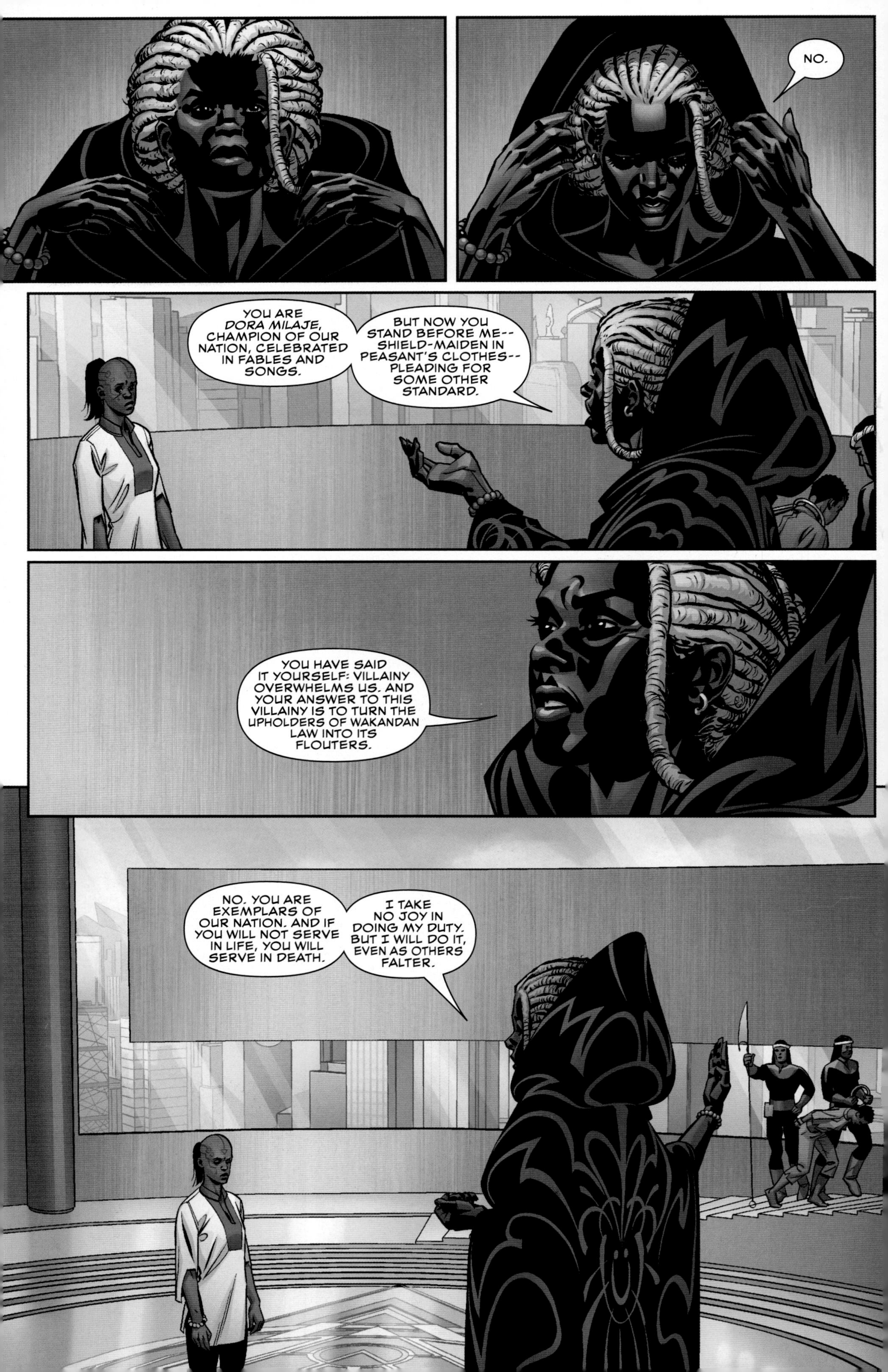
NO.
YOU ARE DORA MILAJE, CHAMPION OF OUR NATION, CELEBRATED IN FABLES AND SONGS.
BUT NOW YOU STAND BEFORE ME-- SHIELD-MAIDEN IN PEASANT'S CLOTHES-- PLEADING FOR SOME OTHER STANDARD.
YOU HAVE SAID IT YOURSELF: VILLAINY OVERWHELMS US. AND YOUR ANSWER TO THIS VILLAINY IS TO TURN THE UPHOLDERS OF WAKANDAN LAW INTO ITS FLOUTERS.
NO. YOU ARE EXEMPLARS OF OUR NATION. AND IF YOU WILL NOT SERVE IN LIFE, YOU WILL SERVE IN DEATH.
I TAKE NO JOY IN DOING MY DUTY. BUT I WILL DO IT, EVEN AS OTHERS FALTER.

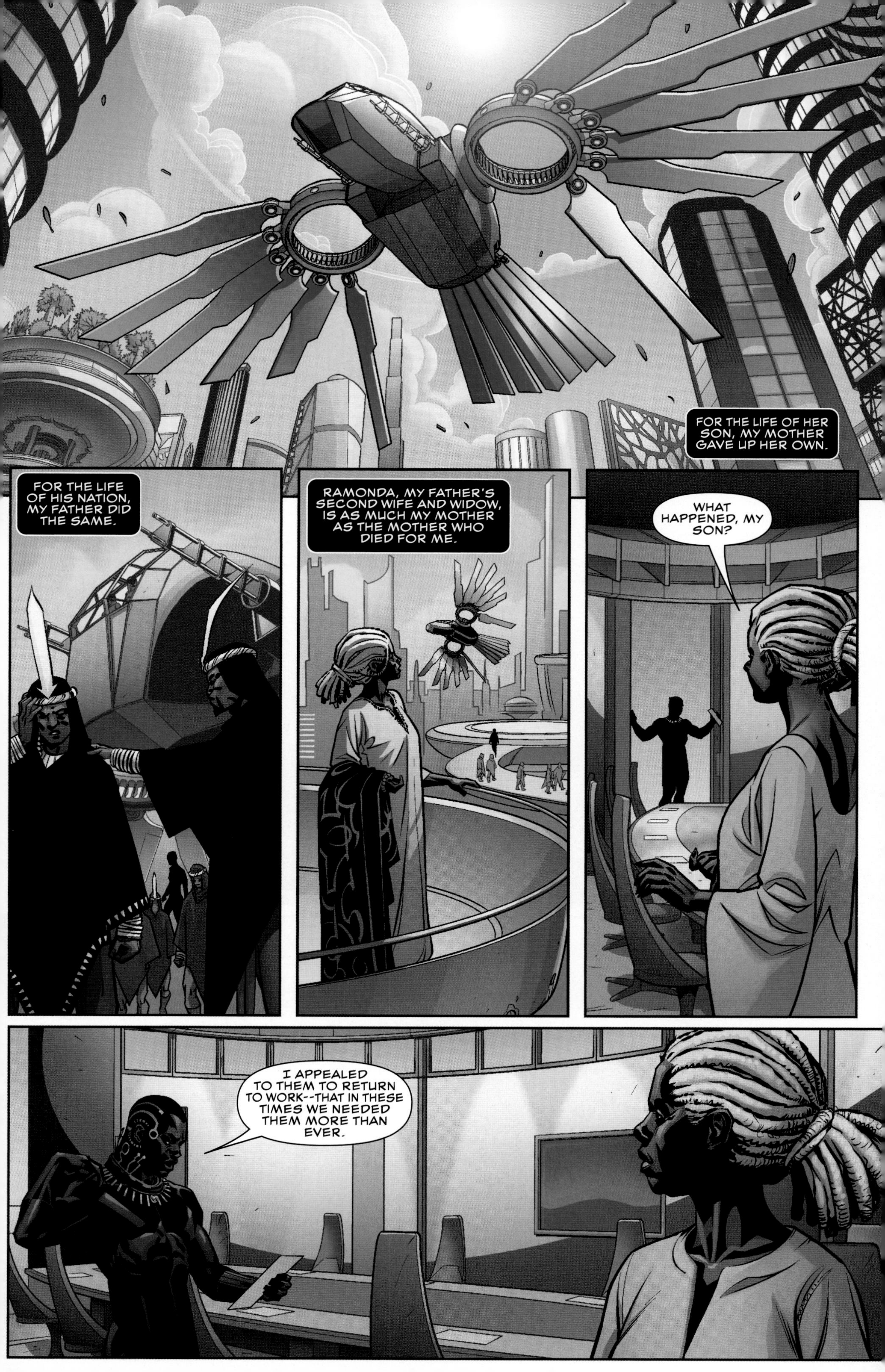
FOR THE LIFE OF HER SON, MY MOTHER GAVE UP HER OWN.
FOR THE LIFE OF HIS NATION, MY FATHER DID THE SAME.
RAMONDA, MY FATHER'S SECOND WIFE AND WIDOW, IS AS MUCH MY MOTHER AS THE MOTHER WHO DIED FOR ME.
WHAT HAPPENED, MY SON?
I APPEALED TO THEM TO RETURN TO WORK--THAT IN THESE TIMES WE NEEDED THEM MORE THAN EVER.

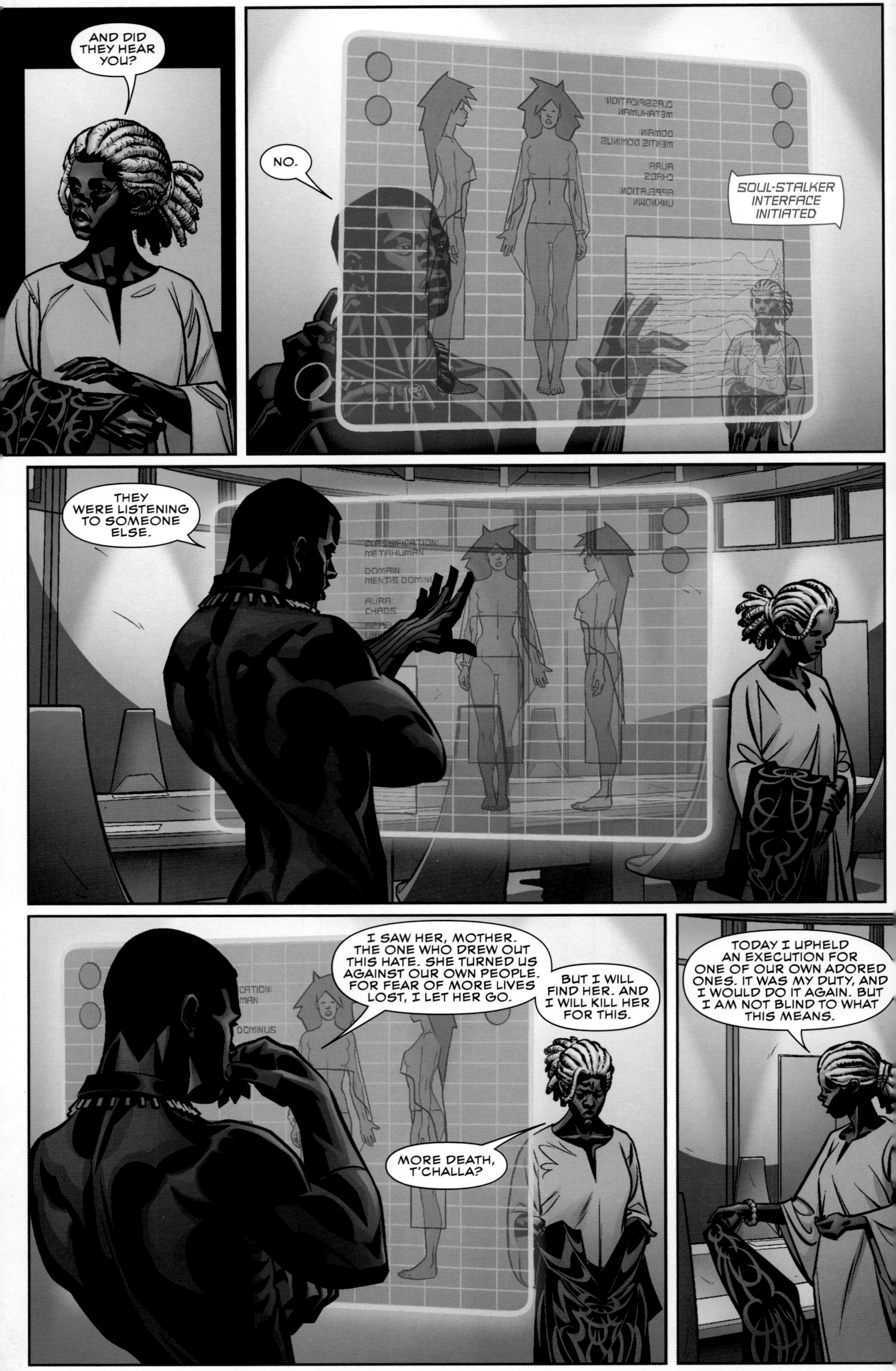
AND DID THEY HEAR YOU?
NO.
SOUL-STALKER INTERFACE INITIATED
THEY WERE LISTENING TO SOMEONE ELSE.
CLASSIFICATION: METAHUMAN
DOMAIN: MENTIS DOMIN
AURA: CHAOS
I SAW HER, MOTHER. THE ONE WHO DREW OUT THIS HATE. SHE TURNED US AGAINST OUR OWN PEOPLE. FOR FEAR OF MORE LIVES LOST, I LET HER GO.
BUT I WILL FIND HER. AND I WILL KILL HER FOR THIS.
MORE DEATH, T'CHALLA?
TODAY I UPHELD AN EXECUTION FOR ONE OF OUR OWN ADORED ONES. IT WAS MY DUTY, AND I WOULD DO IT AGAIN. BUT I AM NOT BLIND TO WHAT THIS MEANS.

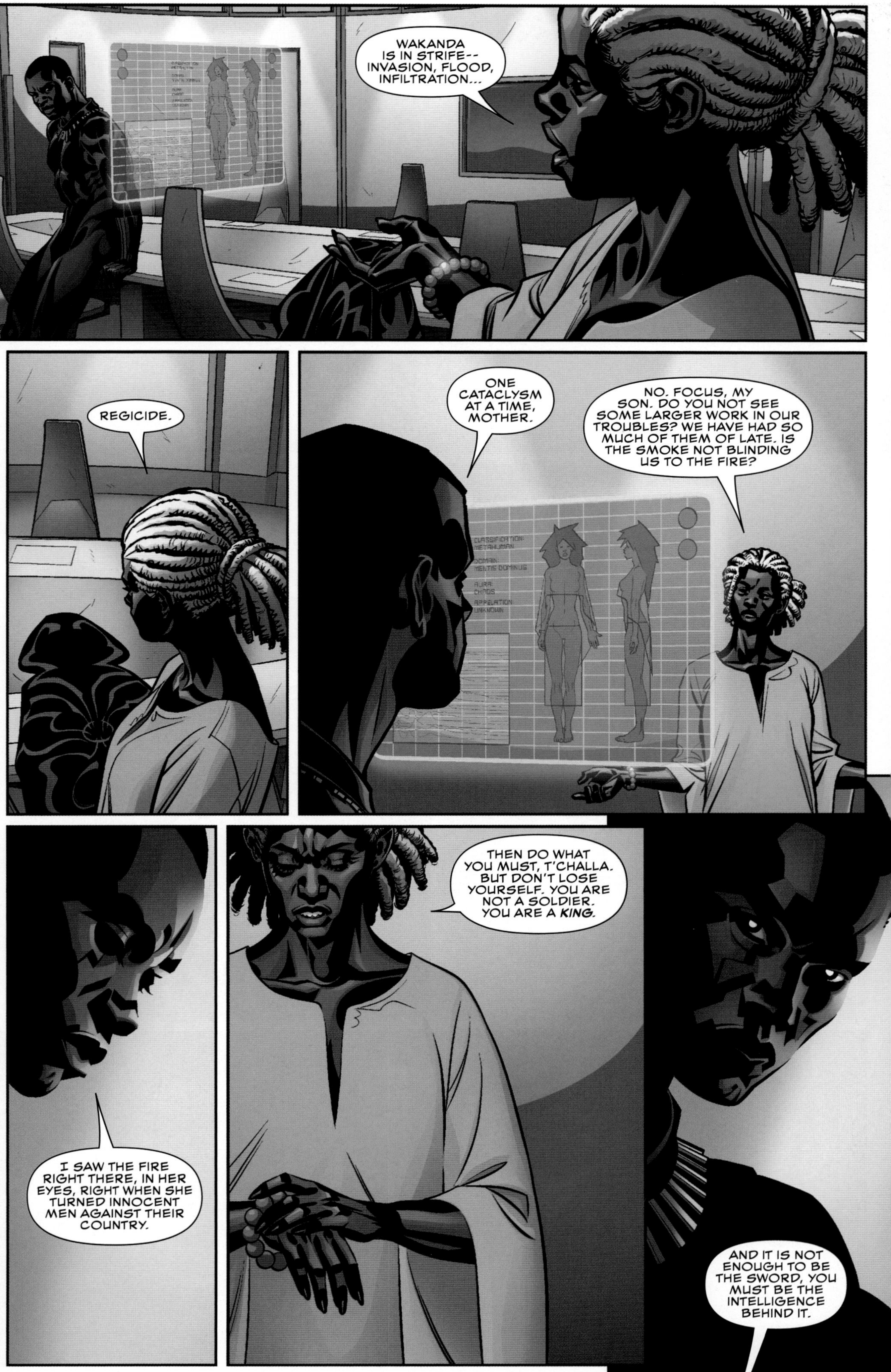
WAKANDA IS IN STRIFE-- INVASION, FLOOD, INFILTRATION...
REGICIDE.
ONE CATACLYSM AT A TIME, MOTHER.
NO. FOCUS, MY SON. DO YOU NOT SEE SOME LARGER WORK IN OUR TROUBLES? WE HAVE HAD SO MUCH OF THEM OF LATE. IS THE SMOKE NOT BLINDING US TO THE FIRE?
CLASSIFICATION: METAHUMAN
DOMAIN: MENTIS DOMINUS
AURA: CHAOS
APPELATION: UNKNOWN
I SAW THE FIRE RIGHT THERE, IN HER EYES, RIGHT WHEN SHE TURNED INNOCENT MEN AGAINST THEIR COUNTRY.
THEN DO WHAT YOU MUST, T'CHALLA. BUT DON'T LOSE YOURSELF. YOU ARE NOT A SOLDIER. YOU ARE A *KING*.
AND IT IS NOT ENOUGH TO BE THE SWORD, YOU MUST BE THE INTELLIGENCE BEHIND IT.

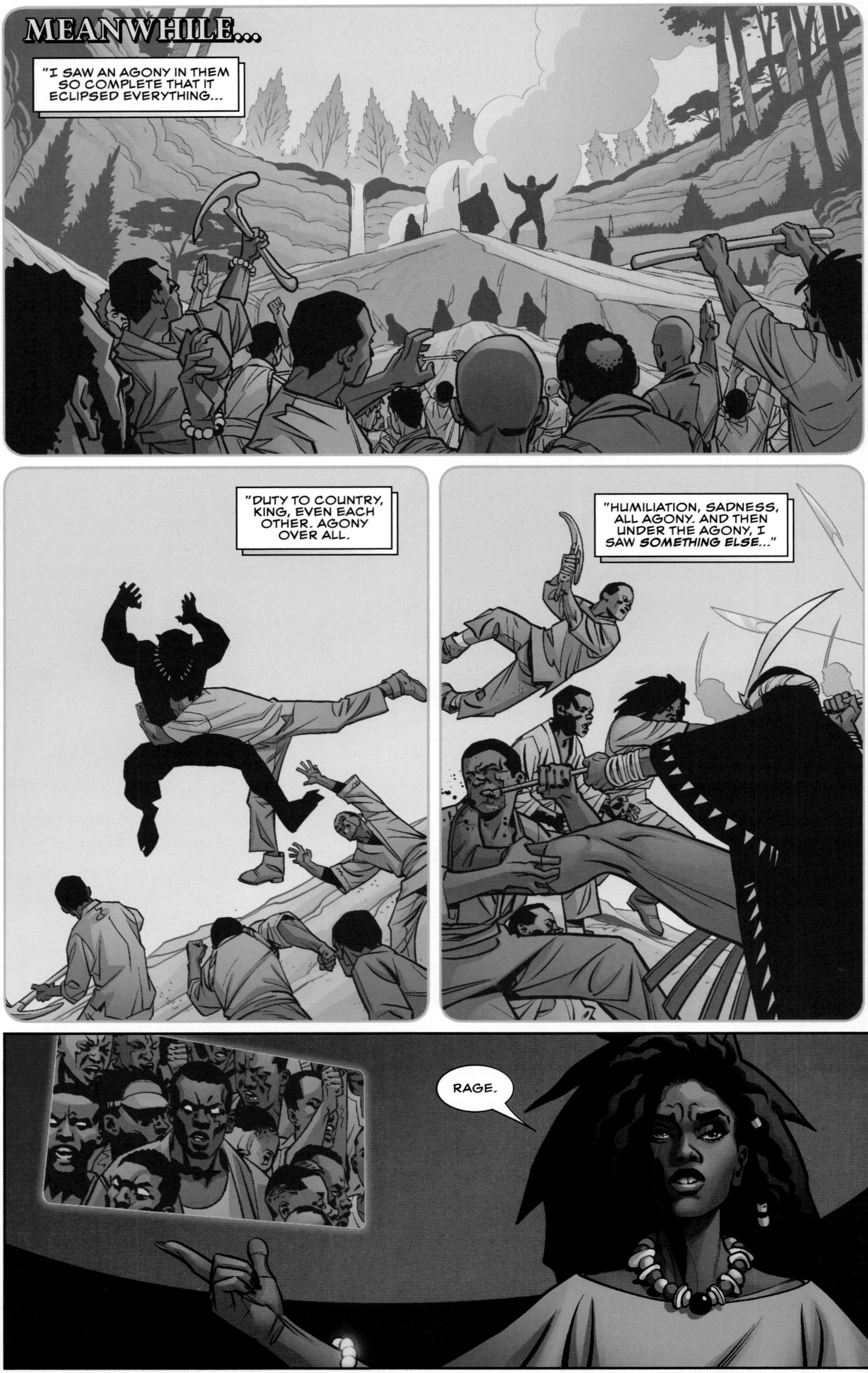
MEANWHILE...
"I SAW AN AGONY IN THEM SO COMPLETE THAT IT ECLIPSED EVERYTHING...
"DUTY TO COUNTRY, KING, EVEN EACH OTHER. AGONY OVER ALL.
"HUMILIATION, SADNESS, ALL AGONY. AND THEN UNDER THE AGONY, I SAW SOMETHING ELSE..."
RAGE.

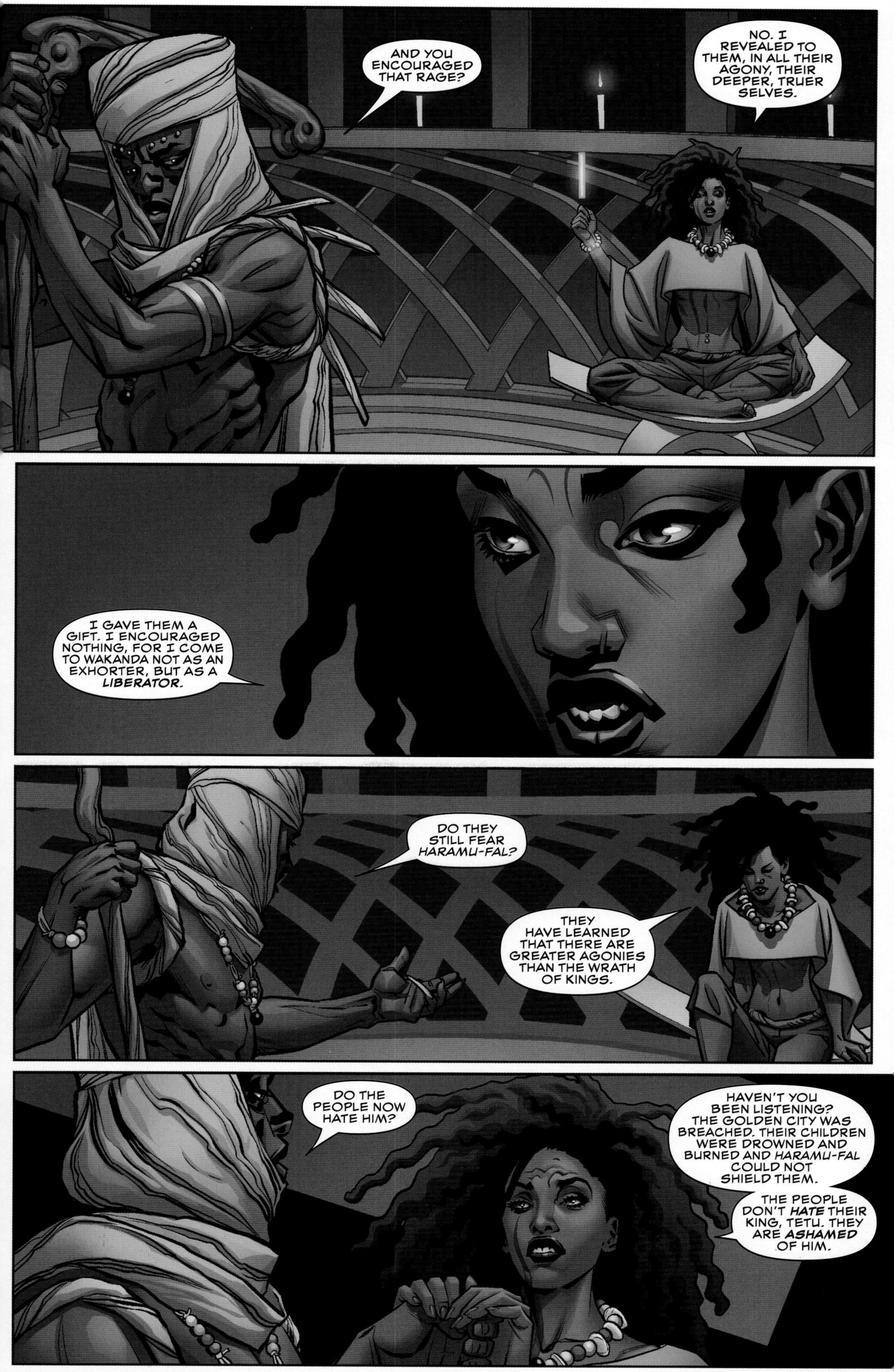

AND YOU ENCOURAGED THAT RAGE?
NO. I REVEALED TO THEM, IN ALL THEIR AGONY, THEIR DEEPER, TRUER SELVES.
I GAVE THEM A GIFT. I ENCOURAGED NOTHING, FOR I COME TO WAKANDA NOT AS AN EXHORTER, BUT AS A LIBERATOR.
DO THEY STILL FEAR HARAMU-FAL?
THEY HAVE LEARNED THAT THERE ARE GREATER AGONIES THAN THE WRATH OF KINGS.
DO THE PEOPLE NOW HATE HIM?
HAVEN'T YOU BEEN LISTENING? THE GOLDEN CITY WAS BREACHED. THEIR CHILDREN WERE DROWNED AND BURNED AND HARAMU-FAL COULD NOT SHIELD THEM.
THE PEOPLE DON'T HATE THEIR KING, TETU. THEY ARE ASHAMED OF HIM.

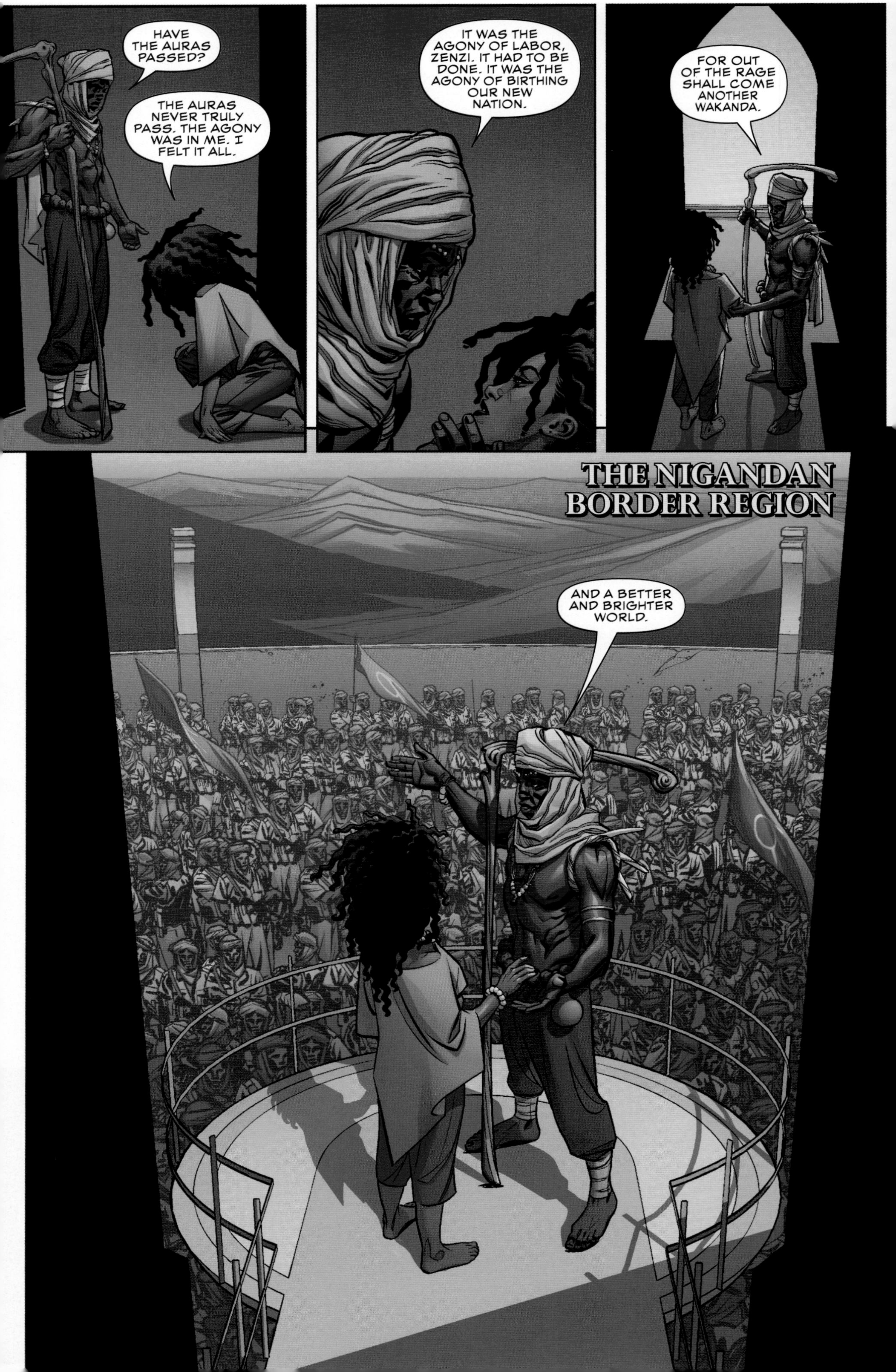
HAVE THE AURAS PASSED?
THE AURAS NEVER TRULY PASS. THE AGONY WAS IN ME. I FELT IT ALL.
IT WAS THE AGONY OF LABOR, ZENZI. IT HAD TO BE DONE. IT WAS THE AGONY OF BIRTHING OUR NEW NATION.
FOR OUT OF THE RAGE SHALL COME ANOTHER WAKANDA.
THE NIGANDAN BORDER REGION
AND A BETTER AND BRIGHTER WORLD.

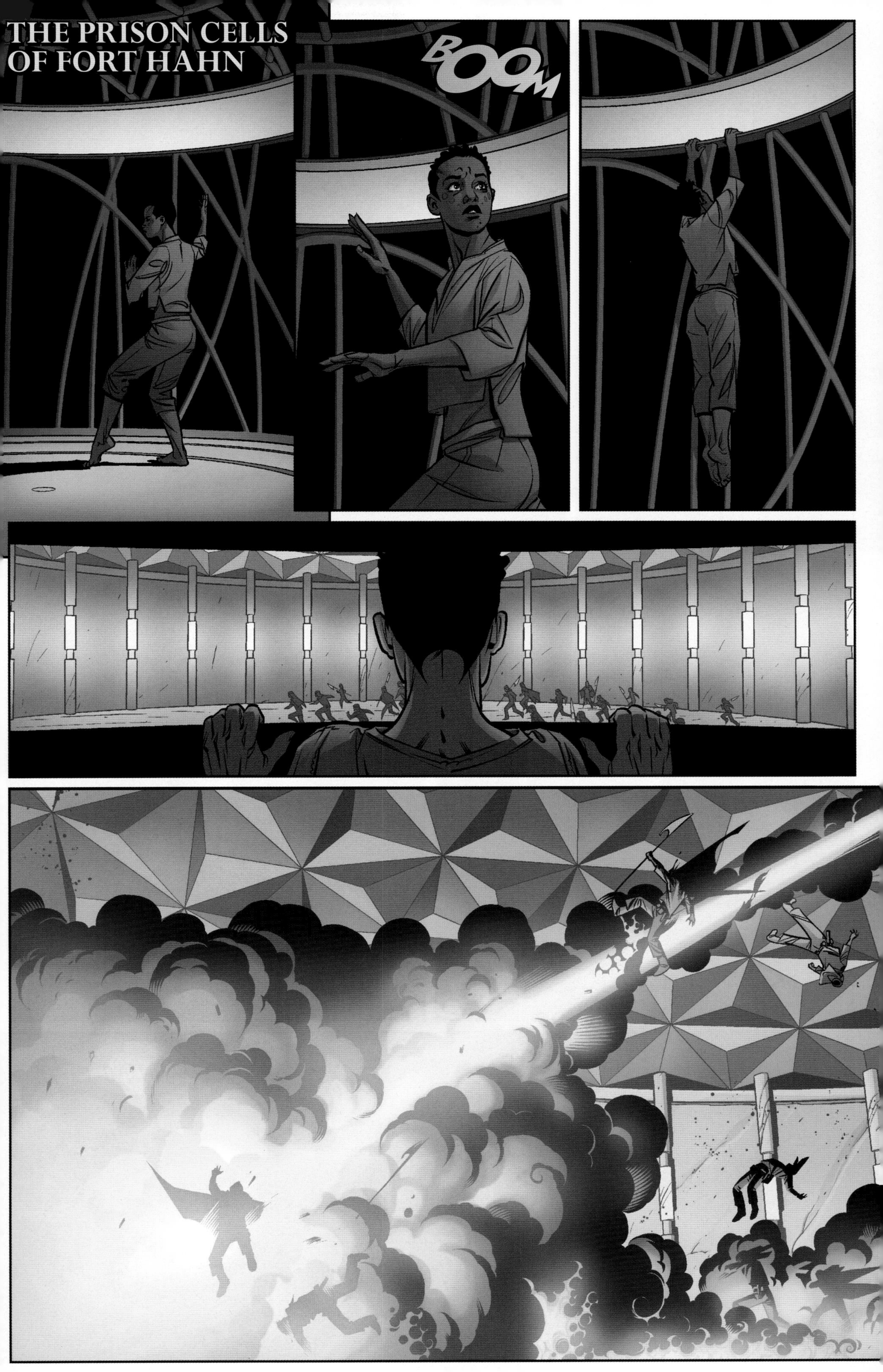
THE PRISON CELLS OF FORT HAHN
BOOM

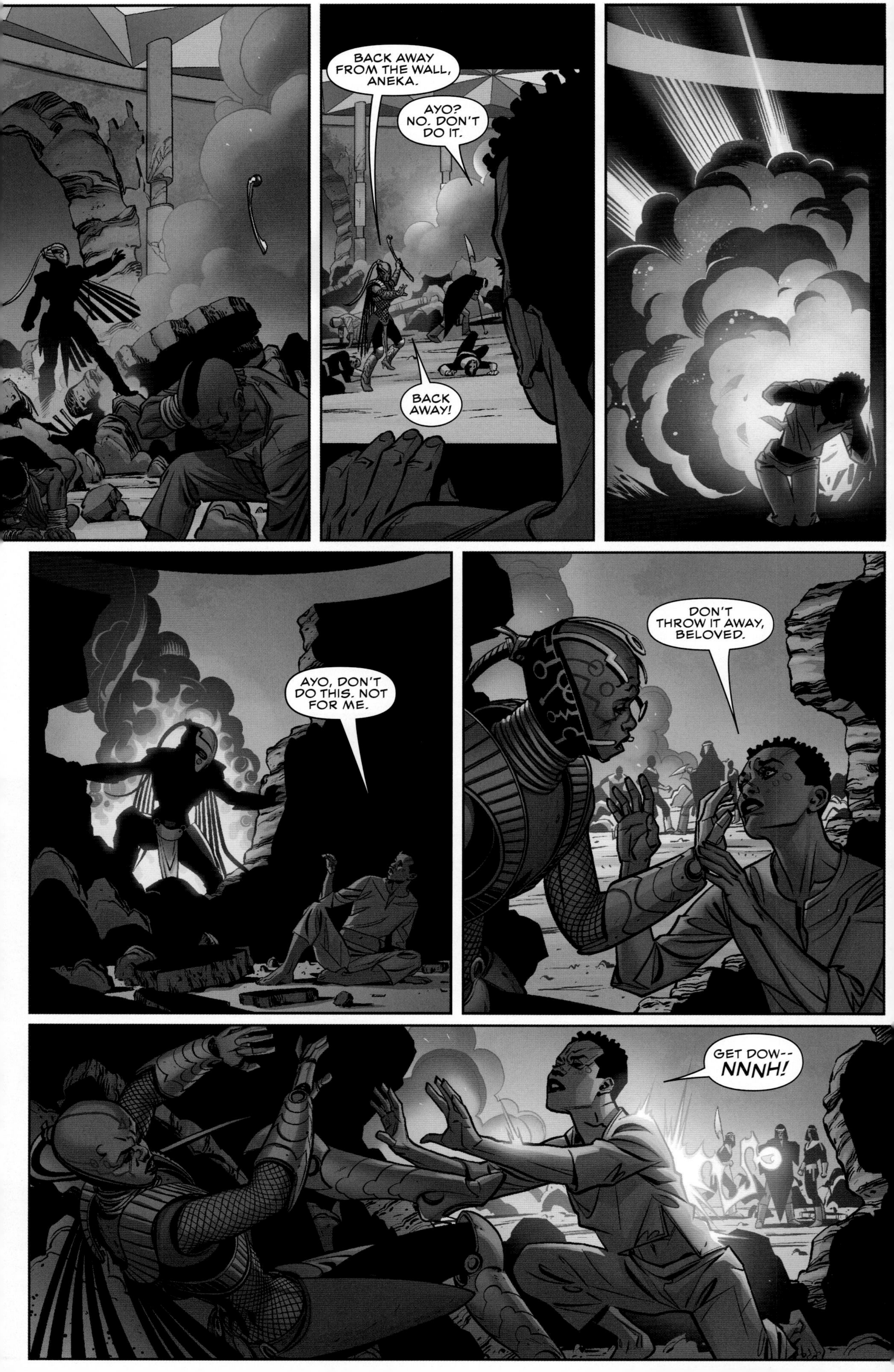
BACK AWAY FROM THE WALL, ANEKA.
AYO? NO. DON'T DO IT.
BACK AWAY!
AYO, DON'T DO THIS. NOT FOR ME.
DON'T THROW IT AWAY, BELOVED.
GET DOW-- NNNH!

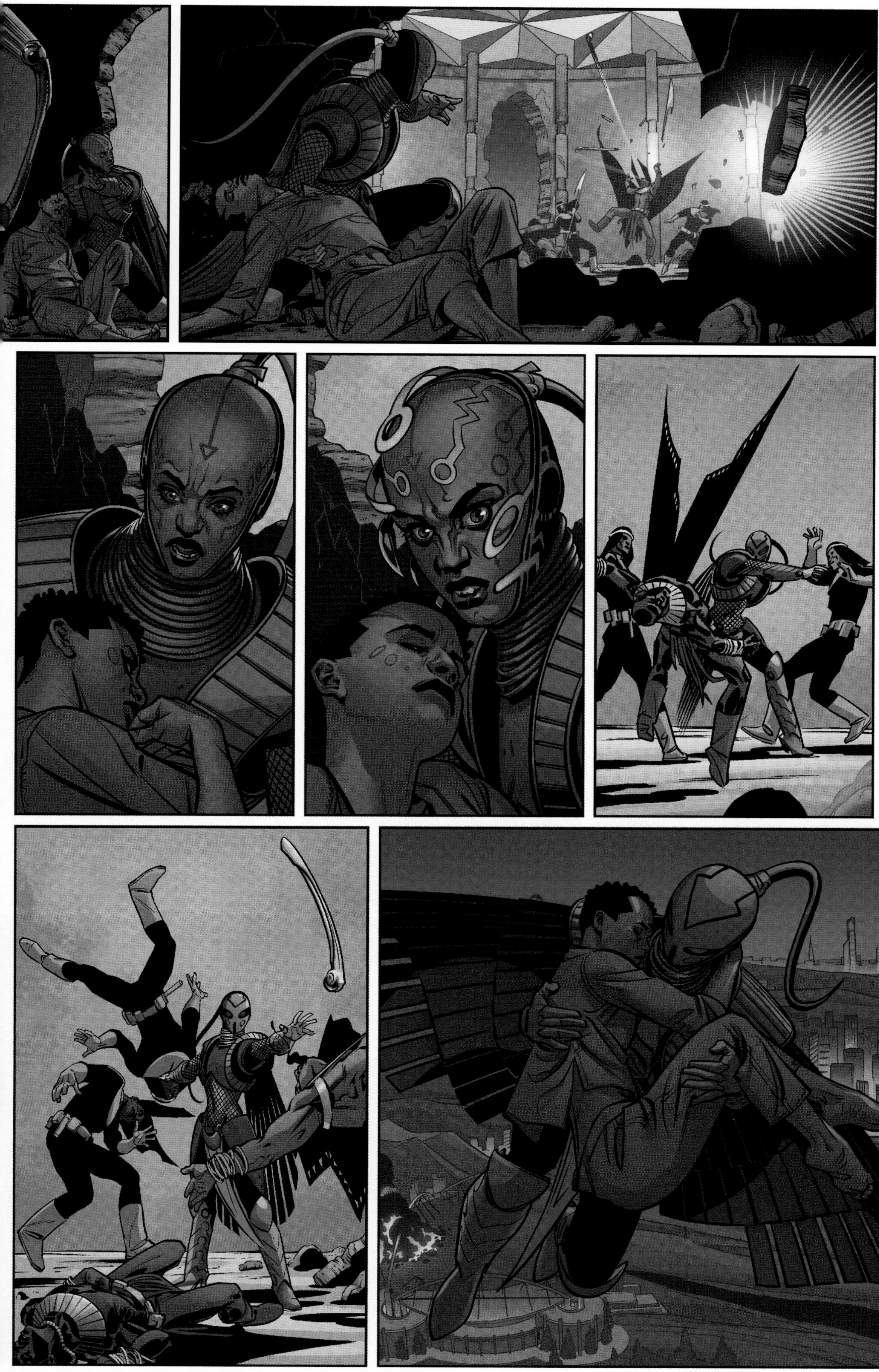

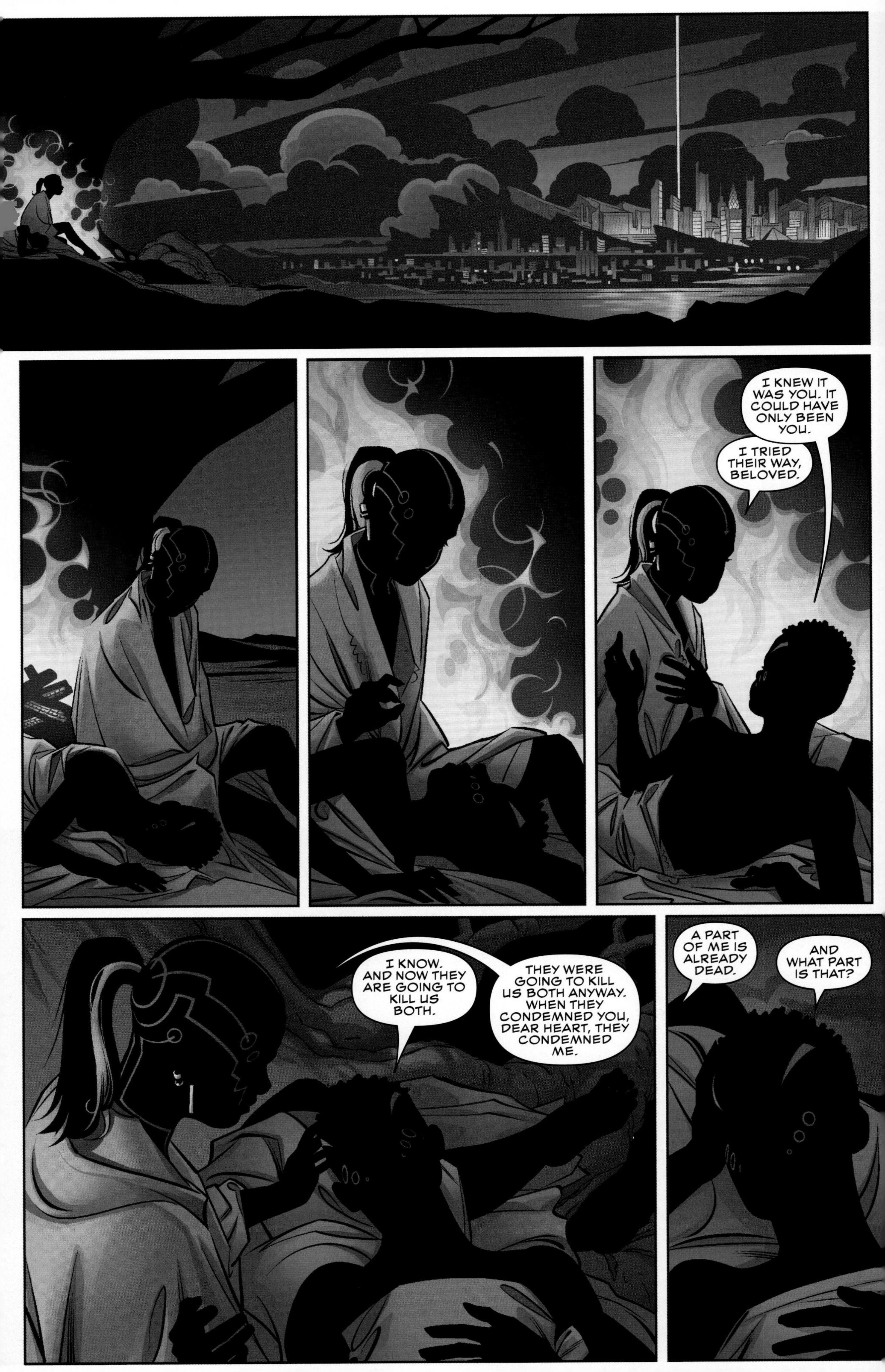
I KNEW IT WAS YOU. IT COULD HAVE ONLY BEEN YOU.
I TRIED THEIR WAY, BELOVED.
I KNOW. AND NOW THEY ARE GOING TO KILL US BOTH.
THEY WERE GOING TO KILL US BOTH ANYWAY. WHEN THEY CONDEMNED YOU, DEAR HEART, THEY CONDEMNED ME.
A PART OF ME IS ALREADY DEAD.
AND WHAT PART IS THAT?

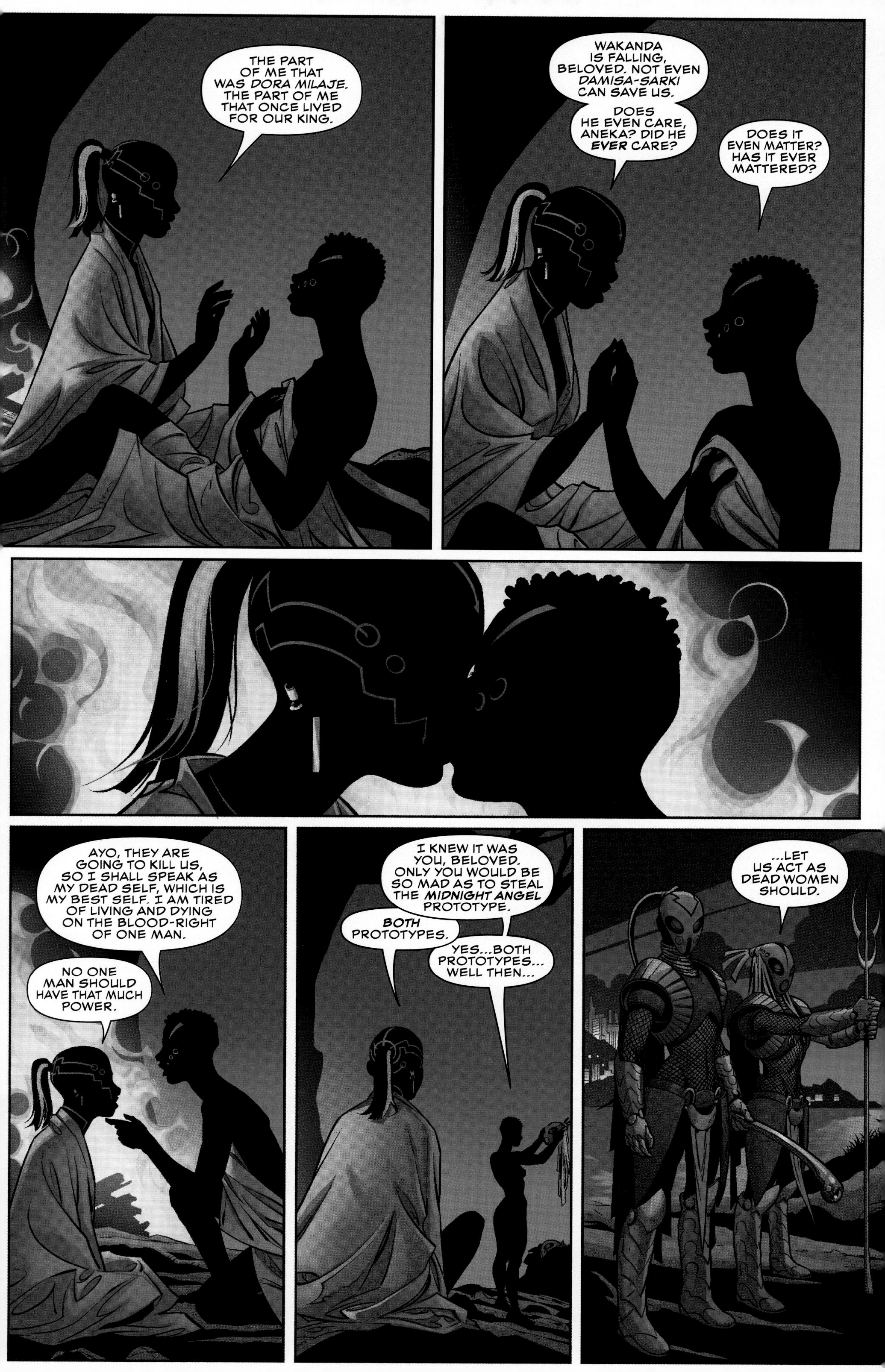
THE PART OF ME THAT WAS DORA MILAJE. THE PART OF ME THAT ONCE LIVED FOR OUR KING.
WAKANDA IS FALLING, BELOVED. NOT EVEN DAMISA-SARKI CAN SAVE US.
DOES HE EVEN CARE, ANEKA? DID HE EVER CARE?
DOES IT EVEN MATTER? HAS IT EVER MATTERED?
AYO, THEY ARE GOING TO KILL US, SO I SHALL SPEAK AS MY DEAD SELF, WHICH IS MY BEST SELF. I AM TIRED OF LIVING AND DYING ON THE BLOOD-RIGHT OF ONE MAN.
NO ONE MAN SHOULD HAVE THAT MUCH POWER.
I KNEW IT WAS YOU, BELOVED. ONLY YOU WOULD BE SO MAD AS TO STEAL THE MIDNIGHT ANGEL PROTOTYPE.
BOTH PROTOTYPES.
YES...BOTH PROTOTYPES... WELL THEN...
...LET US ACT AS DEAD WOMEN SHOULD.

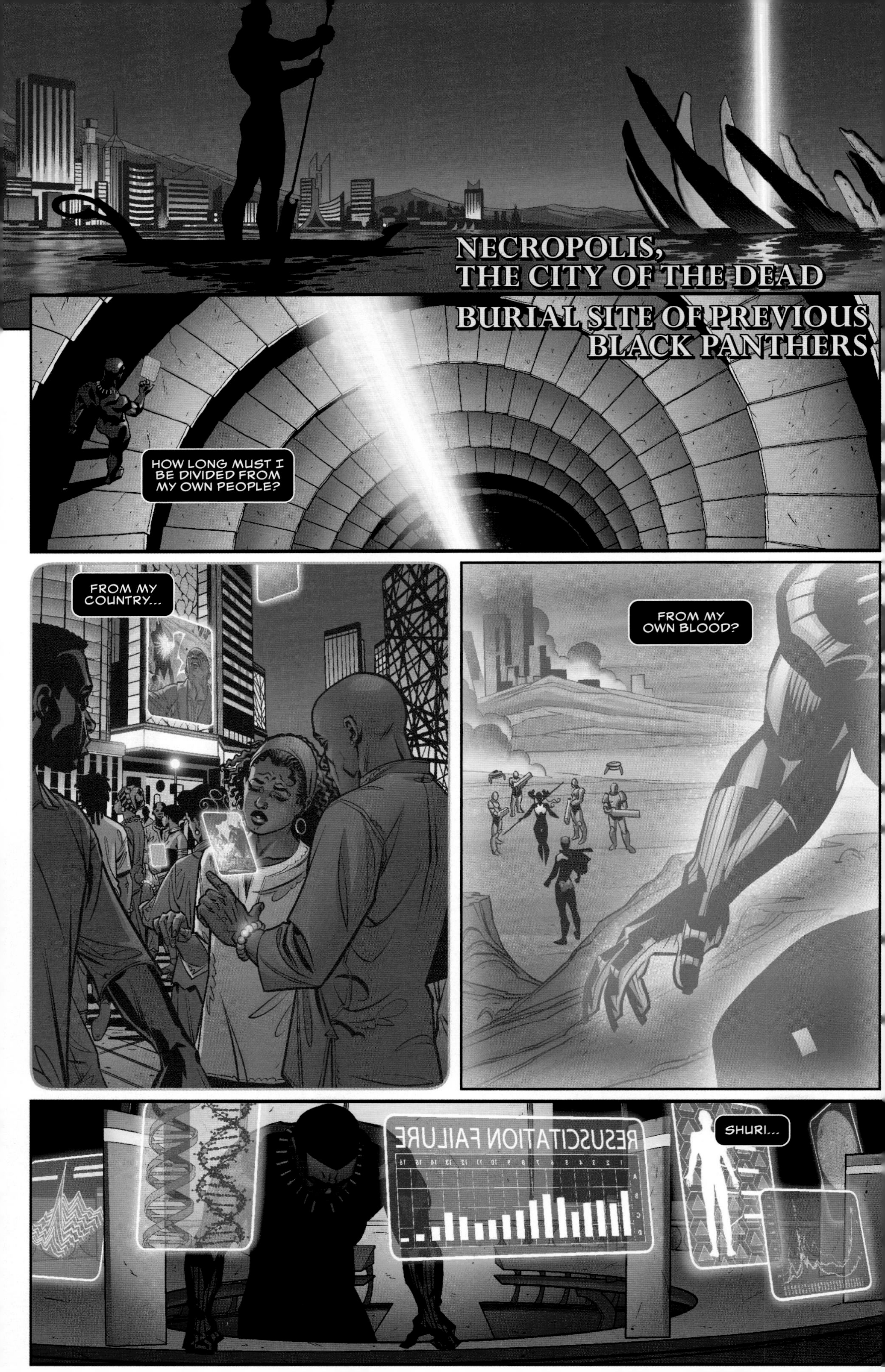
NECROPOLIS, THE CITY OF THE DEAD
BURIAL SITE OF PREVIOUS BLACK PANTHERS
HOW LONG MUST I BE DIVIDED FROM MY OWN PEOPLE?
FROM MY COUNTRY...
FROM MY OWN BLOOD?
RESUSCITATION FAILURE
SHURI...

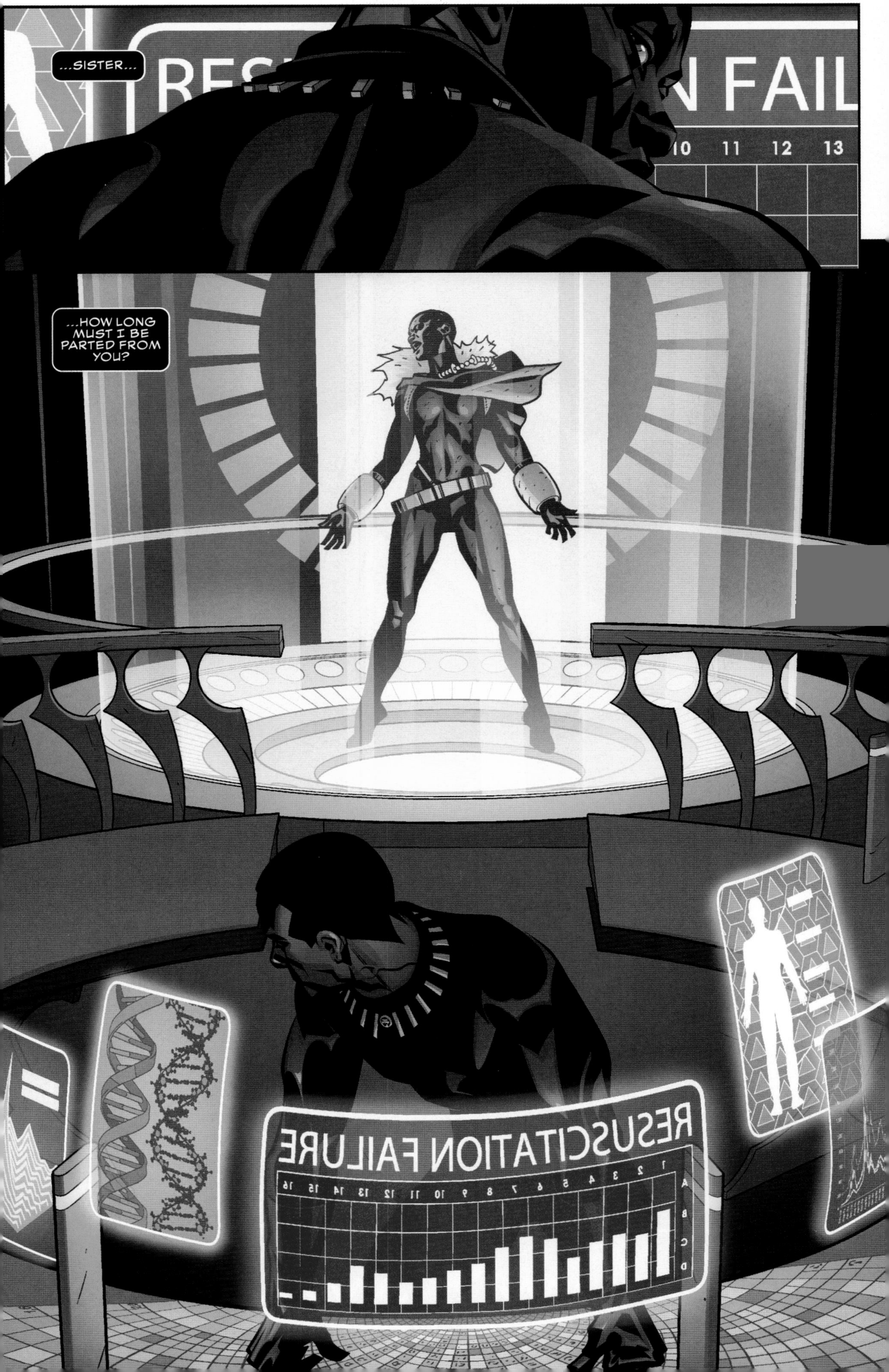
...SISTER...
...HOW LONG MUST I BE PARTED FROM YOU?
RESUSCITATION FAILURE

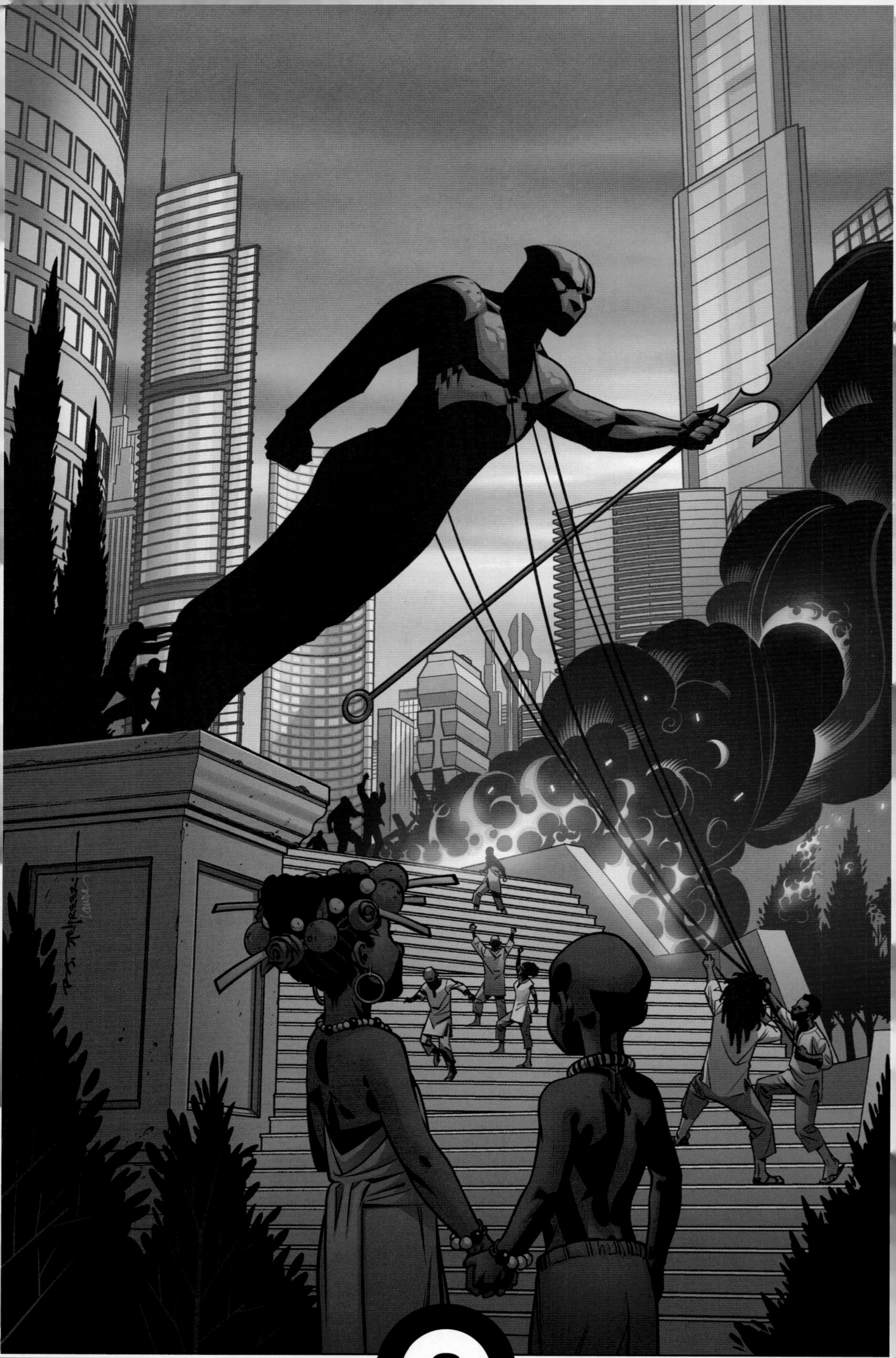

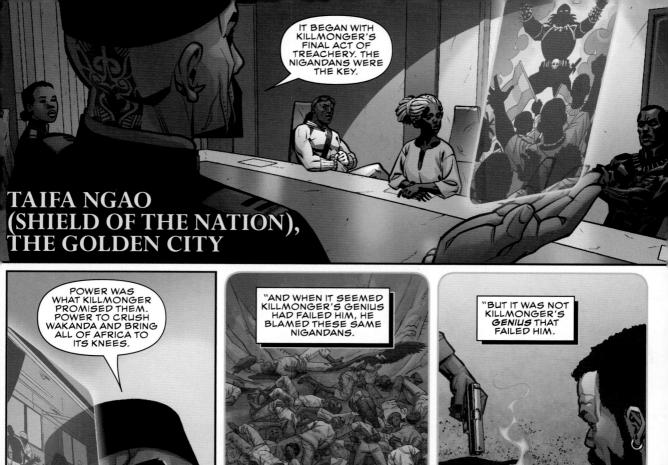

IT BEGAN WITH KILLMONGER'S FINAL ACT OF TREACHERY. THE NIGANDANS WERE THE KEY.

## TAIFA NGAO (SHIELD OF THE NATION), THE GOLDEN CITY

POWER WAS WHAT KILLMONGER PROMISED THEM. POWER TO CRUSH WAKANDA AND BRING ALL OF AFRICA TO ITS KNEES.

"AND WHEN IT SEEMED KILLMONGER'S GENIUS HAD FAILED HIM, HE BLAMED THESE SAME NIGANDANS.

"BUT IT WAS NOT KILLMONGER'S GENIUS THAT FAILED HIM.

"IT WAS HIS PATIENCE."

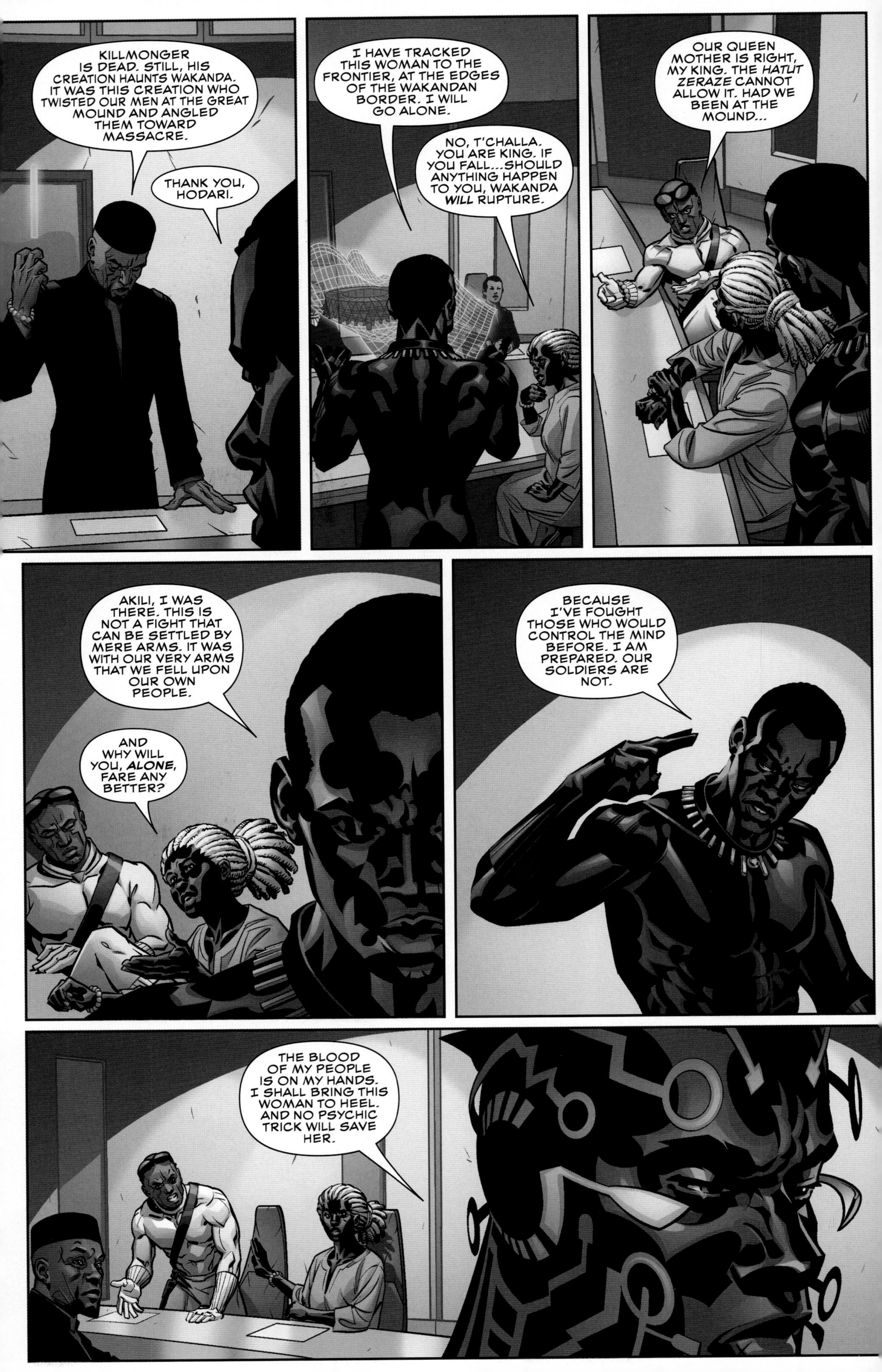
KILLMONGER IS DEAD. STILL, HIS CREATION HAUNTS WAKANDA. IT WAS THIS CREATION WHO TWISTED OUR MEN AT THE GREAT MOUND AND ANGLED THEM TOWARD MASSACRE.
THANK YOU, HODARI.
I HAVE TRACKED THIS WOMAN TO THE FRONTIER, AT THE EDGES OF THE WAKANDAN BORDER. I WILL GO ALONE.
NO, T'CHALLA. YOU ARE KING. IF YOU FALL...SHOULD ANYTHING HAPPEN TO YOU, WAKANDA *WILL* RUPTURE.
OUR QUEEN MOTHER IS RIGHT, MY KING. THE *HATUT ZERAZE* CANNOT ALLOW IT. HAD WE BEEN AT THE MOUND...
AKILI, I WAS THERE. THIS IS NOT A FIGHT THAT CAN BE SETTLED BY MERE ARMS. IT WAS WITH OUR VERY ARMS THAT WE FELL UPON OUR OWN PEOPLE.
AND WHY WILL YOU, *ALONE*, FARE ANY BETTER?
BECAUSE I'VE FOUGHT THOSE WHO WOULD CONTROL THE MIND BEFORE. I AM PREPARED. OUR SOLDIERS ARE NOT.
THE BLOOD OF MY PEOPLE IS ON MY HANDS. I SHALL BRING THIS WOMAN TO HEEL. AND NO PSYCHIC TRICK WILL SAVE HER.

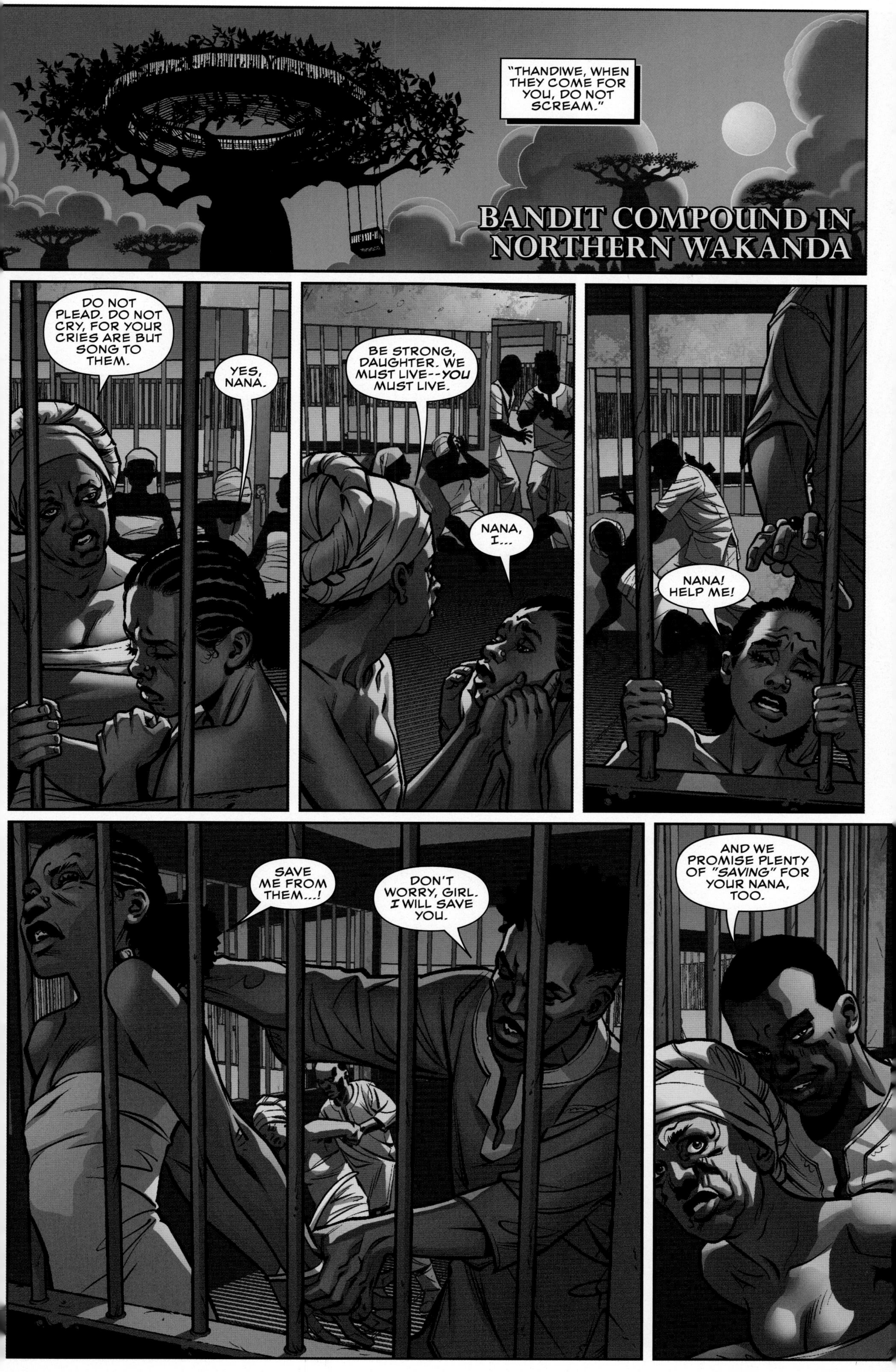
"THANDIWE, WHEN THEY COME FOR YOU, DO NOT SCREAM."
BANDIT COMPOUND IN NORTHERN WAKANDA
DO NOT PLEAD. DO NOT CRY, FOR YOUR CRIES ARE BUT SONG TO THEM.
YES, NANA.
BE STRONG, DAUGHTER. WE MUST LIVE--YOU MUST LIVE.
NANA, I...
NANA! HELP ME!
SAVE ME FROM THEM...!
DON'T WORRY, GIRL. I WILL SAVE YOU.
AND WE PROMISE PLENTY OF "SAVING" FOR YOUR NANA, TOO.

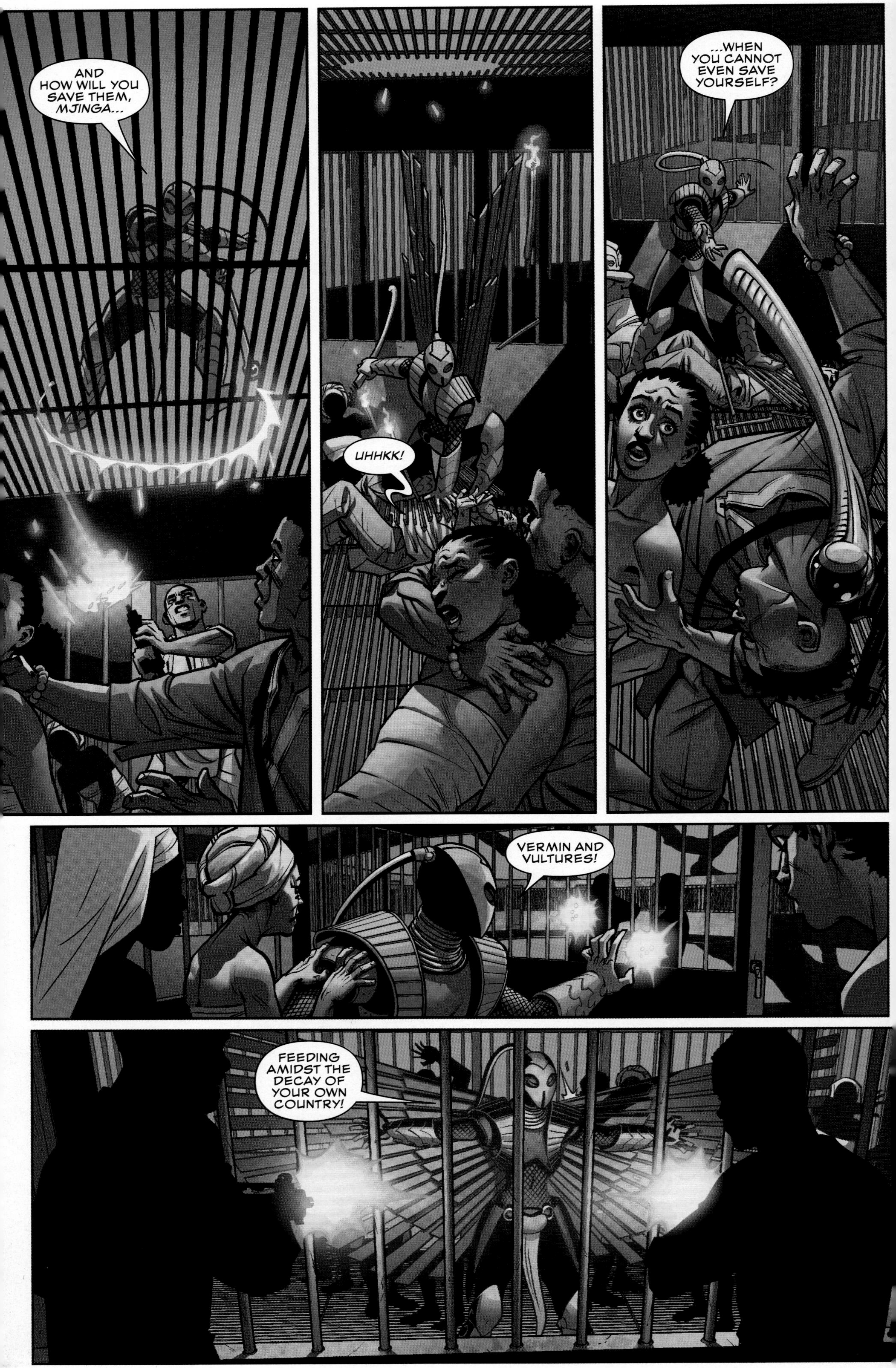
AND HOW WILL YOU SAVE THEM, MJINGA...
UHHKK!
...WHEN YOU CANNOT EVEN SAVE YOURSELF?
VERMIN AND VULTURES!
FEEDING AMIDST THE DECAY OF YOUR OWN COUNTRY!

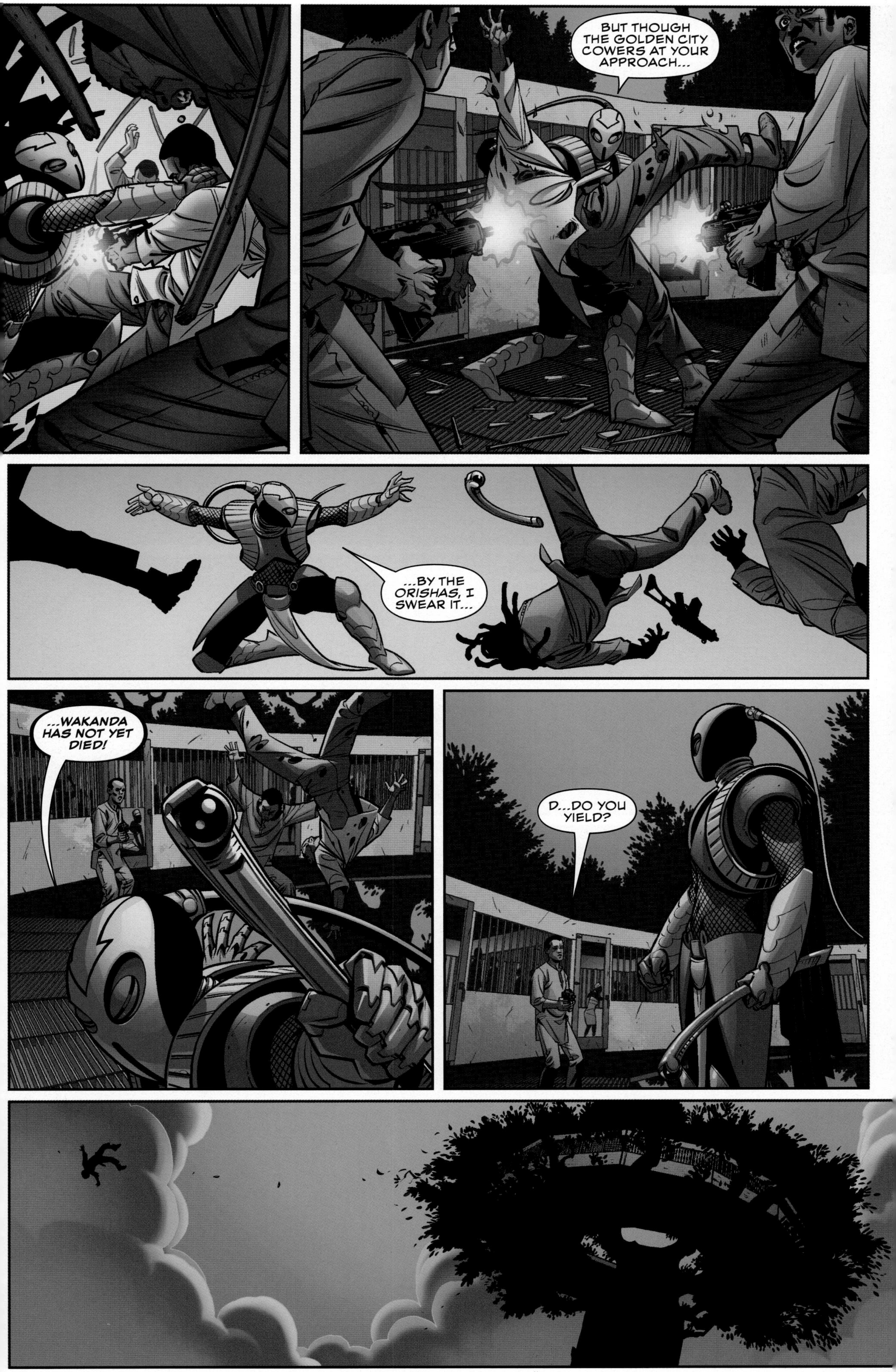
BUT THOUGH THE GOLDEN CITY COWERS AT YOUR APPROACH...
...BY THE ORISHAS, I SWEAR IT...
...WAKANDA HAS NOT YET DIED!
D...DO YOU YIELD?

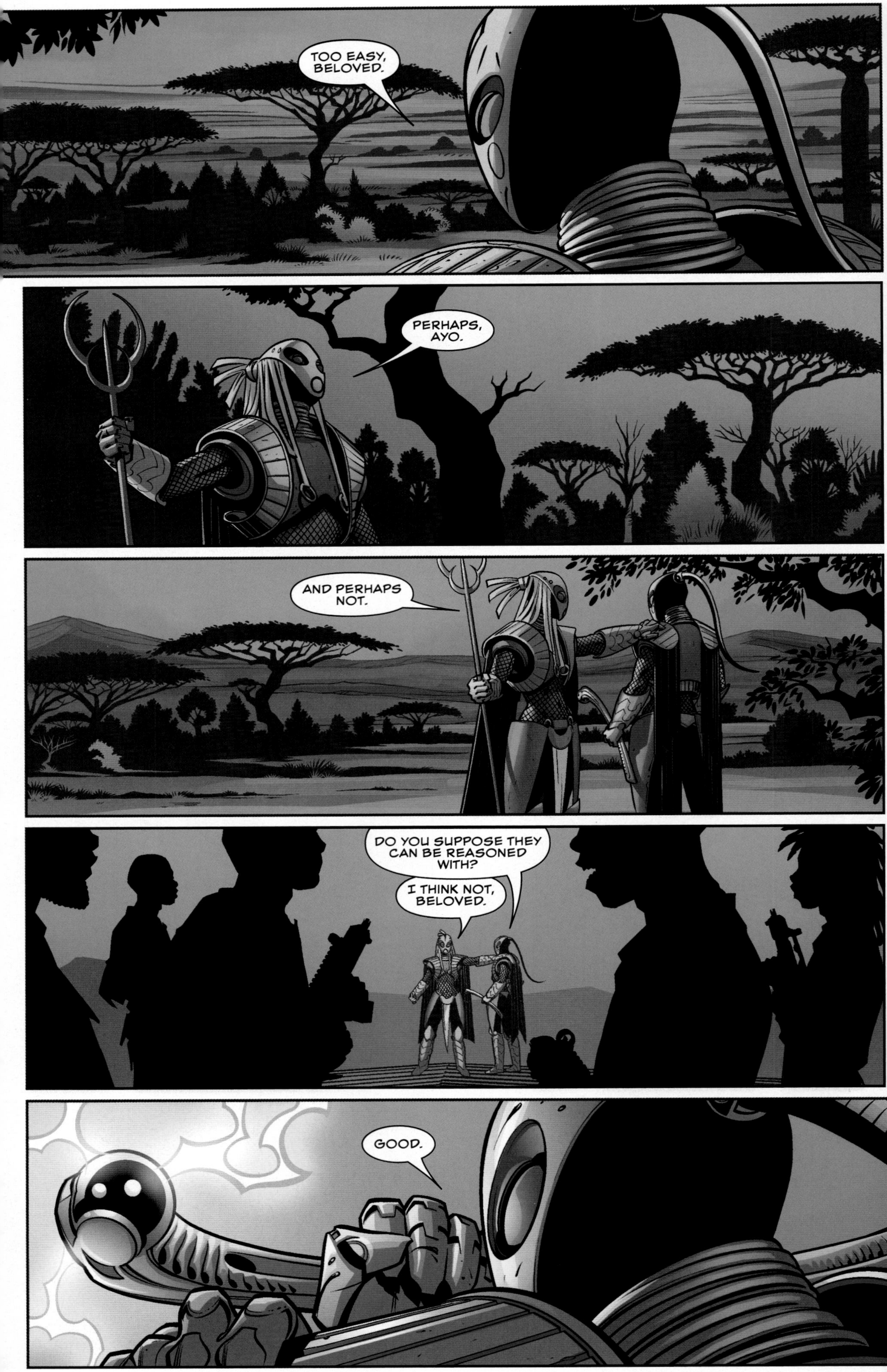
TOO EASY, BELOVED.
PERHAPS, AYO.
AND PERHAPS NOT.
DO YOU SUPPOSE THEY CAN BE REASONED WITH?
I THINK NOT, BELOVED.
GOOD.

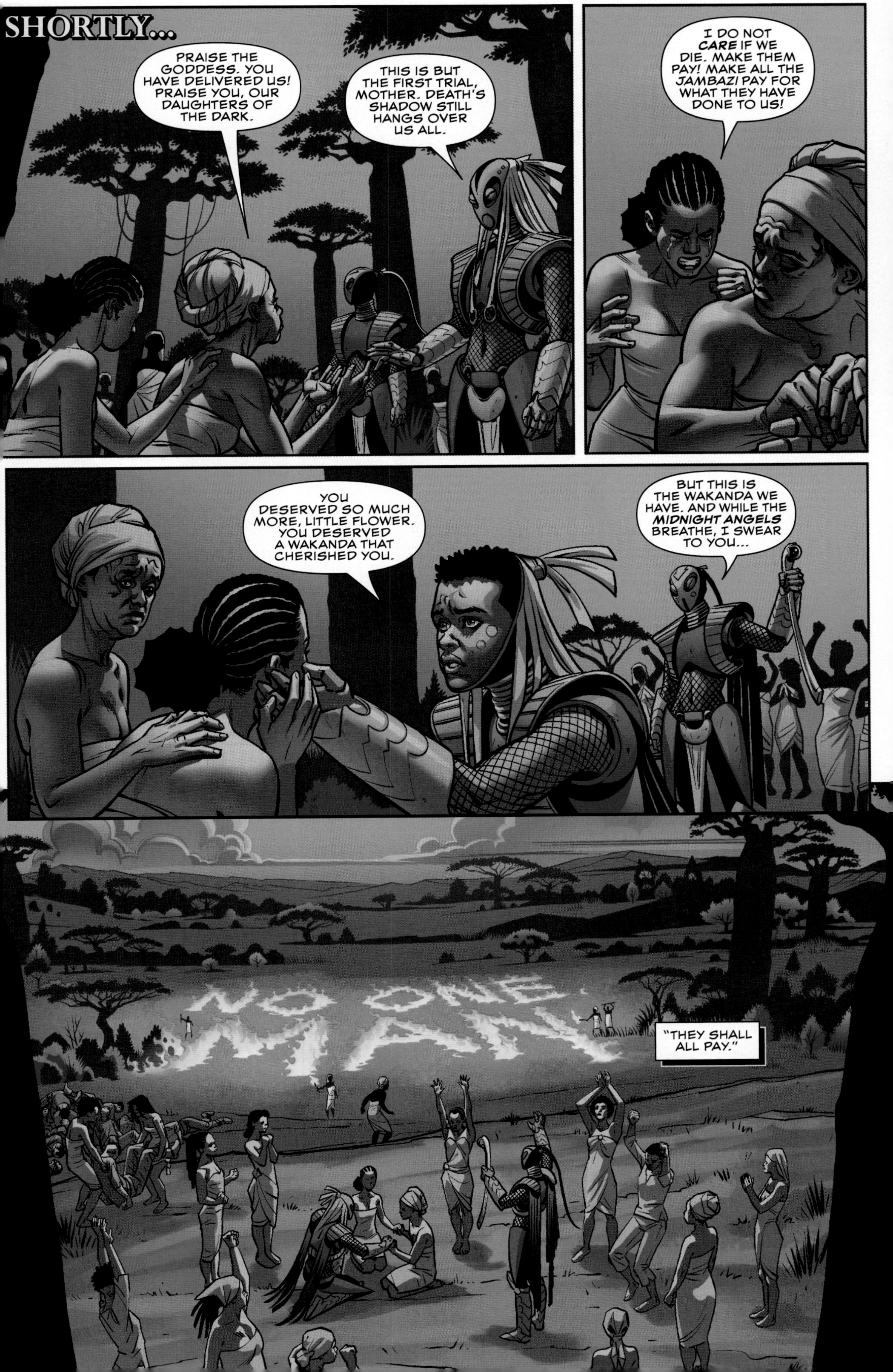
SHORTLY...
PRAISE THE GODDESS. YOU HAVE DELIVERED US! PRAISE YOU, OUR DAUGHTERS OF THE DARK.
THIS IS BUT THE FIRST TRIAL, MOTHER. DEATH'S SHADOW STILL HANGS OVER US ALL.
I DO NOT CARE IF WE DIE. MAKE THEM PAY! MAKE ALL THE JAMBAZI PAY FOR WHAT THEY HAVE DONE TO US!
YOU DESERVED SO MUCH MORE, LITTLE FLOWER. YOU DESERVED A WAKANDA THAT CHERISHED YOU.
BUT THIS IS THE WAKANDA WE HAVE. AND WHILE THE MIDNIGHT ANGELS BREATHE, I SWEAR TO YOU...
NO ONE MAN
"THEY SHALL ALL PAY."

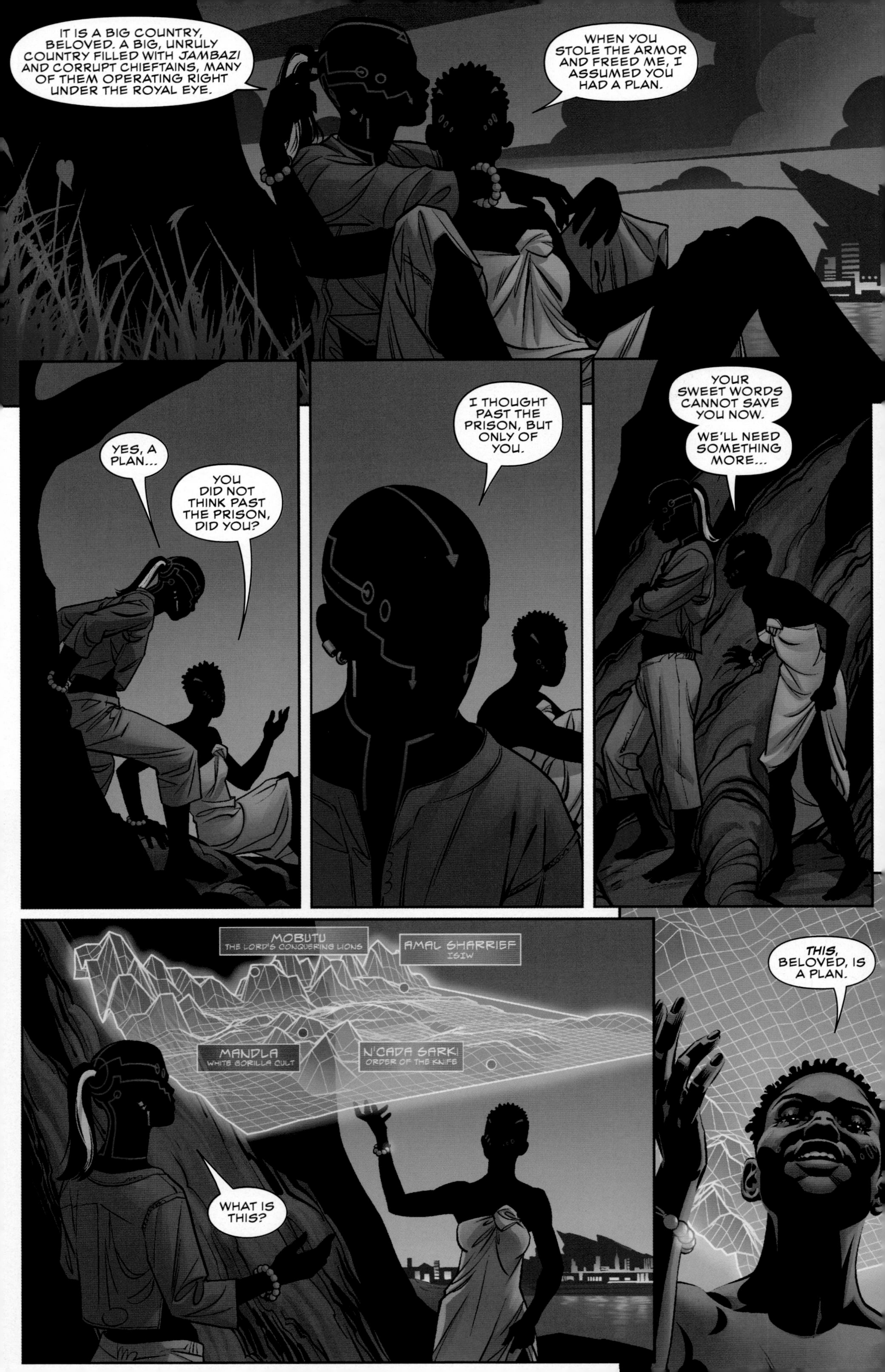
IT IS A BIG COUNTRY, BELOVED. A BIG, UNRULY COUNTRY FILLED WITH JAMBAZI AND CORRUPT CHIEFTAINS, MANY OF THEM OPERATING RIGHT UNDER THE ROYAL EYE.
WHEN YOU STOLE THE ARMOR AND FREED ME, I ASSUMED YOU HAD A PLAN.
YES, A PLAN...
YOU DID NOT THINK PAST THE PRISON, DID YOU?
I THOUGHT PAST THE PRISON, BUT ONLY OF YOU.
YOUR SWEET WORDS CANNOT SAVE YOU NOW.
WE'LL NEED SOMETHING MORE...
MOBUTU
THE LORD'S CONQUERING LIONS
AMAL SHARRIEF
ISIW
MANDLA
WHITE GORILLA CULT
N'CADA SARKI
ORDER OF THE KNIFE
WHAT IS THIS?
THIS, BELOVED, IS A PLAN.

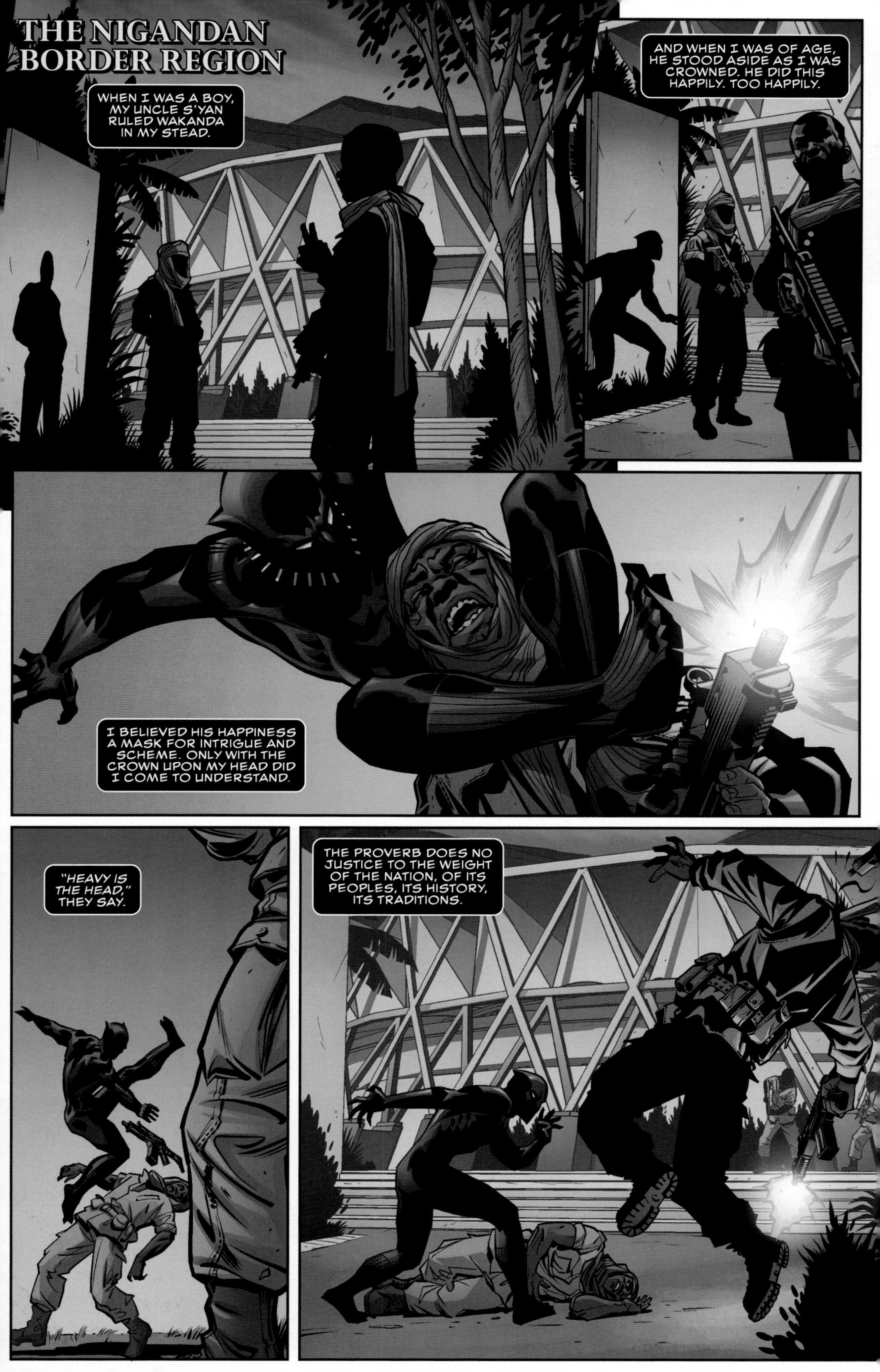
THE NIGANDAN BORDER REGION
WHEN I WAS A BOY, MY UNCLE S'YAN RULED WAKANDA IN MY STEAD.
AND WHEN I WAS OF AGE, HE STOOD ASIDE AS I WAS CROWNED. HE DID THIS HAPPILY. TOO HAPPILY.
I BELIEVED HIS HAPPINESS A MASK FOR INTRIGUE AND SCHEME. ONLY WITH THE CROWN UPON MY HEAD DID I COME TO UNDERSTAND.
"HEAVY IS THE HEAD," THEY SAY.
THE PROVERB DOES NO JUSTICE TO THE WEIGHT OF THE NATION, OF ITS PEOPLES, ITS HISTORY, ITS TRADITIONS.

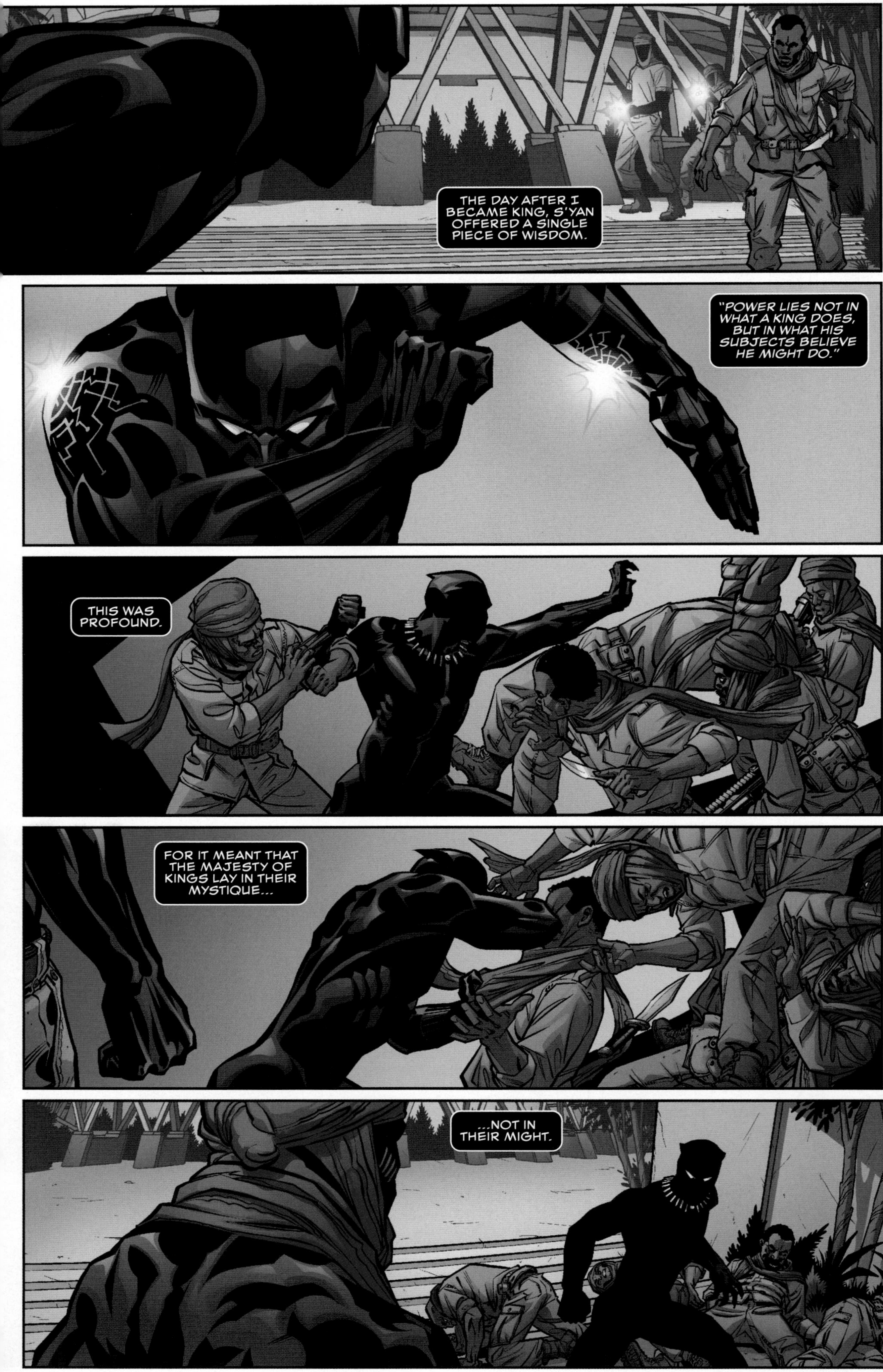
THE DAY AFTER I BECAME KING, S'YAN OFFERED A SINGLE PIECE OF WISDOM.
"POWER LIES NOT IN WHAT A KING DOES, BUT IN WHAT HIS SUBJECTS BELIEVE HE MIGHT DO."
THIS WAS PROFOUND.
FOR IT MEANT THAT THE MAJESTY OF KINGS LAY IN THEIR MYSTIQUE...
...NOT IN THEIR MIGHT.

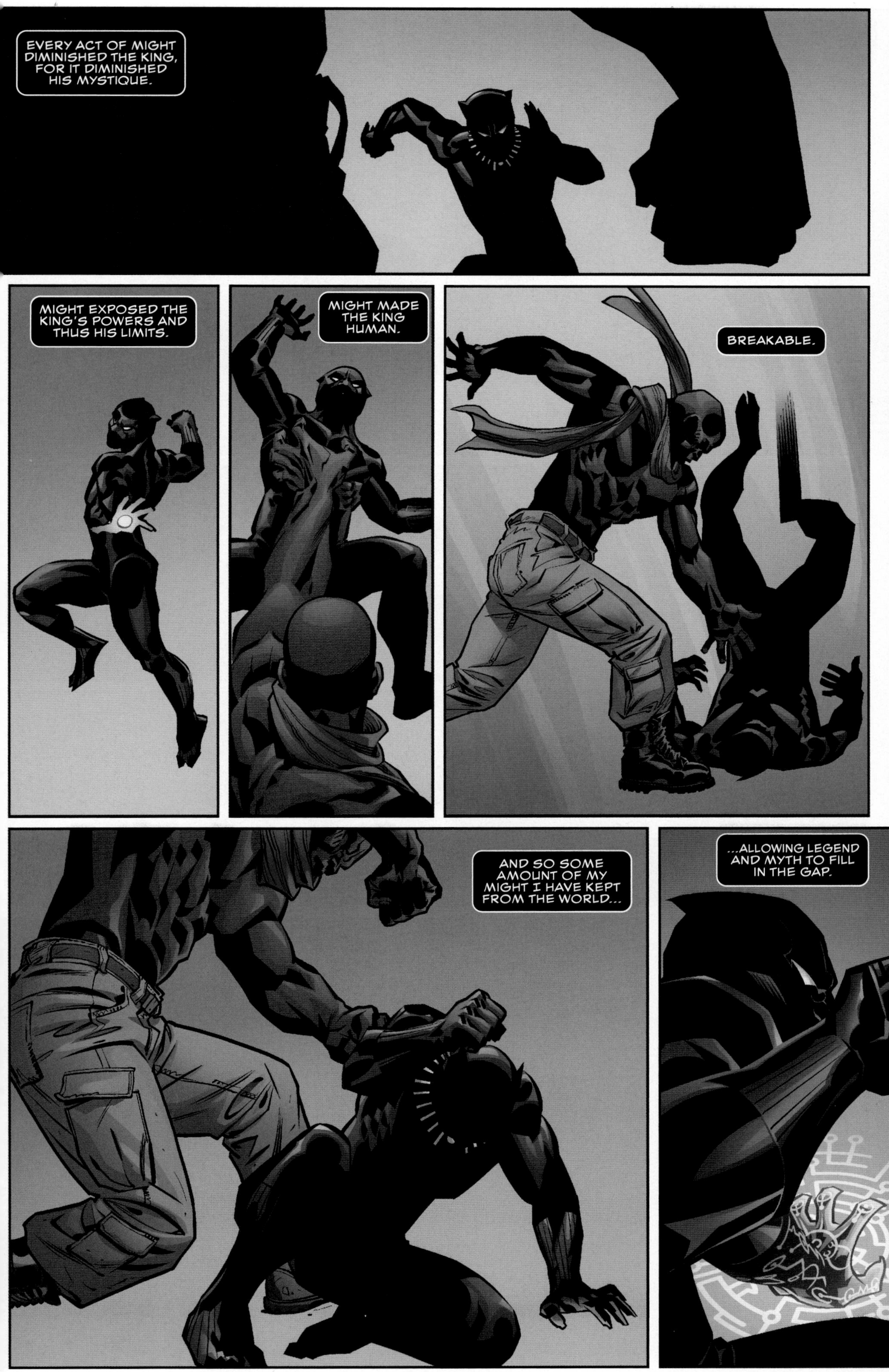

EVERY ACT OF MIGHT DIMINISHED THE KING, FOR IT DIMINISHED HIS MYSTIQUE.
MIGHT EXPOSED THE KING'S POWERS AND THUS HIS LIMITS.
MIGHT MADE THE KING HUMAN.
BREAKABLE.
AND SO SOME AMOUNT OF MY MIGHT I HAVE KEPT FROM THE WORLD...
...ALLOWING LEGEND AND MYTH TO FILL IN THE GAP.

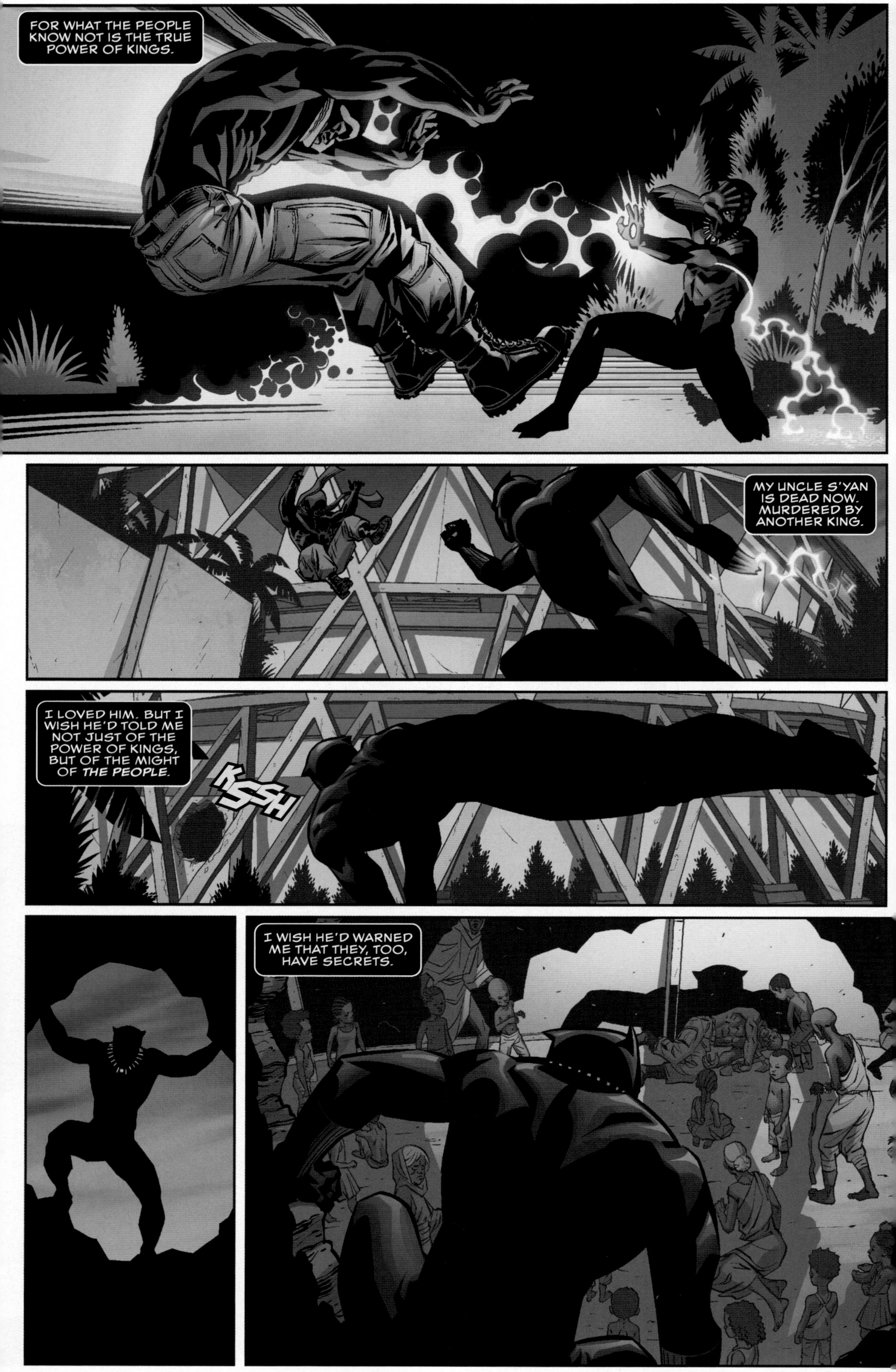
FOR WHAT THE PEOPLE KNOW NOT IS THE TRUE POWER OF KINGS.
MY UNCLE S'YAN IS DEAD NOW. MURDERED BY ANOTHER KING.
I LOVED HIM. BUT I WISH HE'D TOLD ME NOT JUST OF THE POWER OF KINGS, BUT OF THE MIGHT OF *THE PEOPLE*.
KSSH
I WISH HE'D WARNED ME THAT THEY, TOO, HAVE SECRETS.

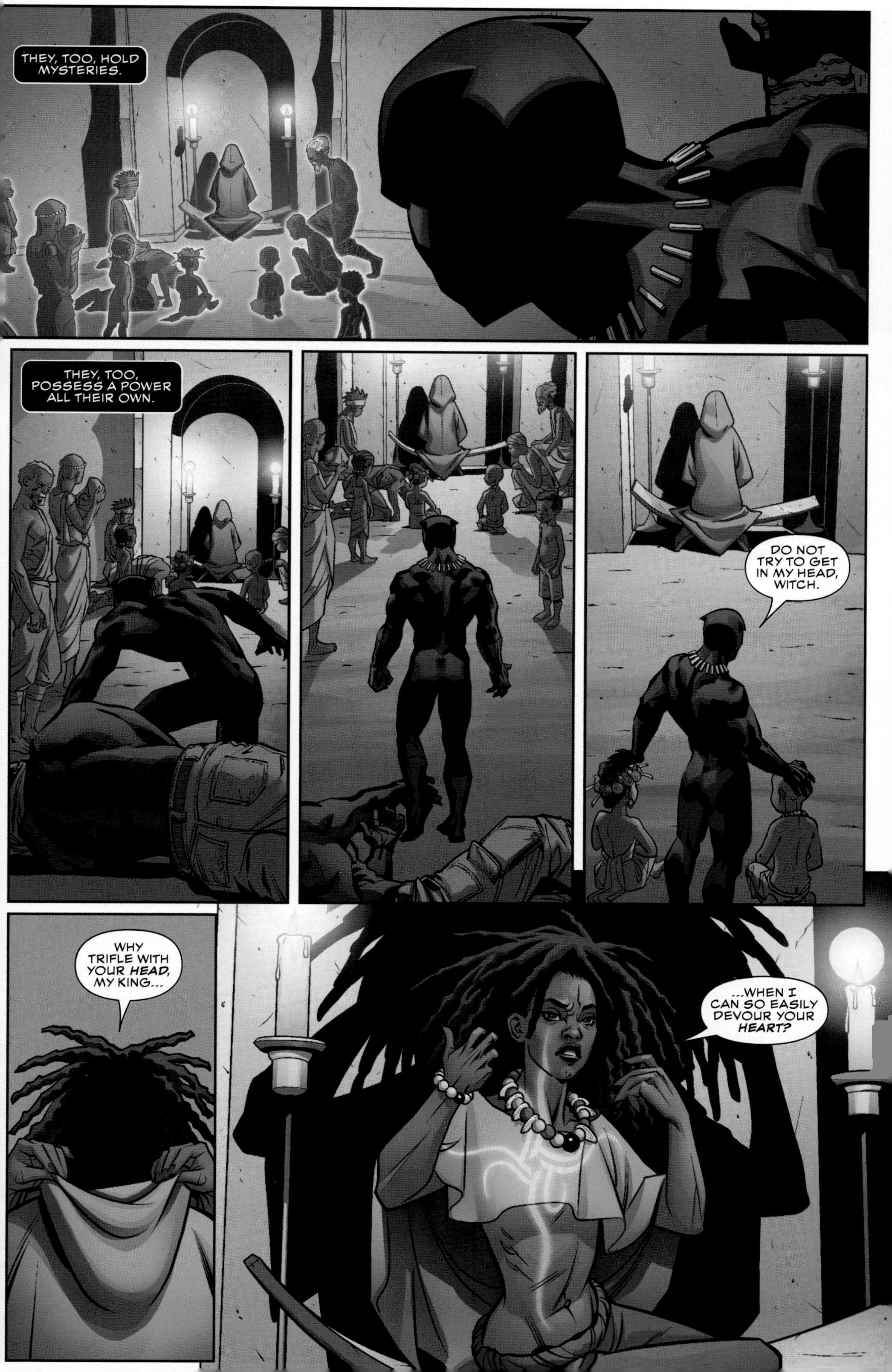
THEY, TOO, HOLD MYSTERIES.
THEY, TOO, POSSESS A POWER ALL THEIR OWN.
DO NOT TRY TO GET IN MY HEAD, WITCH.
WHY TRIFLE WITH YOUR *HEAD*, MY KING...
...WHEN I CAN SO EASILY DEVOUR YOUR *HEART*?

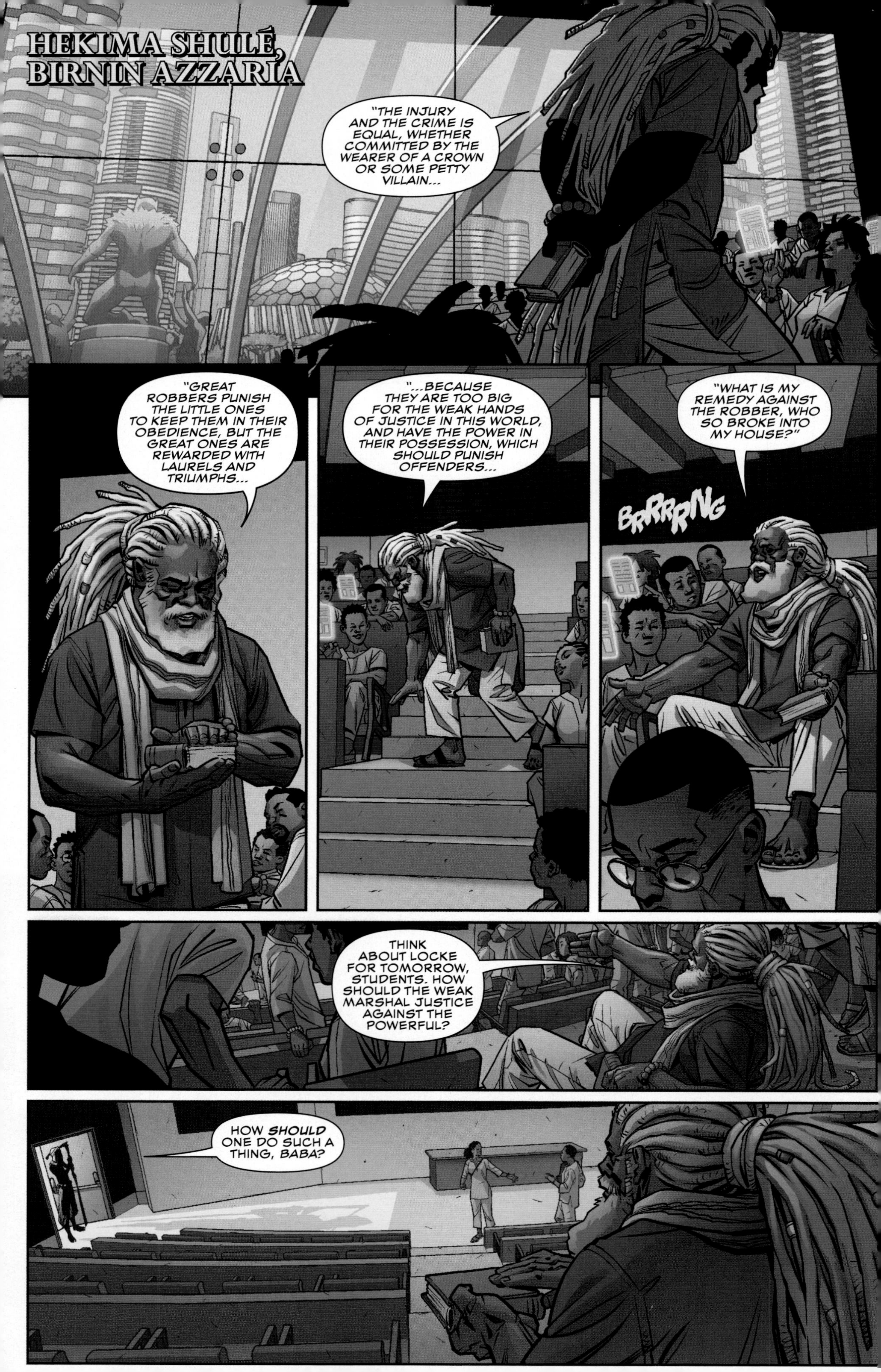
HEKIMA SHULÉ, BIRNIN AZZARIA
"THE INJURY AND THE CRIME IS EQUAL, WHETHER COMMITTED BY THE WEARER OF A CROWN OR SOME PETTY VILLAIN...
"GREAT ROBBERS PUNISH THE LITTLE ONES TO KEEP THEM IN THEIR OBEDIENCE, BUT THE GREAT ONES ARE REWARDED WITH LAURELS AND TRIUMPHS...
"...BECAUSE THEY ARE TOO BIG FOR THE WEAK HANDS OF JUSTICE IN THIS WORLD, AND HAVE THE POWER IN THEIR POSSESSION, WHICH SHOULD PUNISH OFFENDERS...
"WHAT IS MY REMEDY AGAINST THE ROBBER, WHO SO BROKE INTO MY HOUSE?"
BRRRRING
THINK ABOUT LOCKE FOR TOMORROW, STUDENTS. HOW SHOULD THE WEAK MARSHAL JUSTICE AGAINST THE POWERFUL?
HOW SHOULD ONE DO SUCH A THING, BABA?

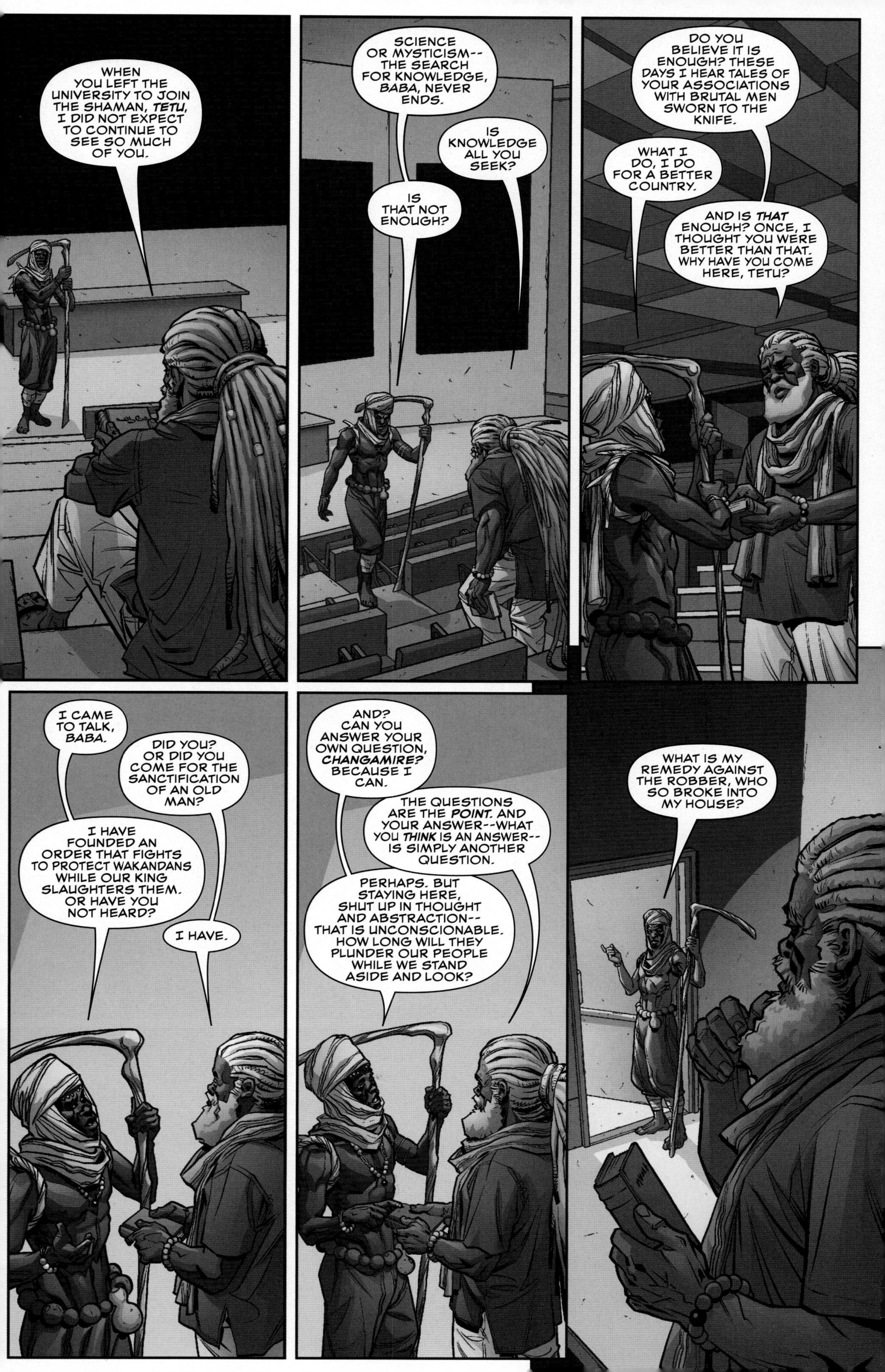
WHEN YOU LEFT THE UNIVERSITY TO JOIN THE SHAMAN, *TETU*, I DID NOT EXPECT TO CONTINUE TO SEE SO MUCH OF YOU.
SCIENCE OR MYSTICISM-- THE SEARCH FOR KNOWLEDGE, *BABA*, NEVER ENDS.
IS KNOWLEDGE ALL YOU SEEK?
IS THAT NOT ENOUGH?
DO YOU BELIEVE IT IS ENOUGH? THESE DAYS I HEAR TALES OF YOUR ASSOCIATIONS WITH BRUTAL MEN SWORN TO THE KNIFE.
WHAT I DO, I DO FOR A BETTER COUNTRY.
AND IS *THAT* ENOUGH? ONCE, I THOUGHT YOU WERE BETTER THAN THAT. WHY HAVE YOU COME HERE, TETU?
I CAME TO TALK, *BABA.*
DID YOU? OR DID YOU COME FOR THE SANCTIFICATION OF AN OLD MAN?
I HAVE FOUNDED AN ORDER THAT FIGHTS TO PROTECT WAKANDANS WHILE OUR KING SLAUGHTERS THEM. OR HAVE YOU NOT HEARD?
I HAVE.
AND? CAN YOU ANSWER YOUR OWN QUESTION, *CHANGAMIRE?* BECAUSE I CAN.
THE QUESTIONS ARE THE *POINT.* AND YOUR ANSWER--WHAT YOU *THINK* IS AN ANSWER-- IS SIMPLY ANOTHER QUESTION.
PERHAPS. BUT STAYING HERE, SHUT UP IN THOUGHT AND ABSTRACTION-- THAT IS UNCONSCIONABLE. HOW LONG WILL THEY PLUNDER OUR PEOPLE WHILE WE STAND ASIDE AND LOOK?
WHAT IS MY REMEDY AGAINST THE ROBBER, WHO SO BROKE INTO MY HOUSE?

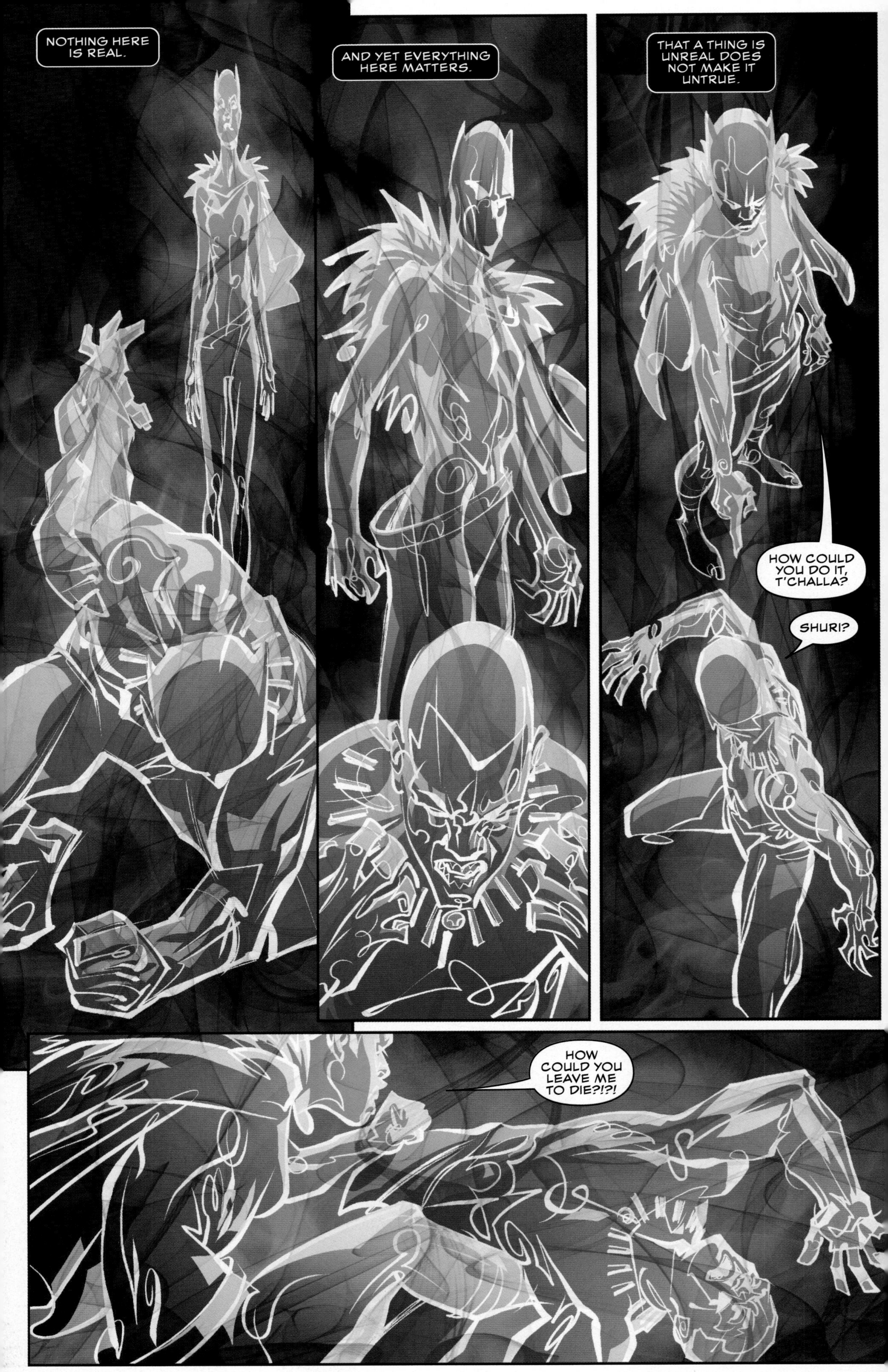
NOTHING HERE IS REAL.
AND YET EVERYTHING HERE MATTERS.
THAT A THING IS UNREAL DOES NOT MAKE IT UNTRUE.
HOW COULD YOU DO IT, T'CHALLA?
SHURI!?
HOW COULD YOU LEAVE ME TO DIE?!?!

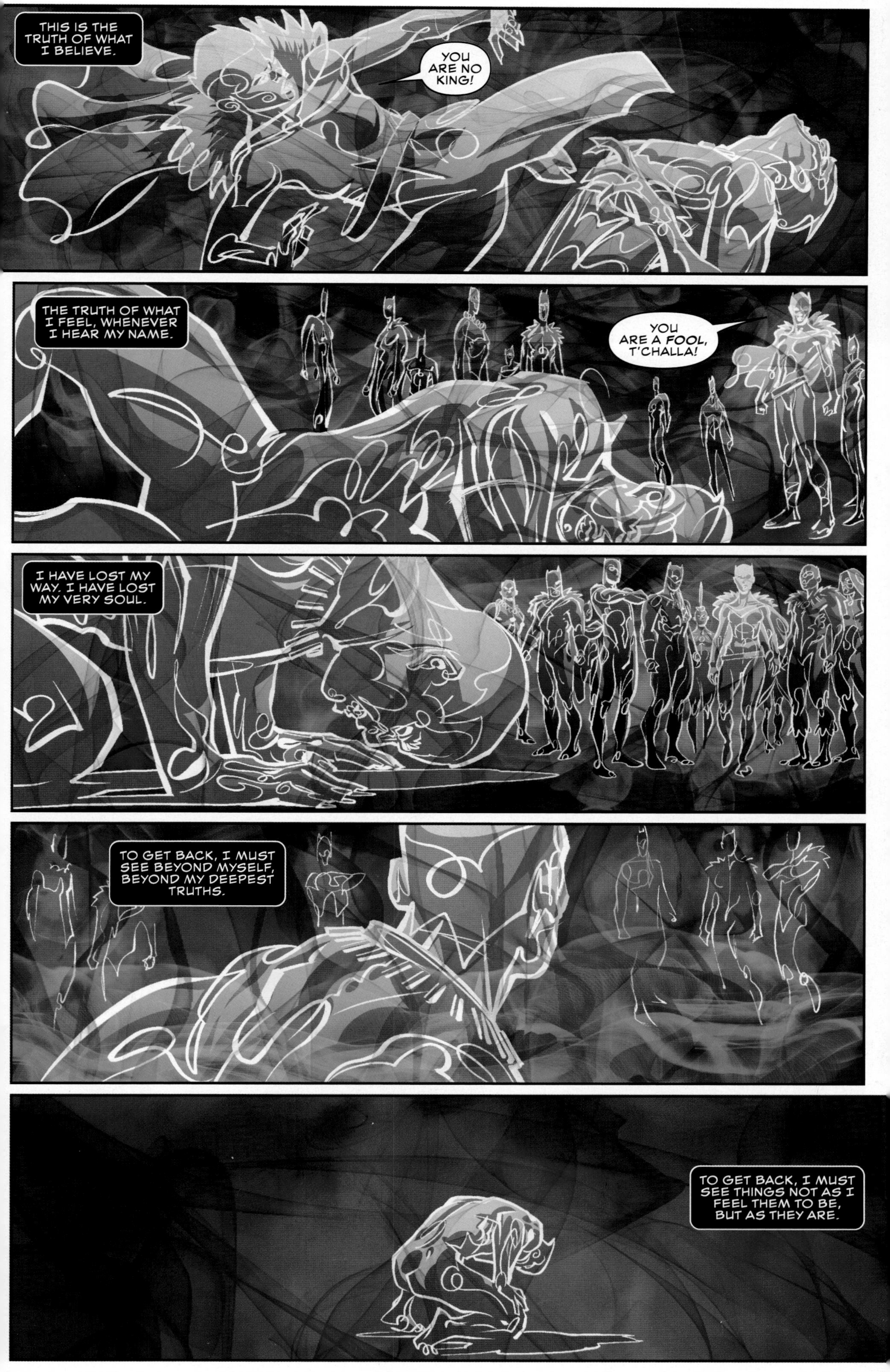
THIS IS THE TRUTH OF WHAT I BELIEVE.
YOU ARE NO KING!
THE TRUTH OF WHAT I FEEL, WHENEVER I HEAR MY NAME.
YOU ARE A FOOL, T'CHALLA!
I HAVE LOST MY WAY. I HAVE LOST MY VERY SOUL.
TO GET BACK, I MUST SEE BEYOND MYSELF, BEYOND MY DEEPEST TRUTHS.
TO GET BACK, I MUST SEE THINGS NOT AS I FEEL THEM TO BE, BUT AS THEY ARE.

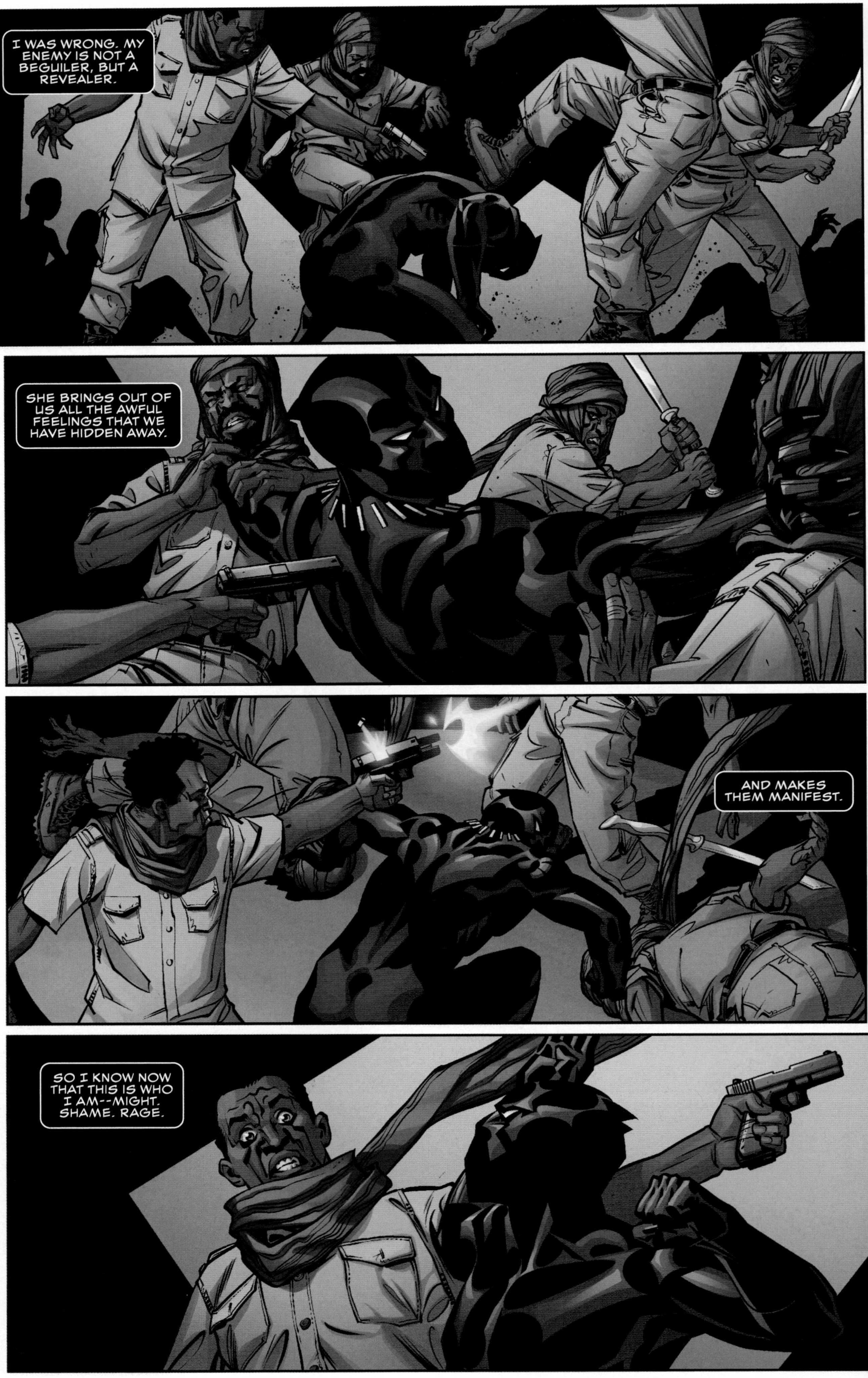
I WAS WRONG. MY ENEMY IS NOT A BEGUILER, BUT A REVEALER.
SHE BRINGS OUT OF US ALL THE AWFUL FEELINGS THAT WE HAVE HIDDEN AWAY.
AND MAKES THEM MANIFEST.
SO I KNOW NOW THAT THIS IS WHO I AM--MIGHT. SHAME. RAGE.

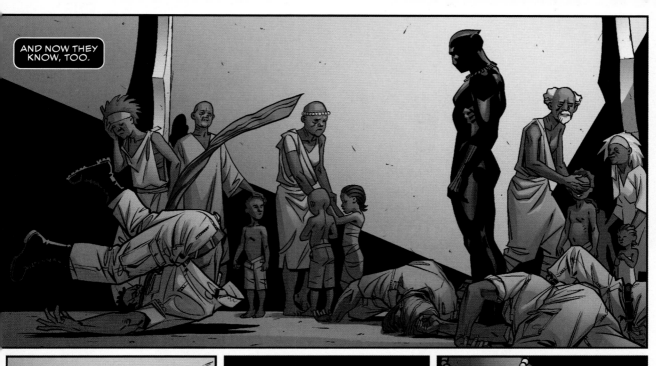

AND NOW THEY KNOW, TOO.

THESE MEN ARE RESPONSIBLE FOR CRIMES AGAINST YOUR COUNTRY. THEY WILL BE BROUGHT TO JUSTICE.

YOUR KING WILL PROVIDE FOR YOU.

THESE MEN WERE PROVIDING FOR US.

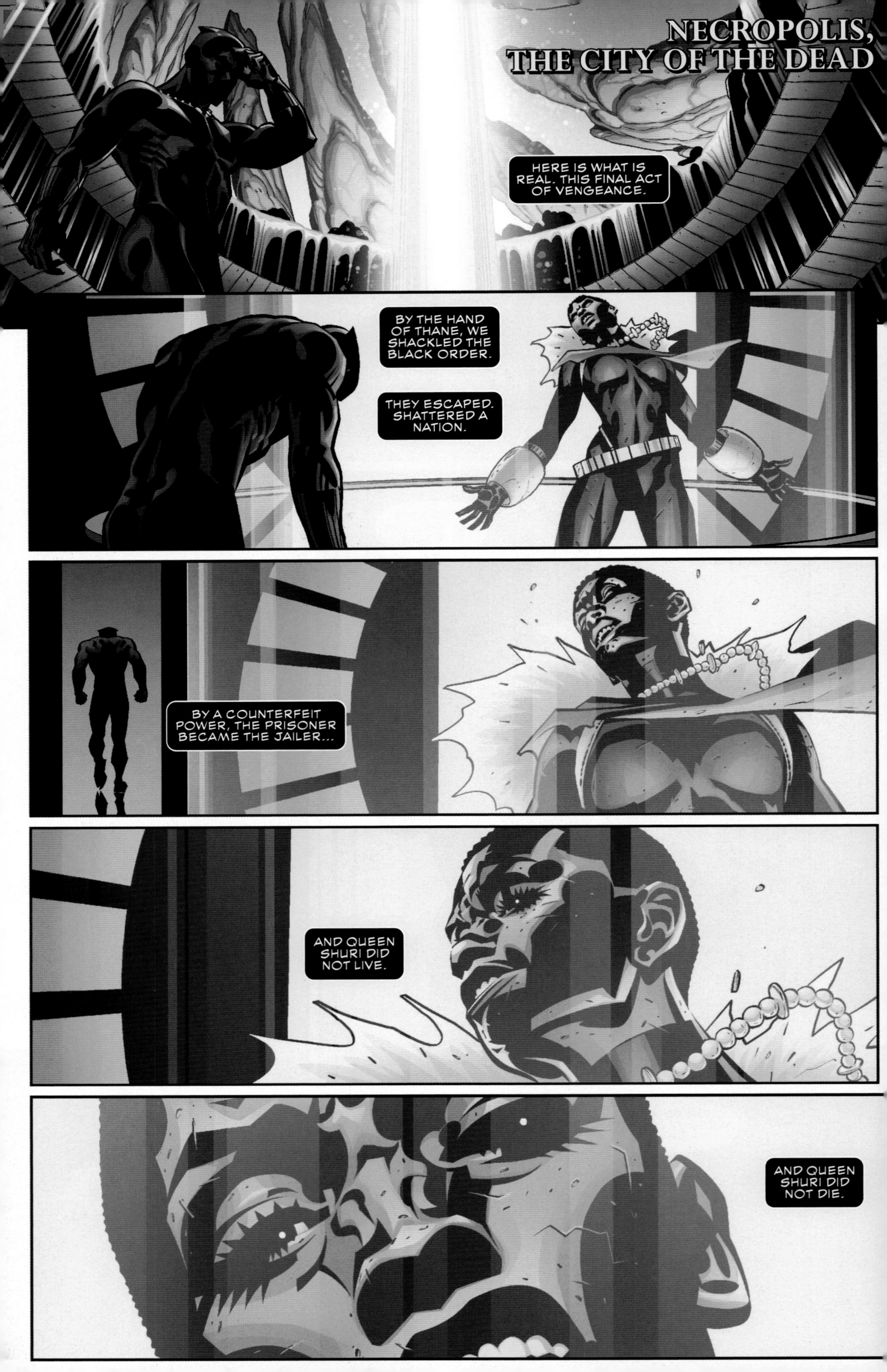
NECROPOLIS, THE CITY OF THE DEAD
HERE IS WHAT IS REAL. THIS FINAL ACT OF VENGEANCE.
BY THE HAND OF THANE, WE SHACKLED THE BLACK ORDER.
THEY ESCAPED. SHATTERED A NATION.
BY A COUNTERFEIT POWER, THE PRISONER BECAME THE JAILER...
AND QUEEN SHURI DID NOT LIVE.
AND QUEEN SHURI DID NOT DIE.

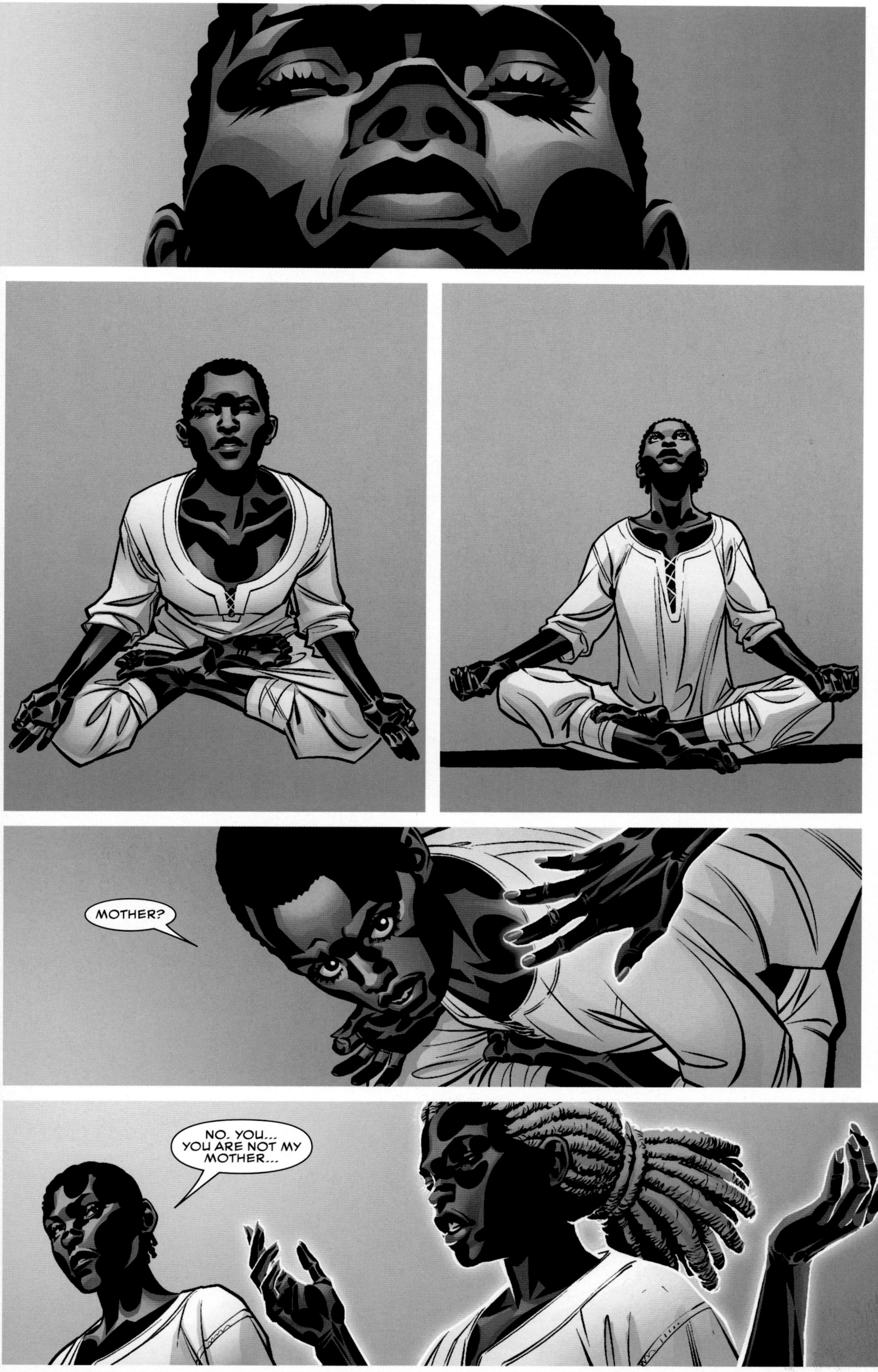
MOTHER?
NO. YOU... YOU ARE NOT MY MOTHER...

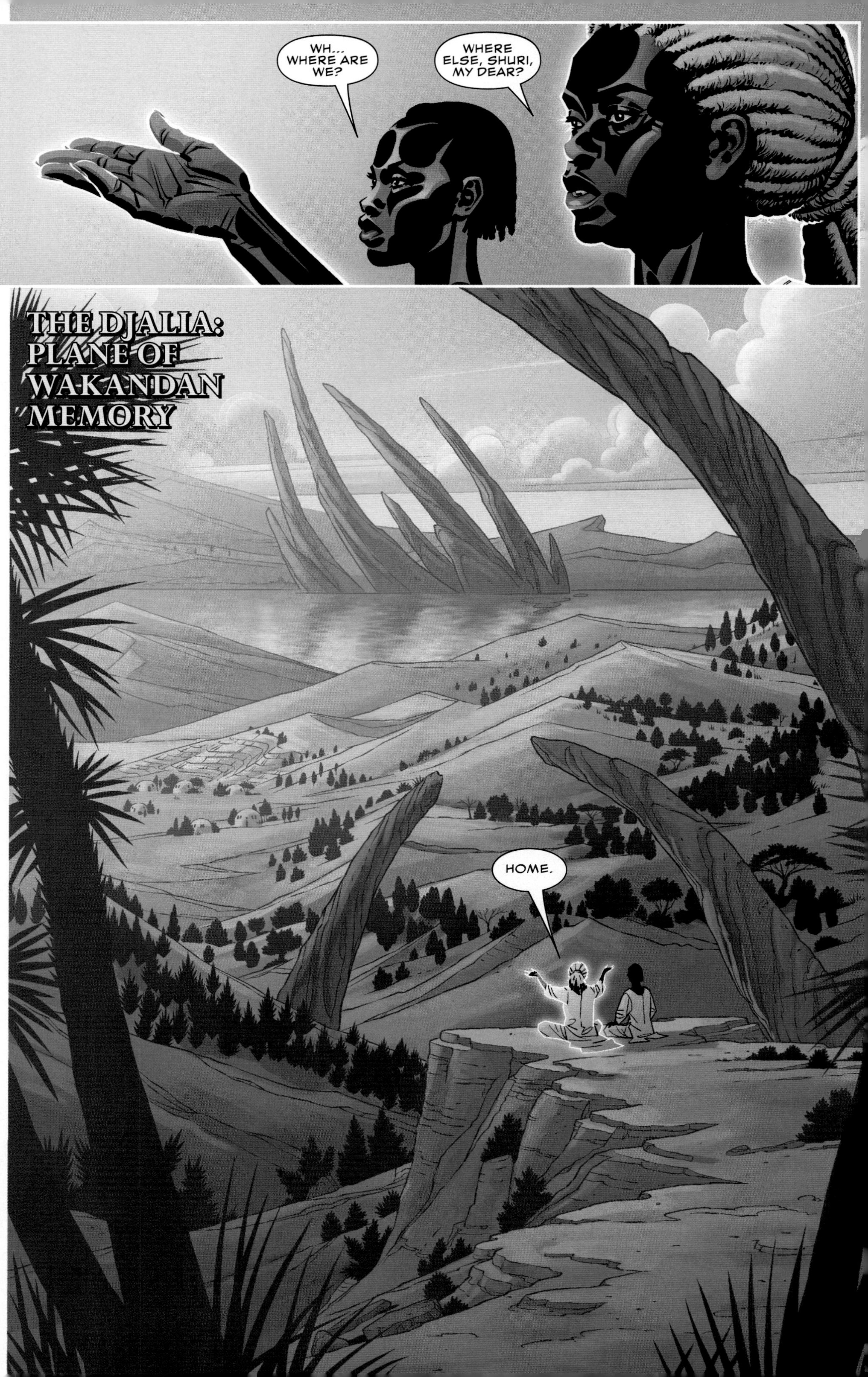
WH... WHERE ARE WE?
WHERE ELSE, SHURI, MY DEAR?
THE DJALIA: PLANE OF WAKANDAN MEMORY
HOME.

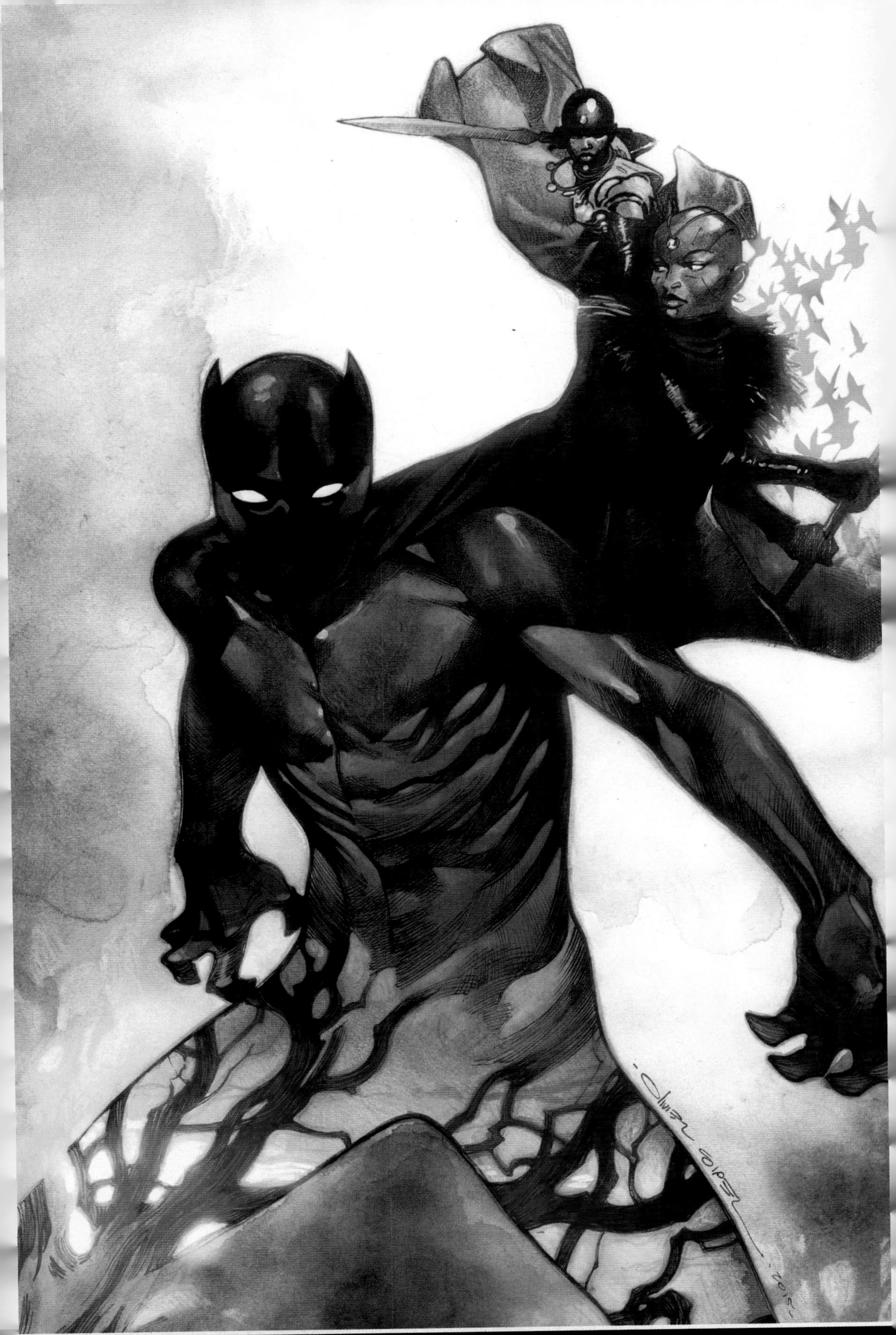

#1 VARIANT BY **OLIVIER COIPEL**

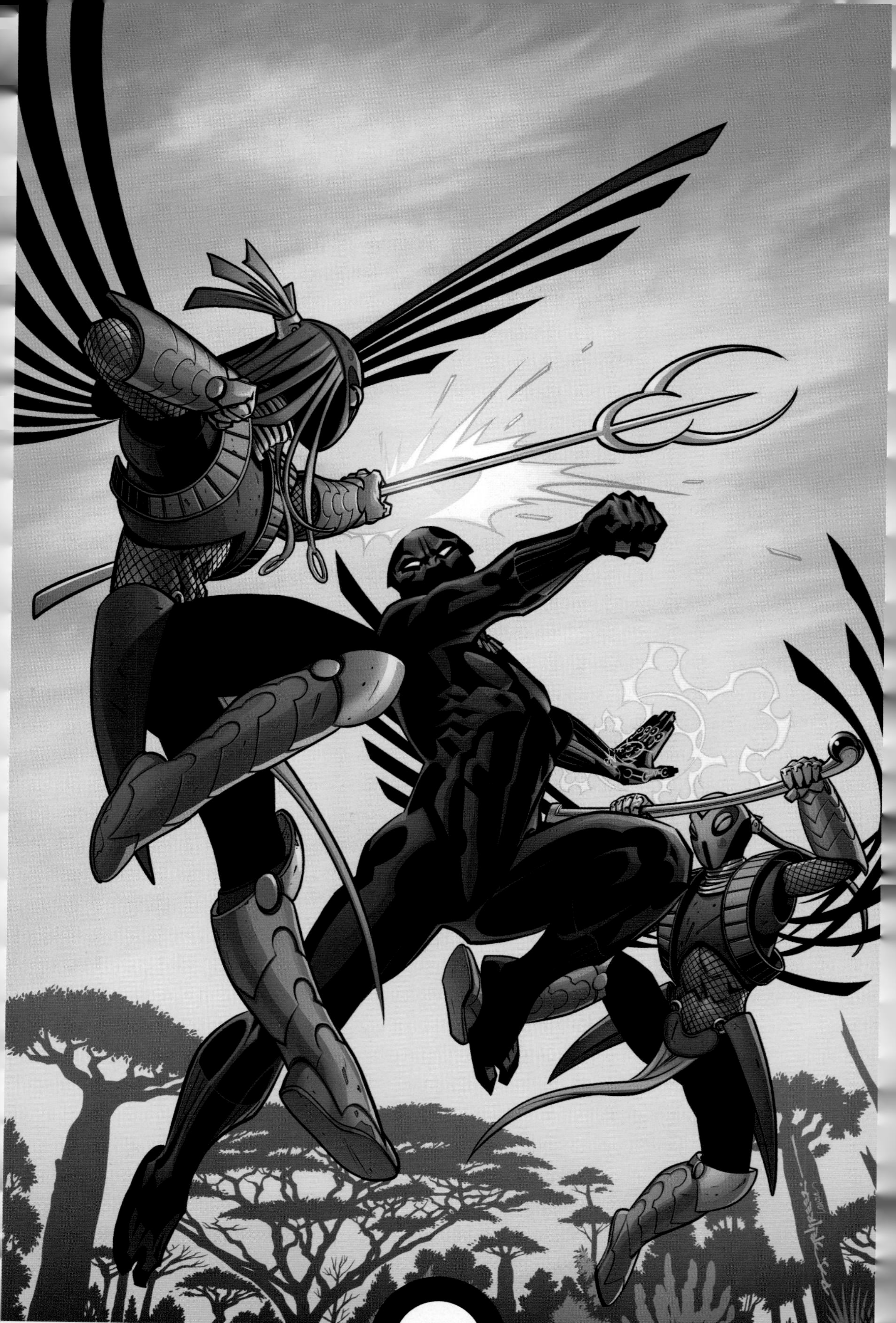

3

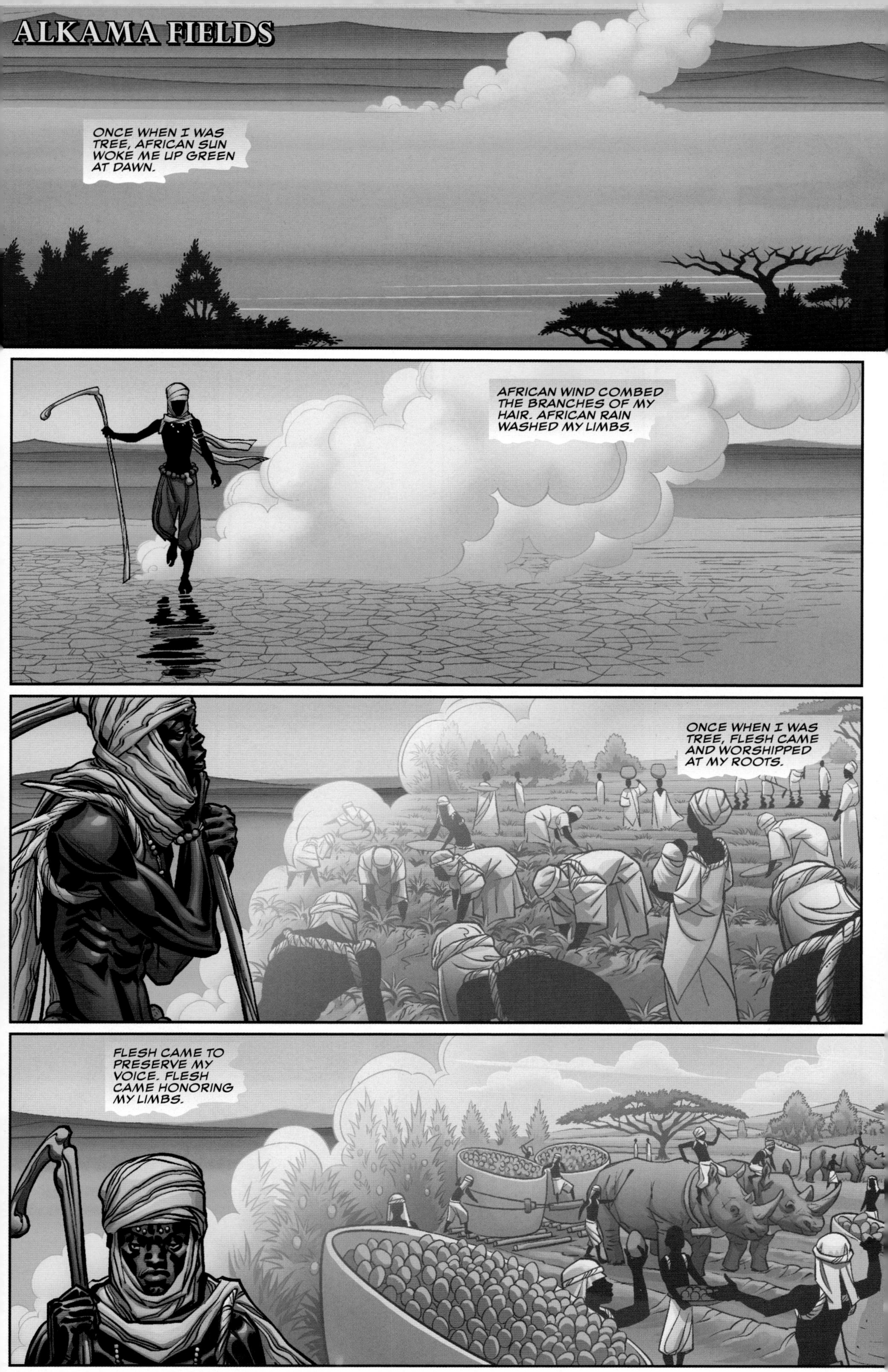
ALKAMA FIELDS
ONCE WHEN I WAS TREE, AFRICAN SUN WOKE ME UP GREEN AT DAWN.
AFRICAN WIND COMBED THE BRANCHES OF MY HAIR. AFRICAN RAIN WASHED MY LIMBS.
ONCE WHEN I WAS TREE, FLESH CAME AND WORSHIPPED AT MY ROOTS.
FLESH CAME TO PRESERVE MY VOICE. FLESH CAME HONORING MY LIMBS.

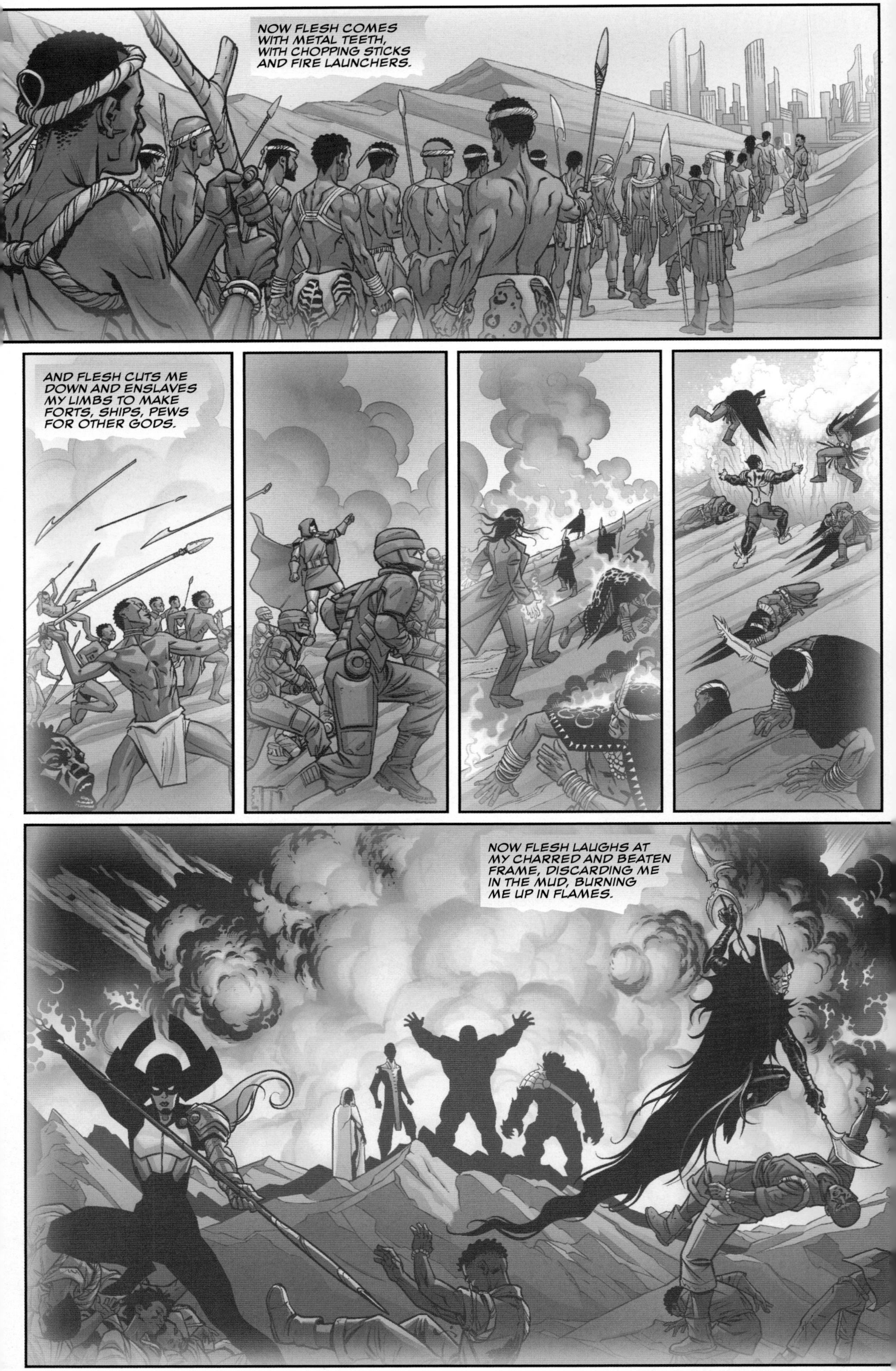
NOW FLESH COMES WITH METAL TEETH, WITH CHOPPING STICKS AND FIRE LAUNCHERS.
AND FLESH CUTS ME DOWN AND ENSLAVES MY LIMBS TO MAKE FORTS, SHIPS, PEWS FOR OTHER GODS.
NOW FLESH LAUGHS AT MY CHARRED AND BEATEN FRAME, DISCARDING ME IN THE MUD, BURNING ME UP IN FLAMES.

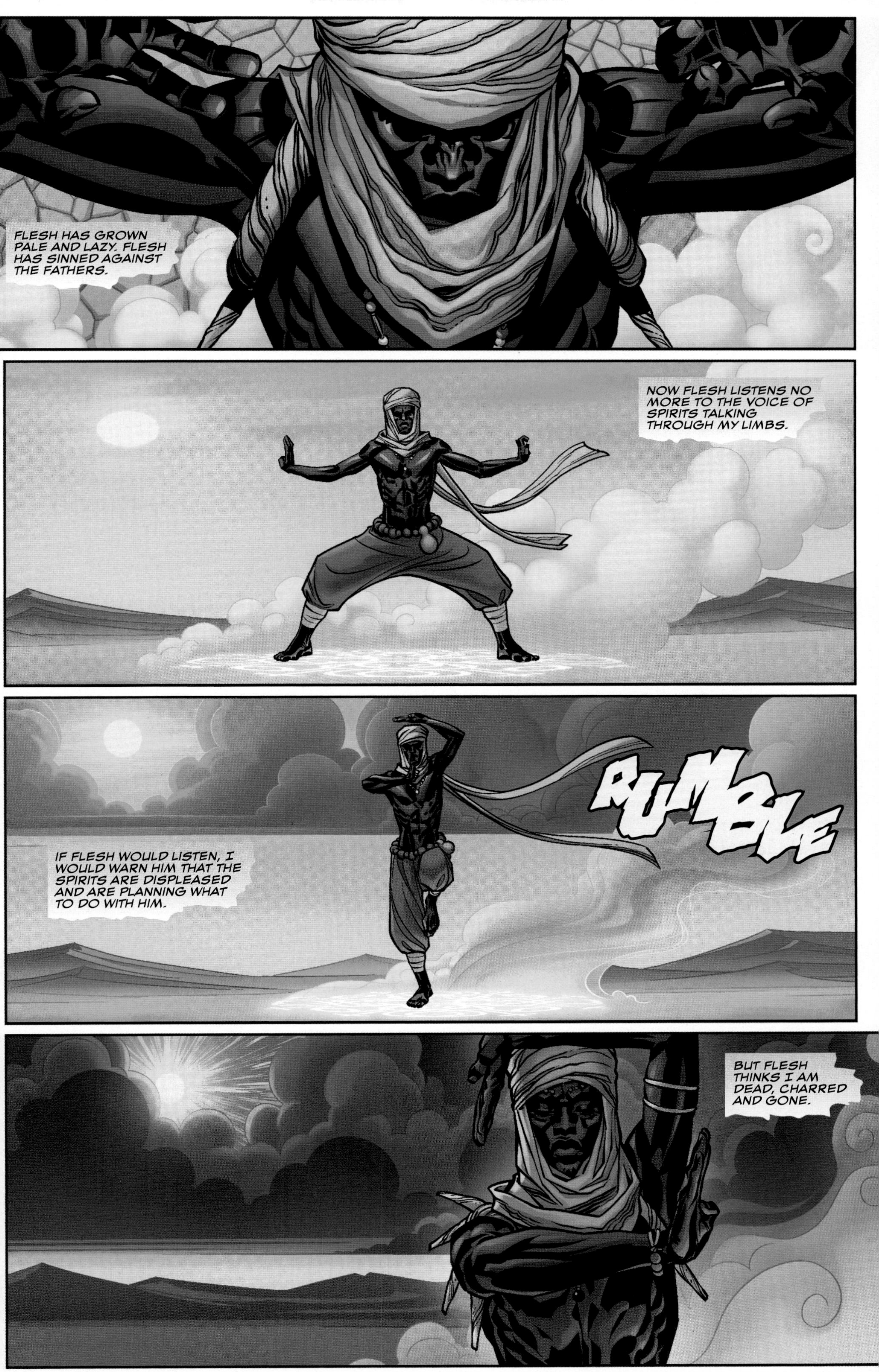
FLESH HAS GROWN PALE AND LAZY. FLESH HAS SINNED AGAINST THE FATHERS.
NOW FLESH LISTENS NO MORE TO THE VOICE OF SPIRITS TALKING THROUGH MY LIMBS.
RUMBLE
IF FLESH WOULD LISTEN, I WOULD WARN HIM THAT THE SPIRITS ARE DISPLEASED AND ARE PLANNING WHAT TO DO WITH HIM.
BUT FLESH THINKS I AM DEAD, CHARRED AND GONE.

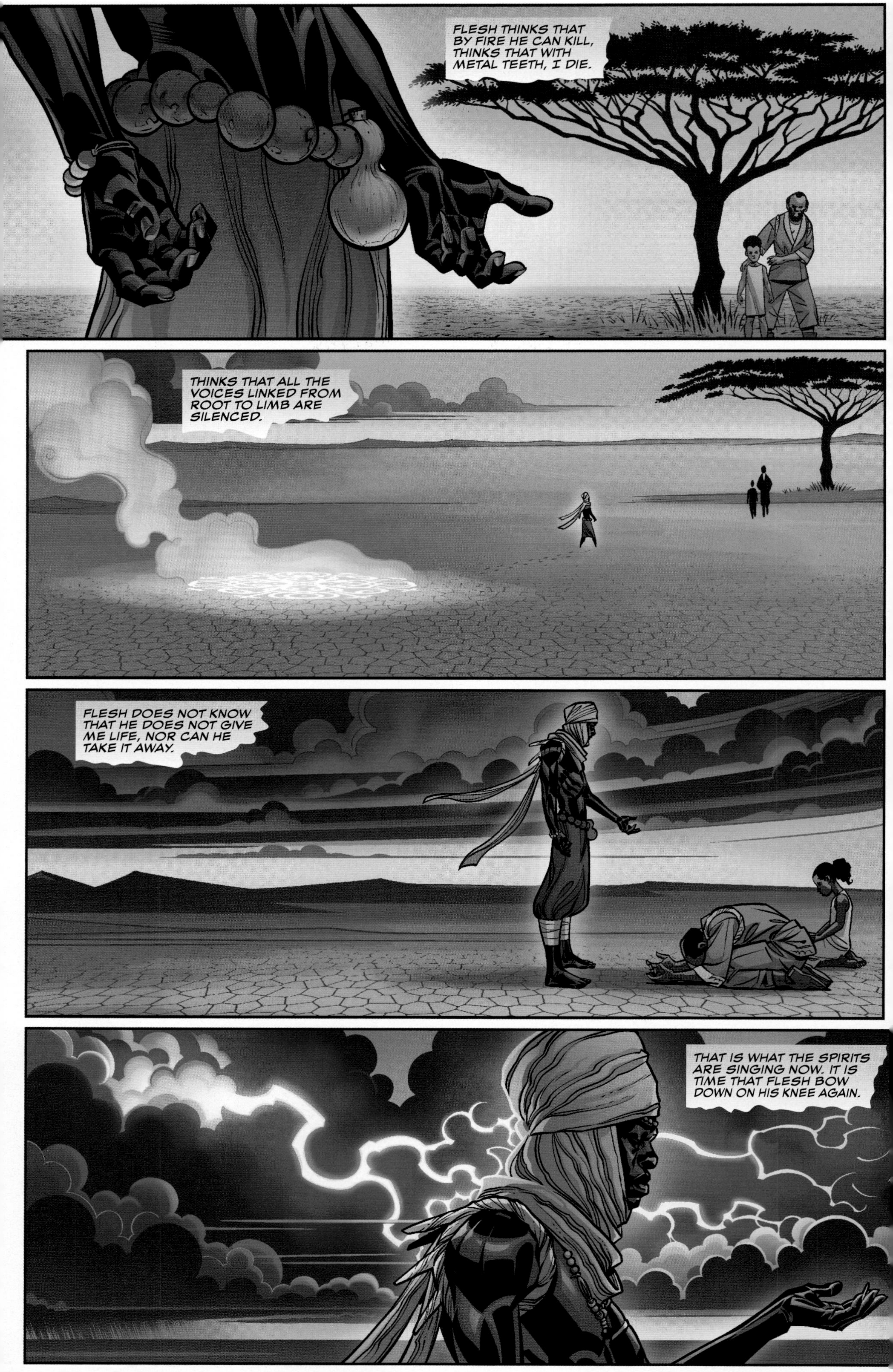
FLESH THINKS THAT BY FIRE HE CAN KILL, THINKS THAT WITH METAL TEETH, I DIE.
THINKS THAT ALL THE VOICES LINKED FROM ROOT TO LIMB ARE SILENCED.
FLESH DOES NOT KNOW THAT HE DOES NOT GIVE ME LIFE, NOR CAN HE TAKE IT AWAY.
THAT IS WHAT THE SPIRITS ARE SINGING NOW. IT IS TIME THAT FLESH BOW DOWN ON HIS KNEE AGAIN.

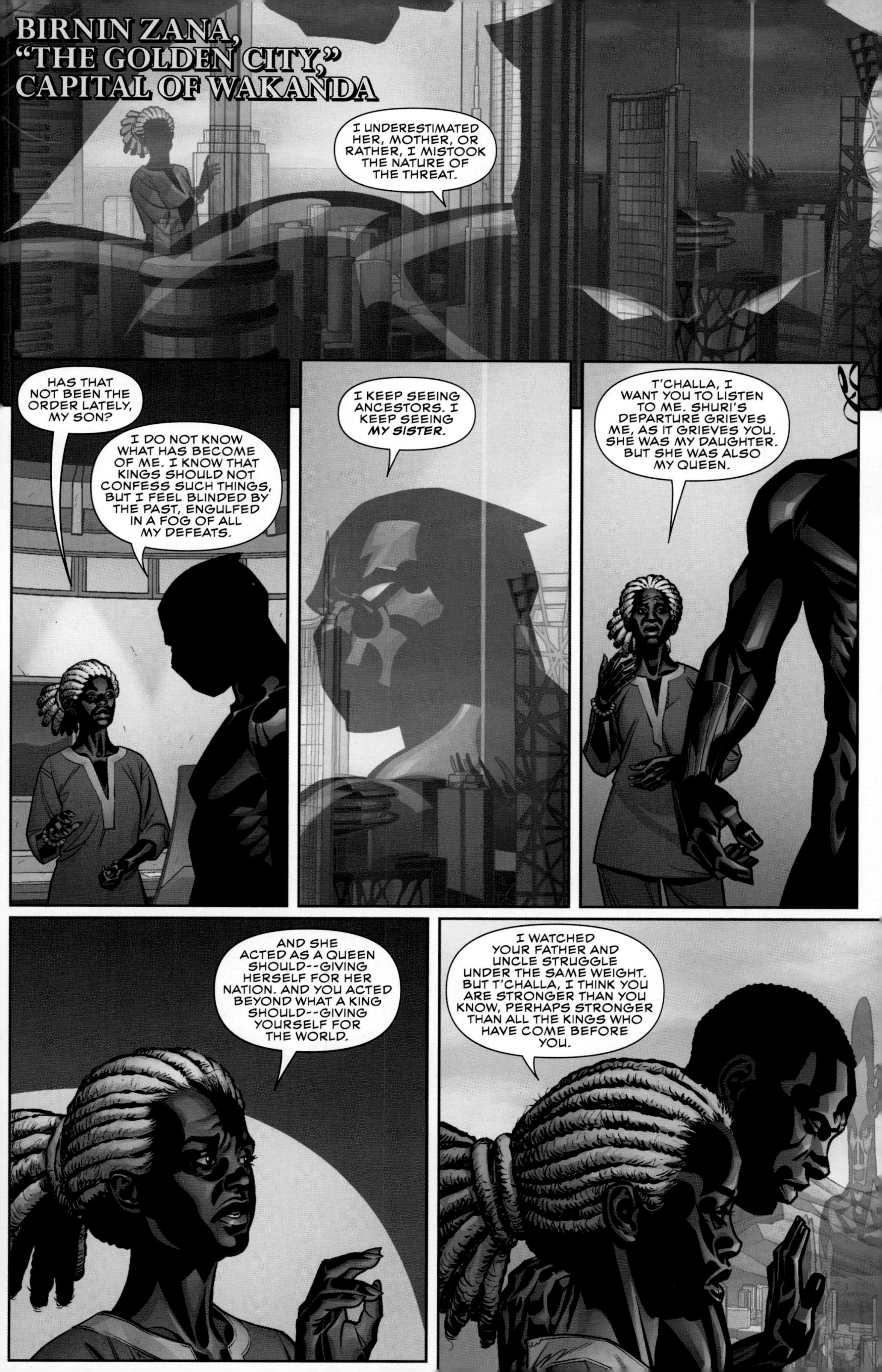
BIRNIN ZANA, "THE GOLDEN CITY," CAPITAL OF WAKANDA
I UNDERESTIMATED HER, MOTHER, OR RATHER, I MISTOOK THE NATURE OF THE THREAT.
HAS THAT NOT BEEN THE ORDER LATELY, MY SON?
I DO NOT KNOW WHAT HAS BECOME OF ME. I KNOW THAT KINGS SHOULD NOT CONFESS SUCH THINGS, BUT I FEEL BLINDED BY THE PAST, ENGULFED IN A FOG OF ALL MY DEFEATS.
I KEEP SEEING ANCESTORS. I KEEP SEEING MY SISTER.
T'CHALLA, I WANT YOU TO LISTEN TO ME. SHURI'S DEPARTURE GRIEVES ME, AS IT GRIEVES YOU. SHE WAS MY DAUGHTER. BUT SHE WAS ALSO MY QUEEN.
AND SHE ACTED AS A QUEEN SHOULD--GIVING HERSELF FOR HER NATION. AND YOU ACTED BEYOND WHAT A KING SHOULD--GIVING YOURSELF FOR THE WORLD.
I WATCHED YOUR FATHER AND UNCLE STRUGGLE UNDER THE SAME WEIGHT. BUT T'CHALLA, I THINK YOU ARE STRONGER THAN YOU KNOW, PERHAPS STRONGER THAN ALL THE KINGS WHO HAVE COME BEFORE YOU.

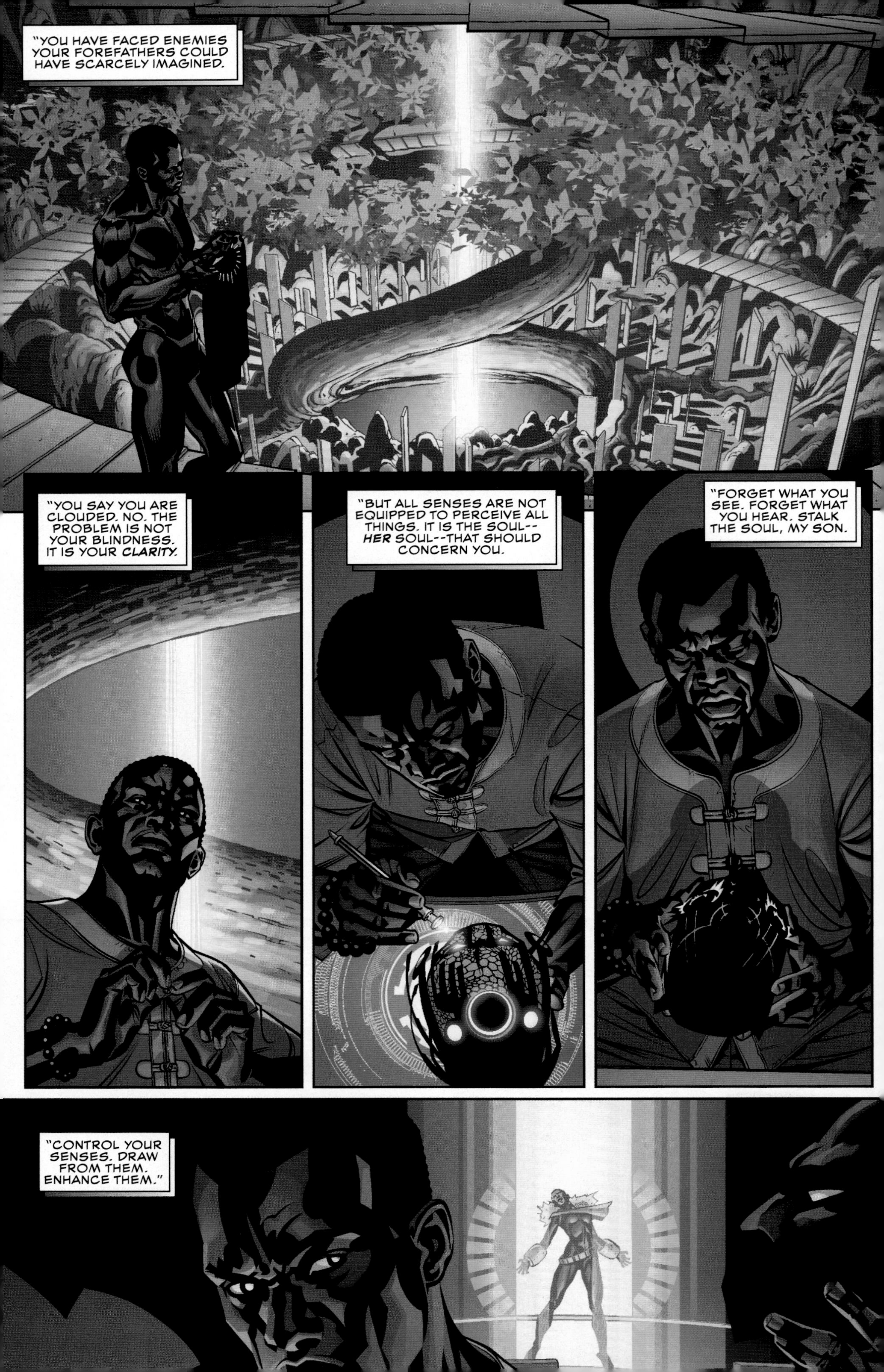
"YOU HAVE FACED ENEMIES YOUR FOREFATHERS COULD HAVE SCARCELY IMAGINED.
"YOU SAY YOU ARE CLOUDED. NO. THE PROBLEM IS NOT YOUR BLINDNESS. IT IS YOUR CLARITY.
"BUT ALL SENSES ARE NOT EQUIPPED TO PERCEIVE ALL THINGS. IT IS THE SOUL-- HER SOUL--THAT SHOULD CONCERN YOU.
"FORGET WHAT YOU SEE. FORGET WHAT YOU HEAR. STALK THE SOUL, MY SON.
"CONTROL YOUR SENSES. DRAW FROM THEM. ENHANCE THEM."

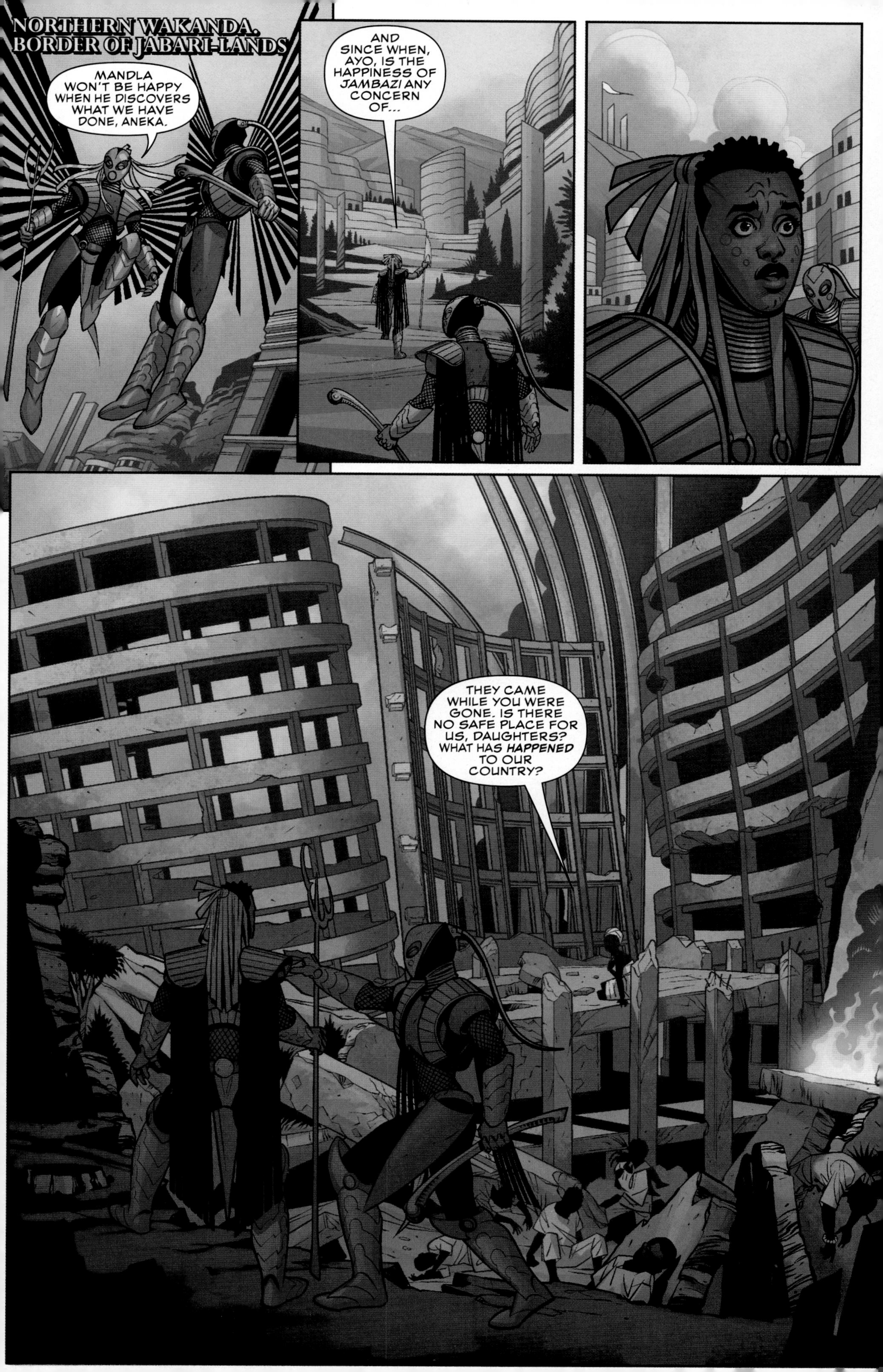
NORTHERN WAKANDA. BORDER OF JABARI-LANDS
MANDLA WON'T BE HAPPY WHEN HE DISCOVERS WHAT WE HAVE DONE, ANEKA.
AND SINCE WHEN, AYO, IS THE HAPPINESS OF JAMBAZI ANY CONCERN OF...
THEY CAME WHILE YOU WERE GONE. IS THERE NO SAFE PLACE FOR US, DAUGHTERS? WHAT HAS HAPPENED TO OUR COUNTRY?

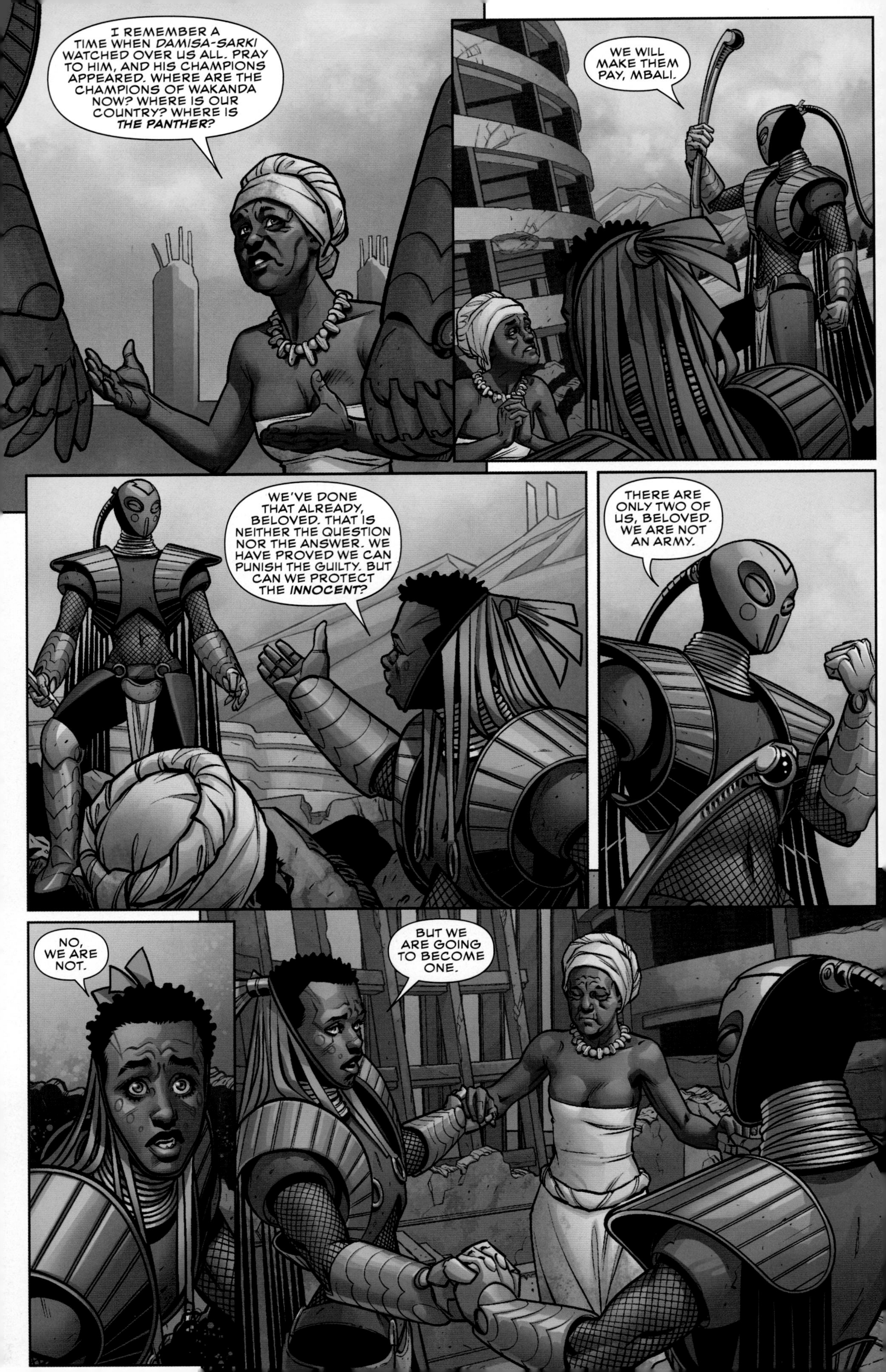
I REMEMBER A TIME WHEN *DAMISA-SARKI* WATCHED OVER US ALL. PRAY TO HIM, AND HIS CHAMPIONS APPEARED. WHERE ARE THE CHAMPIONS OF WAKANDA NOW? WHERE IS OUR COUNTRY? WHERE IS *THE PANTHER?*
WE WILL MAKE THEM PAY, MBALI.
WE'VE DONE THAT ALREADY, BELOVED. THAT IS NEITHER THE QUESTION NOR THE ANSWER. WE HAVE PROVED WE CAN PUNISH THE GUILTY. BUT CAN WE PROTECT THE *INNOCENT?*
THERE ARE ONLY TWO OF US, BELOVED. WE ARE NOT AN ARMY.
NO, WE ARE NOT.
BUT WE ARE GOING TO BECOME ONE.

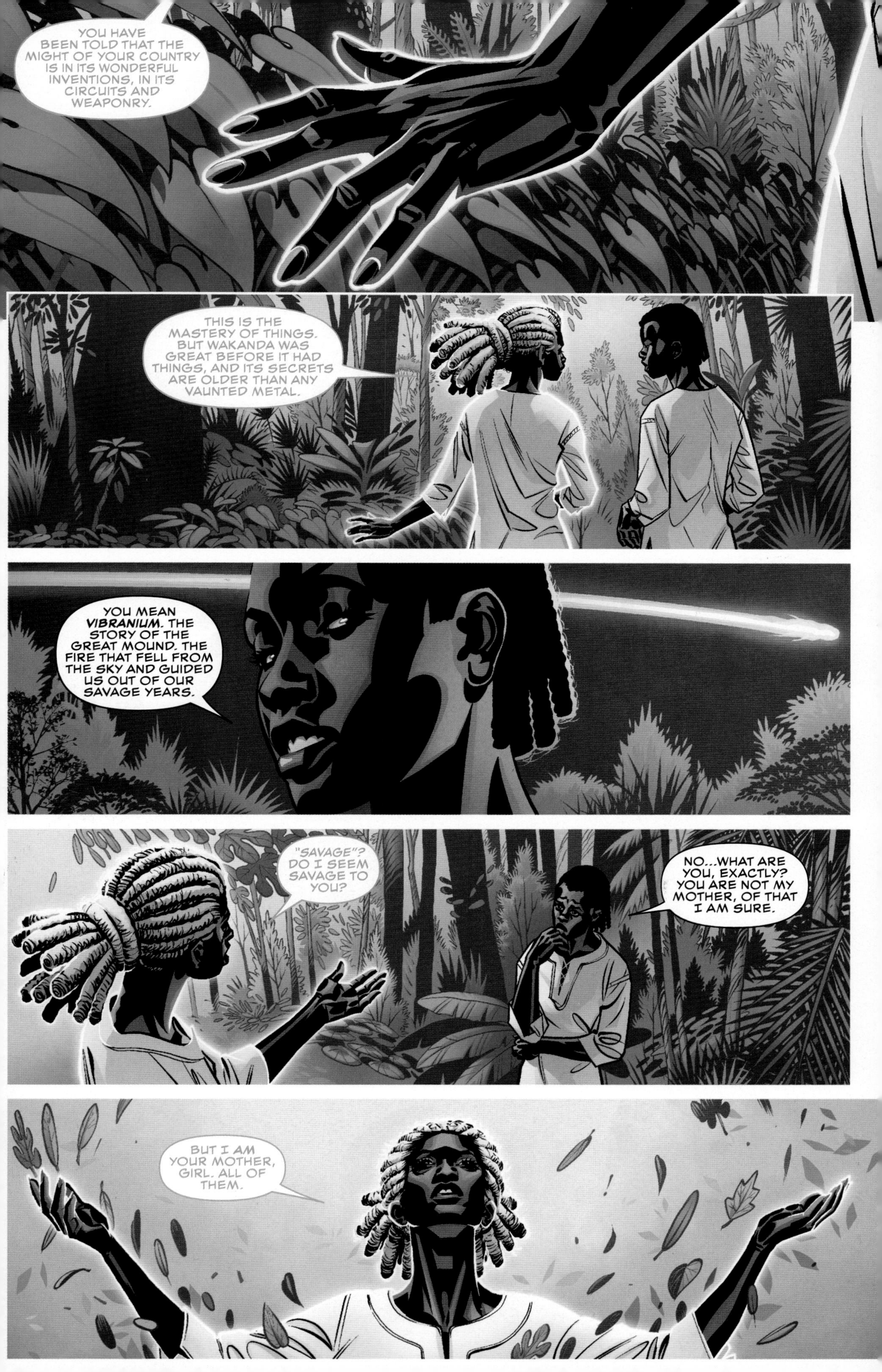
YOU HAVE BEEN TOLD THAT THE MIGHT OF YOUR COUNTRY IS IN ITS WONDERFUL INVENTIONS, IN ITS CIRCUITS AND WEAPONRY.
THIS IS THE MASTERY OF THINGS. BUT WAKANDA WAS GREAT BEFORE IT HAD THINGS, AND ITS SECRETS ARE OLDER THAN ANY VAUNTED METAL.
YOU MEAN VIBRANIUM. THE STORY OF THE GREAT MOUND. THE FIRE THAT FELL FROM THE SKY AND GUIDED US OUT OF OUR SAVAGE YEARS.
"SAVAGE"? DO I SEEM SAVAGE TO YOU?
NO...WHAT ARE YOU, EXACTLY? YOU ARE NOT MY MOTHER, OF THAT I AM SURE.
BUT I AM YOUR MOTHER, GIRL. ALL OF THEM.

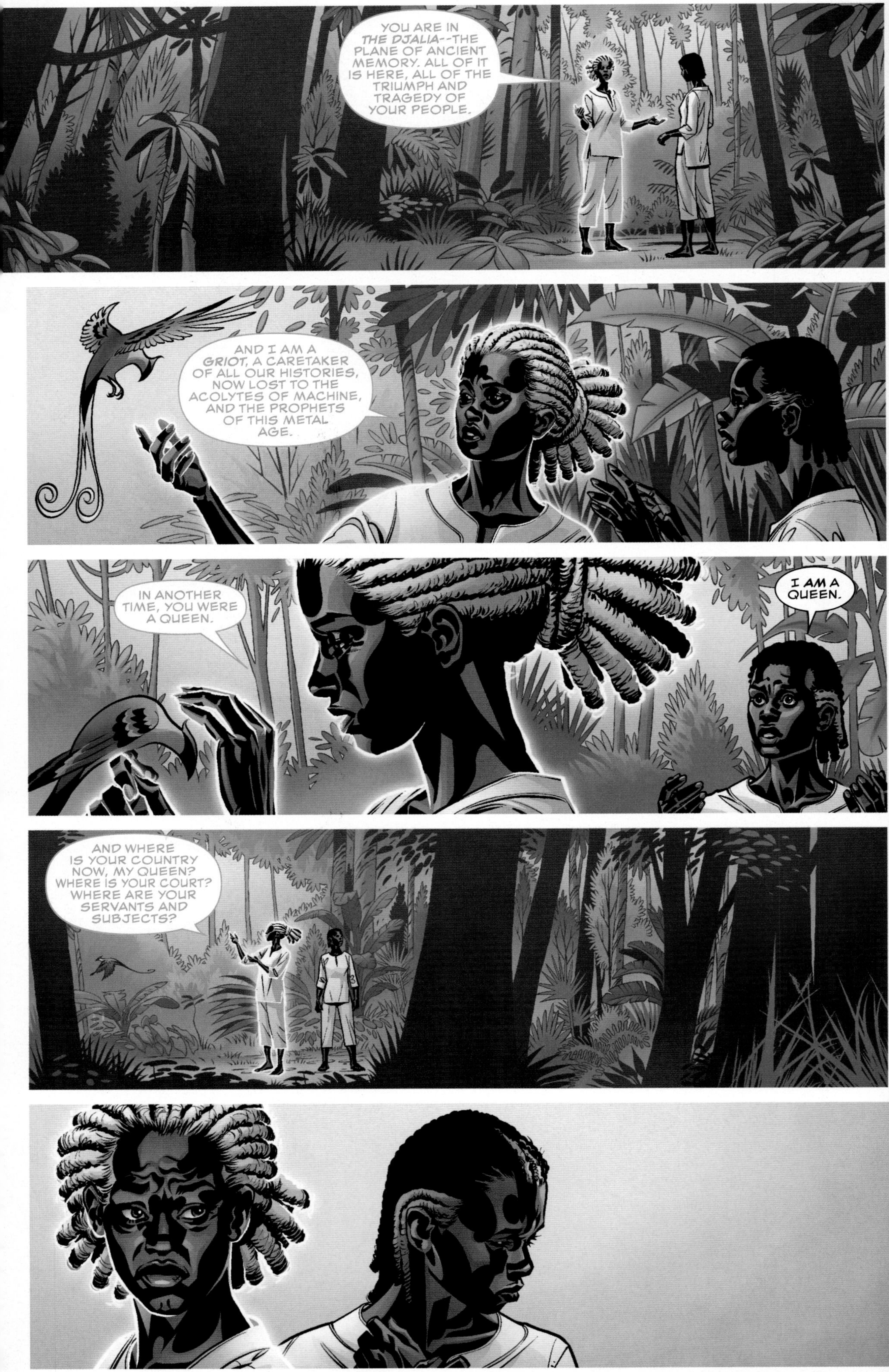
YOU ARE IN THE DJALIA--THE PLANE OF ANCIENT MEMORY. ALL OF IT IS HERE, ALL OF THE TRIUMPH AND TRAGEDY OF YOUR PEOPLE.
AND I AM A GRIOT, A CARETAKER OF ALL OUR HISTORIES, NOW LOST TO THE ACOLYTES OF MACHINE, AND THE PROPHETS OF THIS METAL AGE.
IN ANOTHER TIME, YOU WERE A QUEEN.
I AM A QUEEN.
AND WHERE IS YOUR COUNTRY NOW, MY QUEEN? WHERE IS YOUR COURT? WHERE ARE YOUR SERVANTS AND SUBJECTS?

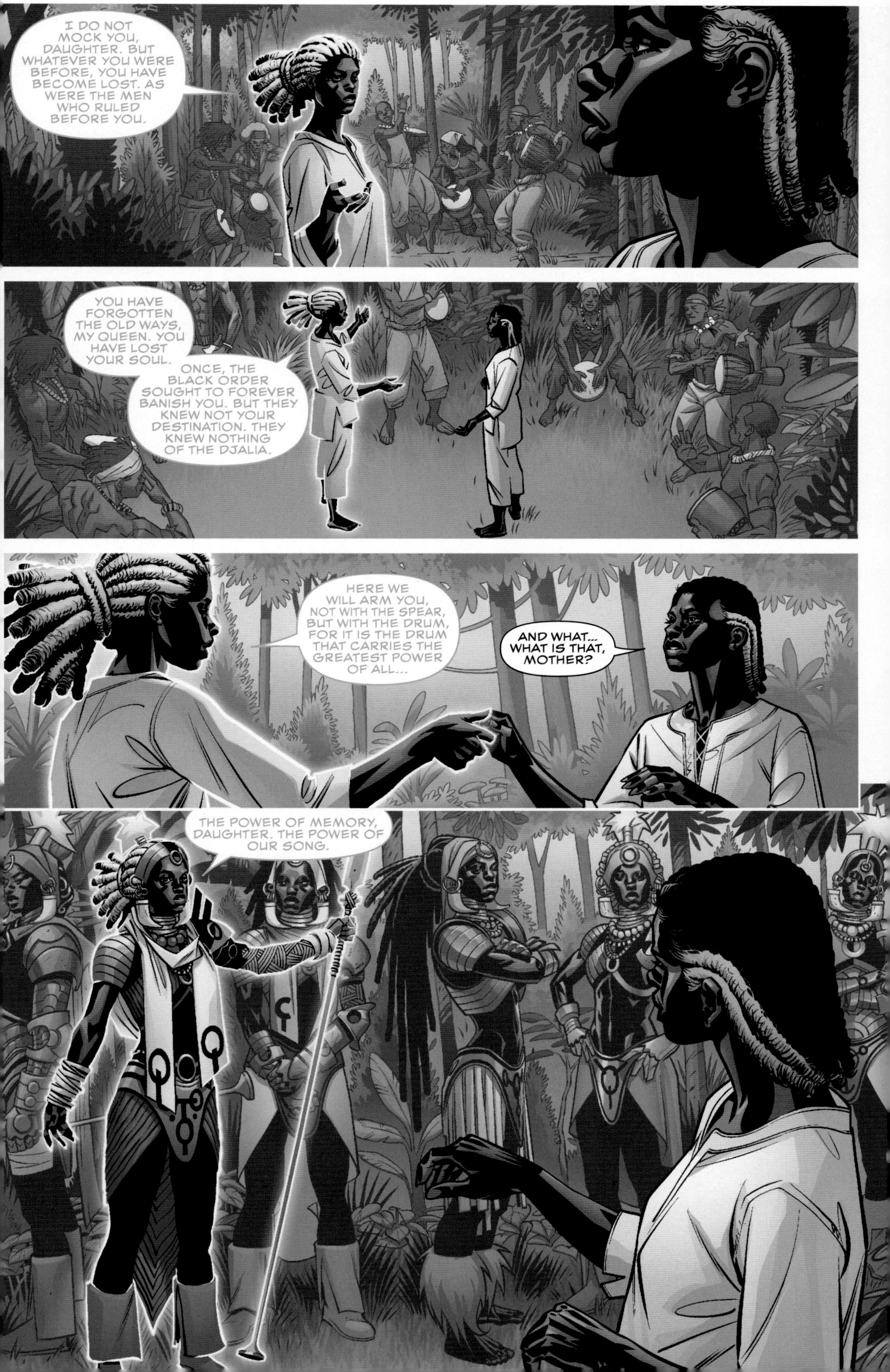
I DO NOT MOCK YOU, DAUGHTER. BUT WHATEVER YOU WERE BEFORE, YOU HAVE BECOME LOST. AS WERE THE MEN WHO RULED BEFORE YOU.
YOU HAVE FORGOTTEN THE OLD WAYS, MY QUEEN. YOU HAVE LOST YOUR SOUL.
ONCE, THE BLACK ORDER SOUGHT TO FOREVER BANISH YOU. BUT THEY KNEW NOT YOUR DESTINATION. THEY KNEW NOTHING OF THE DJALIA.
HERE WE WILL ARM YOU, NOT WITH THE SPEAR, BUT WITH THE DRUM, FOR IT IS THE DRUM THAT CARRIES THE GREATEST POWER OF ALL...
AND WHAT... WHAT IS THAT, MOTHER?
THE POWER OF MEMORY, DAUGHTER. THE POWER OF OUR SONG.

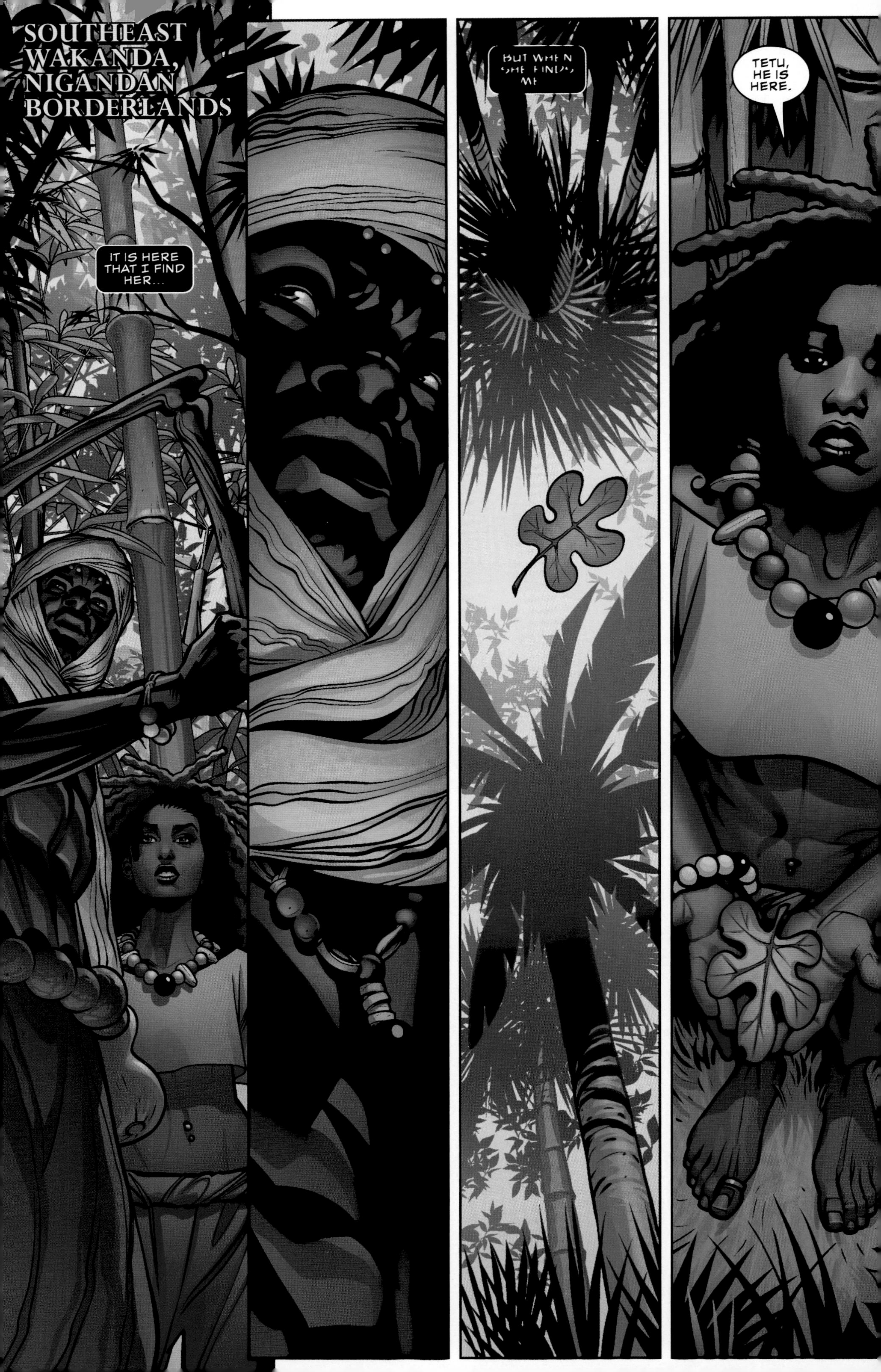
SOUTHEAST WAKANDA, NIGANDAN BORDERLANDS
IT IS HERE THAT I FIND HER...
BUT WHEN SHE FINDS ME
TETU, HE IS HERE.

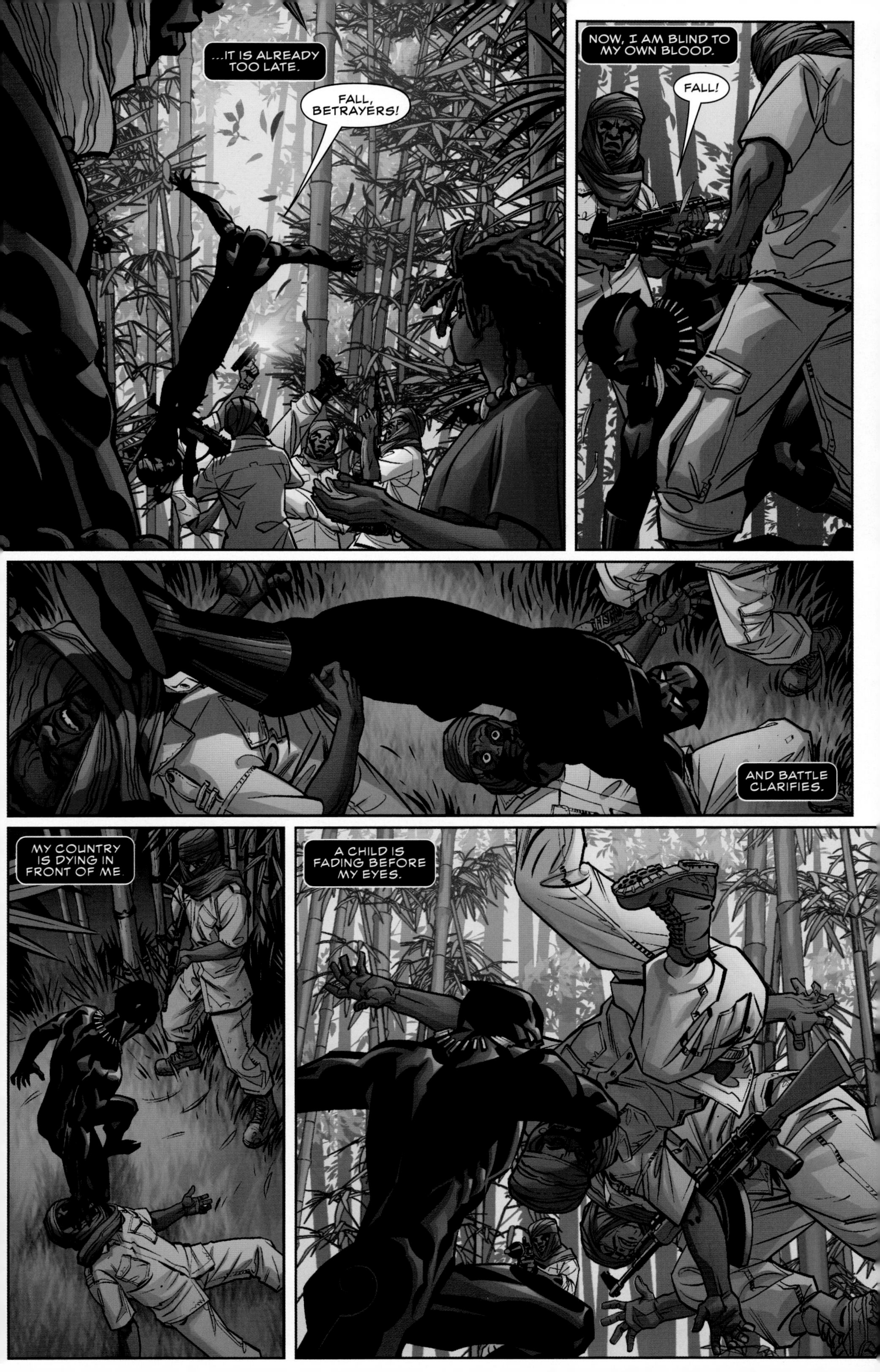
...IT IS ALREADY TOO LATE.
FALL, BETRAYERS!
NOW, I AM BLIND TO MY OWN BLOOD.
FALL!
AND BATTLE CLARIFIES.
MY COUNTRY IS DYING IN FRONT OF ME.
A CHILD IS FADING BEFORE MY EYES.

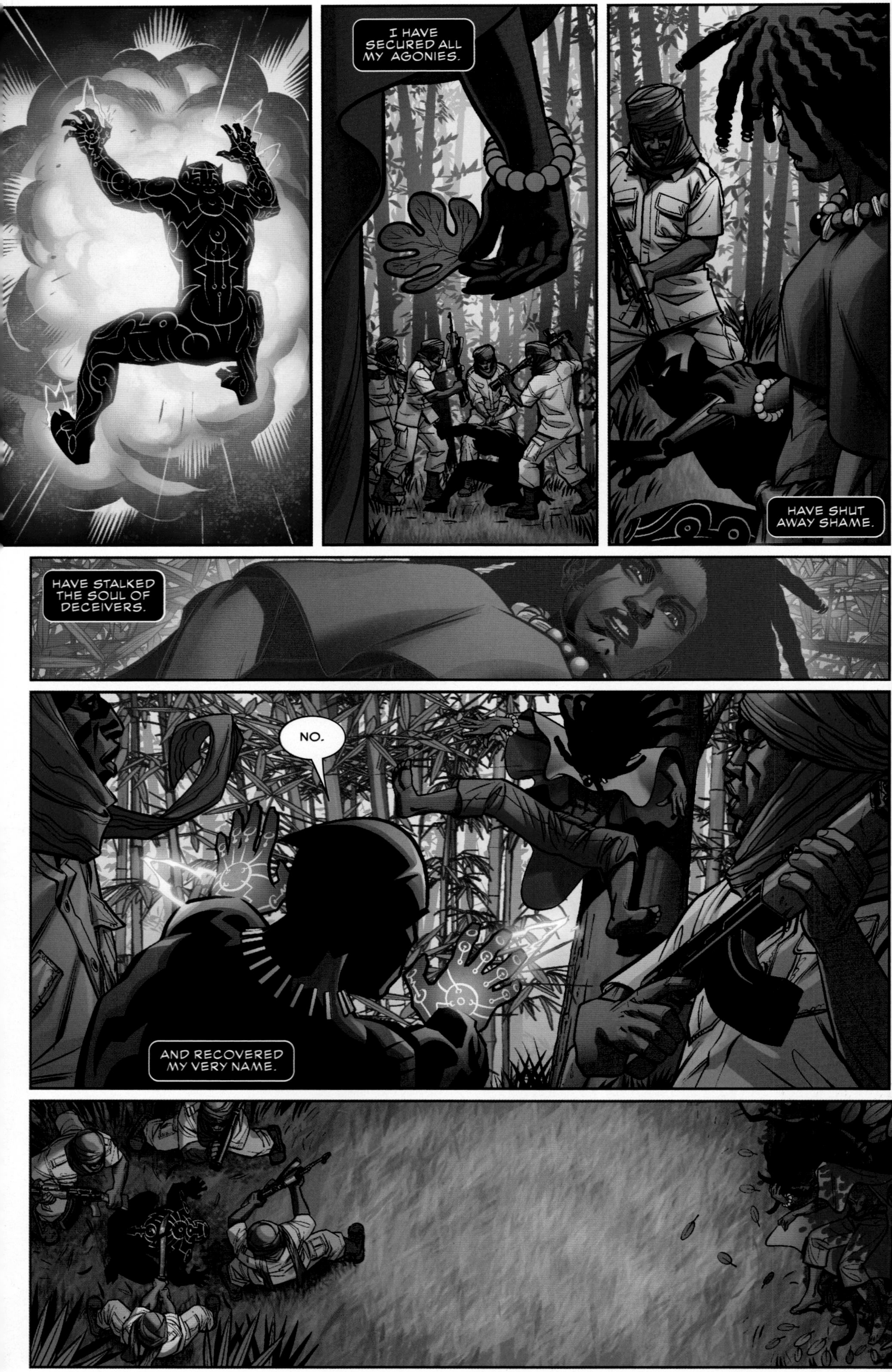
I HAVE SECURED ALL MY AGONIES.
HAVE SHUT AWAY SHAME.
HAVE STALKED THE SOUL OF DECEIVERS.
NO.
AND RECOVERED MY VERY NAME.

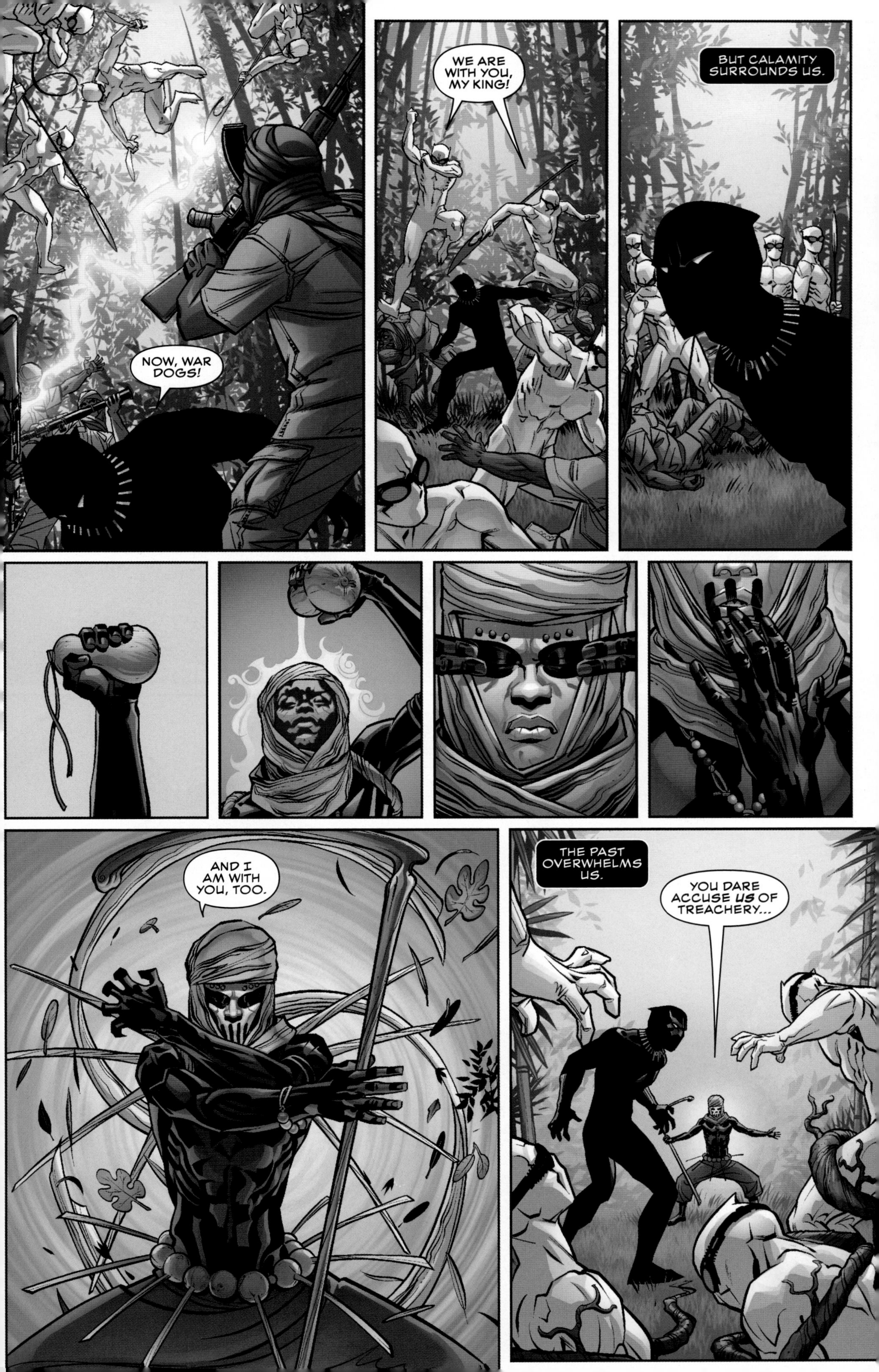
NOW, WAR DOGS!
WE ARE WITH YOU, MY KING!
BUT CALAMITY SURROUNDS US.
AND I AM WITH YOU, TOO.
THE PAST OVERWHELMS US.
YOU DARE ACCUSE US OF TREACHERY...

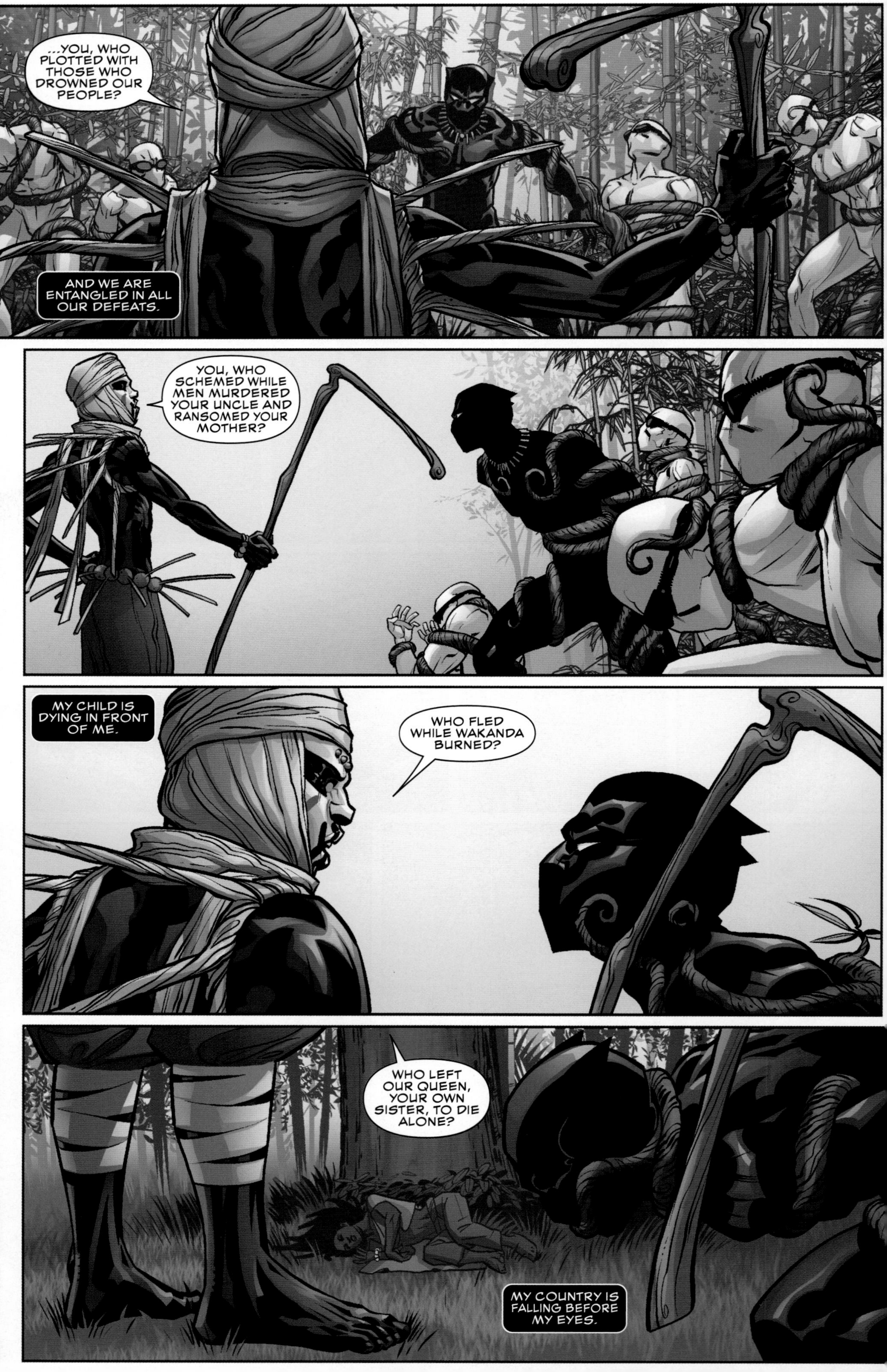
...YOU, WHO PLOTTED WITH THOSE WHO DROWNED OUR PEOPLE?
AND WE ARE ENTANGLED IN ALL OUR DEFEATS.
YOU, WHO SCHEMED WHILE MEN MURDERED YOUR UNCLE AND RANSOMED YOUR MOTHER?
MY CHILD IS DYING IN FRONT OF ME.
WHO FLED WHILE WAKANDA BURNED?
WHO LEFT OUR QUEEN, YOUR OWN SISTER, TO DIE ALONE?
MY COUNTRY IS FALLING BEFORE MY EYES.

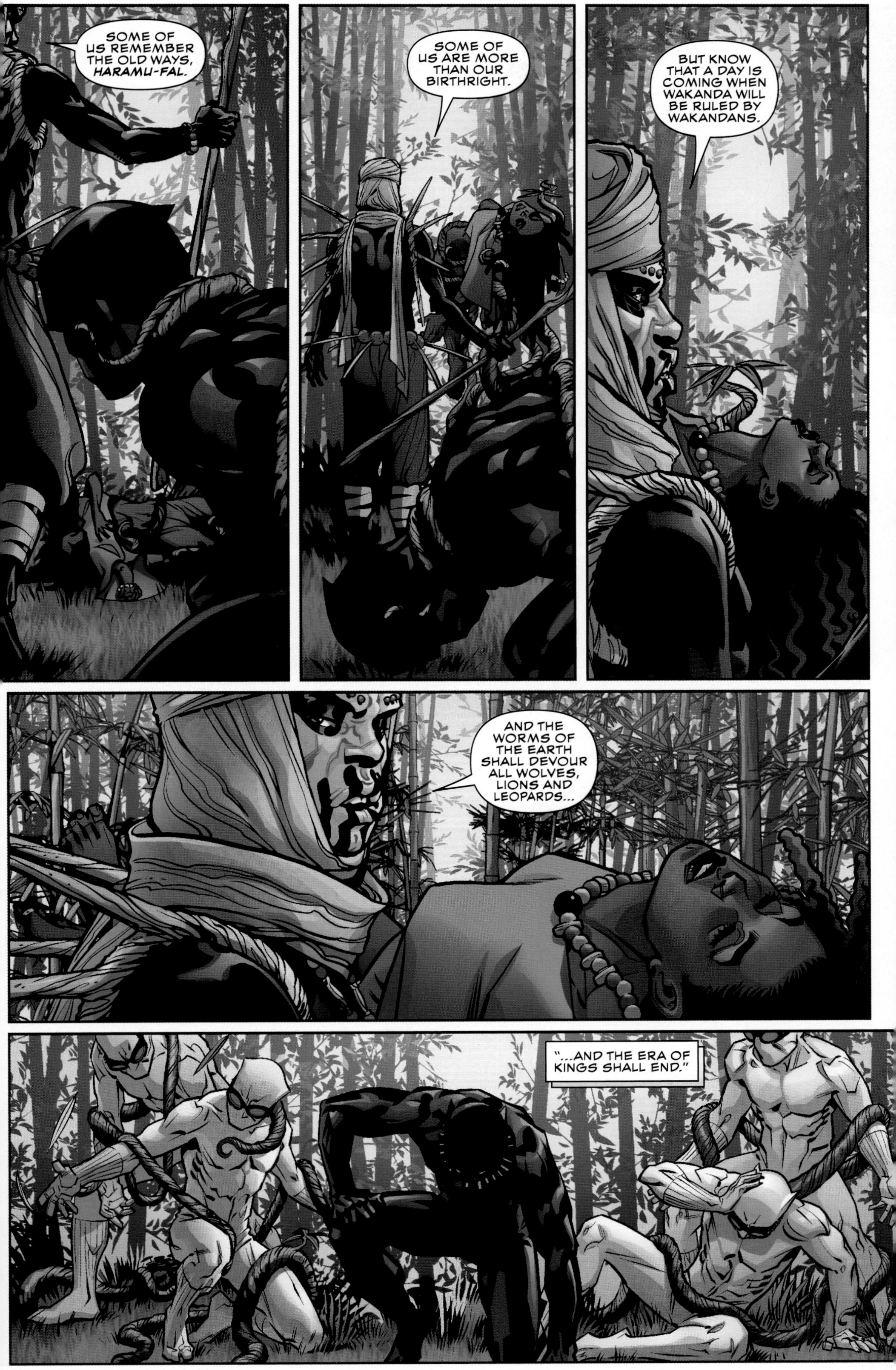
SOME OF US REMEMBER THE OLD WAYS, HARAMU-FAL.
SOME OF US ARE MORE THAN OUR BIRTHRIGHT.
BUT KNOW THAT A DAY IS COMING WHEN WAKANDA WILL BE RULED BY WAKANDANS.
AND THE WORMS OF THE EARTH SHALL DEVOUR ALL WOLVES, LIONS AND LEOPARDS...
"...AND THE ERA OF KINGS SHALL END."

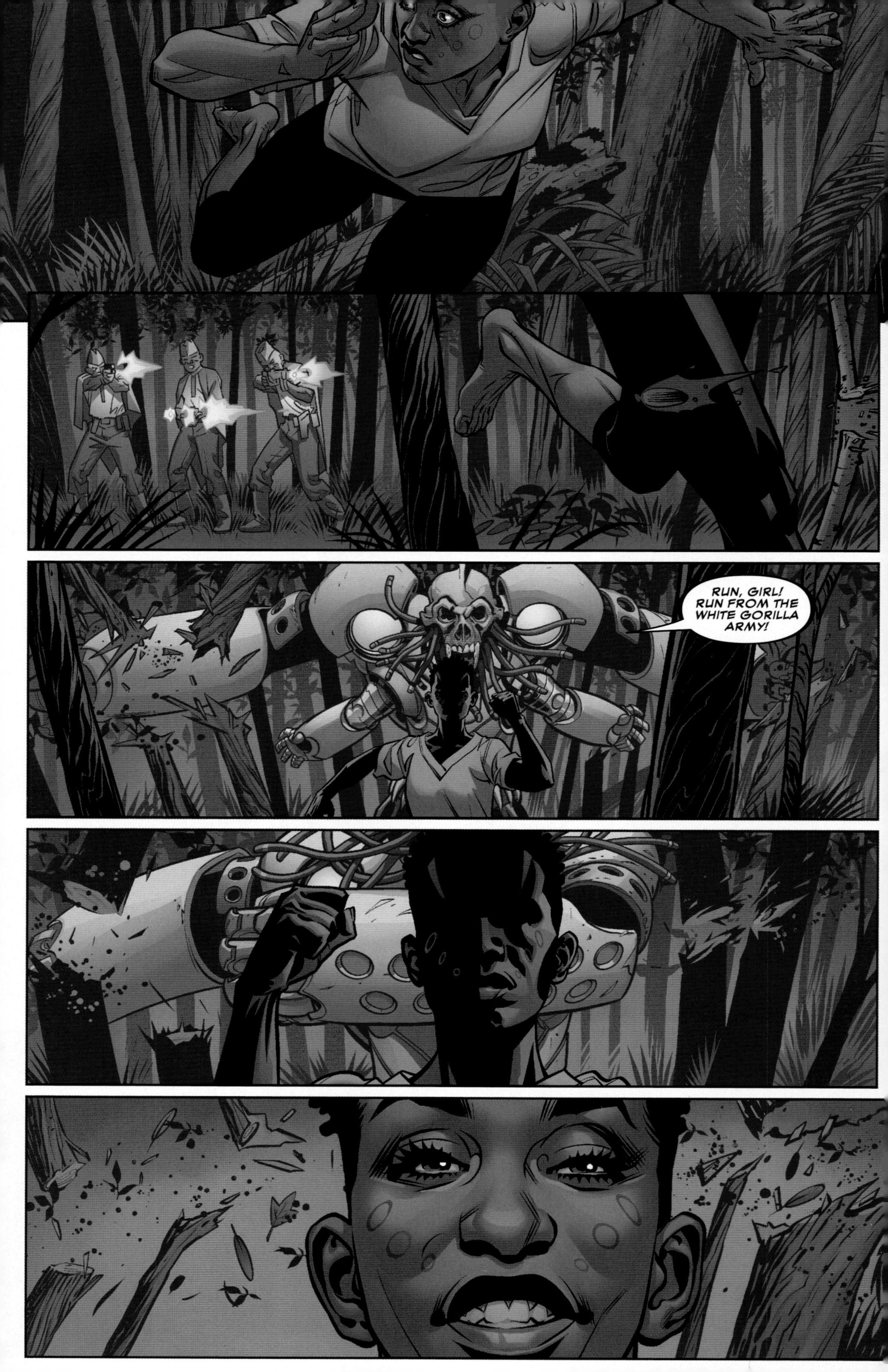
RUN, GIRL! RUN FROM THE WHITE GORILLA ARMY!

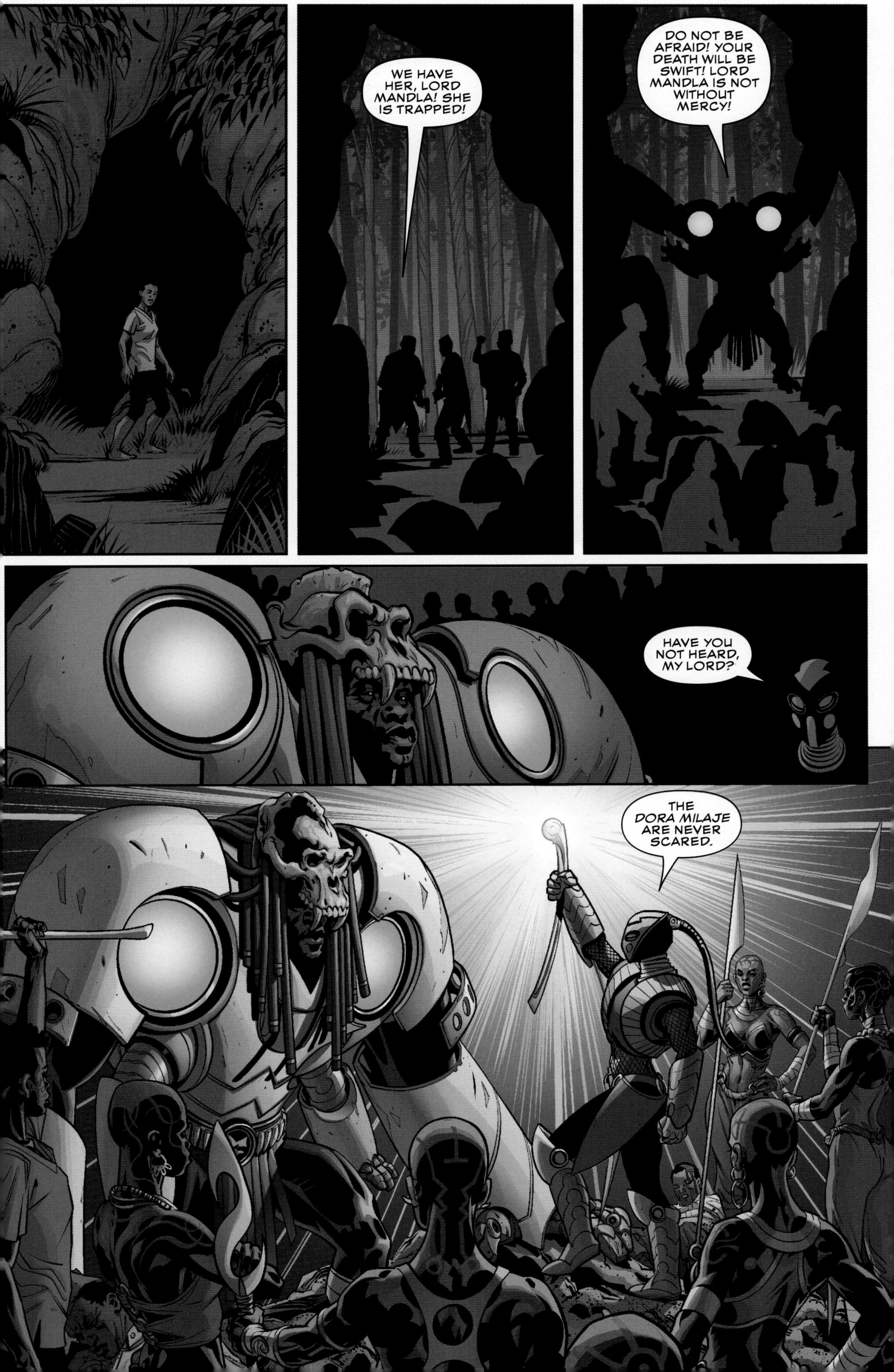
WE HAVE HER, LORD MANDLA! SHE IS TRAPPED!
DO NOT BE AFRAID! YOUR DEATH WILL BE SWIFT! LORD MANDLA IS NOT WITHOUT MERCY!
HAVE YOU NOT HEARD, MY LORD?
THE DORA MILAJE ARE NEVER SCARED.

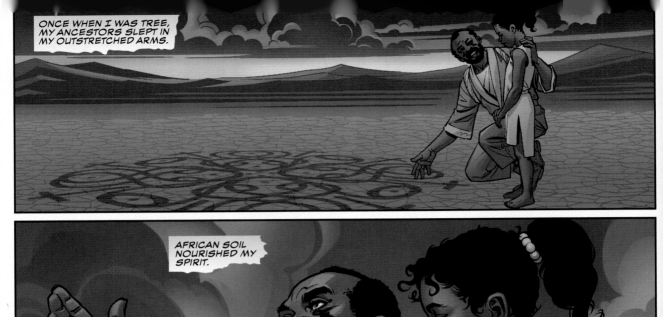

ONCE WHEN I WAS TREE, MY ANCESTORS SLEPT IN MY OUTSTRETCHED ARMS.

AFRICAN SOIL NOURISHED MY SPIRIT.

AFRICAN WIND COMBED THE BRANCHES OF MY HAIR.

ONCE WHEN I WAS TREE, AFRICAN RAIN WASHED MY LIMBS.

AFRICAN SUN WOKE ME UP GREEN AT DAWN.

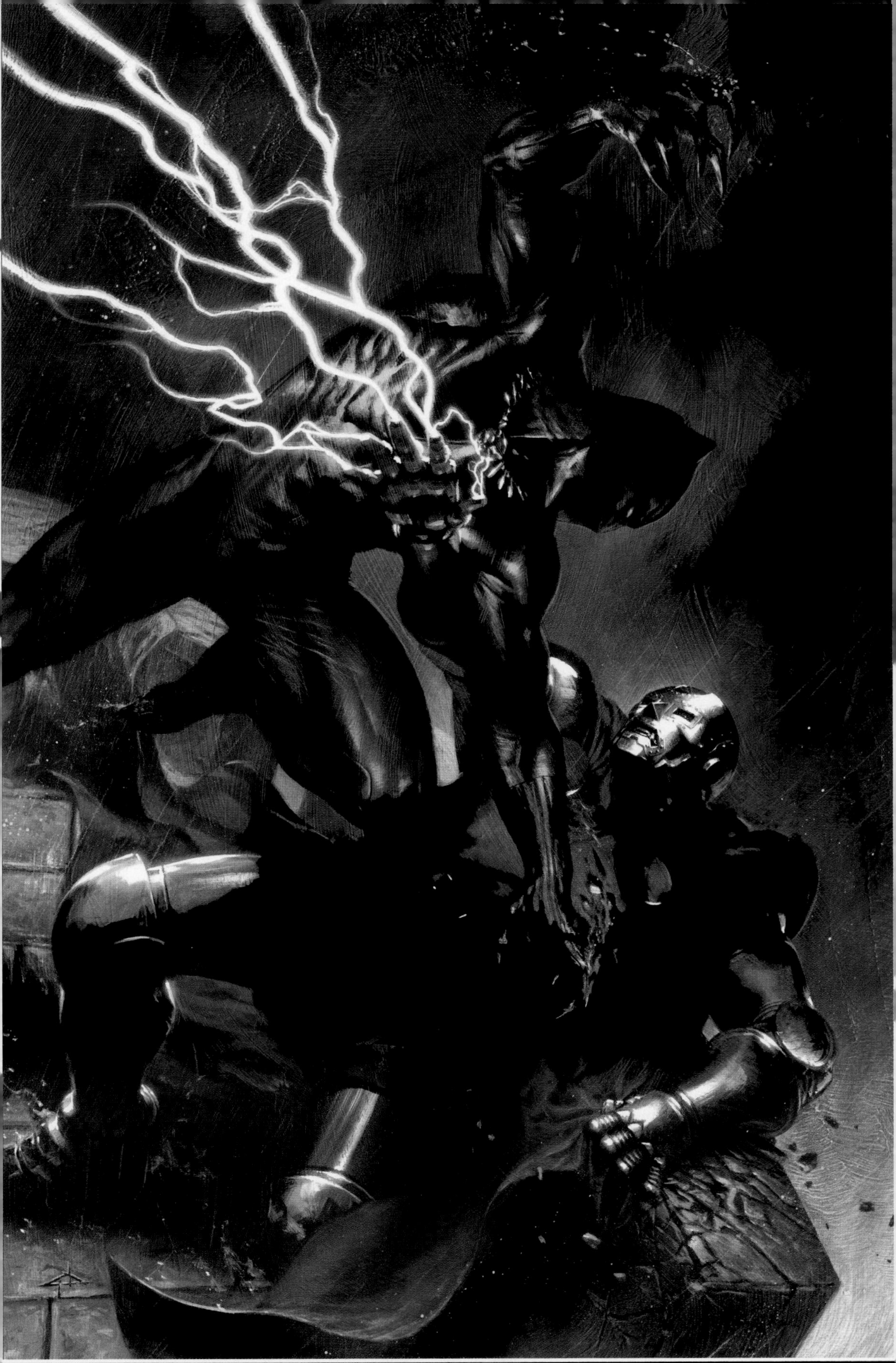

#1 VARIANT BY **GABRIELE DELL'OTTO**

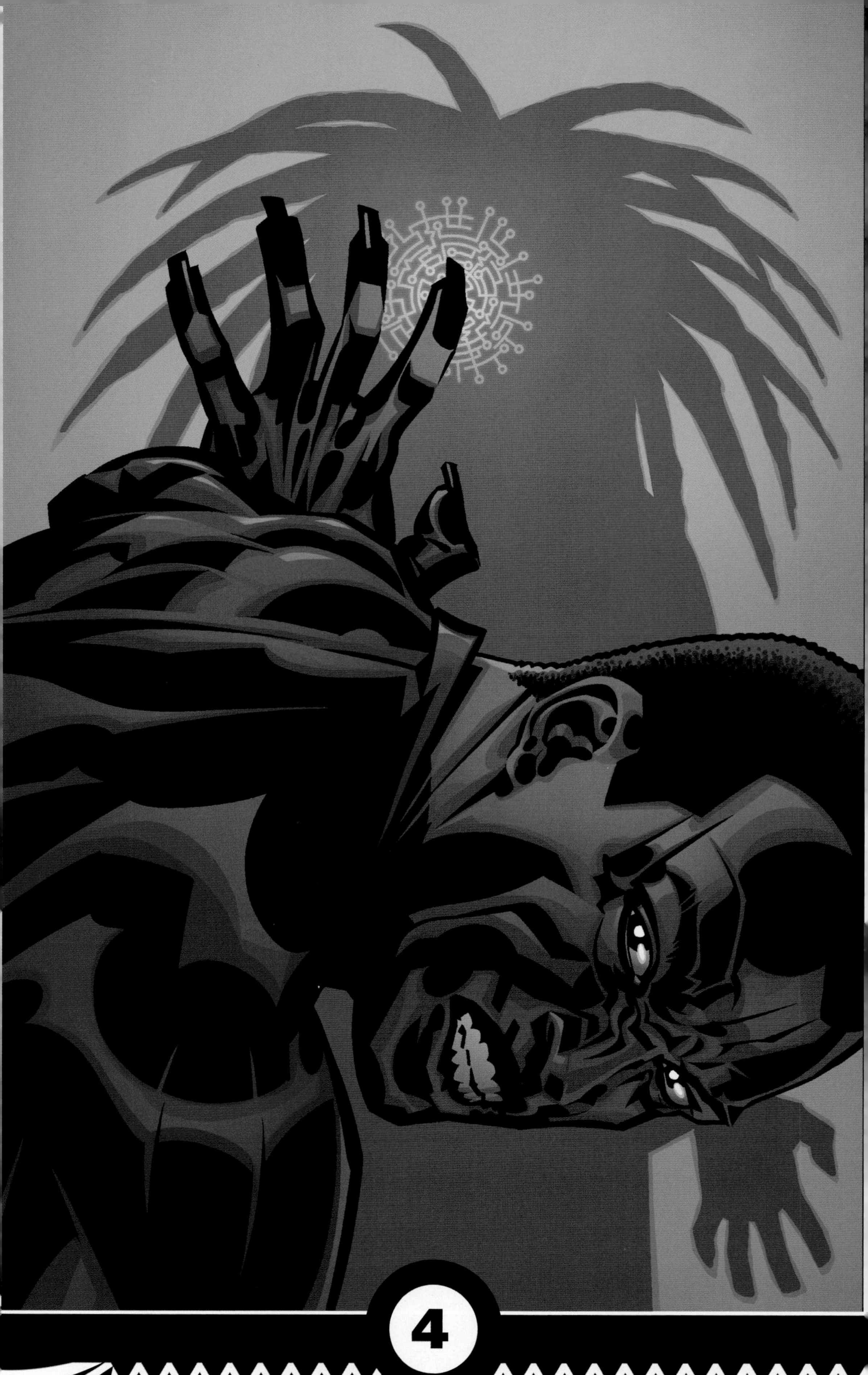

4

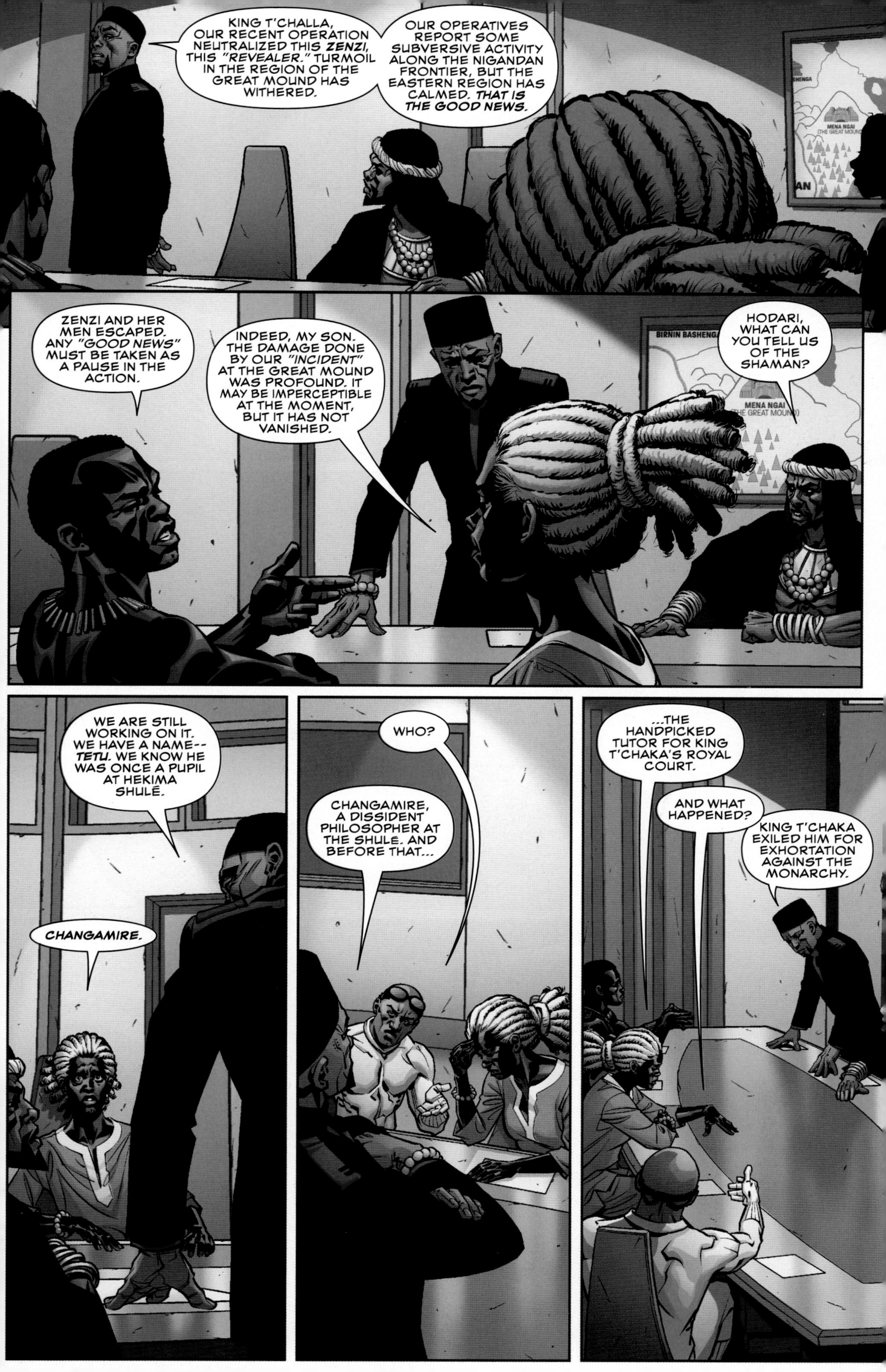
KING T'CHALLA, OUR RECENT OPERATION NEUTRALIZED THIS ZENZI, THIS "REVEALER." TURMOIL IN THE REGION OF THE GREAT MOUND HAS WITHERED.
OUR OPERATIVES REPORT SOME SUBVERSIVE ACTIVITY ALONG THE NIGANDAN FRONTIER, BUT THE EASTERN REGION HAS CALMED. THAT IS THE GOOD NEWS.
MENA NGAI
(THE GREAT MOUND)
ZENZI AND HER MEN ESCAPED. ANY "GOOD NEWS" MUST BE TAKEN AS A PAUSE IN THE ACTION.
INDEED, MY SON. THE DAMAGE DONE BY OUR "INCIDENT" AT THE GREAT MOUND WAS PROFOUND. IT MAY BE IMPERCEPTIBLE AT THE MOMENT, BUT IT HAS NOT VANISHED.
BIRNIN BASHENGA
MENA NGAI
(THE GREAT MOUND)
HODARI, WHAT CAN YOU TELL US OF THE SHAMAN?
WE ARE STILL WORKING ON IT. WE HAVE A NAME--TETU. WE KNOW HE WAS ONCE A PUPIL AT HEKIMA SHULĒ.
CHANGAMIRE.
WHO?
CHANGAMIRE, A DISSIDENT PHILOSOPHER AT THE SHULĒ. AND BEFORE THAT...
...THE HANDPICKED TUTOR FOR KING T'CHAKA'S ROYAL COURT.
AND WHAT HAPPENED?
KING T'CHAKA EXILED HIM FOR EXHORTATION AGAINST THE MONARCHY.

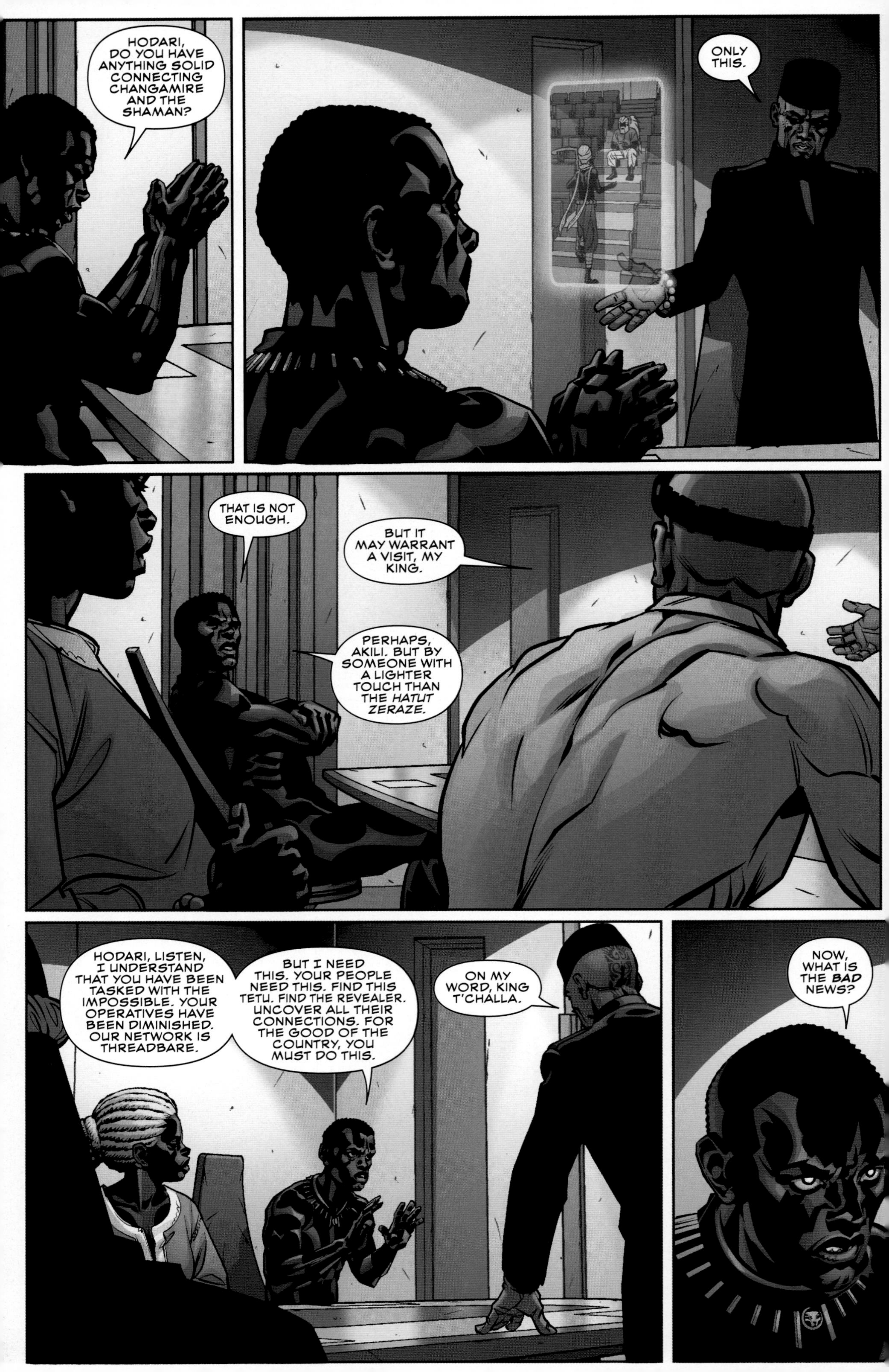
HODARI, DO YOU HAVE ANYTHING SOLID CONNECTING CHANGAMIRE AND THE SHAMAN?
ONLY THIS.
THAT IS NOT ENOUGH.
BUT IT MAY WARRANT A VISIT, MY KING.
PERHAPS, AKILI. BUT BY SOMEONE WITH A LIGHTER TOUCH THAN THE *HATUT ZERAZE.*
HODARI, LISTEN, I UNDERSTAND THAT YOU HAVE BEEN TASKED WITH THE IMPOSSIBLE. YOUR OPERATIVES HAVE BEEN DIMINISHED. OUR NETWORK IS THREADBARE.
BUT I NEED THIS. YOUR PEOPLE NEED THIS. FIND THIS TETU. FIND THE REVEALER. UNCOVER ALL THEIR CONNECTIONS. FOR THE GOOD OF THE COUNTRY, YOU MUST DO THIS.
ON MY WORD, KING T'CHALLA.
NOW, WHAT IS THE *BAD* NEWS?

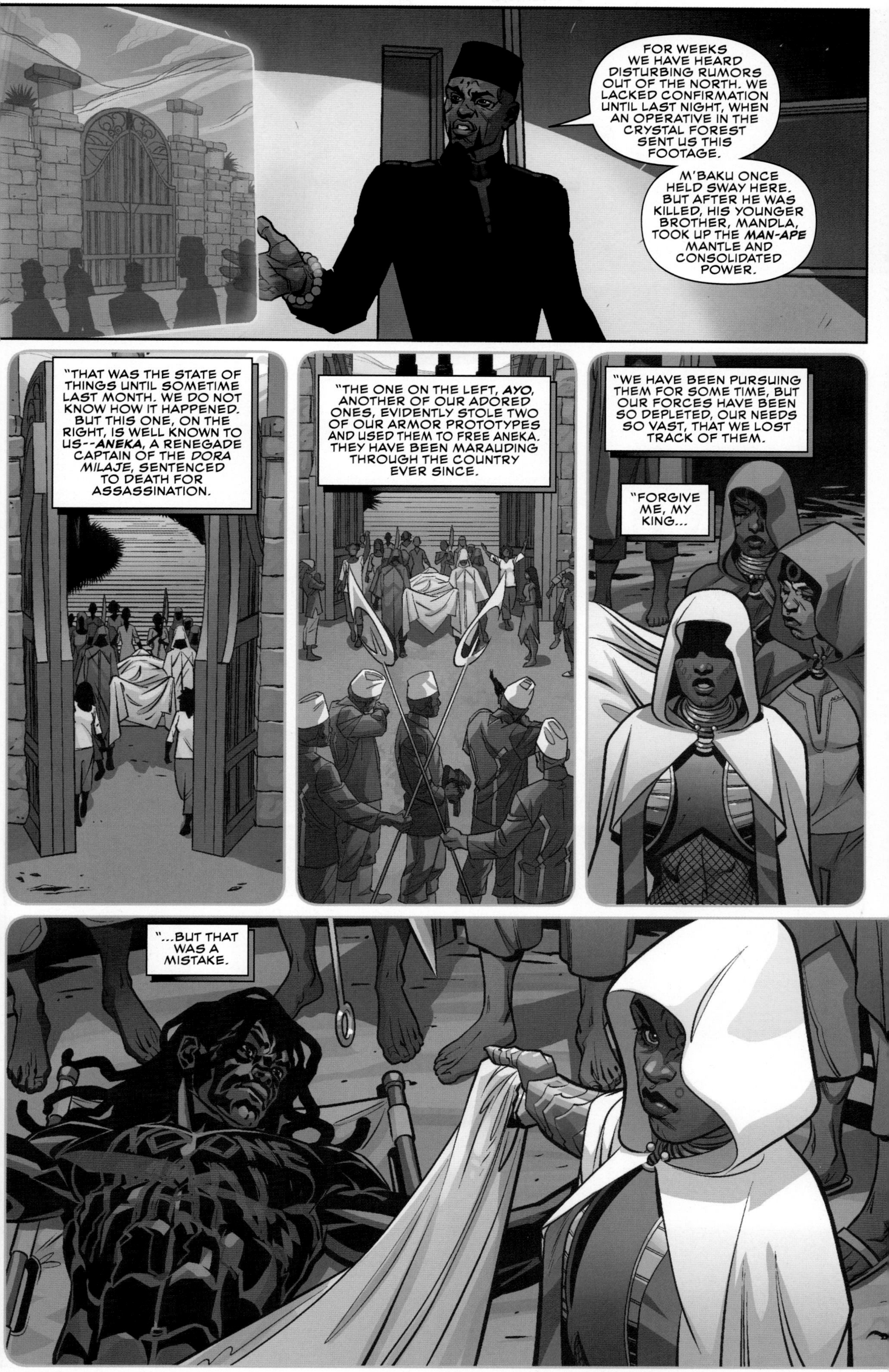
FOR WEEKS WE HAVE HEARD DISTURBING RUMORS OUT OF THE NORTH. WE LACKED CONFIRMATION UNTIL LAST NIGHT, WHEN AN OPERATIVE IN THE CRYSTAL FOREST SENT US THIS FOOTAGE.
M'BAKU ONCE HELD SWAY HERE. BUT AFTER HE WAS KILLED, HIS YOUNGER BROTHER, MANDLA, TOOK UP THE MAN-APE MANTLE AND CONSOLIDATED POWER.
"THAT WAS THE STATE OF THINGS UNTIL SOMETIME LAST MONTH. WE DO NOT KNOW HOW IT HAPPENED. BUT THIS ONE, ON THE RIGHT, IS WELL KNOWN TO US--ANEKA, A RENEGADE CAPTAIN OF THE DORA MILAJE, SENTENCED TO DEATH FOR ASSASSINATION.
"THE ONE ON THE LEFT, AYO, ANOTHER OF OUR ADORED ONES, EVIDENTLY STOLE TWO OF OUR ARMOR PROTOTYPES AND USED THEM TO FREE ANEKA. THEY HAVE BEEN MARAUDING THROUGH THE COUNTRY EVER SINCE.
"WE HAVE BEEN PURSUING THEM FOR SOME TIME, BUT OUR FORCES HAVE BEEN SO DEPLETED, OUR NEEDS SO VAST, THAT WE LOST TRACK OF THEM.
"FORGIVE ME, MY KING...
"...BUT THAT WAS A MISTAKE.

"THESE RENEGADES OVERRAN MANDLA'S FORCES...

"...RAZED THE CITADEL OF THE JABARI FOREFATHERS...

"...AND CONVENED TRIBUNALS."

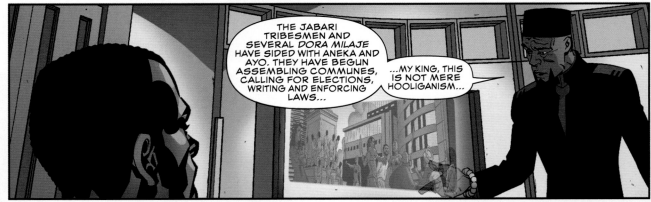

THE JABARI TRIBESMEN AND SEVERAL DORA MILAJE HAVE SIDED WITH ANEKA AND AYO. THEY HAVE BEGUN ASSEMBLING COMMUNES, CALLING FOR ELECTIONS, WRITING AND ENFORCING LAWS...

...MY KING, THIS IS NOT MERE HOOLIGANISM...

...THIS IS REVOLUTION.

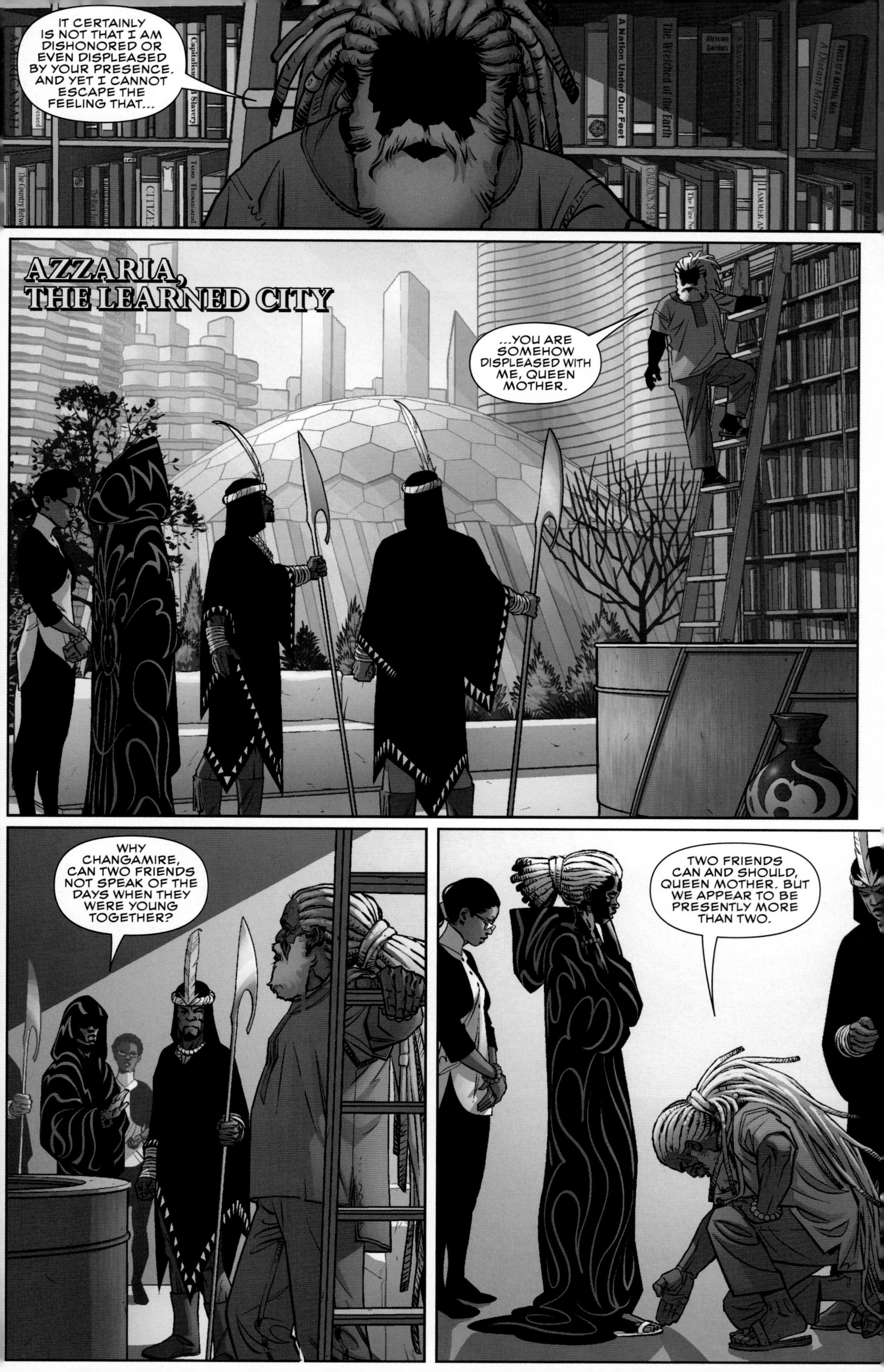
IT CERTAINLY IS NOT THAT I AM DISHONORED OR EVEN DISPLEASED BY YOUR PRESENCE. AND YET I CANNOT ESCAPE THE FEELING THAT...
AZZARIA, THE LEARNED CITY
...YOU ARE SOMEHOW DISPLEASED WITH ME, QUEEN MOTHER.
WHY CHANGAMIRE, CAN TWO FRIENDS NOT SPEAK OF THE DAYS WHEN THEY WERE YOUNG TOGETHER?
TWO FRIENDS CAN AND SHOULD, QUEEN MOTHER. BUT WE APPEAR TO BE PRESENTLY MORE THAN TWO.

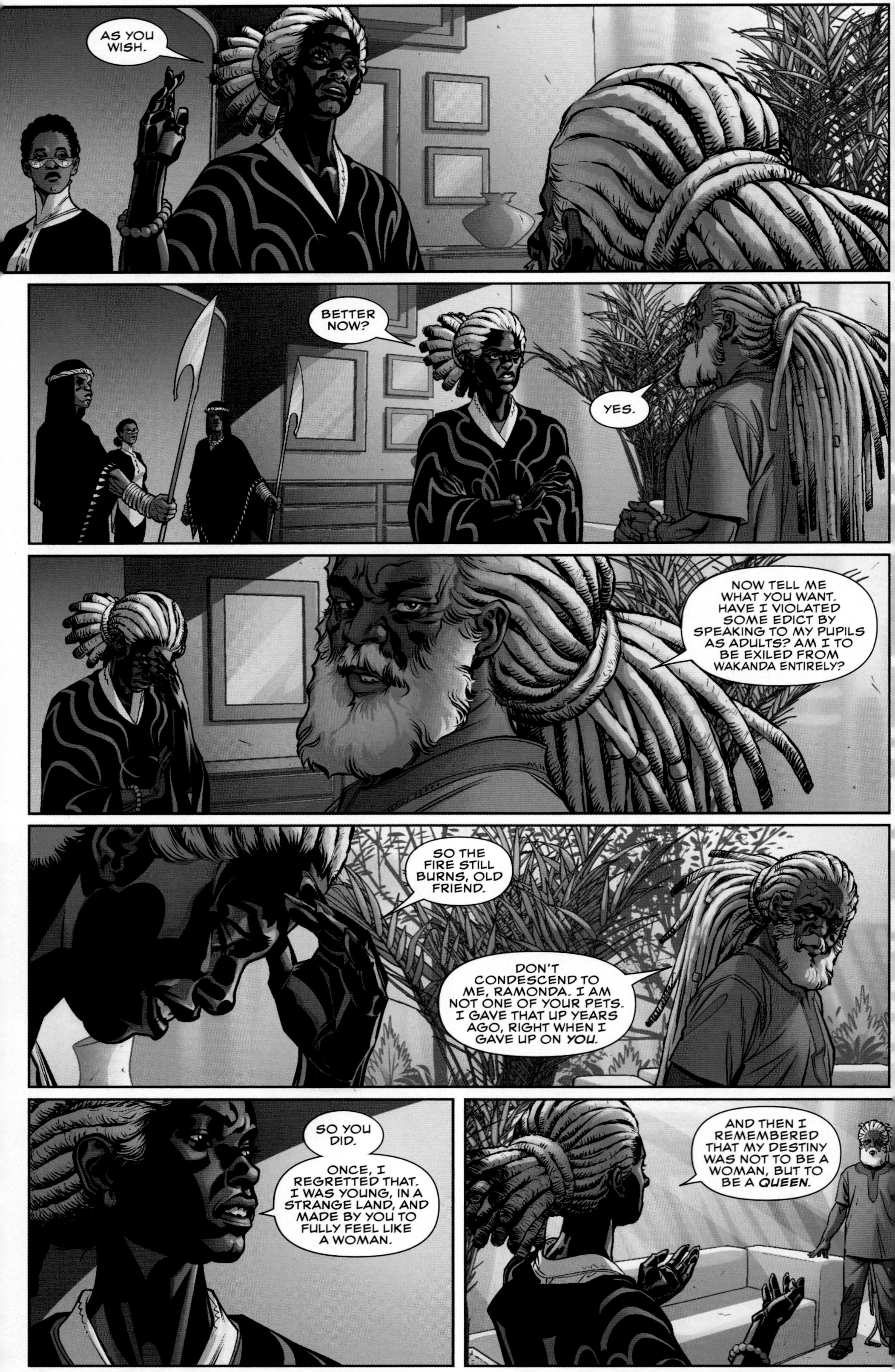
AS YOU WISH.
BETTER NOW?
YES.
NOW TELL ME WHAT YOU WANT. HAVE I VIOLATED SOME EDICT BY SPEAKING TO MY PUPILS AS ADULTS? AM I TO BE EXILED FROM WAKANDA ENTIRELY?
SO THE FIRE STILL BURNS, OLD FRIEND.
DON'T CONDESCEND TO ME, RAMONDA. I AM NOT ONE OF YOUR PETS. I GAVE THAT UP YEARS AGO, RIGHT WHEN I GAVE UP ON *YOU*.
SO YOU DID.
ONCE, I REGRETTED THAT. I WAS YOUNG, IN A STRANGE LAND, AND MADE BY YOU TO FULLY FEEL LIKE A WOMAN.
AND THEN I REMEMBERED THAT MY DESTINY WAS NOT TO BE A WOMAN, BUT TO BE A ***QUEEN***.

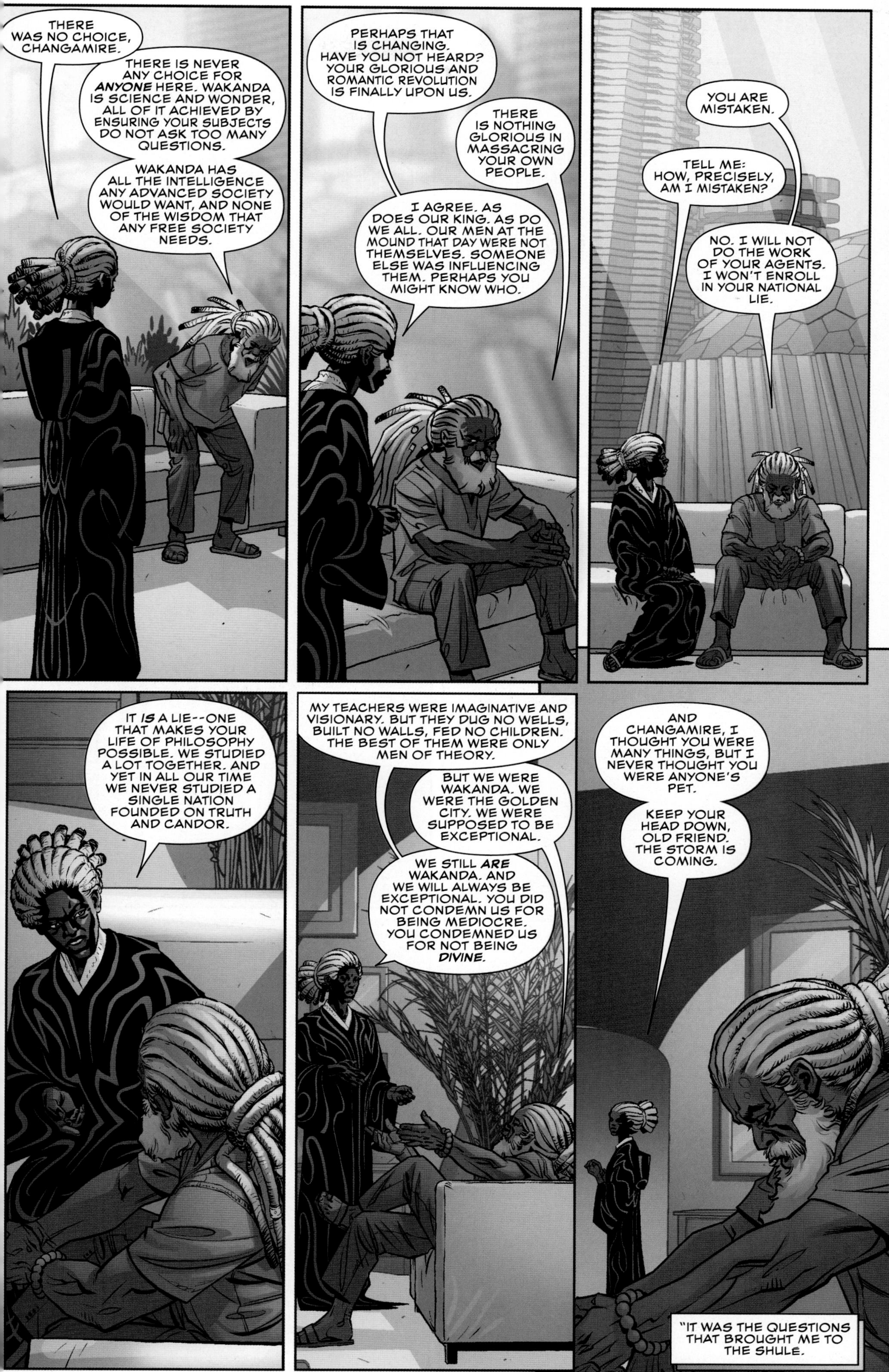
THERE WAS NO CHOICE, CHANGAMIRE.
THERE IS NEVER ANY CHOICE FOR ANYONE HERE. WAKANDA IS SCIENCE AND WONDER, ALL OF IT ACHIEVED BY ENSURING YOUR SUBJECTS DO NOT ASK TOO MANY QUESTIONS.
WAKANDA HAS ALL THE INTELLIGENCE ANY ADVANCED SOCIETY WOULD WANT, AND NONE OF THE WISDOM THAT ANY FREE SOCIETY NEEDS.
PERHAPS THAT IS CHANGING. HAVE YOU NOT HEARD? YOUR GLORIOUS AND ROMANTIC REVOLUTION IS FINALLY UPON US.
THERE IS NOTHING GLORIOUS IN MASSACRING YOUR OWN PEOPLE.
I AGREE. AS DOES OUR KING. AS DO WE ALL. OUR MEN AT THE MOUND THAT DAY WERE NOT THEMSELVES. SOMEONE ELSE WAS INFLUENCING THEM. PERHAPS YOU MIGHT KNOW WHO.
YOU ARE MISTAKEN.
TELL ME: HOW, PRECISELY, AM I MISTAKEN?
NO. I WILL NOT DO THE WORK OF YOUR AGENTS. I WON'T ENROLL IN YOUR NATIONAL LIE.
IT IS A LIE--ONE THAT MAKES YOUR LIFE OF PHILOSOPHY POSSIBLE. WE STUDIED A LOT TOGETHER. AND YET IN ALL OUR TIME WE NEVER STUDIED A SINGLE NATION FOUNDED ON TRUTH AND CANDOR.
MY TEACHERS WERE IMAGINATIVE AND VISIONARY. BUT THEY DUG NO WELLS, BUILT NO WALLS, FED NO CHILDREN. THE BEST OF THEM WERE ONLY MEN OF THEORY.
BUT WE WERE WAKANDA. WE WERE THE GOLDEN CITY. WE WERE SUPPOSED TO BE EXCEPTIONAL.
WE STILL ARE WAKANDA. AND WE WILL ALWAYS BE EXCEPTIONAL. YOU DID NOT CONDEMN US FOR BEING MEDIOCRE. YOU CONDEMNED US FOR NOT BEING DIVINE.
AND CHANGAMIRE, I THOUGHT YOU WERE MANY THINGS, BUT I NEVER THOUGHT YOU WERE ANYONE'S PET.
KEEP YOUR HEAD DOWN, OLD FRIEND. THE STORM IS COMING.
"IT WAS THE QUESTIONS THAT BROUGHT ME TO THE SHULE.

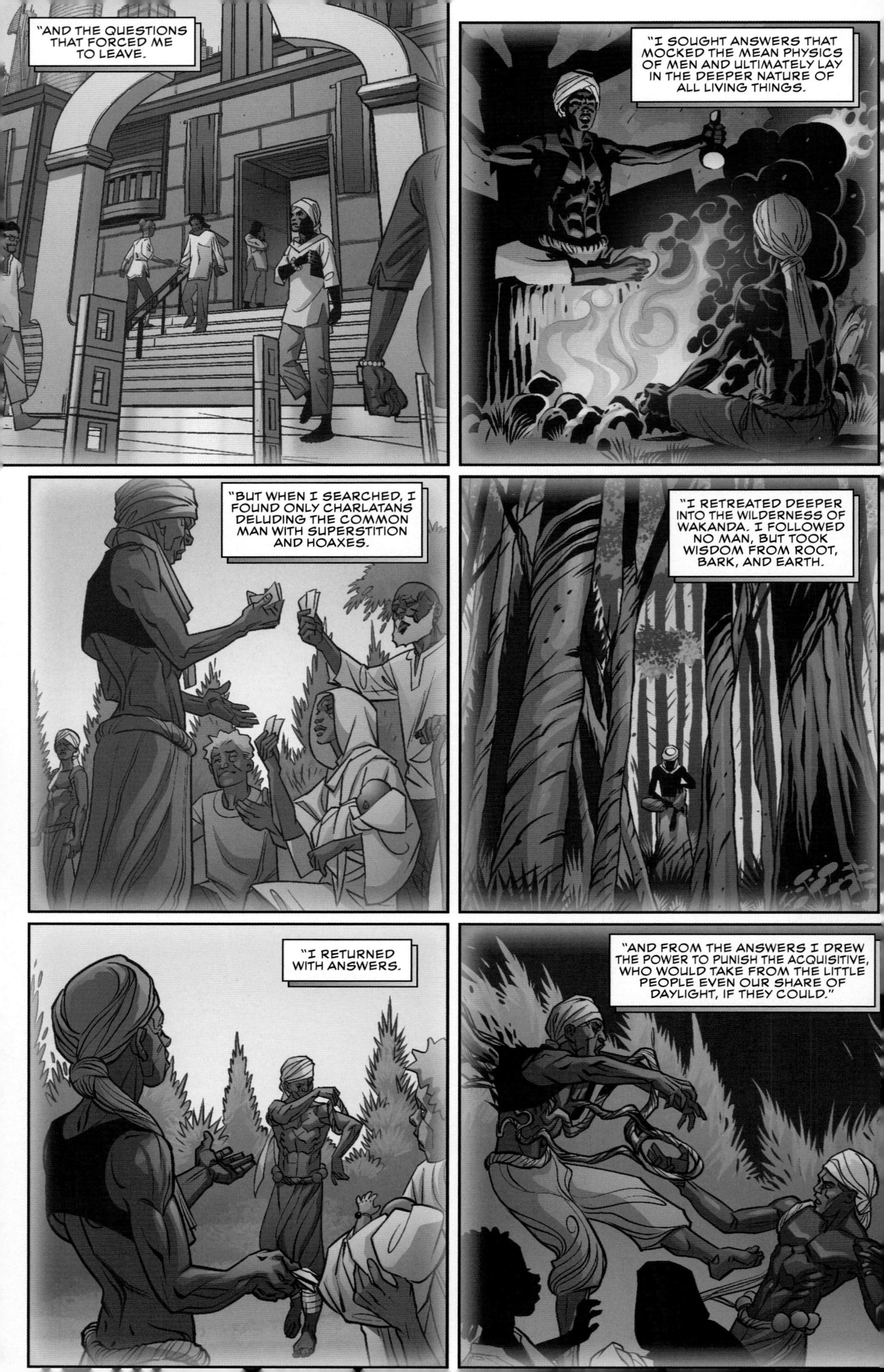
"AND THE QUESTIONS THAT FORCED ME TO LEAVE.
"I SOUGHT ANSWERS THAT MOCKED THE MEAN PHYSICS OF MEN AND ULTIMATELY LAY IN THE DEEPER NATURE OF ALL LIVING THINGS.
"BUT WHEN I SEARCHED, I FOUND ONLY CHARLATANS DELUDING THE COMMON MAN WITH SUPERSTITION AND HOAXES.
"I RETREATED DEEPER INTO THE WILDERNESS OF WAKANDA. I FOLLOWED NO MAN, BUT TOOK WISDOM FROM ROOT, BARK, AND EARTH.
"I RETURNED WITH ANSWERS.
"AND FROM THE ANSWERS I DREW THE POWER TO PUNISH THE ACQUISITIVE, WHO WOULD TAKE FROM THE LITTLE PEOPLE EVEN OUR SHARE OF DAYLIGHT, IF THEY COULD."

I WANTED A NEW COUNTRY, A COUNTRY THAT RESPECTED ALL OF US EQUALLY, AND RESPECTED THE EARTH FROM WHICH WE ALL HAIL, AND THE EARTH TO WHICH WE ALL SHALL RETURN.

I BELIEVE I HAVE FOUND THAT COUNTRY.

I COME TO OFFER YOU MY ADMIRATION. TOPPLING THE JABARI TYRANT WAS A GREAT SERVICE TO THE NATION. BUT MORE, I OFFER YOU MY ARMS. IT WILL NOT END WITH THE JABARI. *WAR* IS COMING.

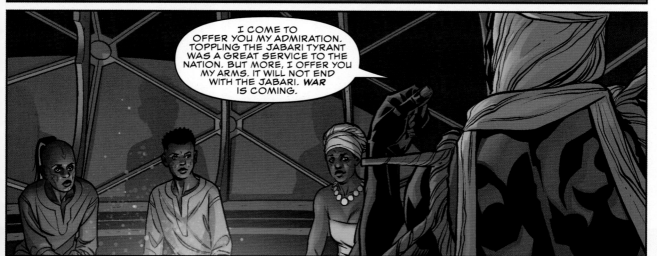

TETU, EACH DAY ANOTHER OF OUR SISTERS JOINS THE CAUSE. EACH DAY WE GROW STRONGER.

THE MIDNIGHT ANGELS WERE ENOUGH FOR MANDLA. THEY WILL BE ENOUGH FOR *DAMISA-SARKI* TOO.

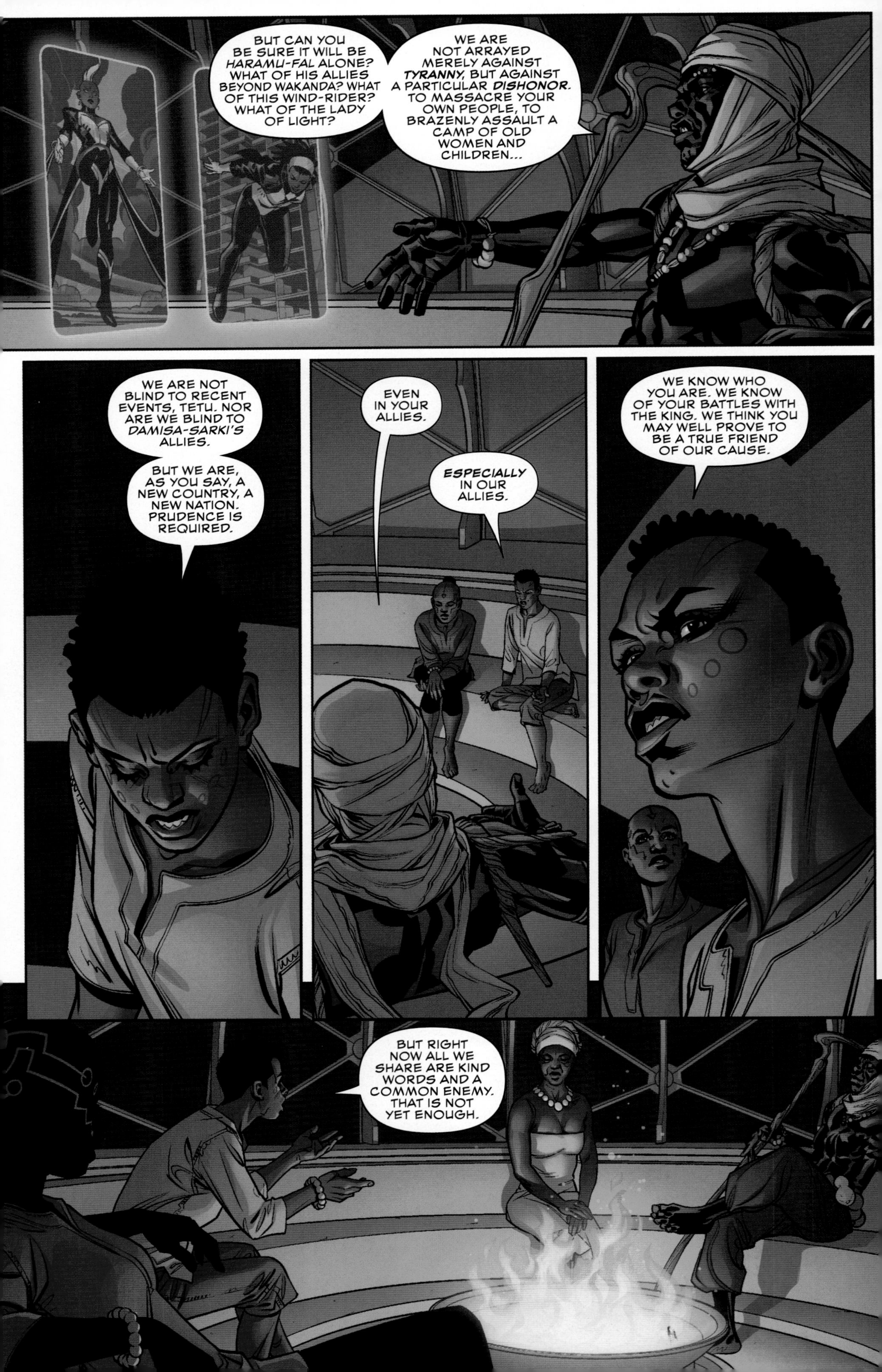
BUT CAN YOU BE SURE IT WILL BE HARAMU-FAL ALONE? WHAT OF HIS ALLIES BEYOND WAKANDA? WHAT OF THIS WIND-RIDER? WHAT OF THE LADY OF LIGHT?
WE ARE NOT ARRAYED MERELY AGAINST TYRANNY, BUT AGAINST A PARTICULAR DISHONOR. TO MASSACRE YOUR OWN PEOPLE, TO BRAZENLY ASSAULT A CAMP OF OLD WOMEN AND CHILDREN...
WE ARE NOT BLIND TO RECENT EVENTS, TETU. NOR ARE WE BLIND TO DAMISA-SARKI'S ALLIES.
BUT WE ARE, AS YOU SAY, A NEW COUNTRY, A NEW NATION. PRUDENCE IS REQUIRED.
EVEN IN YOUR ALLIES.
ESPECIALLY IN OUR ALLIES.
WE KNOW WHO YOU ARE. WE KNOW OF YOUR BATTLES WITH THE KING. WE THINK YOU MAY WELL PROVE TO BE A TRUE FRIEND OF OUR CAUSE.
BUT RIGHT NOW ALL WE SHARE ARE KIND WORDS AND A COMMON ENEMY. THAT IS NOT YET ENOUGH.

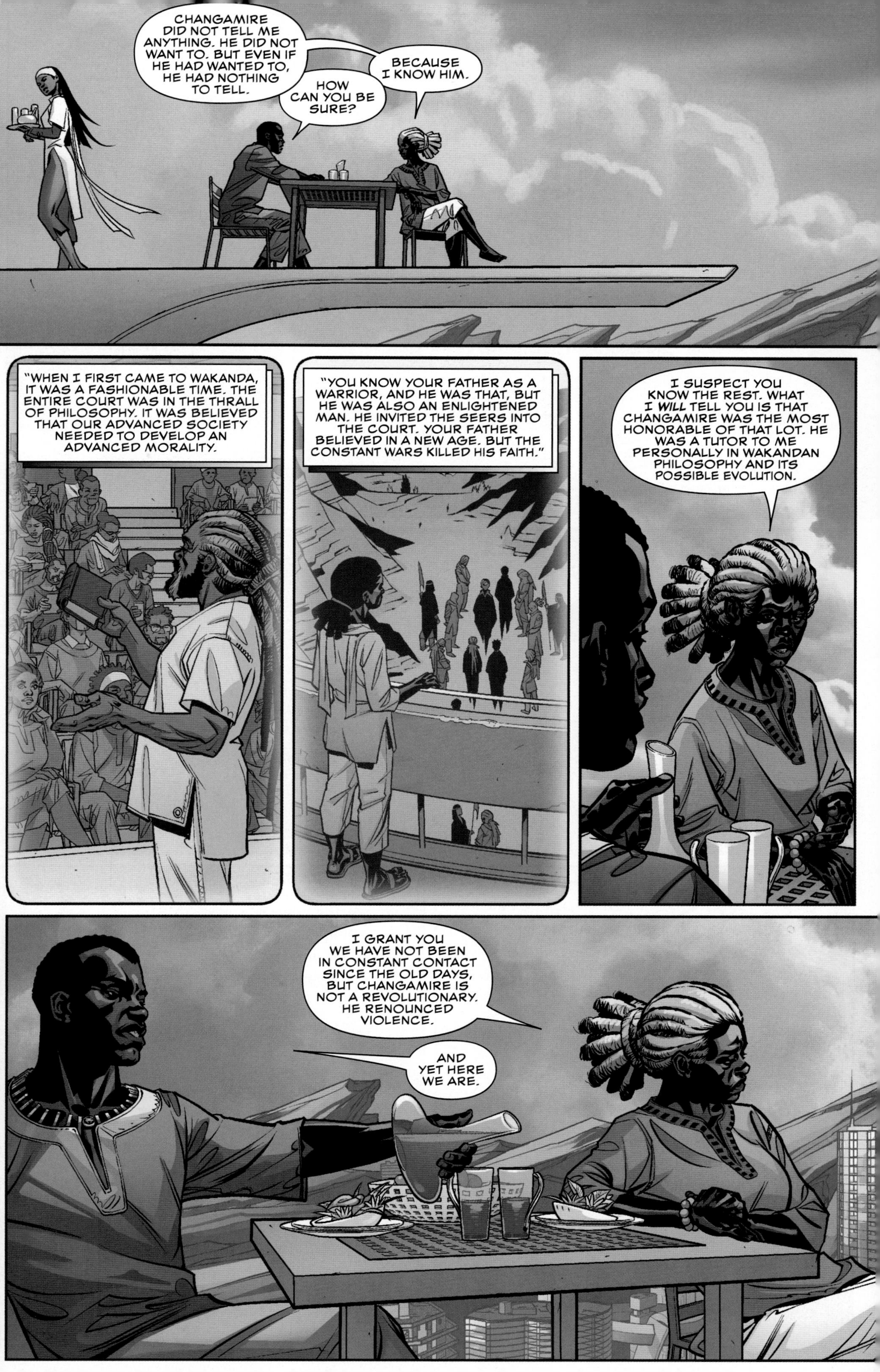
CHANGAMIRE DID NOT TELL ME ANYTHING. HE DID NOT WANT TO. BUT EVEN IF HE HAD WANTED TO, HE HAD NOTHING TO TELL.
HOW CAN YOU BE SURE?
BECAUSE I KNOW HIM.
"WHEN I FIRST CAME TO WAKANDA, IT WAS A FASHIONABLE TIME. THE ENTIRE COURT WAS IN THE THRALL OF PHILOSOPHY. IT WAS BELIEVED THAT OUR ADVANCED SOCIETY NEEDED TO DEVELOP AN ADVANCED MORALITY.
"YOU KNOW YOUR FATHER AS A WARRIOR, AND HE WAS THAT, BUT HE WAS ALSO AN ENLIGHTENED MAN. HE INVITED THE SEERS INTO THE COURT. YOUR FATHER BELIEVED IN A NEW AGE. BUT THE CONSTANT WARS KILLED HIS FAITH."
I SUSPECT YOU KNOW THE REST. WHAT I *WILL* TELL YOU IS THAT CHANGAMIRE WAS THE MOST HONORABLE OF THAT LOT. HE WAS A TUTOR TO ME PERSONALLY IN WAKANDAN PHILOSOPHY AND ITS POSSIBLE EVOLUTION.
I GRANT YOU WE HAVE NOT BEEN IN CONSTANT CONTACT SINCE THE OLD DAYS, BUT CHANGAMIRE IS NOT A REVOLUTIONARY. HE RENOUNCED VIOLENCE.
AND YET HERE WE ARE.

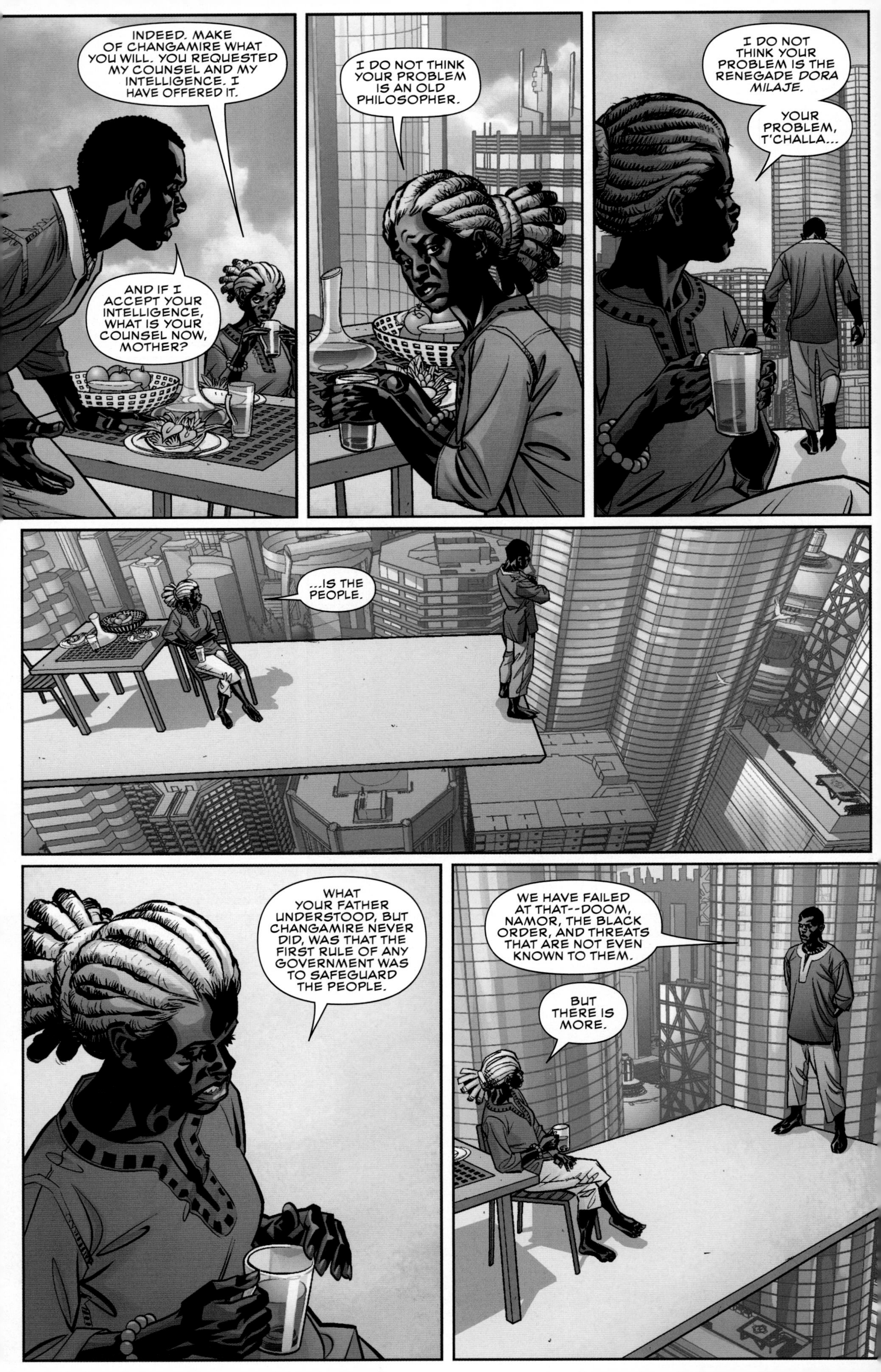
INDEED. MAKE OF CHANGAMIRE WHAT YOU WILL. YOU REQUESTED MY COUNSEL AND MY INTELLIGENCE. I HAVE OFFERED IT.
AND IF I ACCEPT YOUR INTELLIGENCE, WHAT IS YOUR COUNSEL NOW, MOTHER?
I DO NOT THINK YOUR PROBLEM IS AN OLD PHILOSOPHER.
I DO NOT THINK YOUR PROBLEM IS THE RENEGADE *DORA MILAJE.*
YOUR PROBLEM, T'CHALLA...
...IS THE PEOPLE.
WHAT YOUR FATHER UNDERSTOOD, BUT CHANGAMIRE NEVER DID, WAS THAT THE FIRST RULE OF ANY GOVERNMENT WAS TO SAFEGUARD THE PEOPLE.
WE HAVE FAILED AT THAT--DOOM, NAMOR, THE BLACK ORDER, AND THREATS THAT ARE NOT EVEN KNOWN TO THEM.
BUT THERE IS MORE.

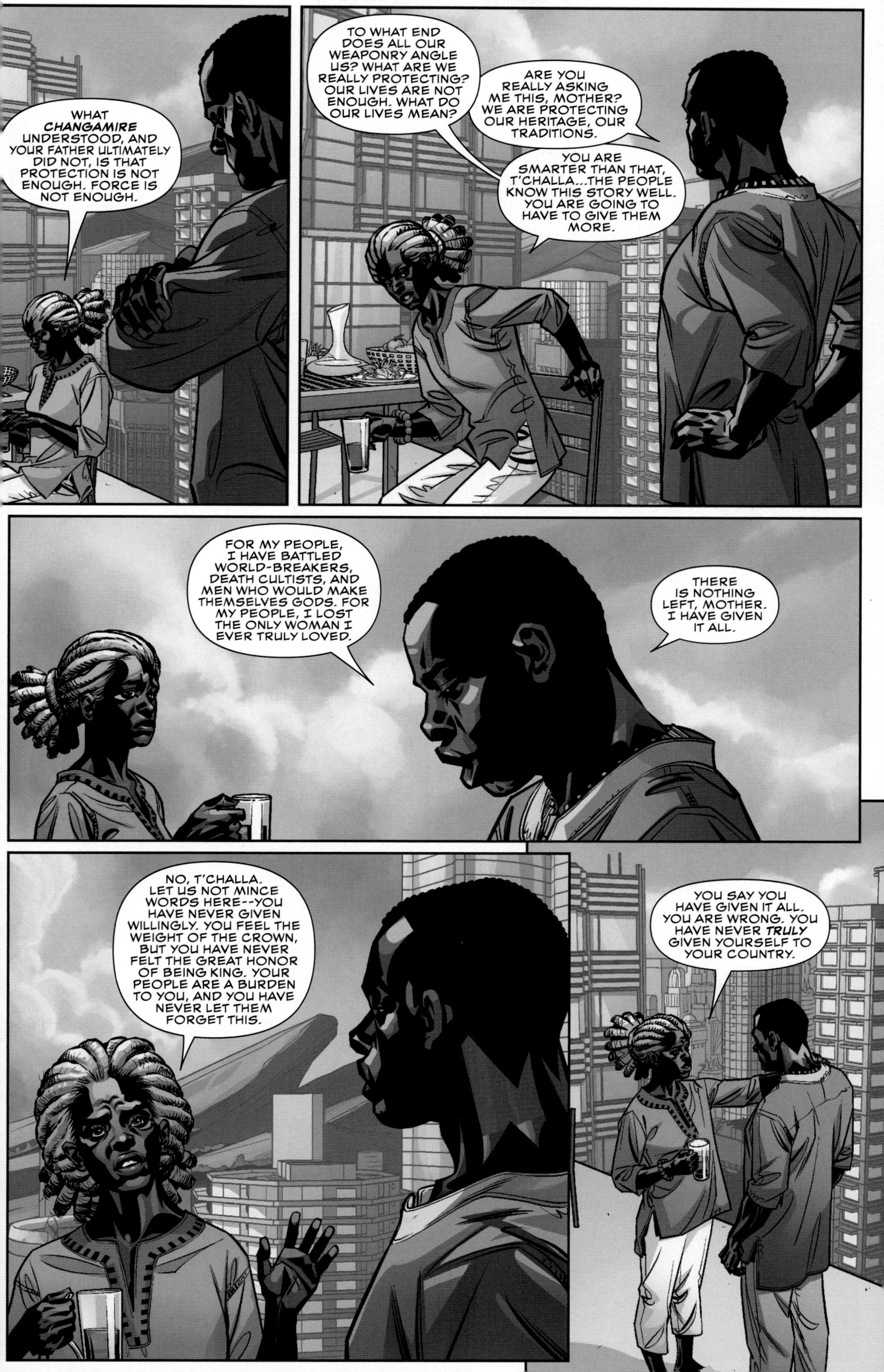

WHAT *CHANGAMIRE* UNDERSTOOD, AND YOUR FATHER ULTIMATELY DID NOT, IS THAT PROTECTION IS NOT ENOUGH. FORCE IS NOT ENOUGH.
TO WHAT END DOES ALL OUR WEAPONRY ANGLE US? WHAT ARE WE REALLY PROTECTING? OUR LIVES ARE NOT ENOUGH. WHAT DO OUR LIVES MEAN?
ARE YOU REALLY ASKING ME THIS, MOTHER? WE ARE PROTECTING OUR HERITAGE, OUR TRADITIONS.
YOU ARE SMARTER THAN THAT, T'CHALLA...THE PEOPLE KNOW THIS STORY WELL. YOU ARE GOING TO HAVE TO GIVE THEM MORE.
FOR MY PEOPLE, I HAVE BATTLED WORLD-BREAKERS, DEATH CULTISTS, AND MEN WHO WOULD MAKE THEMSELVES GODS. FOR MY PEOPLE, I LOST THE ONLY WOMAN I EVER TRULY LOVED.
THERE IS NOTHING LEFT, MOTHER. I HAVE GIVEN IT ALL.
NO, T'CHALLA. LET US NOT MINCE WORDS HERE--YOU HAVE NEVER GIVEN WILLINGLY. YOU FEEL THE WEIGHT OF THE CROWN, BUT YOU HAVE NEVER FELT THE GREAT HONOR OF BEING KING. YOUR PEOPLE ARE A BURDEN TO YOU, AND YOU HAVE NEVER LET THEM FORGET THIS.
YOU SAY YOU HAVE GIVEN IT ALL. YOU ARE WRONG. YOU HAVE NEVER *TRULY* GIVEN YOURSELF TO YOUR COUNTRY.

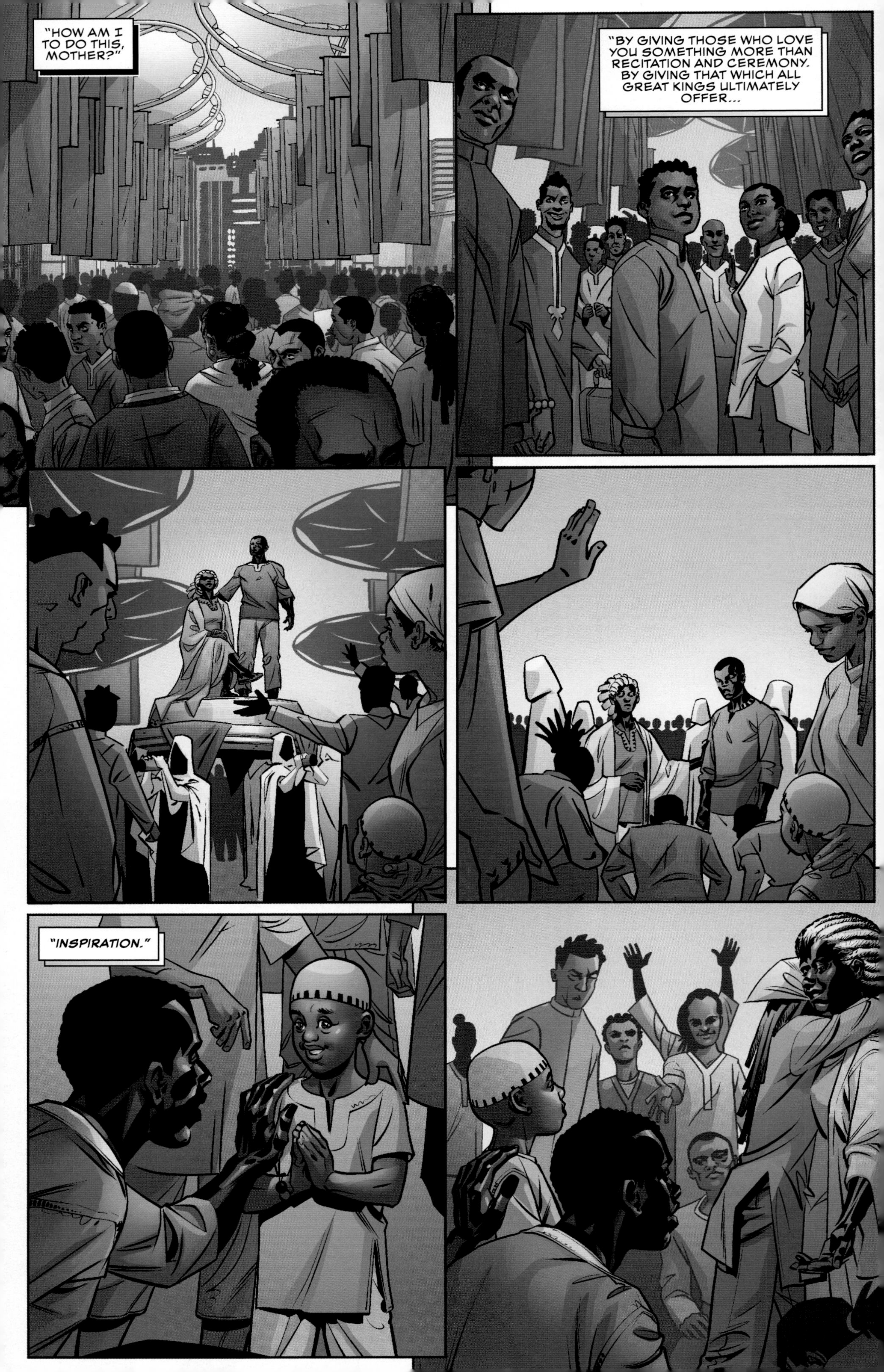
"HOW AM I TO DO THIS, MOTHER?"
"BY GIVING THOSE WHO LOVE YOU SOMETHING MORE THAN RECITATION AND CEREMONY. BY GIVING THAT WHICH ALL GREAT KINGS ULTIMATELY OFFER...
"INSPIRATION."

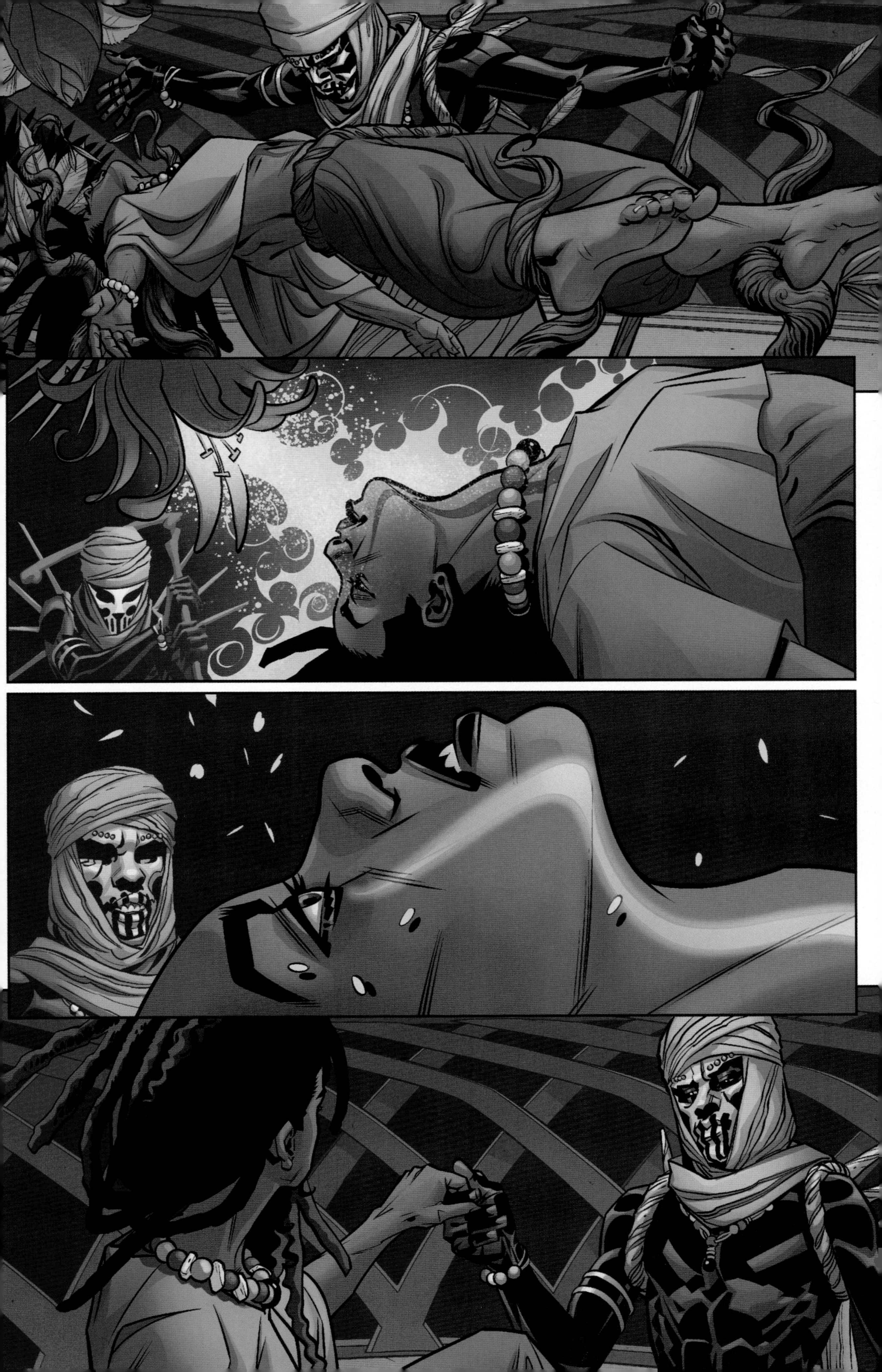

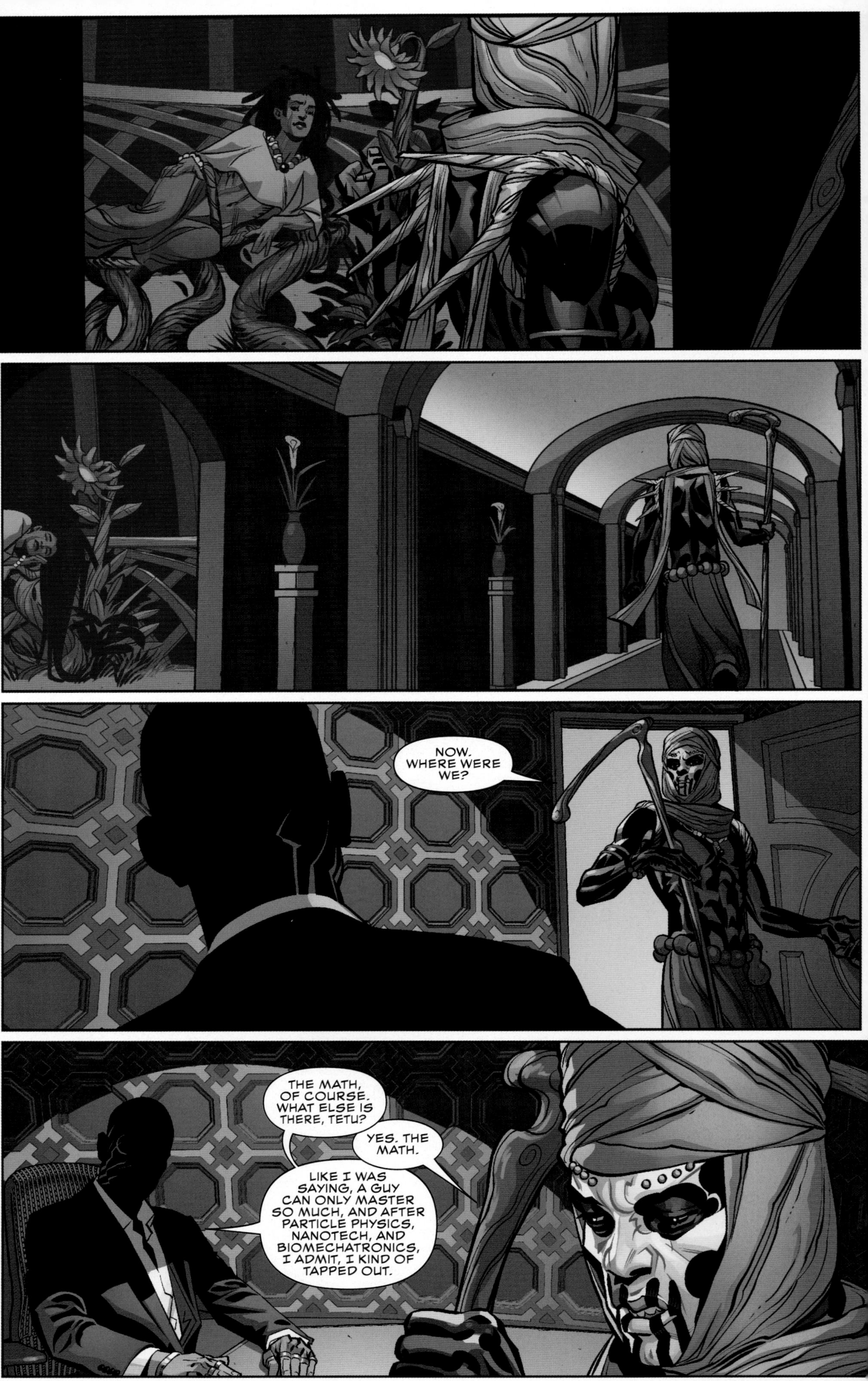
NOW. WHERE WERE WE?
THE MATH, OF COURSE. WHAT ELSE IS THERE, TETU?
YES. THE MATH.
LIKE I WAS SAYING, A GUY CAN ONLY MASTER SO MUCH, AND AFTER PARTICLE PHYSICS, NANOTECH, AND BIOMECHATRONICS, I ADMIT, I KIND OF TAPPED OUT.

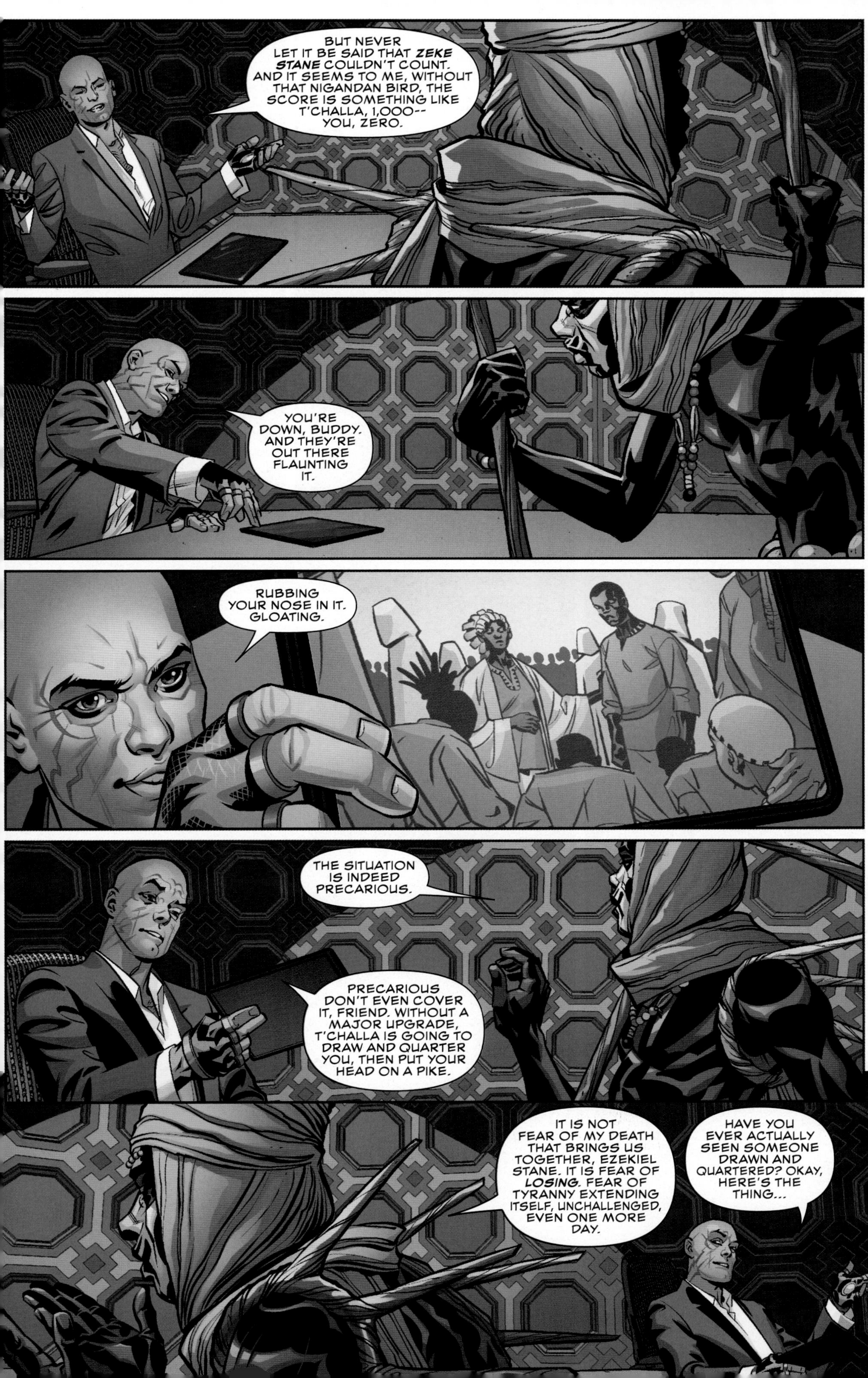
BUT NEVER LET IT BE SAID THAT ZEKE STANE COULDN'T COUNT. AND IT SEEMS TO ME, WITHOUT THAT NIGANDAN BIRD, THE SCORE IS SOMETHING LIKE T'CHALLA, 1,000-- YOU, ZERO.
YOU'RE DOWN, BUDDY. AND THEY'RE OUT THERE FLAUNTING IT.
RUBBING YOUR NOSE IN IT. GLOATING.
THE SITUATION IS INDEED PRECARIOUS.
PRECARIOUS DON'T EVEN COVER IT, FRIEND. WITHOUT A MAJOR UPGRADE, T'CHALLA IS GOING TO DRAW AND QUARTER YOU, THEN PUT YOUR HEAD ON A PIKE.
IT IS NOT FEAR OF MY DEATH THAT BRINGS US TOGETHER, EZEKIEL STANE. IT IS FEAR OF LOSING. FEAR OF TYRANNY EXTENDING ITSELF, UNCHALLENGED, EVEN ONE MORE DAY.
HAVE YOU EVER ACTUALLY SEEN SOMEONE DRAWN AND QUARTERED? OKAY, HERE'S THE THING...

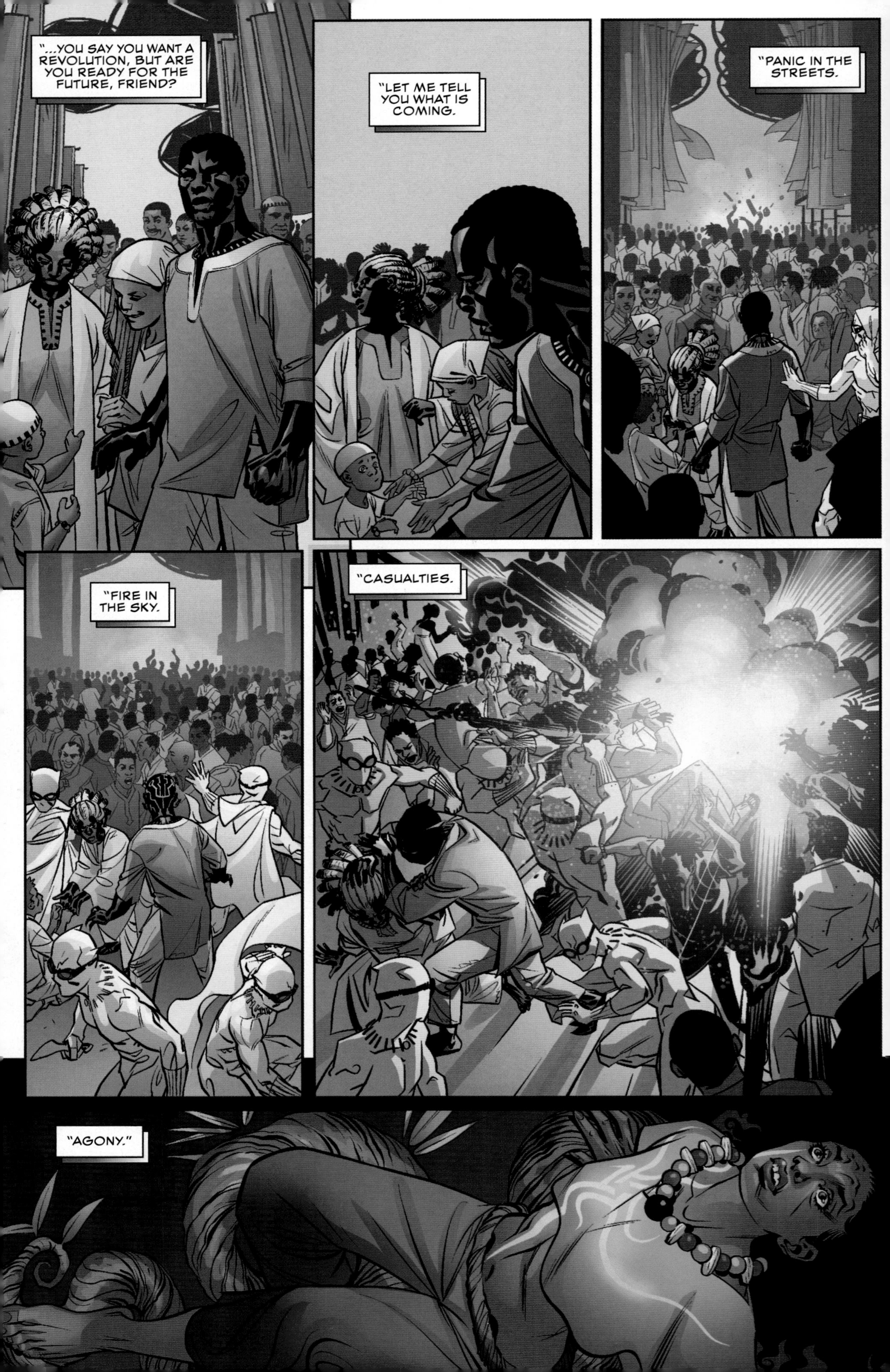
"...YOU SAY YOU WANT A REVOLUTION, BUT ARE YOU READY FOR THE FUTURE, FRIEND?
"LET ME TELL YOU WHAT IS COMING.
"PANIC IN THE STREETS.
"FIRE IN THE SKY.
"CASUALTIES.
"AGONY."

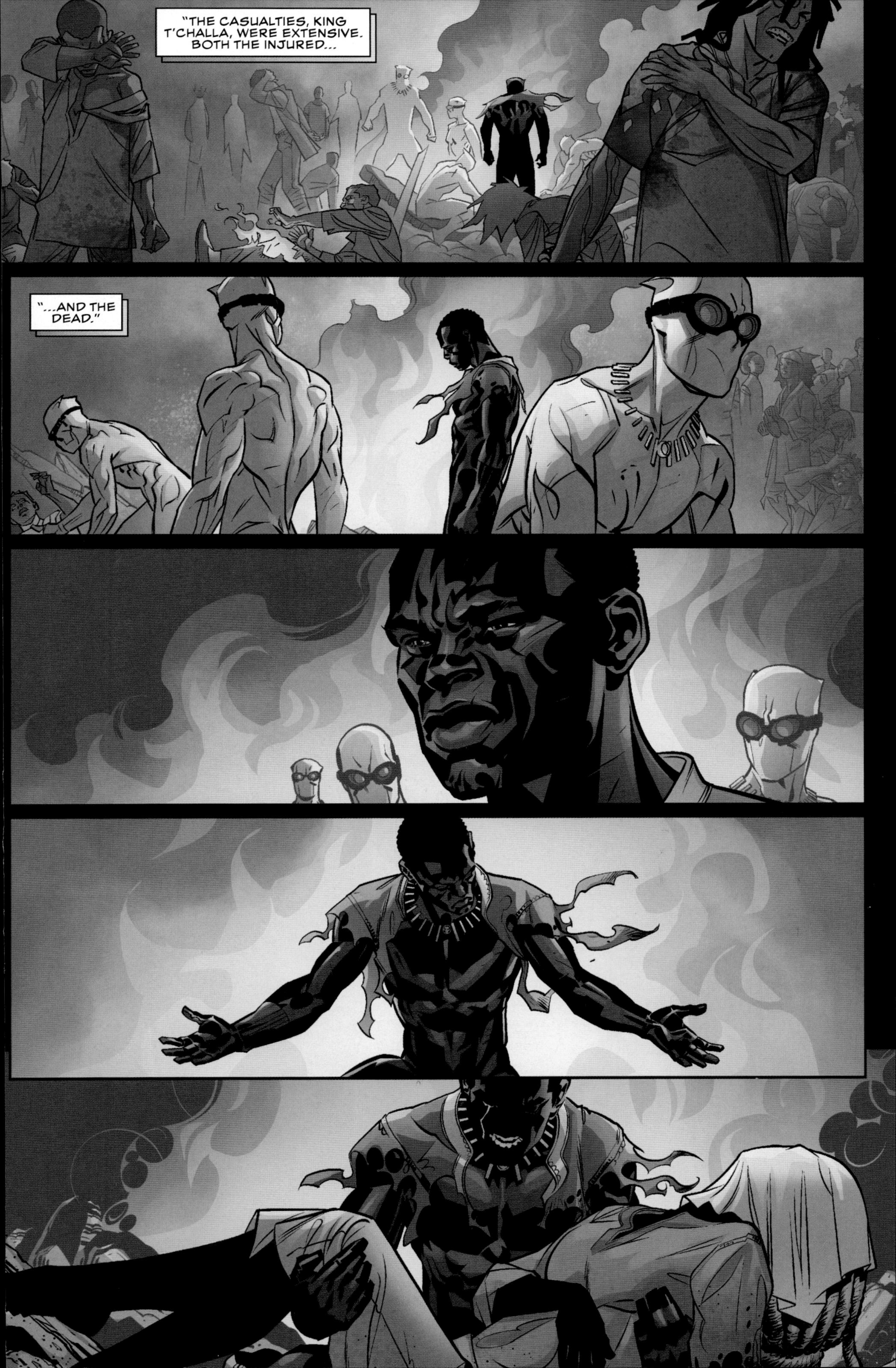
"THE CASUALTIES, KING T'CHALLA, WERE EXTENSIVE. BOTH THE INJURED...
"...AND THE DEAD."

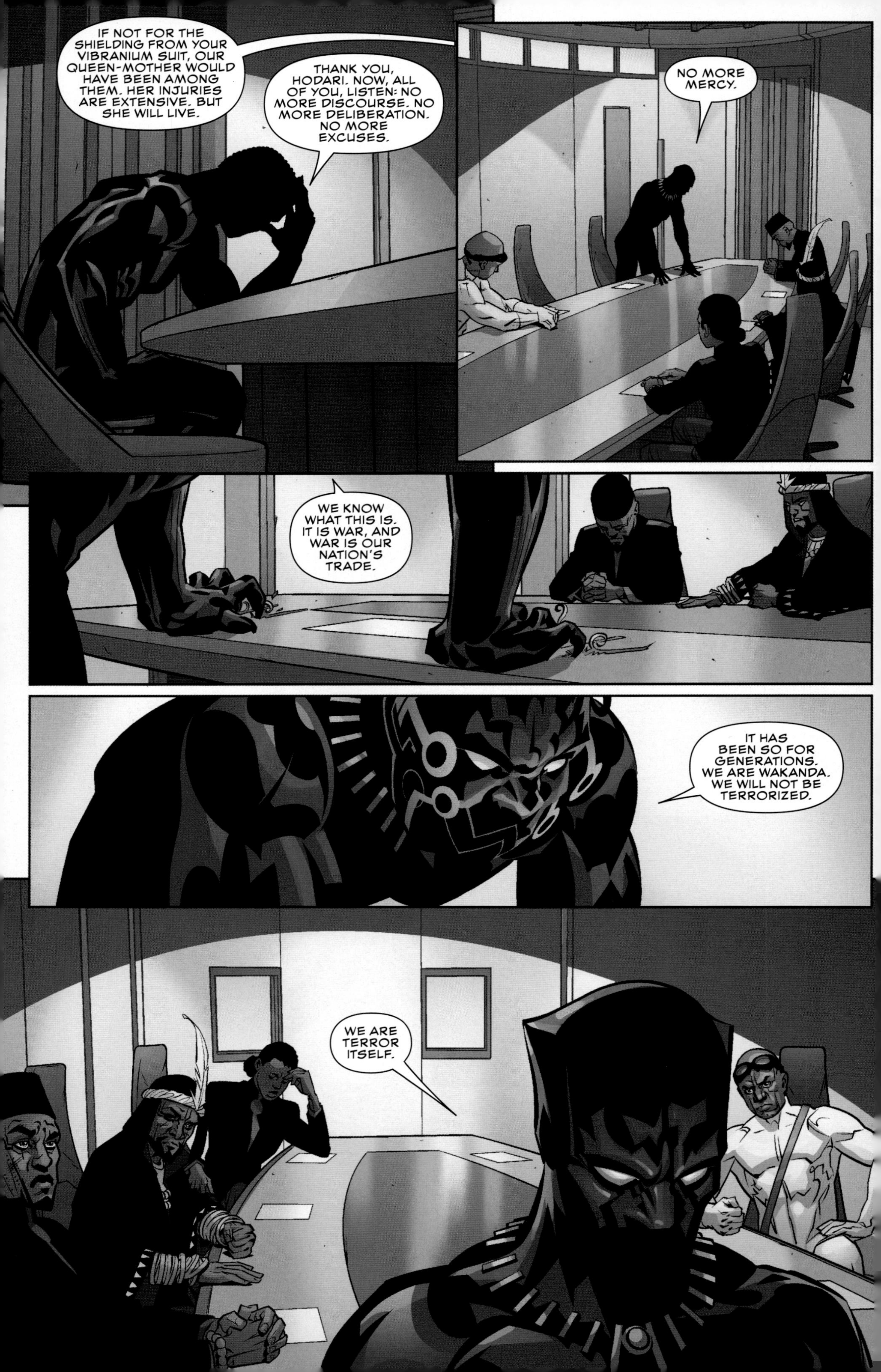
IF NOT FOR THE SHIELDING FROM YOUR VIBRANIUM SUIT, OUR QUEEN-MOTHER WOULD HAVE BEEN AMONG THEM. HER INJURIES ARE EXTENSIVE. BUT SHE WILL LIVE.
THANK YOU, HODARI. NOW, ALL OF YOU, LISTEN: NO MORE DISCOURSE. NO MORE DELIBERATION. NO MORE EXCUSES.
NO MORE MERCY.
WE KNOW WHAT THIS IS. IT IS WAR, AND WAR IS OUR NATION'S TRADE.
IT HAS BEEN SO FOR GENERATIONS. WE ARE WAKANDA. WE WILL NOT BE TERRORIZED.
WE ARE TERROR ITSELF.

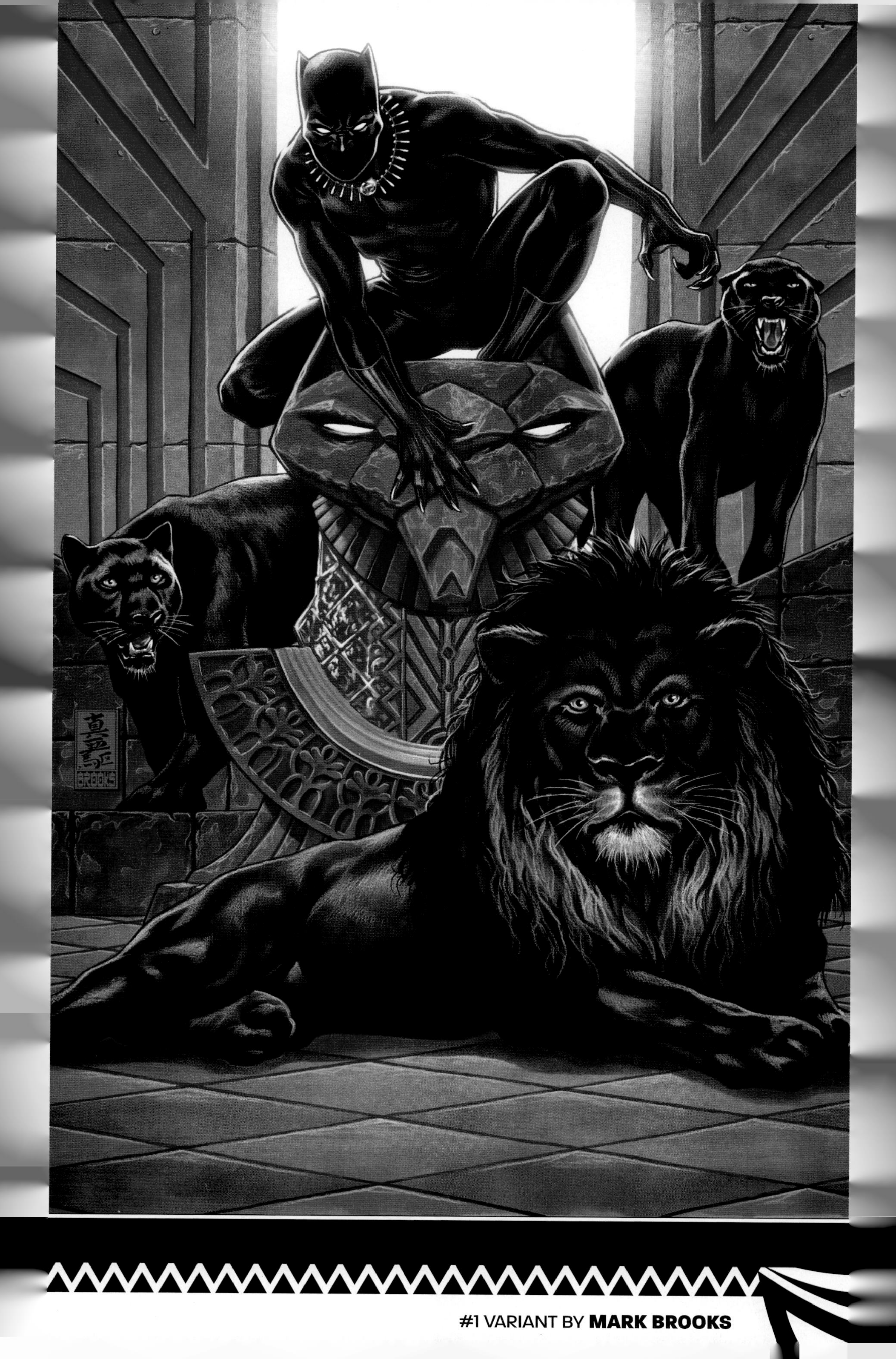
BROOKS

#1 VARIANT BY **MARK BROOKS**

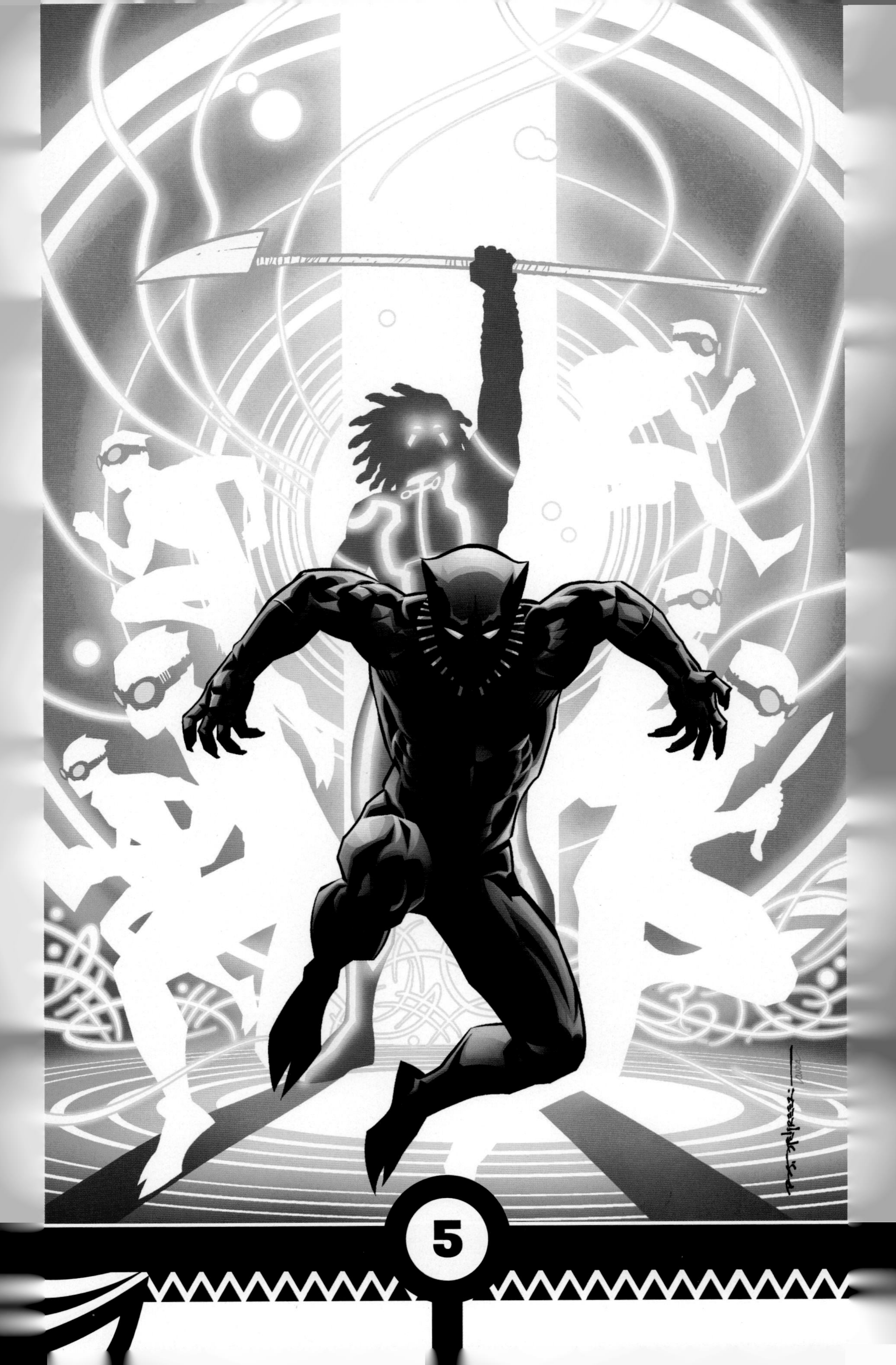
5

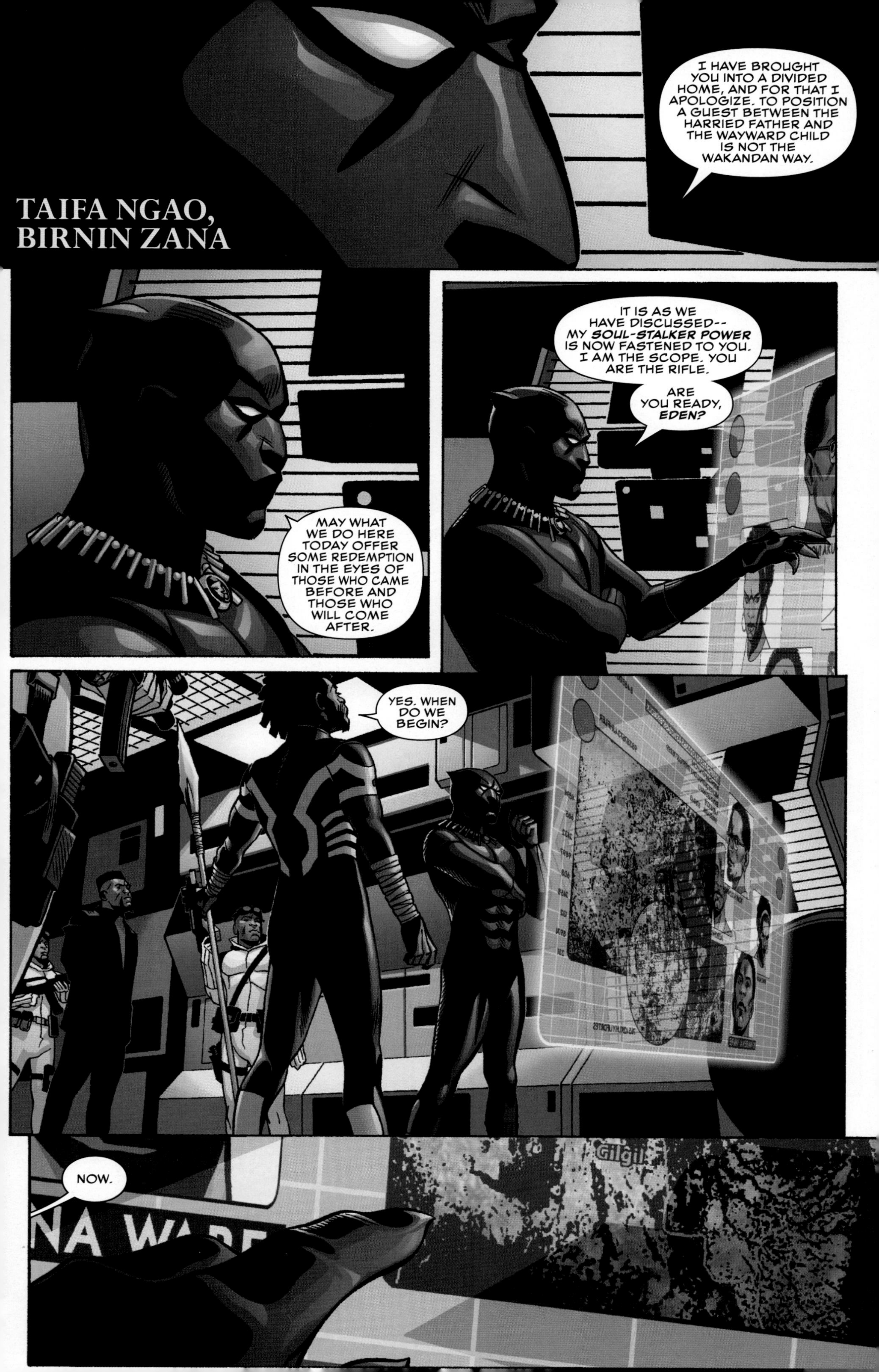
TAIFA NGAO,
BIRNIN ZANA
I HAVE BROUGHT YOU INTO A DIVIDED HOME, AND FOR THAT I APOLOGIZE. TO POSITION A GUEST BETWEEN THE HARRIED FATHER AND THE WAYWARD CHILD IS NOT THE WAKANDAN WAY.
MAY WHAT WE DO HERE TODAY OFFER SOME REDEMPTION IN THE EYES OF THOSE WHO CAME BEFORE AND THOSE WHO WILL COME AFTER.
IT IS AS WE HAVE DISCUSSED-- MY SOUL-STALKER POWER IS NOW FASTENED TO YOU. I AM THE SCOPE. YOU ARE THE RIFLE.
ARE YOU READY, EDEN?
YES. WHEN DO WE BEGIN?
NOW.
Gilgil

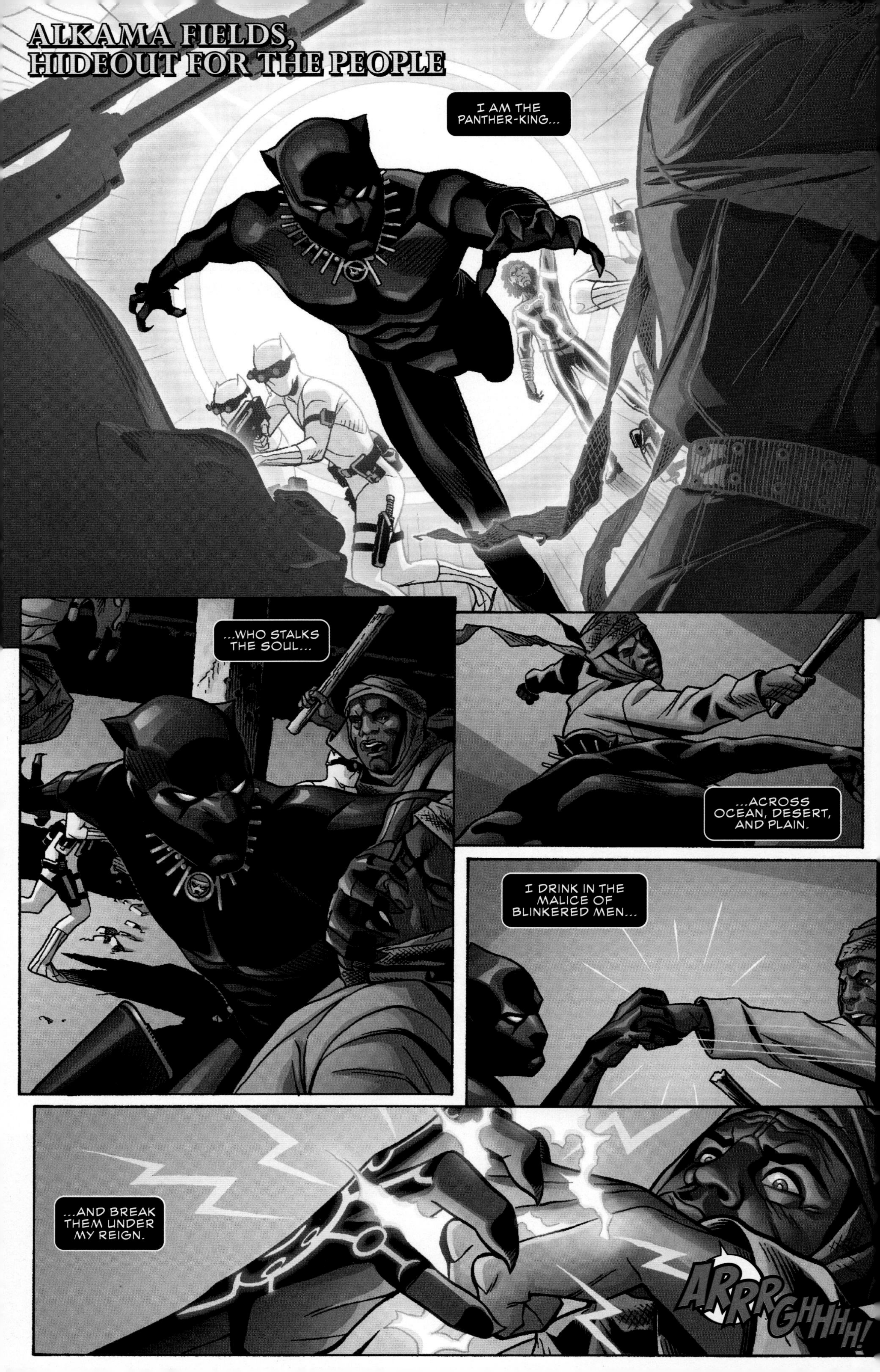
ALKAMA FIELDS, HIDEOUT FOR THE PEOPLE
I AM THE PANTHER-KING...
...WHO STALKS THE SOUL...
...ACROSS OCEAN, DESERT, AND PLAIN.
I DRINK IN THE MALICE OF BLINKERED MEN...
...AND BREAK THEM UNDER MY REIGN.
ARRRGHHHH!

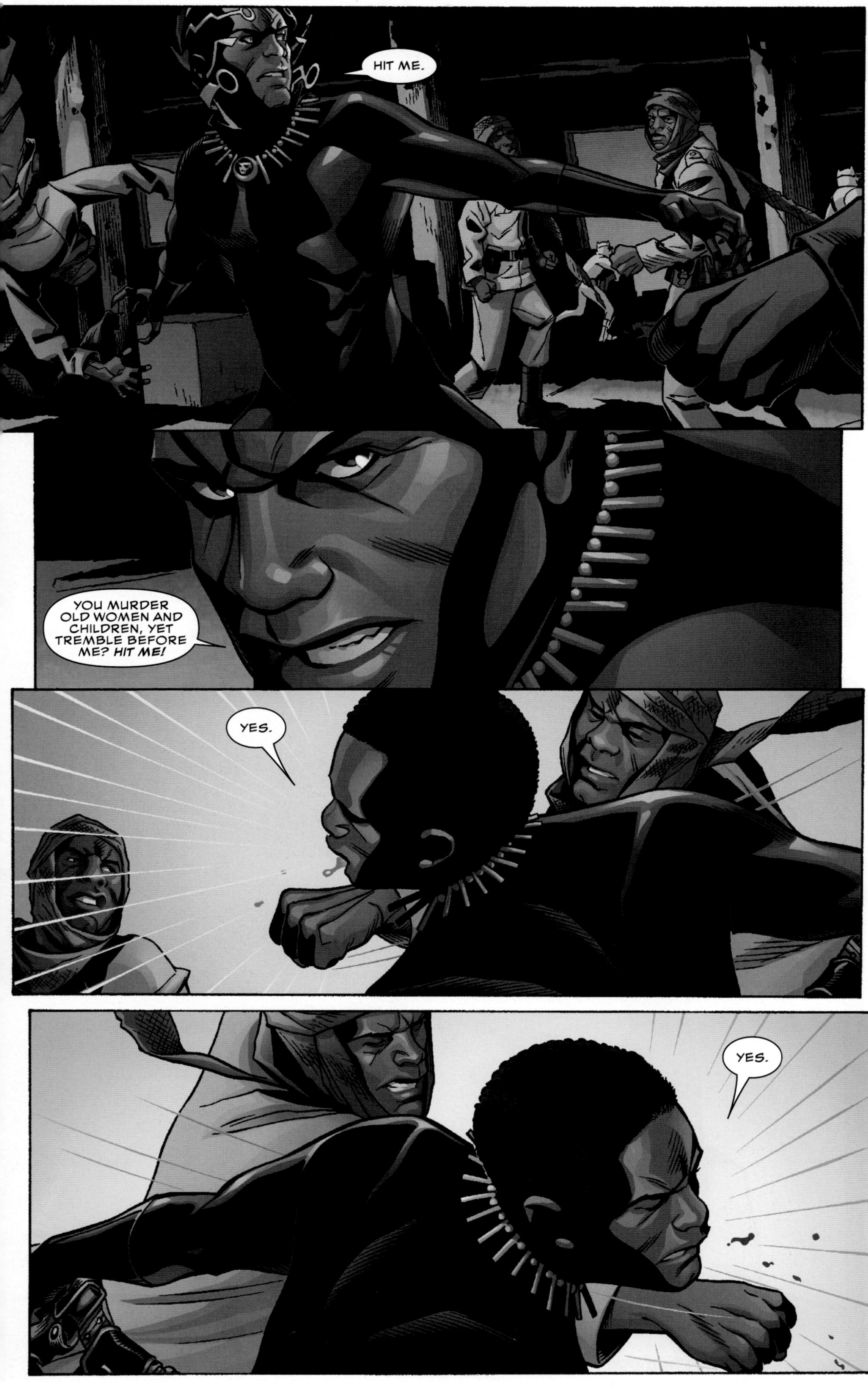
HIT ME.
YOU MURDER OLD WOMEN AND CHILDREN, YET TREMBLE BEFORE ME? *HIT ME!*
YES.
YES.

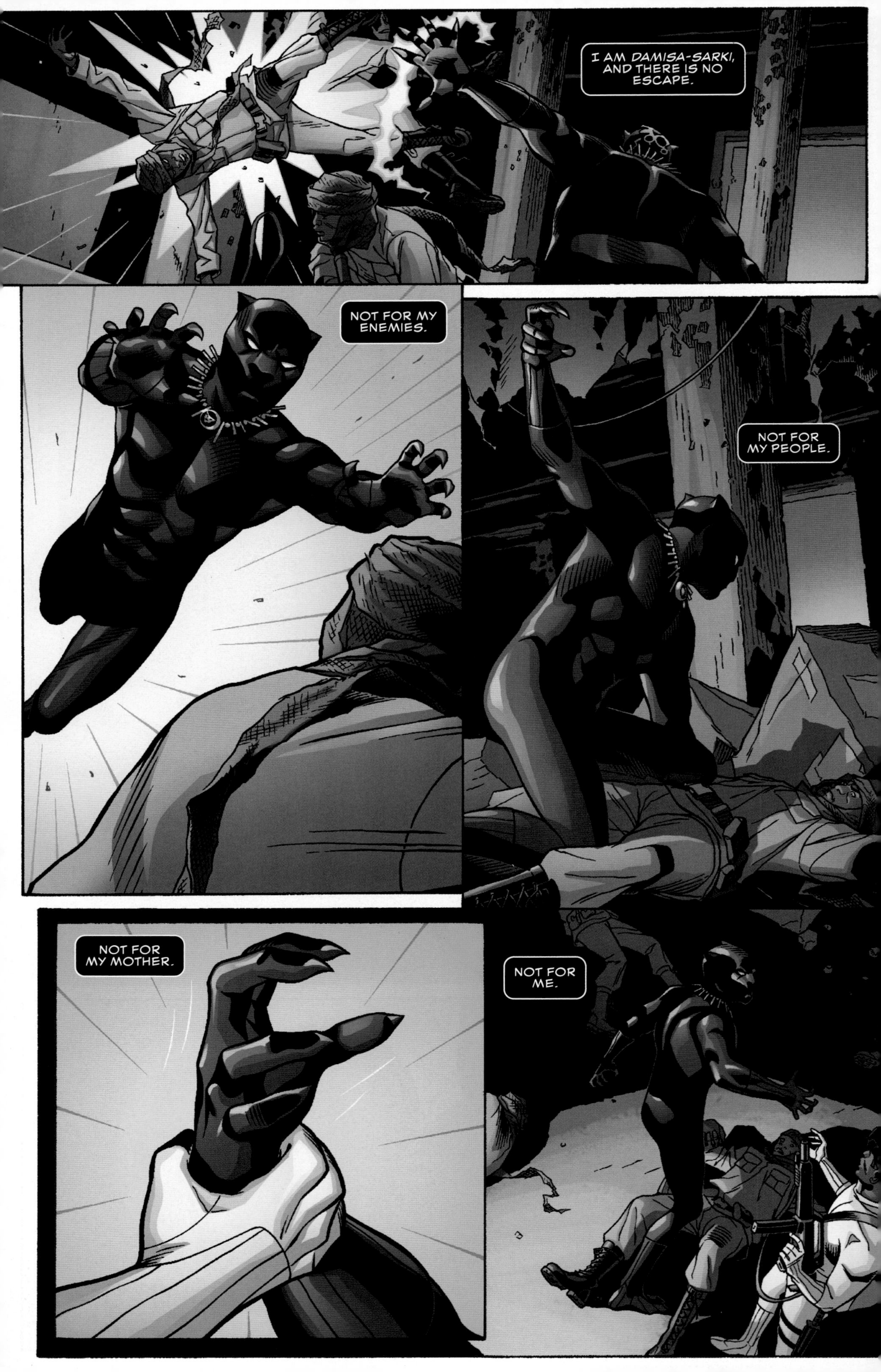
I AM DAMISA-SARKI, AND THERE IS NO ESCAPE.
NOT FOR MY ENEMIES.
NOT FOR MY PEOPLE.
NOT FOR MY MOTHER.
NOT FOR ME.

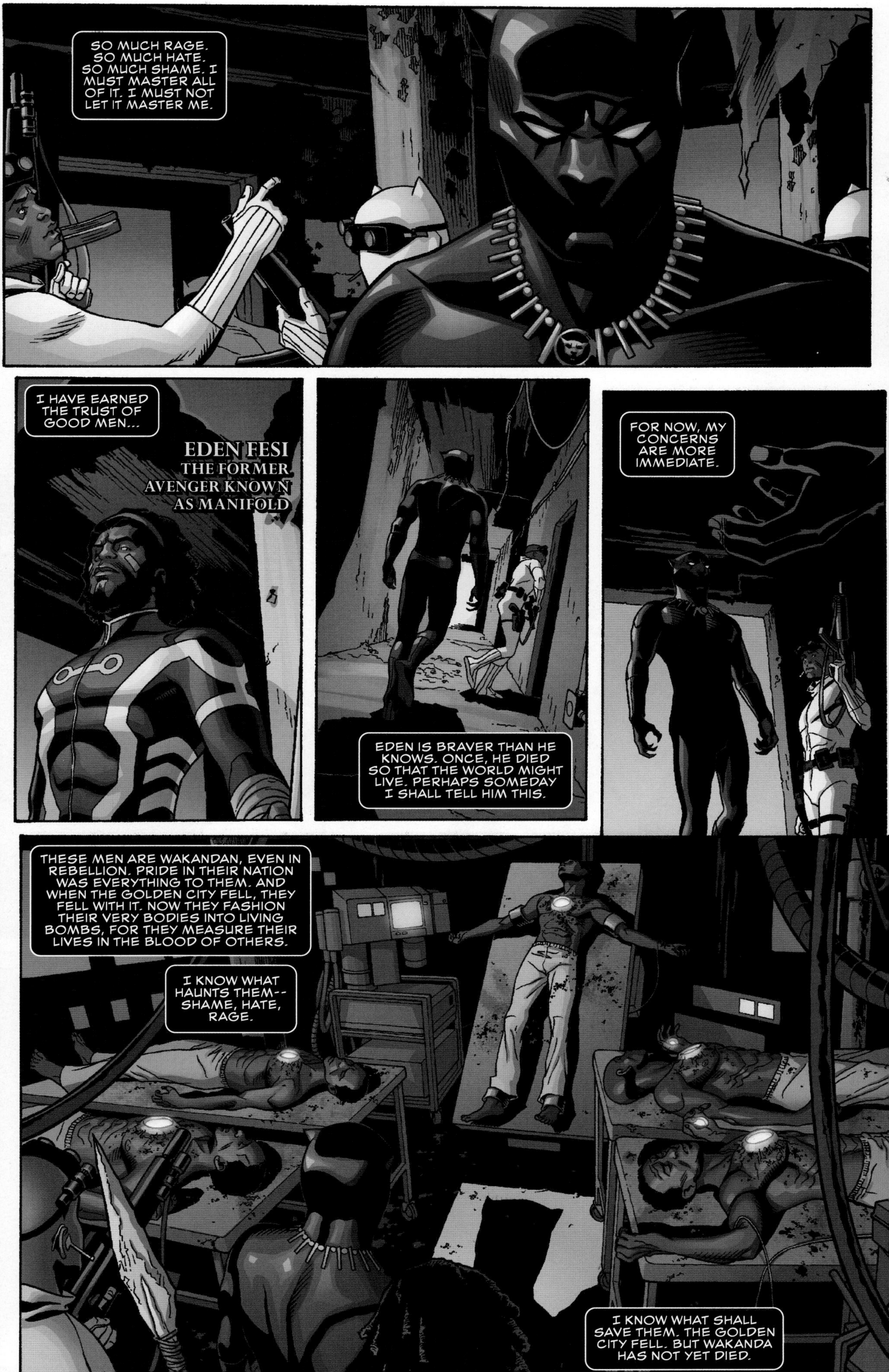
SO MUCH RAGE. SO MUCH HATE. SO MUCH SHAME. I MUST MASTER ALL OF IT. I MUST NOT LET IT MASTER ME.
I HAVE EARNED THE TRUST OF GOOD MEN...
EDEN FESI THE FORMER AVENGER KNOWN AS MANIFOLD
EDEN IS BRAVER THAN HE KNOWS. ONCE, HE DIED SO THAT THE WORLD MIGHT LIVE. PERHAPS SOMEDAY I SHALL TELL HIM THIS.
FOR NOW, MY CONCERNS ARE MORE IMMEDIATE.
THESE MEN ARE WAKANDAN, EVEN IN REBELLION. PRIDE IN THEIR NATION WAS EVERYTHING TO THEM. AND WHEN THE GOLDEN CITY FELL, THEY FELL WITH IT. NOW THEY FASHION THEIR VERY BODIES INTO LIVING BOMBS, FOR THEY MEASURE THEIR LIVES IN THE BLOOD OF OTHERS.
I KNOW WHAT HAUNTS THEM-- SHAME, HATE, RAGE.
I KNOW WHAT SHALL SAVE THEM. THE GOLDEN CITY FELL. BUT WAKANDA HAS NOT YET DIED.

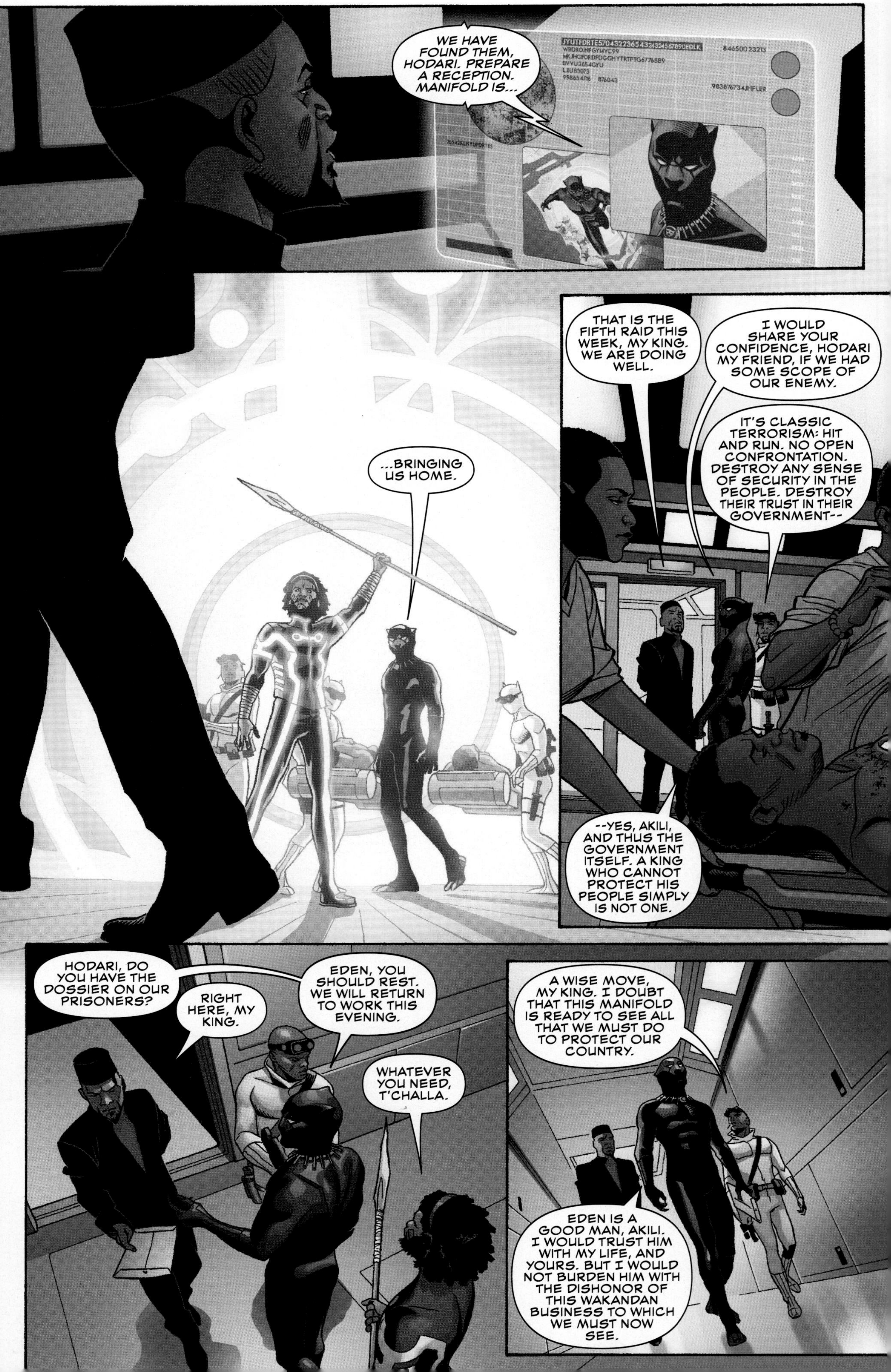
WE HAVE FOUND THEM, HODARI. PREPARE A RECEPTION. MANIFOLD IS...
...BRINGING US HOME.
THAT IS THE FIFTH RAID THIS WEEK, MY KING. WE ARE DOING WELL.
I WOULD SHARE YOUR CONFIDENCE, HODARI MY FRIEND, IF WE HAD SOME SCOPE OF OUR ENEMY.
IT'S CLASSIC TERRORISM: HIT AND RUN. NO OPEN CONFRONTATION. DESTROY ANY SENSE OF SECURITY IN THE PEOPLE. DESTROY THEIR TRUST IN THEIR GOVERNMENT--
--YES, AKILI, AND THUS THE GOVERNMENT ITSELF. A KING WHO CANNOT PROTECT HIS PEOPLE SIMPLY IS NOT ONE.
HODARI, DO YOU HAVE THE DOSSIER ON OUR PRISONERS?
RIGHT HERE, MY KING.
EDEN, YOU SHOULD REST. WE WILL RETURN TO WORK THIS EVENING.
WHATEVER YOU NEED, T'CHALLA.
A WISE MOVE, MY KING. I DOUBT THAT THIS MANIFOLD IS READY TO SEE ALL THAT WE MUST DO TO PROTECT OUR COUNTRY.
EDEN IS A GOOD MAN, AKILI. I WOULD TRUST HIM WITH MY LIFE, AND YOURS. BUT I WOULD NOT BURDEN HIM WITH THE DISHONOR OF THIS WAKANDAN BUSINESS TO WHICH WE MUST NOW SEE.

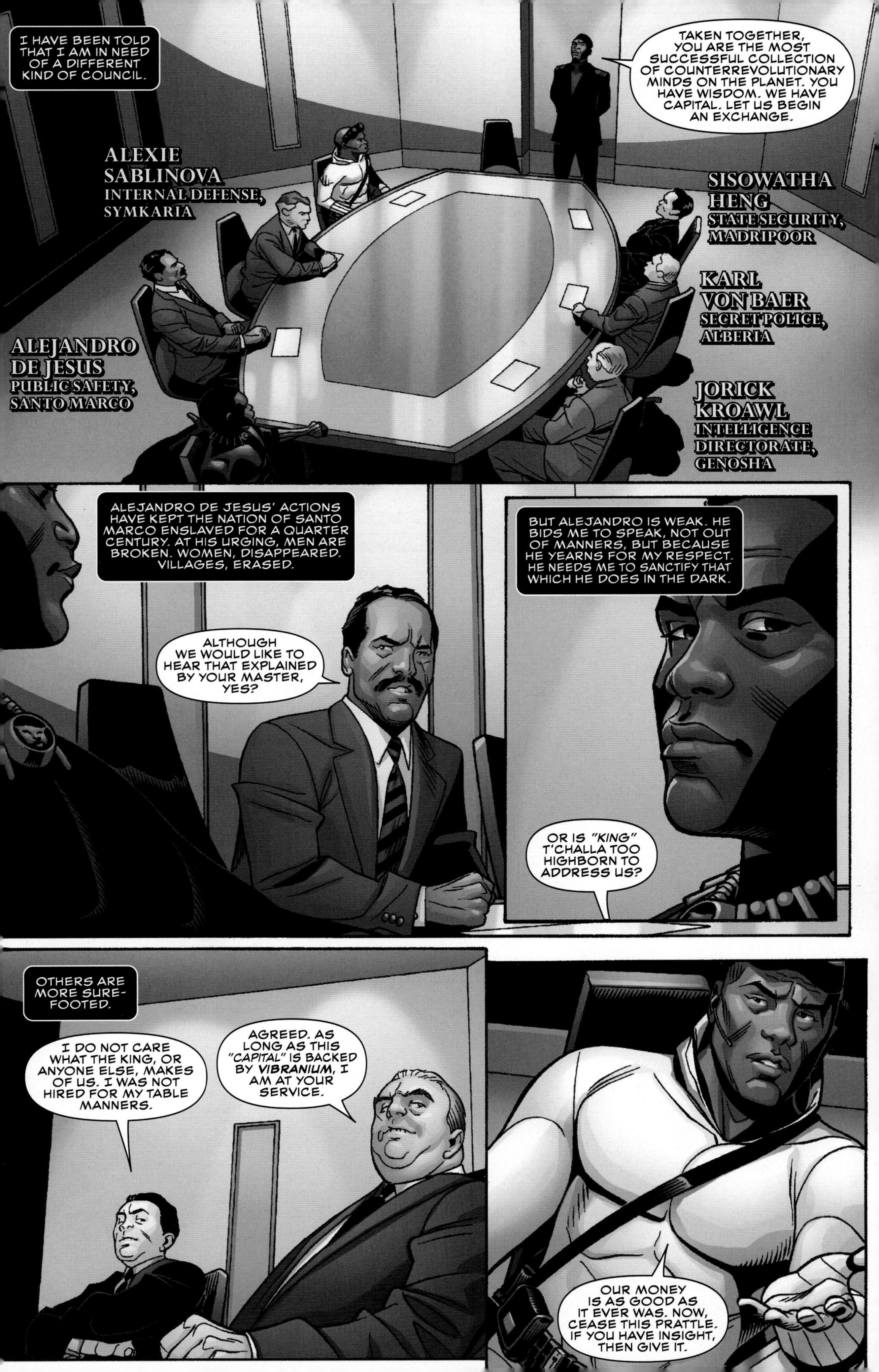

I HAVE BEEN TOLD THAT I AM IN NEED OF A DIFFERENT KIND OF COUNCIL.
TAKEN TOGETHER, YOU ARE THE MOST SUCCESSFUL COLLECTION OF COUNTERREVOLUTIONARY MINDS ON THE PLANET. YOU HAVE WISDOM. WE HAVE CAPITAL. LET US BEGIN AN EXCHANGE.
ALEXIE SABLINOVA INTERNAL DEFENSE, SYMKARIA
SISOWATHA HENG STATE SECURITY, MADRIPOOR
KARL VON BAER SECRET POLICE, ALBERIA
ALEJANDRO DE JESUS PUBLIC SAFETY, SANTO MARCO
JORICK KROAWL INTELLIGENCE DIRECTORATE, GENOSHA
ALEJANDRO DE JESUS' ACTIONS HAVE KEPT THE NATION OF SANTO MARCO ENSLAVED FOR A QUARTER CENTURY. AT HIS URGING, MEN ARE BROKEN. WOMEN, DISAPPEARED. VILLAGES, ERASED.
ALTHOUGH WE WOULD LIKE TO HEAR THAT EXPLAINED BY YOUR MASTER, YES?
BUT ALEJANDRO IS WEAK. HE BIDS ME TO SPEAK, NOT OUT OF MANNERS, BUT BECAUSE HE YEARNS FOR MY RESPECT. HE NEEDS ME TO SANCTIFY THAT WHICH HE DOES IN THE DARK.
OR IS "KING" T'CHALLA TOO HIGHBORN TO ADDRESS US?
OTHERS ARE MORE SURE-FOOTED.
I DO NOT CARE WHAT THE KING, OR ANYONE ELSE, MAKES OF US. I WAS NOT HIRED FOR MY TABLE MANNERS.
AGREED. AS LONG AS THIS "CAPITAL" IS BACKED BY VIBRANIUM, I AM AT YOUR SERVICE.
OUR MONEY IS AS GOOD AS IT EVER WAS. NOW, CEASE THIS PRATTLE. IF YOU HAVE INSIGHT, THEN GIVE IT.

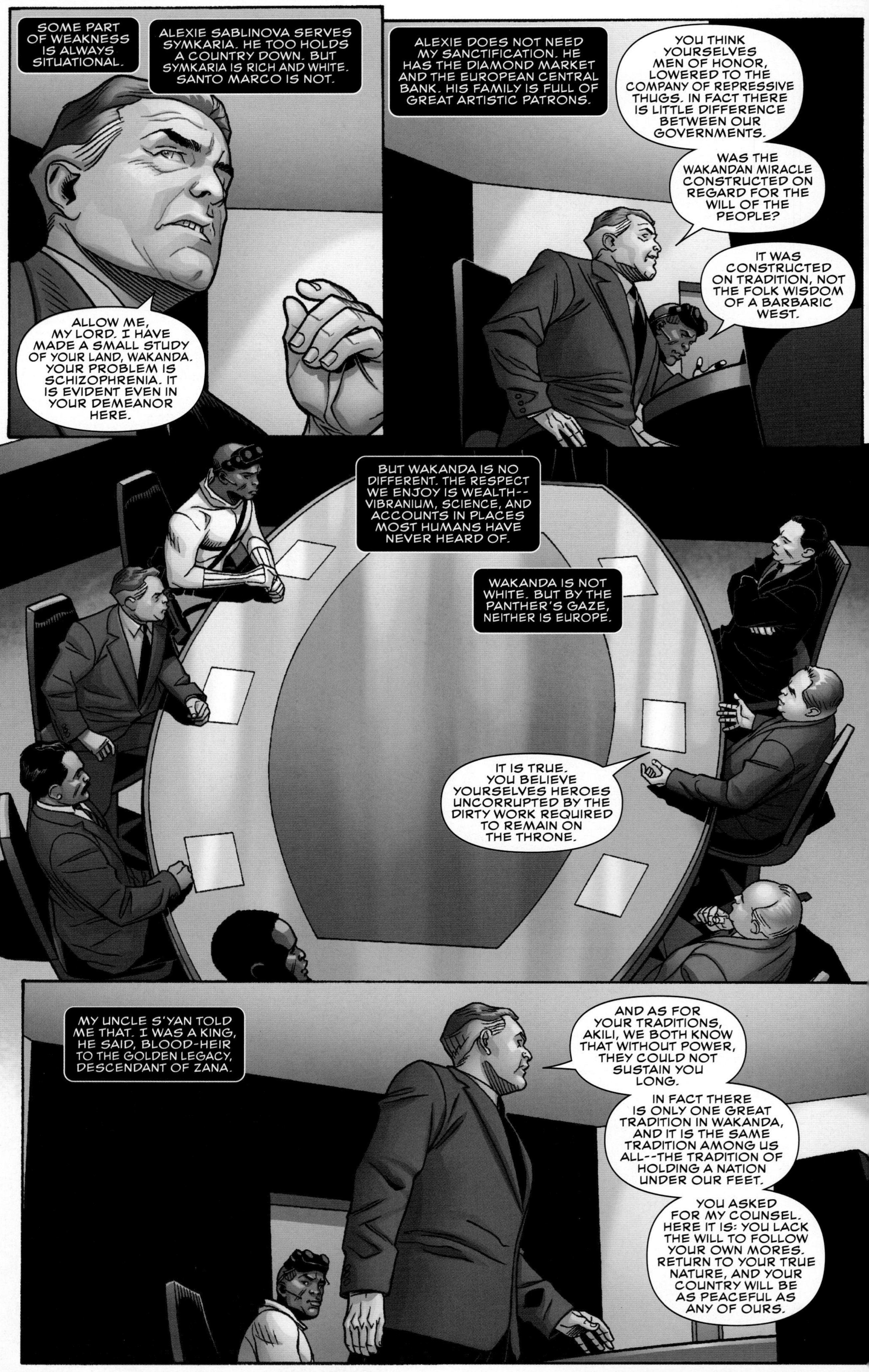
SOME PART OF WEAKNESS IS ALWAYS SITUATIONAL.
ALEXIE SABLINOVA SERVES SYMKARIA. HE TOO HOLDS A COUNTRY DOWN. BUT SYMKARIA IS RICH AND WHITE. SANTO MARCO IS NOT.
ALLOW ME, MY LORD. I HAVE MADE A SMALL STUDY OF YOUR LAND, WAKANDA. YOUR PROBLEM IS SCHIZOPHRENIA. IT IS EVIDENT EVEN IN YOUR DEMEANOR HERE.
ALEXIE DOES NOT NEED MY SANCTIFICATION. HE HAS THE DIAMOND MARKET AND THE EUROPEAN CENTRAL BANK. HIS FAMILY IS FULL OF GREAT ARTISTIC PATRONS.
YOU THINK YOURSELVES MEN OF HONOR, LOWERED TO THE COMPANY OF REPRESSIVE THUGS. IN FACT THERE IS LITTLE DIFFERENCE BETWEEN OUR GOVERNMENTS.
WAS THE WAKANDAN MIRACLE CONSTRUCTED ON REGARD FOR THE WILL OF THE PEOPLE?
IT WAS CONSTRUCTED ON TRADITION, NOT THE FOLK WISDOM OF A BARBARIC WEST.
BUT WAKANDA IS NO DIFFERENT. THE RESPECT WE ENJOY IS WEALTH--VIBRANIUM, SCIENCE, AND ACCOUNTS IN PLACES MOST HUMANS HAVE NEVER HEARD OF.
WAKANDA IS NOT WHITE. BUT BY THE PANTHER'S GAZE, NEITHER IS EUROPE.
IT IS TRUE. YOU BELIEVE YOURSELVES HEROES UNCORRUPTED BY THE DIRTY WORK REQUIRED TO REMAIN ON THE THRONE.
MY UNCLE S'YAN TOLD ME THAT. I WAS A KING, HE SAID, BLOOD-HEIR TO THE GOLDEN LEGACY, DESCENDANT OF ZANA.
AND AS FOR YOUR TRADITIONS, AKILI, WE BOTH KNOW THAT WITHOUT POWER, THEY COULD NOT SUSTAIN YOU LONG.
IN FACT THERE IS ONLY ONE GREAT TRADITION IN WAKANDA, AND IT IS THE SAME TRADITION AMONG US ALL--THE TRADITION OF HOLDING A NATION UNDER OUR FEET.
YOU ASKED FOR MY COUNSEL. HERE IT IS: YOU LACK THE WILL TO FOLLOW YOUR OWN MORES. RETURN TO YOUR TRUE NATURE, AND YOUR COUNTRY WILL BE AS PEACEFUL AS ANY OF OURS.

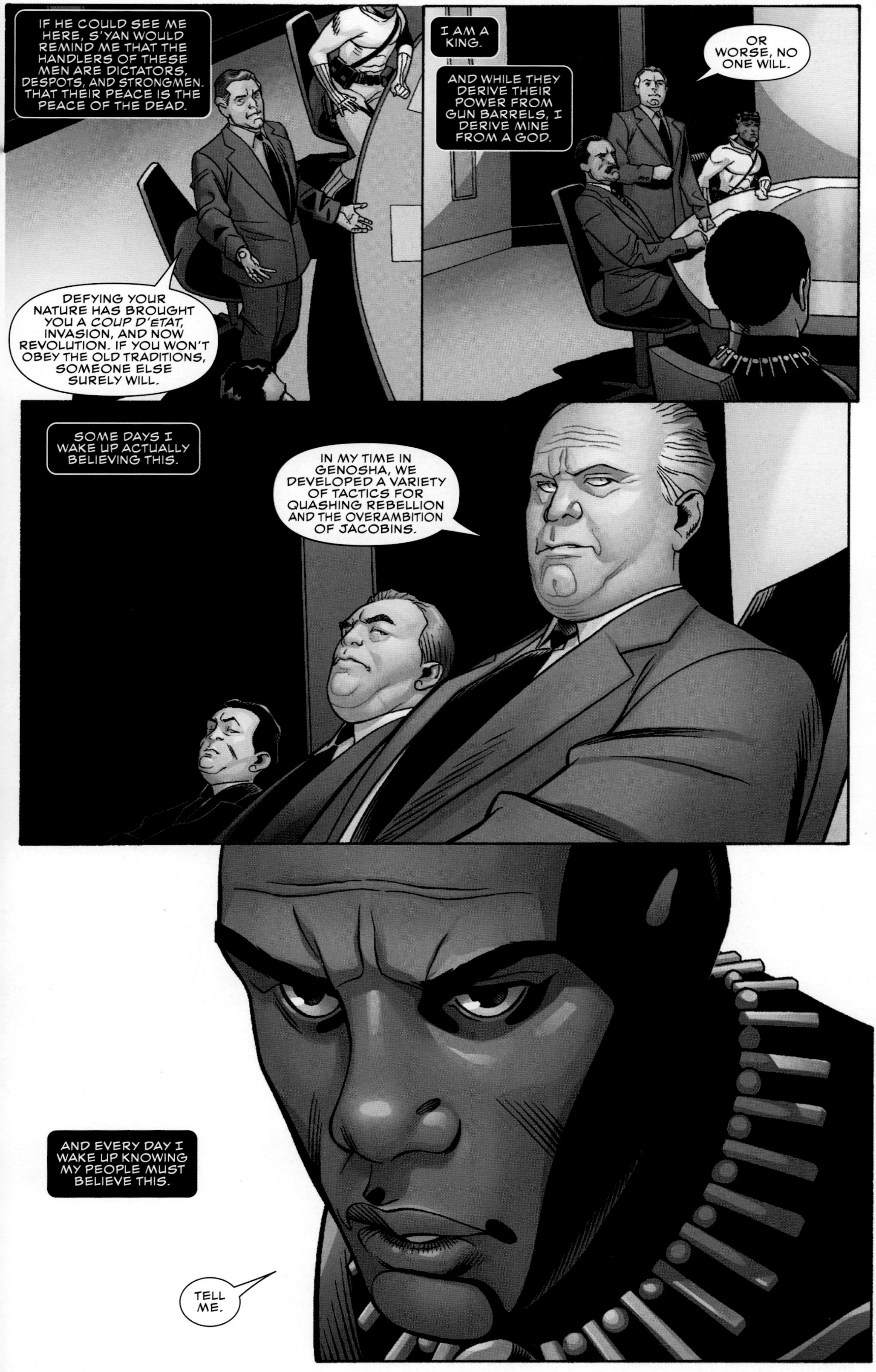
IF HE COULD SEE ME HERE, S'YAN WOULD REMIND ME THAT THE HANDLERS OF THESE MEN ARE DICTATORS, DESPOTS, AND STRONGMEN. THAT THEIR PEACE IS THE PEACE OF THE DEAD.
DEFYING YOUR NATURE HAS BROUGHT YOU A *COUP D'ETAT*, INVASION, AND NOW REVOLUTION. IF YOU WON'T OBEY THE OLD TRADITIONS, SOMEONE ELSE SURELY WILL.
I AM A KING.
AND WHILE THEY DERIVE THEIR POWER FROM GUN BARRELS, I DERIVE MINE FROM A GOD.
OR WORSE, NO ONE WILL.
SOME DAYS I WAKE UP ACTUALLY BELIEVING THIS.
IN MY TIME IN GENOSHA, WE DEVELOPED A VARIETY OF TACTICS FOR QUASHING REBELLION AND THE OVERAMBITION OF JACOBINS.
AND EVERY DAY I WAKE UP KNOWING MY PEOPLE MUST BELIEVE THIS.
TELL ME.

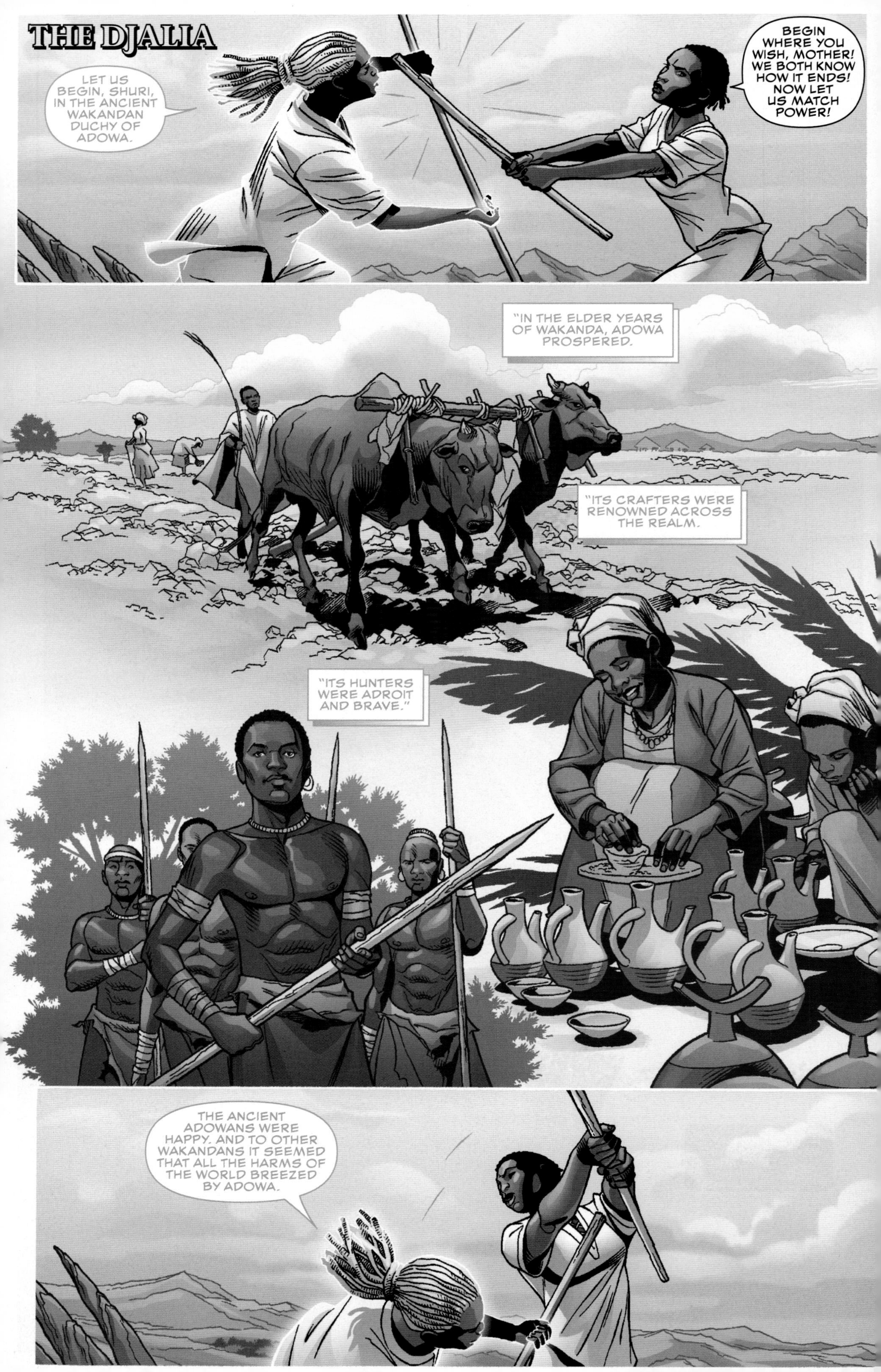
THE DJALIA
LET US BEGIN, SHURI, IN THE ANCIENT WAKANDAN DUCHY OF ADOWA.
BEGIN WHERE YOU WISH, MOTHER! WE BOTH KNOW HOW IT ENDS! NOW LET US MATCH POWER!
"IN THE ELDER YEARS OF WAKANDA, ADOWA PROSPERED.
"ITS CRAFTERS WERE RENOWNED ACROSS THE REALM.
"ITS HUNTERS WERE ADROIT AND BRAVE."
THE ANCIENT ADOWANS WERE HAPPY. AND TO OTHER WAKANDANS IT SEEMED THAT ALL THE HARMS OF THE WORLD BREEZED BY ADOWA.

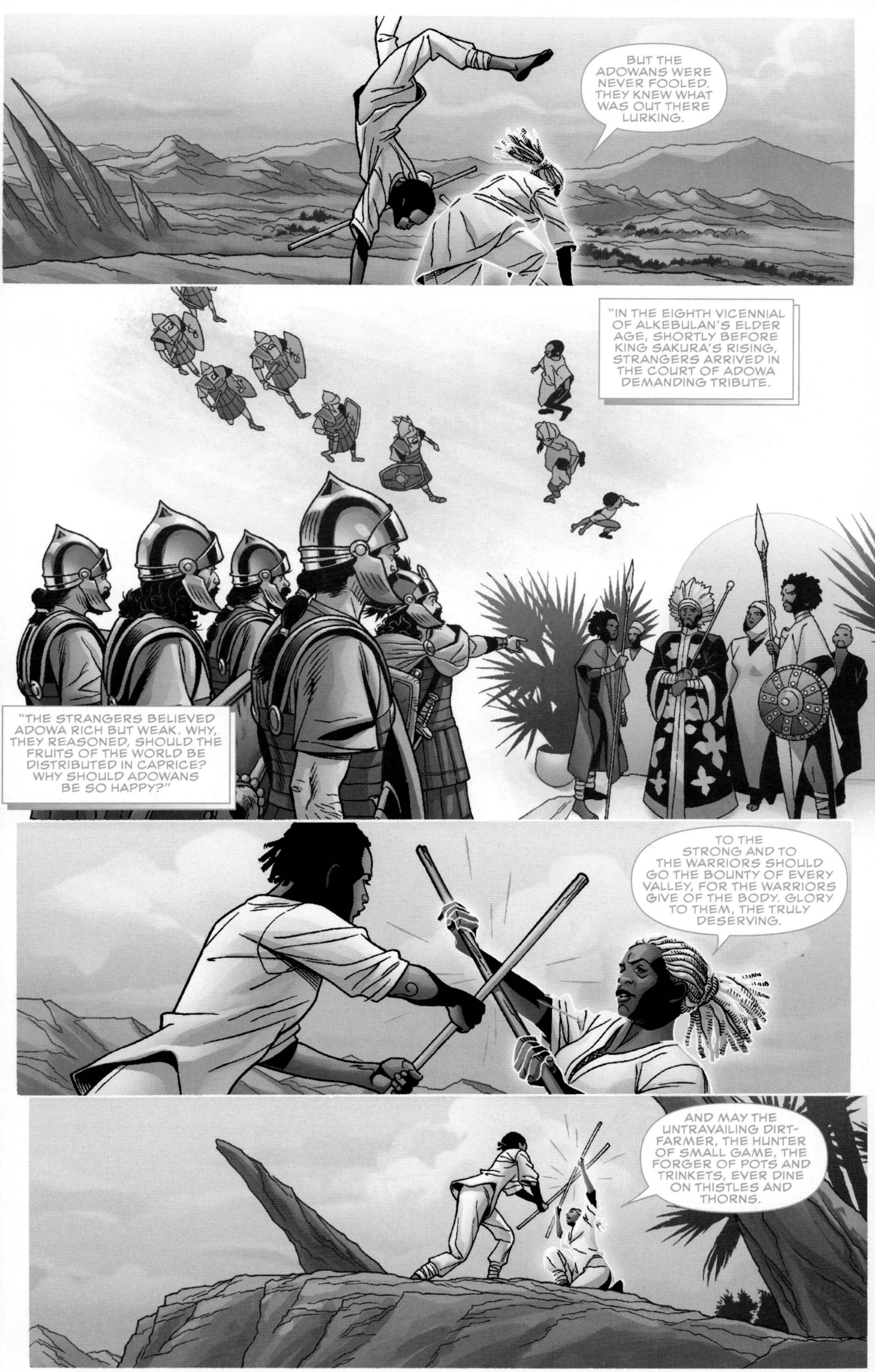
BUT THE ADOWANS WERE NEVER FOOLED. THEY KNEW WHAT WAS OUT THERE LURKING.
"IN THE EIGHTH VICENNIAL OF ALKEBULAN'S ELDER AGE, SHORTLY BEFORE KING SAKURA'S RISING, STRANGERS ARRIVED IN THE COURT OF ADOWA DEMANDING TRIBUTE.
"THE STRANGERS BELIEVED ADOWA RICH BUT WEAK. WHY, THEY REASONED, SHOULD THE FRUITS OF THE WORLD BE DISTRIBUTED IN CAPRICE? WHY SHOULD ADOWANS BE SO HAPPY?"
TO THE STRONG AND TO THE WARRIORS SHOULD GO THE BOUNTY OF EVERY VALLEY, FOR THE WARRIORS GIVE OF THE BODY. GLORY TO THEM, THE TRULY DESERVING.
AND MAY THE UNTRAVAILING DIRT-FARMER, THE HUNTER OF SMALL GAME, THE FORGER OF POTS AND TRINKETS, EVER DINE ON THISTLES AND THORNS.

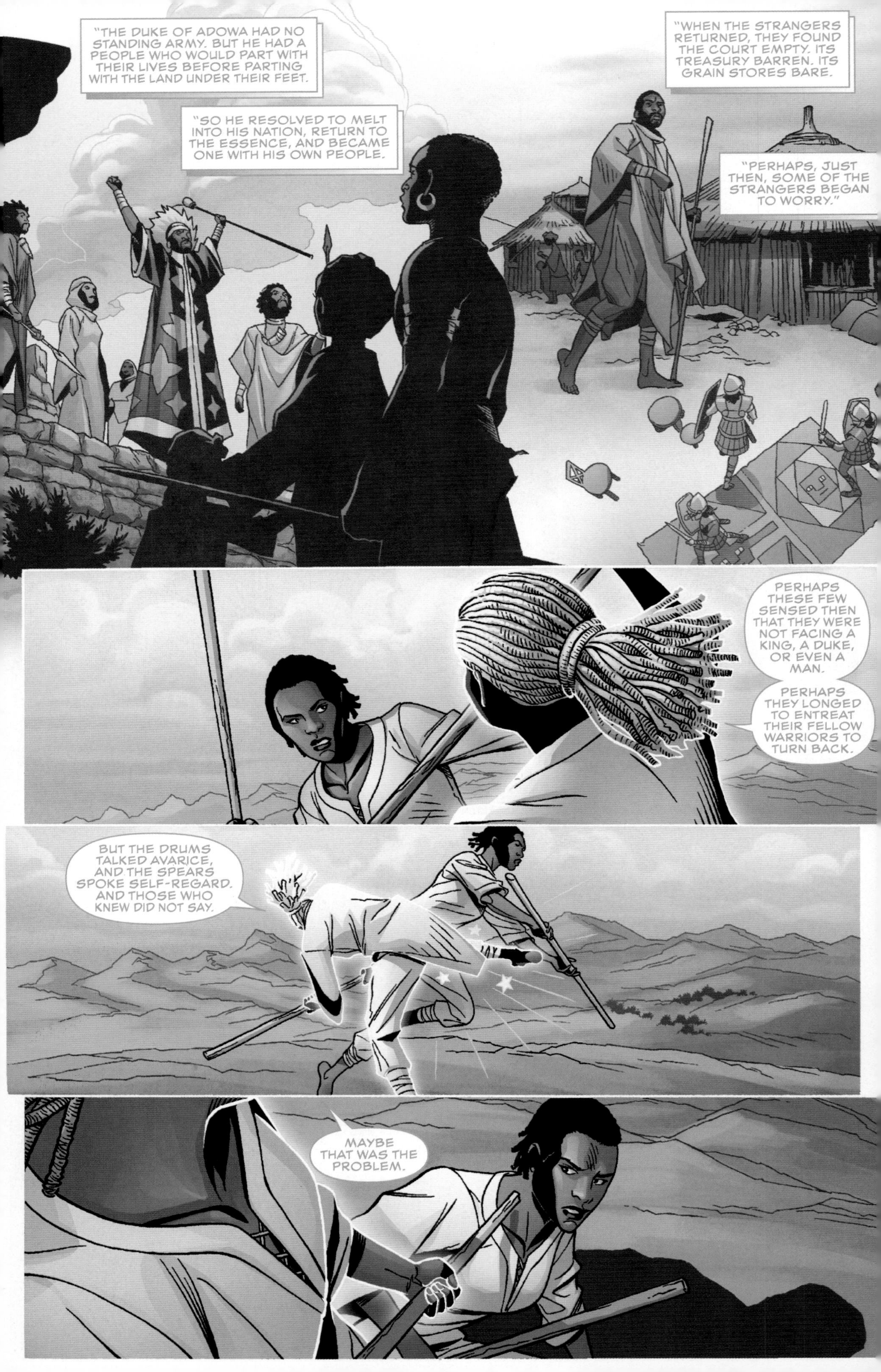
"THE DUKE OF ADOWA HAD NO STANDING ARMY. BUT HE HAD A PEOPLE WHO WOULD PART WITH THEIR LIVES BEFORE PARTING WITH THE LAND UNDER THEIR FEET.
"SO HE RESOLVED TO MELT INTO HIS NATION, RETURN TO THE ESSENCE, AND BECAME ONE WITH HIS OWN PEOPLE.
"WHEN THE STRANGERS RETURNED, THEY FOUND THE COURT EMPTY. ITS TREASURY BARREN. ITS GRAIN STORES BARE.
"PERHAPS, JUST THEN, SOME OF THE STRANGERS BEGAN TO WORRY."
PERHAPS THESE FEW SENSED THEN THAT THEY WERE NOT FACING A KING, A DUKE, OR EVEN A MAN.
PERHAPS THEY LONGED TO ENTREAT THEIR FELLOW WARRIORS TO TURN BACK.
BUT THE DRUMS TALKED AVARICE, AND THE SPEARS SPOKE SELF-REGARD. AND THOSE WHO KNEW DID NOT SAY.
MAYBE THAT WAS THE PROBLEM.

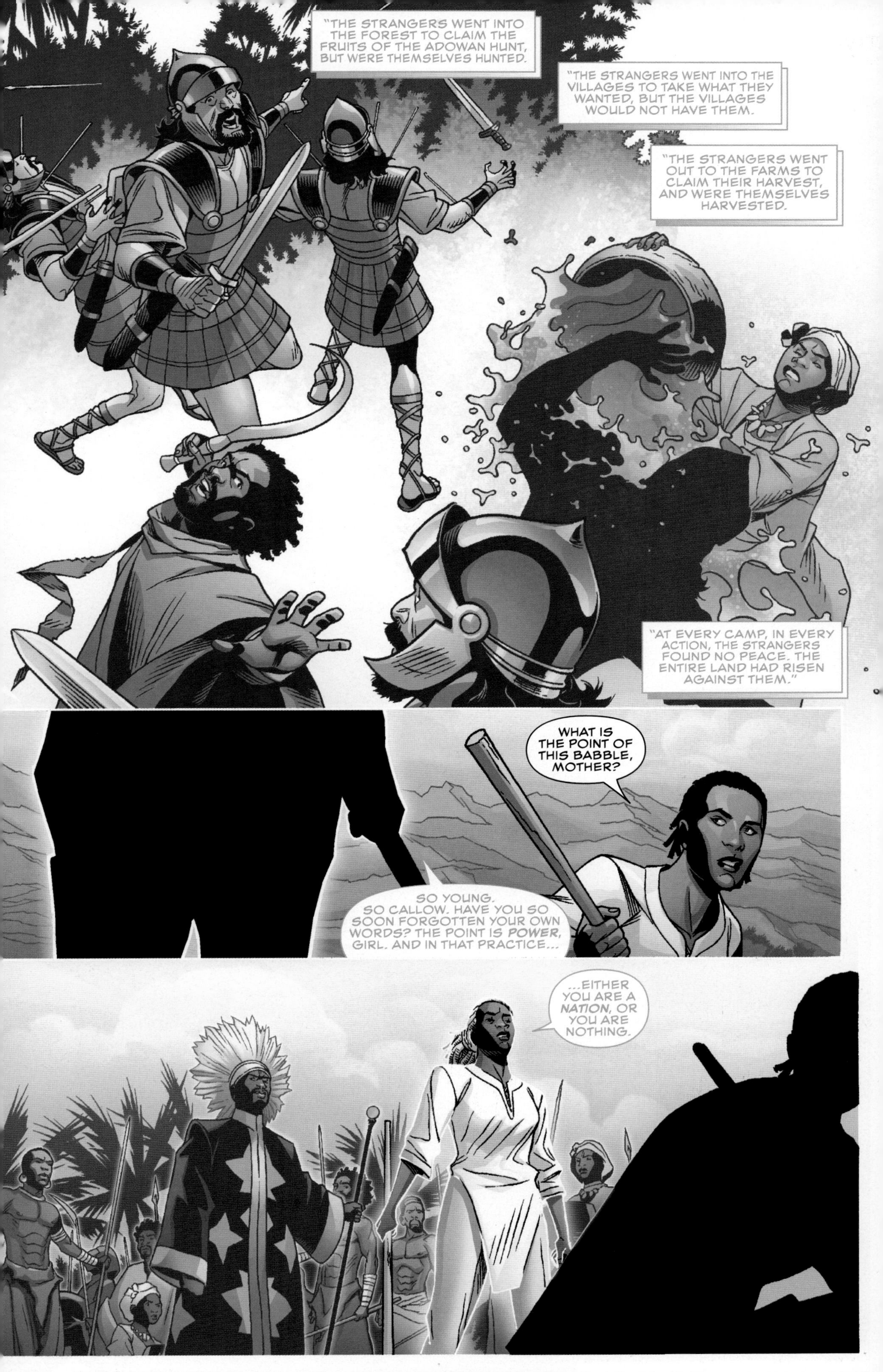
"THE STRANGERS WENT INTO THE FOREST TO CLAIM THE FRUITS OF THE ADOWAN HUNT, BUT WERE THEMSELVES HUNTED.
"THE STRANGERS WENT INTO THE VILLAGES TO TAKE WHAT THEY WANTED, BUT THE VILLAGES WOULD NOT HAVE THEM.
"THE STRANGERS WENT OUT TO THE FARMS TO CLAIM THEIR HARVEST, AND WERE THEMSELVES HARVESTED.
"AT EVERY CAMP, IN EVERY ACTION, THE STRANGERS FOUND NO PEACE. THE ENTIRE LAND HAD RISEN AGAINST THEM."
WHAT IS THE POINT OF THIS BABBLE, MOTHER?
SO YOUNG. SO CALLOW. HAVE YOU SO SOON FORGOTTEN YOUR OWN WORDS? THE POINT IS *POWER*, GIRL. AND IN THAT PRACTICE...
...EITHER YOU ARE A *NATION*, OR YOU ARE NOTHING.

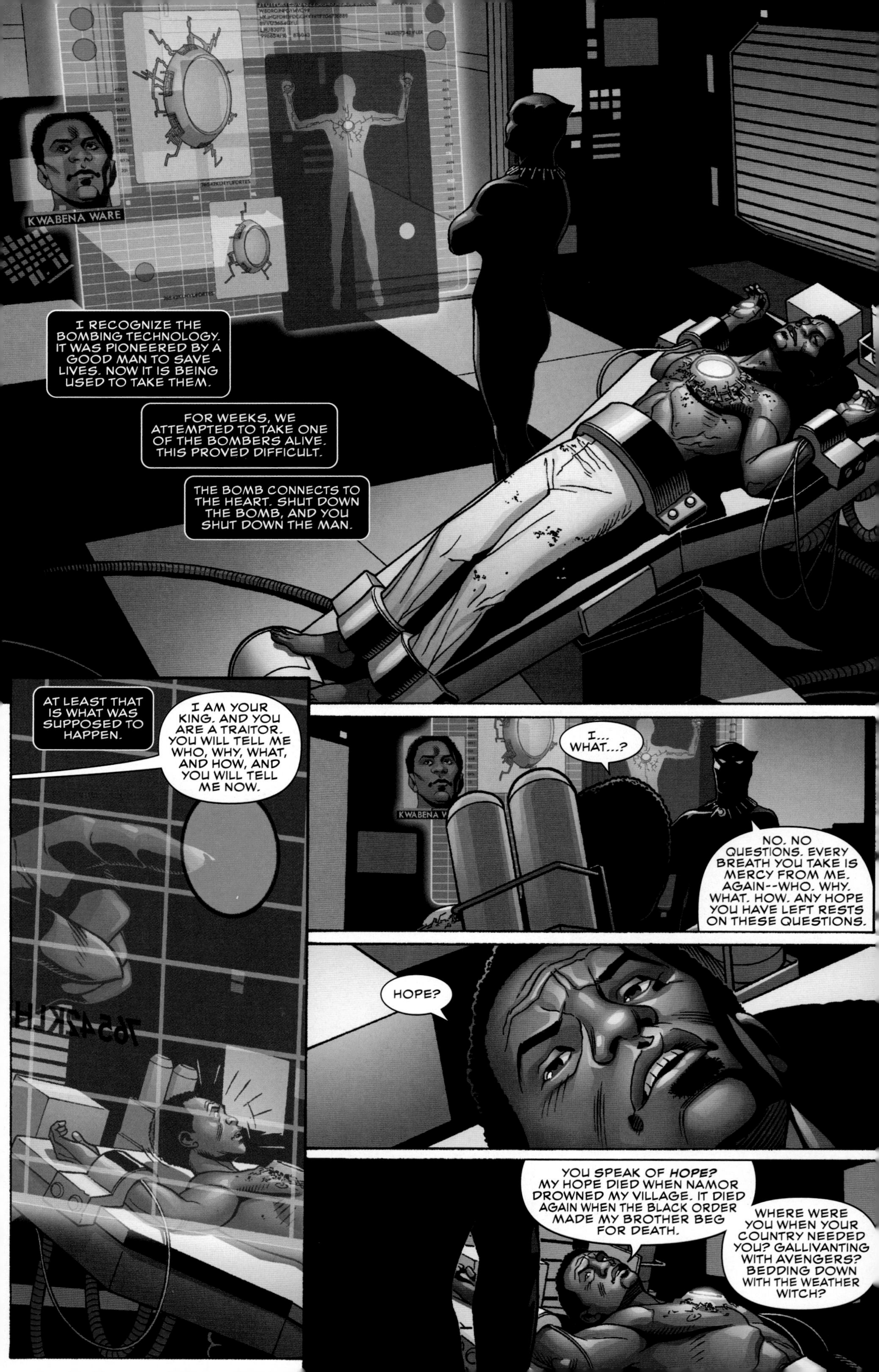
KWABENA WARE
I RECOGNIZE THE BOMBING TECHNOLOGY. IT WAS PIONEERED BY A GOOD MAN TO SAVE LIVES. NOW IT IS BEING USED TO TAKE THEM.
FOR WEEKS, WE ATTEMPTED TO TAKE ONE OF THE BOMBERS ALIVE. THIS PROVED DIFFICULT.
THE BOMB CONNECTS TO THE HEART. SHUT DOWN THE BOMB, AND YOU SHUT DOWN THE MAN.
AT LEAST THAT IS WHAT WAS SUPPOSED TO HAPPEN.
I AM YOUR KING. AND YOU ARE A TRAITOR. YOU WILL TELL ME WHO, WHY, WHAT, AND HOW, AND YOU WILL TELL ME NOW.
I... WHAT...?
NO. NO QUESTIONS. EVERY BREATH YOU TAKE IS MERCY FROM ME. AGAIN--WHO. WHY. WHAT. HOW. ANY HOPE YOU HAVE LEFT RESTS ON THESE QUESTIONS.
HOPE?
YOU SPEAK OF *HOPE?* MY HOPE DIED WHEN NAMOR DROWNED MY VILLAGE. IT DIED AGAIN WHEN THE BLACK ORDER MADE MY BROTHER BEG FOR DEATH.
WHERE WERE YOU WHEN YOUR COUNTRY NEEDED YOU? GALLIVANTING WITH AVENGERS? BEDDING DOWN WITH THE WEATHER WITCH?

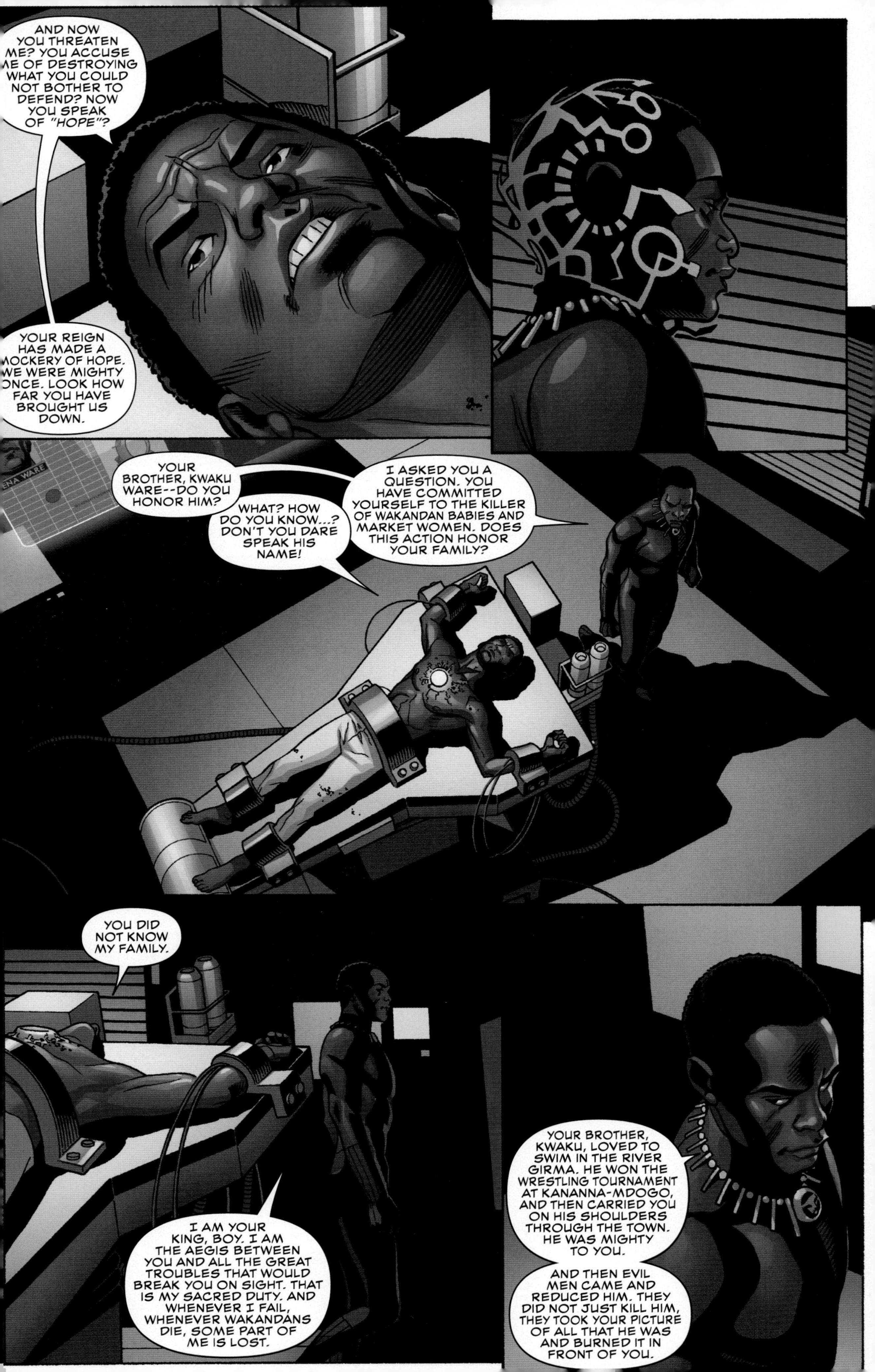
AND NOW YOU THREATEN ME? YOU ACCUSE ME OF DESTROYING WHAT YOU COULD NOT BOTHER TO DEFEND? NOW YOU SPEAK OF "HOPE"?
YOUR REIGN HAS MADE A MOCKERY OF HOPE. WE WERE MIGHTY ONCE. LOOK HOW FAR YOU HAVE BROUGHT US DOWN.
YOUR BROTHER, KWAKU WARE--DO YOU HONOR HIM?
WHAT? HOW DO YOU KNOW...? DON'T YOU DARE SPEAK HIS NAME!
I ASKED YOU A QUESTION. YOU HAVE COMMITTED YOURSELF TO THE KILLER OF WAKANDAN BABIES AND MARKET WOMEN. DOES THIS ACTION HONOR YOUR FAMILY?
YOU DID NOT KNOW MY FAMILY.
I AM YOUR KING, BOY. I AM THE AEGIS BETWEEN YOU AND ALL THE GREAT TROUBLES THAT WOULD BREAK YOU ON SIGHT. THAT IS MY SACRED DUTY. AND WHENEVER I FAIL, WHENEVER WAKANDANS DIE, SOME PART OF ME IS LOST.
YOUR BROTHER, KWAKU, LOVED TO SWIM IN THE RIVER GIRMA. HE WON THE WRESTLING TOURNAMENT AT KANANNA-MDOGO, AND THEN CARRIED YOU ON HIS SHOULDERS THROUGH THE TOWN. HE WAS MIGHTY TO YOU.
AND THEN EVIL MEN CAME AND REDUCED HIM. THEY DID NOT JUST KILL HIM, THEY TOOK YOUR PICTURE OF ALL THAT HE WAS AND BURNED IT IN FRONT OF YOU.

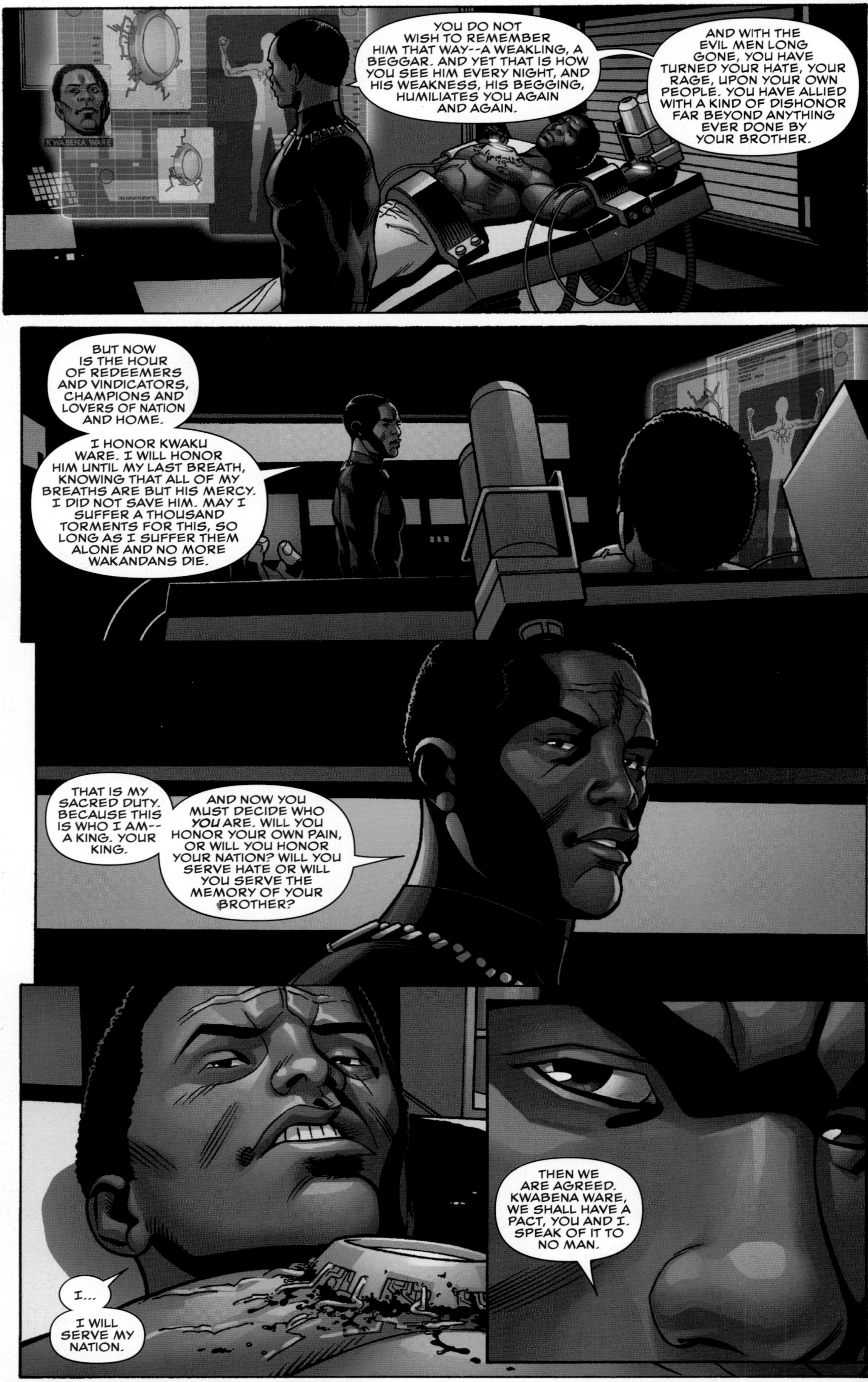
KWABENA WARE
YOU DO NOT WISH TO REMEMBER HIM THAT WAY--A WEAKLING, A BEGGAR. AND YET THAT IS HOW YOU SEE HIM EVERY NIGHT, AND HIS WEAKNESS, HIS BEGGING, HUMILIATES YOU AGAIN AND AGAIN.
AND WITH THE EVIL MEN LONG GONE, YOU HAVE TURNED YOUR HATE, YOUR RAGE, UPON YOUR OWN PEOPLE. YOU HAVE ALLIED WITH A KIND OF DISHONOR FAR BEYOND ANYTHING EVER DONE BY YOUR BROTHER.
BUT NOW IS THE HOUR OF REDEEMERS AND VINDICATORS, CHAMPIONS AND LOVERS OF NATION AND HOME.
I HONOR KWAKU WARE. I WILL HONOR HIM UNTIL MY LAST BREATH, KNOWING THAT ALL OF MY BREATHS ARE BUT HIS MERCY. I DID NOT SAVE HIM. MAY I SUFFER A THOUSAND TORMENTS FOR THIS, SO LONG AS I SUFFER THEM ALONE AND NO MORE WAKANDANS DIE.
THAT IS MY SACRED DUTY. BECAUSE THIS IS WHO I AM-- A KING. YOUR KING.
AND NOW YOU MUST DECIDE WHO *YOU* ARE. WILL YOU HONOR YOUR OWN PAIN, OR WILL YOU HONOR YOUR NATION? WILL YOU SERVE HATE OR WILL YOU SERVE THE MEMORY OF YOUR BROTHER?
I...
I WILL SERVE MY NATION.
THEN WE ARE AGREED. KWABENA WARE, WE SHALL HAVE A PACT, YOU AND I. SPEAK OF IT TO NO MAN.

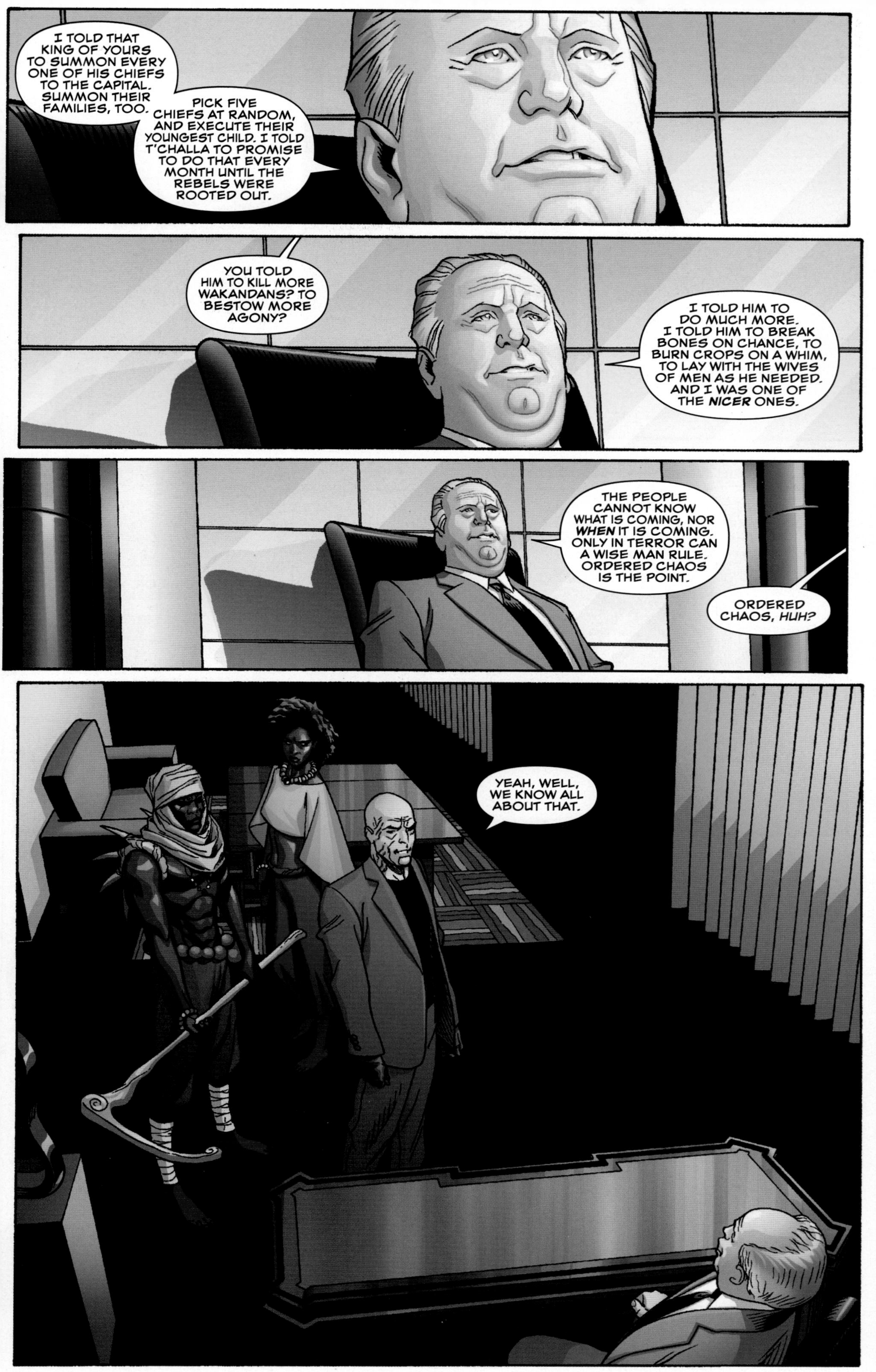
I TOLD THAT KING OF YOURS TO SUMMON EVERY ONE OF HIS CHIEFS TO THE CAPITAL. SUMMON THEIR FAMILIES, TOO.
PICK FIVE CHIEFS AT RANDOM, AND EXECUTE THEIR YOUNGEST CHILD. I TOLD T'CHALLA TO PROMISE TO DO THAT EVERY MONTH UNTIL THE REBELS WERE ROOTED OUT.
YOU TOLD HIM TO KILL MORE WAKANDANS? TO BESTOW MORE AGONY?
I TOLD HIM TO DO MUCH MORE. I TOLD HIM TO BREAK BONES ON CHANCE, TO BURN CROPS ON A WHIM, TO LAY WITH THE WIVES OF MEN AS HE NEEDED. AND I WAS ONE OF THE *NICER* ONES.
THE PEOPLE CANNOT KNOW WHAT IS COMING, NOR *WHEN* IT IS COMING. ONLY IN TERROR CAN A WISE MAN RULE. ORDERED CHAOS IS THE POINT.
ORDERED CHAOS, *HUH?*
YEAH, WELL, WE KNOW ALL ABOUT THAT.

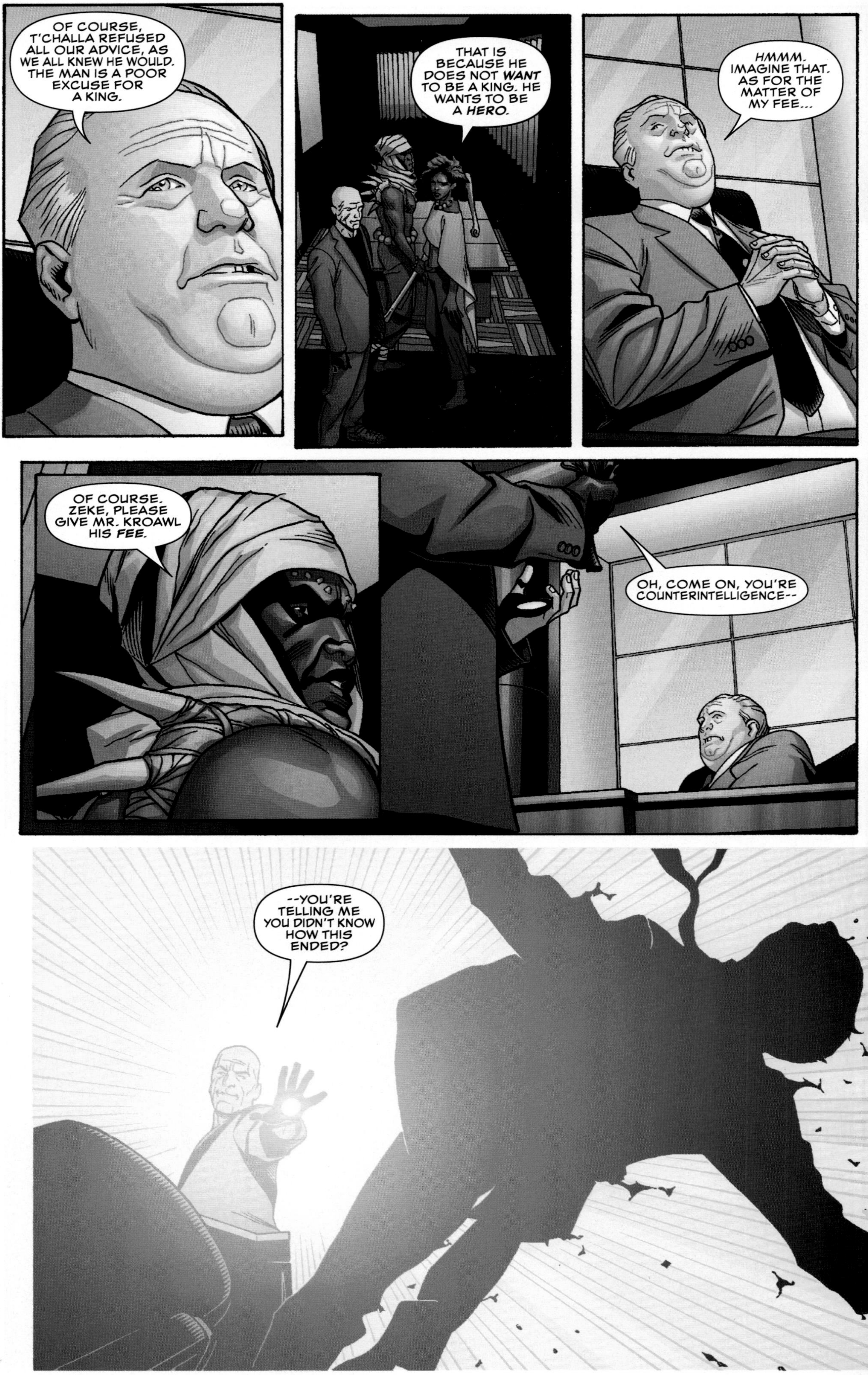
OF COURSE, T'CHALLA REFUSED ALL OUR ADVICE, AS WE ALL KNEW HE WOULD. THE MAN IS A POOR EXCUSE FOR A KING.
THAT IS BECAUSE HE DOES NOT *WANT* TO BE A KING. HE WANTS TO BE A *HERO*.
*HMMM.* IMAGINE THAT. AS FOR THE MATTER OF MY FEE...
OF COURSE. ZEKE, PLEASE GIVE MR. KROAWL HIS *FEE*.
OH, COME ON, YOU'RE COUNTERINTELLIGENCE--
--YOU'RE TELLING ME YOU DIDN'T KNOW HOW THIS ENDED?

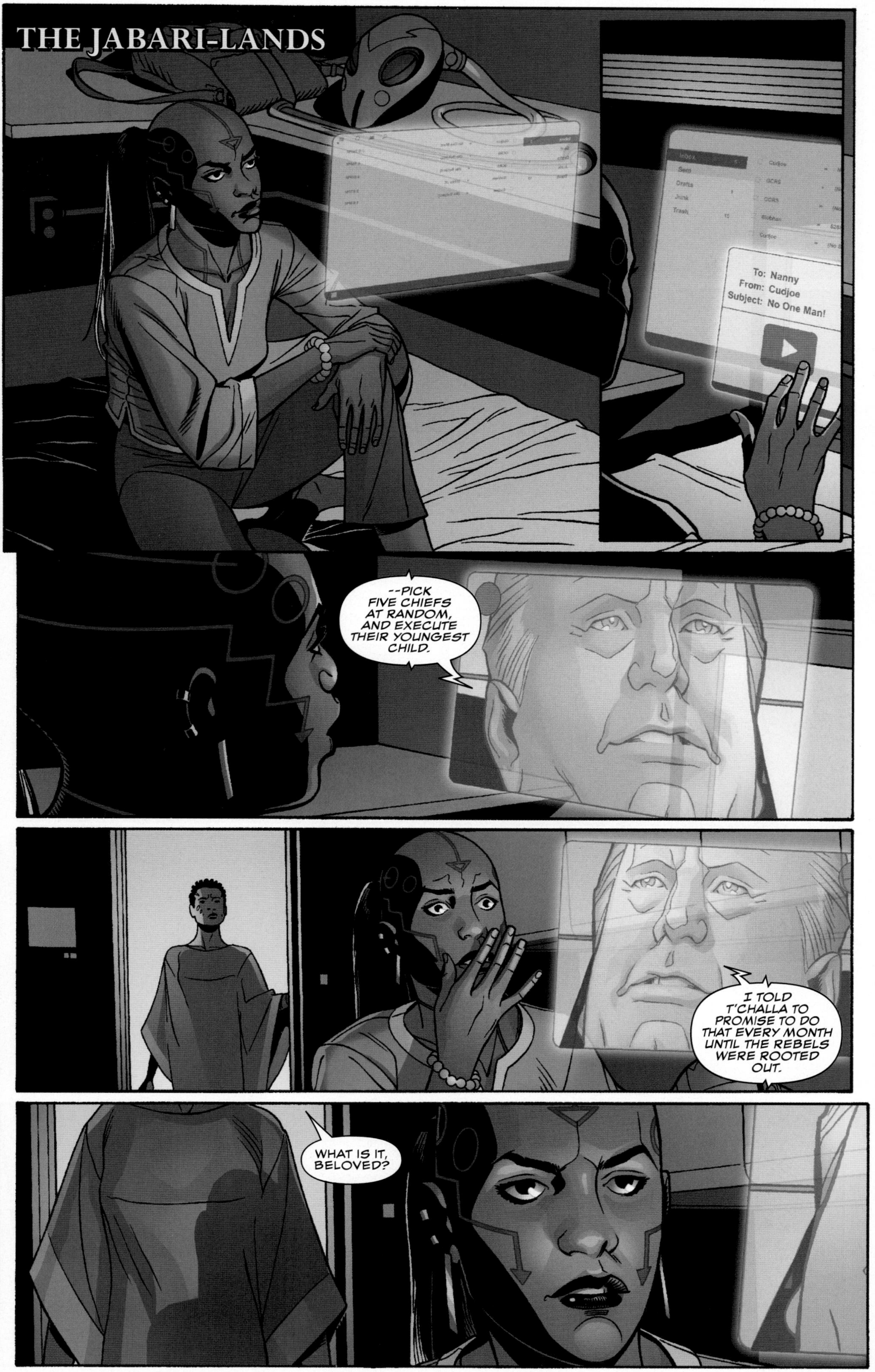
THE JABARI-LANDS
To: Nanny
From: Cudjoe
Subject: No One Man!
--PICK FIVE CHIEFS AT RANDOM, AND EXECUTE THEIR YOUNGEST CHILD.
I TOLD T'CHALLA TO PROMISE TO DO THAT EVERY MONTH UNTIL THE REBELS WERE ROOTED OUT.
WHAT IS IT, BELOVED?

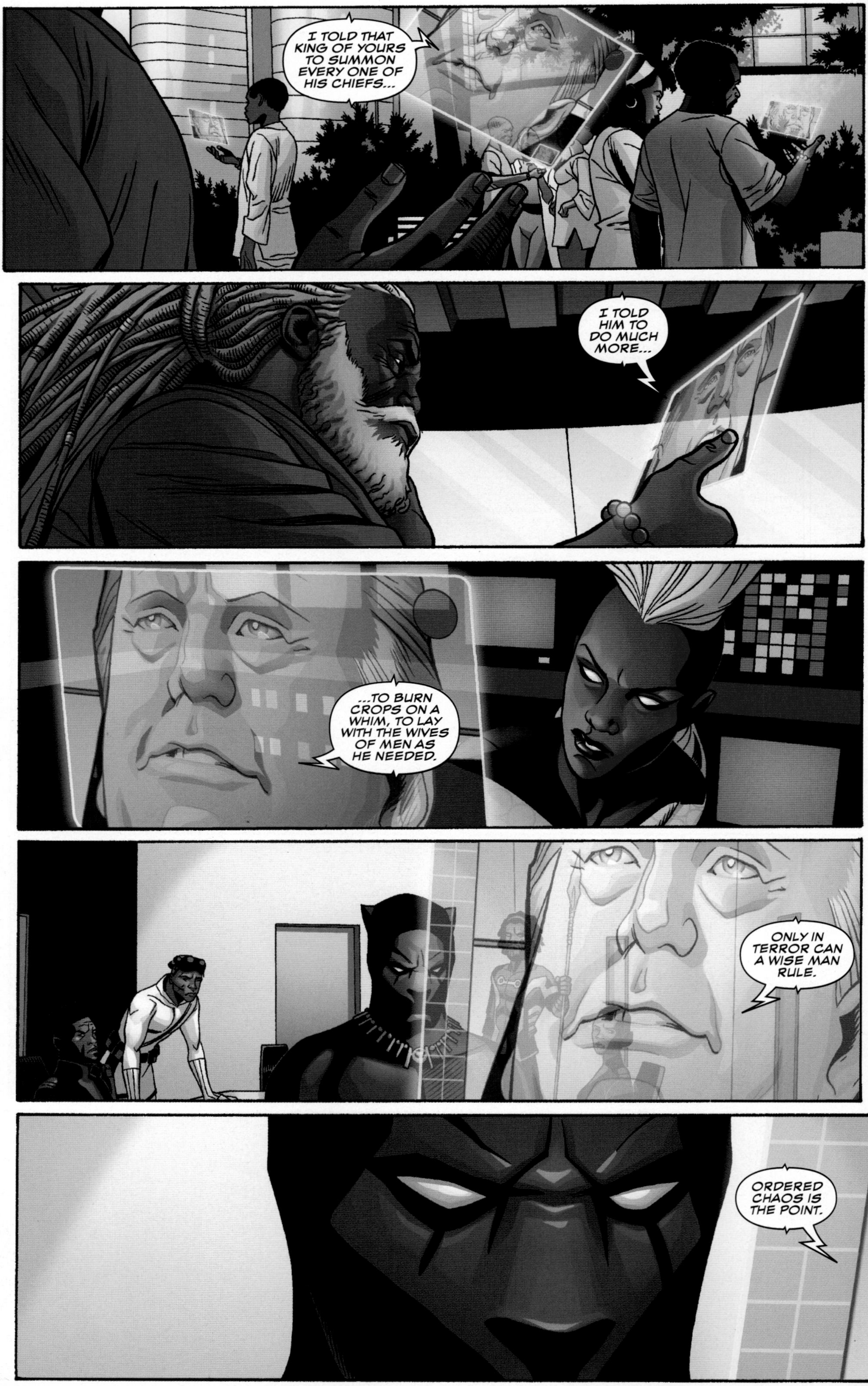
I TOLD THAT KING OF YOURS TO SUMMON EVERY ONE OF HIS CHIEFS...
I TOLD HIM TO DO MUCH MORE...
...TO BURN CROPS ON A WHIM, TO LAY WITH THE WIVES OF MEN AS HE NEEDED.
ONLY IN TERROR CAN A WISE MAN RULE.
ORDERED CHAOS IS THE POINT.

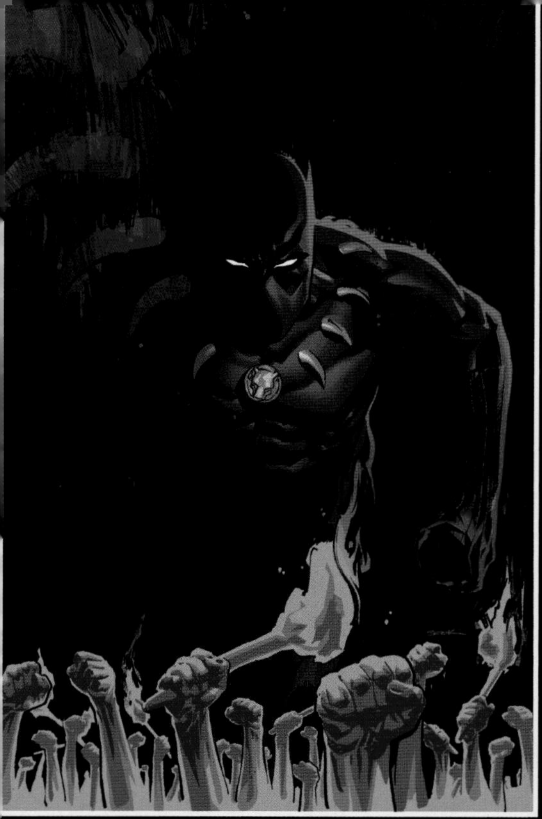

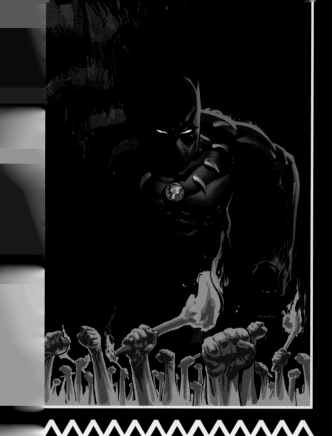

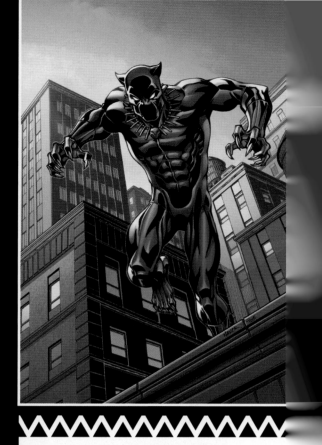

#1 VARIANT BY **RYAN SOOK**

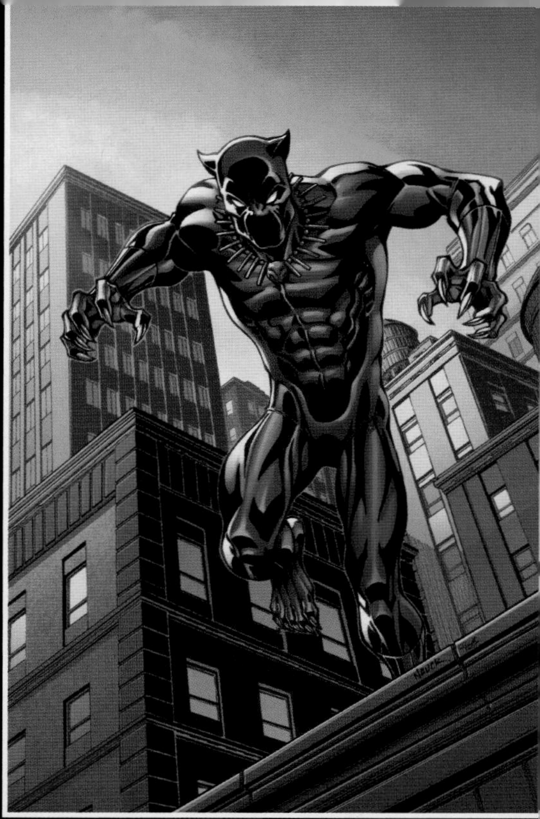

#1 VARIANT BY **TODD NAUCK & RACHELLE ROSENBERG**

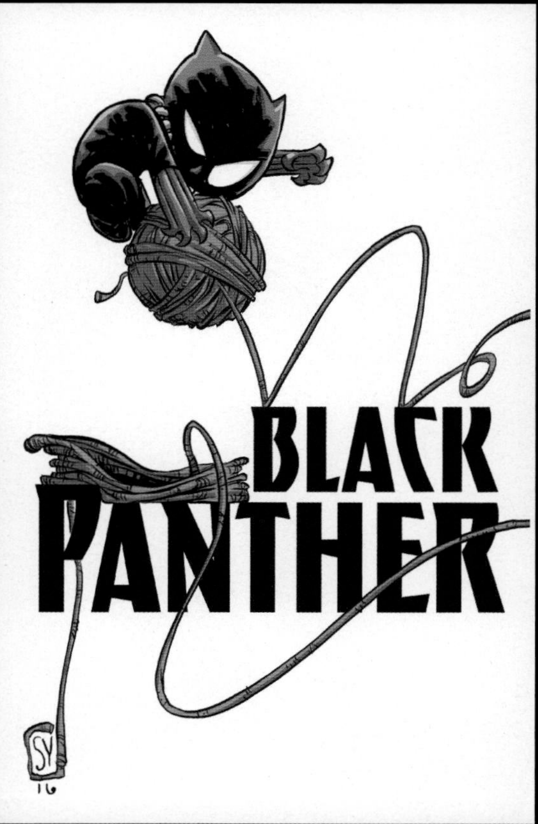
BLACK
PANTHER

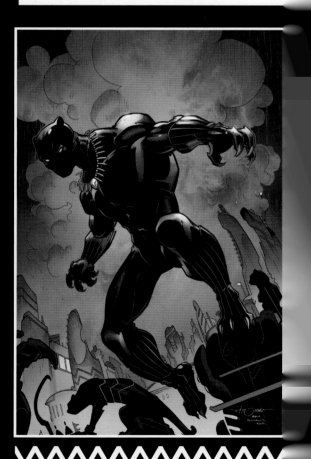

#1 VARIANT BY **SKOTTIE YOUNG**

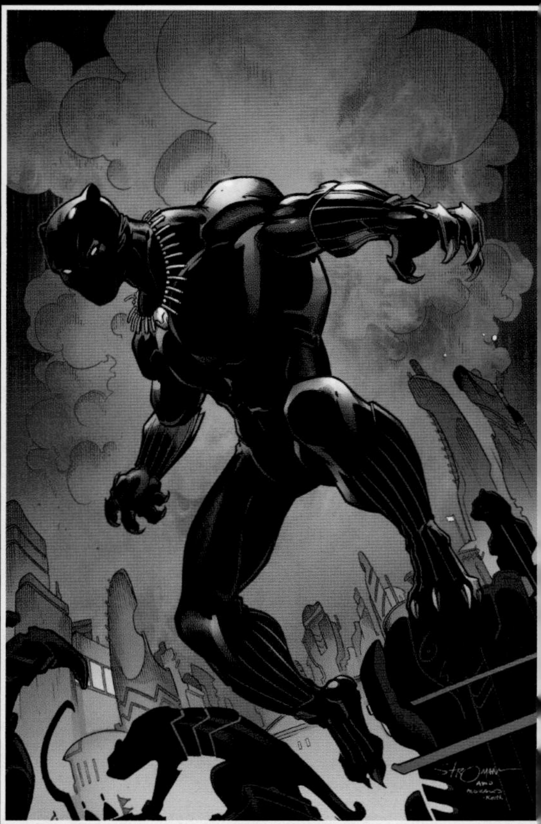

#1 VARIANT BY **LARRY STROMAN, MARK MORALES & JASON KEITH**

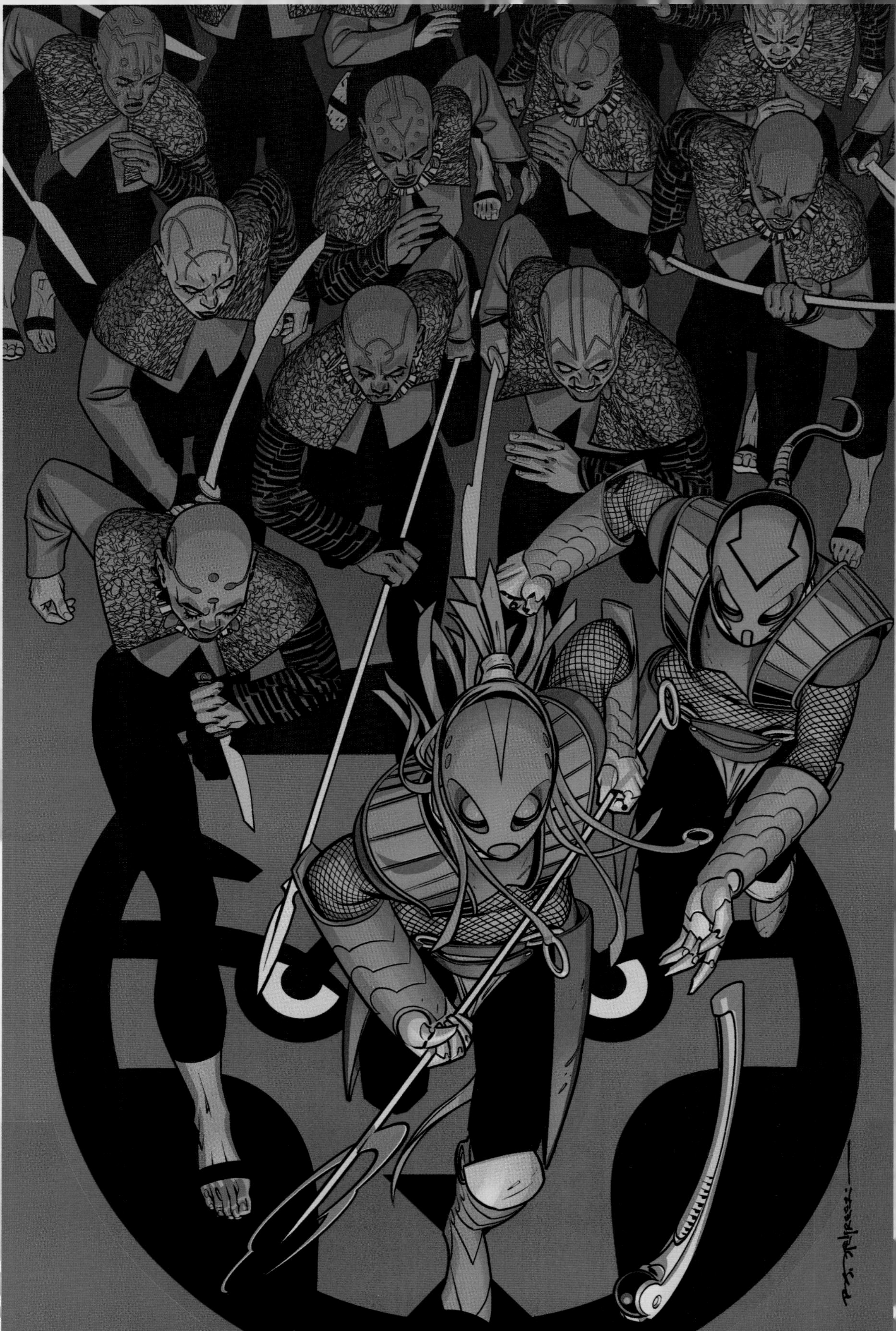

6

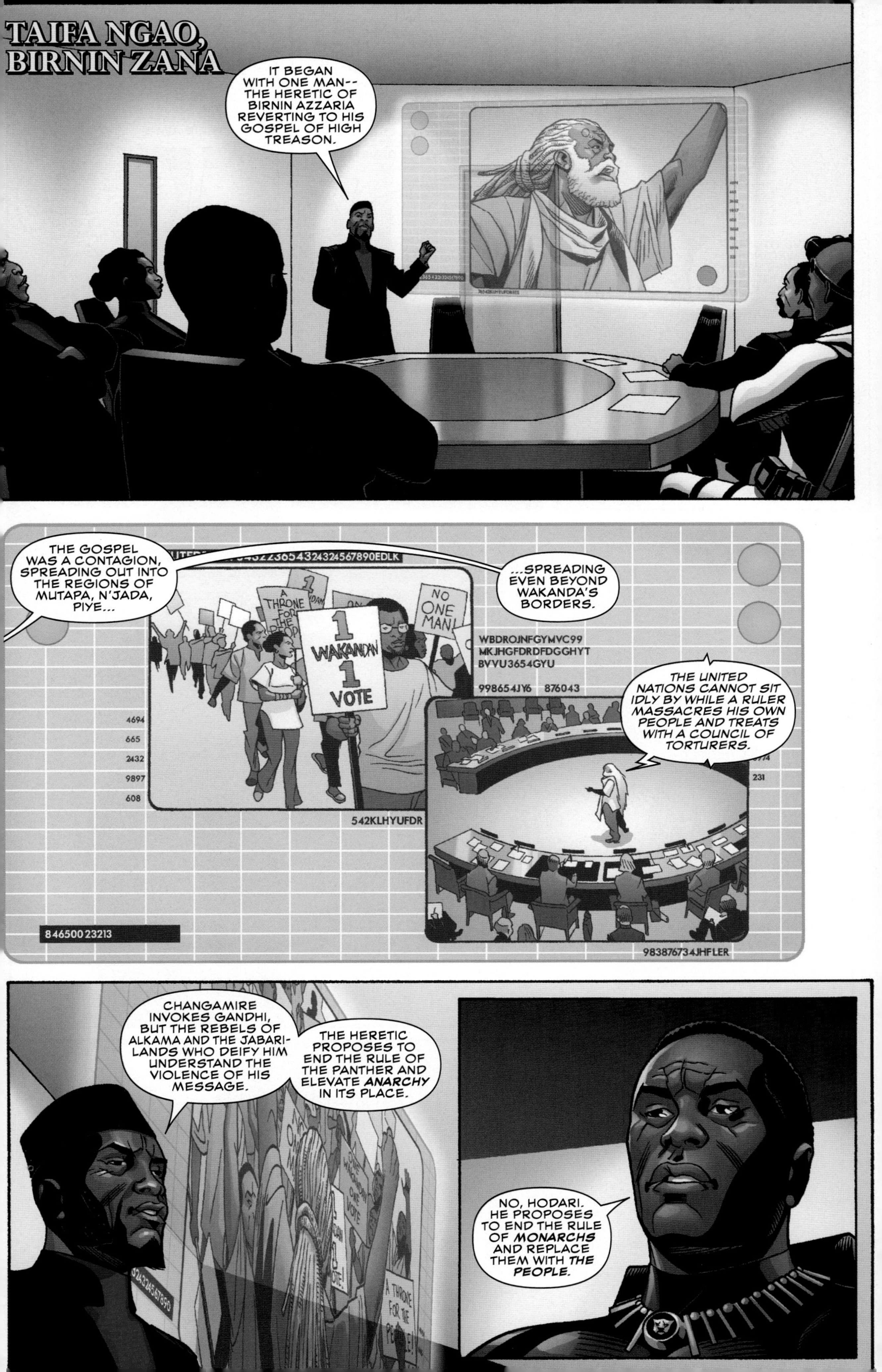
TAIFA NGAO, BIRNIN ZANA
IT BEGAN WITH ONE MAN-- THE HERETIC OF BIRNIN AZZARIA REVERTING TO HIS GOSPEL OF HIGH TREASON.
THE GOSPEL WAS A CONTAGION, SPREADING OUT INTO THE REGIONS OF MUTAPA, N'JADA, PIYE...
...SPREADING EVEN BEYOND WAKANDA'S BORDERS.
A THRONE FOR THE PEOPLE
NO ONE MAN!
1 WAKANDAN 1 VOTE
WBDROJNFGYMVC99
MKJHGFDRDFDGGHYT
BVVU3654GYU
998654JY6 876043
4694
665
2432
9897
608
542KLHYUFDR
231
84650023213
983876734JHFLER
THE UNITED NATIONS CANNOT SIT IDLY BY WHILE A RULER MASSACRES HIS OWN PEOPLE AND TREATS WITH A COUNCIL OF TORTURERS.
CHANGAMIRE INVOKES GANDHI, BUT THE REBELS OF ALKAMA AND THE JABARI-LANDS WHO DEIFY HIM UNDERSTAND THE VIOLENCE OF HIS MESSAGE.
THE HERETIC PROPOSES TO END THE RULE OF THE PANTHER AND ELEVATE ANARCHY IN ITS PLACE.
NO, HODARI. HE PROPOSES TO END THE RULE OF MONARCHS AND REPLACE THEM WITH THE PEOPLE.

I HAVE STUDIED HIS WRITINGS. CHANGAMIRE BELIEVES THAT WISDOM ULTIMATELY RESTS WITHIN THE PEOPLE THEMSELVES.

RUBBISH. THE THRONE OF WAKANDA IS THE EMBODIMENT OF THE GODDESS *BAST*, AND YOU ARE HER EXALTED SERVANT.

AND YET WE FIND THIS EXALTED SERVANT POWERLESS BEFORE ALL OUR MIGHTY TROUBLES AND TREATING WITH CRAVEN THUGS.

MY APOLOGIES, KING T'CHALLA. I CONFESS I ERRED IN MY COUCIL.

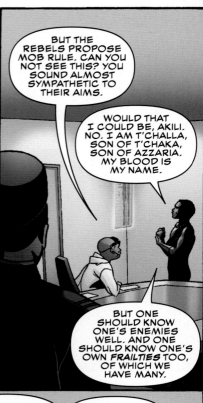

BUT THE REBELS PROPOSE MOB RULE. CAN YOU NOT SEE THIS? YOU SOUND ALMOST SYMPATHETIC TO THEIR AIMS.

WOULD THAT I COULD BE, AKILI. NO. I AM T'CHALLA, SON OF T'CHAKA, SON OF AZZARIA. MY BLOOD IS MY NAME.

BUT ONE SHOULD KNOW ONE'S ENEMIES WELL. AND ONE SHOULD KNOW ONE'S OWN *FRAILTIES* TOO, OF WHICH WE HAVE MANY.

ZEKE STANE

DESIGNATION: Metahuman

DOMAIN: Partis Acceleratus

AURA: Malice

KWABENA WARE

STILL, WE ARE NOT WITHOUT OUR OWN RESOURCES. OUR MAN IS LOOSE. I HAVE HIS SCENT AND THE SCENT OF HIS MASTER.

WHEN THE TWO CROSS, WE SHALL KNOW, AND THEN I WILL ATTACK.

IN THE MEANTIME, PROCEED WITH YOUR PLANNED STRIKE IN THE JABARI-LANDS.

CHAOS IS THE AIR OF THIS REVOLT. WE WILL SMOTHER IT WITH ORDER-- *OUR ORDER.*

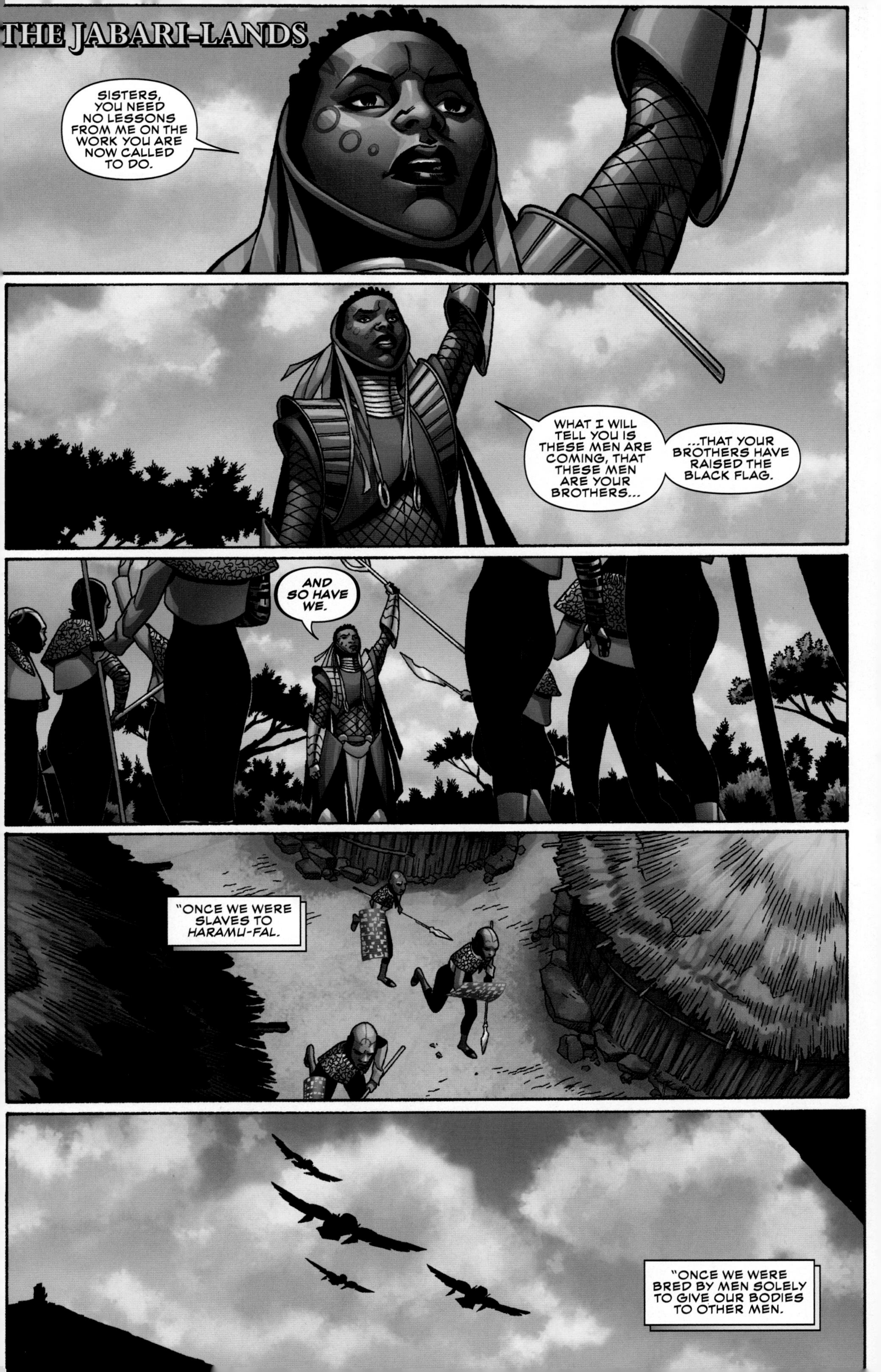
THE JABARI-LANDS
SISTERS, YOU NEED NO LESSONS FROM ME ON THE WORK YOU ARE NOW CALLED TO DO.
WHAT I WILL TELL YOU IS THESE MEN ARE COMING, THAT THESE MEN ARE YOUR BROTHERS...
...THAT YOUR BROTHERS HAVE RAISED THE BLACK FLAG.
AND SO HAVE WE.
"ONCE WE WERE SLAVES TO HARAMU-FAL.
"ONCE WE WERE BRED BY MEN SOLELY TO GIVE OUR BODIES TO OTHER MEN.

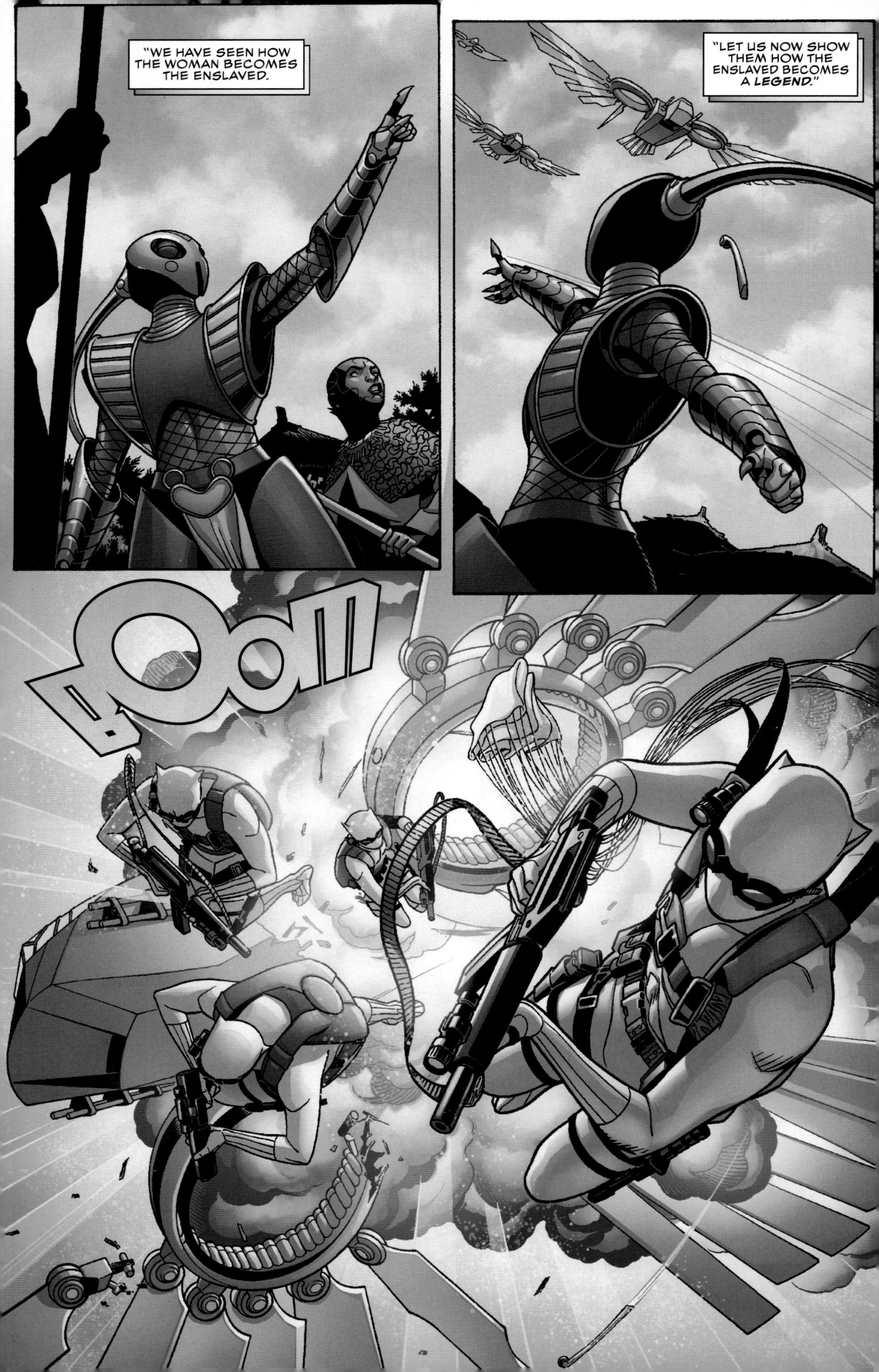
"WE HAVE SEEN HOW THE WOMAN BECOMES THE ENSLAVED.
"LET US NOW SHOW THEM HOW THE ENSLAVED BECOMES A *LEGEND*."
BOOM

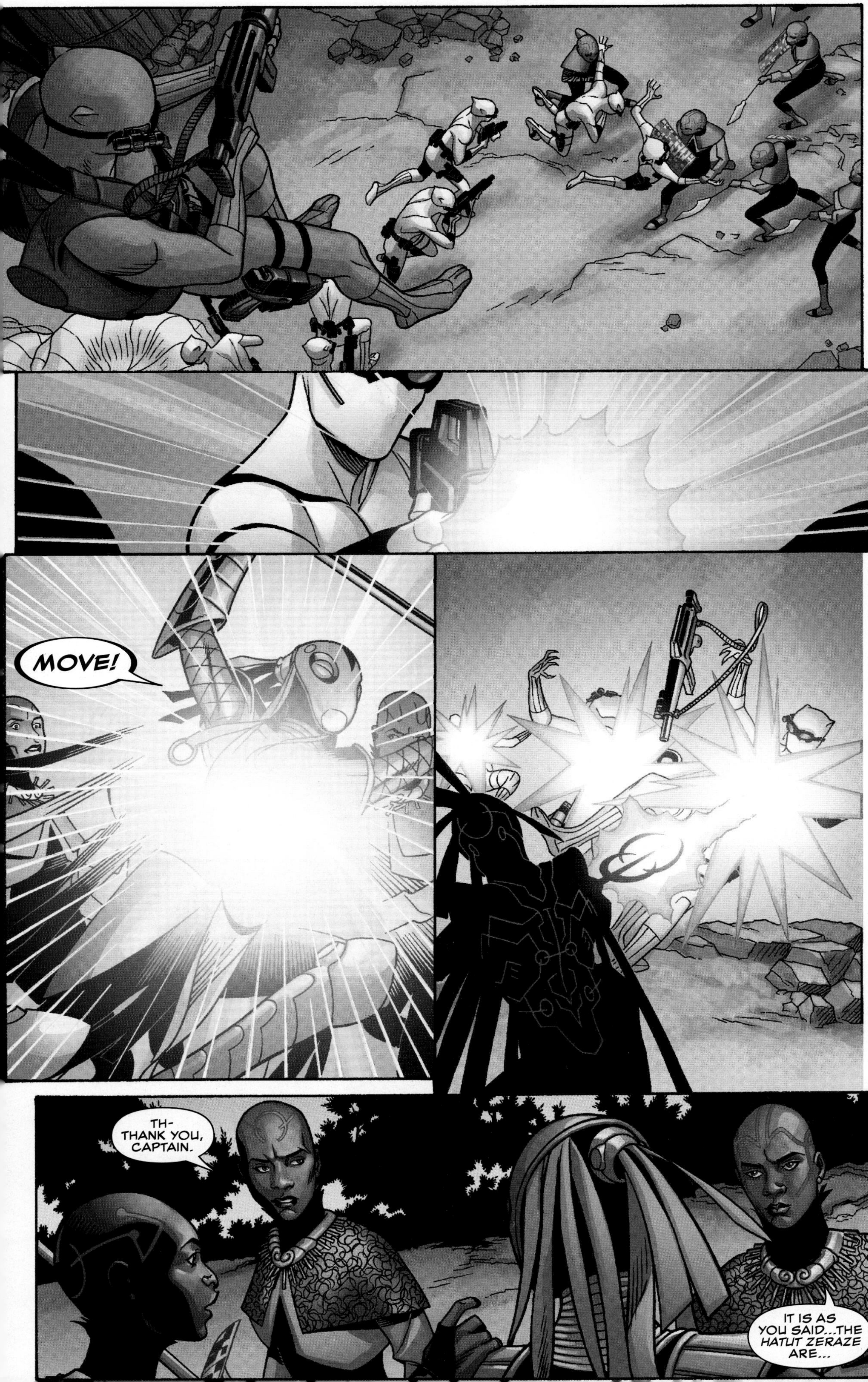
MOVE!
TH- THANK YOU, CAPTAIN.
IT IS AS YOU SAID...THE HATUT ZERAZE ARE...

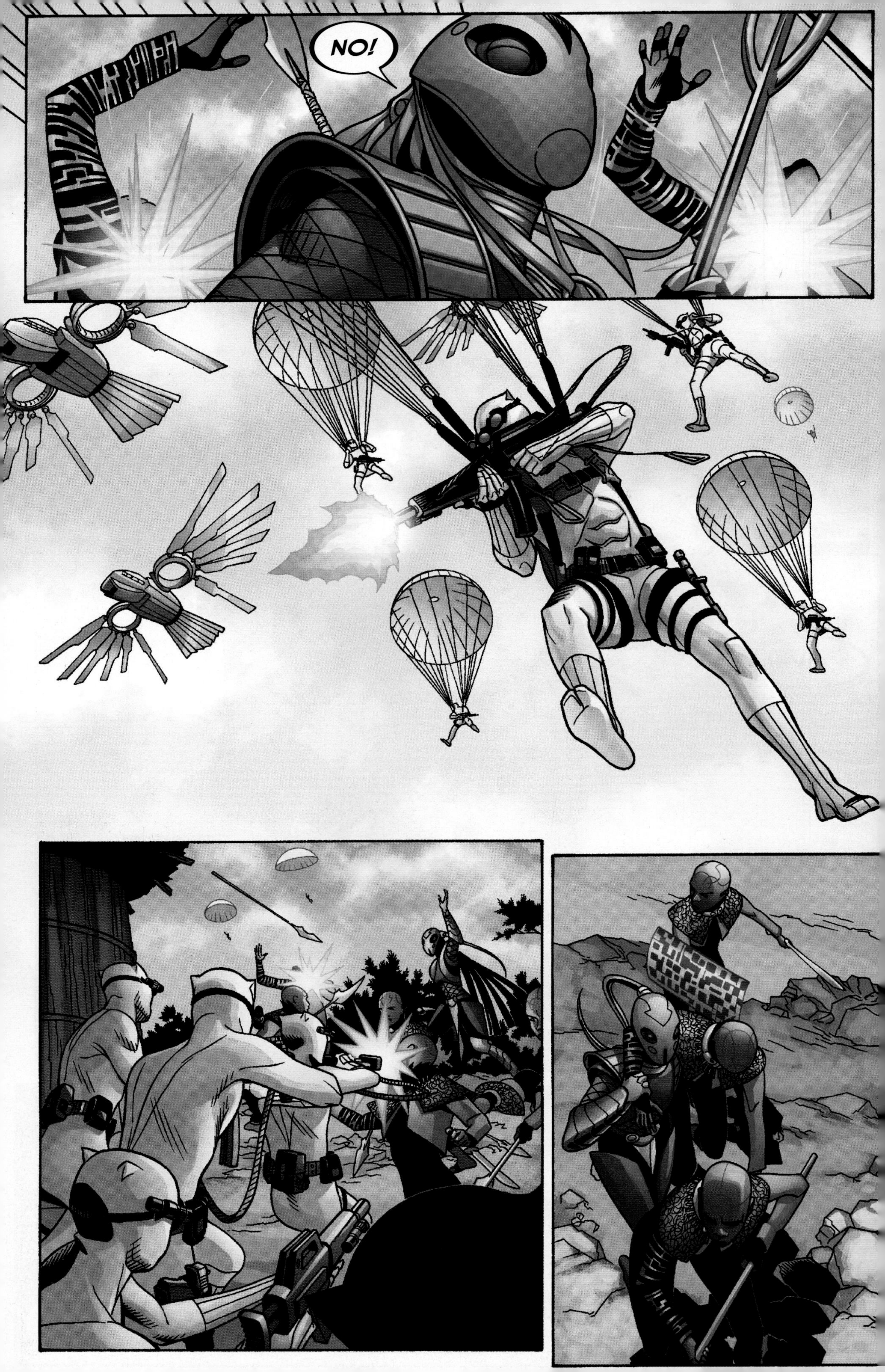
NO!

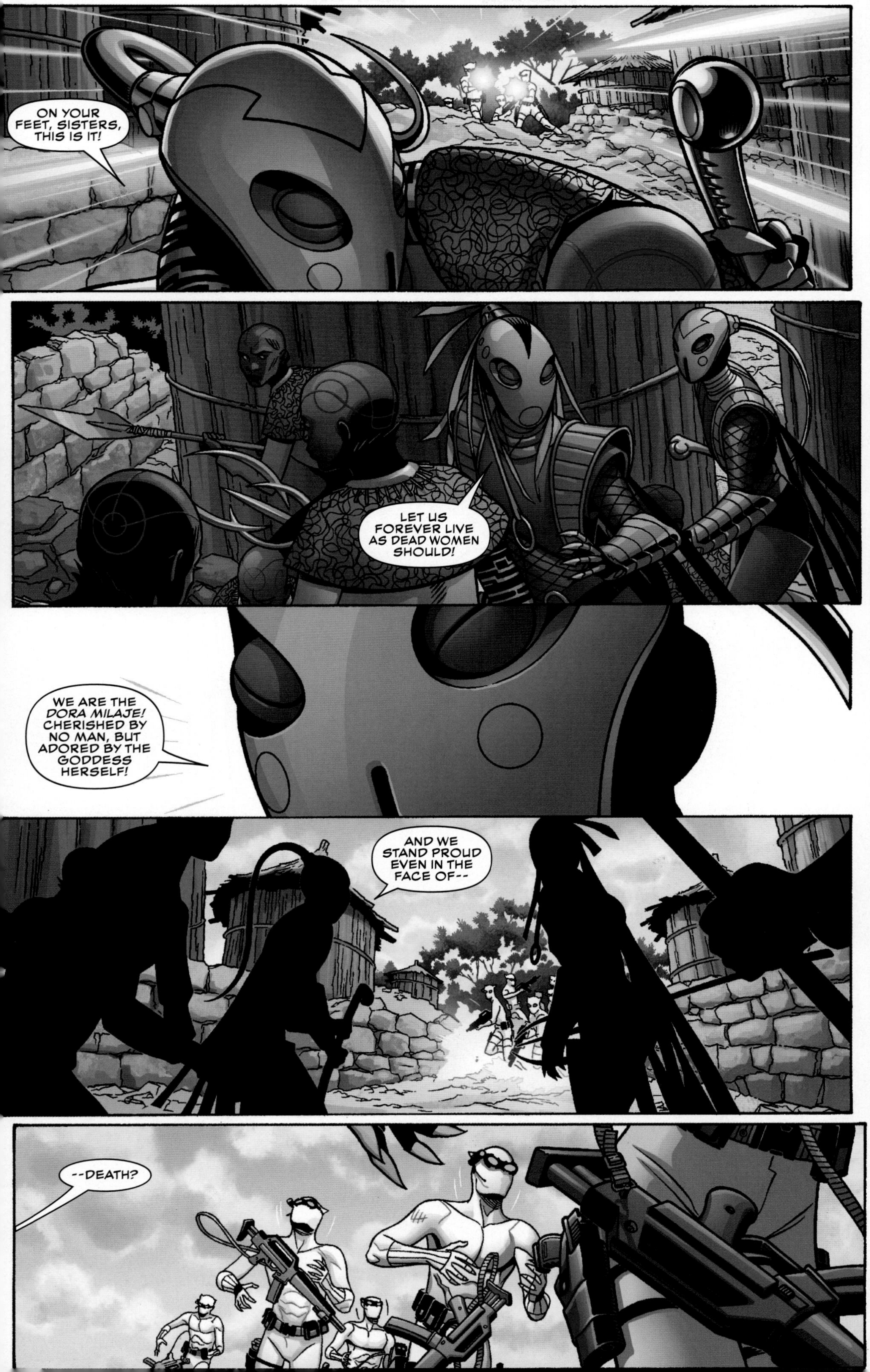
ON YOUR FEET, SISTERS, THIS IS IT!
LET US FOREVER LIVE AS DEAD WOMEN SHOULD!
WE ARE THE *DORA MILAJE!* CHERISHED BY NO MAN, BUT ADORED BY THE GODDESS HERSELF!
AND WE STAND PROUD EVEN IN THE FACE OF--
--DEATH?

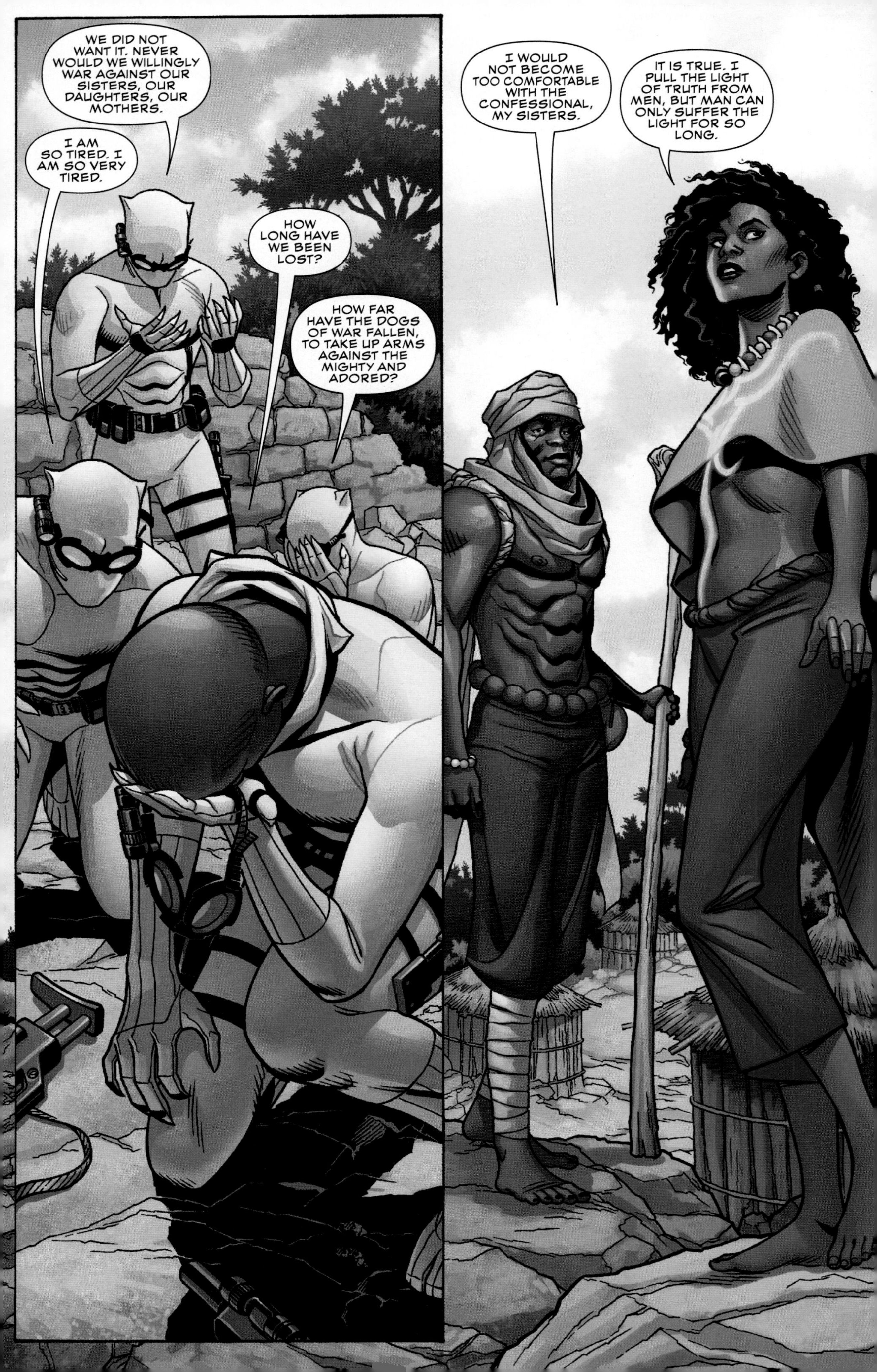
WE DID NOT WANT IT. NEVER WOULD WE WILLINGLY WAR AGAINST OUR SISTERS, OUR DAUGHTERS, OUR MOTHERS.
I AM SO TIRED. I AM SO VERY TIRED.
HOW LONG HAVE WE BEEN LOST?
HOW FAR HAVE THE DOGS OF WAR FALLEN, TO TAKE UP ARMS AGAINST THE MIGHTY AND ADORED?
I WOULD NOT BECOME TOO COMFORTABLE WITH THE CONFESSIONAL, MY SISTERS.
IT IS TRUE. I PULL THE LIGHT OF TRUTH FROM MEN, BUT MAN CAN ONLY SUFFER THE LIGHT FOR SO LONG.

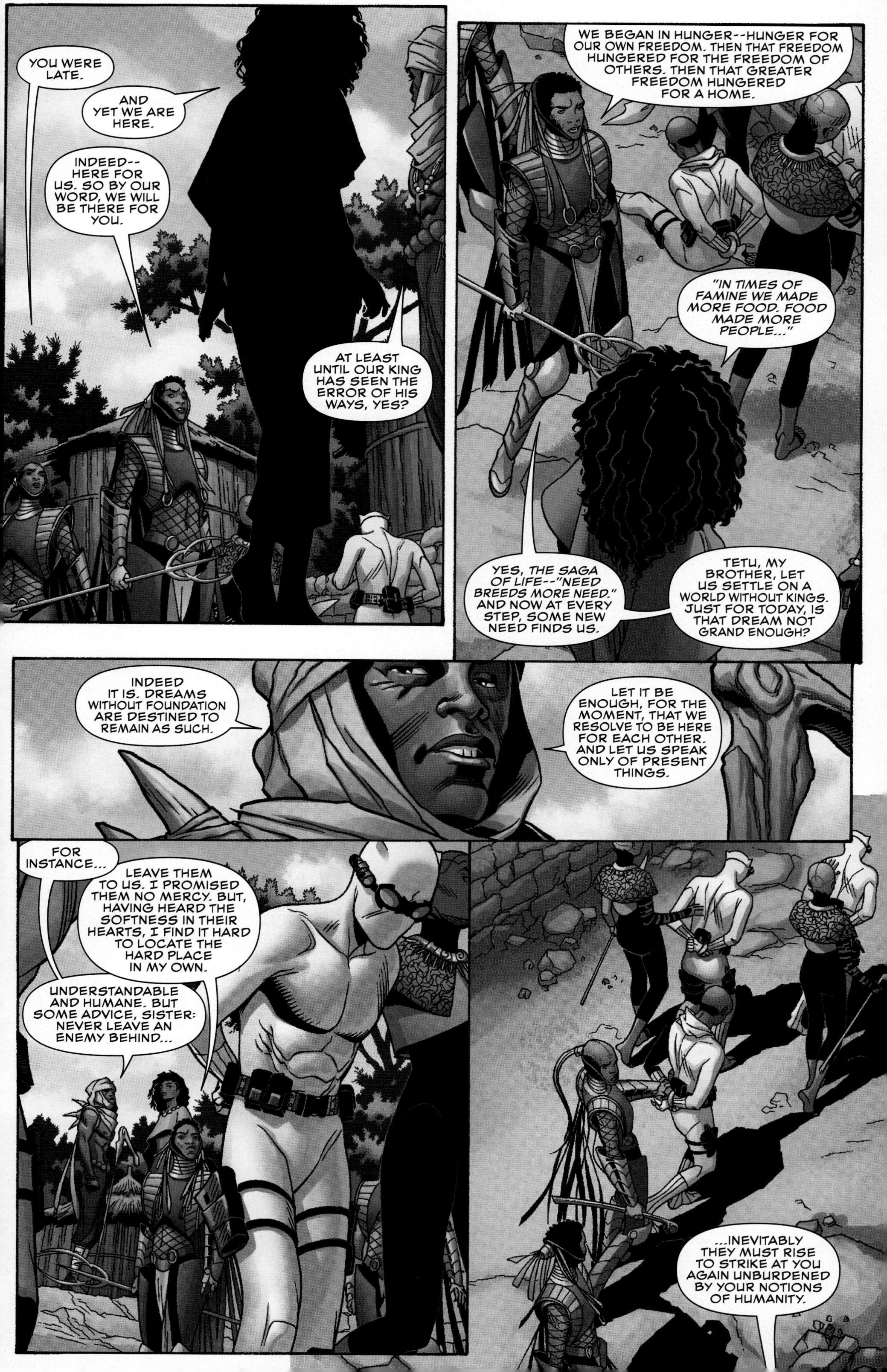
YOU WERE LATE.
AND YET WE ARE HERE.
INDEED--HERE FOR US. SO BY OUR WORD, WE WILL BE THERE FOR YOU.
AT LEAST UNTIL OUR KING HAS SEEN THE ERROR OF HIS WAYS, YES?
WE BEGAN IN HUNGER--HUNGER FOR OUR OWN FREEDOM. THEN THAT FREEDOM HUNGERED FOR THE FREEDOM OF OTHERS. THEN THAT GREATER FREEDOM HUNGERED FOR A HOME.
"IN TIMES OF FAMINE WE MADE MORE FOOD. FOOD MADE MORE PEOPLE..."
YES, THE SAGA OF LIFE--"NEED BREEDS MORE NEED." AND NOW AT EVERY STEP, SOME NEW NEED FINDS US.
TETU, MY BROTHER, LET US SETTLE ON A WORLD WITHOUT KINGS. JUST FOR TODAY, IS THAT DREAM NOT GRAND ENOUGH?
INDEED IT IS. DREAMS WITHOUT FOUNDATION ARE DESTINED TO REMAIN AS SUCH.
LET IT BE ENOUGH, FOR THE MOMENT, THAT WE RESOLVE TO BE HERE FOR EACH OTHER. AND LET US SPEAK ONLY OF PRESENT THINGS.
FOR INSTANCE...
LEAVE THEM TO US. I PROMISED THEM NO MERCY. BUT, HAVING HEARD THE SOFTNESS IN THEIR HEARTS, I FIND IT HARD TO LOCATE THE HARD PLACE IN MY OWN.
UNDERSTANDABLE AND HUMANE. BUT SOME ADVICE, SISTER: NEVER LEAVE AN ENEMY BEHIND...
...INEVITABLY THEY MUST RISE TO STRIKE AT YOU AGAIN UNBURDENED BY YOUR NOTIONS OF HUMANITY.

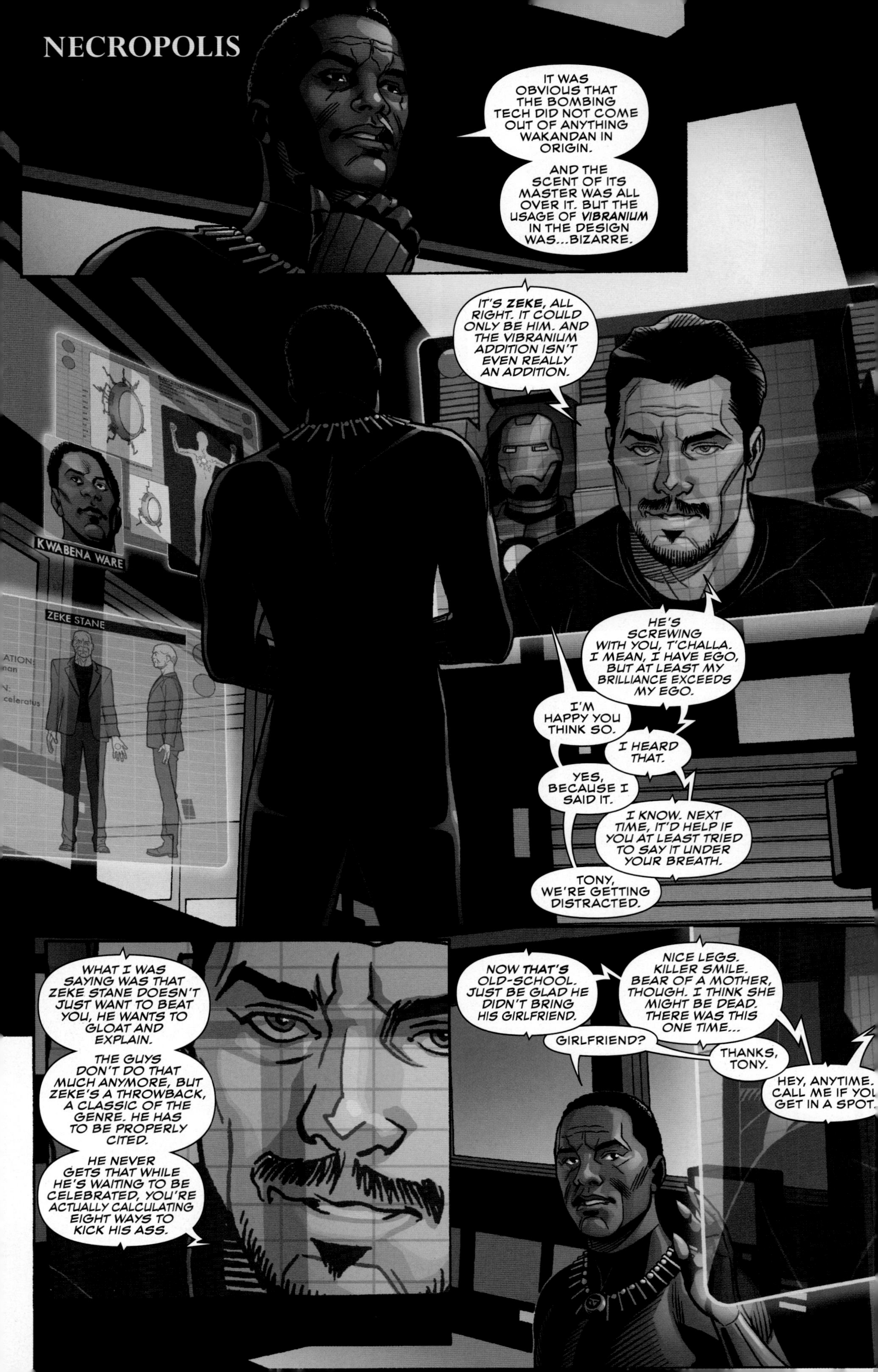
IT WAS OBVIOUS THAT THE BOMBING TECH DID NOT COME OUT OF ANYTHING WAKANDAN IN ORIGIN.
AND THE SCENT OF ITS MASTER WAS ALL OVER IT. BUT THE USAGE OF VIBRANIUM IN THE DESIGN WAS...BIZARRE.
IT'S ZEKE, ALL RIGHT. IT COULD ONLY BE HIM. AND THE VIBRANIUM ADDITION ISN'T EVEN REALLY AN ADDITION.
KWABENA WARE
ZEKE STANE
HE'S SCREWING WITH YOU, T'CHALLA. I MEAN, I HAVE EGO, BUT AT LEAST MY BRILLIANCE EXCEEDS MY EGO.
I'M HAPPY YOU THINK SO.
I HEARD THAT.
YES, BECAUSE I SAID IT.
I KNOW. NEXT TIME, IT'D HELP IF YOU AT LEAST TRIED TO SAY IT UNDER YOUR BREATH.
TONY, WE'RE GETTING DISTRACTED.
WHAT I WAS SAYING WAS THAT ZEKE STANE DOESN'T JUST WANT TO BEAT YOU, HE WANTS TO GLOAT AND EXPLAIN.
THE GUYS DON'T DO THAT MUCH ANYMORE, BUT ZEKE'S A THROWBACK, A CLASSIC OF THE GENRE. HE HAS TO BE PROPERLY CITED.
HE NEVER GETS THAT WHILE HE'S WAITING TO BE CELEBRATED, YOU'RE ACTUALLY CALCULATING EIGHT WAYS TO KICK HIS ASS.
NOW THAT'S OLD-SCHOOL. JUST BE GLAD HE DIDN'T BRING HIS GIRLFRIEND.
GIRLFRIEND?
NICE LEGS. KILLER SMILE. BEAR OF A MOTHER, THOUGH. I THINK SHE MIGHT BE DEAD. THERE WAS THIS ONE TIME...
THANKS, TONY.
HEY, ANYTIME. CALL ME IF YOU GET IN A SPOT.

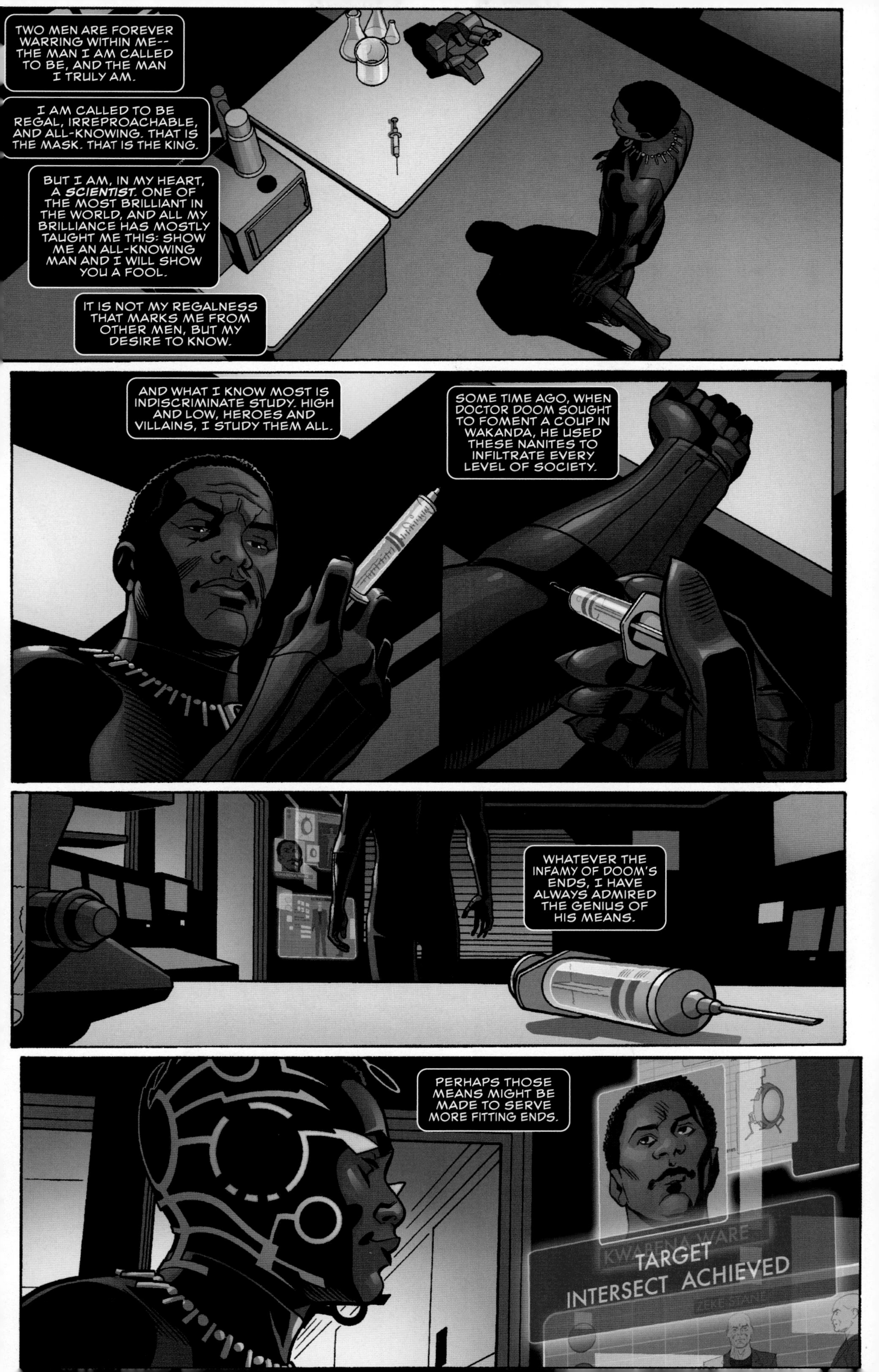
TWO MEN ARE FOREVER WARRING WITHIN ME-- THE MAN I AM CALLED TO BE, AND THE MAN I TRULY AM.
I AM CALLED TO BE REGAL, IRREPROACHABLE, AND ALL-KNOWING. THAT IS THE MASK. THAT IS THE KING.
BUT I AM, IN MY HEART, A ***SCIENTIST.*** ONE OF THE MOST BRILLIANT IN THE WORLD, AND ALL MY BRILLIANCE HAS MOSTLY TAUGHT ME THIS: SHOW ME AN ALL-KNOWING MAN AND I WILL SHOW YOU A FOOL.
IT IS NOT MY REGALNESS THAT MARKS ME FROM OTHER MEN, BUT MY DESIRE TO KNOW.
AND WHAT I KNOW MOST IS INDISCRIMINATE STUDY. HIGH AND LOW, HEROES AND VILLAINS, I STUDY THEM ALL.
SOME TIME AGO, WHEN DOCTOR DOOM SOUGHT TO FOMENT A COUP IN WAKANDA, HE USED THESE NANITES TO INFILTRATE EVERY LEVEL OF SOCIETY.
WHATEVER THE INFAMY OF DOOM'S ENDS, I HAVE ALWAYS ADMIRED THE GENIUS OF HIS MEANS.
PERHAPS THOSE MEANS MIGHT BE MADE TO SERVE MORE FITTING ENDS.
TARGET
INTERSECT ACHIEVED

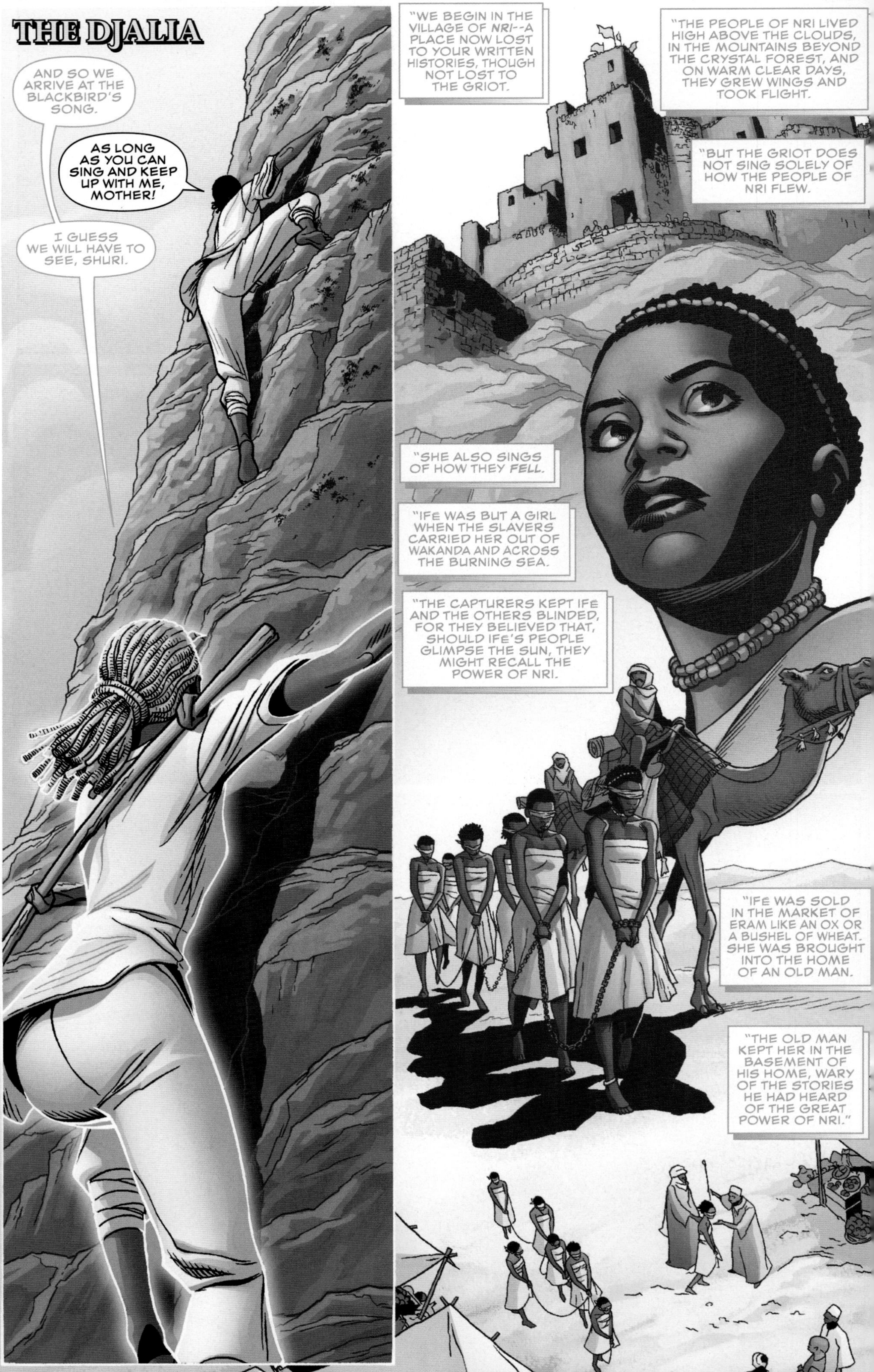
THE DJALIA
AND SO WE ARRIVE AT THE BLACKBIRD'S SONG.
AS LONG AS YOU CAN SING AND KEEP UP WITH ME, MOTHER!
I GUESS WE WILL HAVE TO SEE, SHURI.
"WE BEGIN IN THE VILLAGE OF NRI--A PLACE NOW LOST TO YOUR WRITTEN HISTORIES, THOUGH NOT LOST TO THE GRIOT.
"THE PEOPLE OF NRI LIVED HIGH ABOVE THE CLOUDS, IN THE MOUNTAINS BEYOND THE CRYSTAL FOREST, AND ON WARM CLEAR DAYS, THEY GREW WINGS AND TOOK FLIGHT.
"BUT THE GRIOT DOES NOT SING SOLELY OF HOW THE PEOPLE OF NRI FLEW.
"SHE ALSO SINGS OF HOW THEY FELL.
"IFE WAS BUT A GIRL WHEN THE SLAVERS CARRIED HER OUT OF WAKANDA AND ACROSS THE BURNING SEA.
"THE CAPTURERS KEPT IFE AND THE OTHERS BLINDED, FOR THEY BELIEVED THAT, SHOULD IFE'S PEOPLE GLIMPSE THE SUN, THEY MIGHT RECALL THE POWER OF NRI.
"IFE WAS SOLD IN THE MARKET OF ERAM LIKE AN OX OR A BUSHEL OF WHEAT. SHE WAS BROUGHT INTO THE HOME OF AN OLD MAN.
"THE OLD MAN KEPT HER IN THE BASEMENT OF HIS HOME, WARY OF THE STORIES HE HAD HEARD OF THE GREAT POWER OF NRI."

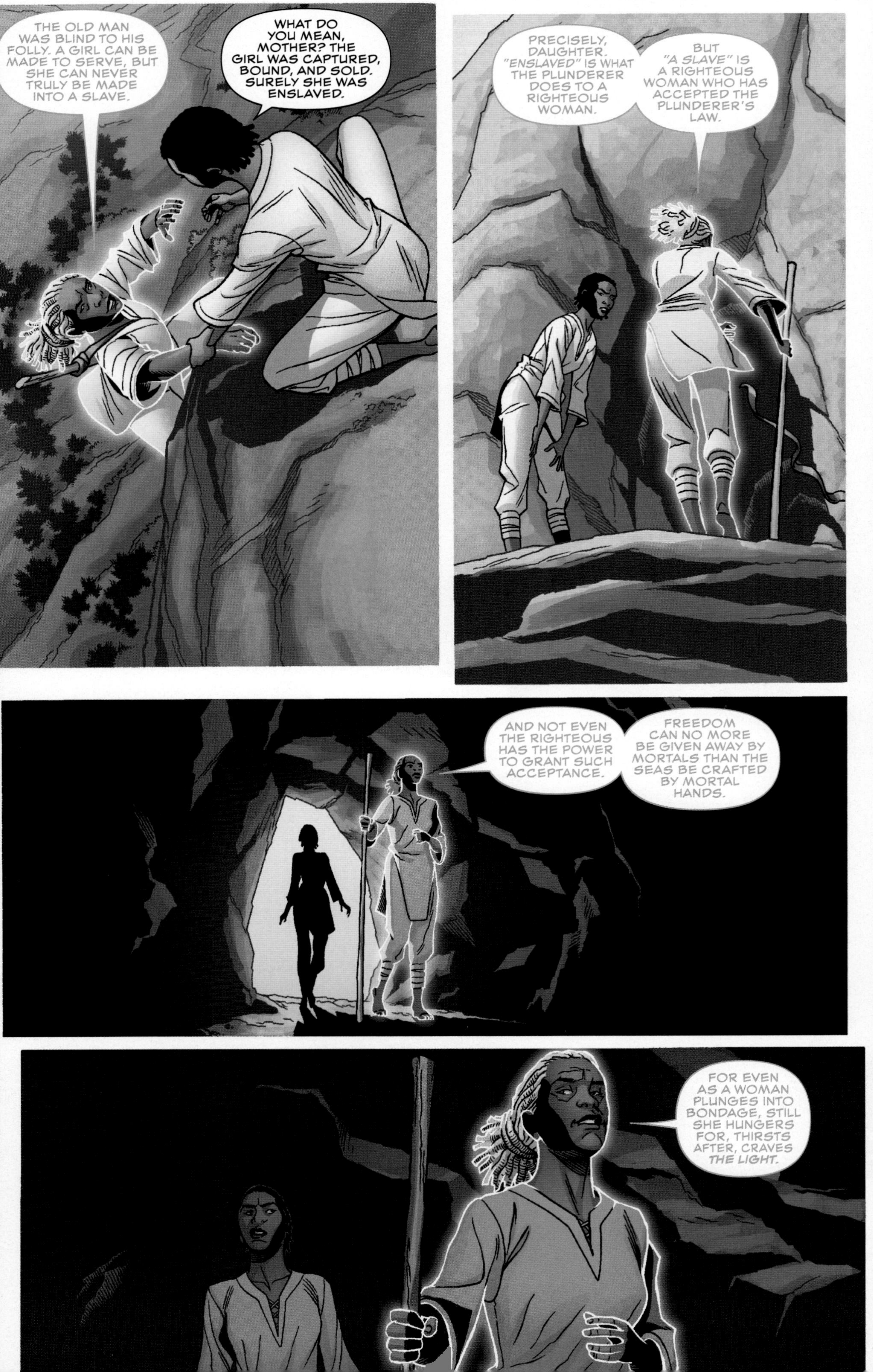
THE OLD MAN WAS BLIND TO HIS FOLLY. A GIRL CAN BE MADE TO SERVE, BUT SHE CAN NEVER TRULY BE MADE INTO A SLAVE.
WHAT DO YOU MEAN, MOTHER? THE GIRL WAS CAPTURED, BOUND, AND SOLD. SURELY SHE WAS ENSLAVED.
PRECISELY, DAUGHTER. "ENSLAVED" IS WHAT THE PLUNDERER DOES TO A RIGHTEOUS WOMAN.
BUT "A SLAVE" IS A RIGHTEOUS WOMAN WHO HAS ACCEPTED THE PLUNDERER'S LAW.
AND NOT EVEN THE RIGHTEOUS HAS THE POWER TO GRANT SUCH ACCEPTANCE.
FREEDOM CAN NO MORE BE GIVEN AWAY BY MORTALS THAN THE SEAS BE CRAFTED BY MORTAL HANDS.
FOR EVEN AS A WOMAN PLUNGES INTO BONDAGE, STILL SHE HUNGERS FOR, THIRSTS AFTER, CRAVES THE LIGHT.

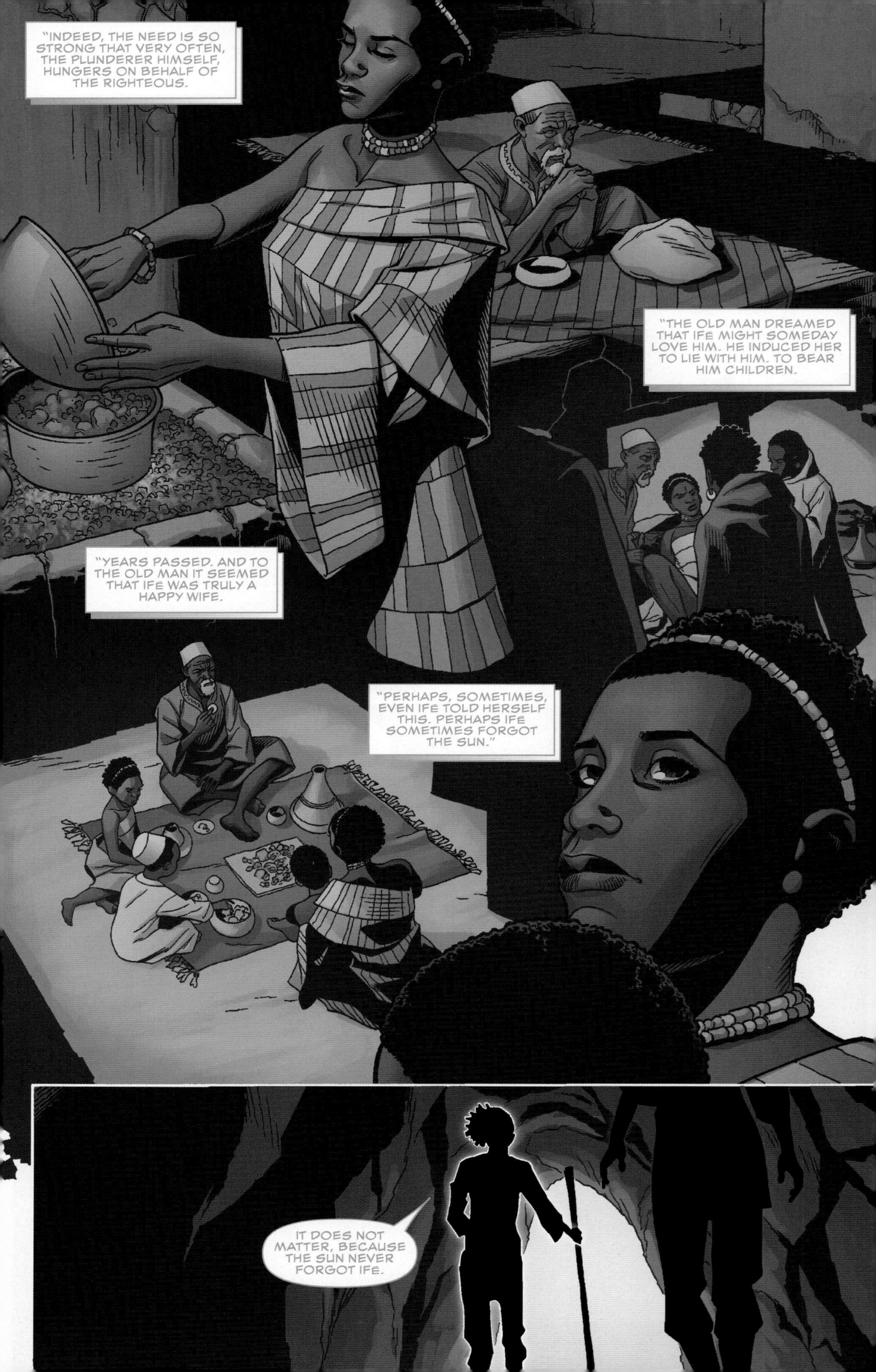
"INDEED, THE NEED IS SO STRONG THAT VERY OFTEN, THE PLUNDERER HIMSELF, HUNGERS ON BEHALF OF THE RIGHTEOUS.
"THE OLD MAN DREAMED THAT IFE MIGHT SOMEDAY LOVE HIM. HE INDUCED HER TO LIE WITH HIM. TO BEAR HIM CHILDREN.
"YEARS PASSED. AND TO THE OLD MAN IT SEEMED THAT IFE WAS TRULY A HAPPY WIFE.
"PERHAPS, SOMETIMES, EVEN IFE TOLD HERSELF THIS. PERHAPS IFE SOMETIMES FORGOT THE SUN."
IT DOES NOT MATTER, BECAUSE THE SUN NEVER FORGOT IFE.

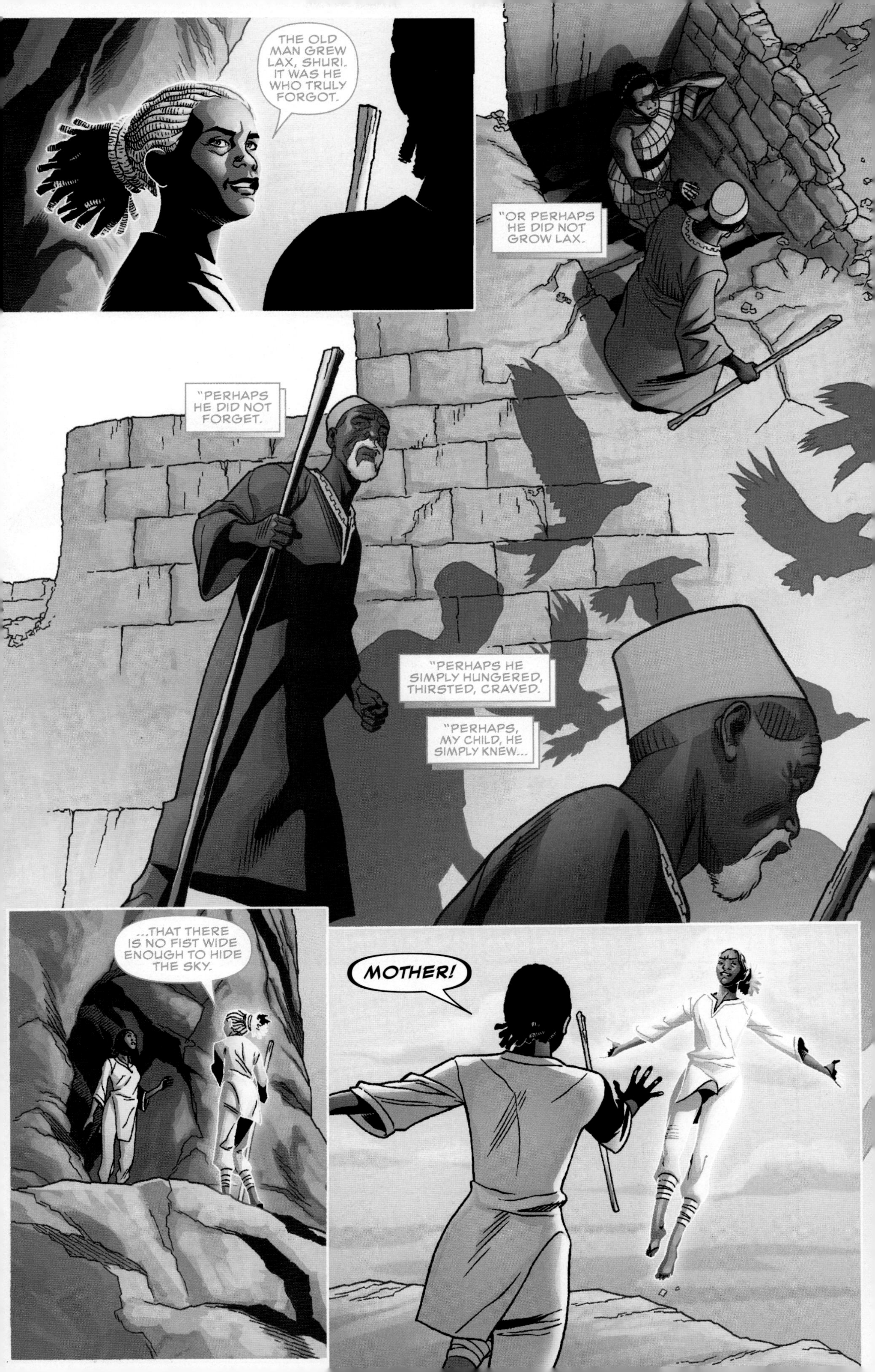
THE OLD MAN GREW LAX, SHURI. IT WAS HE WHO TRULY FORGOT.
"OR PERHAPS HE DID NOT GROW LAX.
"PERHAPS HE DID NOT FORGET.
"PERHAPS HE SIMPLY HUNGERED, THIRSTED, CRAVED.
"PERHAPS, MY CHILD, HE SIMPLY KNEW...
...THAT THERE IS NO FIST WIDE ENOUGH TO HIDE THE SKY.
MOTHER!

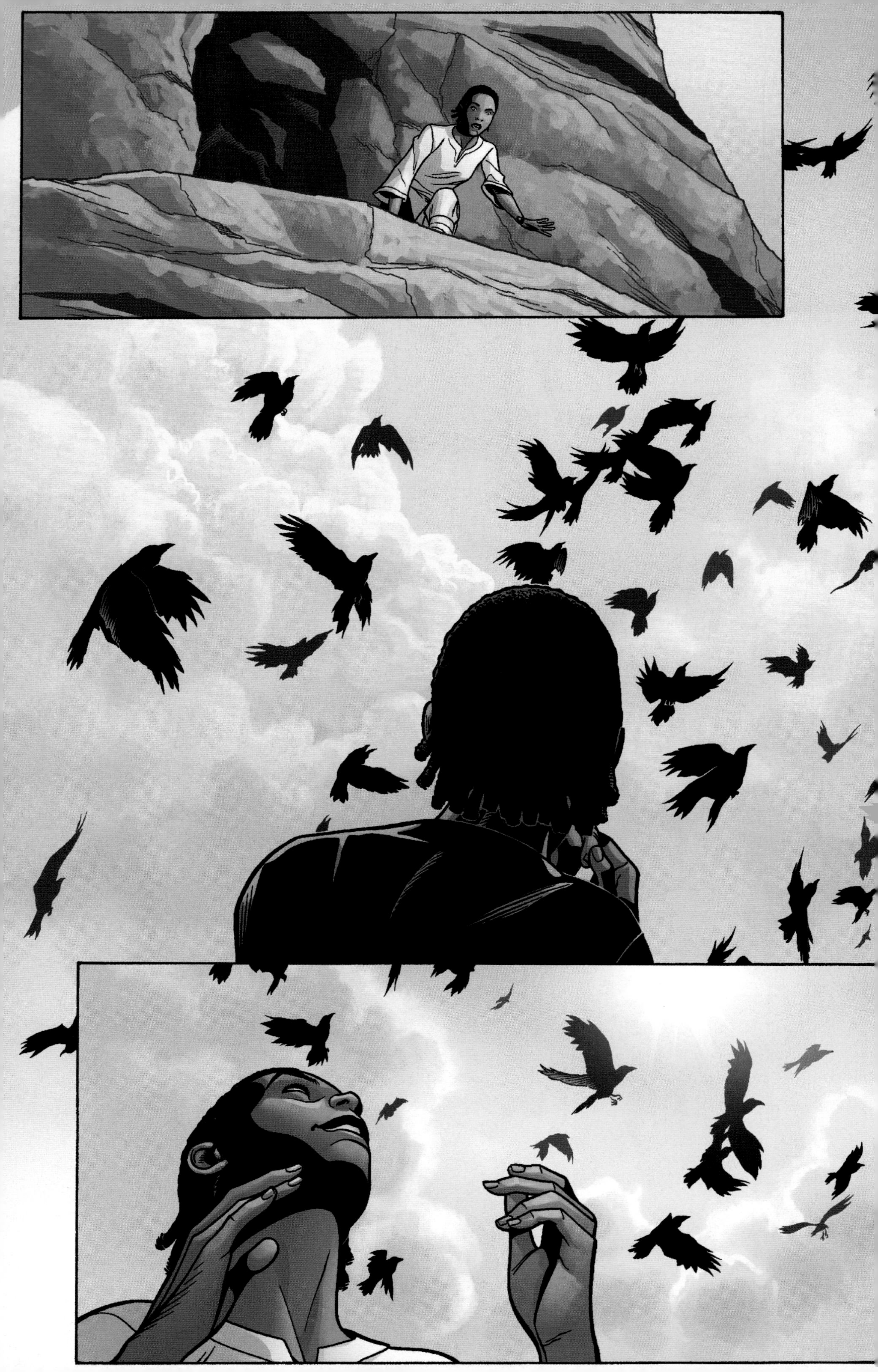

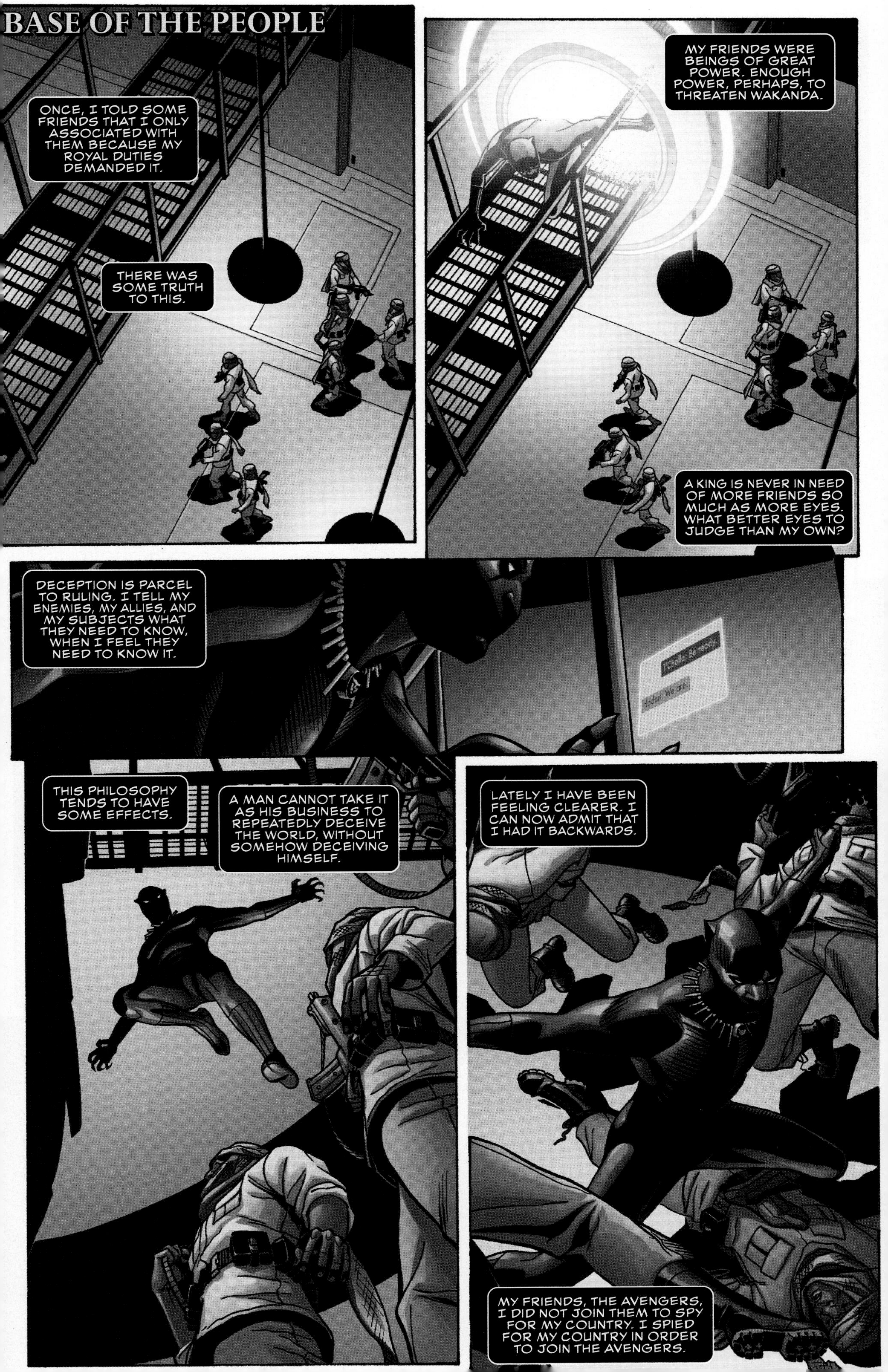
BASE OF THE PEOPLE
ONCE, I TOLD SOME FRIENDS THAT I ONLY ASSOCIATED WITH THEM BECAUSE MY ROYAL DUTIES DEMANDED IT.
THERE WAS SOME TRUTH TO THIS.
MY FRIENDS WERE BEINGS OF GREAT POWER. ENOUGH POWER, PERHAPS, TO THREATEN WAKANDA.
A KING IS NEVER IN NEED OF MORE FRIENDS SO MUCH AS MORE EYES. WHAT BETTER EYES TO JUDGE THAN MY OWN?
DECEPTION IS PARCEL TO RULING. I TELL MY ENEMIES, MY ALLIES, AND MY SUBJECTS WHAT THEY NEED TO KNOW, WHEN I FEEL THEY NEED TO KNOW IT.
T'Challa: Be ready.
Hodari: We are.
THIS PHILOSOPHY TENDS TO HAVE SOME EFFECTS.
A MAN CANNOT TAKE IT AS HIS BUSINESS TO REPEATEDLY DECEIVE THE WORLD, WITHOUT SOMEHOW DECEIVING HIMSELF.
LATELY I HAVE BEEN FEELING CLEARER. I CAN NOW ADMIT THAT I HAD IT BACKWARDS.
MY FRIENDS, THE AVENGERS, I DID NOT JOIN THEM TO SPY FOR MY COUNTRY. I SPIED FOR MY COUNTRY IN ORDER TO JOIN THE AVENGERS.

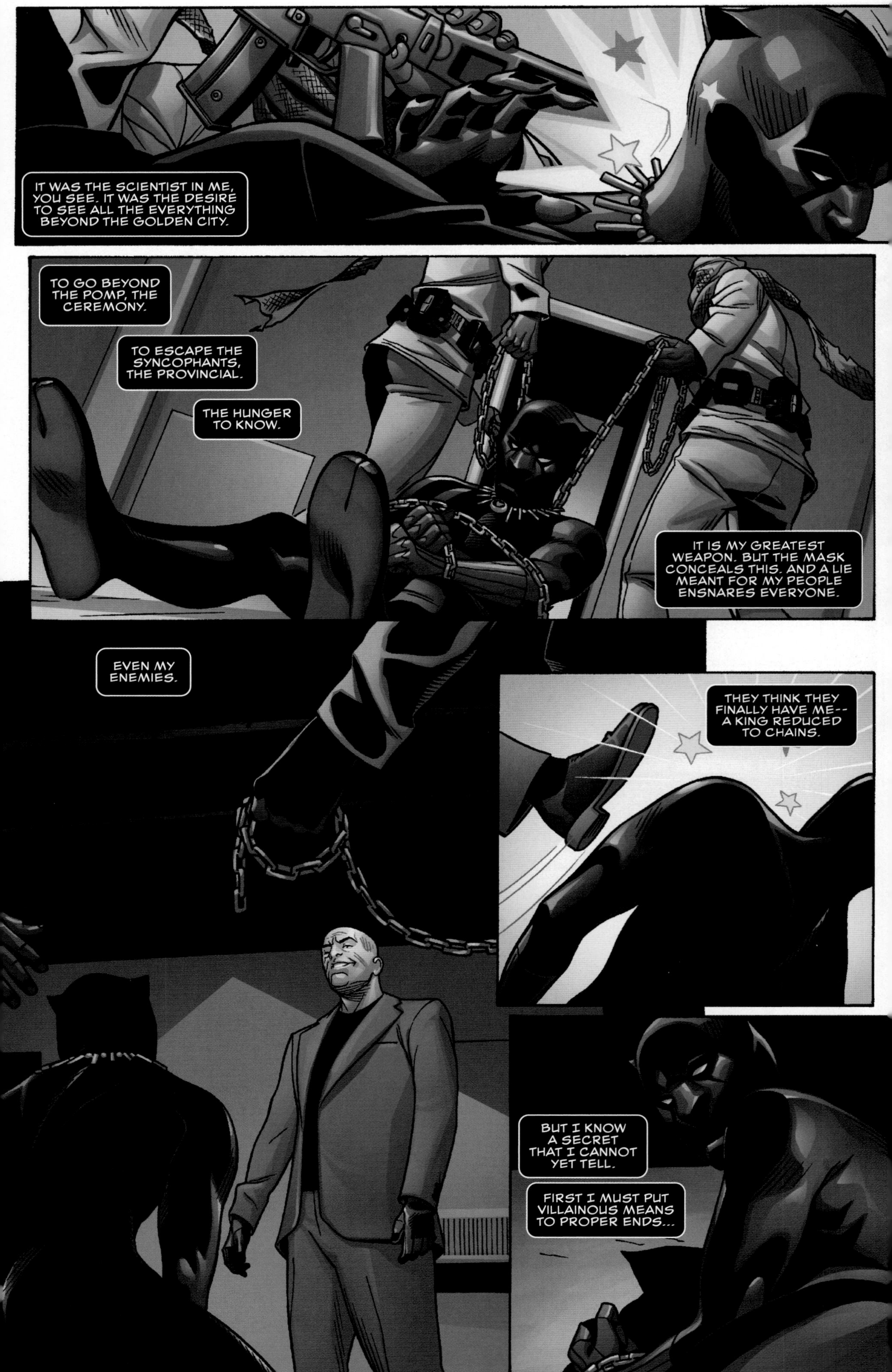
IT WAS THE SCIENTIST IN ME, YOU SEE. IT WAS THE DESIRE TO SEE ALL THE EVERYTHING BEYOND THE GOLDEN CITY.
TO GO BEYOND THE POMP, THE CEREMONY.
TO ESCAPE THE SYNCOPHANTS, THE PROVINCIAL.
THE HUNGER TO KNOW.
IT IS MY GREATEST WEAPON. BUT THE MASK CONCEALS THIS. AND A LIE MEANT FOR MY PEOPLE ENSNARES EVERYONE.
EVEN MY ENEMIES.
THEY THINK THEY FINALLY HAVE ME-- A KING REDUCED TO CHAINS.
BUT I KNOW A SECRET THAT I CANNOT YET TELL.
FIRST I MUST PUT VILLAINOUS MEANS TO PROPER ENDS...

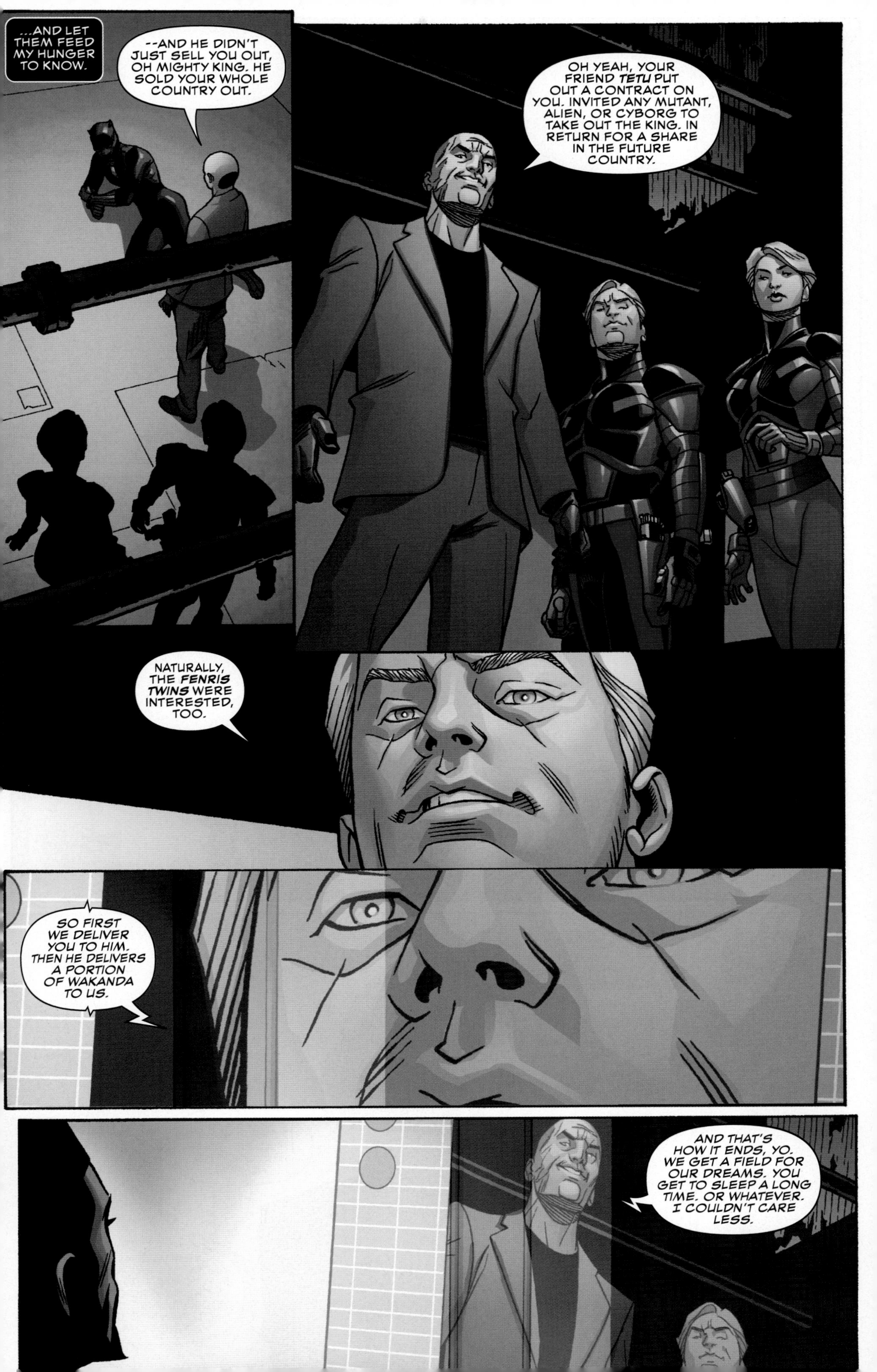
...AND LET THEM FEED MY HUNGER TO KNOW.
--AND HE DIDN'T JUST SELL YOU OUT, OH MIGHTY KING. HE SOLD YOUR WHOLE COUNTRY OUT.
OH YEAH, YOUR FRIEND TETU PUT OUT A CONTRACT ON YOU. INVITED ANY MUTANT, ALIEN, OR CYBORG TO TAKE OUT THE KING. IN RETURN FOR A SHARE IN THE FUTURE COUNTRY.
NATURALLY, THE FENRIS TWINS WERE INTERESTED, TOO.
SO FIRST WE DELIVER YOU TO HIM. THEN HE DELIVERS A PORTION OF WAKANDA TO US.
AND THAT'S HOW IT ENDS, YO. WE GET A FIELD FOR OUR DREAMS. YOU GET TO SLEEP A LONG TIME. OR WHATEVER. I COULDN'T CARE LESS.

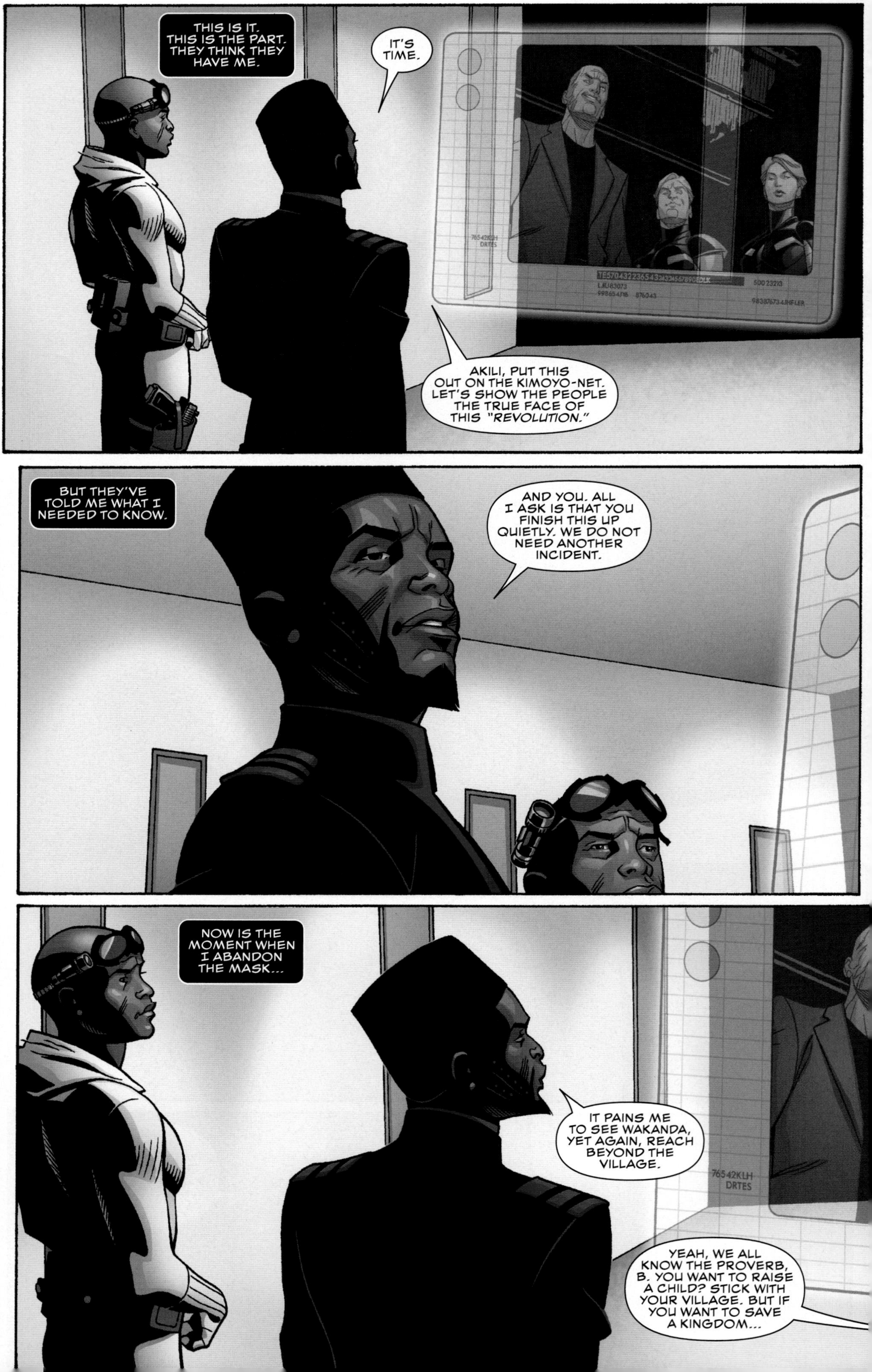

THIS IS IT. THIS IS THE PART. THEY THINK THEY HAVE ME.
IT'S TIME.
AKILI, PUT THIS OUT ON THE KIMOYO-NET. LET'S SHOW THE PEOPLE THE TRUE FACE OF THIS "REVOLUTION."
BUT THEY'VE TOLD ME WHAT I NEEDED TO KNOW.
AND YOU. ALL I ASK IS THAT YOU FINISH THIS UP QUIETLY. WE DO NOT NEED ANOTHER INCIDENT.
NOW IS THE MOMENT WHEN I ABANDON THE MASK...
IT PAINS ME TO SEE WAKANDA, YET AGAIN, REACH BEYOND THE VILLAGE.
YEAH, WE ALL KNOW THE PROVERB, B. YOU WANT TO RAISE A CHILD? STICK WITH YOUR VILLAGE. BUT IF YOU WANT TO SAVE A KINGDOM...

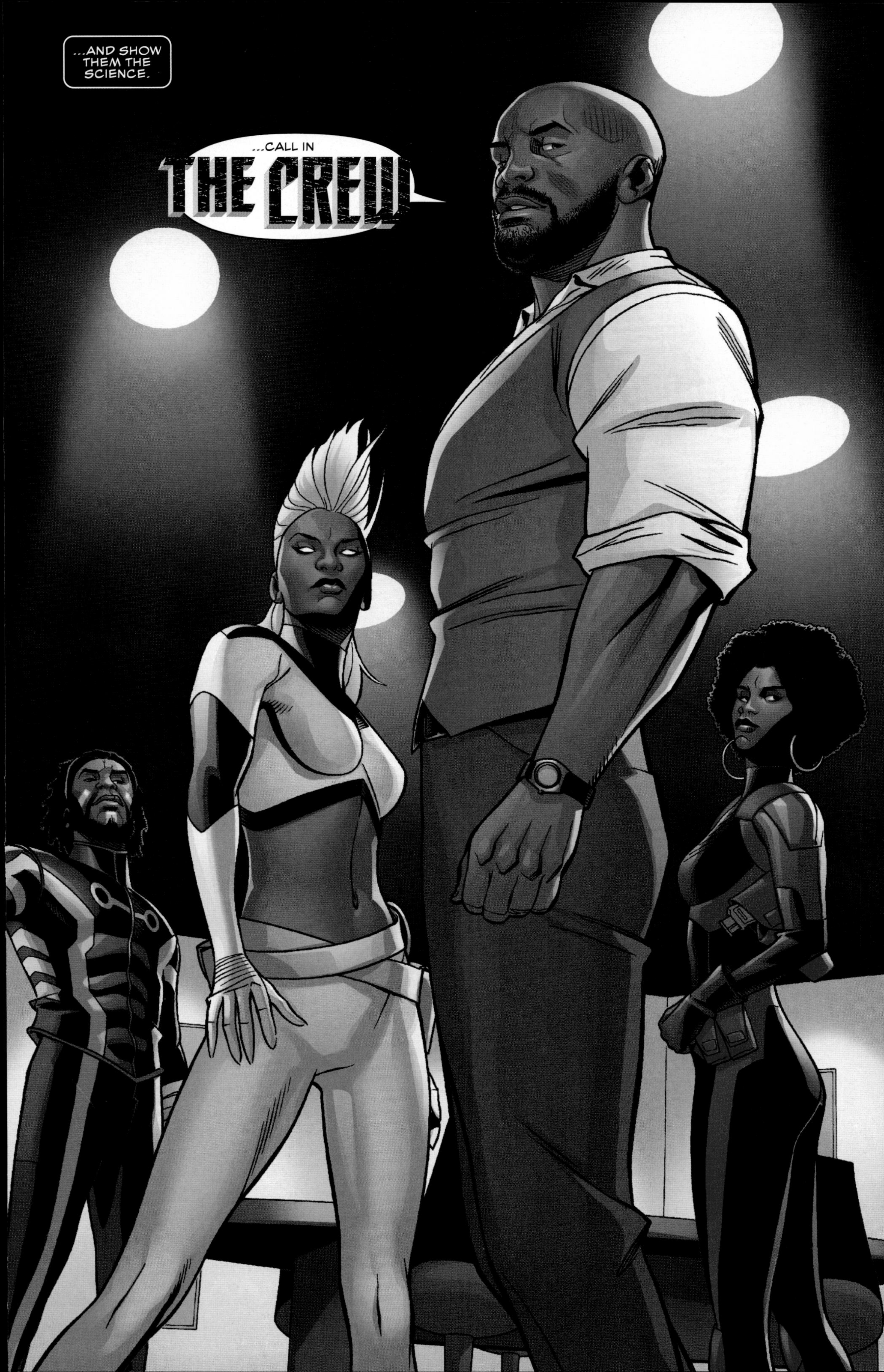
...AND SHOW THEM THE SCIENCE.
...CALL IN THE CREW

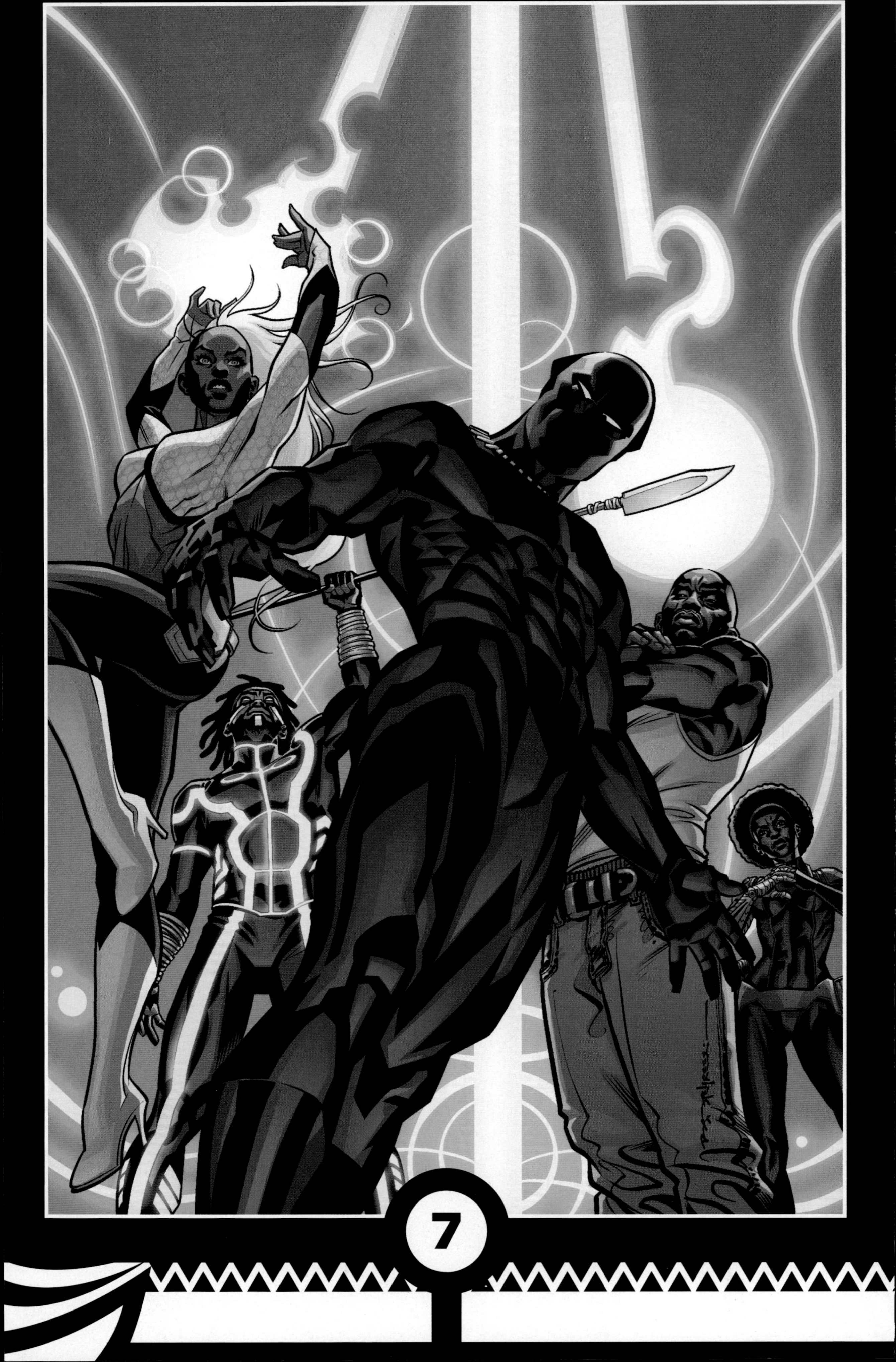
7

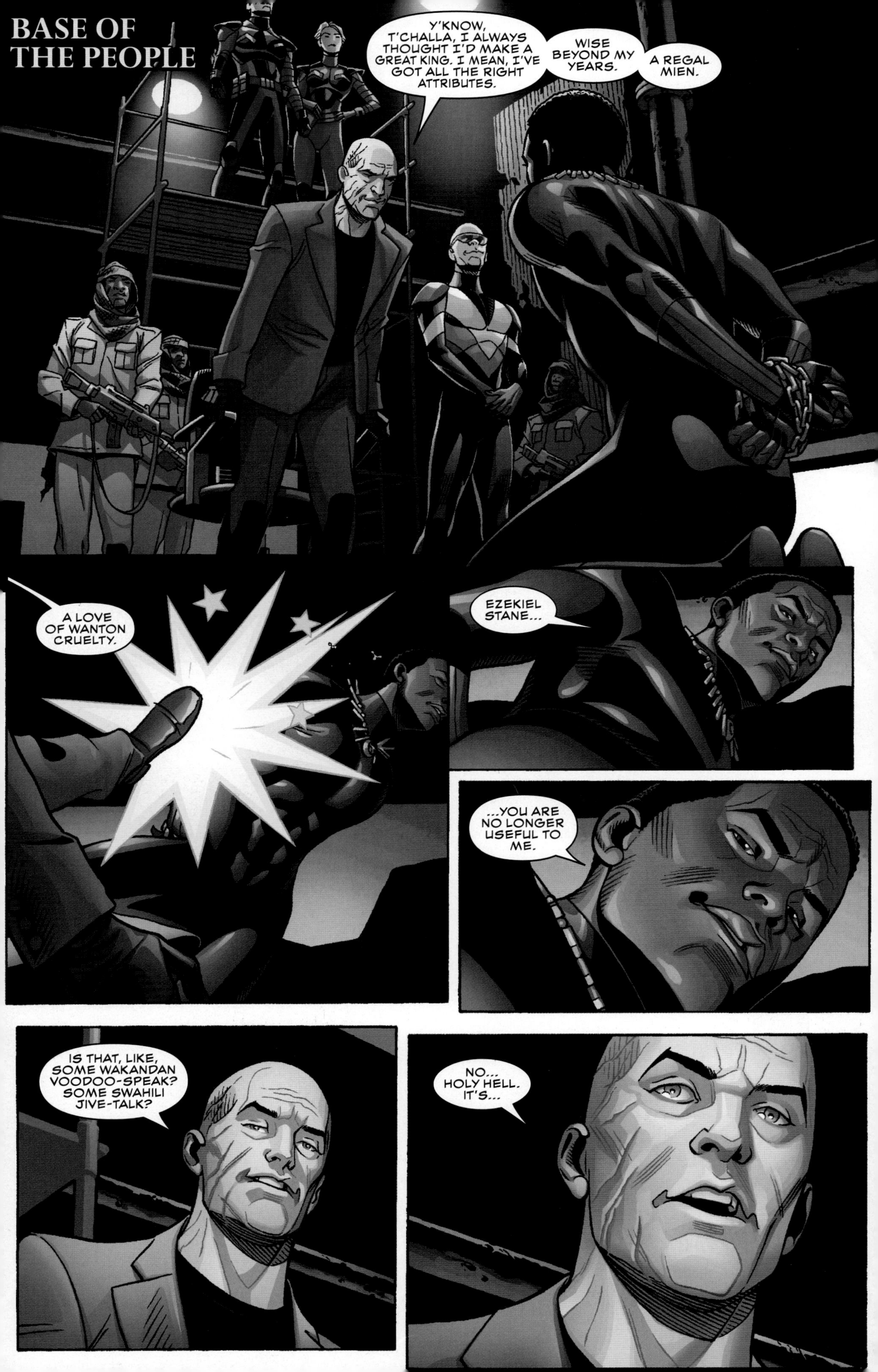
BASE OF THE PEOPLE
Y'KNOW, T'CHALLA, I ALWAYS THOUGHT I'D MAKE A GREAT KING. I MEAN, I'VE GOT ALL THE RIGHT ATTRIBUTES.
WISE BEYOND MY YEARS.
A REGAL MIEN.
A LOVE OF WANTON CRUELTY.
EZEKIEL STANE...
...YOU ARE NO LONGER USEFUL TO ME.
IS THAT, LIKE, SOME WAKANDAN VOODOO-SPEAK? SOME SWAHILI JIVE-TALK?
NO... HOLY HELL. IT'S...

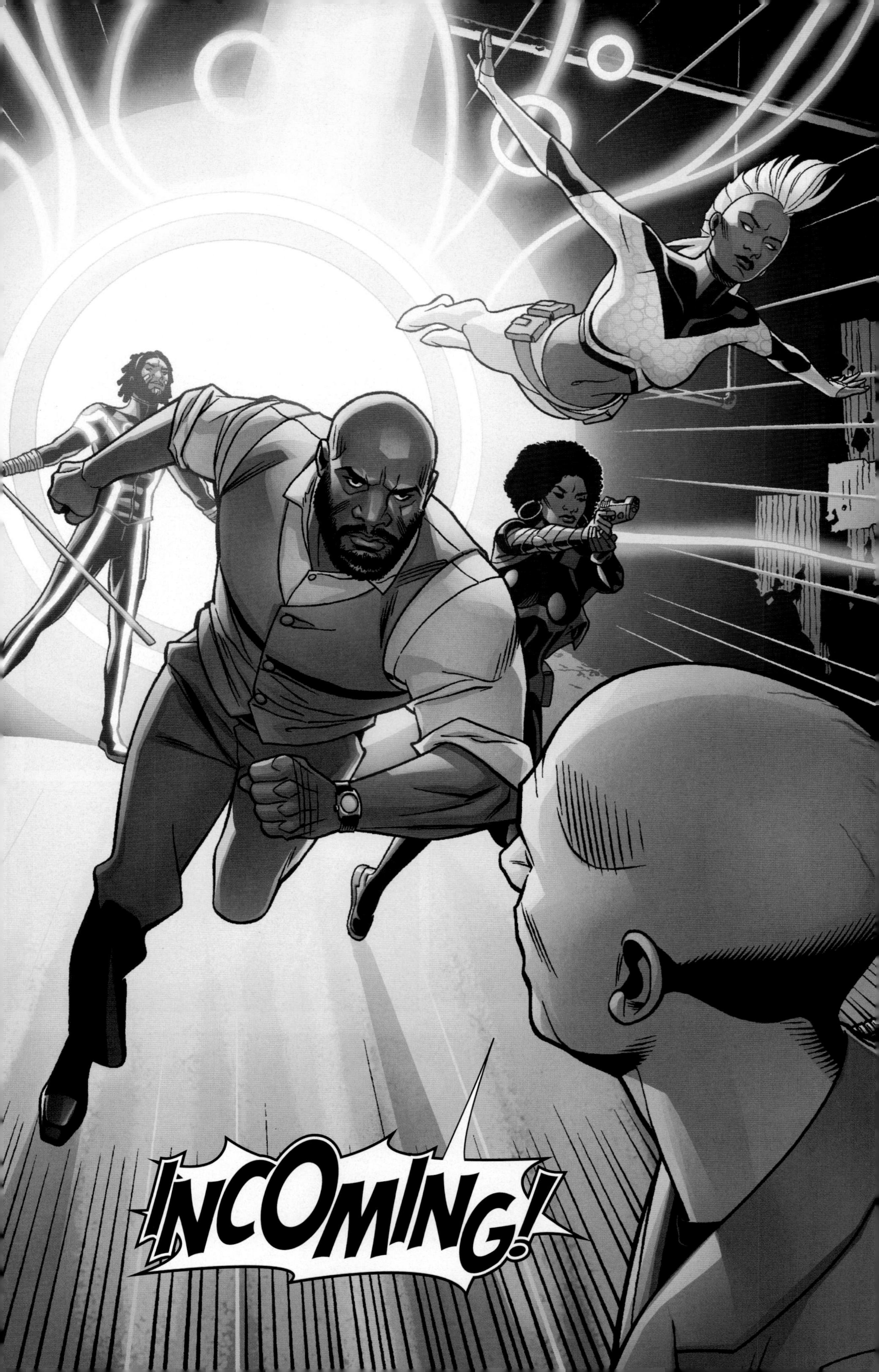
INCOMING!

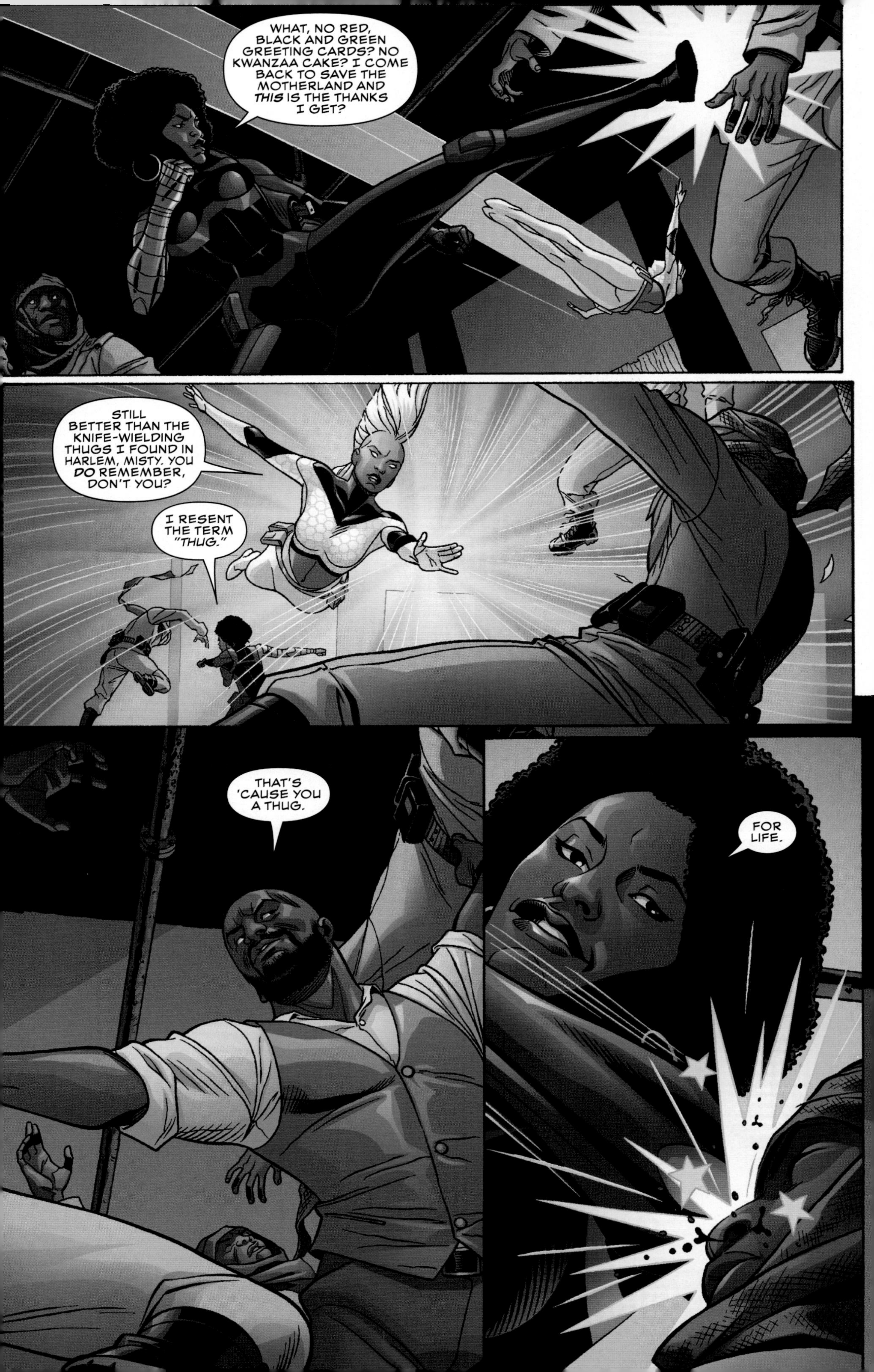
WHAT, NO RED, BLACK AND GREEN GREETING CARDS? NO KWANZAA CAKE? I COME BACK TO SAVE THE MOTHERLAND AND THIS IS THE THANKS I GET?
STILL BETTER THAN THE KNIFE-WIELDING THUGS I FOUND IN HARLEM, MISTY. YOU DO REMEMBER, DON'T YOU?
I RESENT THE TERM "THUG."
THAT'S 'CAUSE YOU A THUG.
FOR LIFE.

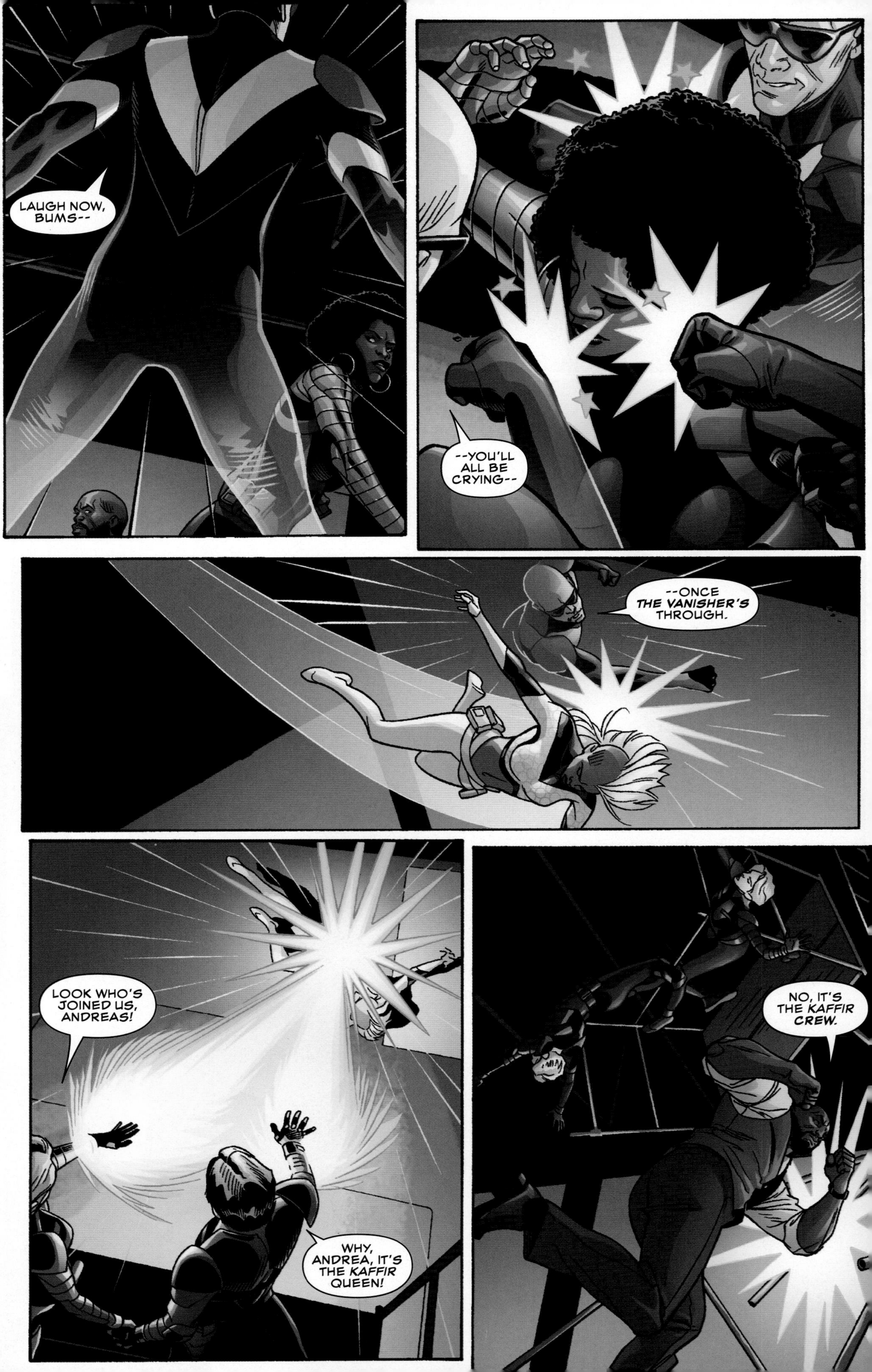
LAUGH NOW, BUMS--
--YOU'LL ALL BE CRYING--
--ONCE *THE VANISHER'S* THROUGH.
LOOK WHO'S JOINED US, ANDREAS!
WHY, ANDREA, IT'S THE *KAFFIR* QUEEN!
NO, IT'S THE *KAFFIR* CREW.

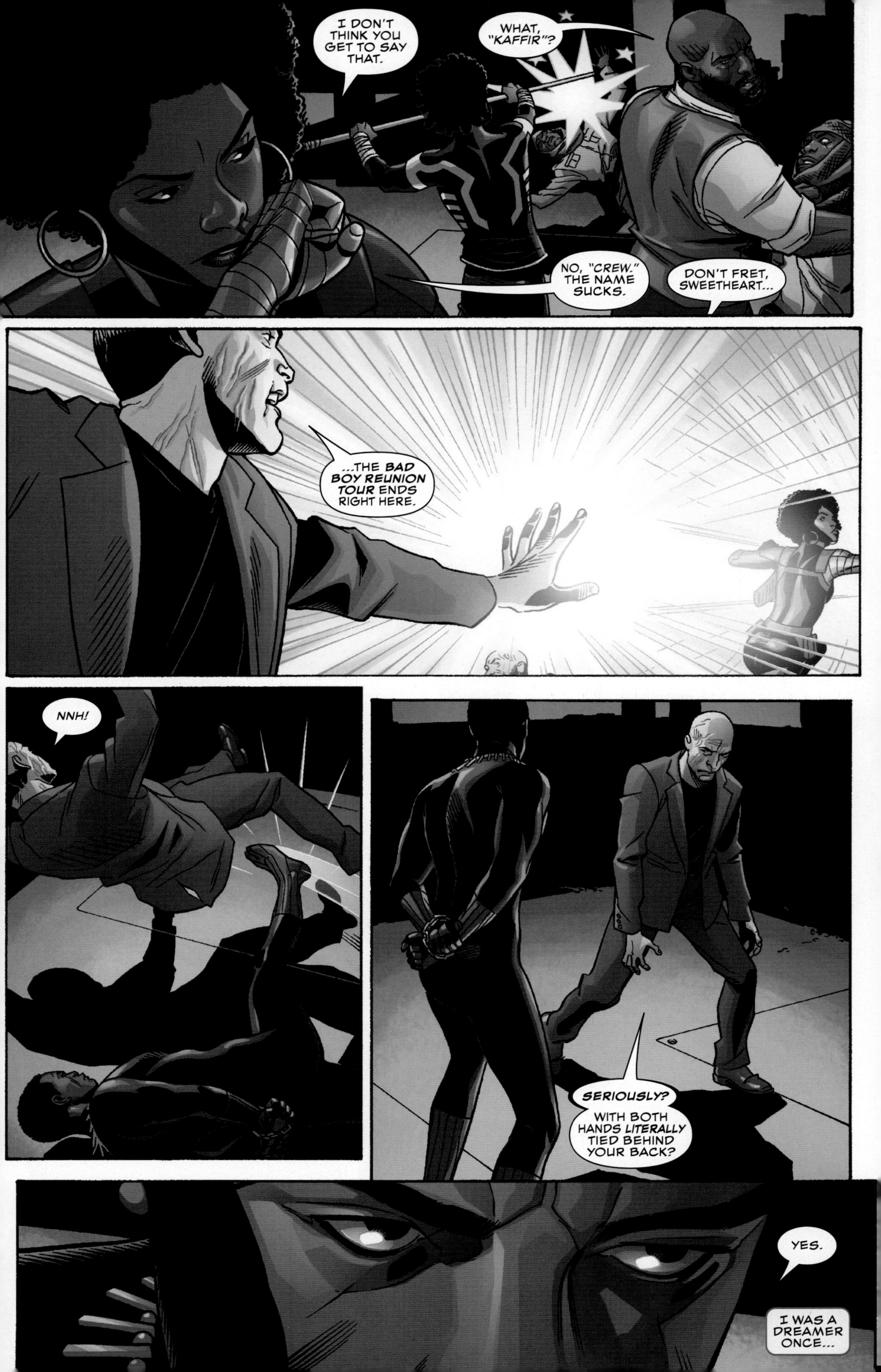
I DON'T THINK YOU GET TO SAY THAT.
WHAT, "KAFFIR"?
NO, "CREW." THE NAME SUCKS.
DON'T FRET, SWEETHEART...
...THE BAD BOY REUNION TOUR ENDS RIGHT HERE.
NNH!
SERIOUSLY? WITH BOTH HANDS LITERALLY TIED BEHIND YOUR BACK?
YES.
I WAS A DREAMER ONCE...

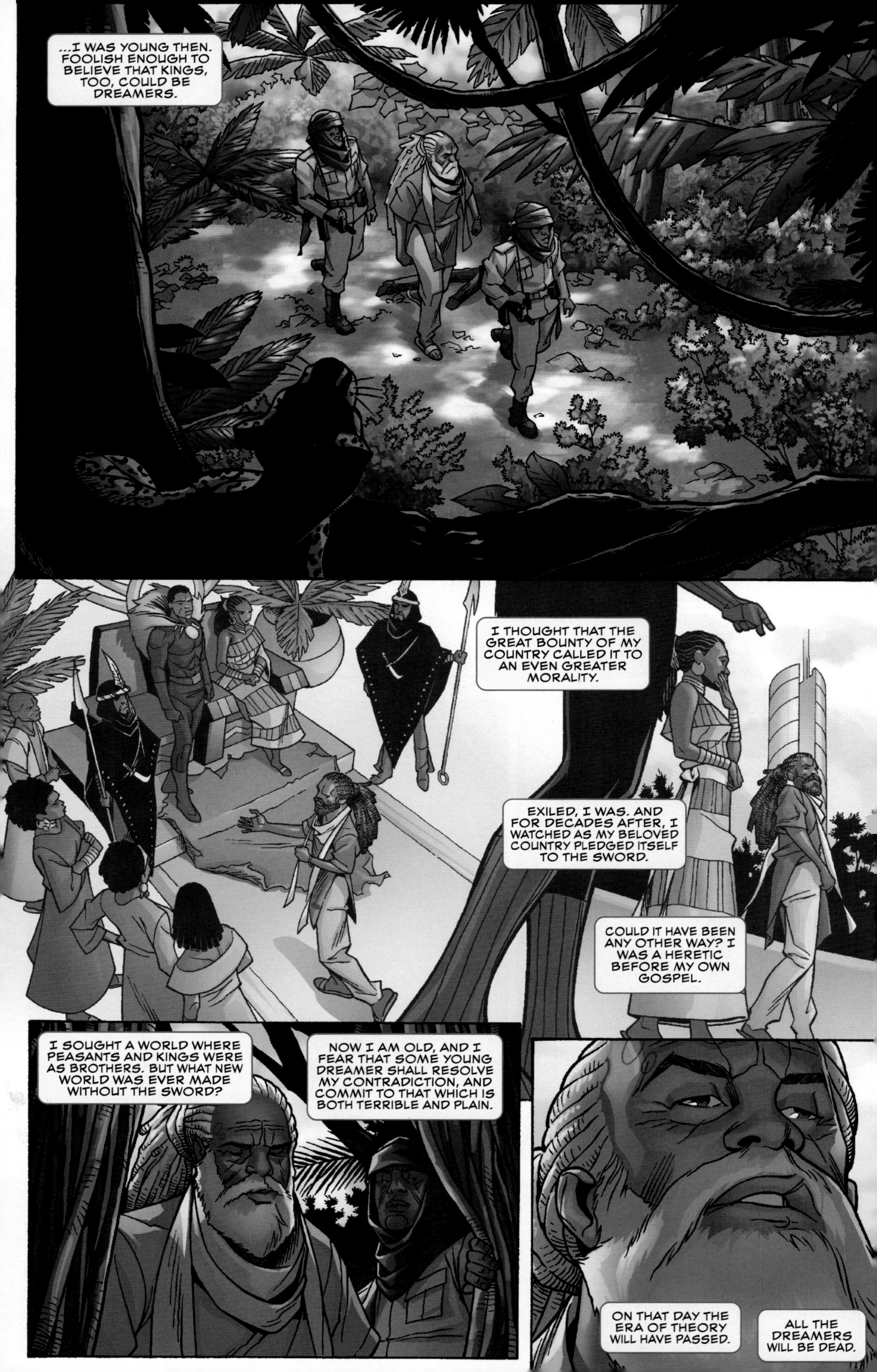
...I WAS YOUNG THEN. FOOLISH ENOUGH TO BELIEVE THAT KINGS, TOO, COULD BE DREAMERS.
I THOUGHT THAT THE GREAT BOUNTY OF MY COUNTRY CALLED IT TO AN EVEN GREATER MORALITY.
EXILED, I WAS. AND FOR DECADES AFTER, I WATCHED AS MY BELOVED COUNTRY PLEDGED ITSELF TO THE SWORD.
COULD IT HAVE BEEN ANY OTHER WAY? I WAS A HERETIC BEFORE MY OWN GOSPEL.
I SOUGHT A WORLD WHERE PEASANTS AND KINGS WERE AS BROTHERS. BUT WHAT NEW WORLD WAS EVER MADE WITHOUT THE SWORD?
NOW I AM OLD, AND I FEAR THAT SOME YOUNG DREAMER SHALL RESOLVE MY CONTRADICTION, AND COMMIT TO THAT WHICH IS BOTH TERRIBLE AND PLAIN.
ON THAT DAY THE ERA OF THEORY WILL HAVE PASSED.
ALL THE DREAMERS WILL BE DEAD.

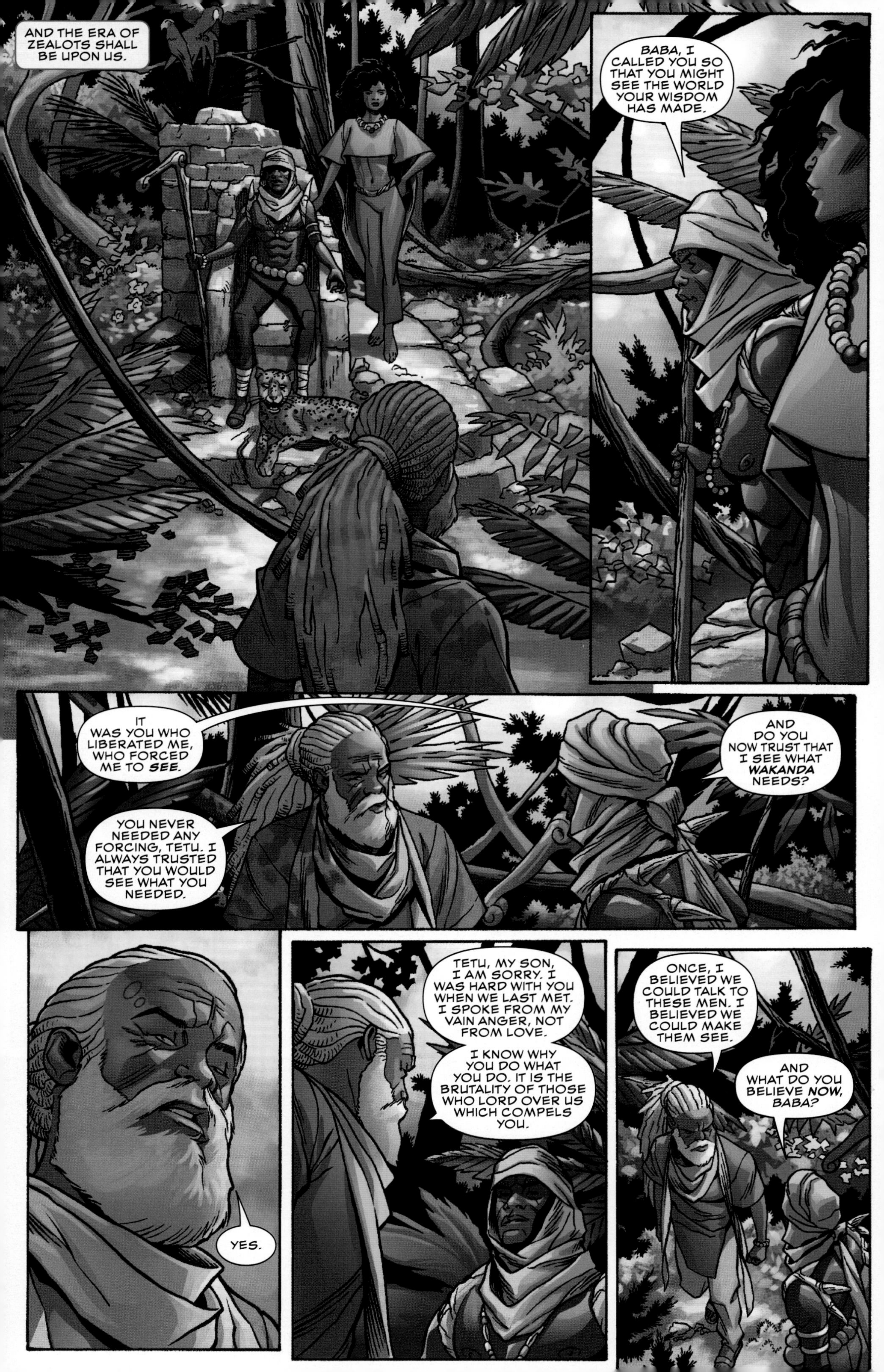
AND THE ERA OF ZEALOTS SHALL BE UPON US.
BABA, I CALLED YOU SO THAT YOU MIGHT SEE THE WORLD YOUR WISDOM HAS MADE.
IT WAS YOU WHO LIBERATED ME, WHO FORCED ME TO SEE.
YOU NEVER NEEDED ANY FORCING, TETU. I ALWAYS TRUSTED THAT YOU WOULD SEE WHAT YOU NEEDED.
AND DO YOU NOW TRUST THAT I SEE WHAT WAKANDA NEEDS?
YES.
TETU, MY SON, I AM SORRY. I WAS HARD WITH YOU WHEN WE LAST MET. I SPOKE FROM MY VAIN ANGER, NOT FROM LOVE.
I KNOW WHY YOU DO WHAT YOU DO. IT IS THE BRUTALITY OF THOSE WHO LORD OVER US WHICH COMPELS YOU.
ONCE, I BELIEVED WE COULD TALK TO THESE MEN. I BELIEVED WE COULD MAKE THEM SEE.
AND WHAT DO YOU BELIEVE NOW, BABA?

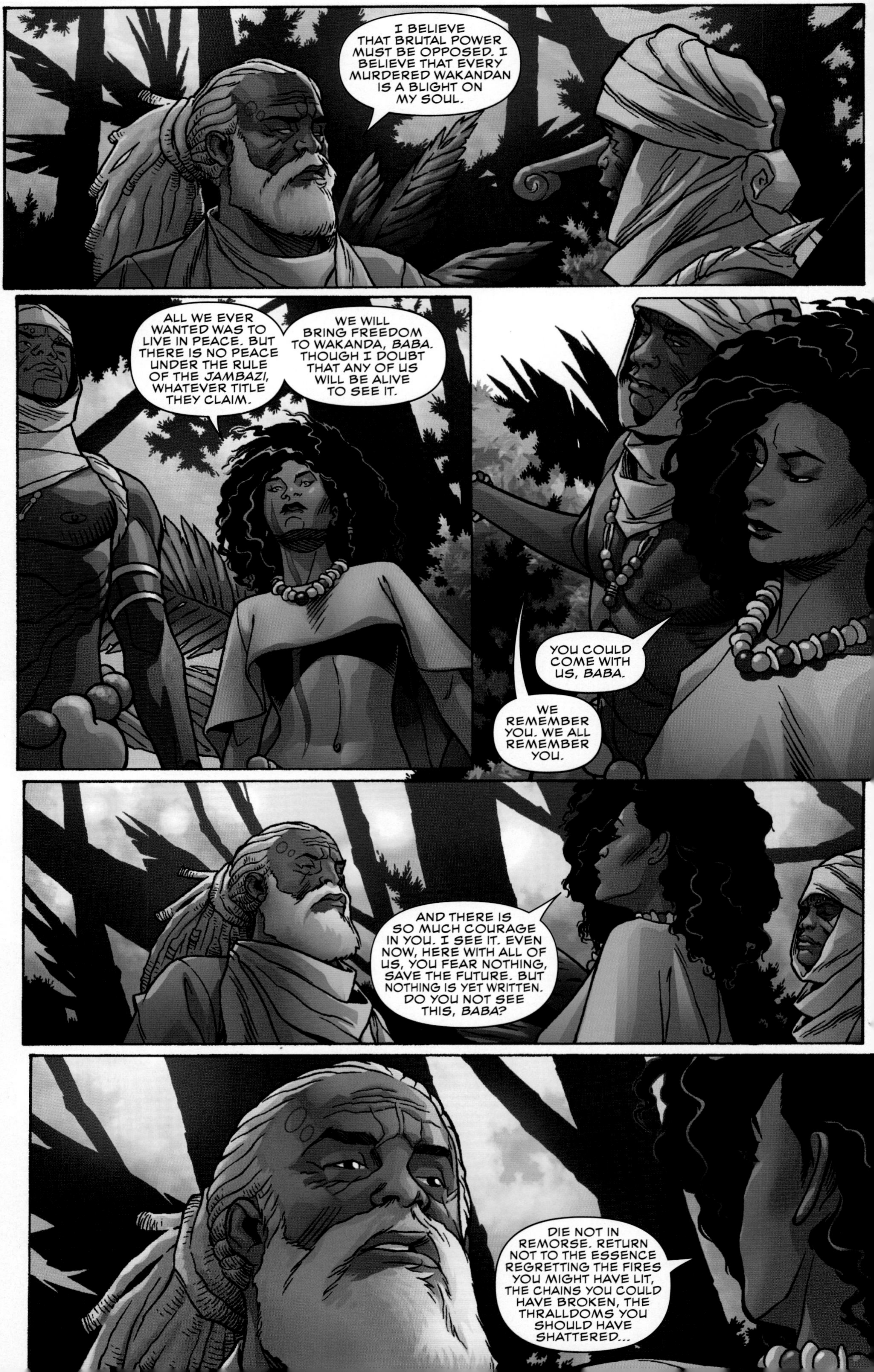
I BELIEVE THAT BRUTAL POWER MUST BE OPPOSED. I BELIEVE THAT EVERY MURDERED WAKANDAN IS A BLIGHT ON MY SOUL.
ALL WE EVER WANTED WAS TO LIVE IN PEACE. BUT THERE IS NO PEACE UNDER THE RULE OF THE *JAMBAZI*, WHATEVER TITLE THEY CLAIM.
WE WILL BRING FREEDOM TO WAKANDA, *BABA*. THOUGH I DOUBT THAT ANY OF US WILL BE ALIVE TO SEE IT.
YOU COULD COME WITH US, *BABA*.
WE REMEMBER YOU. WE ALL REMEMBER YOU.
AND THERE IS SO MUCH COURAGE IN YOU. I SEE IT. EVEN NOW, HERE WITH ALL OF US, YOU FEAR NOTHING, SAVE THE FUTURE. BUT NOTHING IS YET WRITTEN. DO YOU NOT SEE THIS, *BABA*?
DIE NOT IN REMORSE. RETURN NOT TO THE ESSENCE REGRETTING THE FIRES YOU MIGHT HAVE LIT, THE CHAINS YOU COULD HAVE BROKEN, THE THRALLDOMS YOU SHOULD HAVE SHATTERED...

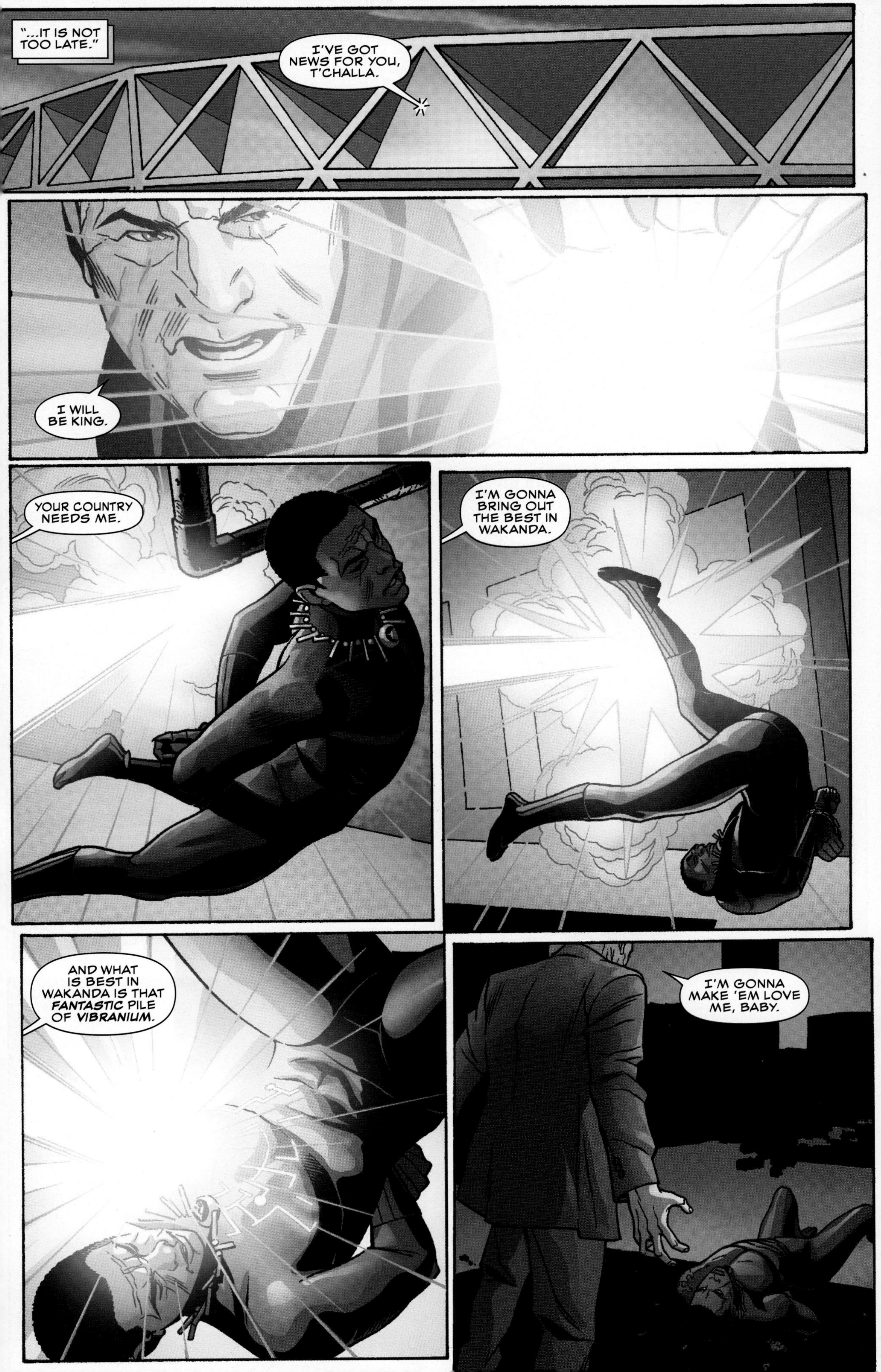

"...IT IS NOT TOO LATE."
I'VE GOT NEWS FOR YOU, T'CHALLA.
I WILL BE KING.
YOUR COUNTRY NEEDS ME.
I'M GONNA BRING OUT THE BEST IN WAKANDA.
AND WHAT IS BEST IN WAKANDA IS THAT *FANTASTIC* PILE OF *VIBRANIUM*.
I'M GONNA MAKE 'EM LOVE ME, BABY.

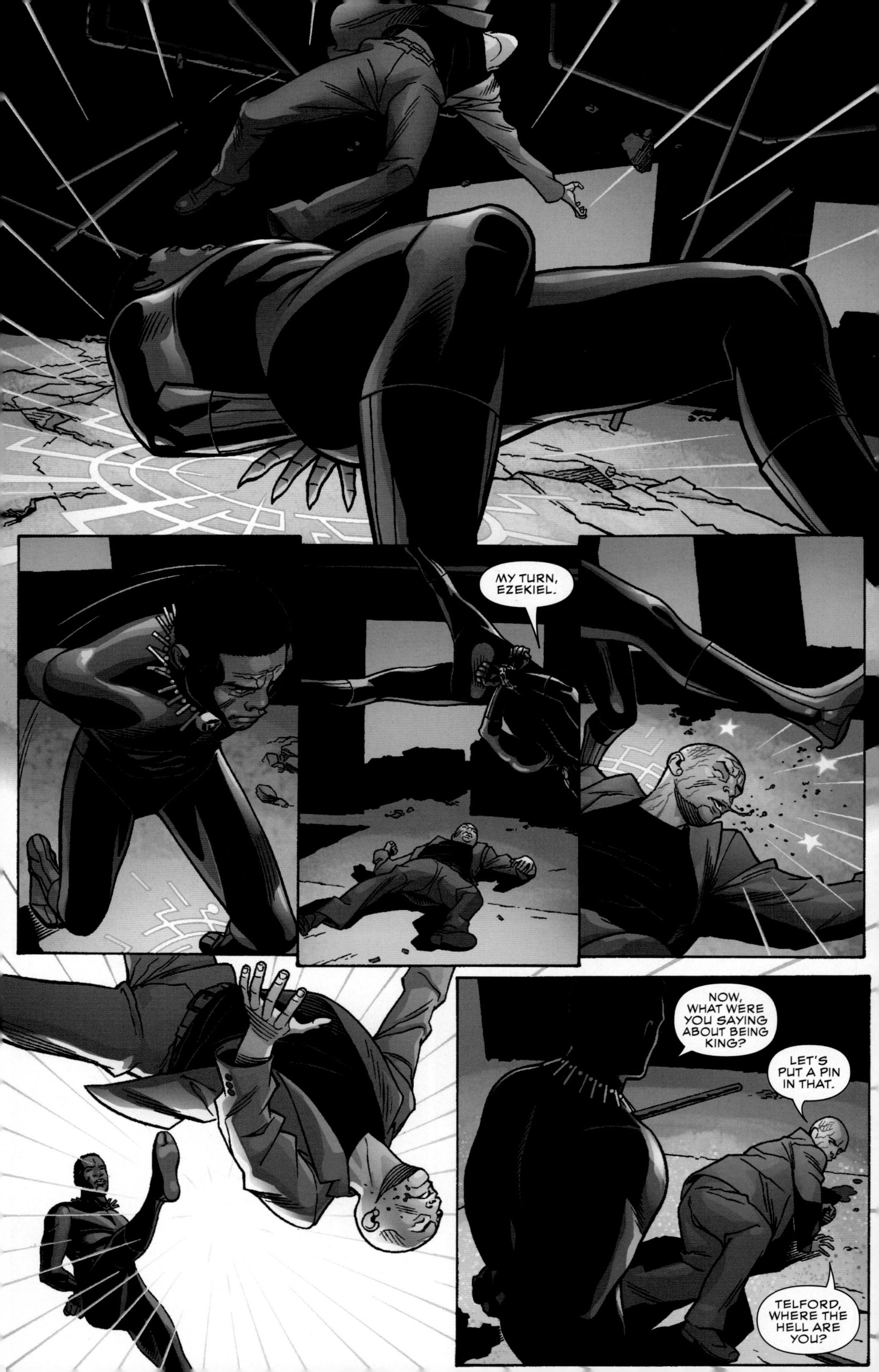
MY TURN, EZEKIEL.
NOW, WHAT WERE YOU SAYING ABOUT BEING KING?
LET'S PUT A PIN IN THAT.
TELFORD, WHERE THE HELL ARE YOU?

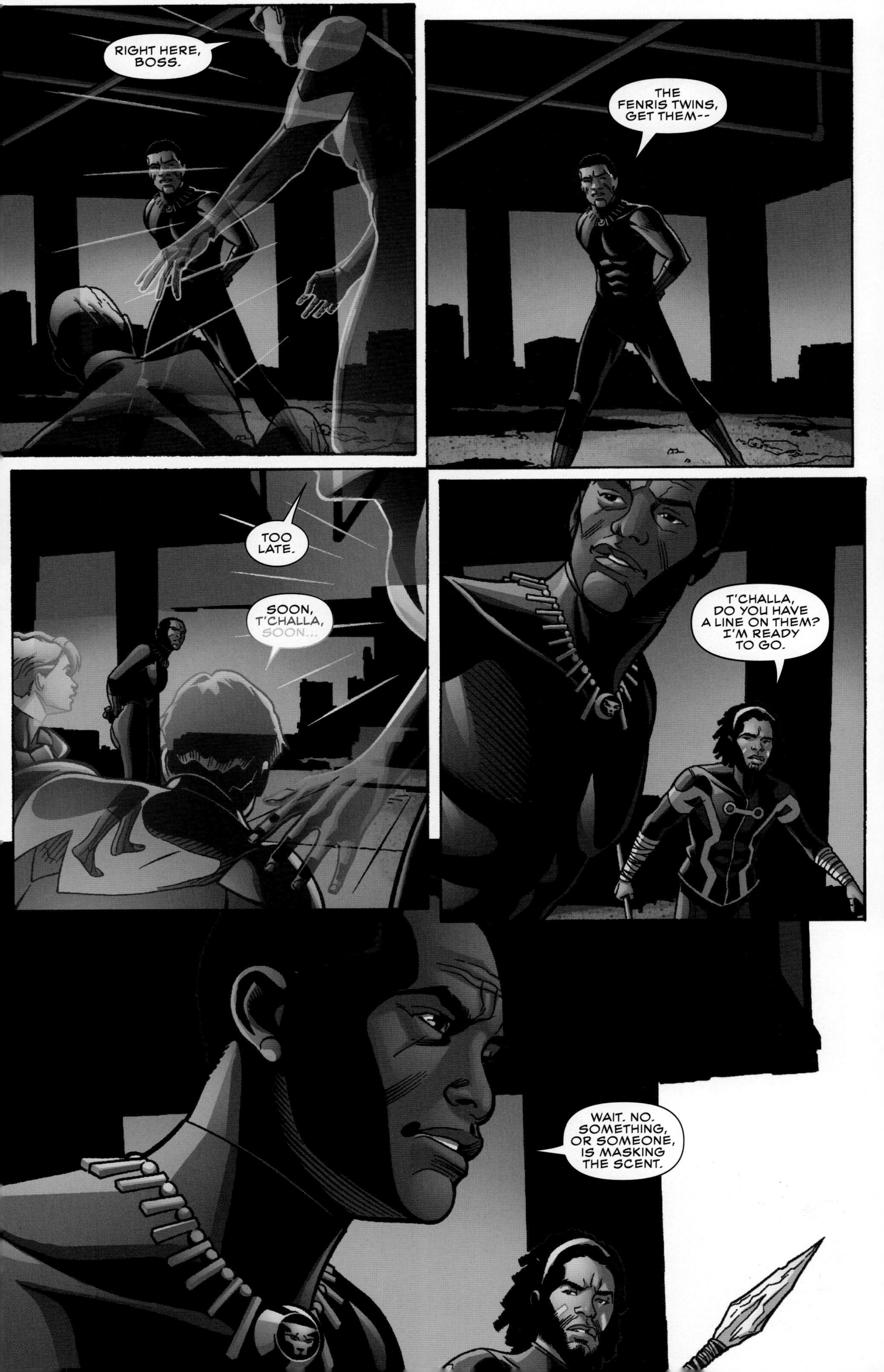
RIGHT HERE, BOSS.
THE FENRIS TWINS, GET THEM--
TOO LATE.
SOON, T'CHALLA, SOON...
T'CHALLA, DO YOU HAVE A LINE ON THEM? I'M READY TO GO.
WAIT. NO. SOMETHING, OR SOMEONE, IS MASKING THE SCENT.

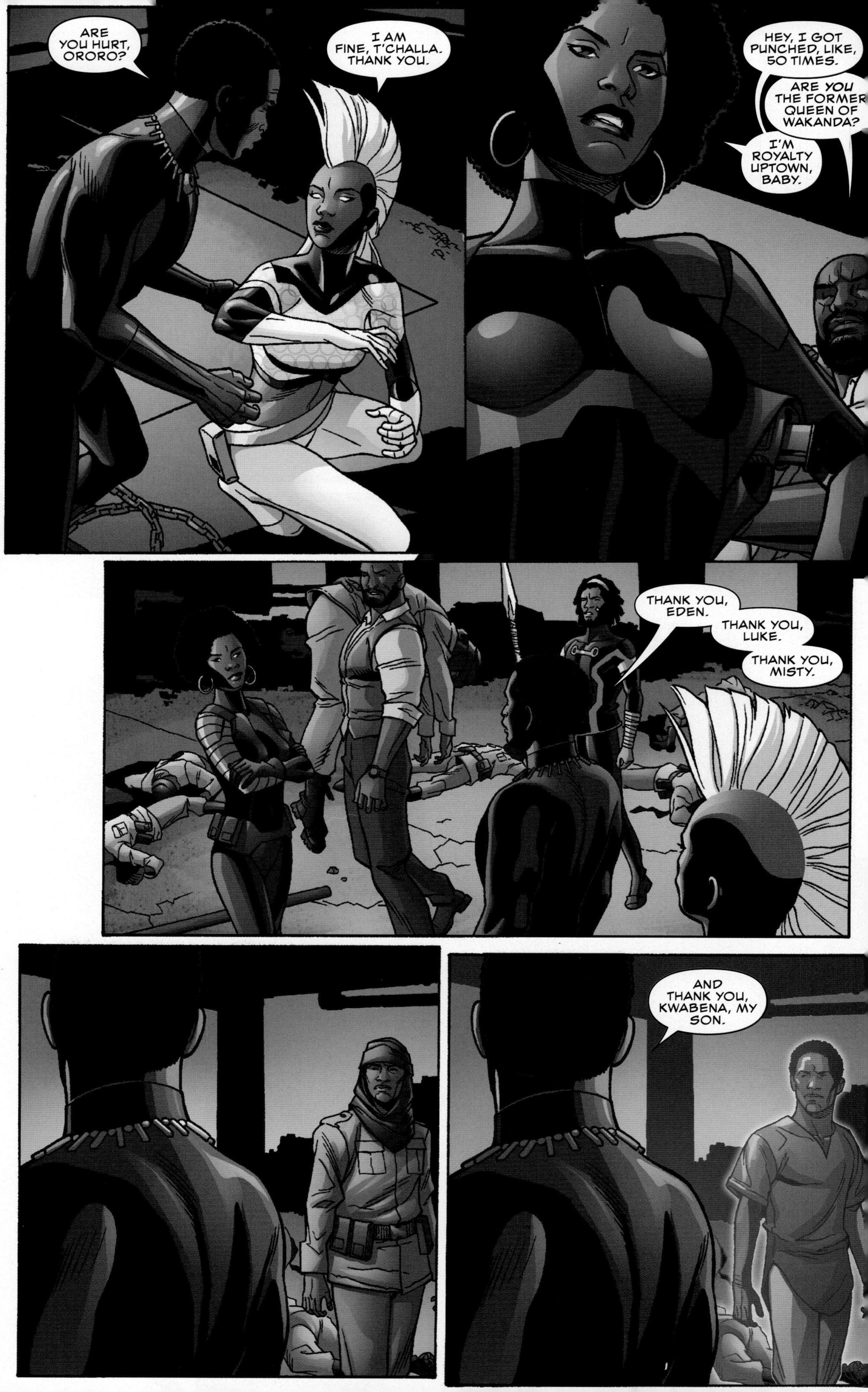
ARE YOU HURT, ORORO?
I AM FINE, T'CHALLA. THANK YOU.
HEY, I GOT PUNCHED, LIKE, 50 TIMES.
ARE YOU THE FORMER QUEEN OF WAKANDA?
I'M ROYALTY UPTOWN, BABY.
THANK YOU, EDEN.
THANK YOU, LUKE.
THANK YOU, MISTY.
AND THANK YOU, KWABENA, MY SON.

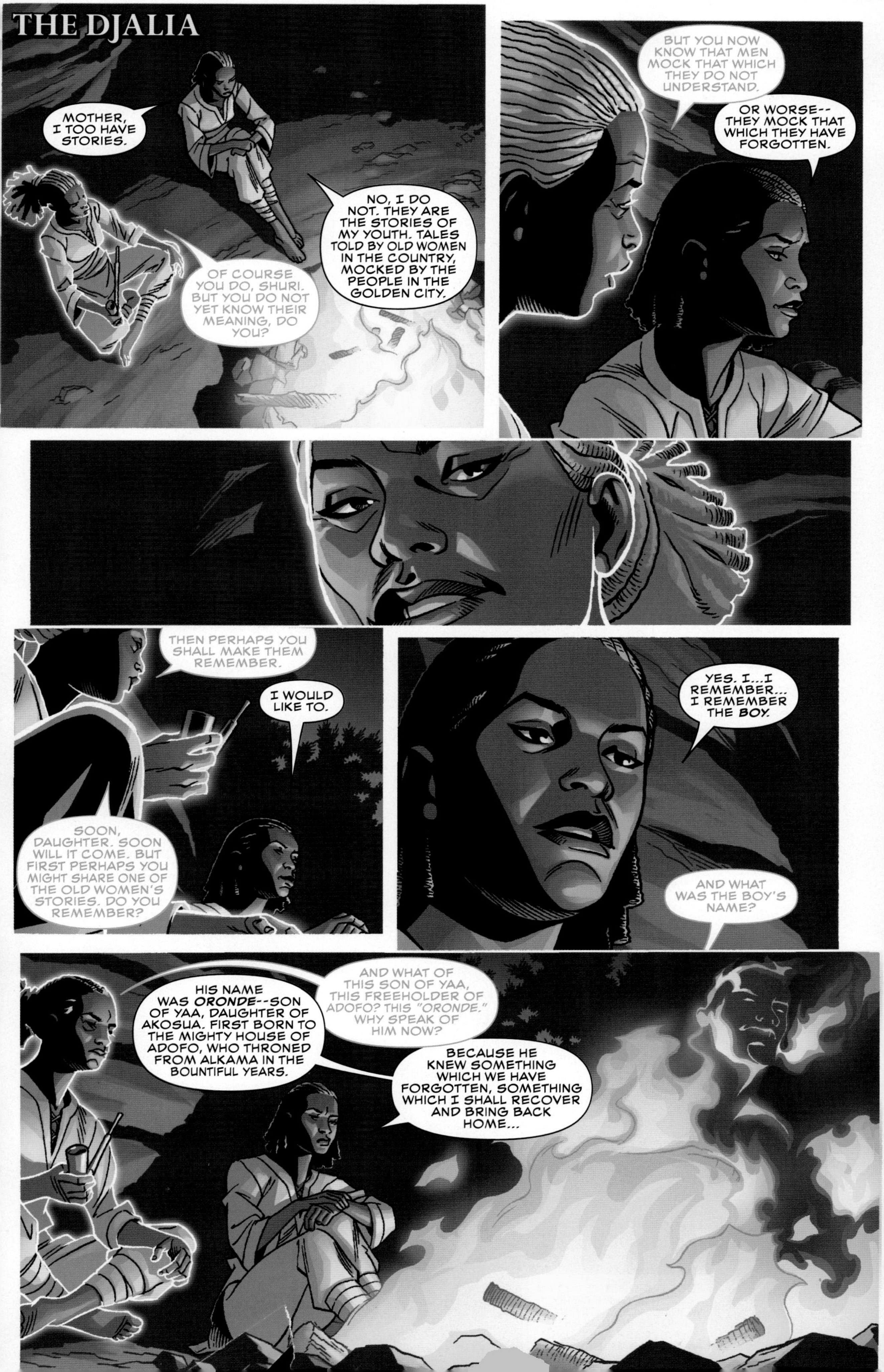
THE DJALIA
MOTHER, I TOO HAVE STORIES.
OF COURSE YOU DO, SHURI. BUT YOU DO NOT YET KNOW THEIR MEANING, DO YOU?
NO, I DO NOT. THEY ARE THE STORIES OF MY YOUTH. TALES TOLD BY OLD WOMEN IN THE COUNTRY, MOCKED BY THE PEOPLE IN THE GOLDEN CITY.
BUT YOU NOW KNOW THAT MEN MOCK THAT WHICH THEY DO NOT UNDERSTAND.
OR WORSE-- THEY MOCK THAT WHICH THEY HAVE FORGOTTEN.
THEN PERHAPS YOU SHALL MAKE THEM REMEMBER.
I WOULD LIKE TO.
SOON, DAUGHTER. SOON WILL IT COME. BUT FIRST PERHAPS YOU MIGHT SHARE ONE OF THE OLD WOMEN'S STORIES. DO YOU REMEMBER?
YES. I...I REMEMBER... I REMEMBER THE BOY.
AND WHAT WAS THE BOY'S NAME?
HIS NAME WAS ORONDE--SON OF YAA, DAUGHTER OF AKOSUA. FIRST BORN TO THE MIGHTY HOUSE OF ADOFO, WHO THRONED FROM ALKAMA IN THE BOUNTIFUL YEARS.
AND WHAT OF THIS SON OF YAA, THIS FREEHOLDER OF ADOFO? THIS "ORONDE." WHY SPEAK OF HIM NOW?
BECAUSE HE KNEW SOMETHING WHICH WE HAVE FORGOTTEN, SOMETHING WHICH I SHALL RECOVER AND BRING BACK HOME...

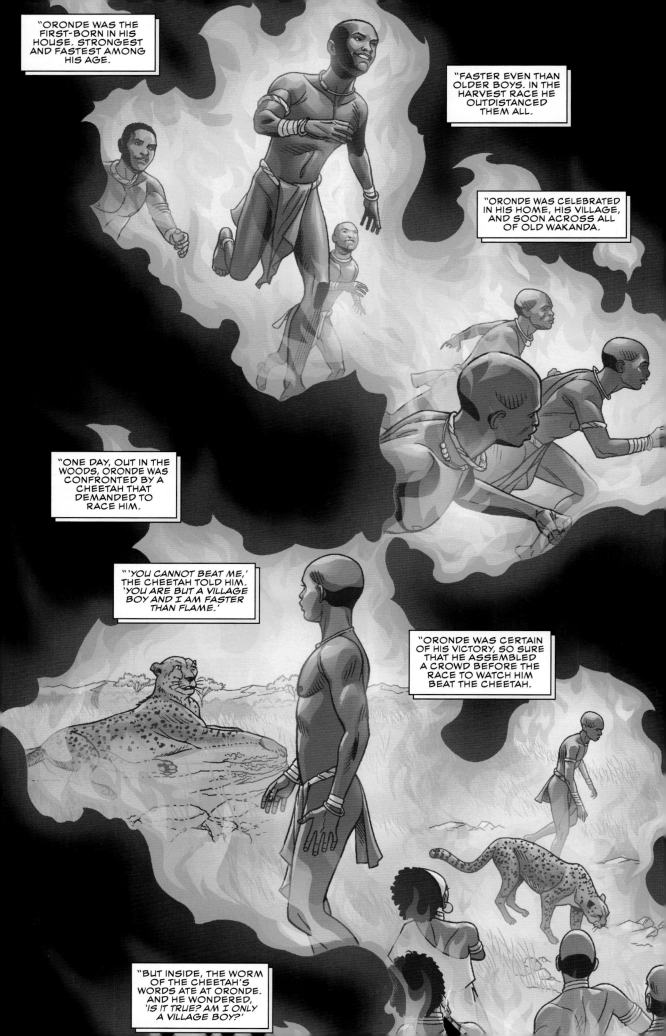

"ORONDE WAS THE FIRST-BORN IN HIS HOUSE. STRONGEST AND FASTEST AMONG HIS AGE.

"FASTER EVEN THAN OLDER BOYS. IN THE HARVEST RACE HE OUTDISTANCED THEM ALL.

"ORONDE WAS CELEBRATED IN HIS HOME, HIS VILLAGE, AND SOON ACROSS ALL OF OLD WAKANDA.

"ONE DAY, OUT IN THE WOODS, ORONDE WAS CONFRONTED BY A CHEETAH THAT DEMANDED TO RACE HIM.

"'YOU CANNOT BEAT ME,' THE CHEETAH TOLD HIM. 'YOU ARE BUT A VILLAGE BOY AND I AM FASTER THAN FLAME.'

"ORONDE WAS CERTAIN OF HIS VICTORY, SO SURE THAT HE ASSEMBLED A CROWD BEFORE THE RACE TO WATCH HIM BEAT THE CHEETAH.

"BUT INSIDE, THE WORM OF THE CHEETAH'S WORDS ATE AT ORONDE. AND HE WONDERED, 'IS IT TRUE? AM I ONLY A VILLAGE BOY?'

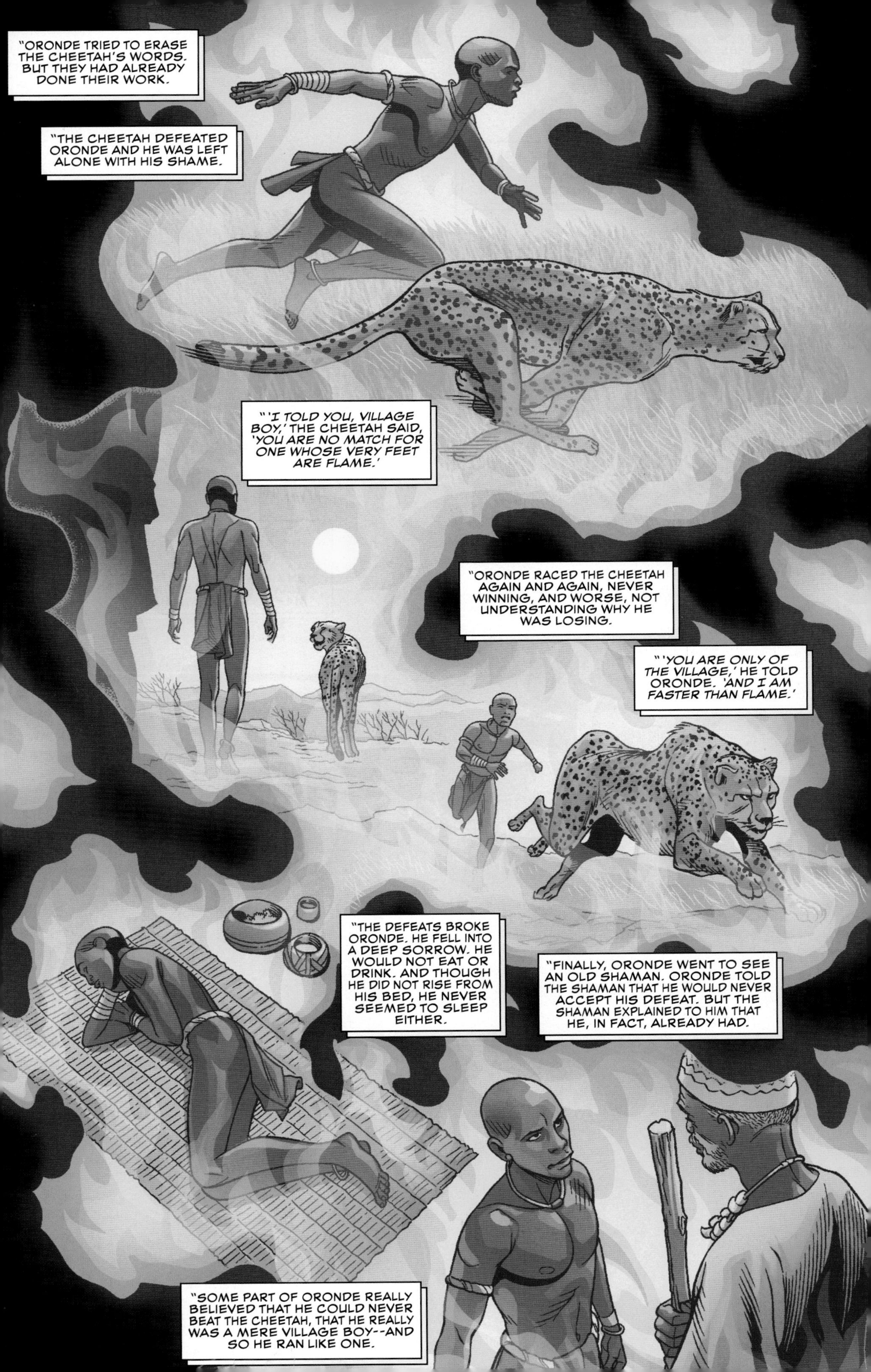
"ORONDE TRIED TO ERASE THE CHEETAH'S WORDS. BUT THEY HAD ALREADY DONE THEIR WORK.
"THE CHEETAH DEFEATED ORONDE AND HE WAS LEFT ALONE WITH HIS SHAME.
"'I TOLD YOU, VILLAGE BOY,' THE CHEETAH SAID, 'YOU ARE NO MATCH FOR ONE WHOSE VERY FEET ARE FLAME.'
"ORONDE RACED THE CHEETAH AGAIN AND AGAIN, NEVER WINNING, AND WORSE, NOT UNDERSTANDING WHY HE WAS LOSING.
"'YOU ARE ONLY OF THE VILLAGE,' HE TOLD ORONDE. 'AND I AM FASTER THAN FLAME.'
"THE DEFEATS BROKE ORONDE. HE FELL INTO A DEEP SORROW. HE WOULD NOT EAT OR DRINK. AND THOUGH HE DID NOT RISE FROM HIS BED, HE NEVER SEEMED TO SLEEP EITHER.
"FINALLY, ORONDE WENT TO SEE AN OLD SHAMAN. ORONDE TOLD THE SHAMAN THAT HE WOULD NEVER ACCEPT HIS DEFEAT. BUT THE SHAMAN EXPLAINED TO HIM THAT HE, IN FACT, ALREADY HAD.
"SOME PART OF ORONDE REALLY BELIEVED THAT HE COULD NEVER BEAT THE CHEETAH, THAT HE REALLY WAS A MERE VILLAGE BOY--AND SO HE RAN LIKE ONE.

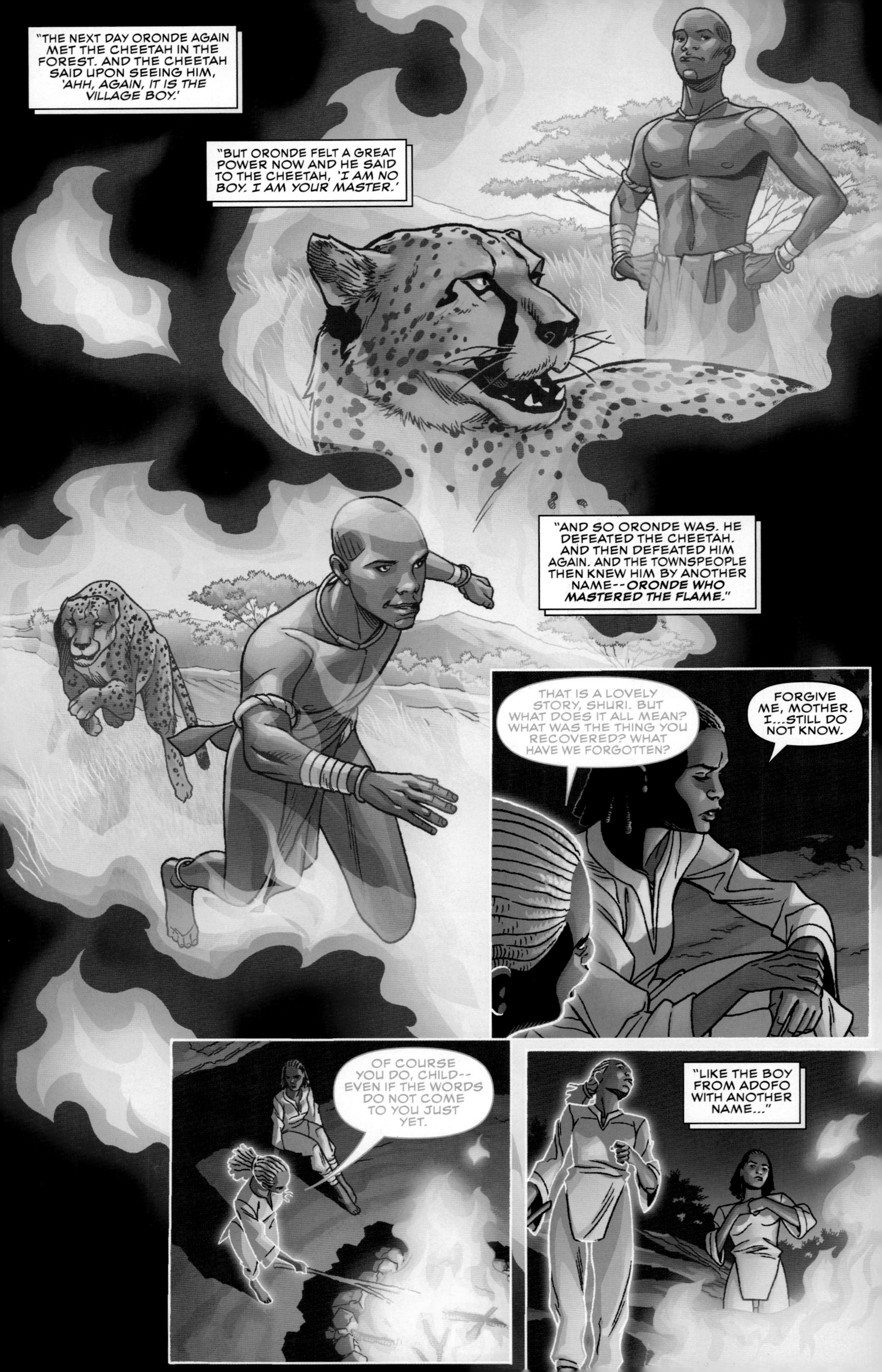
"THE NEXT DAY ORONDE AGAIN MET THE CHEETAH IN THE FOREST. AND THE CHEETAH SAID UPON SEEING HIM, 'AHH, AGAIN, IT IS THE VILLAGE BOY.'
"BUT ORONDE FELT A GREAT POWER NOW AND HE SAID TO THE CHEETAH, 'I AM NO BOY. I AM YOUR MASTER.'
"AND SO ORONDE WAS. HE DEFEATED THE CHEETAH. AND THEN DEFEATED HIM AGAIN. AND THE TOWNSPEOPLE THEN KNEW HIM BY ANOTHER NAME--ORONDE WHO MASTERED THE FLAME."
THAT IS A LOVELY STORY, SHURI. BUT WHAT DOES IT ALL MEAN? WHAT WAS THE THING YOU RECOVERED? WHAT HAVE WE FORGOTTEN?
FORGIVE ME, MOTHER. I...STILL DO NOT KNOW.
OF COURSE YOU DO, CHILD-- EVEN IF THE WORDS DO NOT COME TO YOU JUST YET.
"LIKE THE BOY FROM ADOFO WITH ANOTHER NAME..."

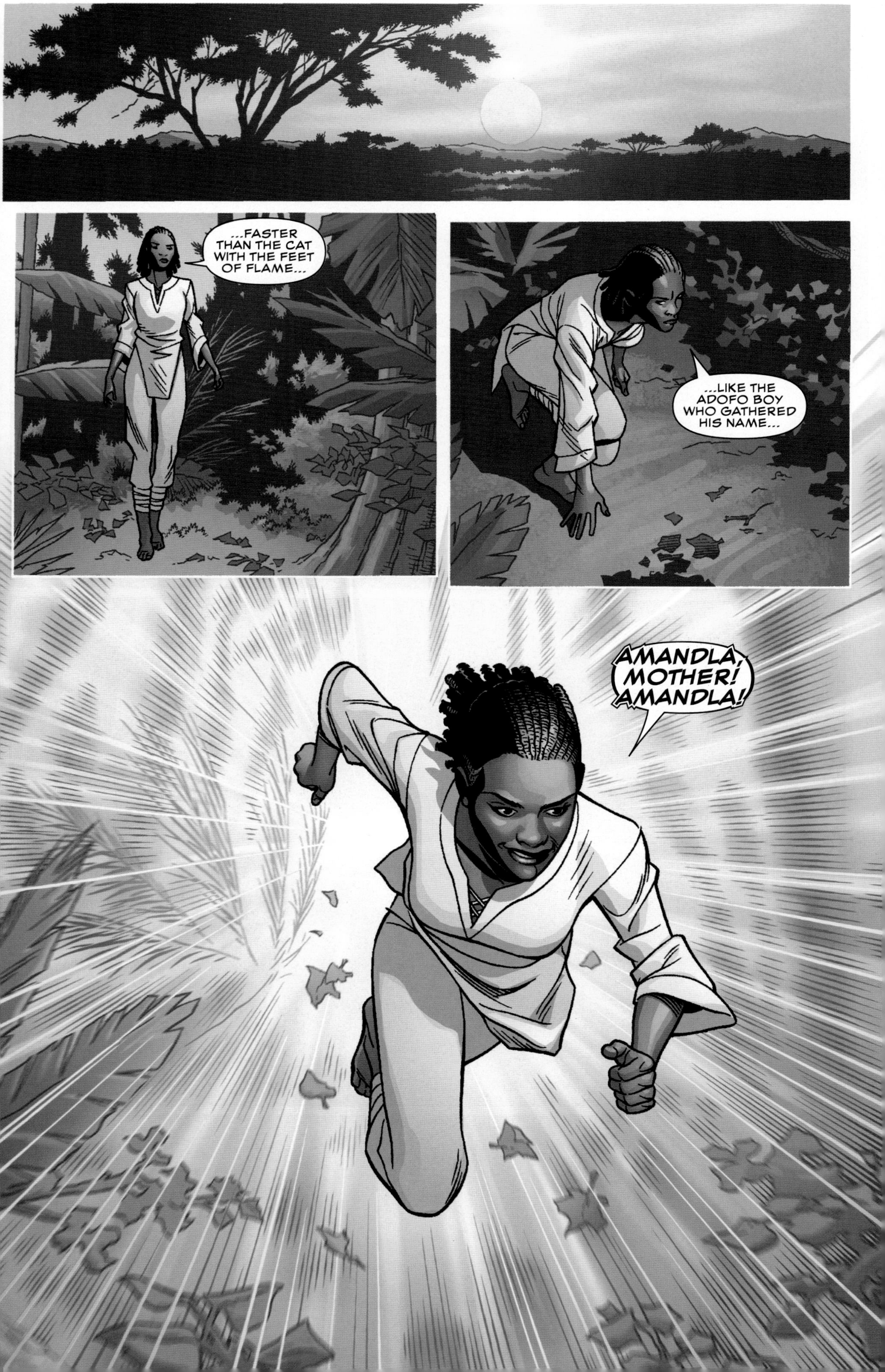
...FASTER THAN THE CAT WITH THE FEET OF FLAME...
...LIKE THE ADOFO BOY WHO GATHERED HIS NAME...
AMANDLA, MOTHER! AMANDLA!

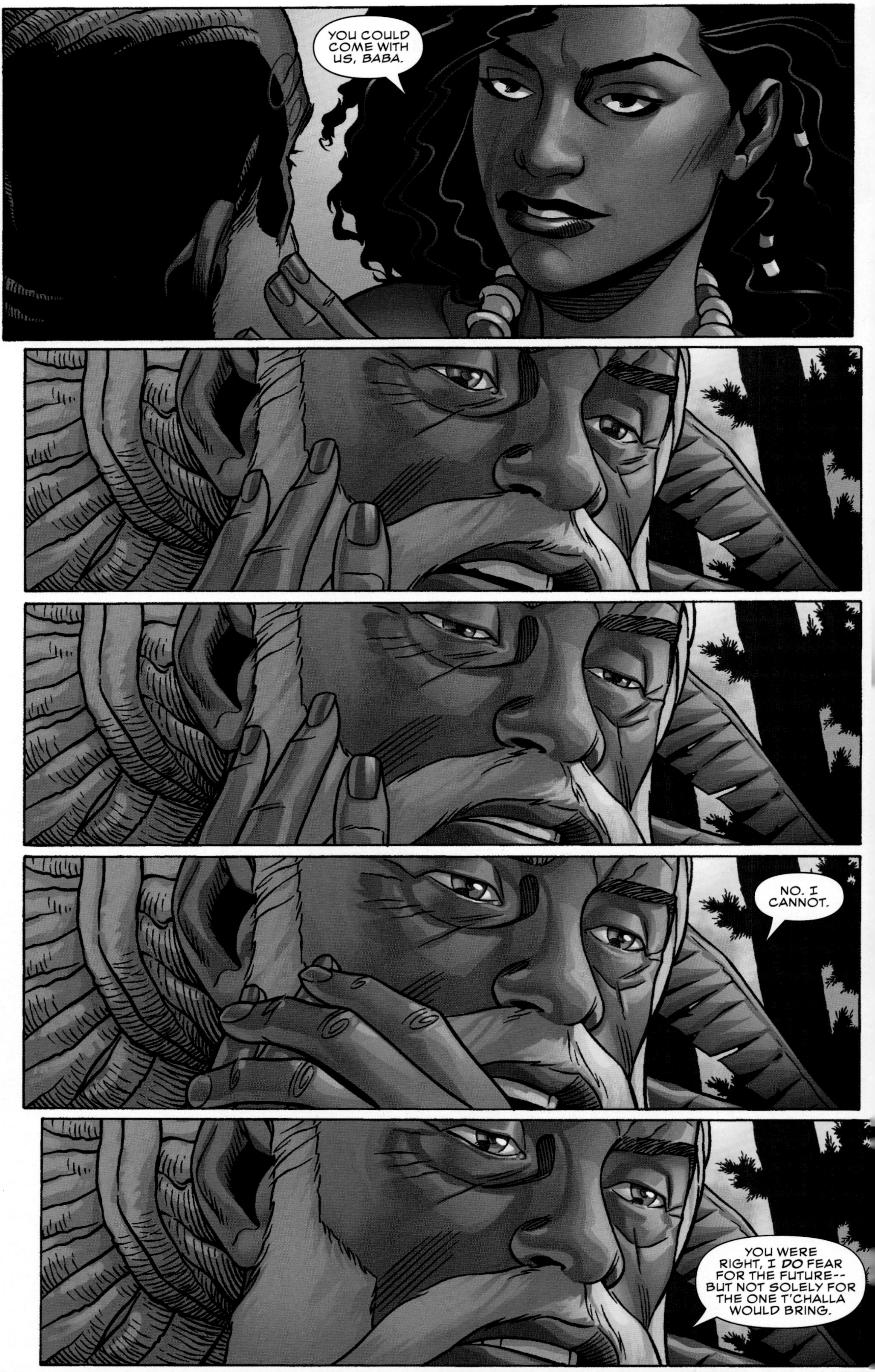
YOU COULD COME WITH US, BABA.
NO. I CANNOT.
YOU WERE RIGHT, I *DO* FEAR FOR THE FUTURE-- BUT NOT SOLELY FOR THE ONE T'CHALLA WOULD BRING.

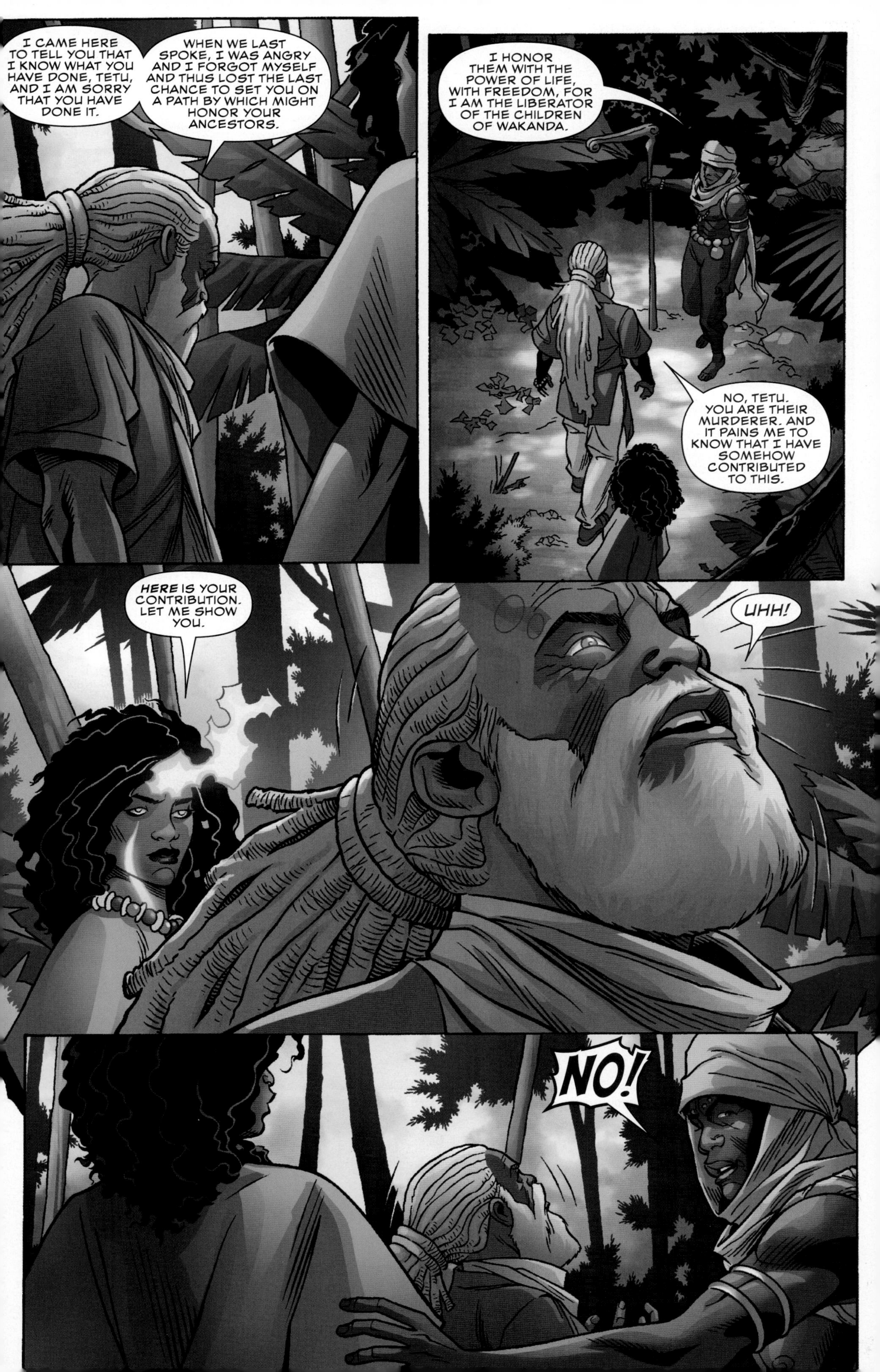
I CAME HERE TO TELL YOU THAT I KNOW WHAT YOU HAVE DONE, TETU, AND I AM SORRY THAT YOU HAVE DONE IT.
WHEN WE LAST SPOKE, I WAS ANGRY AND I FORGOT MYSELF AND THUS LOST THE LAST CHANCE TO SET YOU ON A PATH BY WHICH MIGHT HONOR YOUR ANCESTORS.
I HONOR THEM WITH THE POWER OF LIFE, WITH FREEDOM, FOR I AM THE LIBERATOR OF THE CHILDREN OF WAKANDA.
NO, TETU. YOU ARE THEIR MURDERER. AND IT PAINS ME TO KNOW THAT I HAVE SOMEHOW CONTRIBUTED TO THIS.
HERE IS YOUR CONTRIBUTION. LET ME SHOW YOU.
UHH!
NO!

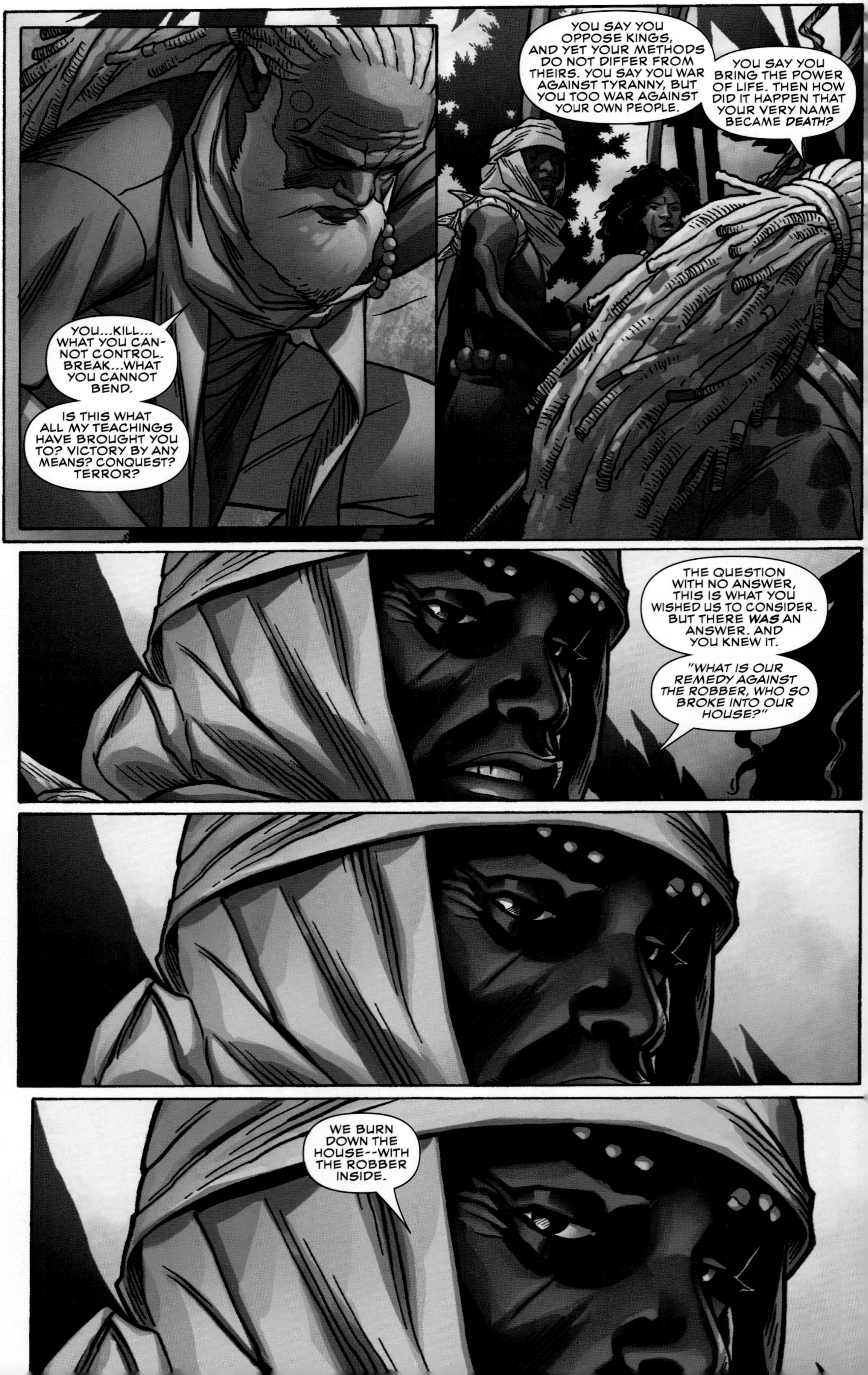
YOU...KILL... WHAT YOU CAN-NOT CONTROL. BREAK...WHAT YOU CANNOT BEND.
IS THIS WHAT ALL MY TEACHINGS HAVE BROUGHT YOU TO? VICTORY BY ANY MEANS? CONQUEST? TERROR?
YOU SAY YOU OPPOSE KINGS, AND YET YOUR METHODS DO NOT DIFFER FROM THEIRS. YOU SAY YOU WAR AGAINST TYRANNY, BUT YOU TOO WAR AGAINST YOUR OWN PEOPLE.
YOU SAY YOU BRING THE POWER OF LIFE. THEN HOW DID IT HAPPEN THAT YOUR VERY NAME BECAME DEATH?
THE QUESTION WITH NO ANSWER, THIS IS WHAT YOU WISHED US TO CONSIDER. BUT THERE WAS AN ANSWER. AND YOU KNEW IT.
"WHAT IS OUR REMEDY AGAINST THE ROBBER, WHO SO BROKE INTO OUR HOUSE?"
WE BURN DOWN THE HOUSE--WITH THE ROBBER INSIDE.

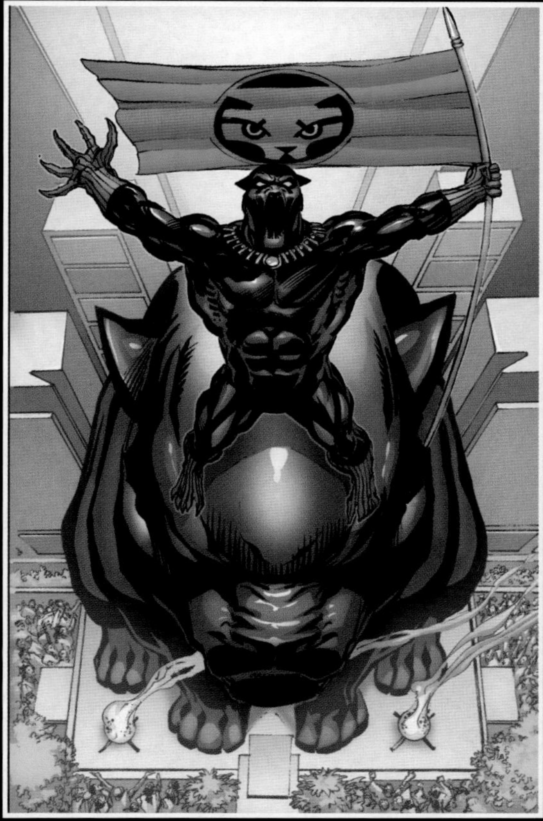

#1 VARIANT BY **NEAL ADAMS**

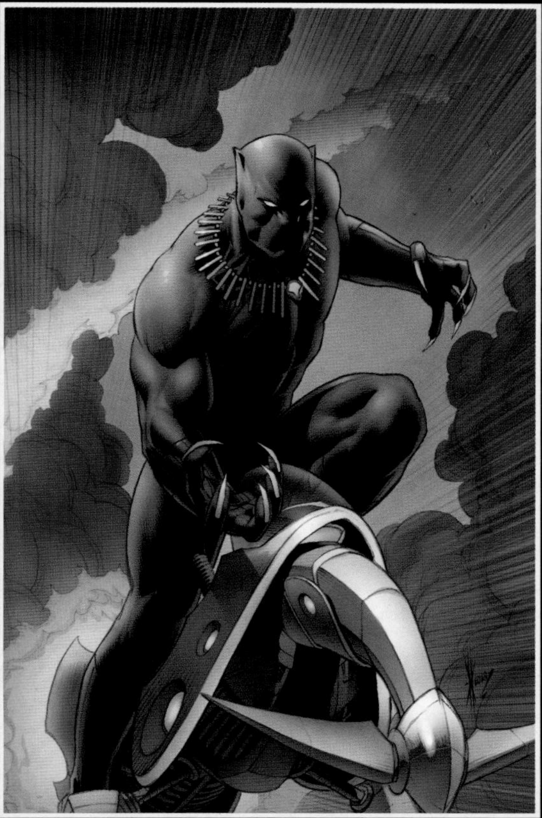

#1 VARIANT BY **DALE KEOWN**

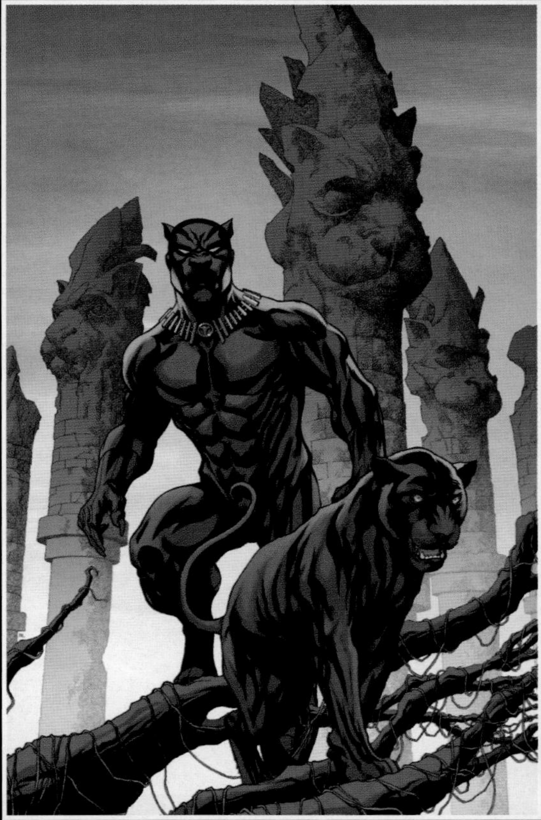

#1 VARIANT BY **MIKE McKONE**
**& FRANK MARTIN**

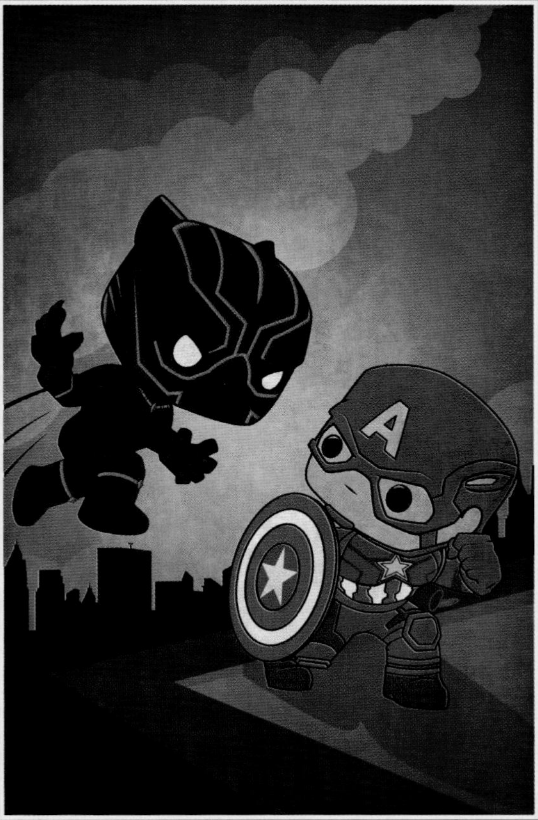
A

#1 FUNKO VARIANT

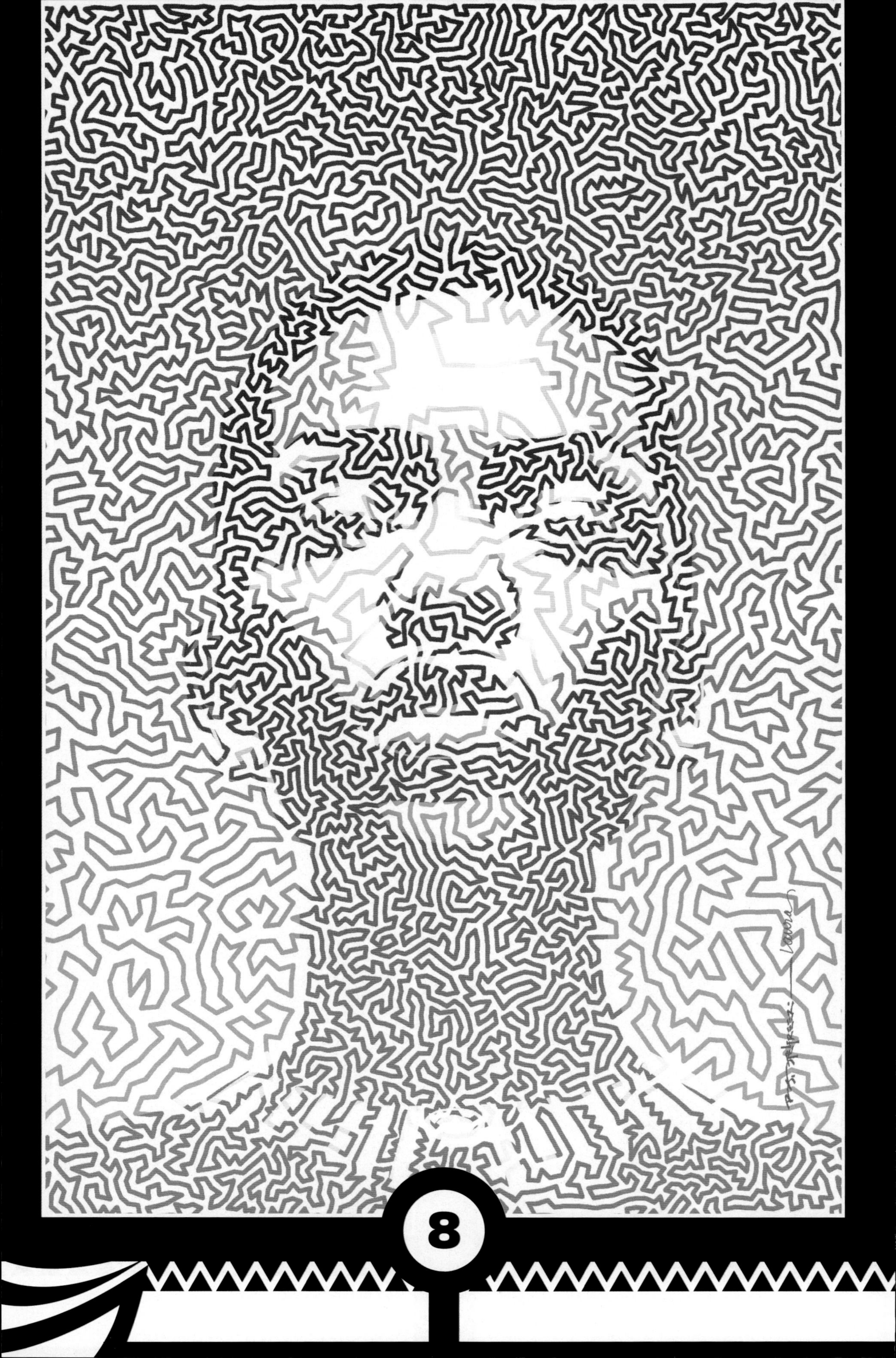

8

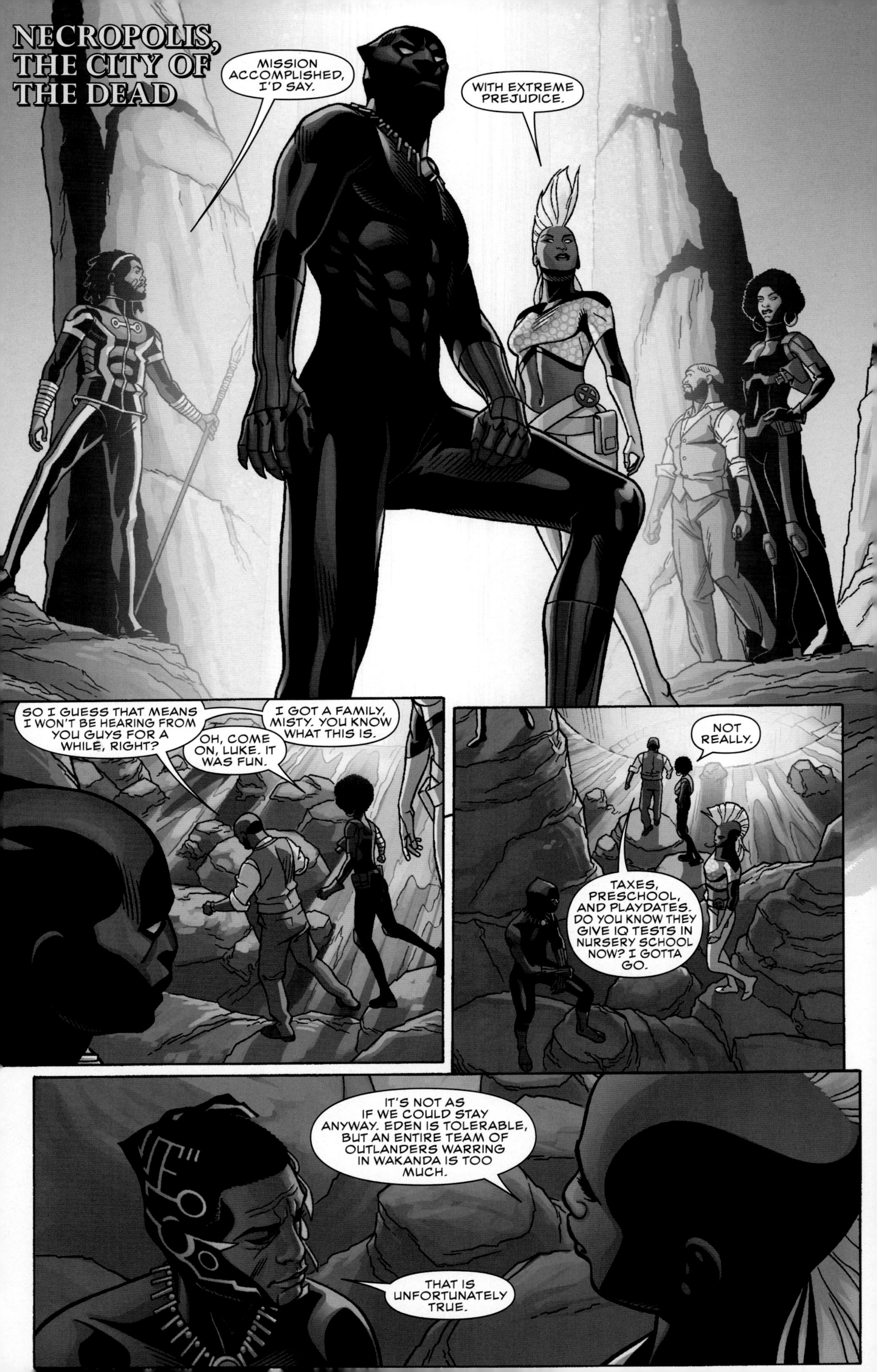
NECROPOLIS, THE CITY OF THE DEAD
MISSION ACCOMPLISHED, I'D SAY.
WITH EXTREME PREJUDICE.
SO I GUESS THAT MEANS I WON'T BE HEARING FROM YOU GUYS FOR A WHILE, RIGHT?
I GOT A FAMILY, MISTY. YOU KNOW WHAT THIS IS.
OH, COME ON, LUKE. IT WAS FUN.
NOT REALLY.
TAXES, PRESCHOOL, AND PLAYDATES. DO YOU KNOW THEY GIVE IQ TESTS IN NURSERY SCHOOL NOW? I GOTTA GO.
IT'S NOT AS IF WE COULD STAY ANYWAY. EDEN IS TOLERABLE, BUT AN ENTIRE TEAM OF OUTLANDERS WARRING IN WAKANDA IS TOO MUCH.
THAT IS UNFORTUNATELY TRUE.

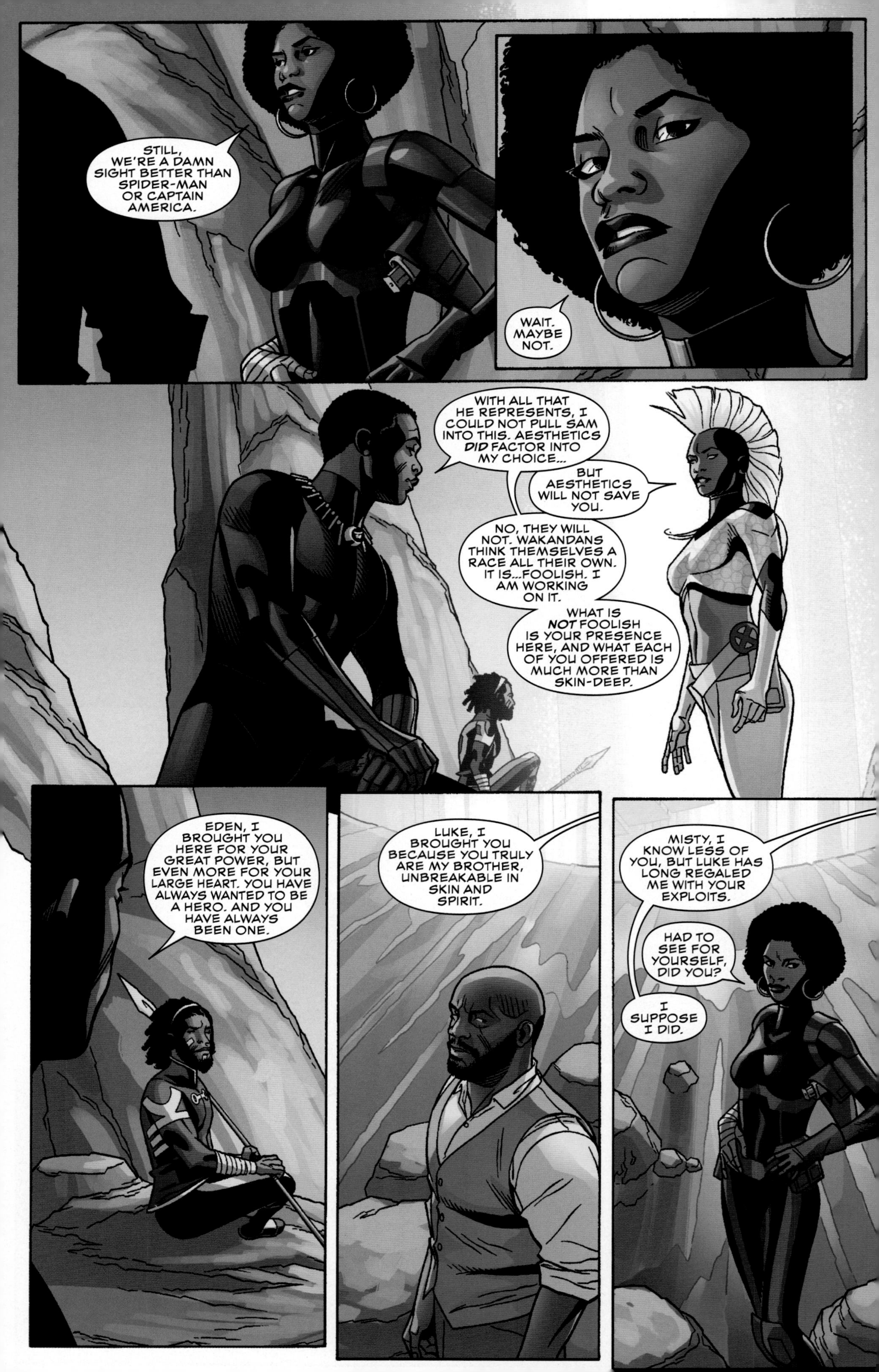
STILL, WE'RE A DAMN SIGHT BETTER THAN SPIDER-MAN OR CAPTAIN AMERICA.
WAIT. MAYBE NOT.
WITH ALL THAT HE REPRESENTS, I COULD NOT PULL SAM INTO THIS. AESTHETICS *DID* FACTOR INTO MY CHOICE...
BUT AESTHETICS WILL NOT SAVE YOU.
NO, THEY WILL NOT. WAKANDANS THINK THEMSELVES A RACE ALL THEIR OWN. IT IS...FOOLISH. I AM WORKING ON IT.
WHAT IS *NOT* FOOLISH IS YOUR PRESENCE HERE, AND WHAT EACH OF YOU OFFERED IS MUCH MORE THAN SKIN-DEEP.
EDEN, I BROUGHT YOU HERE FOR YOUR GREAT POWER, BUT EVEN MORE FOR YOUR LARGE HEART. YOU HAVE ALWAYS WANTED TO BE A HERO. AND YOU HAVE ALWAYS BEEN ONE.
LUKE, I BROUGHT YOU BECAUSE YOU TRULY ARE MY BROTHER, UNBREAKABLE IN SKIN AND SPIRIT.
MISTY, I KNOW LESS OF YOU, BUT LUKE HAS LONG REGALED ME WITH YOUR EXPLOITS.
HAD TO SEE FOR YOURSELF, DID YOU?
I SUPPOSE I DID.

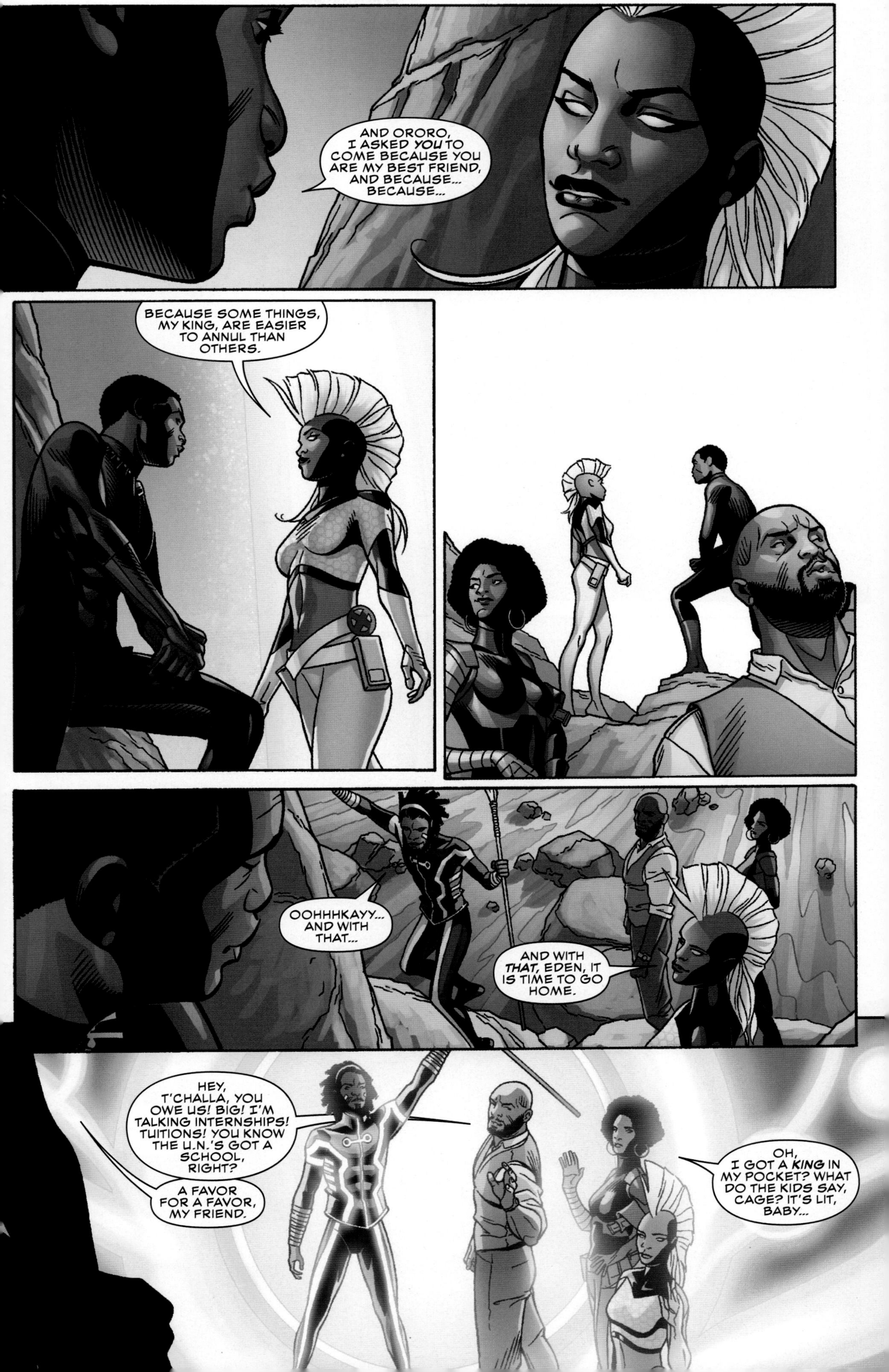
AND ORORO, I ASKED YOU TO COME BECAUSE YOU ARE MY BEST FRIEND, AND BECAUSE... BECAUSE...
BECAUSE SOME THINGS, MY KING, ARE EASIER TO ANNUL THAN OTHERS.
OOHHHKAYY... AND WITH THAT...
AND WITH THAT, EDEN, IT IS TIME TO GO HOME.
HEY, T'CHALLA, YOU OWE US! BIG! I'M TALKING INTERNSHIPS! TUITIONS! YOU KNOW THE U.N.'S GOT A SCHOOL, RIGHT?
A FAVOR FOR A FAVOR, MY FRIEND.
OH, I GOT A KING IN MY POCKET? WHAT DO THE KIDS SAY, CAGE? IT'S LIT, BABY...

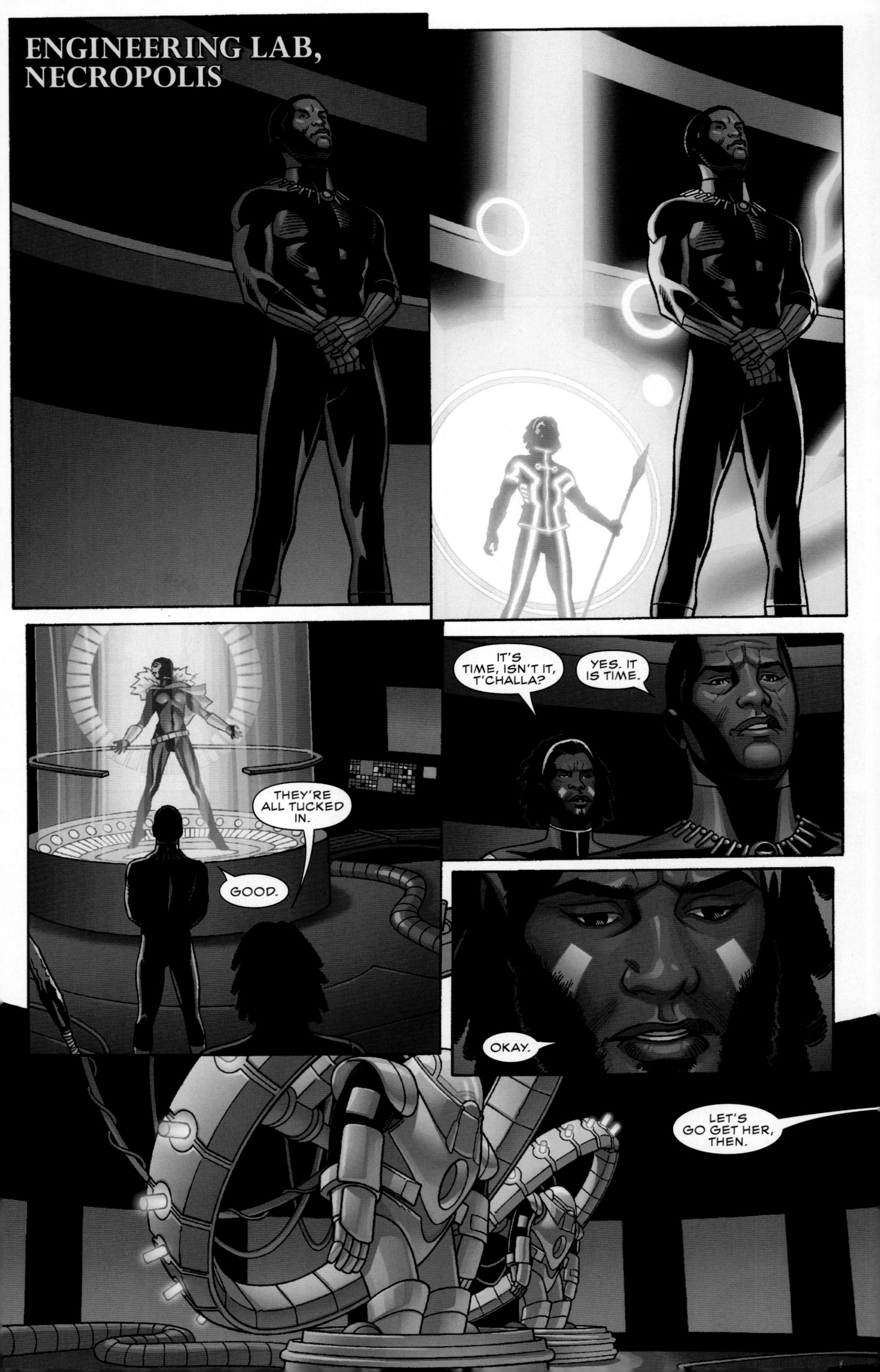
ENGINEERING LAB, NECROPOLIS
THEY'RE ALL TUCKED IN.
GOOD.
IT'S TIME, ISN'T IT, T'CHALLA?
YES. IT IS TIME.
OKAY.
LET'S GO GET HER, THEN.

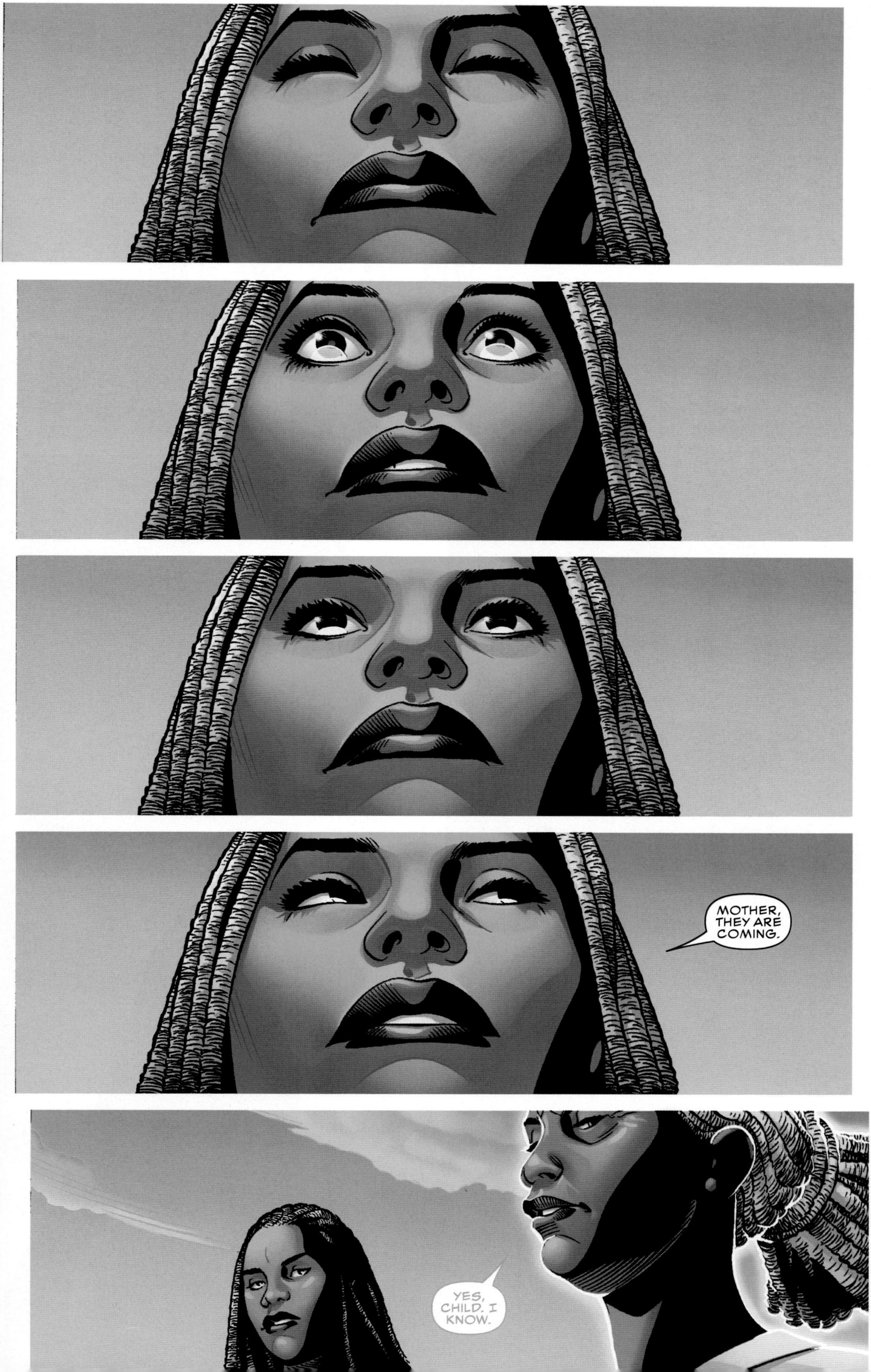
MOTHER, THEY ARE COMING.
YES, CHILD. I KNOW.

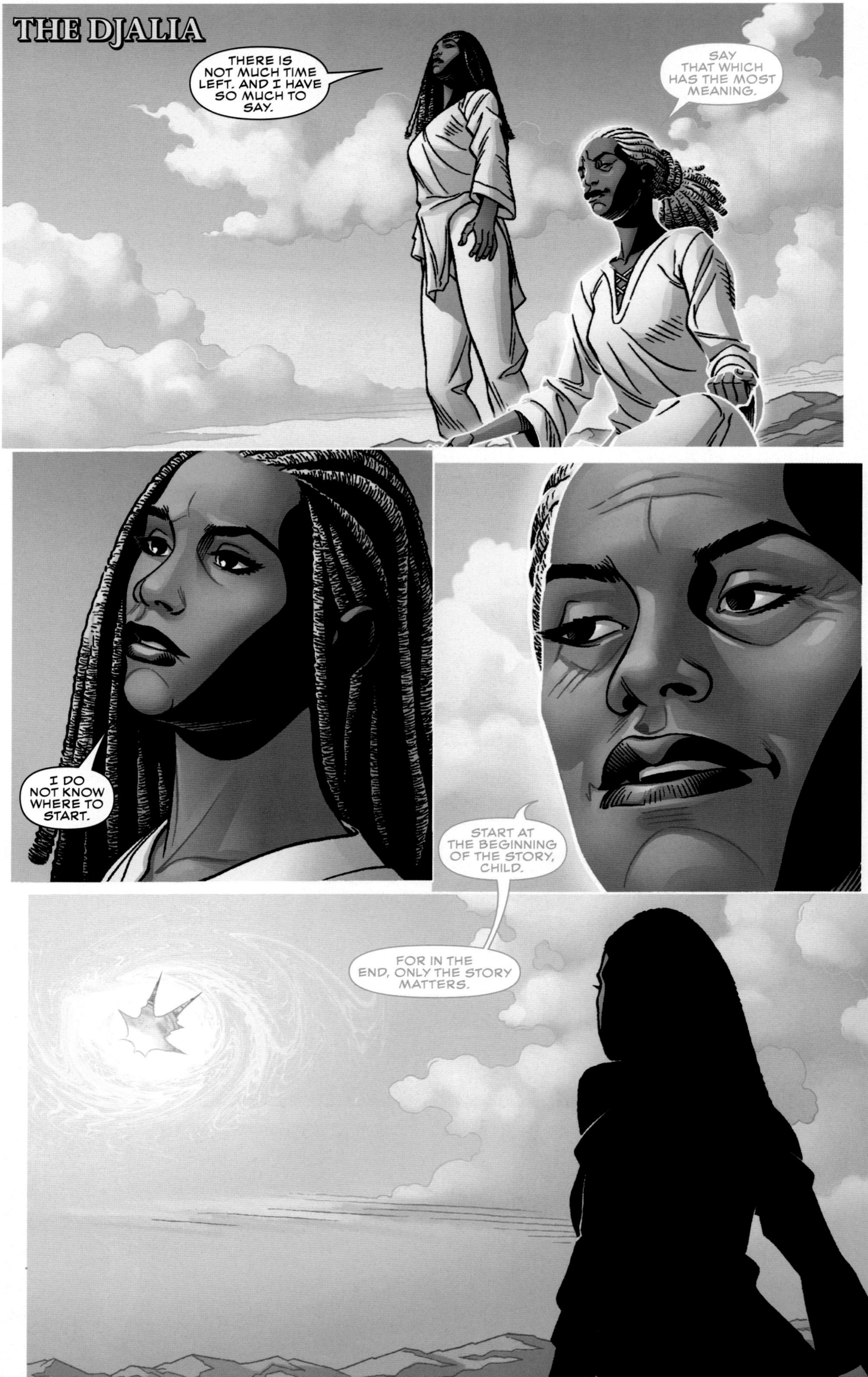
THE DJALIA
THERE IS NOT MUCH TIME LEFT. AND I HAVE SO MUCH TO SAY.
SAY THAT WHICH HAS THE MOST MEANING.
I DO NOT KNOW WHERE TO START.
START AT THE BEGINNING OF THE STORY, CHILD.
FOR IN THE END, ONLY THE STORY MATTERS.

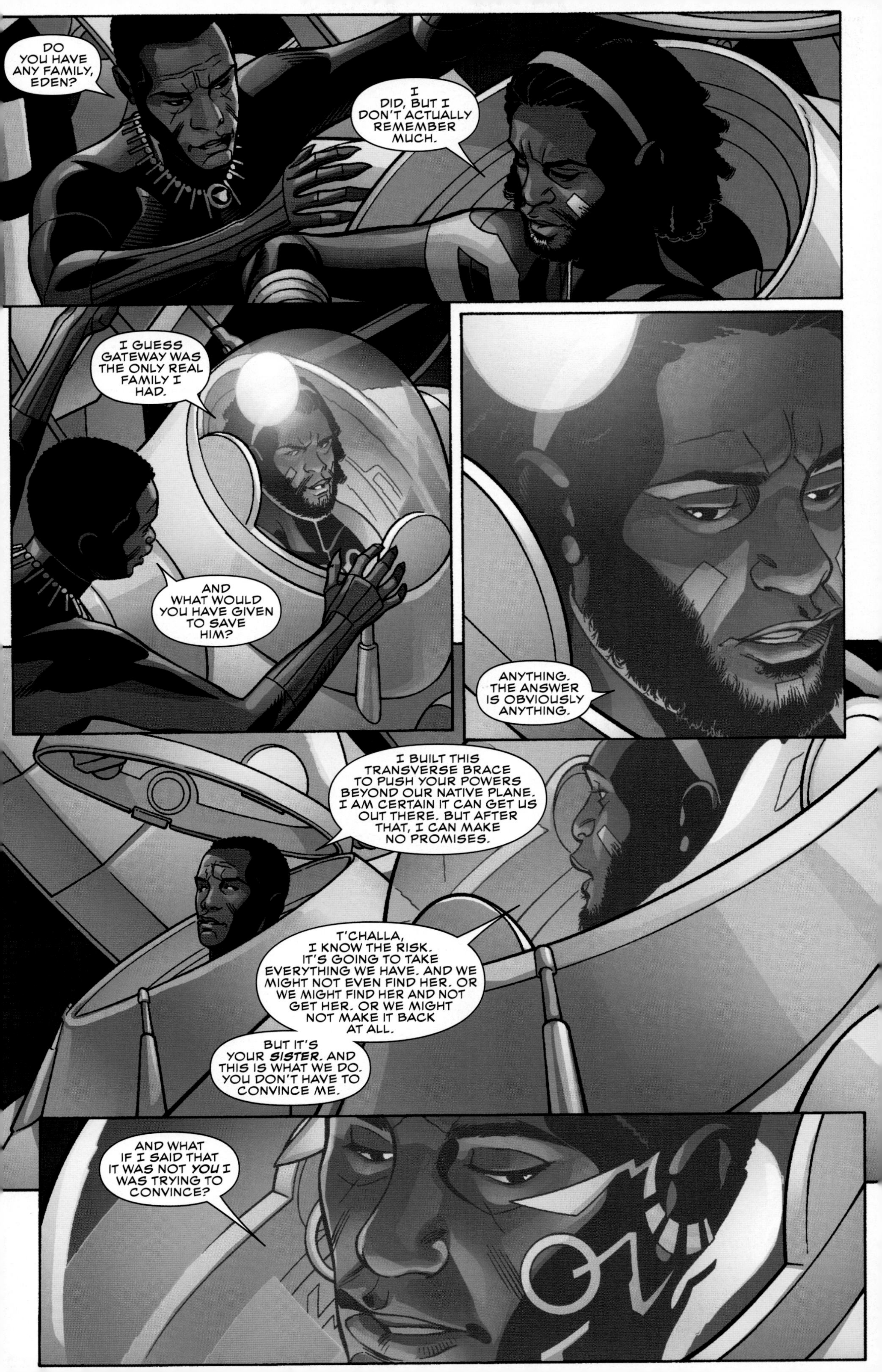

DO YOU HAVE ANY FAMILY, EDEN?
I DID, BUT I DON'T ACTUALLY REMEMBER MUCH.
I GUESS GATEWAY WAS THE ONLY REAL FAMILY I HAD.
AND WHAT WOULD YOU HAVE GIVEN TO SAVE HIM?
ANYTHING. THE ANSWER IS OBVIOUSLY ANYTHING.
I BUILT THIS TRANSVERSE BRACE TO PUSH YOUR POWERS BEYOND OUR NATIVE PLANE. I AM CERTAIN IT CAN GET US OUT THERE. BUT AFTER THAT, I CAN MAKE NO PROMISES.
T'CHALLA, I KNOW THE RISK. IT'S GOING TO TAKE EVERYTHING WE HAVE. AND WE MIGHT NOT EVEN FIND HER. OR WE MIGHT FIND HER AND NOT GET HER. OR WE MIGHT NOT MAKE IT BACK AT ALL.
BUT IT'S YOUR *SISTER*. AND THIS IS WHAT WE DO. YOU DON'T HAVE TO CONVINCE ME.
AND WHAT IF I SAID THAT IT WAS NOT *YOU* I WAS TRYING TO CONVINCE?

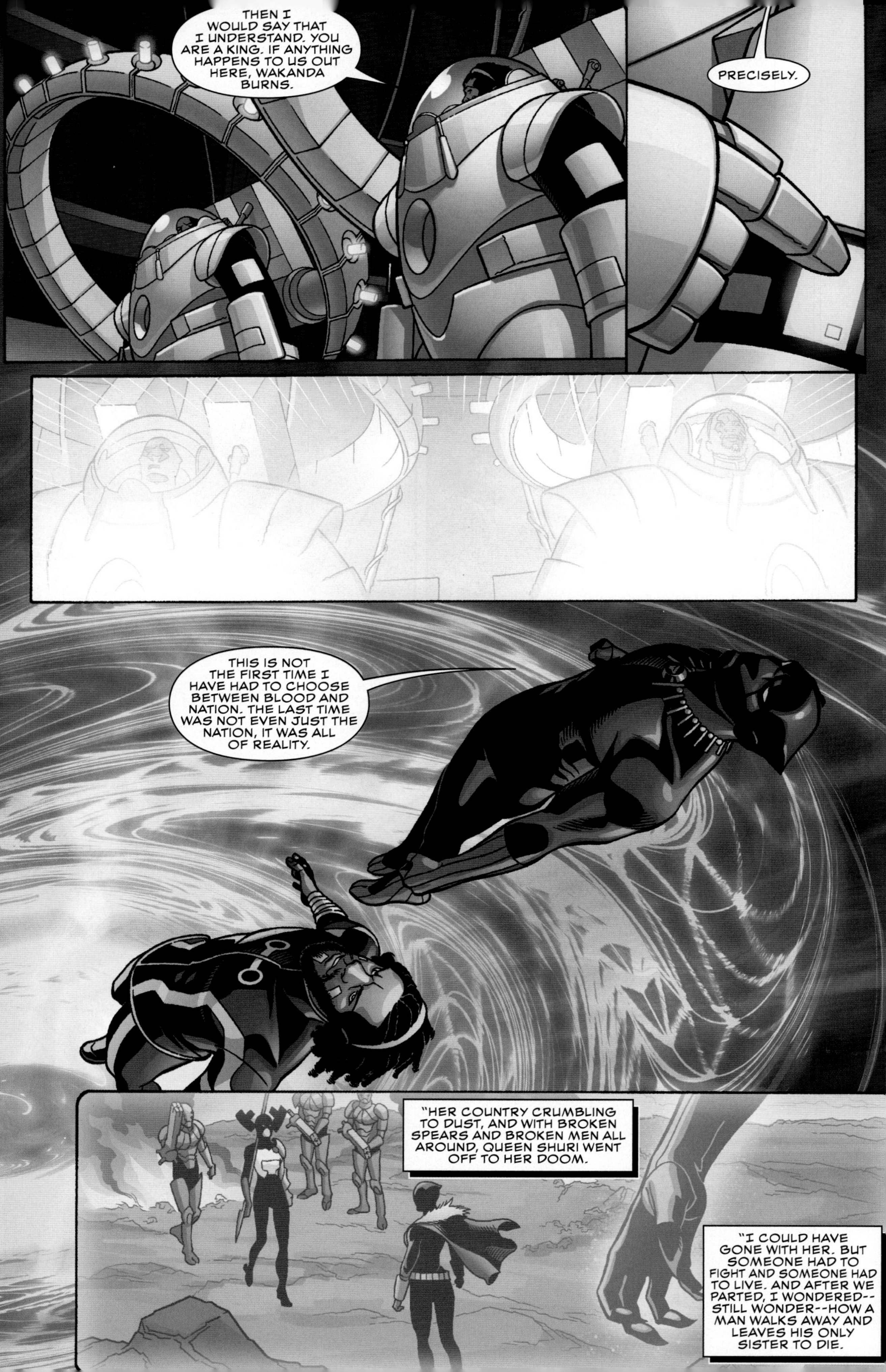
THEN I WOULD SAY THAT I UNDERSTAND. YOU ARE A KING. IF ANYTHING HAPPENS TO US OUT HERE, WAKANDA BURNS.
PRECISELY.
THIS IS NOT THE FIRST TIME I HAVE HAD TO CHOOSE BETWEEN BLOOD AND NATION. THE LAST TIME WAS NOT EVEN JUST THE NATION, IT WAS ALL OF REALITY.
"HER COUNTRY CRUMBLING TO DUST, AND WITH BROKEN SPEARS AND BROKEN MEN ALL AROUND, QUEEN SHURI WENT OFF TO HER DOOM.
"I COULD HAVE GONE WITH HER. BUT SOMEONE HAD TO FIGHT AND SOMEONE HAD TO LIVE. AND AFTER WE PARTED, I WONDERED--STILL WONDER--HOW A MAN WALKS AWAY AND LEAVES HIS ONLY SISTER TO DIE.

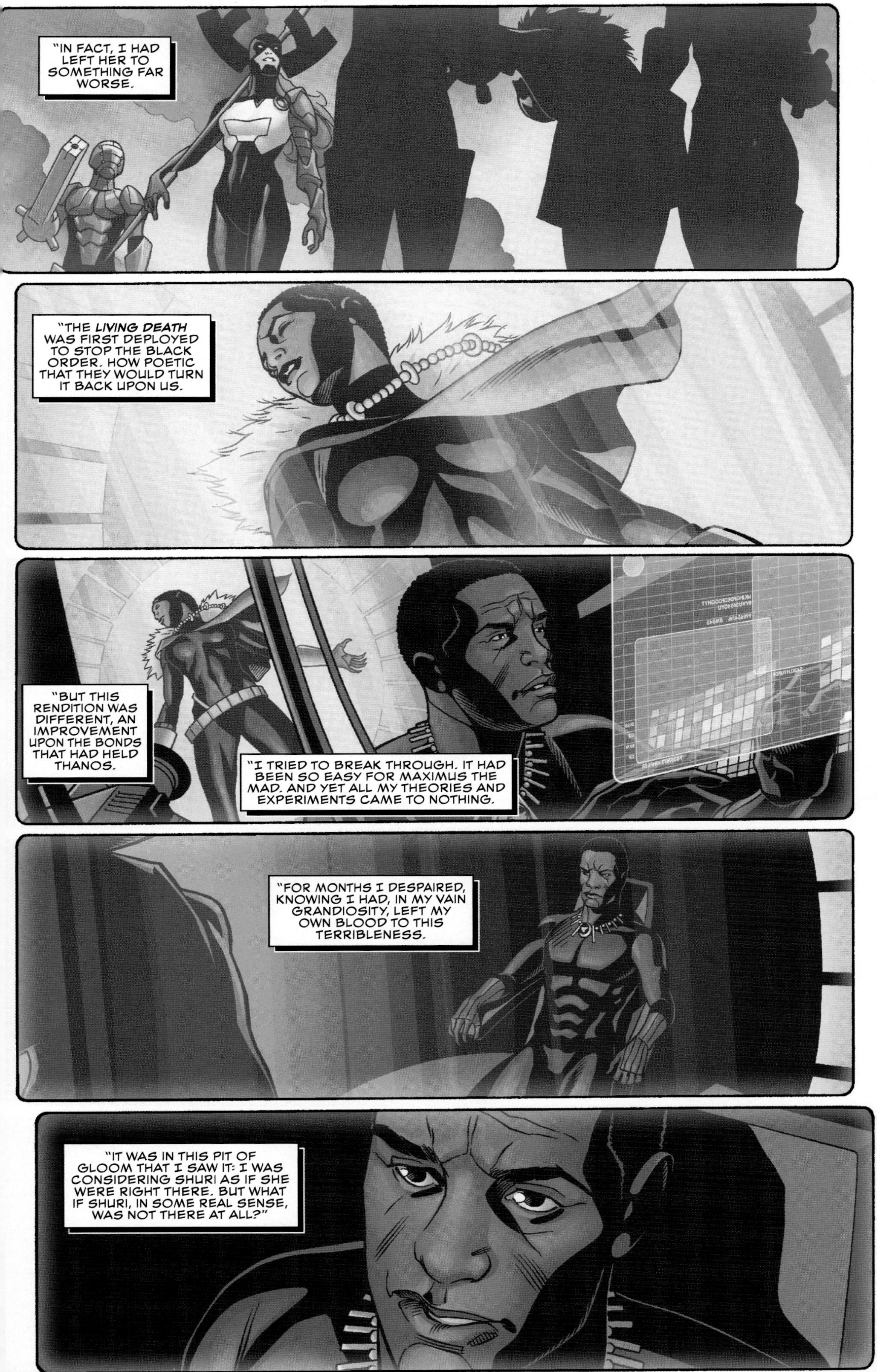
"IN FACT, I HAD LEFT HER TO SOMETHING FAR WORSE.
"THE *LIVING DEATH* WAS FIRST DEPLOYED TO STOP THE BLACK ORDER. HOW POETIC THAT THEY WOULD TURN IT BACK UPON US.
"BUT THIS RENDITION WAS DIFFERENT, AN IMPROVEMENT UPON THE BONDS THAT HAD HELD THANOS.
"I TRIED TO BREAK THROUGH. IT HAD BEEN SO EASY FOR MAXIMUS THE MAD. AND YET ALL MY THEORIES AND EXPERIMENTS CAME TO NOTHING.
"FOR MONTHS I DESPAIRED, KNOWING I HAD, IN MY VAIN GRANDIOSITY, LEFT MY OWN BLOOD TO THIS TERRIBLENESS.
"IT WAS IN THIS PIT OF GLOOM THAT I SAW IT: I WAS CONSIDERING SHURI AS IF SHE WERE RIGHT THERE. BUT WHAT IF SHURI, IN SOME REAL SENSE, WAS NOT THERE AT ALL?"

WHEN I RETURNED, AFTER THE FINAL INCURSION, I WAS DIFFERENT. MY PANTHER SENSES WERE AUGMENTED EVEN MORE. I SAW AS NO OTHER DID, SAW ACROSS GREAT SEAS AND OPEN PLAINS.

THE MORE FAMILIAR THE SCENT, THE FARTHER I COULD TRACK.

I HAD KNOWN SHURI ALL MY LIFE. AND YET THERE WAS NO SCENT, NO TRAIL ABOUT HER.

THE WOMAN FROZEN BEFORE ME WAS NOT SHURI. SHE WAS NOT EVEN A WOMAN. SHE WAS A DOOR.

I LOOKED THROUGH THIS DOOR, OUT ACROSS TIME AND SPACE, PAST GALACTIC WONDERS AND FALLEN DYNASTIES, AND I FOUND HER IN A PLACE LONG FORGOTTEN.

BUT I COULD ONLY LOOK THROUGH THE DOOR. TO WALK THROUGH IT, I NEEDED YOU.

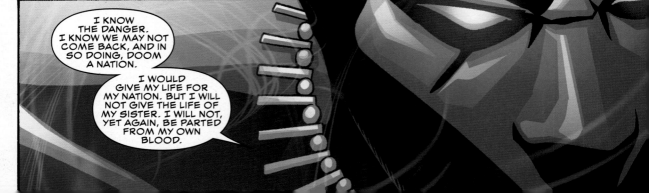

I KNOW THE DANGER. I KNOW WE MAY NOT COME BACK, AND IN SO DOING, DOOM A NATION.

I WOULD GIVE MY LIFE FOR MY NATION. BUT I WILL NOT GIVE THE LIFE OF MY SISTER. I WILL NOT, YET AGAIN, BE PARTED FROM MY OWN BLOOD.

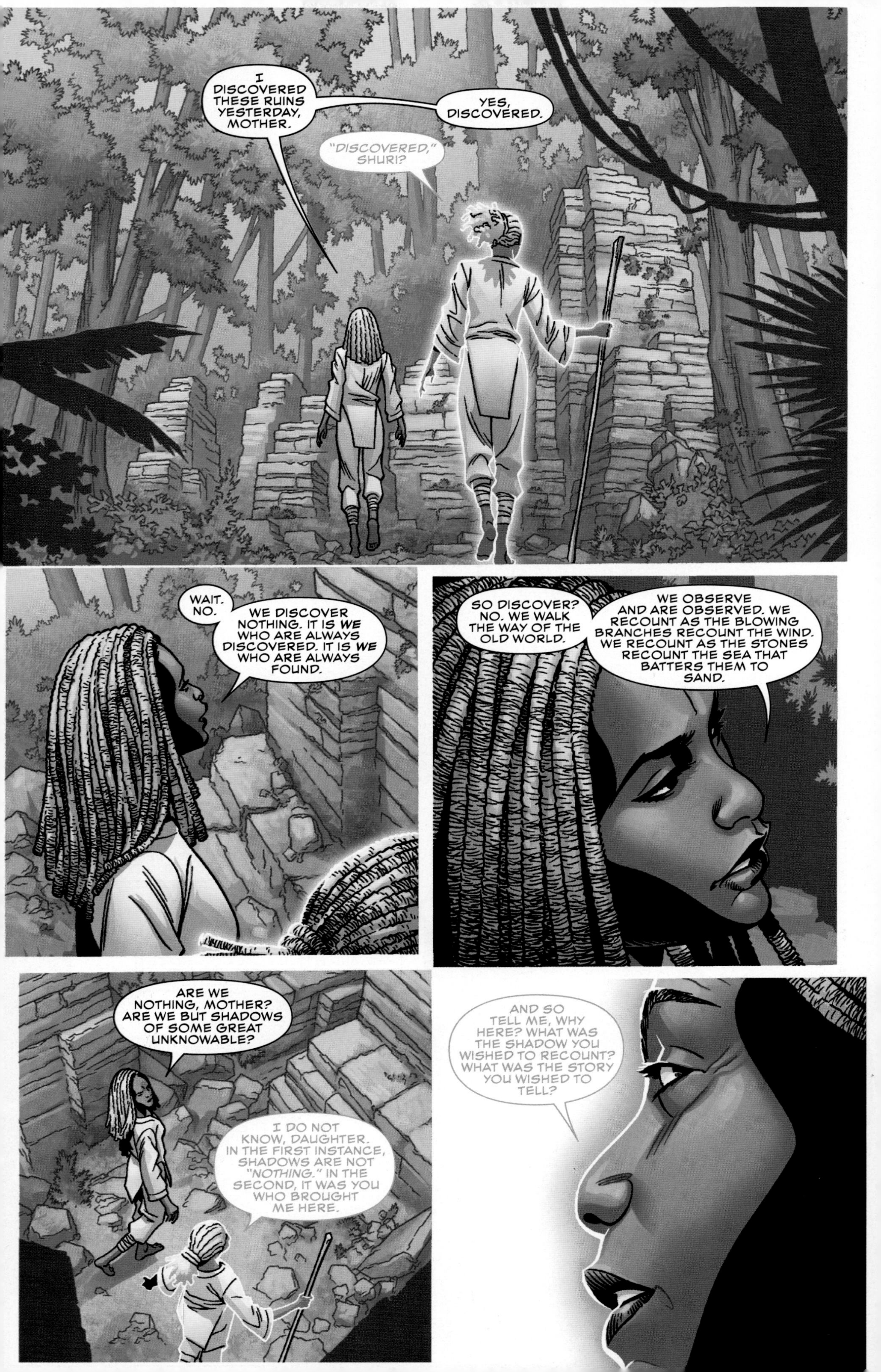

I DISCOVERED THESE RUINS YESTERDAY, MOTHER.
YES, DISCOVERED.
"DISCOVERED," SHURI?
WAIT. NO.
WE DISCOVER NOTHING. IT IS *WE* WHO ARE ALWAYS DISCOVERED. IT IS *WE* WHO ARE ALWAYS FOUND.
SO DISCOVER? NO. WE WALK THE WAY OF THE OLD WORLD.
WE OBSERVE AND ARE OBSERVED. WE RECOUNT AS THE BLOWING BRANCHES RECOUNT THE WIND. WE RECOUNT AS THE STONES RECOUNT THE SEA THAT BATTERS THEM TO SAND.
ARE WE NOTHING, MOTHER? ARE WE BUT SHADOWS OF SOME GREAT UNKNOWABLE?
I DO NOT KNOW, DAUGHTER. IN THE FIRST INSTANCE, SHADOWS ARE NOT *"NOTHING."* IN THE SECOND, IT WAS YOU WHO BROUGHT ME HERE.
AND SO TELL ME, WHY HERE? WHAT WAS THE SHADOW YOU WISHED TO RECOUNT? WHAT WAS THE STORY YOU WISHED TO TELL?

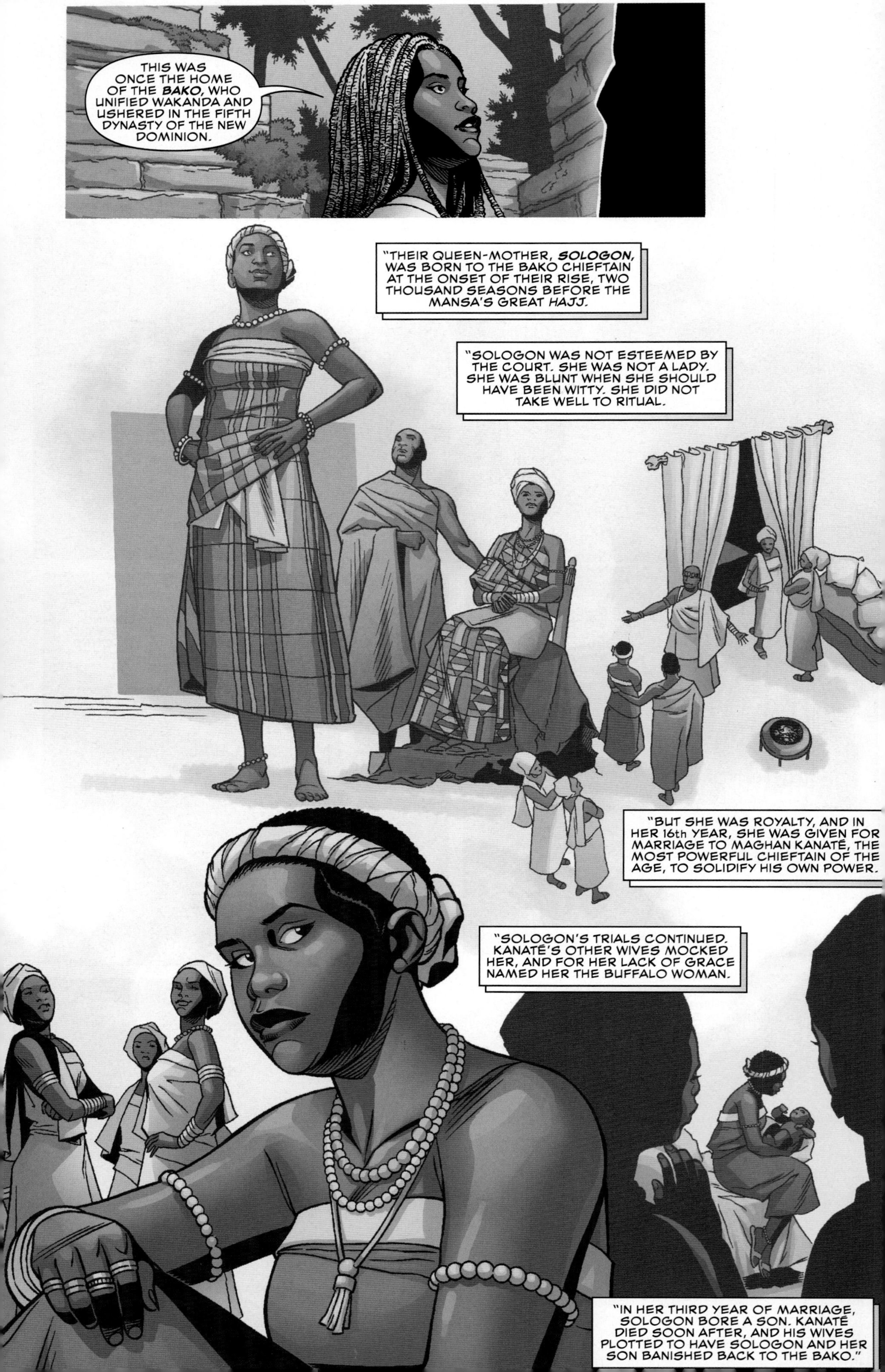
THIS WAS ONCE THE HOME OF THE BAKO, WHO UNIFIED WAKANDA AND USHERED IN THE FIFTH DYNASTY OF THE NEW DOMINION.
"THEIR QUEEN-MOTHER, SOLOGON, WAS BORN TO THE BAKO CHIEFTAIN AT THE ONSET OF THEIR RISE, TWO THOUSAND SEASONS BEFORE THE MANSA'S GREAT HAJJ.
"SOLOGON WAS NOT ESTEEMED BY THE COURT. SHE WAS NOT A LADY. SHE WAS BLUNT WHEN SHE SHOULD HAVE BEEN WITTY. SHE DID NOT TAKE WELL TO RITUAL.
"BUT SHE WAS ROYALTY, AND IN HER 16th YEAR, SHE WAS GIVEN FOR MARRIAGE TO MAGHAN KANATÉ, THE MOST POWERFUL CHIEFTAIN OF THE AGE, TO SOLIDIFY HIS OWN POWER.
"SOLOGON'S TRIALS CONTINUED. KANATÉ'S OTHER WIVES MOCKED HER, AND FOR HER LACK OF GRACE NAMED HER THE BUFFALO WOMAN.
"IN HER THIRD YEAR OF MARRIAGE, SOLOGON BORE A SON. KANATÉ DIED SOON AFTER, AND HIS WIVES PLOTTED TO HAVE SOLOGON AND HER SON BANISHED BACK TO THE BAKO."

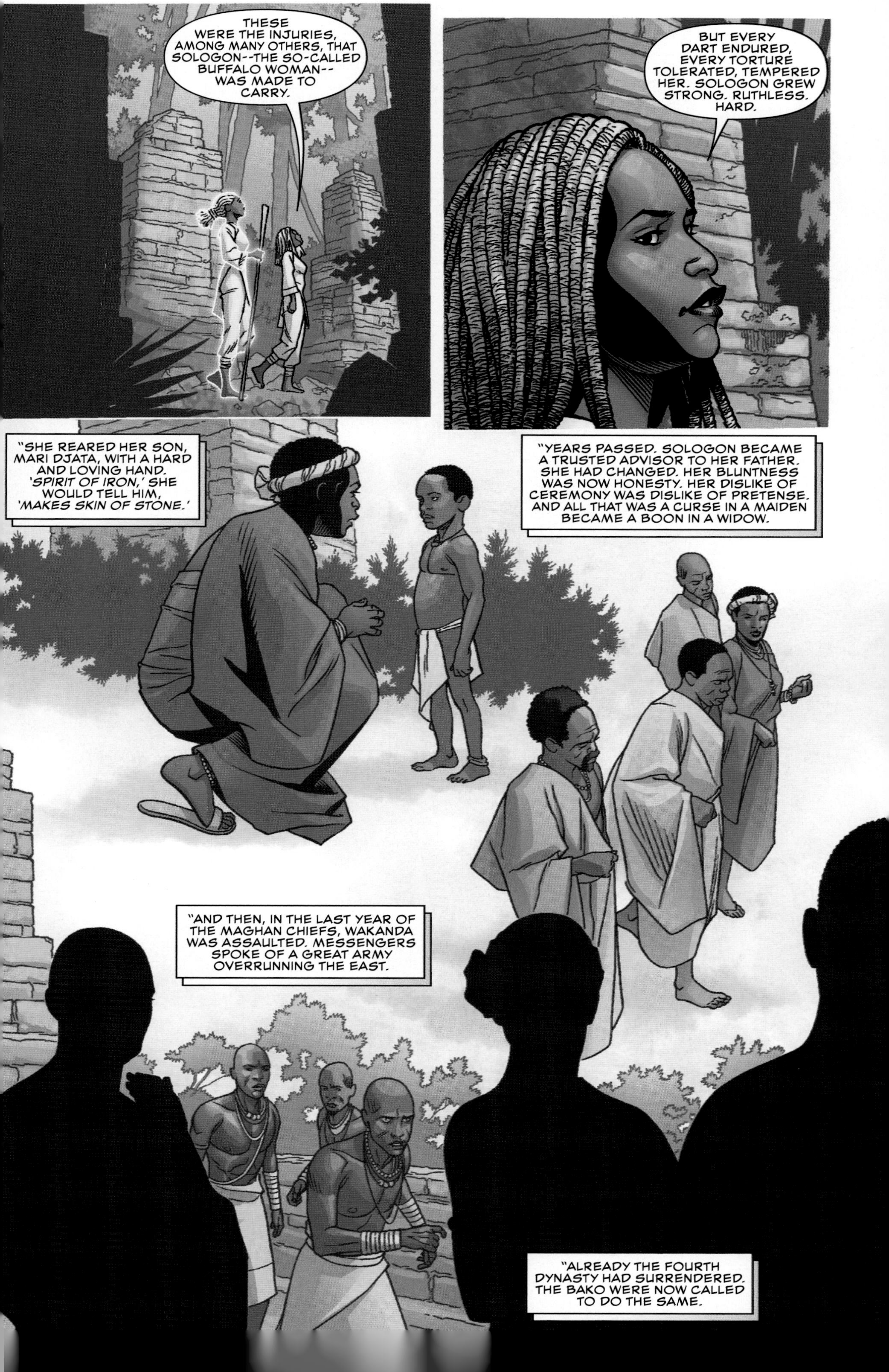
THESE WERE THE INJURIES, AMONG MANY OTHERS, THAT SOLOGON--THE SO-CALLED BUFFALO WOMAN--WAS MADE TO CARRY.
BUT EVERY DART ENDURED, EVERY TORTURE TOLERATED, TEMPERED HER. SOLOGON GREW STRONG. RUTHLESS. HARD.
"SHE REARED HER SON, MARI DJATA, WITH A HARD AND LOVING HAND. *'SPIRIT OF IRON,'* SHE WOULD TELL HIM, *'MAKES SKIN OF STONE.'*
"YEARS PASSED. SOLOGON BECAME A TRUSTED ADVISOR TO HER FATHER. SHE HAD CHANGED. HER BLUNTNESS WAS NOW HONESTY. HER DISLIKE OF CEREMONY WAS DISLIKE OF PRETENSE. AND ALL THAT WAS A CURSE IN A MAIDEN BECAME A BOON IN A WIDOW.
"AND THEN, IN THE LAST YEAR OF THE MAGHAN CHIEFS, WAKANDA WAS ASSAULTED. MESSENGERS SPOKE OF A GREAT ARMY OVERRUNNING THE EAST.
"ALREADY THE FOURTH DYNASTY HAD SURRENDERED. THE BAKO WERE NOW CALLED TO DO THE SAME.

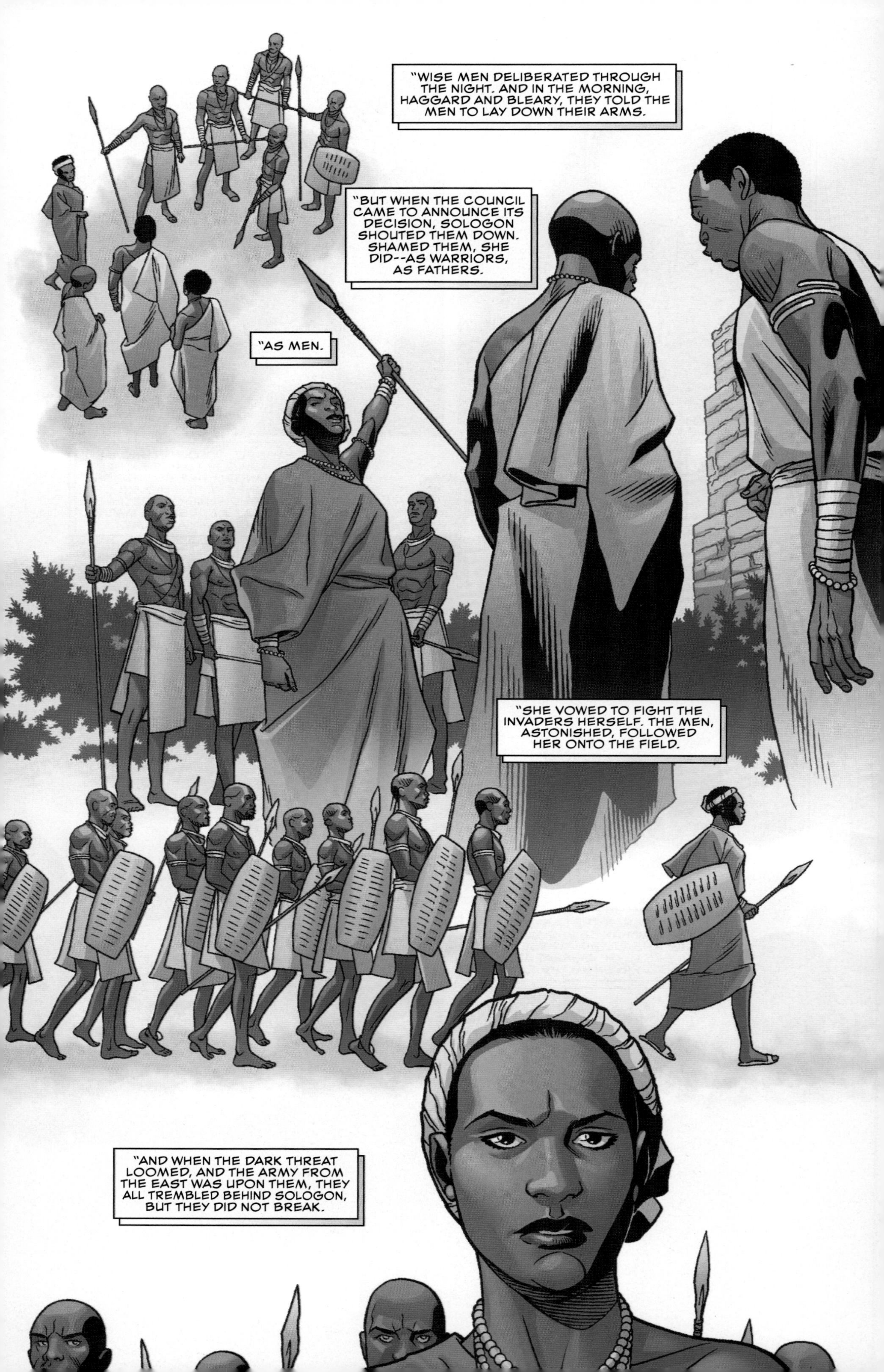
"WISE MEN DELIBERATED THROUGH THE NIGHT. AND IN THE MORNING, HAGGARD AND BLEARY, THEY TOLD THE MEN TO LAY DOWN THEIR ARMS.
"BUT WHEN THE COUNCIL CAME TO ANNOUNCE ITS DECISION, SOLOGON SHOUTED THEM DOWN. SHAMED THEM, SHE DID--AS WARRIORS, AS FATHERS.
"AS MEN.
"SHE VOWED TO FIGHT THE INVADERS HERSELF. THE MEN, ASTONISHED, FOLLOWED HER ONTO THE FIELD.
"AND WHEN THE DARK THREAT LOOMED, AND THE ARMY FROM THE EAST WAS UPON THEM, THEY ALL TREMBLED BEHIND SOLOGON, BUT THEY DID NOT BREAK.

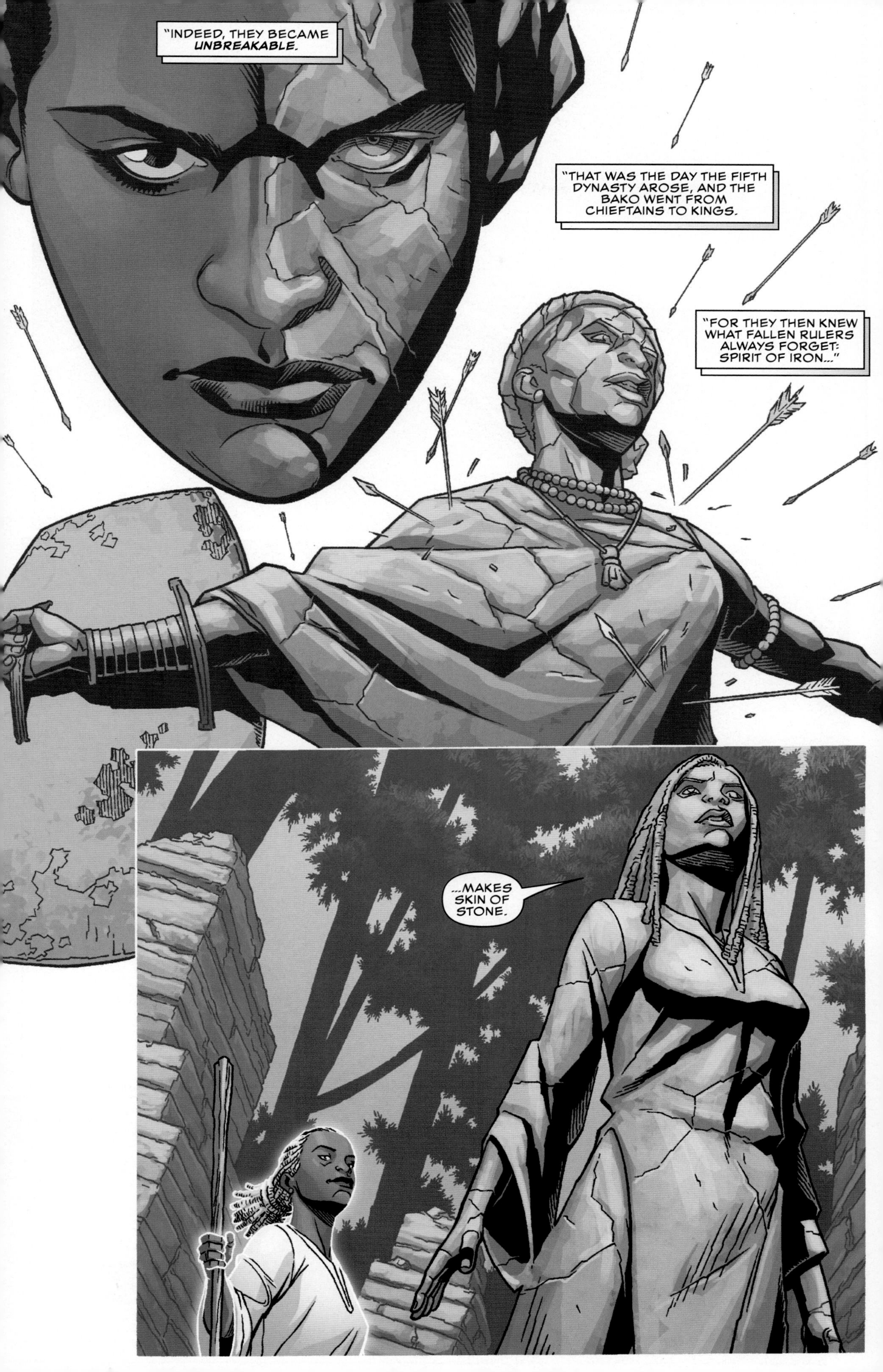
"INDEED, THEY BECAME UNBREAKABLE.
"THAT WAS THE DAY THE FIFTH DYNASTY AROSE, AND THE BAKO WENT FROM CHIEFTAINS TO KINGS.
"FOR THEY THEN KNEW WHAT FALLEN RULERS ALWAYS FORGET: SPIRIT OF IRON..."
...MAKES SKIN OF STONE.

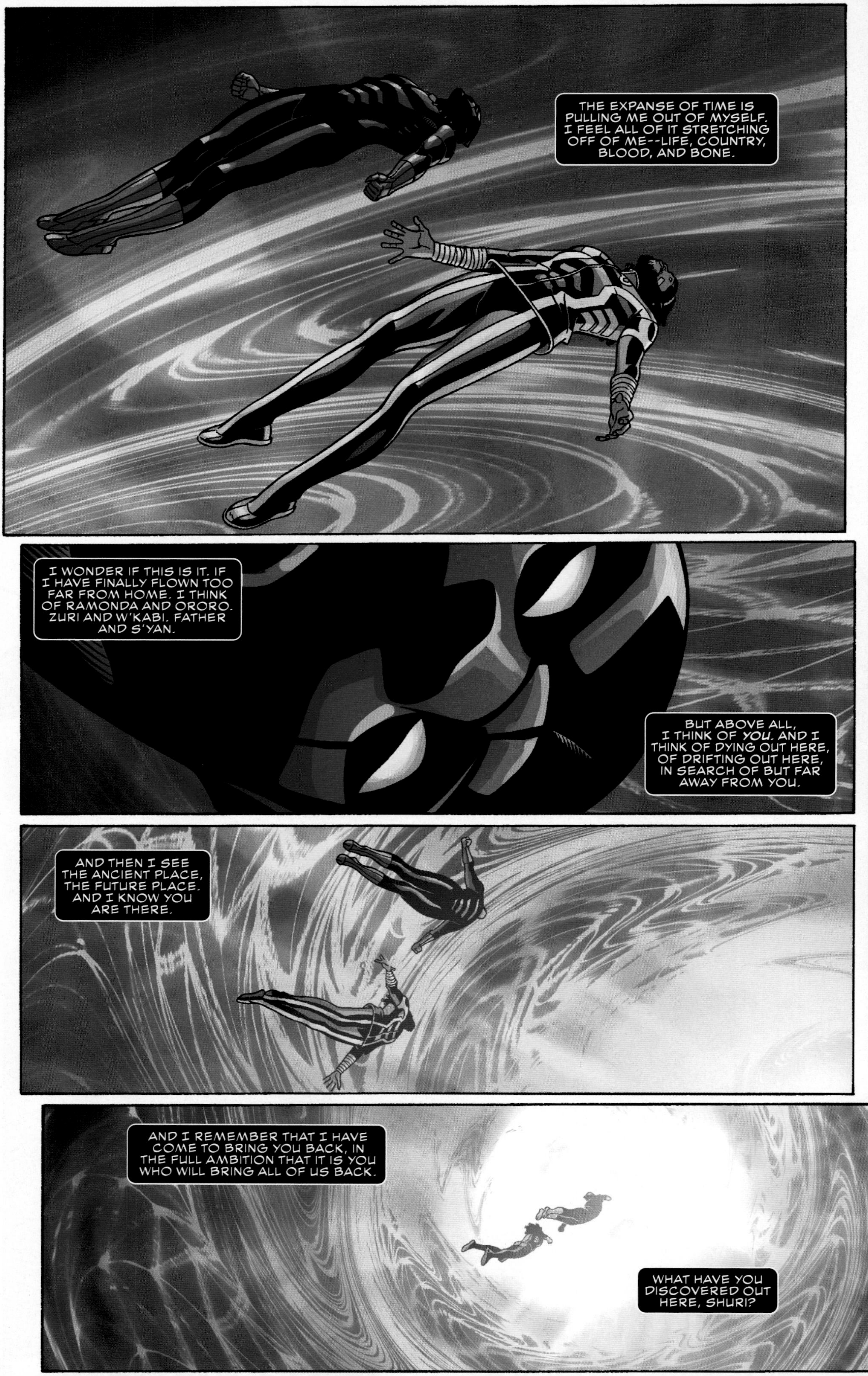
THE EXPANSE OF TIME IS PULLING ME OUT OF MYSELF. I FEEL ALL OF IT STRETCHING OFF OF ME--LIFE, COUNTRY, BLOOD, AND BONE.
I WONDER IF THIS IS IT. IF I HAVE FINALLY FLOWN TOO FAR FROM HOME. I THINK OF RAMONDA AND ORORO. ZURI AND W'KABI. FATHER AND S'YAN.
BUT ABOVE ALL, I THINK OF *YOU*. AND I THINK OF DYING OUT HERE, OF DRIFTING OUT HERE, IN SEARCH OF BUT FAR AWAY FROM YOU.
AND THEN I SEE THE ANCIENT PLACE, THE FUTURE PLACE. AND I KNOW YOU ARE THERE.
AND I REMEMBER THAT I HAVE COME TO BRING YOU BACK, IN THE FULL AMBITION THAT IT IS YOU WHO WILL BRING ALL OF US BACK.
WHAT HAVE YOU DISCOVERED OUT HERE, SHURI?

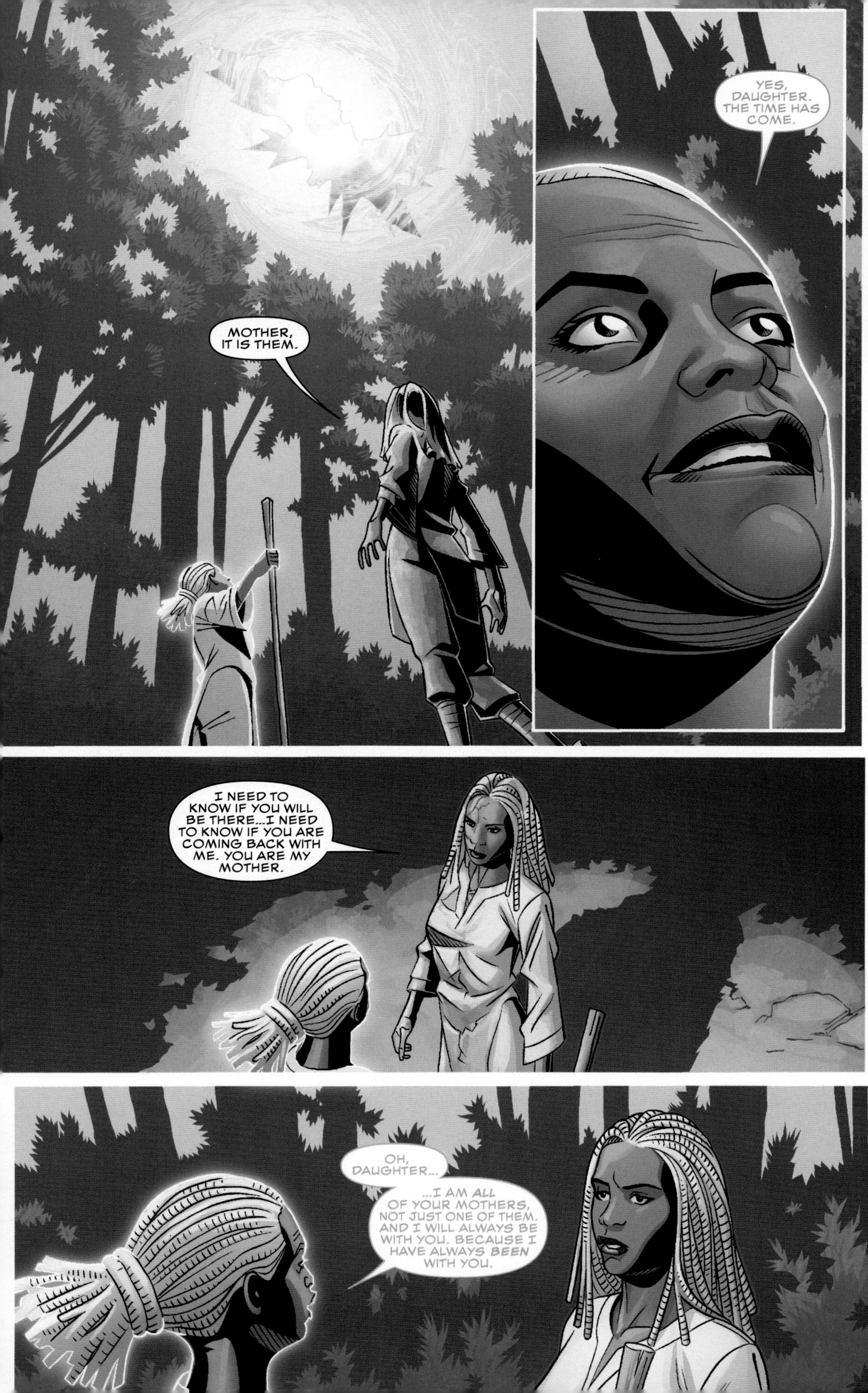
MOTHER, IT IS THEM.
YES, DAUGHTER. THE TIME HAS COME.
I NEED TO KNOW IF YOU WILL BE THERE...I NEED TO KNOW IF YOU ARE COMING BACK WITH ME. YOU ARE MY MOTHER.
OH, DAUGHTER...
...I AM ALL OF YOUR MOTHERS, NOT JUST ONE OF THEM. AND I WILL ALWAYS BE WITH YOU. BECAUSE I HAVE ALWAYS BEEN WITH YOU.

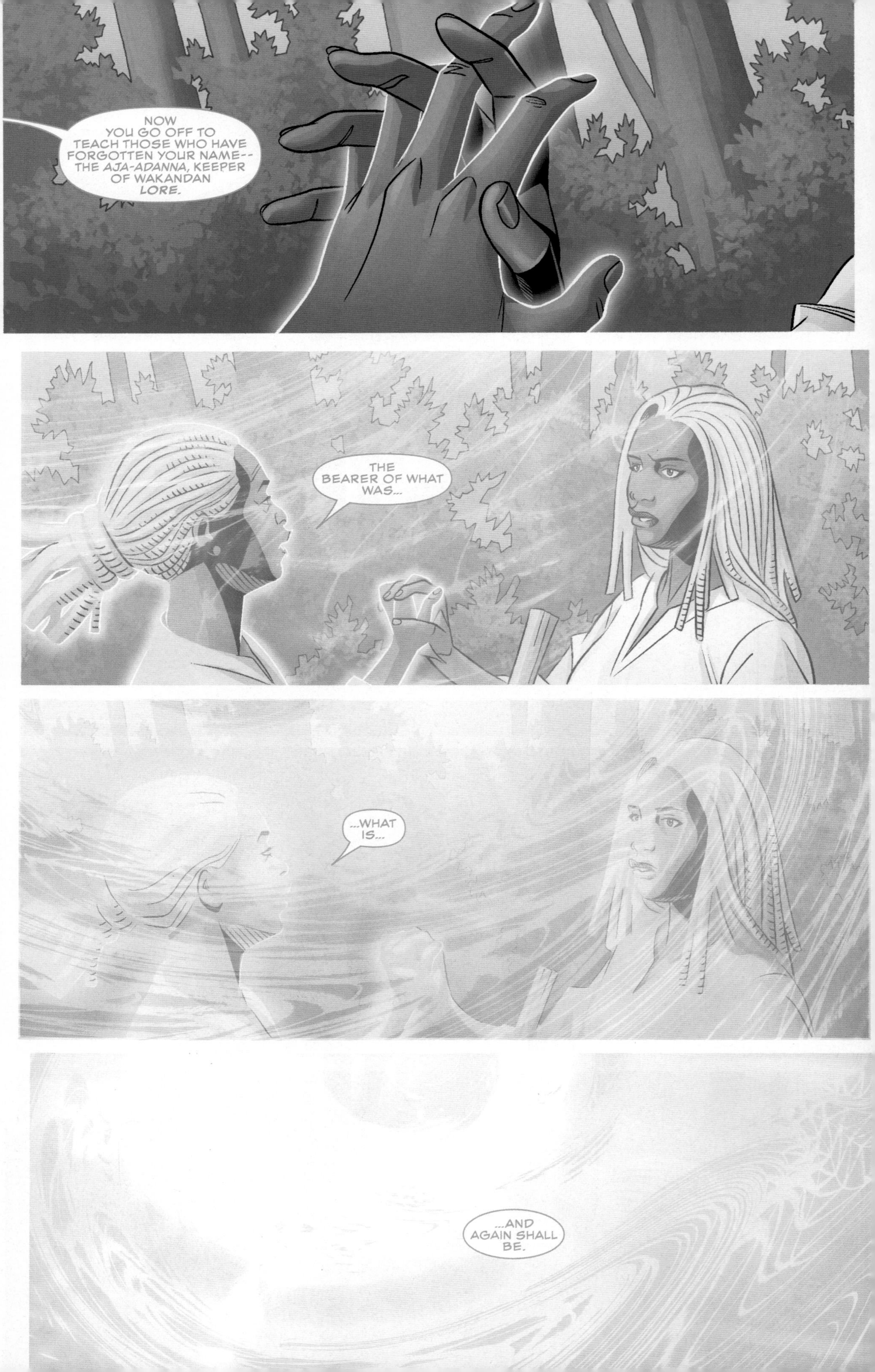
NOW YOU GO OFF TO TEACH THOSE WHO HAVE FORGOTTEN YOUR NAME-- THE AJA-ADANNA, KEEPER OF WAKANDAN LORE.
THE BEARER OF WHAT WAS...
...WHAT IS...
...AND AGAIN SHALL BE.

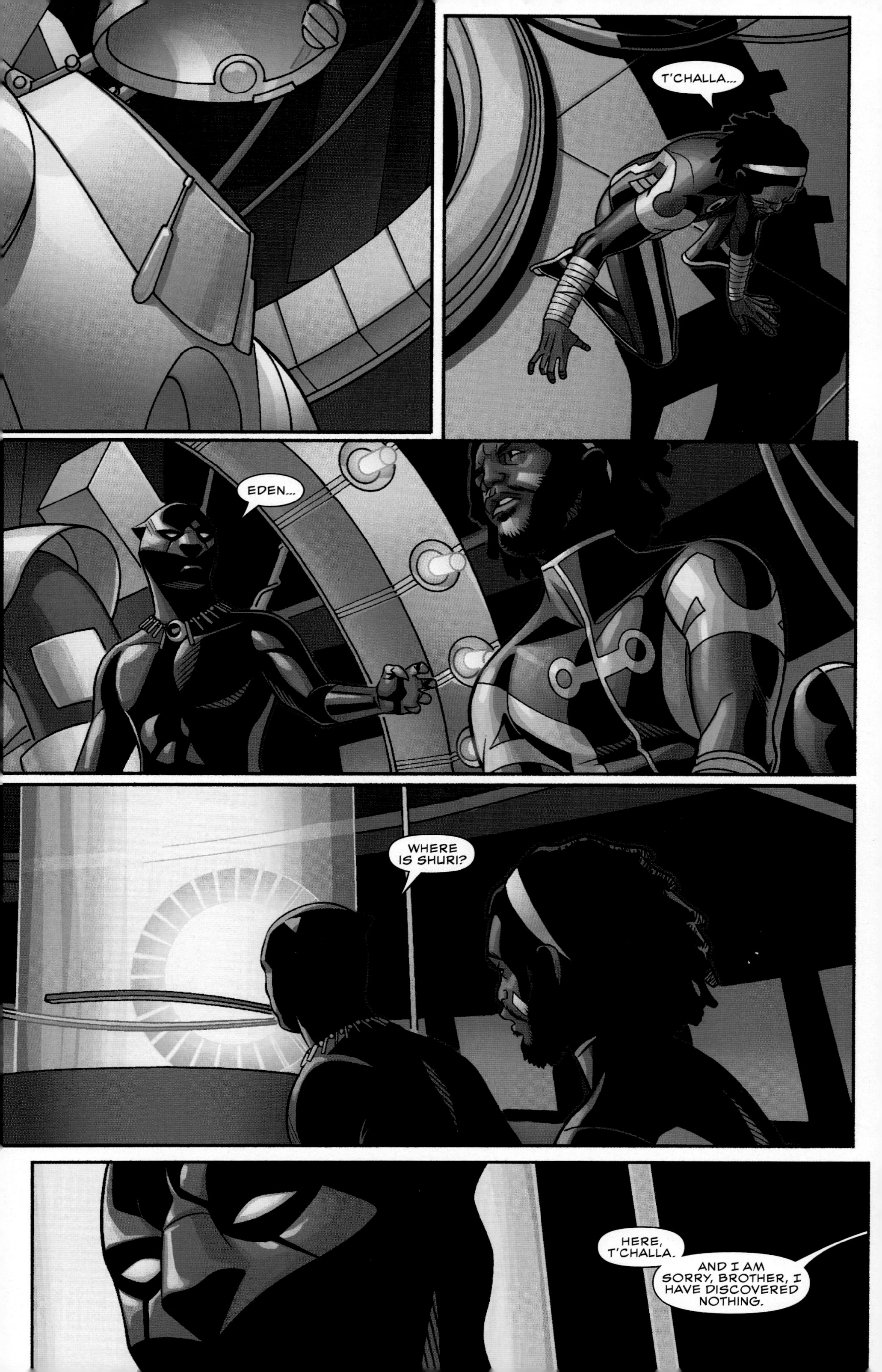
T'CHALLA...
EDEN...
WHERE IS SHURI?
HERE, T'CHALLA.
AND I AM SORRY, BROTHER, I HAVE DISCOVERED NOTHING.

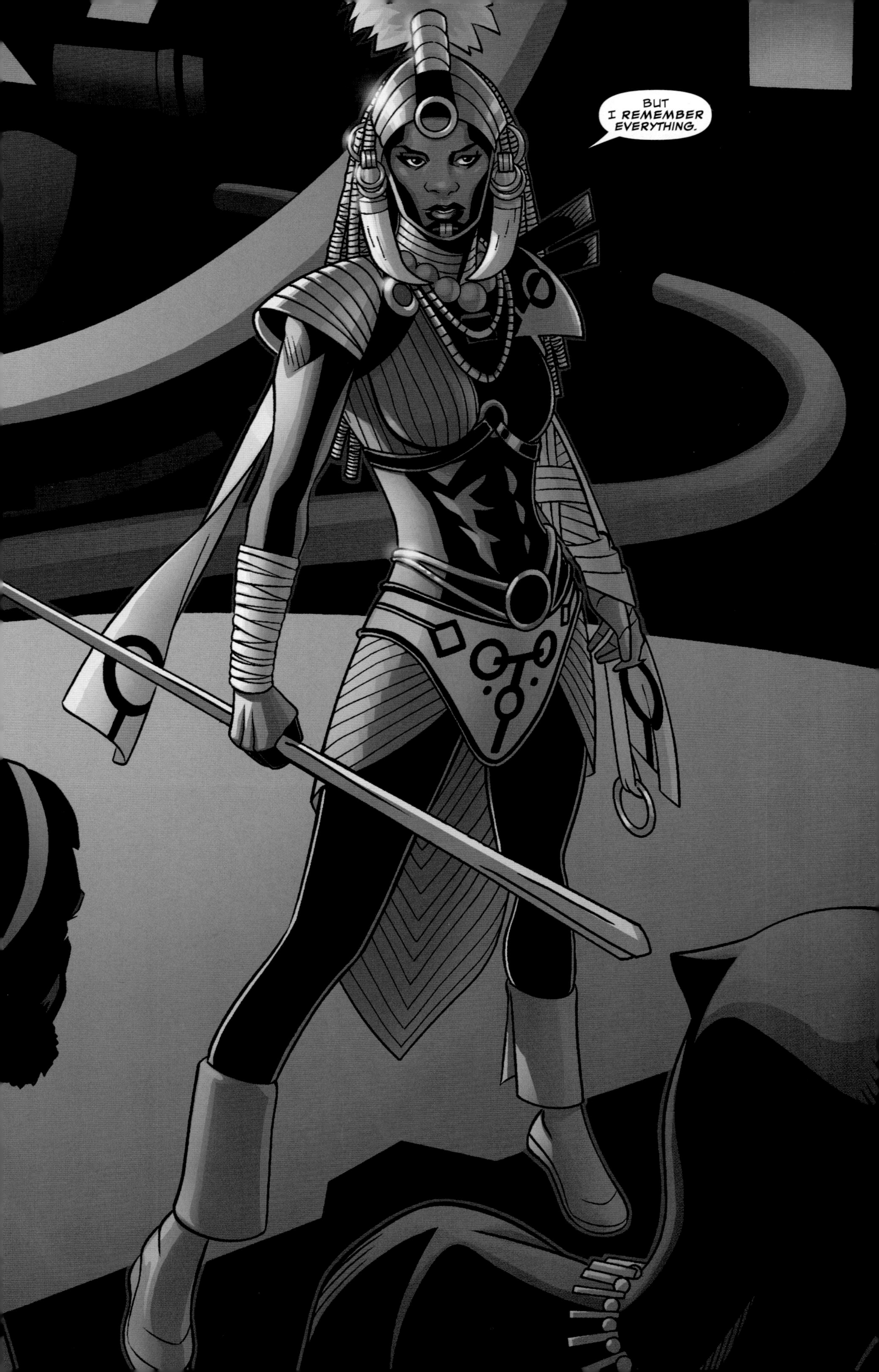
BUT I REMEMBER EVERYTHING.

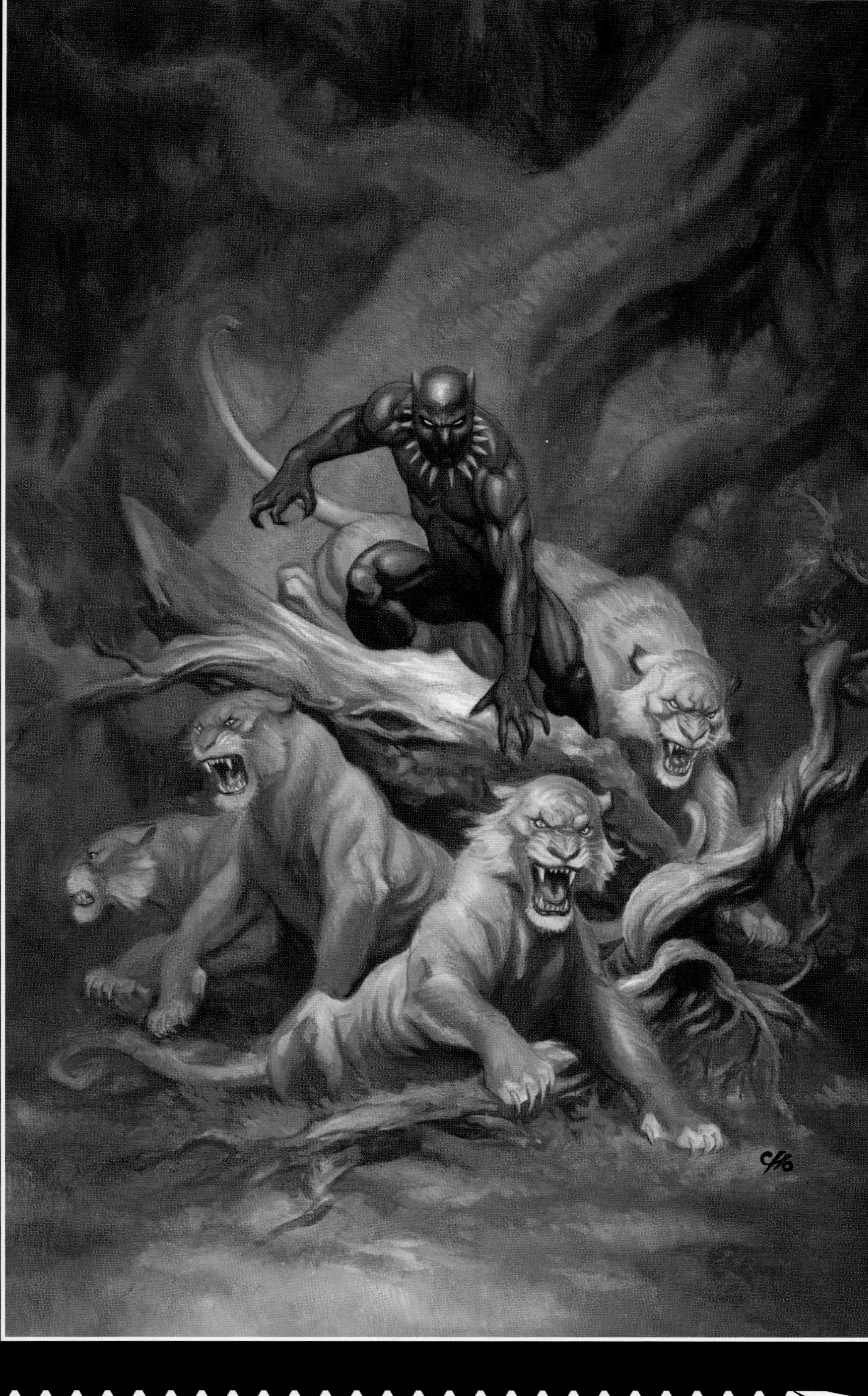
CHO

#2 VARIANT BY **FRANK CHO**

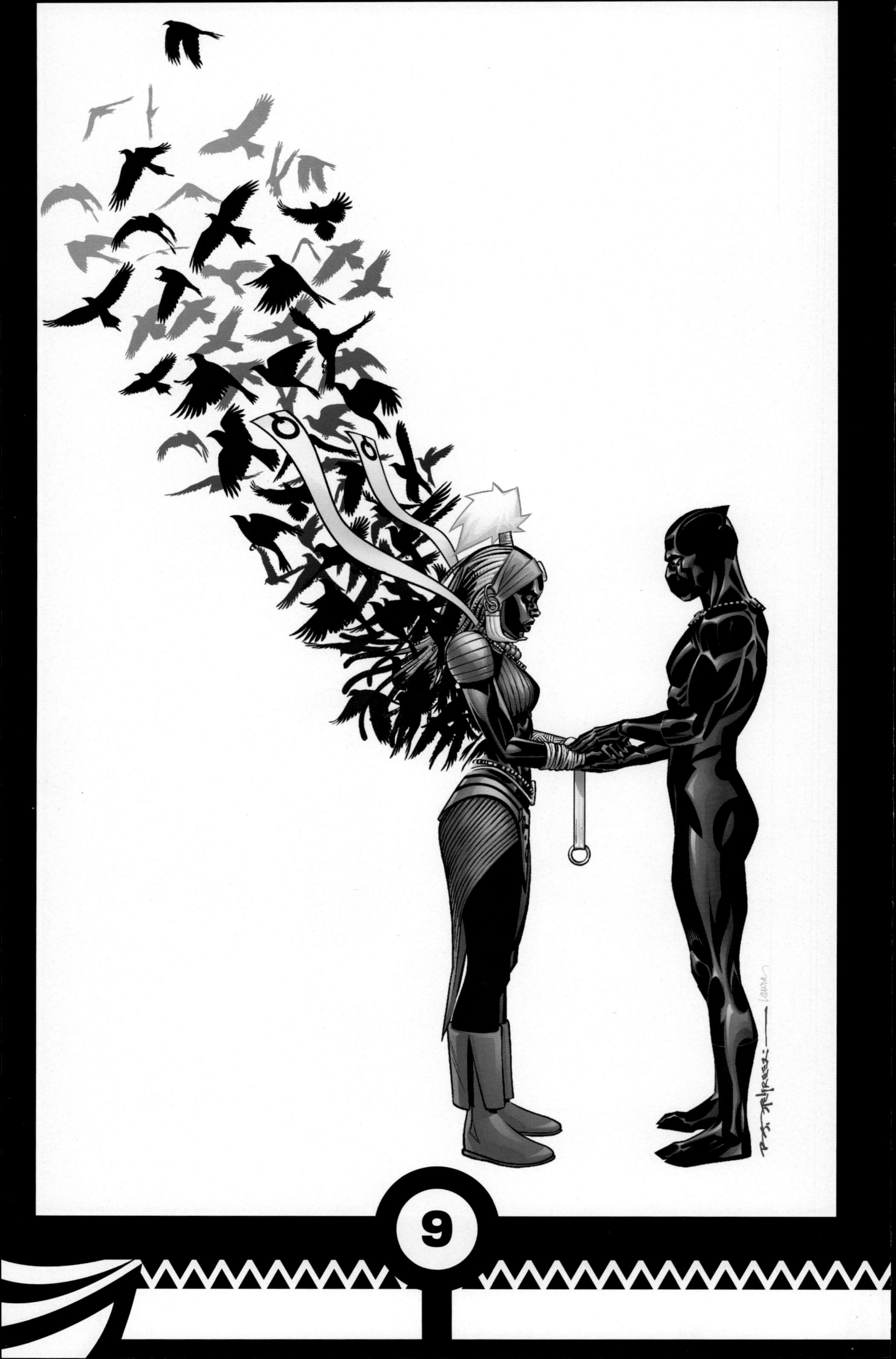
9

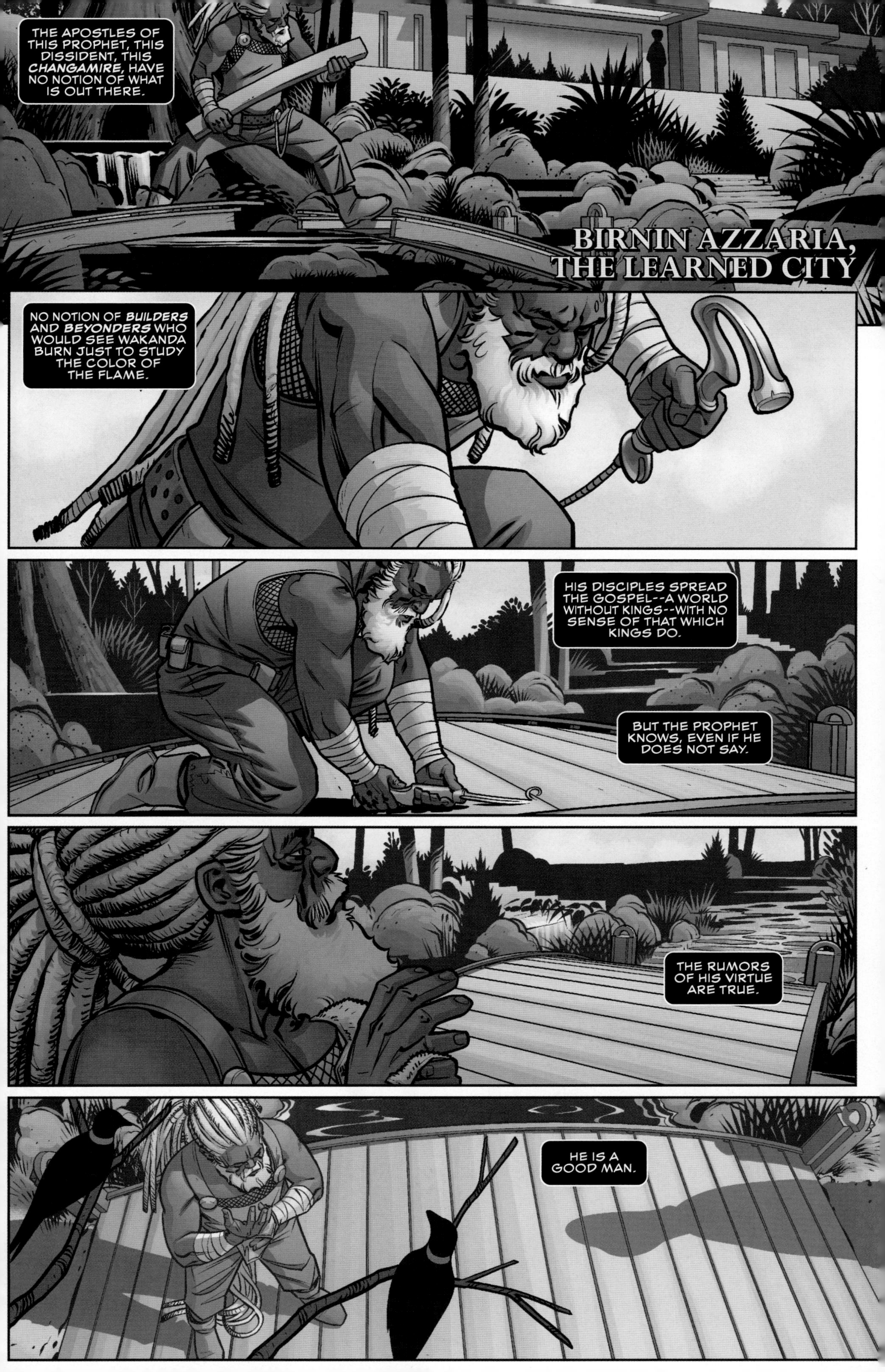
THE APOSTLES OF THIS PROPHET, THIS DISSIDENT, THIS CHANGAMIRE, HAVE NO NOTION OF WHAT IS OUT THERE.
BIRNIN AZZARIA, THE LEARNED CITY
NO NOTION OF BUILDERS AND BEYONDERS WHO WOULD SEE WAKANDA BURN JUST TO STUDY THE COLOR OF THE FLAME.
HIS DISCIPLES SPREAD THE GOSPEL--A WORLD WITHOUT KINGS--WITH NO SENSE OF THAT WHICH KINGS DO.
BUT THE PROPHET KNOWS, EVEN IF HE DOES NOT SAY.
THE RUMORS OF HIS VIRTUE ARE TRUE.
HE IS A GOOD MAN.

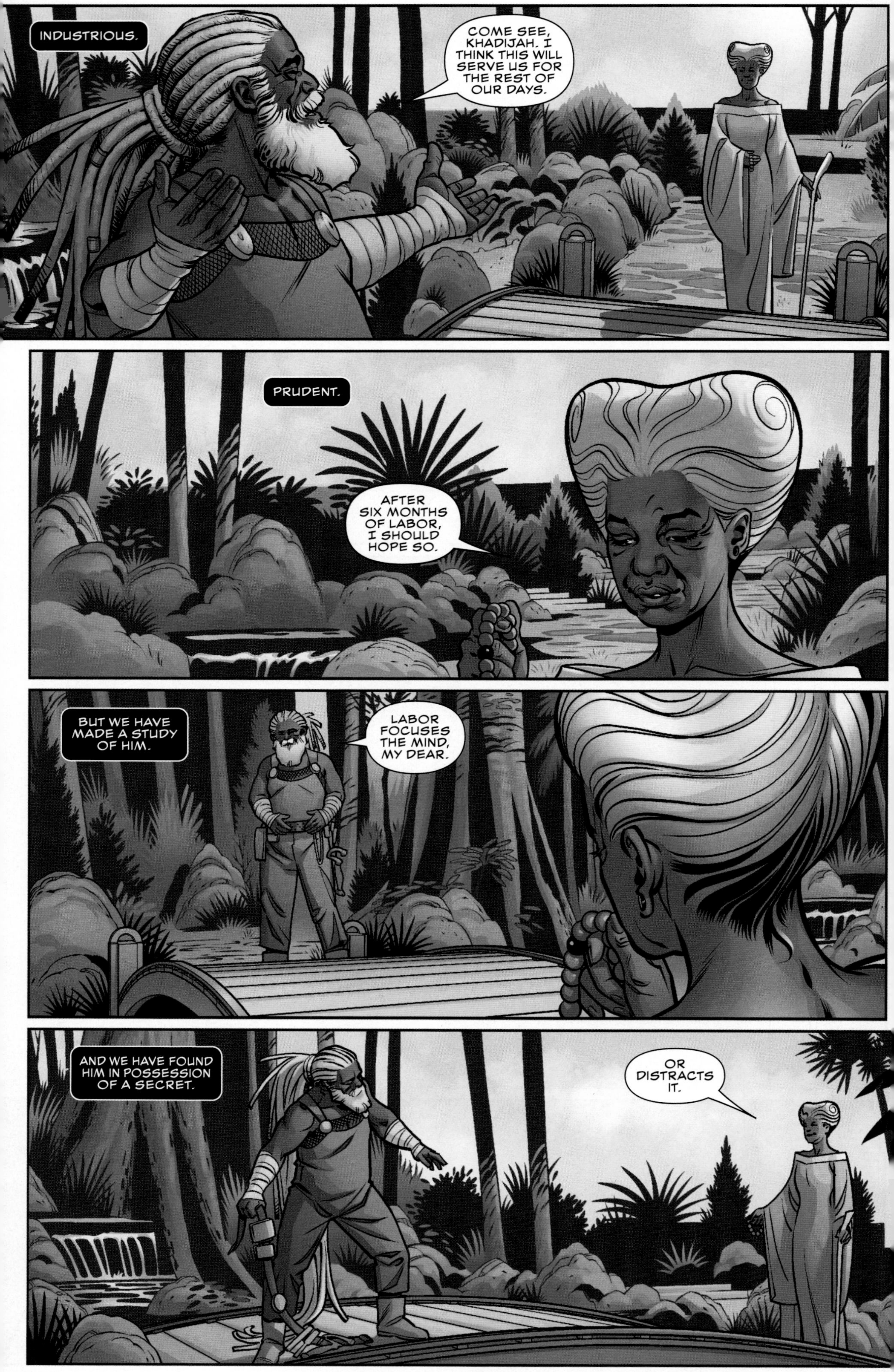
INDUSTRIOUS.
COME SEE, KHADIJAH. I THINK THIS WILL SERVE US FOR THE REST OF OUR DAYS.
PRUDENT.
AFTER SIX MONTHS OF LABOR, I SHOULD HOPE SO.
BUT WE HAVE MADE A STUDY OF HIM.
LABOR FOCUSES THE MIND, MY DEAR.
AND WE HAVE FOUND HIM IN POSSESSION OF A SECRET.
OR DISTRACTS IT.

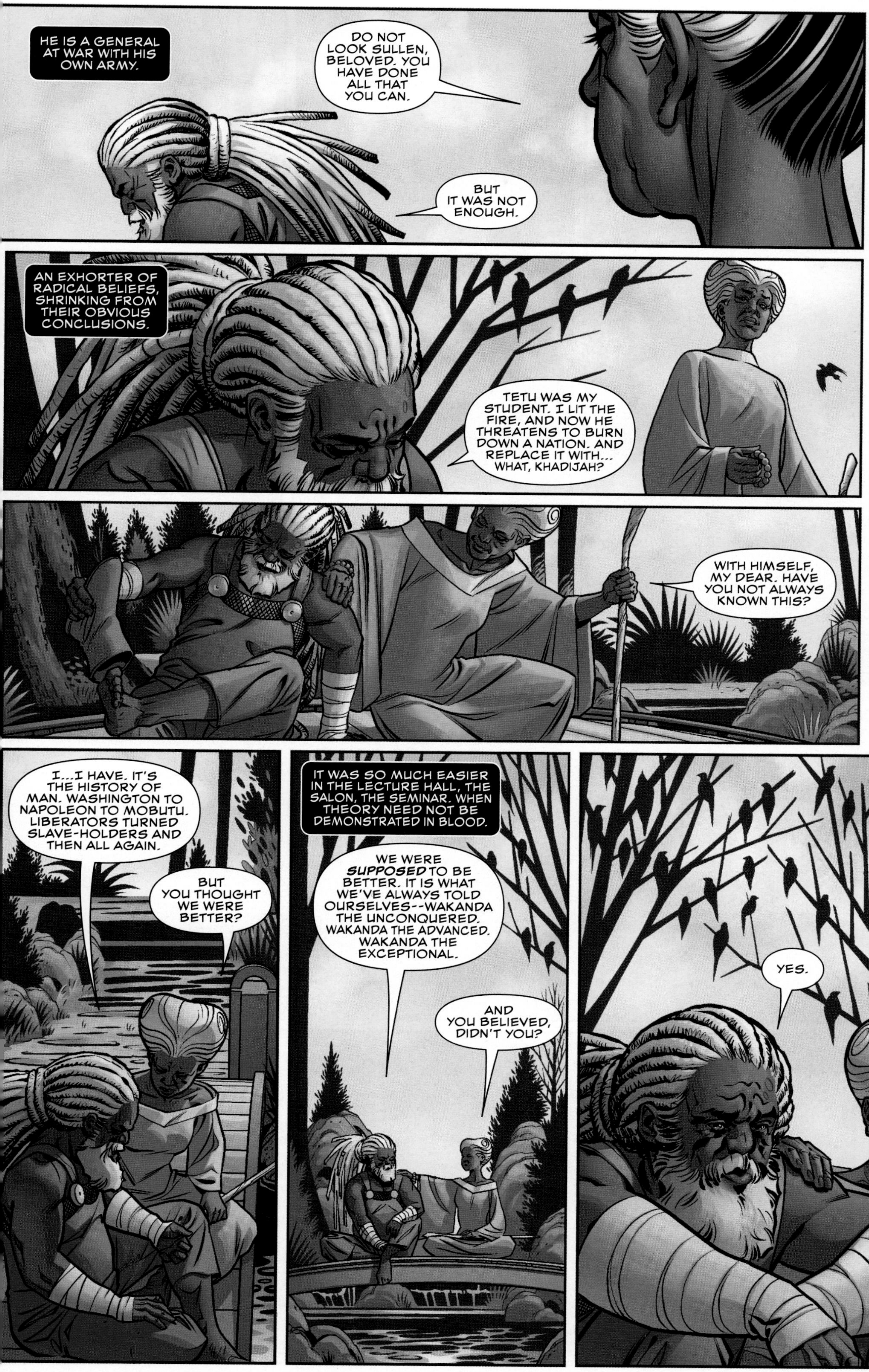
HE IS A GENERAL AT WAR WITH HIS OWN ARMY.
DO NOT LOOK SULLEN, BELOVED. YOU HAVE DONE ALL THAT YOU CAN.
BUT IT WAS NOT ENOUGH.
AN EXHORTER OF RADICAL BELIEFS, SHRINKING FROM THEIR OBVIOUS CONCLUSIONS.
TETU WAS MY STUDENT. I LIT THE FIRE, AND NOW HE THREATENS TO BURN DOWN A NATION. AND REPLACE IT WITH... WHAT, KHADIJAH?
WITH HIMSELF, MY DEAR. HAVE YOU NOT ALWAYS KNOWN THIS?
I...I HAVE. IT'S THE HISTORY OF MAN. WASHINGTON TO NAPOLEON TO MOBUTU. LIBERATORS TURNED SLAVE-HOLDERS AND THEN ALL AGAIN.
BUT YOU THOUGHT WE WERE BETTER?
IT WAS SO MUCH EASIER IN THE LECTURE HALL, THE SALON, THE SEMINAR. WHEN THEORY NEED NOT BE DEMONSTRATED IN BLOOD.
WE WERE *SUPPOSED* TO BE BETTER. IT IS WHAT WE'VE ALWAYS TOLD OURSELVES--WAKANDA THE UNCONQUERED. WAKANDA THE ADVANCED. WAKANDA THE EXCEPTIONAL.
AND YOU BELIEVED, DIDN'T YOU?
YES.

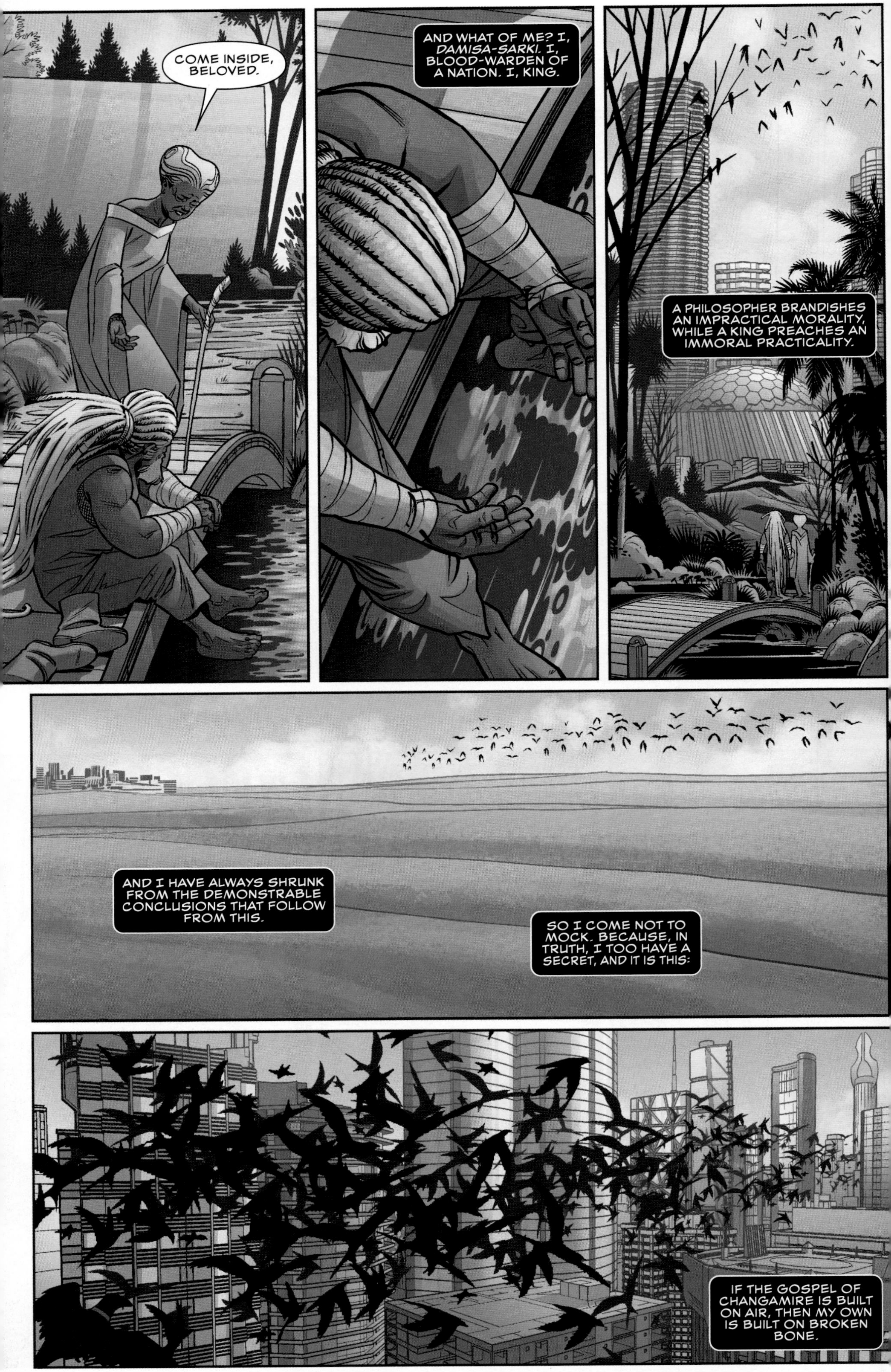
COME INSIDE, BELOVED.
AND WHAT OF ME? I, *DAMISA-SARKI*. I, BLOOD-WARDEN OF A NATION. I, KING.
A PHILOSOPHER BRANDISHES AN IMPRACTICAL MORALITY, WHILE A KING PREACHES AN IMMORAL PRACTICALITY.
AND I HAVE ALWAYS SHRUNK FROM THE DEMONSTRABLE CONCLUSIONS THAT FOLLOW FROM THIS.
SO I COME NOT TO MOCK. BECAUSE, IN TRUTH, I TOO HAVE A SECRET, AND IT IS THIS:
IF THE GOSPEL OF CHANGAMIRE IS BUILT ON AIR, THEN MY OWN IS BUILT ON BROKEN BONE.

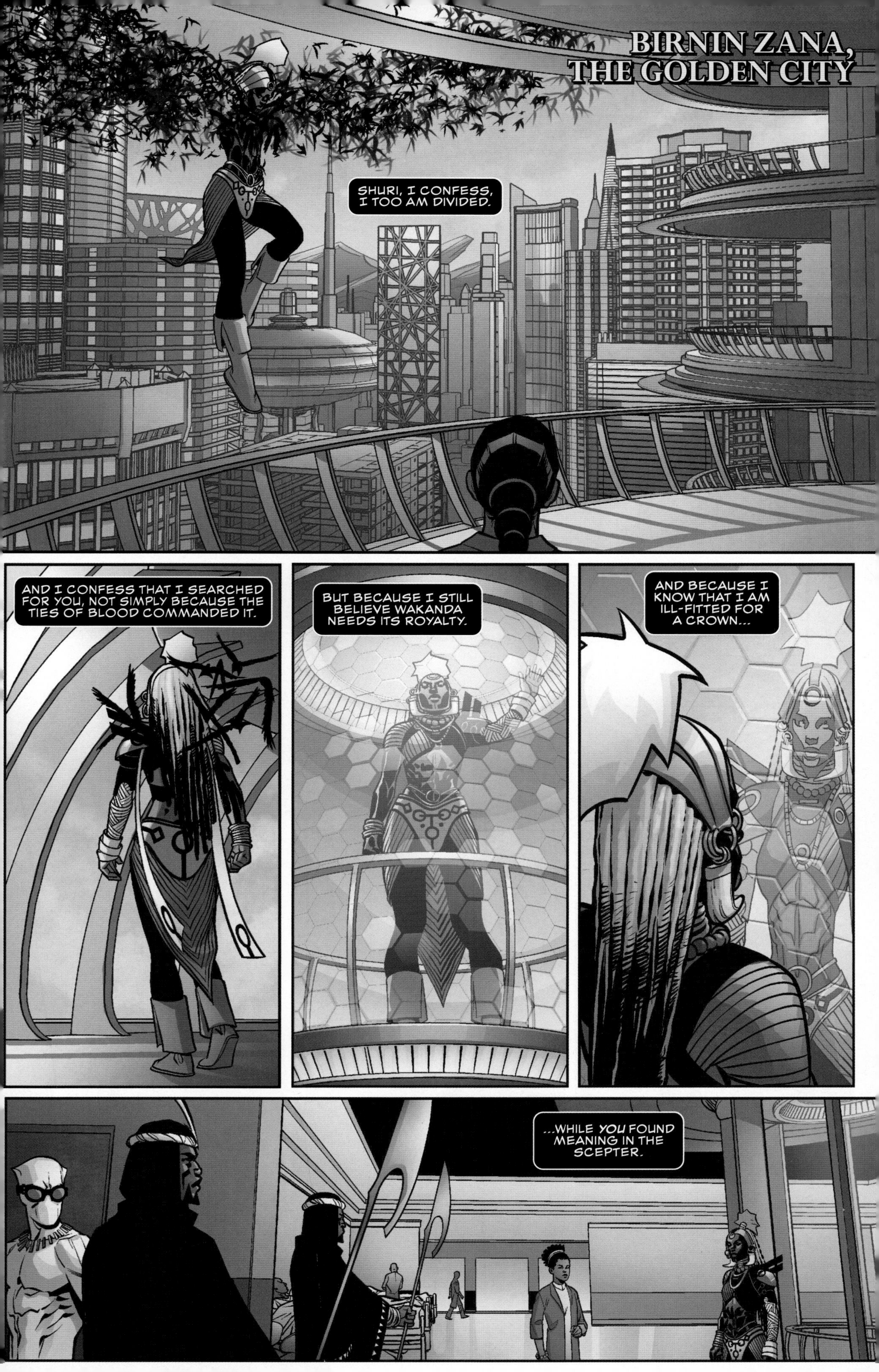
BIRNIN ZANA, THE GOLDEN CITY
SHURI, I CONFESS, I TOO AM DIVIDED.
AND I CONFESS THAT I SEARCHED FOR YOU, NOT SIMPLY BECAUSE THE TIES OF BLOOD COMMANDED IT.
BUT BECAUSE I STILL BELIEVE WAKANDA NEEDS ITS ROYALTY.
AND BECAUSE I KNOW THAT I AM ILL-FITTED FOR A CROWN...
...WHILE *YOU* FOUND MEANING IN THE SCEPTER.

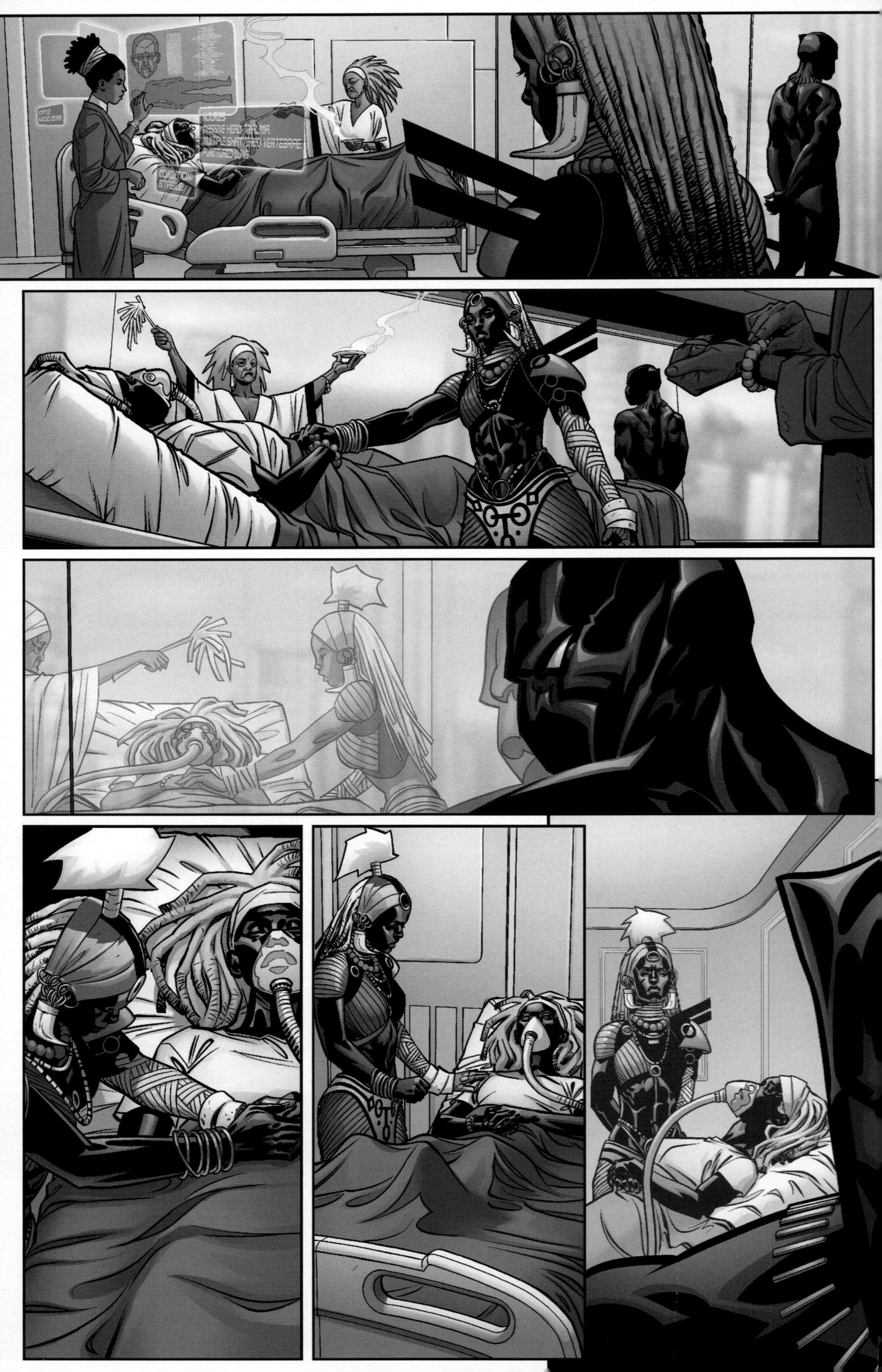
INJURIES
MASSIVE HEAD TRAUMA.
MULTIPLE SHATTERED VERTEBRAE.
PUNCTURED LUNG.
CONDITION:
STABLE.

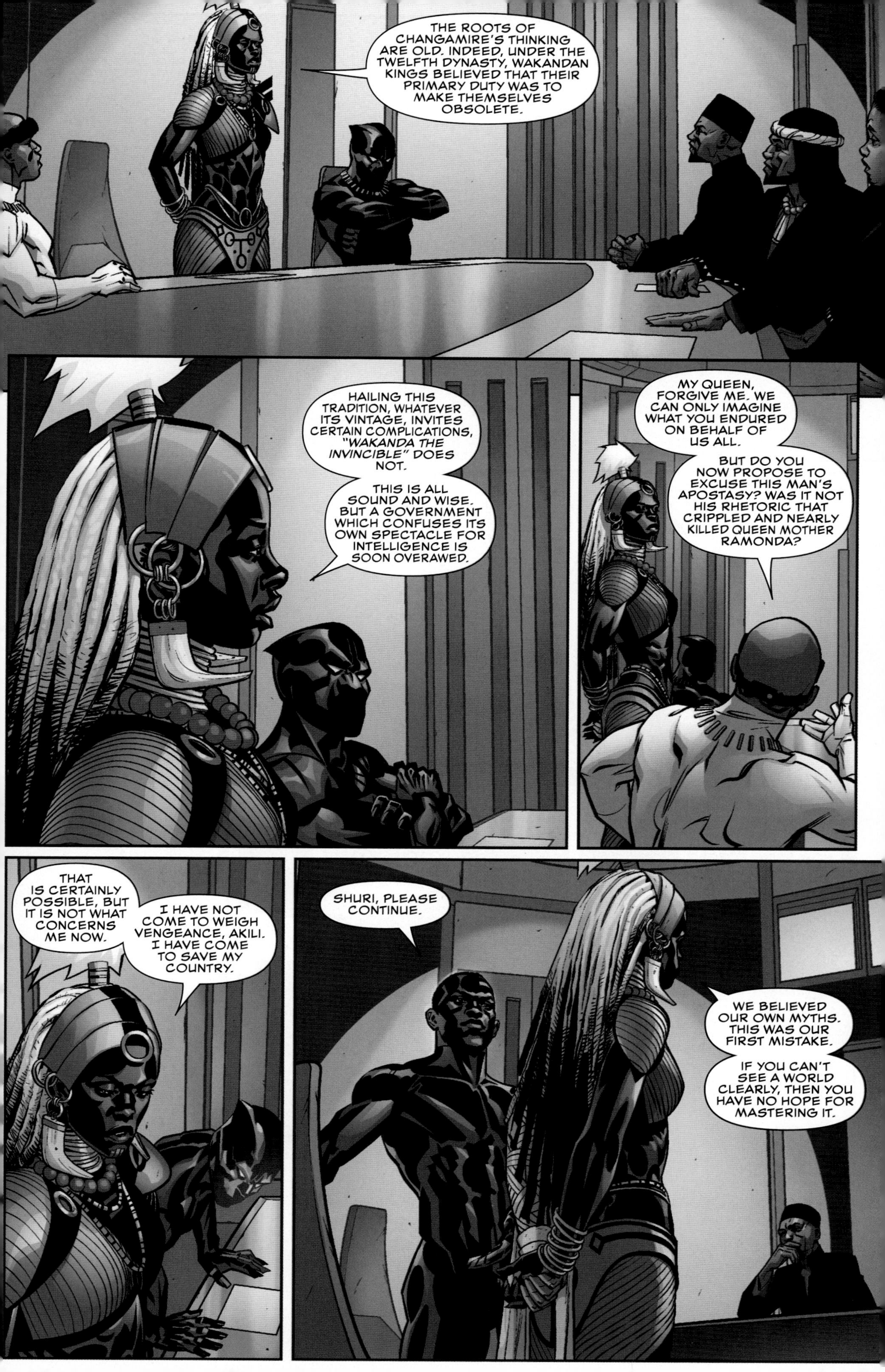
THE ROOTS OF CHANGAMIRE'S THINKING ARE OLD. INDEED, UNDER THE TWELFTH DYNASTY, WAKANDAN KINGS BELIEVED THAT THEIR PRIMARY DUTY WAS TO MAKE THEMSELVES OBSOLETE.
HAILING THIS TRADITION, WHATEVER ITS VINTAGE, INVITES CERTAIN COMPLICATIONS, "WAKANDA THE INVINCIBLE" DOES NOT.
THIS IS ALL SOUND AND WISE. BUT A GOVERNMENT WHICH CONFUSES ITS OWN SPECTACLE FOR INTELLIGENCE IS SOON OVERAWED.
MY QUEEN, FORGIVE ME. WE CAN ONLY IMAGINE WHAT YOU ENDURED ON BEHALF OF US ALL.
BUT DO YOU NOW PROPOSE TO EXCUSE THIS MAN'S APOSTASY? WAS IT NOT HIS RHETORIC THAT CRIPPLED AND NEARLY KILLED QUEEN MOTHER RAMONDA?
THAT IS CERTAINLY POSSIBLE, BUT IT IS NOT WHAT CONCERNS ME NOW.
I HAVE NOT COME TO WEIGH VENGEANCE, AKILI. I HAVE COME TO SAVE MY COUNTRY.
SHURI, PLEASE CONTINUE.
WE BELIEVED OUR OWN MYTHS. THIS WAS OUR FIRST MISTAKE.
IF YOU CAN'T SEE A WORLD CLEARLY, THEN YOU HAVE NO HOPE FOR MASTERING IT.

SEEN CLEARLY, CHANGAMIRE IS NO APOSTATE. INDEED, HE IS THE BEARER OF A TRADITION AS OLD, AND AS WAKANDAN, AS OUR OWN.

WHAT GOOD IS THIS, MY QUEEN? WE ARE AT WAR! A REGIMENT OF *HATUT ZERAZE* ARE IMPRISONED IN THE NORTH. TETU AMASSES FORCES TO THE SOUTH. HOW CAN WE SIT HERE IN CONFERENCE WITH OUR NATION, OUR HONOR, ON THE BRINK?

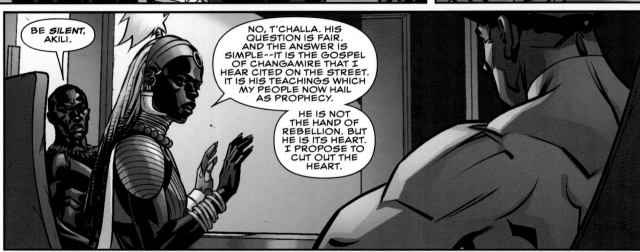

BE *SILENT*, AKILI.

NO, T'CHALLA. HIS QUESTION IS FAIR. AND THE ANSWER IS SIMPLE--IT IS THE GOSPEL OF CHANGAMIRE THAT I HEAR CITED ON THE STREET. IT IS HIS TEACHINGS WHICH MY PEOPLE NOW HAIL AS PROPHECY.

HE IS NOT THE HAND OF REBELLION. BUT HE IS ITS HEART. I PROPOSE TO CUT OUT THE HEART.

THIS WILL NOT BE HARD. CHANGAMIRE IS NOW BEING FORCED TO ACKNOWLEDGE THAT WHICH ALWAYS FOLLOWS REVOLUTION.

HE TOO BELIEVED HIS OWN MYTHS. AND NOW ALL HIS PHILOSOPHY IS CRACKING UNDER THE WEIGHT OF REALITY.

CHANGAMIRE IS NOT REBELLING. HE IS *MOURNING*.

I UNDERSTAND. BUT HOW THEN DO YOU SUGGEST WE HANDLE THIS MOURNER?

IN THE SAME WAY YOU WOULD HANDLE ANY OTHER MAN IN MOURNING...

...BY CONSOLING HIM, OF COURSE.

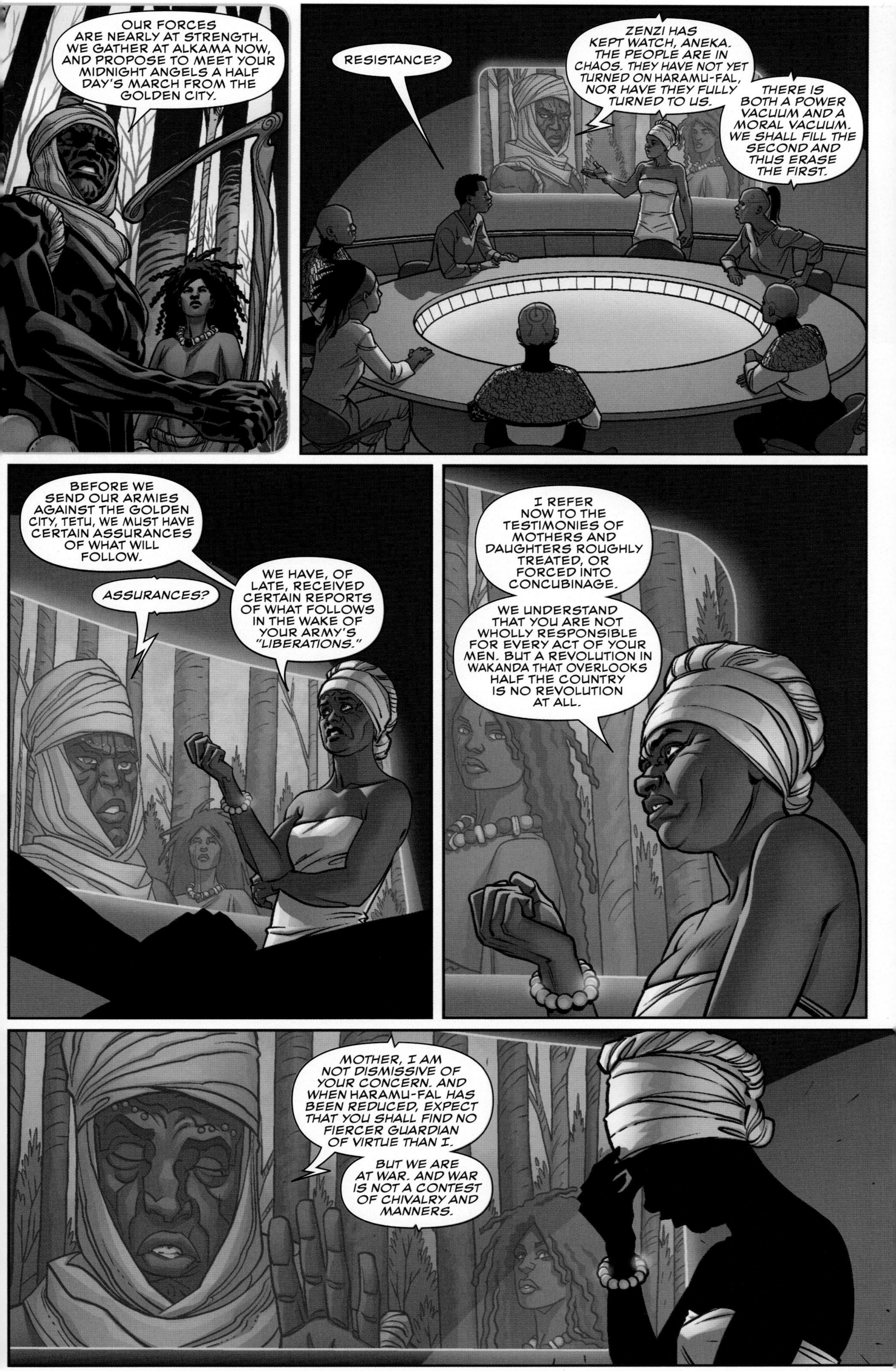
OUR FORCES ARE NEARLY AT STRENGTH. WE GATHER AT ALKAMA NOW, AND PROPOSE TO MEET YOUR MIDNIGHT ANGELS A HALF DAY'S MARCH FROM THE GOLDEN CITY.
RESISTANCE?
ZENZI HAS KEPT WATCH, ANEKA. THE PEOPLE ARE IN CHAOS. THEY HAVE NOT YET TURNED ON HARAMU-FAL, NOR HAVE THEY FULLY TURNED TO US.
THERE IS BOTH A POWER VACUUM AND A MORAL VACUUM. WE SHALL FILL THE SECOND AND THUS ERASE THE FIRST.
BEFORE WE SEND OUR ARMIES AGAINST THE GOLDEN CITY, TETU, WE MUST HAVE CERTAIN ASSURANCES OF WHAT WILL FOLLOW.
ASSURANCES?
WE HAVE, OF LATE, RECEIVED CERTAIN REPORTS OF WHAT FOLLOWS IN THE WAKE OF YOUR ARMY'S "LIBERATIONS."
I REFER NOW TO THE TESTIMONIES OF MOTHERS AND DAUGHTERS ROUGHLY TREATED, OR FORCED INTO CONCUBINAGE.
WE UNDERSTAND THAT YOU ARE NOT WHOLLY RESPONSIBLE FOR EVERY ACT OF YOUR MEN. BUT A REVOLUTION IN WAKANDA THAT OVERLOOKS HALF THE COUNTRY IS NO REVOLUTION AT ALL.
MOTHER, I AM NOT DISMISSIVE OF YOUR CONCERN. AND WHEN HARAMU-FAL HAS BEEN REDUCED, EXPECT THAT YOU SHALL FIND NO FIERCER GUARDIAN OF VIRTUE THAN I.
BUT WE ARE AT WAR. AND WAR IS NOT A CONTEST OF CHIVALRY AND MANNERS.

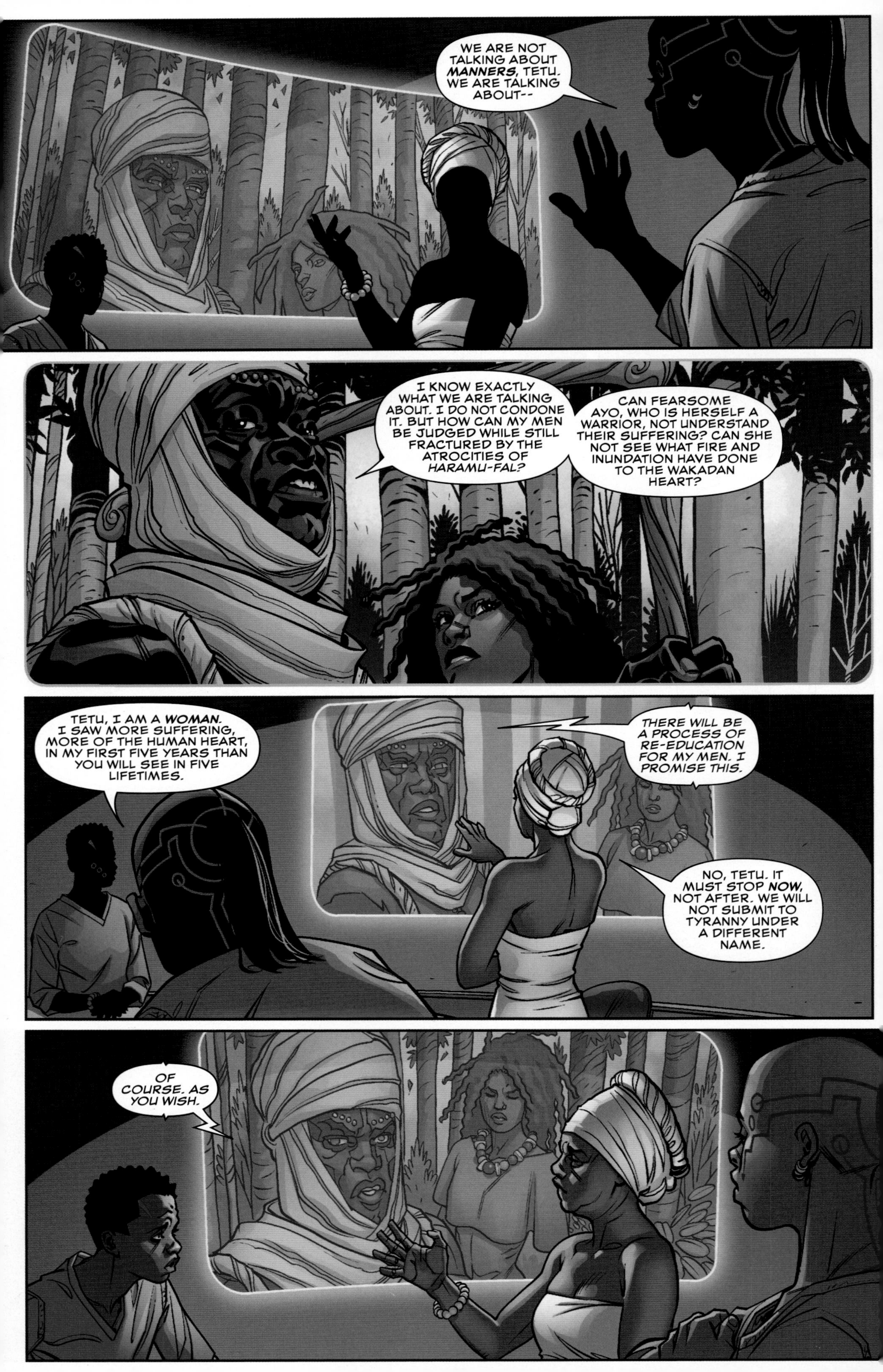
WE ARE NOT TALKING ABOUT MANNERS, TETU. WE ARE TALKING ABOUT--
I KNOW EXACTLY WHAT WE ARE TALKING ABOUT. I DO NOT CONDONE IT. BUT HOW CAN MY MEN BE JUDGED WHILE STILL FRACTURED BY THE ATROCITIES OF HARAMU-FAL?
CAN FEARSOME AYO, WHO IS HERSELF A WARRIOR, NOT UNDERSTAND THEIR SUFFERING? CAN SHE NOT SEE WHAT FIRE AND INUNDATION HAVE DONE TO THE WAKADAN HEART?
TETU, I AM A WOMAN. I SAW MORE SUFFERING, MORE OF THE HUMAN HEART, IN MY FIRST FIVE YEARS THAN YOU WILL SEE IN FIVE LIFETIMES.
THERE WILL BE A PROCESS OF RE-EDUCATION FOR MY MEN. I PROMISE THIS.
NO, TETU. IT MUST STOP NOW, NOT AFTER. WE WILL NOT SUBMIT TO TYRANNY UNDER A DIFFERENT NAME.
OF COURSE. AS YOU WISH.

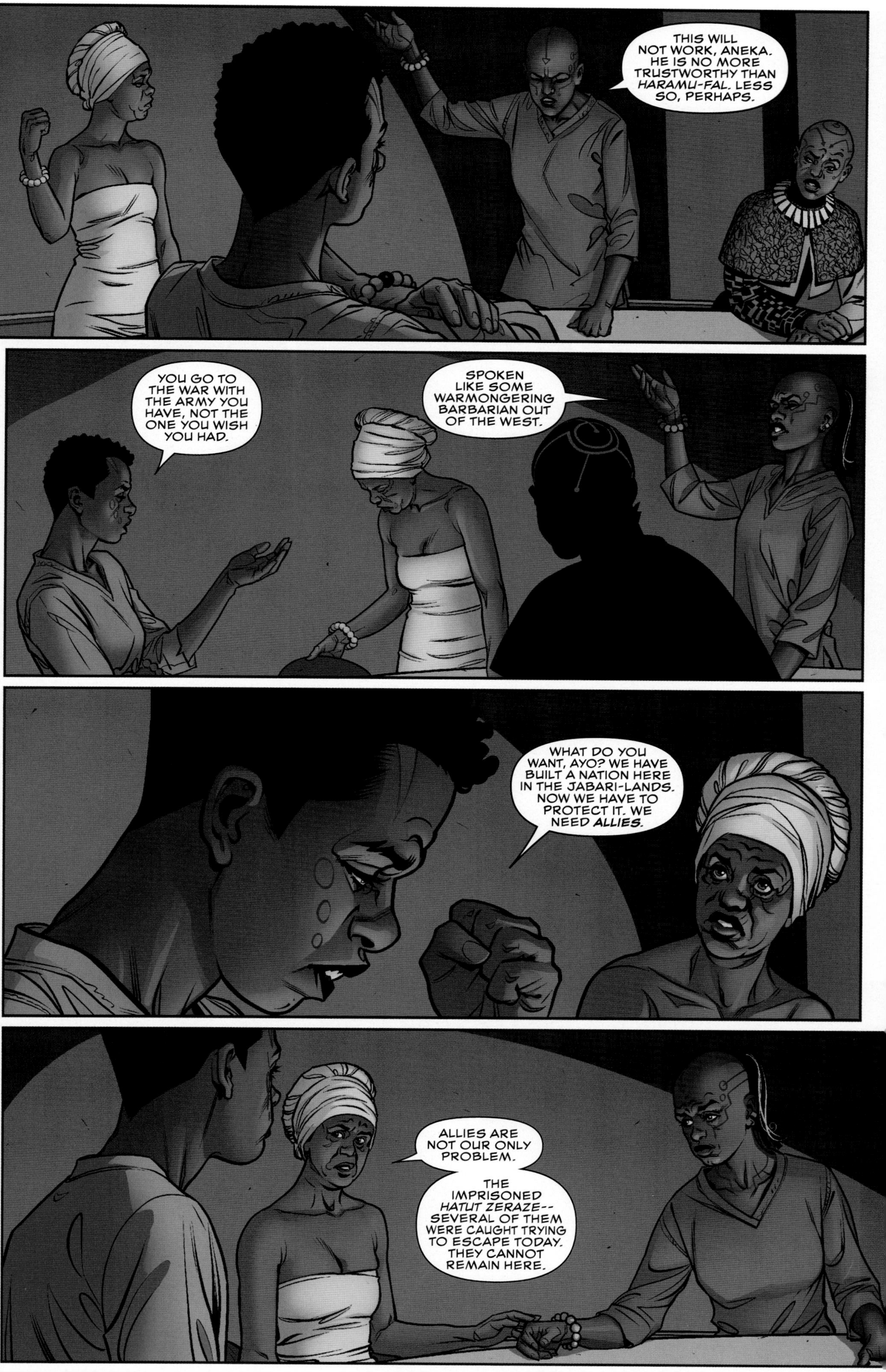
THIS WILL NOT WORK, ANEKA. HE IS NO MORE TRUSTWORTHY THAN *HARAMU-FAL*. LESS SO, PERHAPS.
YOU GO TO THE WAR WITH THE ARMY YOU HAVE, NOT THE ONE YOU WISH YOU HAD.
SPOKEN LIKE SOME WARMONGERING BARBARIAN OUT OF THE WEST.
WHAT DO YOU WANT, AYO? WE HAVE BUILT A NATION HERE IN THE JABARI-LANDS. NOW WE HAVE TO PROTECT IT. WE NEED ***ALLIES***.
ALLIES ARE NOT OUR ONLY PROBLEM.
THE IMPRISONED *HATUT ZERAZE*--SEVERAL OF THEM WERE CAUGHT TRYING TO ESCAPE TODAY. THEY CANNOT REMAIN HERE.

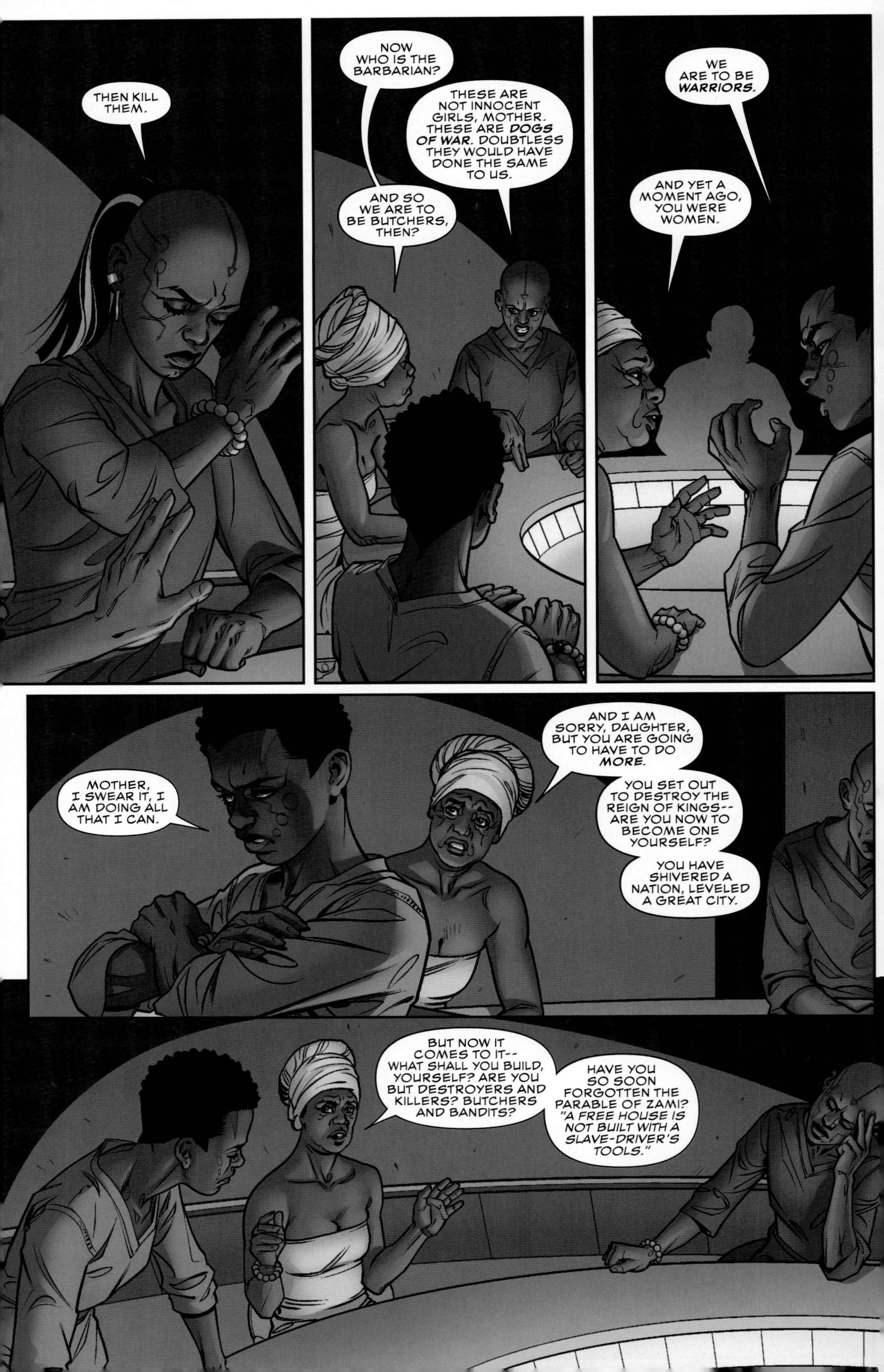
THEN KILL THEM.
NOW WHO IS THE BARBARIAN?
THESE ARE NOT INNOCENT GIRLS, MOTHER. THESE ARE DOGS OF WAR. DOUBTLESS THEY WOULD HAVE DONE THE SAME TO US.
AND SO WE ARE TO BE BUTCHERS, THEN?
WE ARE TO BE WARRIORS.
AND YET A MOMENT AGO, YOU WERE WOMEN.
MOTHER, I SWEAR IT, I AM DOING ALL THAT I CAN.
AND I AM SORRY, DAUGHTER, BUT YOU ARE GOING TO HAVE TO DO MORE.
YOU SET OUT TO DESTROY THE REIGN OF KINGS-- ARE YOU NOW TO BECOME ONE YOURSELF?
YOU HAVE SHIVERED A NATION, LEVELED A GREAT CITY.
BUT NOW IT COMES TO IT-- WHAT SHALL YOU BUILD, YOURSELF? ARE YOU BUT DESTROYERS AND KILLERS? BUTCHERS AND BANDITS?
HAVE YOU SO SOON FORGOTTEN THE PARABLE OF ZAMI? "A FREE HOUSE IS NOT BUILT WITH A SLAVE-DRIVER'S TOOLS."

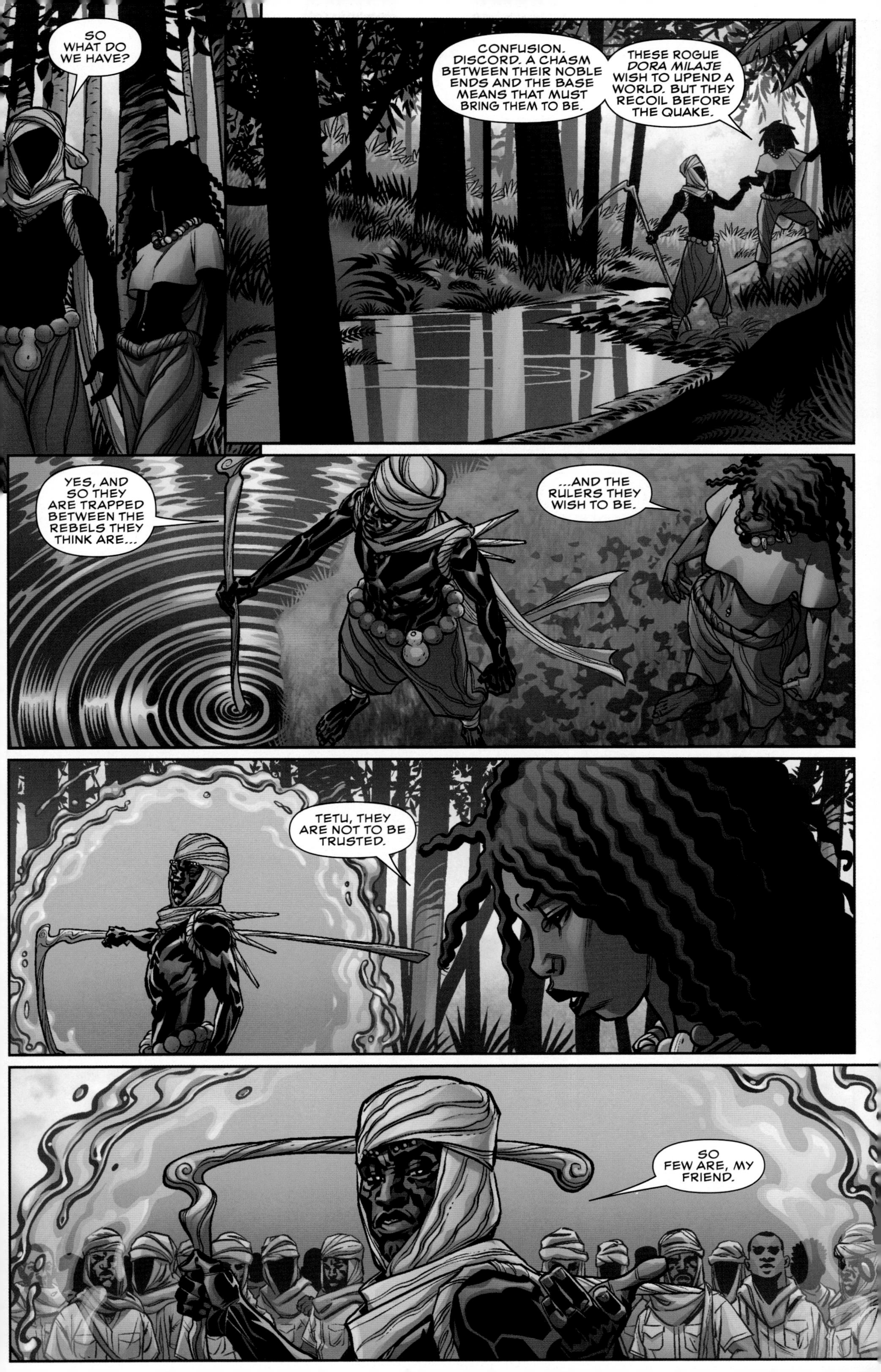
SO WHAT DO WE HAVE?
CONFUSION. DISCORD. A CHASM BETWEEN THEIR NOBLE ENDS AND THE BASE MEANS THAT MUST BRING THEM TO BE.
THESE ROGUE *DORA MILAJE* WISH TO UPEND A WORLD. BUT THEY RECOIL BEFORE THE QUAKE.
YES, AND SO THEY ARE TRAPPED BETWEEN THE REBELS THEY THINK ARE...
...AND THE RULERS THEY WISH TO BE.
TETU, THEY ARE NOT TO BE TRUSTED.
SO FEW ARE, MY FRIEND.

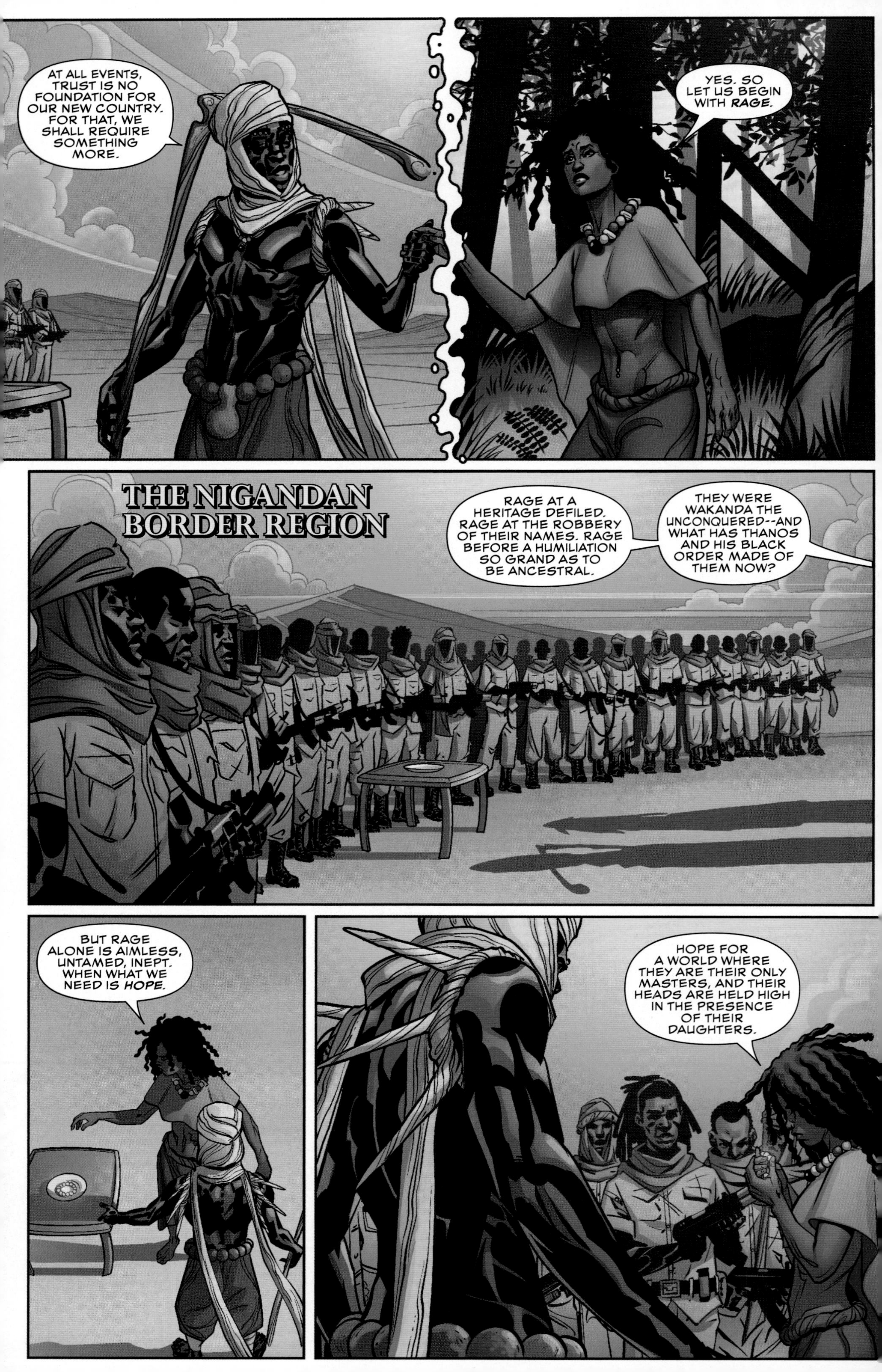
AT ALL EVENTS, TRUST IS NO FOUNDATION FOR OUR NEW COUNTRY. FOR THAT, WE SHALL REQUIRE SOMETHING MORE.
YES. SO LET US BEGIN WITH RAGE.
THE NIGANDAN BORDER REGION
RAGE AT A HERITAGE DEFILED. RAGE AT THE ROBBERY OF THEIR NAMES. RAGE BEFORE A HUMILIATION SO GRAND AS TO BE ANCESTRAL.
THEY WERE WAKANDA THE UNCONQUERED--AND WHAT HAS THANOS AND HIS BLACK ORDER MADE OF THEM NOW?
BUT RAGE ALONE IS AIMLESS, UNTAMED, INEPT. WHEN WHAT WE NEED IS HOPE.
HOPE FOR A WORLD WHERE THEY ARE THEIR ONLY MASTERS, AND THEIR HEADS ARE HELD HIGH IN THE PRESENCE OF THEIR DAUGHTERS.

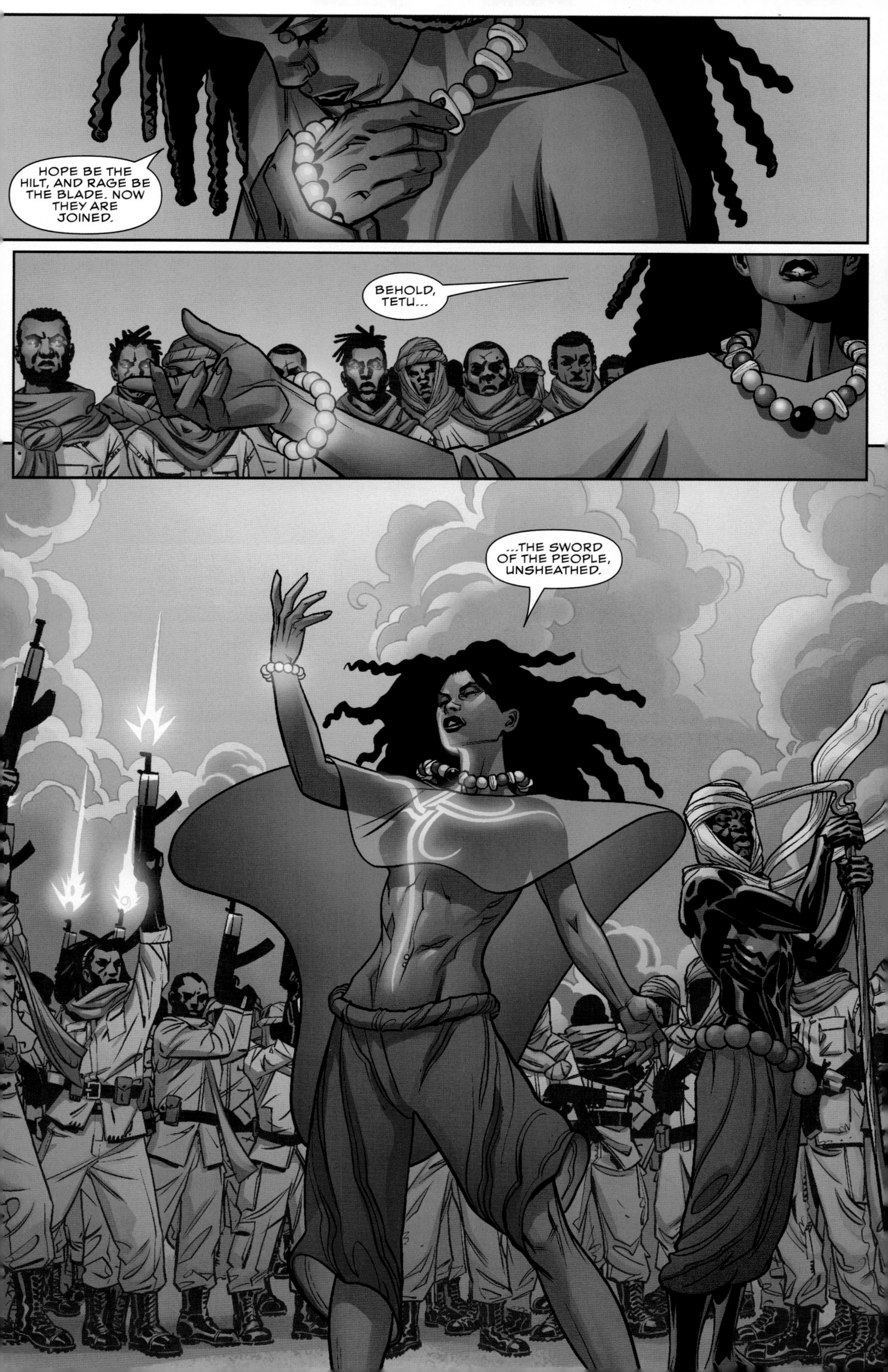
HOPE BE THE HILT, AND RAGE BE THE BLADE. NOW THEY ARE JOINED.
BEHOLD, TETU...
...THE SWORD OF THE PEOPLE, UNSHEATHED.

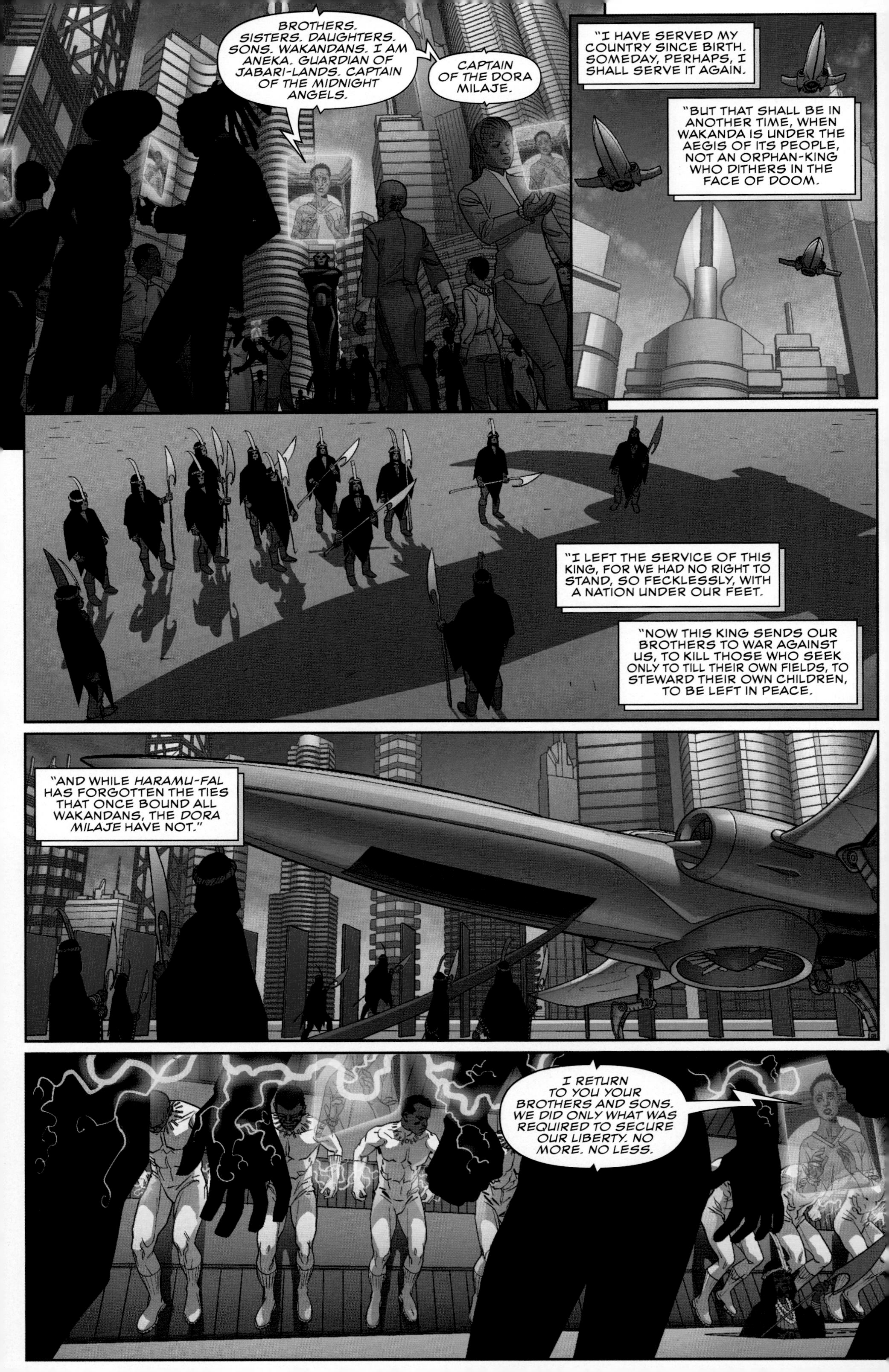

BROTHERS. SISTERS. DAUGHTERS. SONS. WAKANDANS. I AM ANEKA. GUARDIAN OF JABARI-LANDS. CAPTAIN OF THE MIDNIGHT ANGELS.
CAPTAIN OF THE DORA MILAJE.
"I HAVE SERVED MY COUNTRY SINCE BIRTH. SOMEDAY, PERHAPS, I SHALL SERVE IT AGAIN.
"BUT THAT SHALL BE IN ANOTHER TIME, WHEN WAKANDA IS UNDER THE AEGIS OF ITS PEOPLE, NOT AN ORPHAN-KING WHO DITHERS IN THE FACE OF DOOM.
"I LEFT THE SERVICE OF THIS KING, FOR WE HAD NO RIGHT TO STAND, SO FECKLESSLY, WITH A NATION UNDER OUR FEET.
"NOW THIS KING SENDS OUR BROTHERS TO WAR AGAINST US, TO KILL THOSE WHO SEEK ONLY TO TILL THEIR OWN FIELDS, TO STEWARD THEIR OWN CHILDREN, TO BE LEFT IN PEACE.
"AND WHILE *HARAMU-FAL* HAS FORGOTTEN THE TIES THAT ONCE BOUND ALL WAKANDANS, THE *DORA MILAJE* HAVE NOT."
I RETURN TO YOU YOUR BROTHERS AND SONS. WE DID ONLY WHAT WAS REQUIRED TO SECURE OUR LIBERTY. NO MORE. NO LESS.

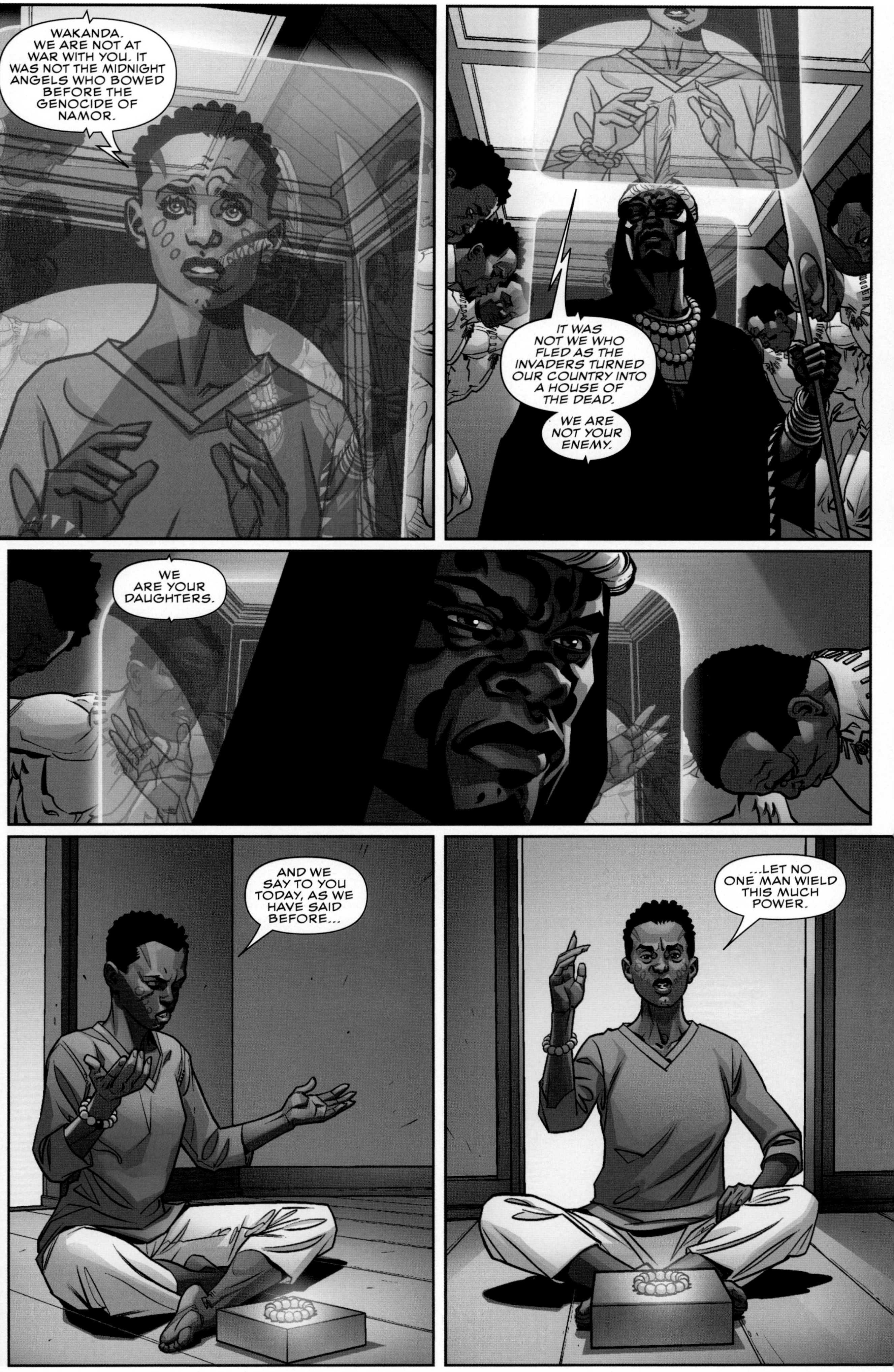
WAKANDA. WE ARE NOT AT WAR WITH YOU. IT WAS NOT THE MIDNIGHT ANGELS WHO BOWED BEFORE THE GENOCIDE OF NAMOR.
IT WAS NOT WE WHO FLED AS THE INVADERS TURNED OUR COUNTRY INTO A HOUSE OF THE DEAD.
WE ARE NOT YOUR ENEMY.
WE ARE YOUR DAUGHTERS.
AND WE SAY TO YOU TODAY, AS WE HAVE SAID BEFORE...
...LET NO ONE MAN WIELD THIS MUCH POWER.

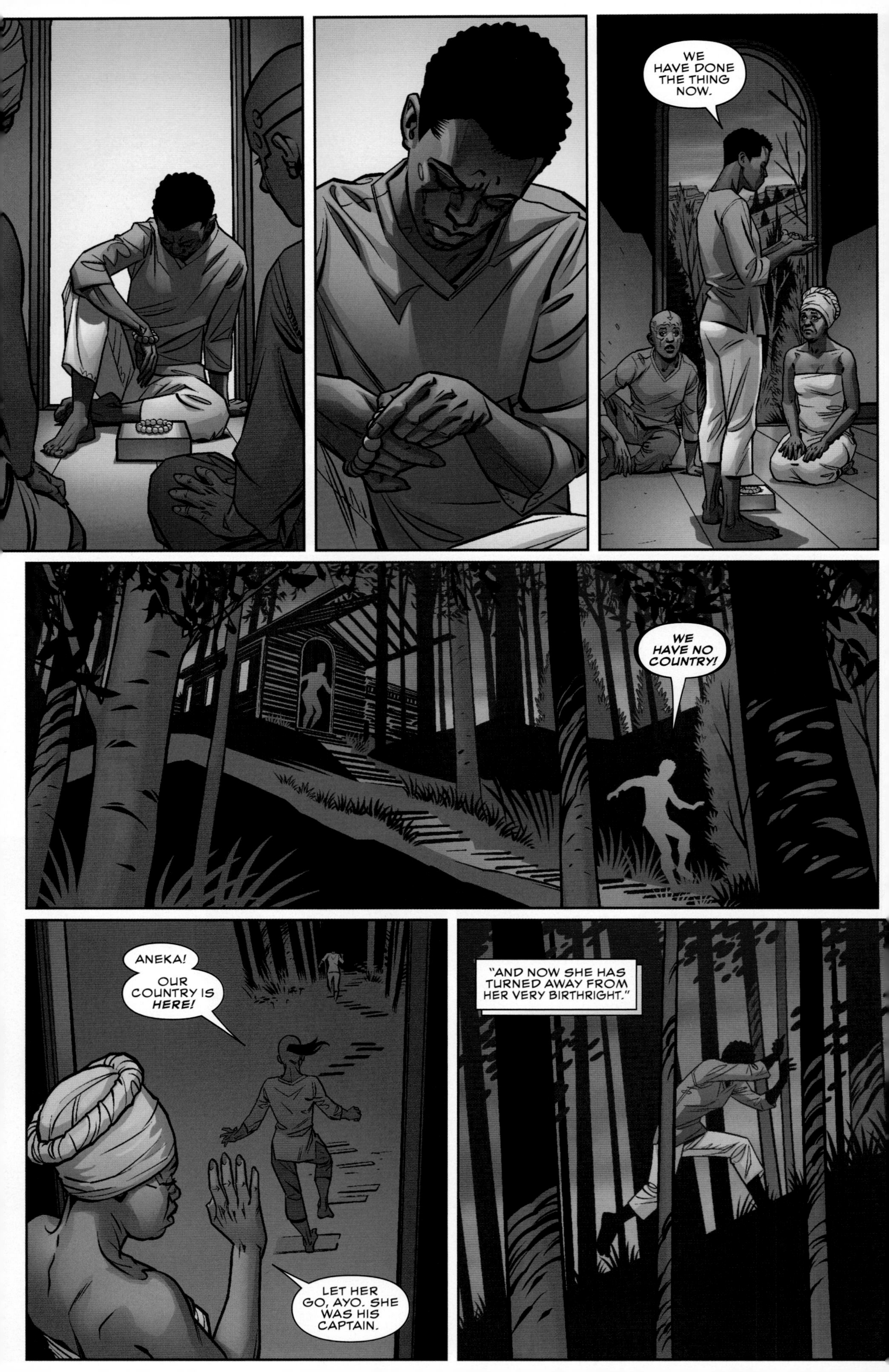
WE HAVE DONE THE THING NOW.
WE HAVE NO COUNTRY!
ANEKA!
OUR COUNTRY IS *HERE!*
"AND NOW SHE HAS TURNED AWAY FROM HER VERY BIRTHRIGHT."
LET HER GO, AYO. SHE WAS HIS CAPTAIN.

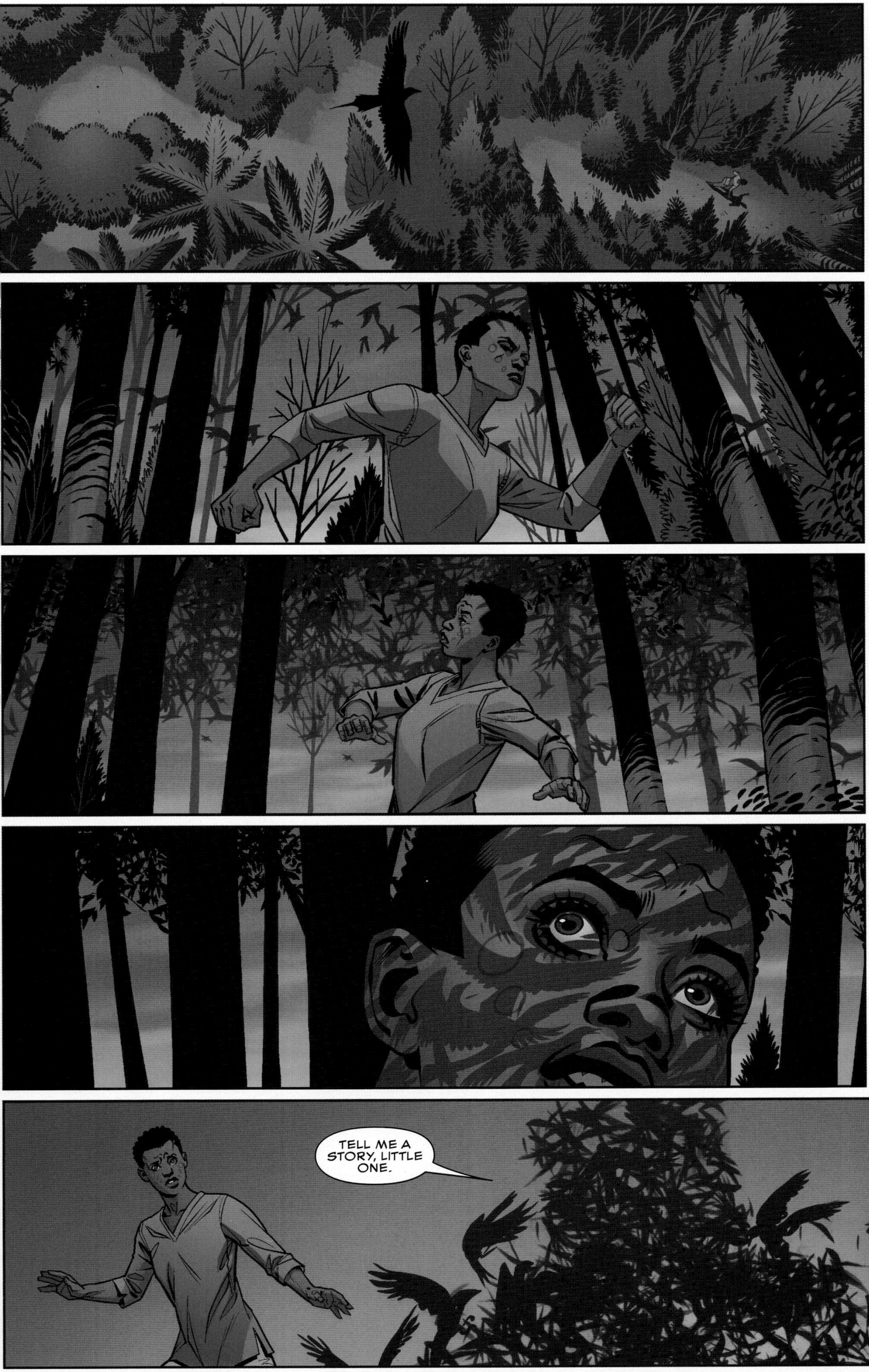
TELL ME A STORY, LITTLE ONE.

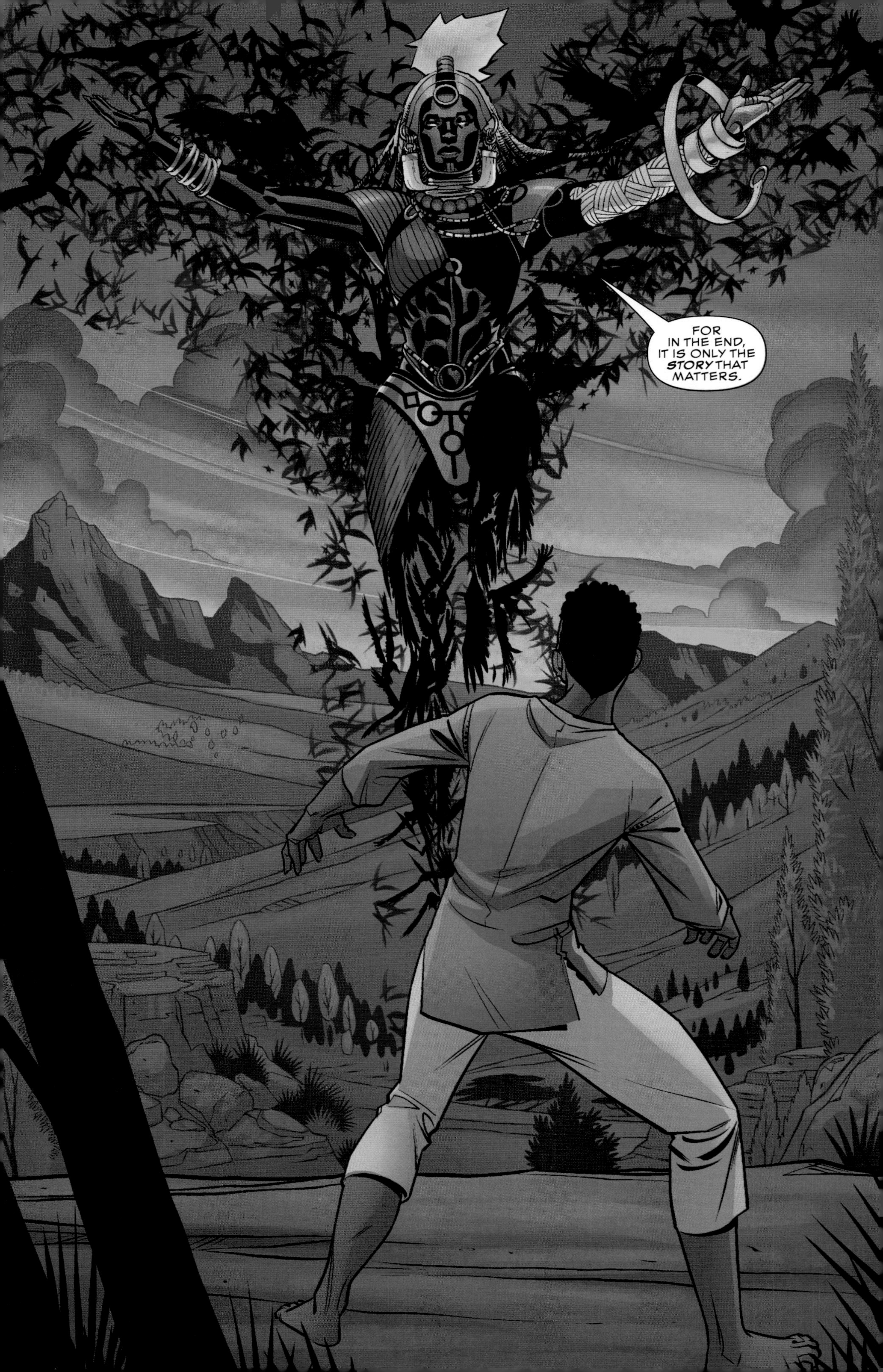
FOR IN THE END, IT IS ONLY THE STORY THAT MATTERS.

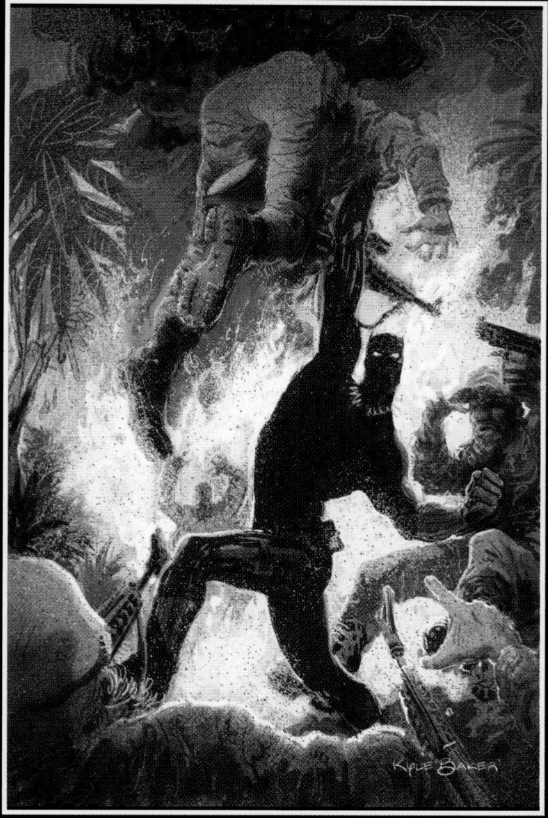
KYLE BAKER

#3 VARIANT BY **KYLE BAKER**

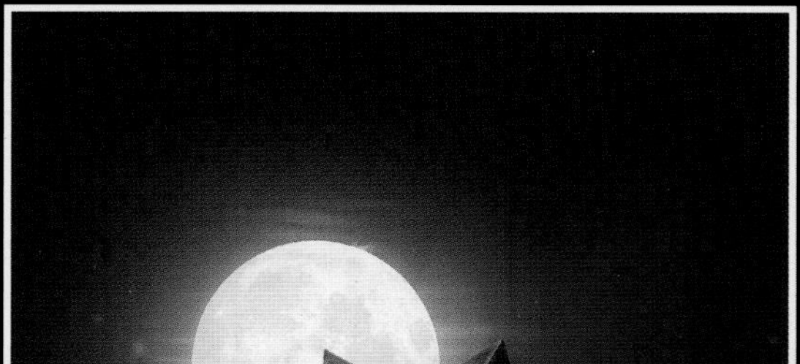

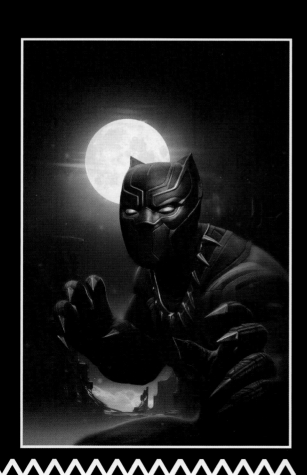

#5 CONTEST OF CHAMPIONS GAME VARIANT
BY **KABAM** WITH **GABRIEL FRIZZERA**

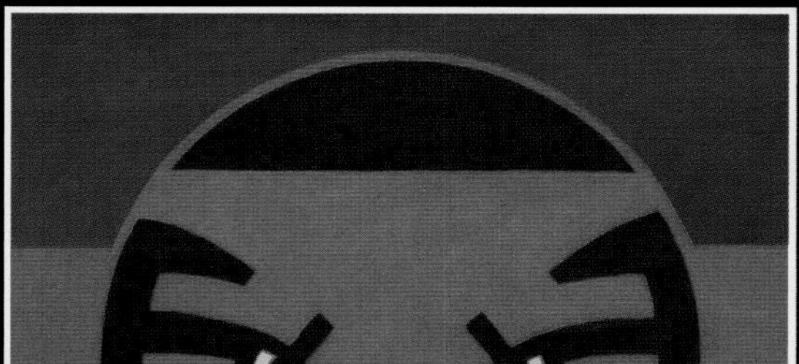
GREG HILDEBRANDT

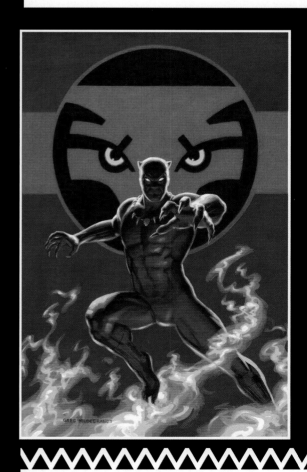

#5 CLASSIC VARIANT
BY **GREG HILDEBRANDT**

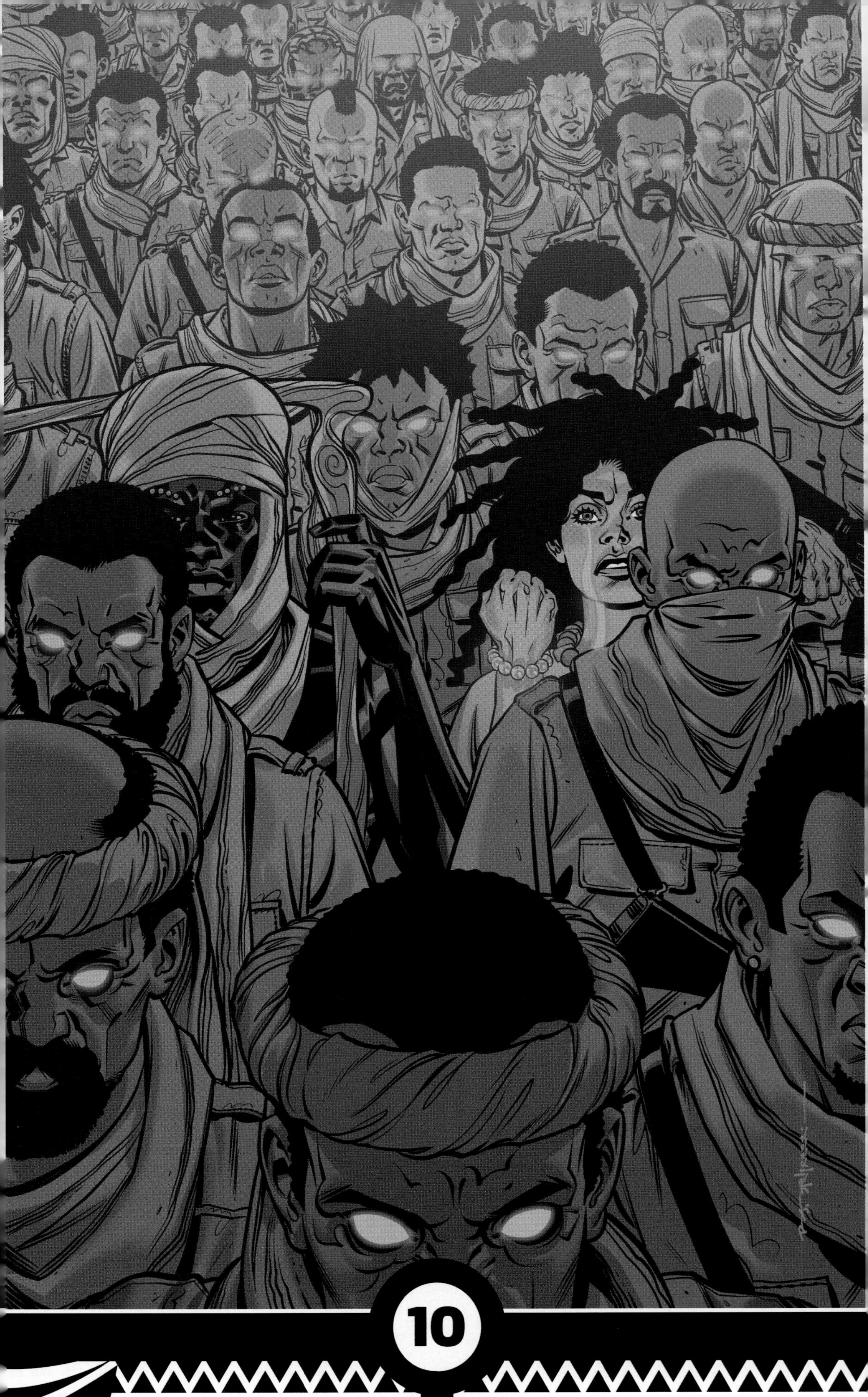

10

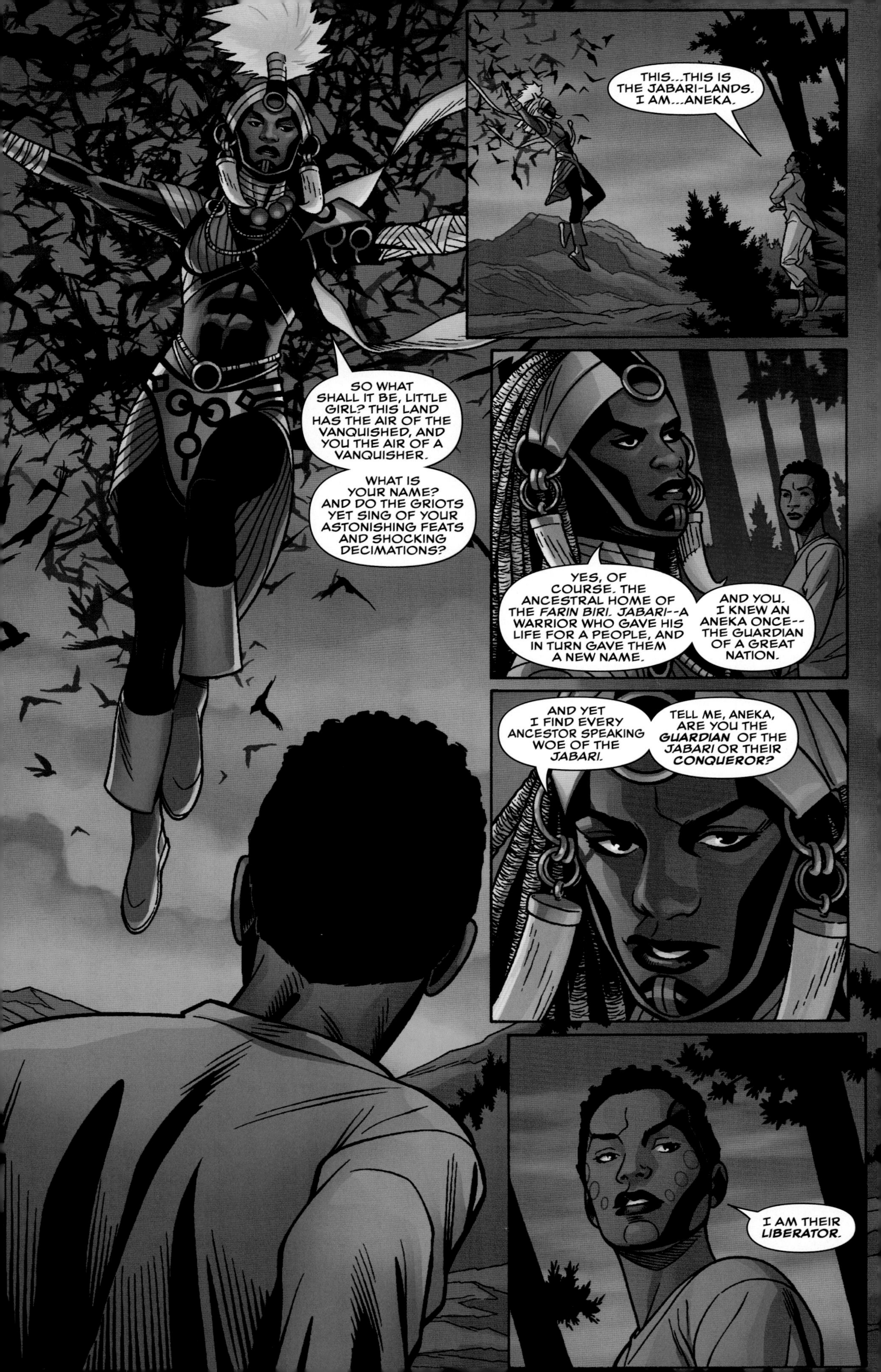
THIS...THIS IS THE JABARI-LANDS. I AM...ANEKA.
SO WHAT SHALL IT BE, LITTLE GIRL? THIS LAND HAS THE AIR OF THE VANQUISHED, AND YOU THE AIR OF A VANQUISHER.
WHAT IS YOUR NAME? AND DO THE GRIOTS YET SING OF YOUR ASTONISHING FEATS AND SHOCKING DECIMATIONS?
YES, OF COURSE. THE ANCESTRAL HOME OF THE FARIN BIRI. JABARI--A WARRIOR WHO GAVE HIS LIFE FOR A PEOPLE, AND IN TURN GAVE THEM A NEW NAME.
AND YOU. I KNEW AN ANEKA ONCE-- THE GUARDIAN OF A GREAT NATION.
AND YET I FIND EVERY ANCESTOR SPEAKING WOE OF THE JABARI.
TELL ME, ANEKA, ARE YOU THE GUARDIAN OF THE JABARI OR THEIR CONQUEROR?
I AM THEIR LIBERATOR.

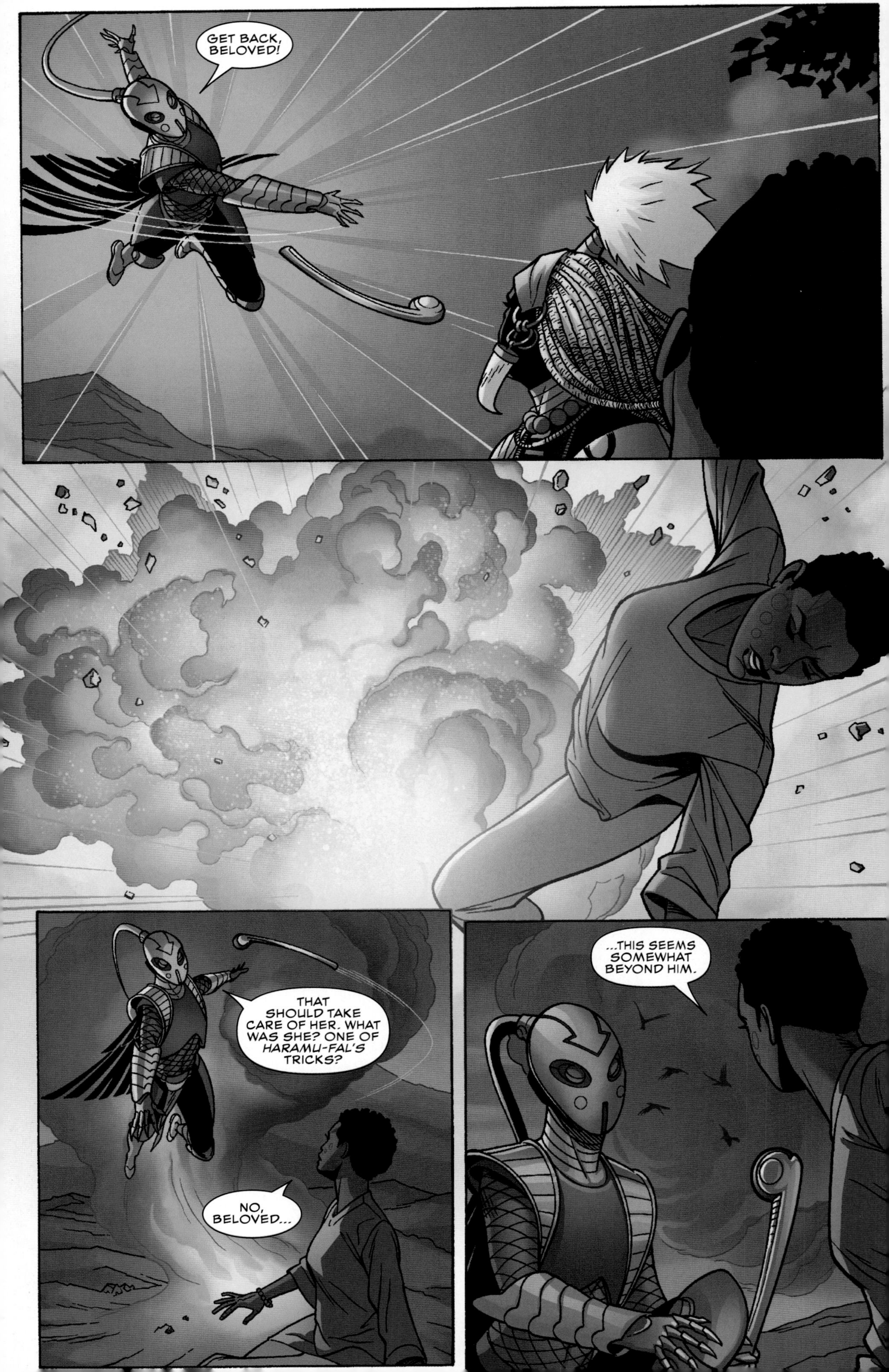
GET BACK, BELOVED!
THAT SHOULD TAKE CARE OF HER. WHAT WAS SHE? ONE OF HARAMU-FAL'S TRICKS?
NO, BELOVED...
...THIS SEEMS SOMEWHAT BEYOND HIM.

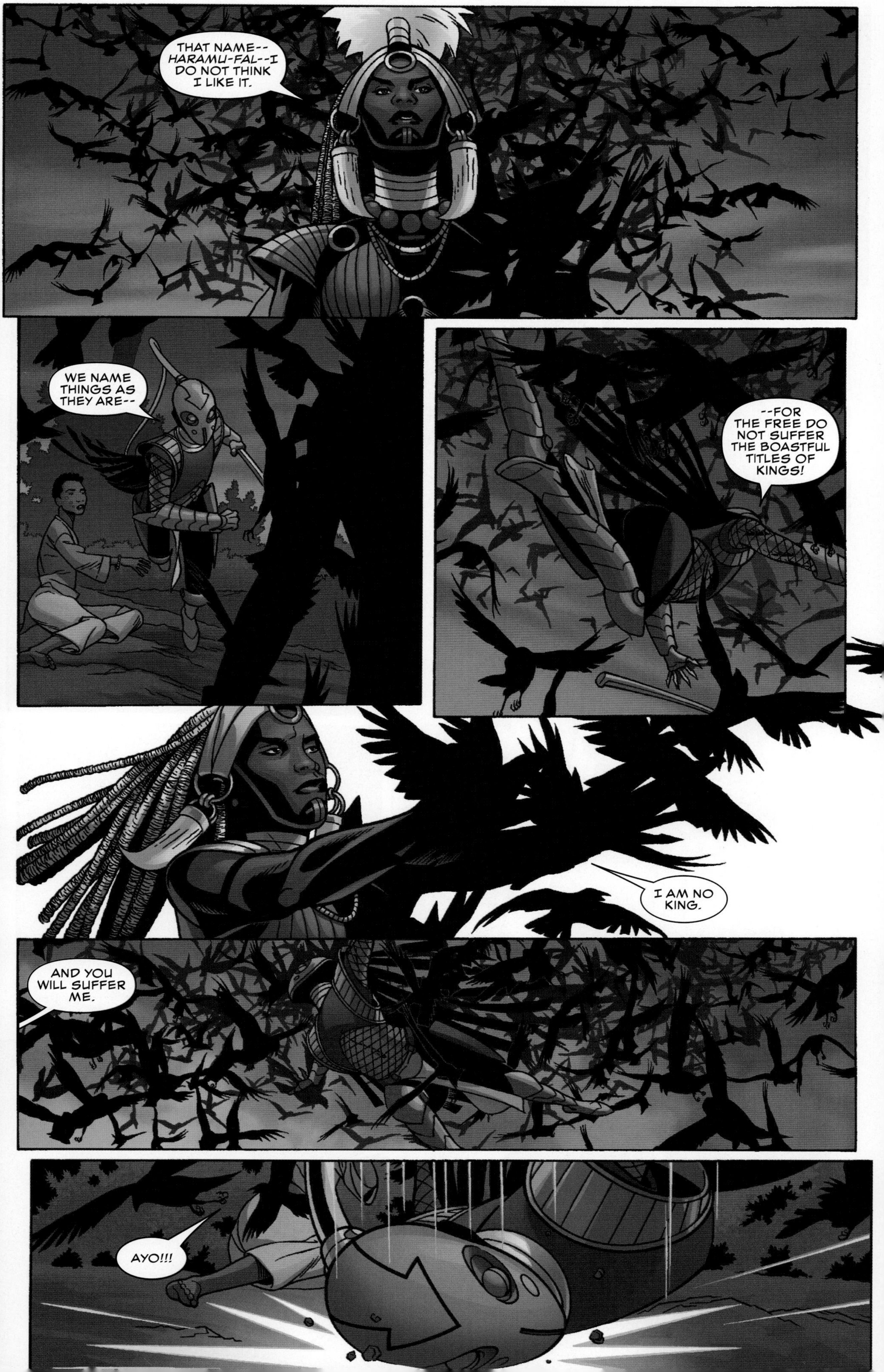
THAT NAME-- HARAMU-FAL--I DO NOT THINK I LIKE IT.
WE NAME THINGS AS THEY ARE--
--FOR THE FREE DO NOT SUFFER THE BOASTFUL TITLES OF KINGS!
I AM NO KING.
AND YOU WILL SUFFER ME.
AYO!!!

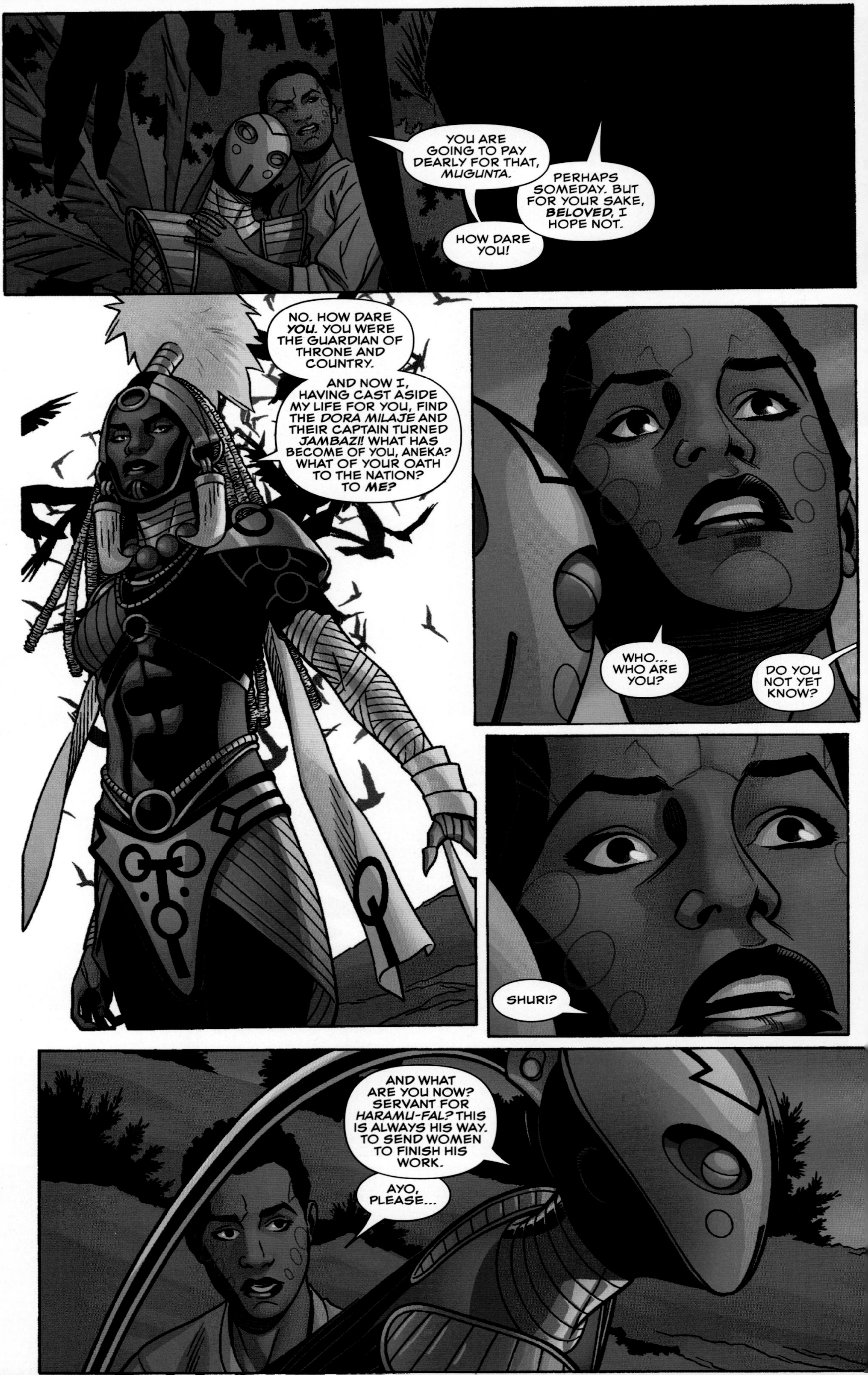
YOU ARE GOING TO PAY DEARLY FOR THAT, MUGUNTA.
PERHAPS SOMEDAY. BUT FOR YOUR SAKE, BELOVED, I HOPE NOT.
HOW DARE YOU!
NO. HOW DARE YOU. YOU WERE THE GUARDIAN OF THRONE AND COUNTRY.
AND NOW I, HAVING CAST ASIDE MY LIFE FOR YOU, FIND THE DORA MILAJE AND THEIR CAPTAIN TURNED JAMBAZI! WHAT HAS BECOME OF YOU, ANEKA? WHAT OF YOUR OATH TO THE NATION? TO ME?
WHO... WHO ARE YOU?
DO YOU NOT YET KNOW?
SHURI?
AND WHAT ARE YOU NOW? SERVANT FOR HARAMU-FAL? THIS IS ALWAYS HIS WAY. TO SEND WOMEN TO FINISH HIS WORK.
AYO, PLEASE...

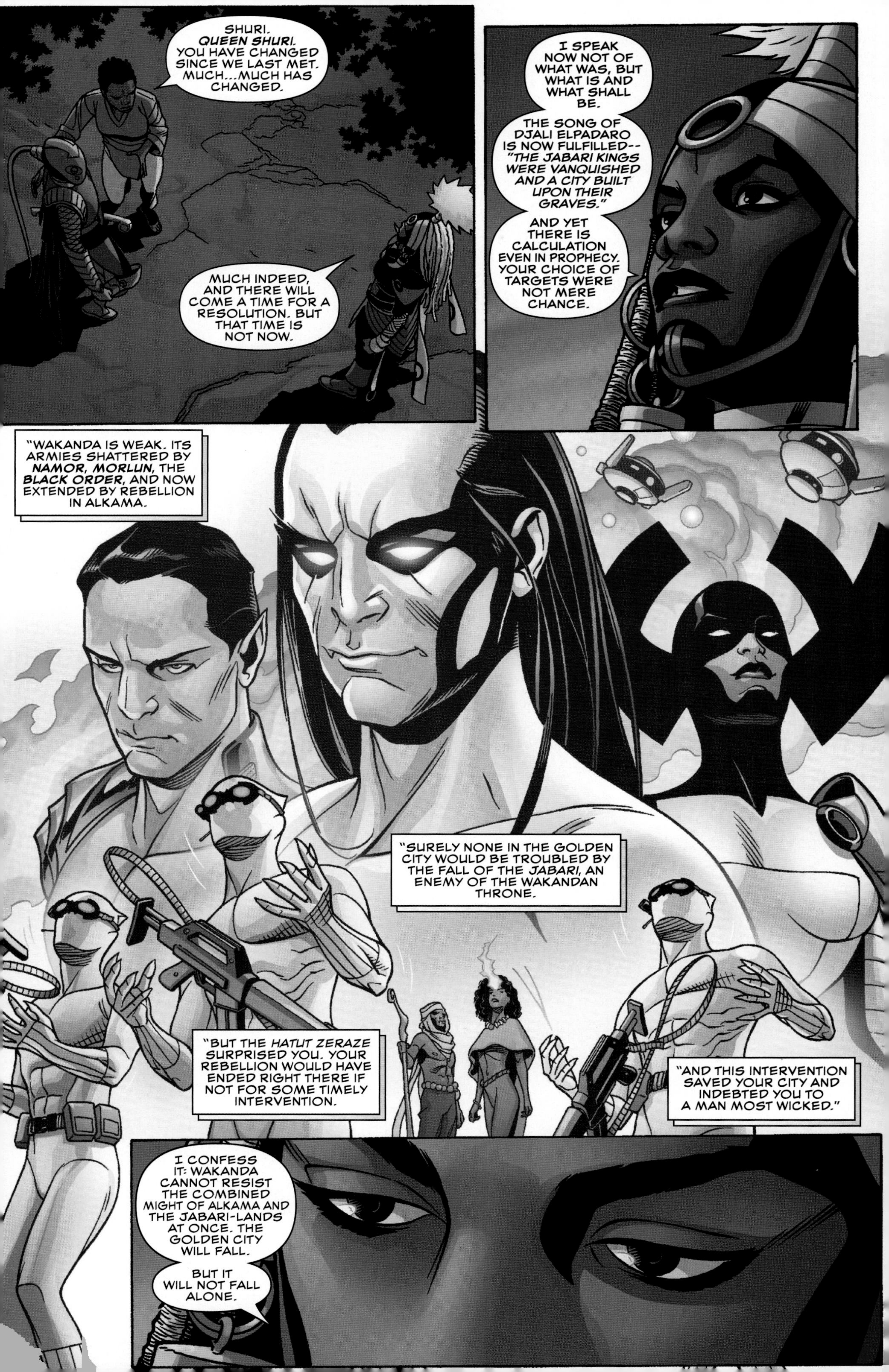
SHURI. QUEEN SHURI. YOU HAVE CHANGED SINCE WE LAST MET. MUCH... MUCH HAS CHANGED.
MUCH INDEED, AND THERE WILL COME A TIME FOR A RESOLUTION. BUT THAT TIME IS NOT NOW.
I SPEAK NOW NOT OF WHAT WAS, BUT WHAT IS AND WHAT SHALL BE.
THE SONG OF DJALI ELPADARO IS NOW FULFILLED-- "THE JABARI KINGS WERE VANQUISHED AND A CITY BUILT UPON THEIR GRAVES."
AND YET THERE IS CALCULATION EVEN IN PROPHECY. YOUR CHOICE OF TARGETS WERE NOT MERE CHANCE.
"WAKANDA IS WEAK. ITS ARMIES SHATTERED BY NAMOR, MORLUN, THE BLACK ORDER, AND NOW EXTENDED BY REBELLION IN ALKAMA.
"SURELY NONE IN THE GOLDEN CITY WOULD BE TROUBLED BY THE FALL OF THE JABARI, AN ENEMY OF THE WAKANDAN THRONE.
"BUT THE HATUT ZERAZE SURPRISED YOU. YOUR REBELLION WOULD HAVE ENDED RIGHT THERE IF NOT FOR SOME TIMELY INTERVENTION.
"AND THIS INTERVENTION SAVED YOUR CITY AND INDEBTED YOU TO A MAN MOST WICKED."
I CONFESS IT: WAKANDA CANNOT RESIST THE COMBINED MIGHT OF ALKAMA AND THE JABARI-LANDS AT ONCE. THE GOLDEN CITY WILL FALL.
BUT IT WILL NOT FALL ALONE.

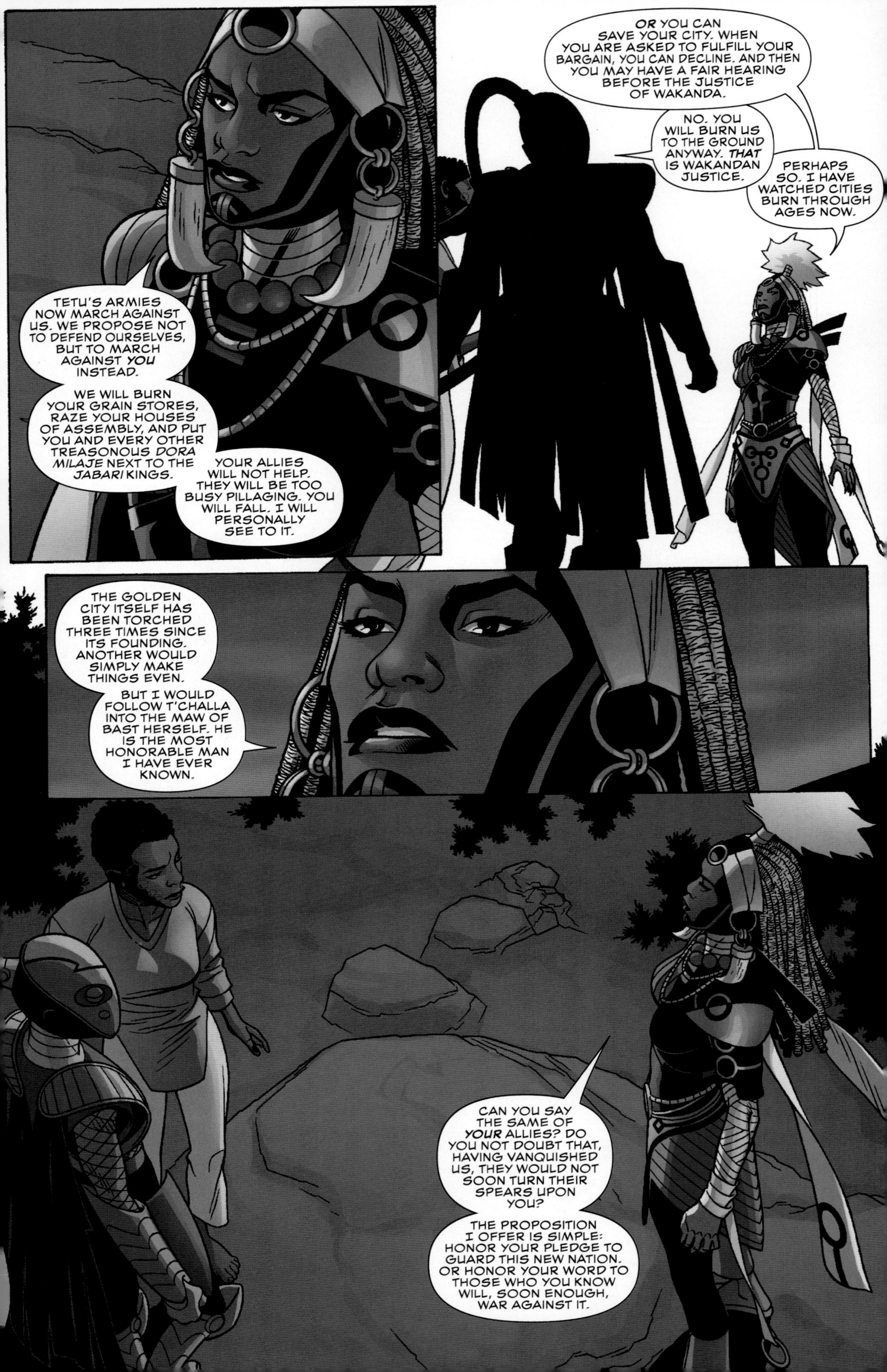
TETU'S ARMIES NOW MARCH AGAINST US. WE PROPOSE NOT TO DEFEND OURSELVES, BUT TO MARCH AGAINST *YOU* INSTEAD.
WE WILL BURN YOUR GRAIN STORES, RAZE YOUR HOUSES OF ASSEMBLY, AND PUT YOU AND EVERY OTHER TREASONOUS *DORA MILAJE* NEXT TO THE *JABARI* KINGS.
YOUR ALLIES WILL NOT HELP. THEY WILL BE TOO BUSY PILLAGING. YOU WILL FALL. I WILL PERSONALLY SEE TO IT.
***OR*** YOU CAN SAVE YOUR CITY. WHEN YOU ARE ASKED TO FULFILL YOUR BARGAIN, YOU CAN DECLINE. AND THEN YOU MAY HAVE A FAIR HEARING BEFORE THE JUSTICE OF WAKANDA.
NO. YOU WILL BURN US TO THE GROUND ANYWAY. ***THAT*** IS WAKANDAN JUSTICE.
PERHAPS SO. I HAVE WATCHED CITIES BURN THROUGH AGES NOW.
THE GOLDEN CITY ITSELF HAS BEEN TORCHED THREE TIMES SINCE ITS FOUNDING. ANOTHER WOULD SIMPLY MAKE THINGS EVEN.
BUT I WOULD FOLLOW T'CHALLA INTO THE MAW OF BAST HERSELF. HE IS THE MOST HONORABLE MAN I HAVE EVER KNOWN.
CAN YOU SAY THE SAME OF ***YOUR*** ALLIES? DO YOU NOT DOUBT THAT, HAVING VANQUISHED US, THEY WOULD NOT SOON TURN THEIR SPEARS UPON YOU?
THE PROPOSITION I OFFER IS SIMPLE: HONOR YOUR PLEDGE TO GUARD THIS NEW NATION. OR HONOR YOUR WORD TO THOSE WHO YOU KNOW WILL, SOON ENOUGH, WAR AGAINST IT.

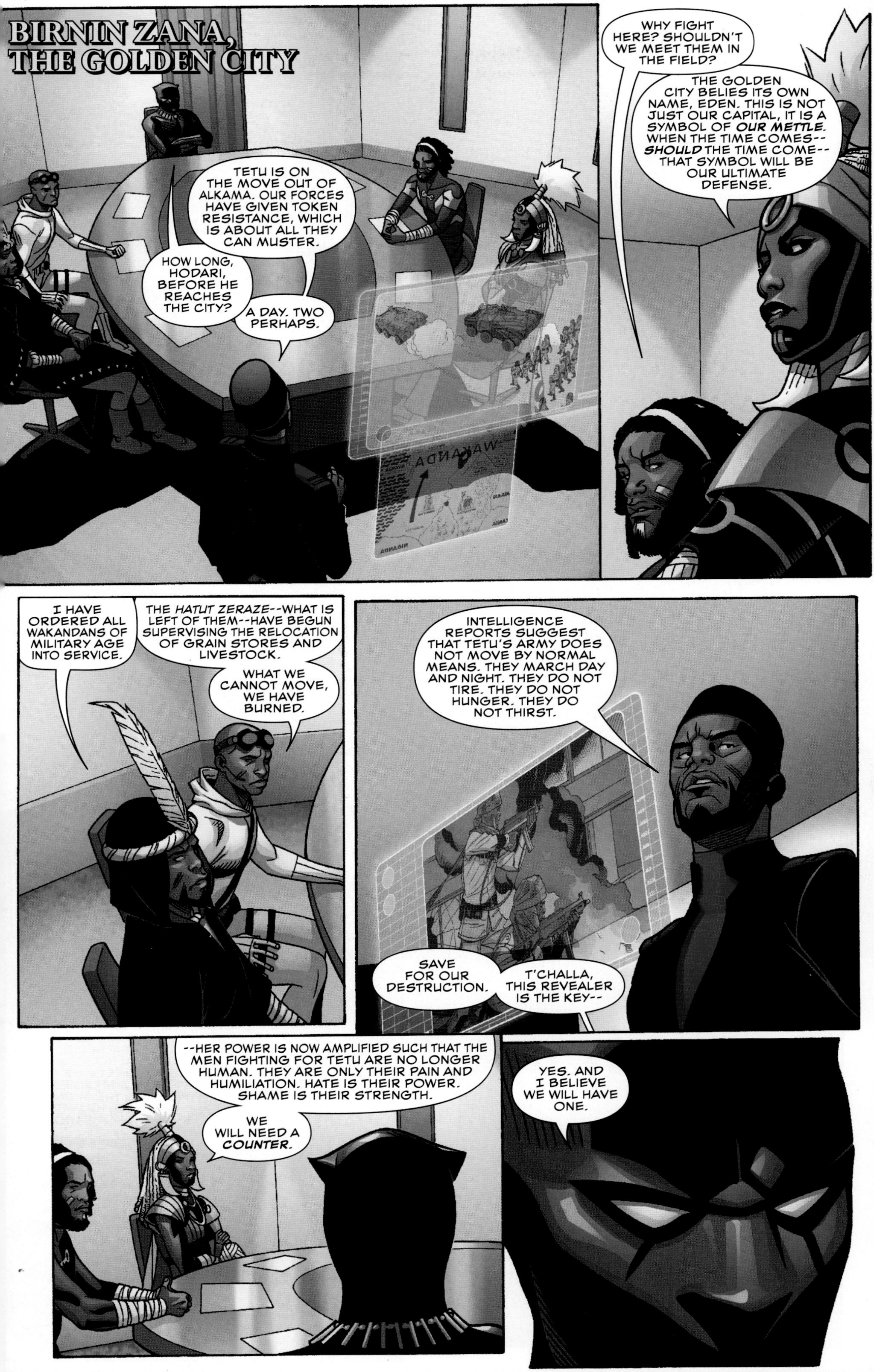
BIRNIN ZANA, THE GOLDEN CITY
TETU IS ON THE MOVE OUT OF ALKAMA. OUR FORCES HAVE GIVEN TOKEN RESISTANCE, WHICH IS ABOUT ALL THEY CAN MUSTER.
HOW LONG, HODARI, BEFORE HE REACHES THE CITY?
A DAY. TWO PERHAPS.
WHY FIGHT HERE? SHOULDN'T WE MEET THEM IN THE FIELD?
THE GOLDEN CITY BELIES ITS OWN NAME, EDEN. THIS IS NOT JUST OUR CAPITAL, IT IS A SYMBOL OF OUR METTLE. WHEN THE TIME COMES-- SHOULD THE TIME COME-- THAT SYMBOL WILL BE OUR ULTIMATE DEFENSE.
I HAVE ORDERED ALL WAKANDANS OF MILITARY AGE INTO SERVICE.
THE HATUT ZERAZE--WHAT IS LEFT OF THEM--HAVE BEGUN SUPERVISING THE RELOCATION OF GRAIN STORES AND LIVESTOCK.
WHAT WE CANNOT MOVE, WE HAVE BURNED.
INTELLIGENCE REPORTS SUGGEST THAT TETU'S ARMY DOES NOT MOVE BY NORMAL MEANS. THEY MARCH DAY AND NIGHT. THEY DO NOT TIRE. THEY DO NOT HUNGER. THEY DO NOT THIRST.
SAVE FOR OUR DESTRUCTION.
T'CHALLA, THIS REVEALER IS THE KEY--
--HER POWER IS NOW AMPLIFIED SUCH THAT THE MEN FIGHTING FOR TETU ARE NO LONGER HUMAN. THEY ARE ONLY THEIR PAIN AND HUMILIATION. HATE IS THEIR POWER. SHAME IS THEIR STRENGTH.
WE WILL NEED A COUNTER.
YES. AND I BELIEVE WE WILL HAVE ONE.

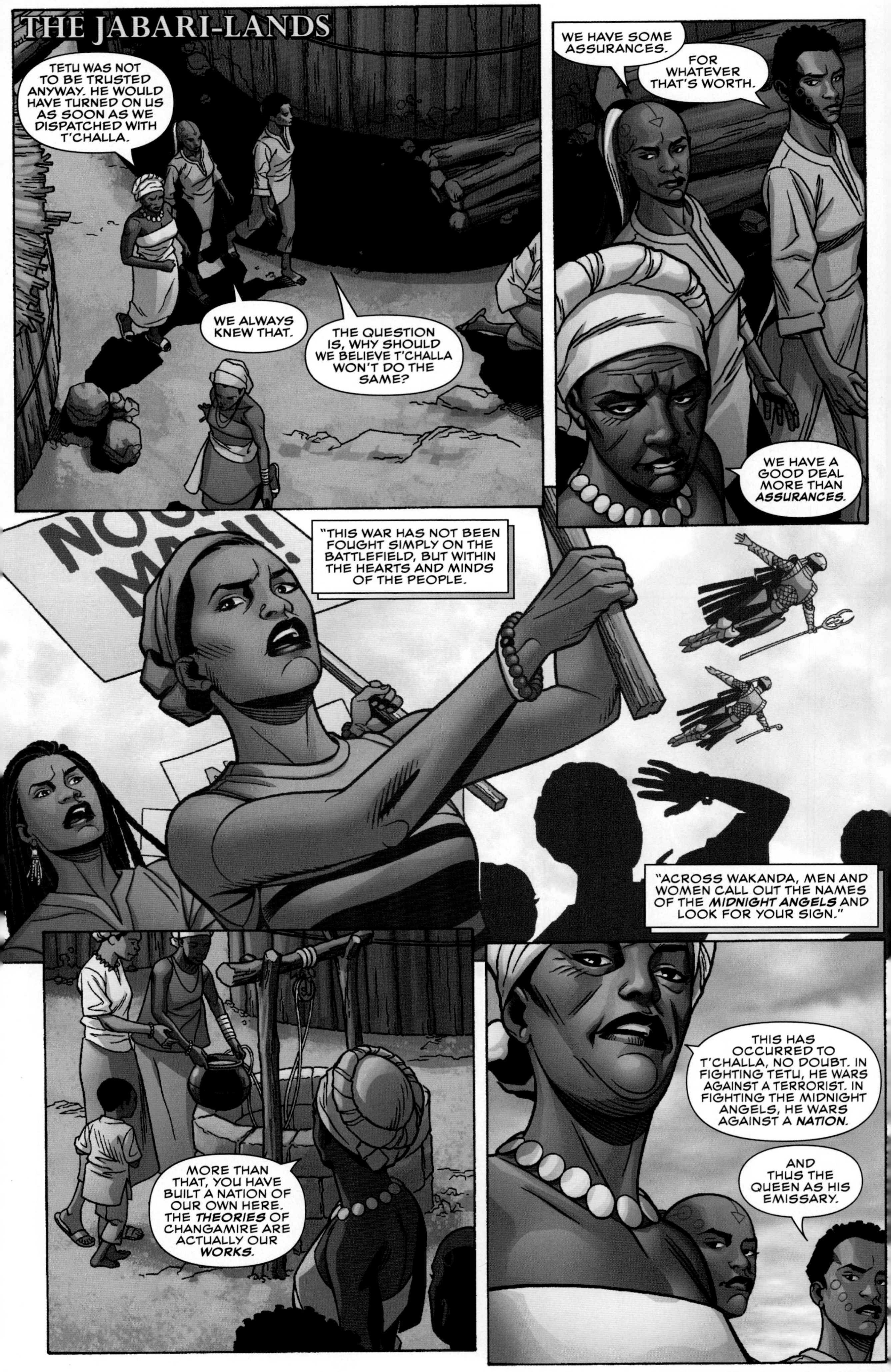
THE JABARI-LANDS
TETU WAS NOT TO BE TRUSTED ANYWAY. HE WOULD HAVE TURNED ON US AS SOON AS WE DISPATCHED WITH T'CHALLA.
WE ALWAYS KNEW THAT.
THE QUESTION IS, WHY SHOULD WE BELIEVE T'CHALLA WON'T DO THE SAME?
WE HAVE SOME ASSURANCES.
FOR WHATEVER THAT'S WORTH.
WE HAVE A GOOD DEAL MORE THAN ASSURANCES.
"THIS WAR HAS NOT BEEN FOUGHT SIMPLY ON THE BATTLEFIELD, BUT WITHIN THE HEARTS AND MINDS OF THE PEOPLE.
"ACROSS WAKANDA, MEN AND WOMEN CALL OUT THE NAMES OF THE MIDNIGHT ANGELS AND LOOK FOR YOUR SIGN."
MORE THAN THAT, YOU HAVE BUILT A NATION OF OUR OWN HERE. THE THEORIES OF CHANGAMIRE ARE ACTUALLY OUR WORKS.
THIS HAS OCCURRED TO T'CHALLA, NO DOUBT. IN FIGHTING TETU, HE WARS AGAINST A TERRORIST. IN FIGHTING THE MIDNIGHT ANGELS, HE WARS AGAINST A NATION.
AND THUS THE QUEEN AS HIS EMISSARY.

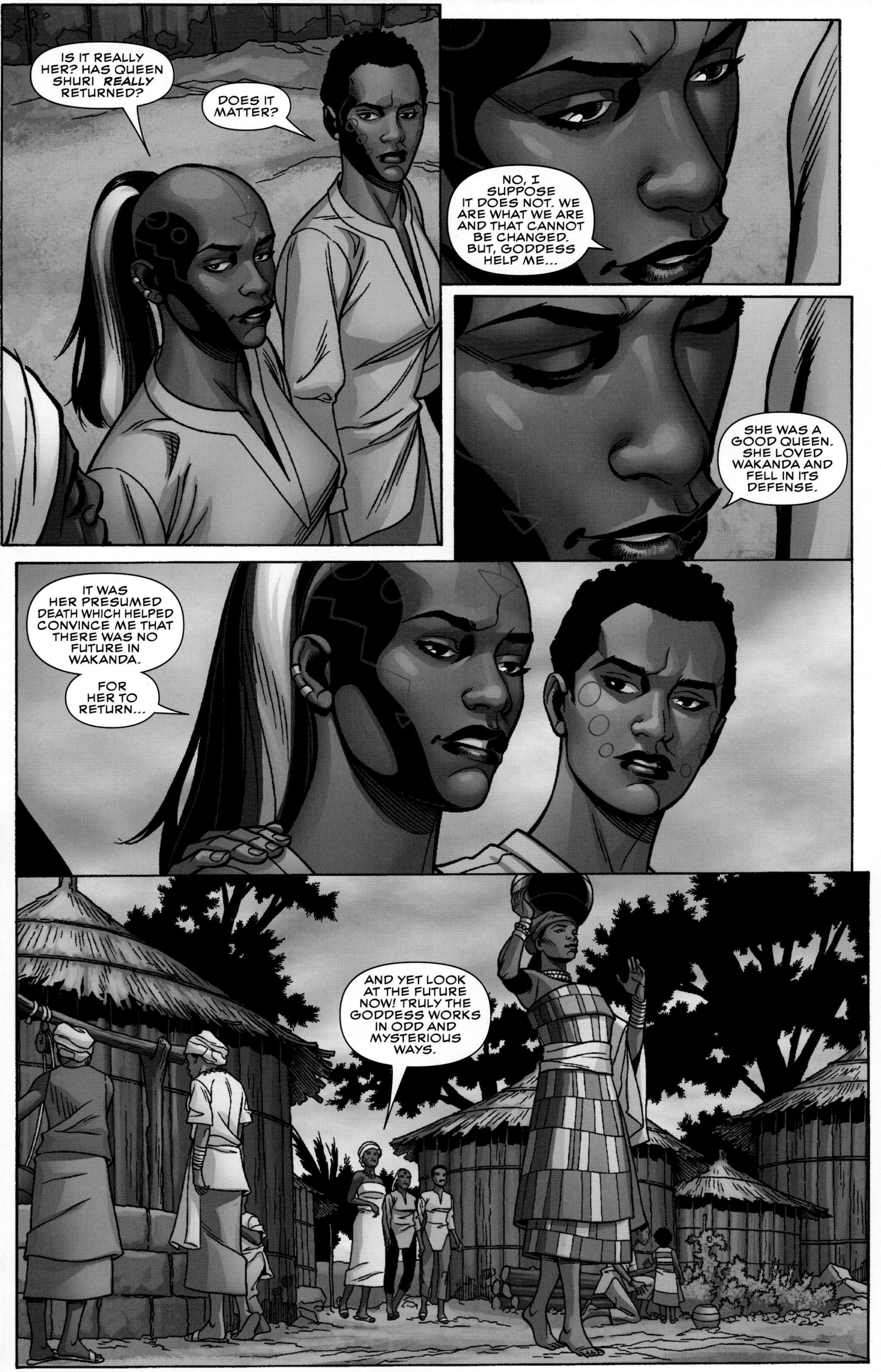
IS IT REALLY HER? HAS QUEEN SHURI REALLY RETURNED?
DOES IT MATTER?
NO, I SUPPOSE IT DOES NOT. WE ARE WHAT WE ARE AND THAT CANNOT BE CHANGED. BUT, GODDESS HELP ME...
SHE WAS A GOOD QUEEN. SHE LOVED WAKANDA AND FELL IN ITS DEFENSE.
IT WAS HER PRESUMED DEATH WHICH HELPED CONVINCE ME THAT THERE WAS NO FUTURE IN WAKANDA.
FOR HER TO RETURN...
AND YET LOOK AT THE FUTURE NOW! TRULY THE GODDESS WORKS IN ODD AND MYSTERIOUS WAYS.

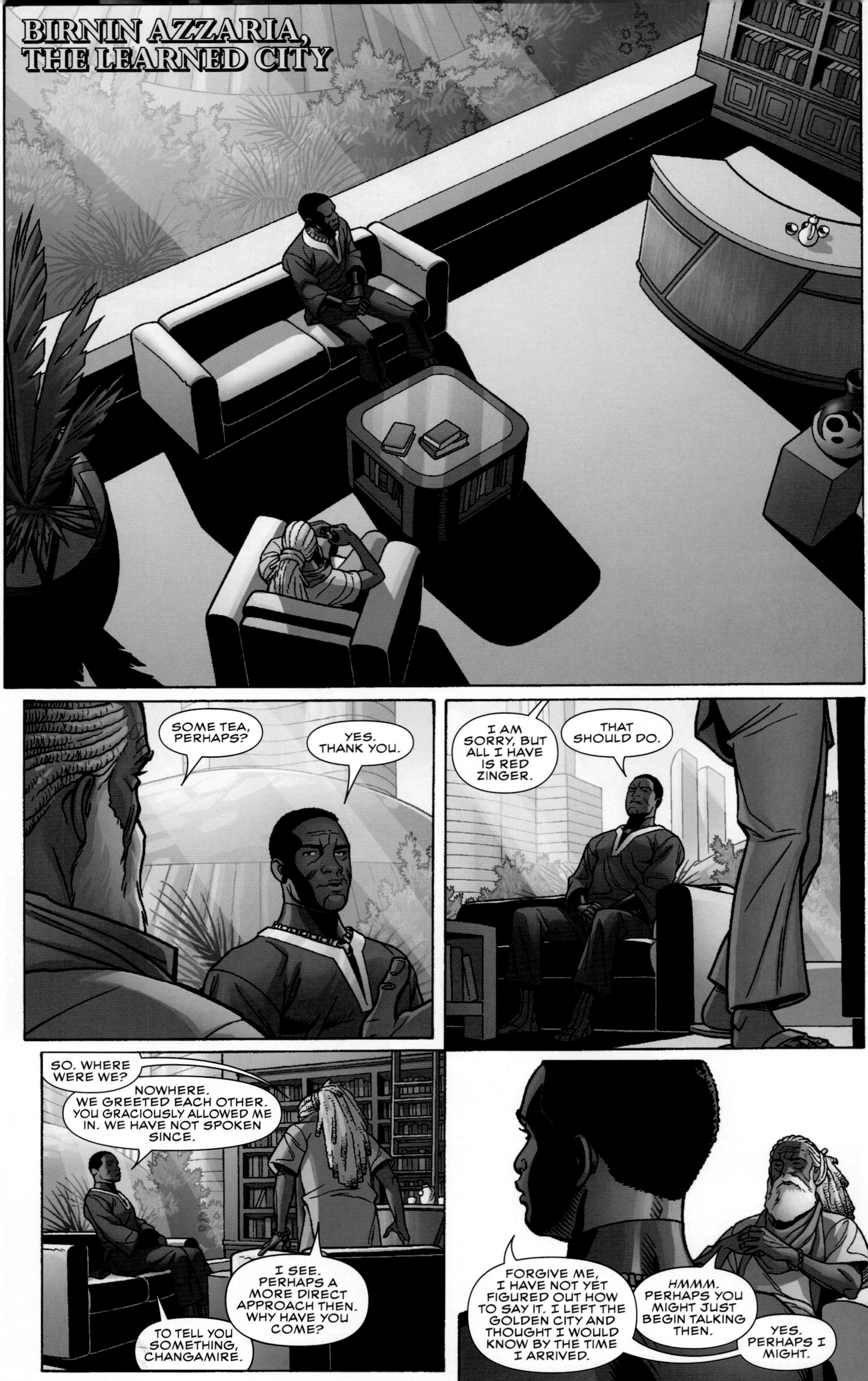
BIRNIN AZZARIA, THE LEARNED CITY
SOME TEA, PERHAPS?
YES. THANK YOU.
I AM SORRY, BUT ALL I HAVE IS RED ZINGER.
THAT SHOULD DO.
SO. WHERE WERE WE?
NOWHERE. WE GREETED EACH OTHER. YOU GRACIOUSLY ALLOWED ME IN. WE HAVE NOT SPOKEN SINCE.
I SEE. PERHAPS A MORE DIRECT APPROACH THEN. WHY HAVE YOU COME?
TO TELL YOU SOMETHING, CHANGAMIRE.
FORGIVE ME, I HAVE NOT YET FIGURED OUT HOW TO SAY IT. I LEFT THE GOLDEN CITY AND THOUGHT I WOULD KNOW BY THE TIME I ARRIVED.
*HMMM.* PERHAPS YOU MIGHT JUST BEGIN TALKING THEN.
YES. PERHAPS I MIGHT.

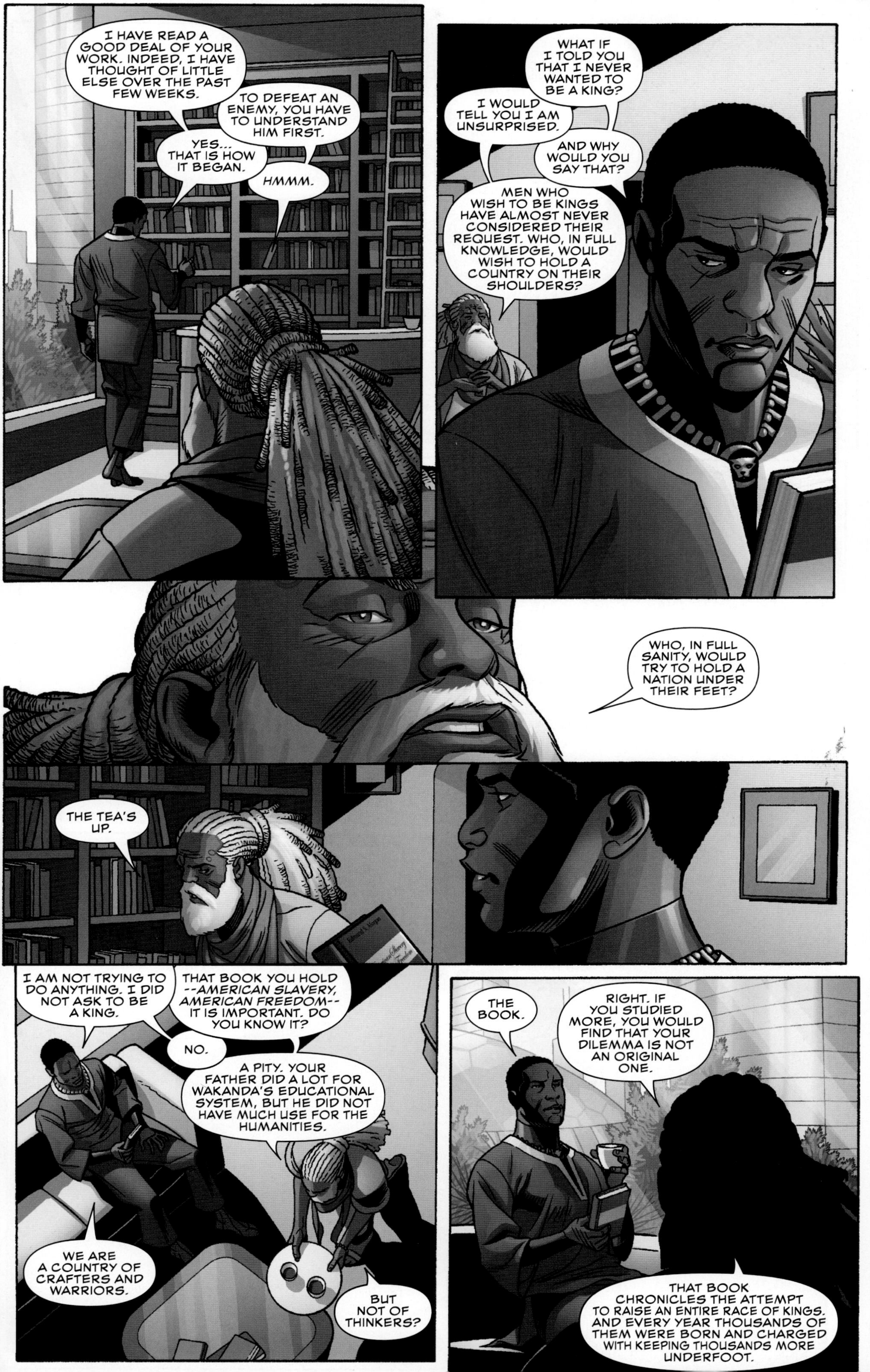
I HAVE READ A GOOD DEAL OF YOUR WORK. INDEED, I HAVE THOUGHT OF LITTLE ELSE OVER THE PAST FEW WEEKS.
TO DEFEAT AN ENEMY, YOU HAVE TO UNDERSTAND HIM FIRST.
YES... THAT IS HOW IT BEGAN.
HMMM.
WHAT IF I TOLD YOU THAT I NEVER WANTED TO BE A KING?
I WOULD TELL YOU I AM UNSURPRISED.
AND WHY WOULD YOU SAY THAT?
MEN WHO WISH TO BE KINGS HAVE ALMOST NEVER CONSIDERED THEIR REQUEST. WHO, IN FULL KNOWLEDGE, WOULD WISH TO HOLD A COUNTRY ON THEIR SHOULDERS?
WHO, IN FULL SANITY, WOULD TRY TO HOLD A NATION UNDER THEIR FEET?
THE TEA'S UP.
I AM NOT TRYING TO DO ANYTHING. I DID NOT ASK TO BE A KING.
THAT BOOK YOU HOLD --AMERICAN SLAVERY, AMERICAN FREEDOM-- IT IS IMPORTANT. DO YOU KNOW IT?
NO.
A PITY. YOUR FATHER DID A LOT FOR WAKANDA'S EDUCATIONAL SYSTEM, BUT HE DID NOT HAVE MUCH USE FOR THE HUMANITIES.
WE ARE A COUNTRY OF CRAFTERS AND WARRIORS.
BUT NOT OF THINKERS?
THE BOOK.
RIGHT. IF YOU STUDIED MORE, YOU WOULD FIND THAT YOUR DILEMMA IS NOT AN ORIGINAL ONE.
THAT BOOK CHRONICLES THE ATTEMPT TO RAISE AN ENTIRE RACE OF KINGS. AND EVERY YEAR THOUSANDS OF THEM WERE BORN AND CHARGED WITH KEEPING THOUSANDS MORE UNDERFOOT.

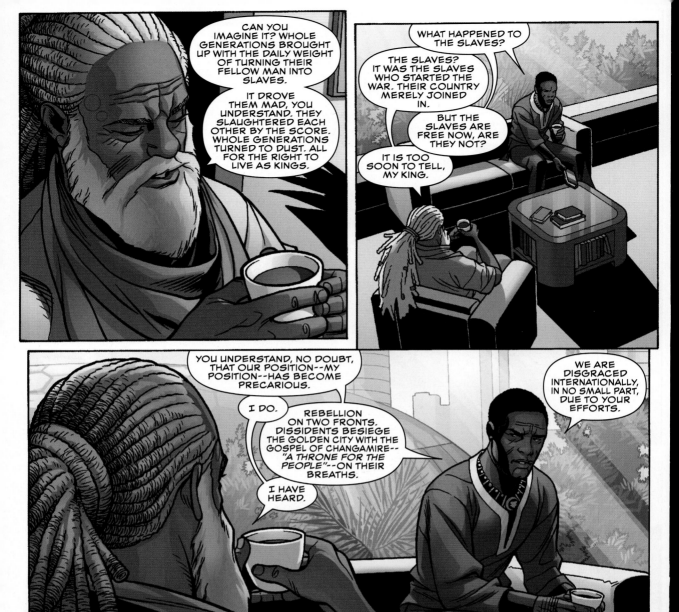

CAN YOU IMAGINE IT? WHOLE GENERATIONS BROUGHT UP WITH THE DAILY WEIGHT OF TURNING THEIR FELLOW MAN INTO SLAVES.

IT DROVE THEM MAD, YOU UNDERSTAND. THEY SLAUGHTERED EACH OTHER BY THE SCORE. WHOLE GENERATIONS TURNED TO DUST. ALL FOR THE RIGHT TO LIVE AS KINGS.

WHAT HAPPENED TO THE SLAVES?

THE SLAVES? IT WAS THE SLAVES WHO STARTED THE WAR. THEIR COUNTRY MERELY JOINED IN.

BUT THE SLAVES ARE FREE NOW, ARE THEY NOT?

IT IS TOO SOON TO TELL, MY KING.

YOU UNDERSTAND, NO DOUBT, THAT OUR POSITION--MY POSITION--HAS BECOME PRECARIOUS.

I DO.

REBELLION ON TWO FRONTS. DISSIDENTS BESIEGE THE GOLDEN CITY WITH THE GOSPEL OF CHANGAMIRE-- "A THRONE FOR THE PEOPLE"--ON THEIR BREATHS.

I HAVE HEARD.

WE ARE DISGRACED INTERNATIONALLY, IN NO SMALL PART, DUE TO YOUR EFFORTS.

HAVE YOU COME TO ARREST ME?

NO. I THINK NOT. ON THE CONTRARY, I HAVE COME TO ASK FOR YOUR HELP.

AND HOW COULD I HELP?

YOU CAN TELL ME WHAT I SHOULD DO.

FRANKLY, I HAVE NO IDEA.

YES. I KNOW.

YOU ARE A VOYAGER WITHOUT A SHIP. DREAMING OF DISTANT LANDS BUT WITH NO MEANS TO REACH THEM.

AND YOU ARE AN INDUSTRIALIST BORN TO A THOUSAND SHIPS. MAROONED HERE WITH THE WEST AND THE REST OF US.

INDEED.

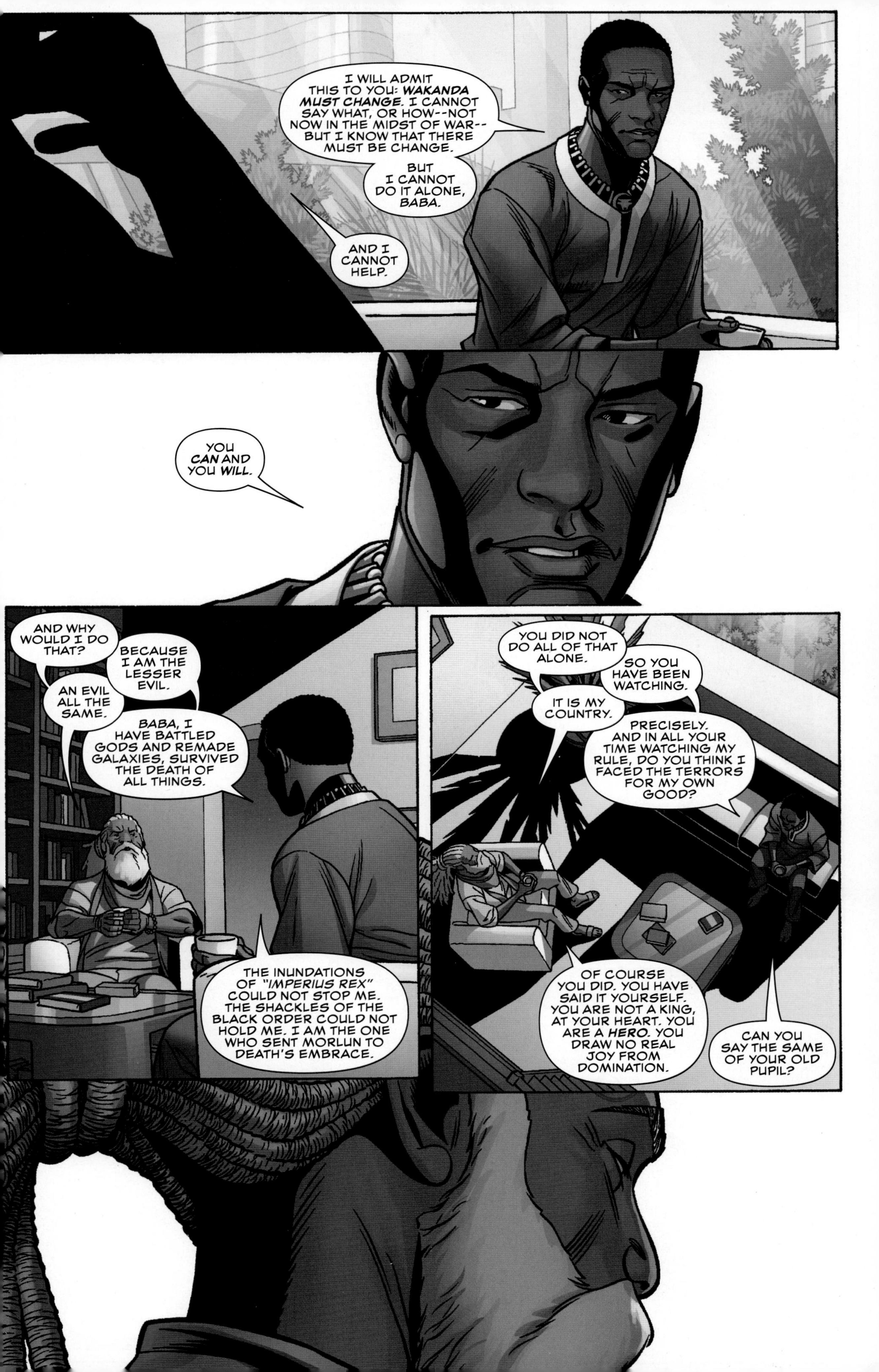

I WILL ADMIT THIS TO YOU: *WAKANDA MUST CHANGE*. I CANNOT SAY WHAT, OR HOW--NOT NOW IN THE MIDST OF WAR--BUT I KNOW THAT THERE MUST BE CHANGE.
BUT I CANNOT DO IT ALONE, *BABA*.
AND I CANNOT HELP.
YOU *CAN* AND YOU *WILL*.
AND WHY WOULD I DO THAT?
BECAUSE I AM THE LESSER EVIL.
AN EVIL ALL THE SAME.
*BABA*, I HAVE BATTLED GODS AND REMADE GALAXIES, SURVIVED THE DEATH OF ALL THINGS.
THE INUNDATIONS OF "*IMPERIUS REX*" COULD NOT STOP ME. THE SHACKLES OF THE BLACK ORDER COULD NOT HOLD ME. I AM THE ONE WHO SENT MORLUN TO DEATH'S EMBRACE.
YOU DID NOT DO ALL OF THAT ALONE.
SO YOU HAVE BEEN WATCHING.
IT IS MY COUNTRY.
PRECISELY. AND IN ALL YOUR TIME WATCHING MY RULE, DO YOU THINK I FACED THE TERRORS FOR MY OWN GOOD?
OF COURSE YOU DID. YOU HAVE SAID IT YOURSELF. YOU ARE NOT A KING, AT YOUR HEART. YOU ARE A *HERO*. YOU DRAW NO REAL JOY FROM DOMINATION.
CAN YOU SAY THE SAME OF YOUR OLD PUPIL?

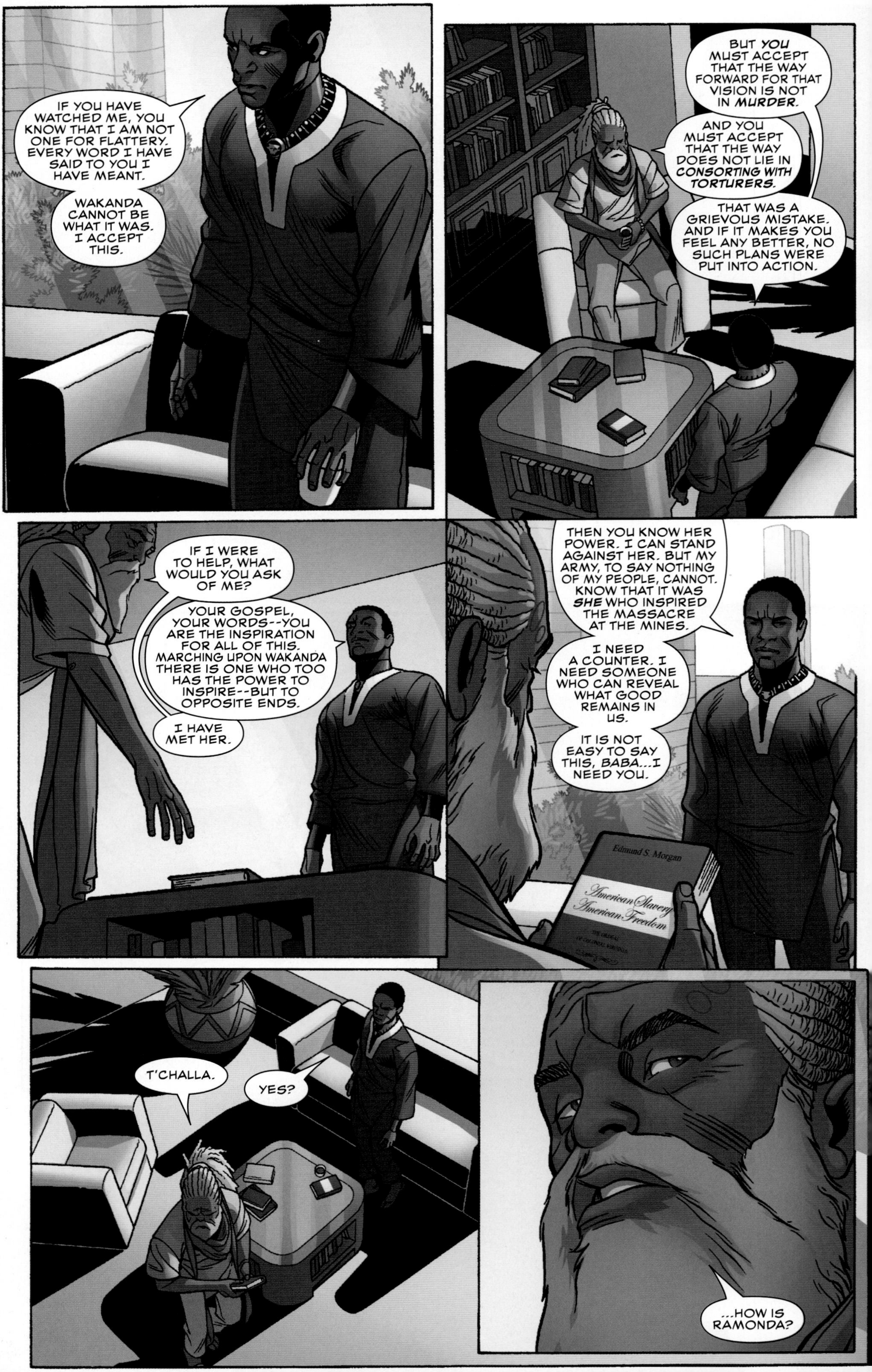
IF YOU HAVE WATCHED ME, YOU KNOW THAT I AM NOT ONE FOR FLATTERY. EVERY WORD I HAVE SAID TO YOU I HAVE MEANT.
WAKANDA CANNOT BE WHAT IT WAS. I ACCEPT THIS.
BUT *YOU* MUST ACCEPT THAT THE WAY FORWARD FOR THAT VISION IS NOT IN ***MURDER.***
AND YOU MUST ACCEPT THAT THE WAY DOES NOT LIE IN ***CONSORTING WITH TORTURERS.***
THAT WAS A GRIEVOUS MISTAKE. AND IF IT MAKES YOU FEEL ANY BETTER, NO SUCH PLANS WERE PUT INTO ACTION.
IF I WERE TO HELP, WHAT WOULD YOU ASK OF ME?
YOUR GOSPEL, YOUR WORDS--YOU ARE THE INSPIRATION FOR ALL OF THIS. MARCHING UPON WAKANDA THERE IS ONE WHO TOO HAS THE POWER TO INSPIRE--BUT TO OPPOSITE ENDS.
I HAVE MET HER.
THEN YOU KNOW HER POWER. I CAN STAND AGAINST HER. BUT MY ARMY, TO SAY NOTHING OF MY PEOPLE, CANNOT. KNOW THAT IT WAS *SHE* WHO INSPIRED THE MASSACRE AT THE MINES.
I NEED A COUNTER. I NEED SOMEONE WHO CAN REVEAL WHAT GOOD REMAINS IN US.
IT IS NOT EASY TO SAY THIS, *BABA*...I NEED YOU.
Edmund S. Morgan
American Slavery American Freedom
T'CHALLA.
YES?
...HOW IS RAMONDA?

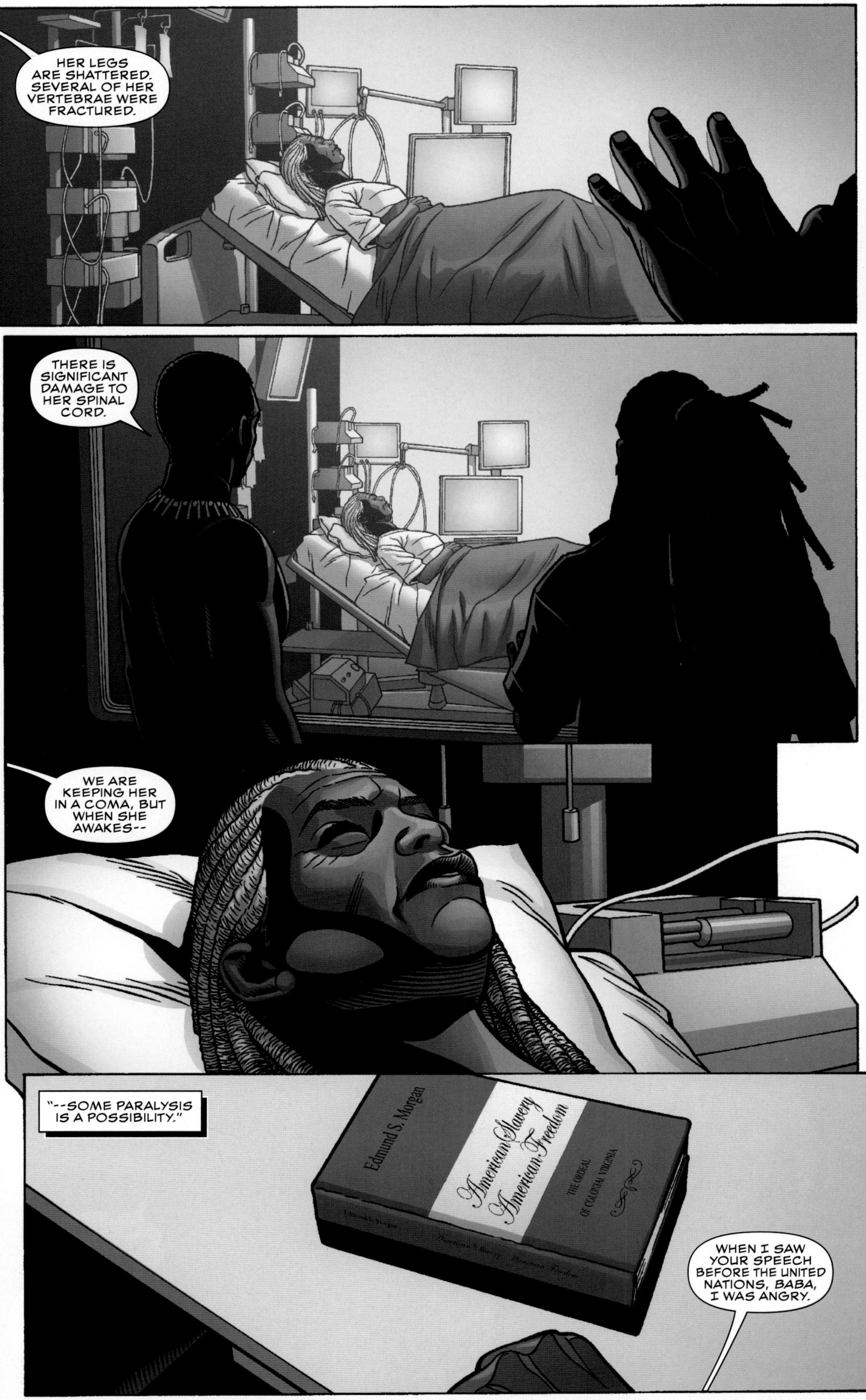
HER LEGS ARE SHATTERED. SEVERAL OF HER VERTEBRAE WERE FRACTURED.
THERE IS SIGNIFICANT DAMAGE TO HER SPINAL CORD.
WE ARE KEEPING HER IN A COMA, BUT WHEN SHE AWAKES--
"--SOME PARALYSIS IS A POSSIBILITY."
Edmund S. Morgan
American Slavery American Freedom
THE ORDEAL OF COLONIAL VIRGINIA
WHEN I SAW YOUR SPEECH BEFORE THE UNITED NATIONS, BABA, I WAS ANGRY.

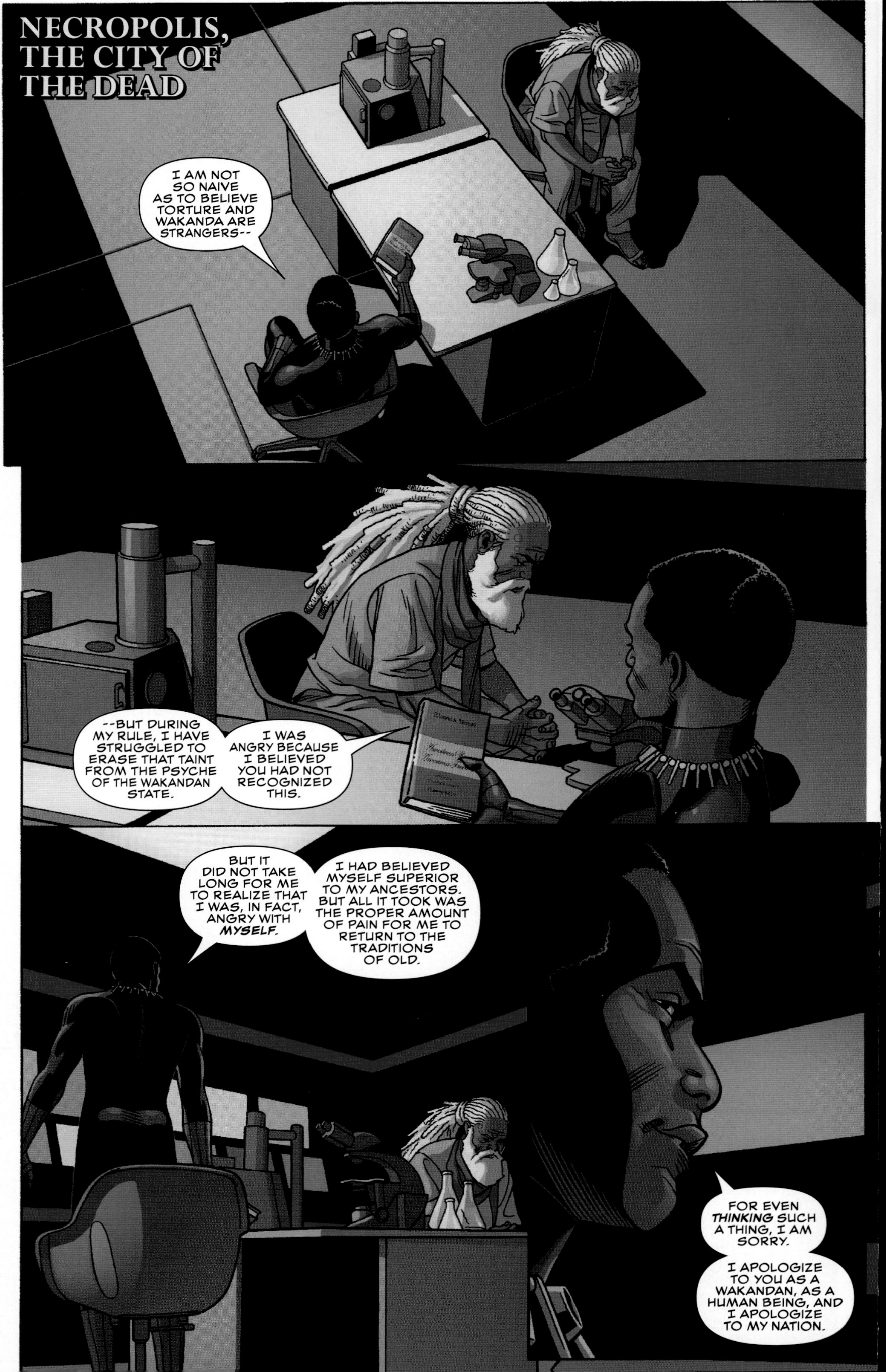
NECROPOLIS, THE CITY OF THE DEAD
I AM NOT SO NAIVE AS TO BELIEVE TORTURE AND WAKANDA ARE STRANGERS--
--BUT DURING MY RULE, I HAVE STRUGGLED TO ERASE THAT TAINT FROM THE PSYCHE OF THE WAKANDAN STATE.
I WAS ANGRY BECAUSE I BELIEVED YOU HAD NOT RECOGNIZED THIS.
BUT IT DID NOT TAKE LONG FOR ME TO REALIZE THAT I WAS, IN FACT, ANGRY WITH *MYSELF*.
I HAD BELIEVED MYSELF SUPERIOR TO MY ANCESTORS. BUT ALL IT TOOK WAS THE PROPER AMOUNT OF PAIN FOR ME TO RETURN TO THE TRADITIONS OF OLD.
FOR EVEN *THINKING* SUCH A THING, I AM SORRY.
I APOLOGIZE TO YOU AS A WAKANDAN, AS A HUMAN BEING, AND I APOLOGIZE TO MY NATION.

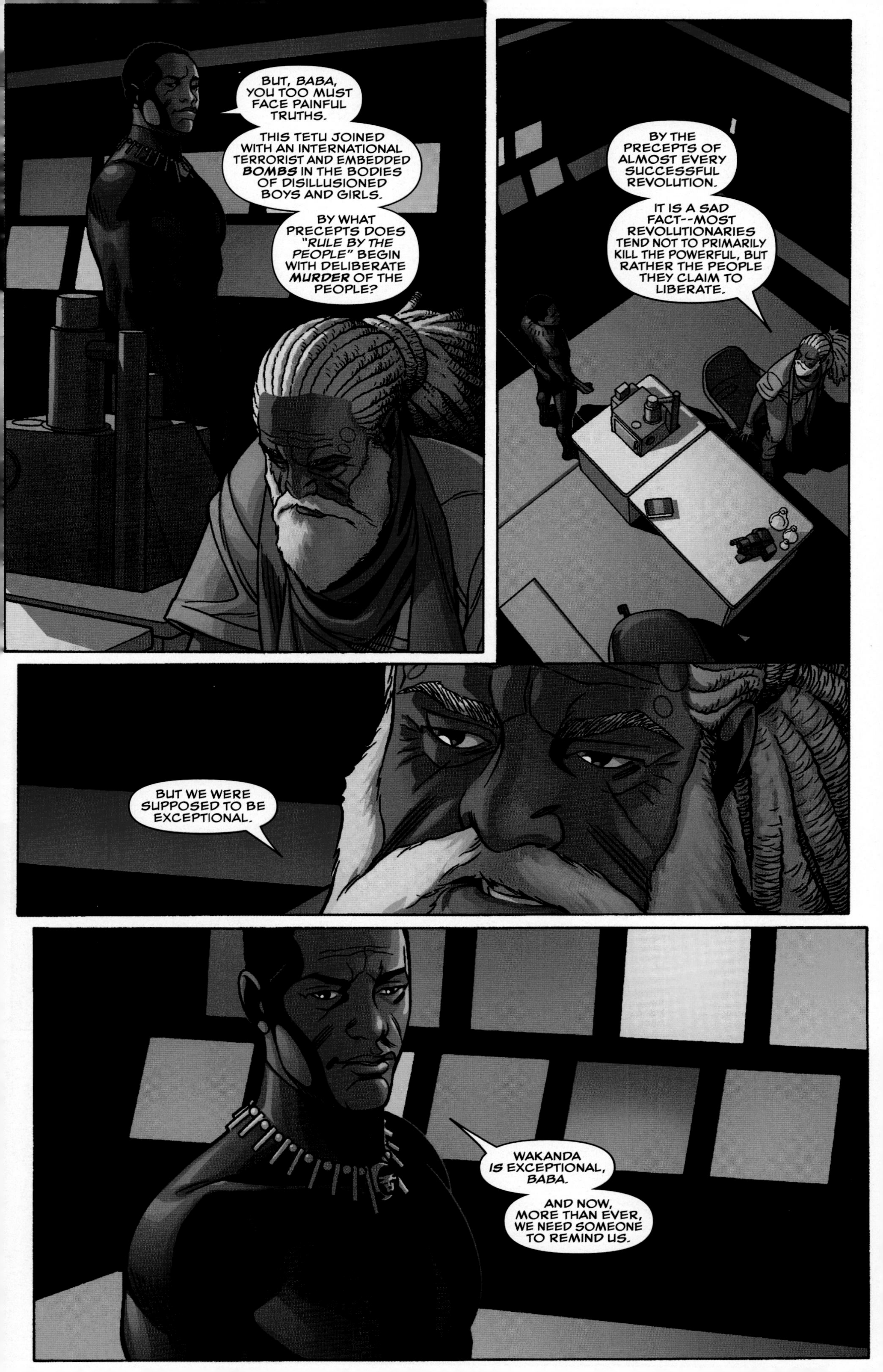

BUT, BABA, YOU TOO MUST FACE PAINFUL TRUTHS.
THIS TETU JOINED WITH AN INTERNATIONAL TERRORIST AND EMBEDDED BOMBS IN THE BODIES OF DISILLUSIONED BOYS AND GIRLS.
BY WHAT PRECEPTS DOES "RULE BY THE PEOPLE" BEGIN WITH DELIBERATE MURDER OF THE PEOPLE?
BY THE PRECEPTS OF ALMOST EVERY SUCCESSFUL REVOLUTION.
IT IS A SAD FACT--MOST REVOLUTIONARIES TEND NOT TO PRIMARILY KILL THE POWERFUL, BUT RATHER THE PEOPLE THEY CLAIM TO LIBERATE.
BUT WE WERE SUPPOSED TO BE EXCEPTIONAL.
WAKANDA IS EXCEPTIONAL, BABA.
AND NOW, MORE THAN EVER, WE NEED SOMEONE TO REMIND US.

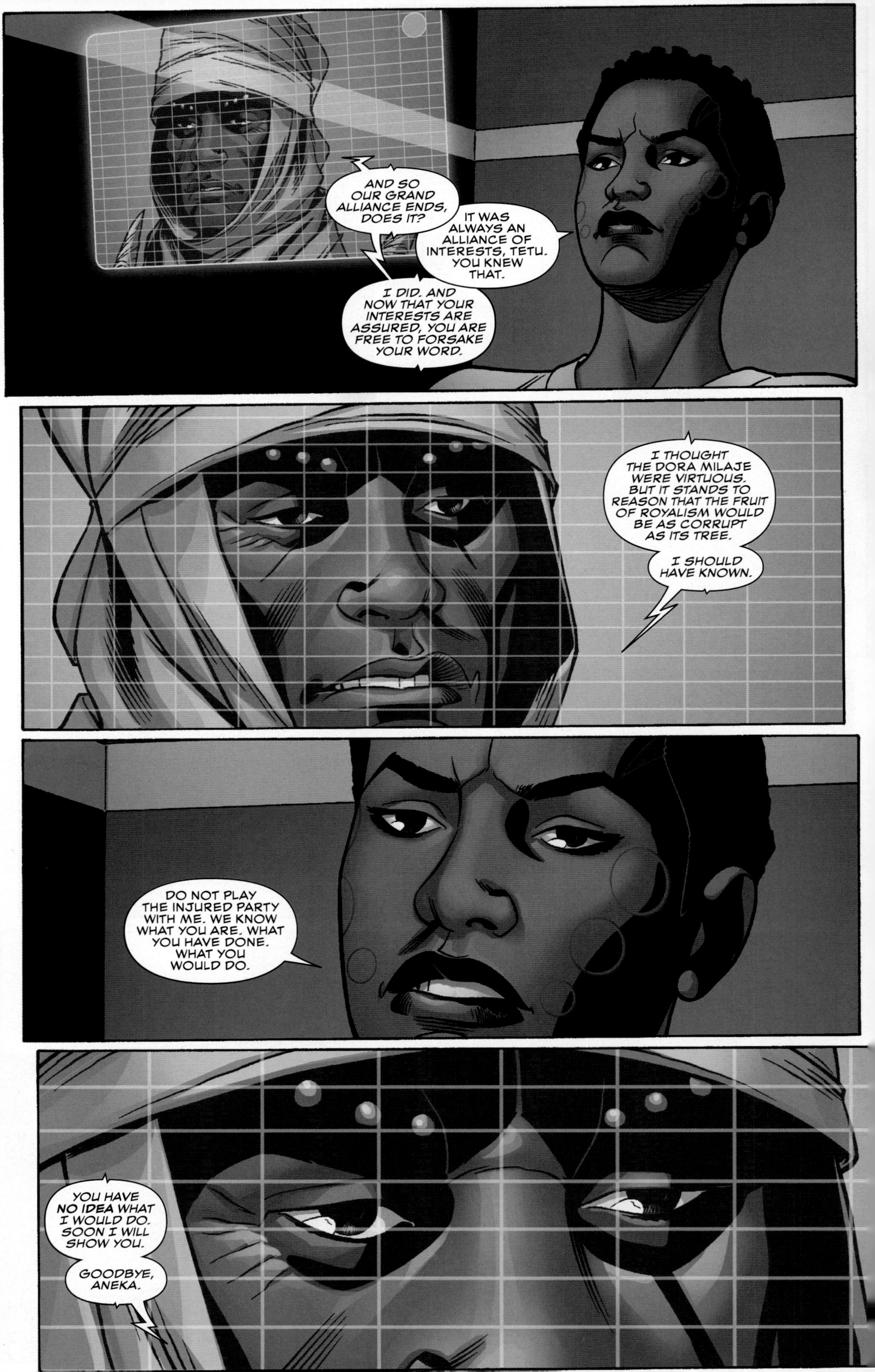
AND SO OUR GRAND ALLIANCE ENDS, DOES IT?
IT WAS ALWAYS AN ALLIANCE OF INTERESTS, TETU. YOU KNEW THAT.
I DID. AND NOW THAT YOUR INTERESTS ARE ASSURED, YOU ARE FREE TO FORSAKE YOUR WORD.
I THOUGHT THE DORA MILAJE WERE VIRTUOUS. BUT IT STANDS TO REASON THAT THE FRUIT OF ROYALISM WOULD BE AS CORRUPT AS ITS TREE.
I SHOULD HAVE KNOWN.
DO NOT PLAY THE INJURED PARTY WITH ME. WE KNOW WHAT YOU ARE. WHAT YOU HAVE DONE. WHAT YOU WOULD DO.
YOU HAVE **NO IDEA** WHAT I WOULD DO. SOON I WILL SHOW YOU.
GOODBYE, ANEKA.

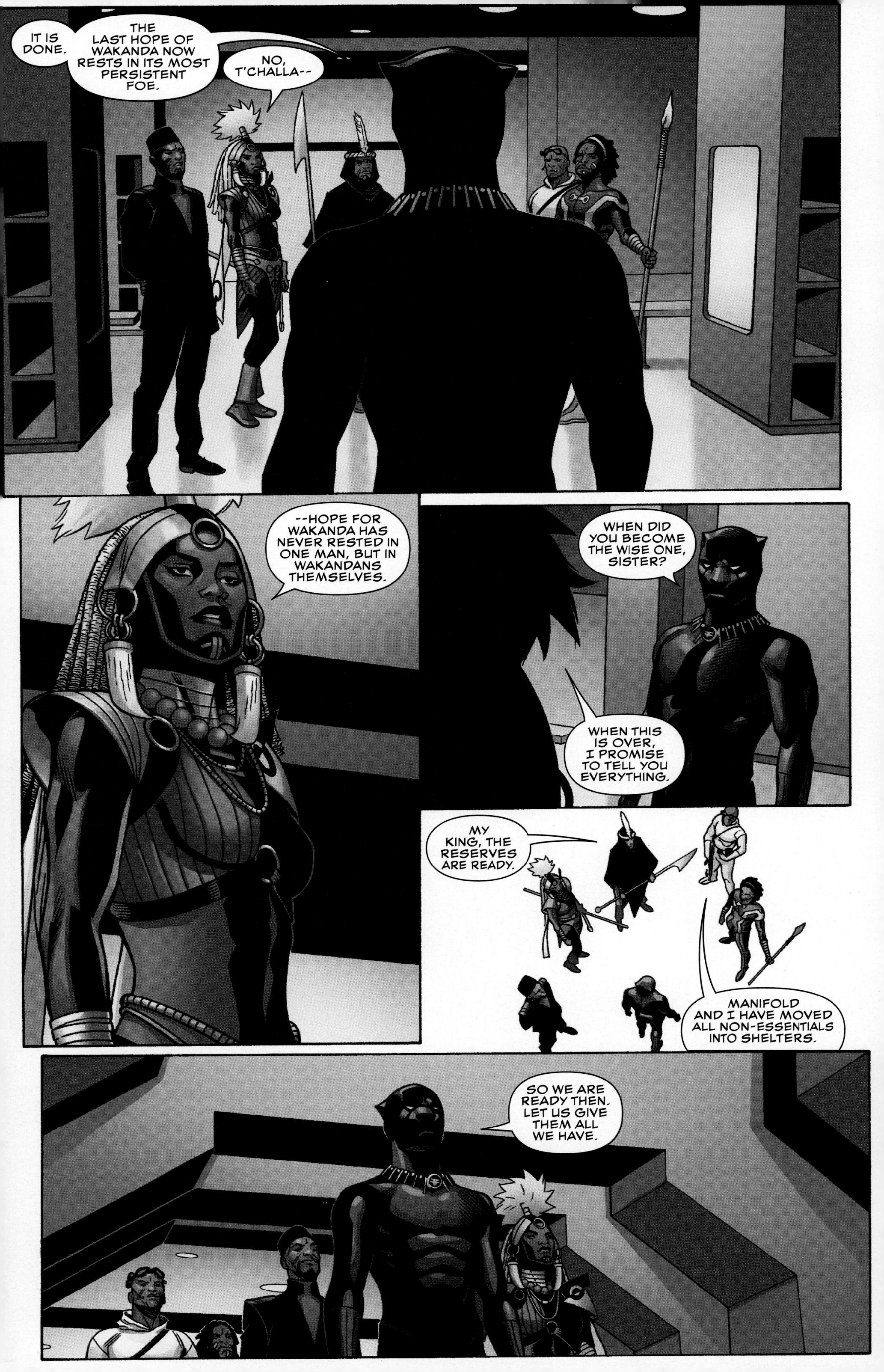
IT IS DONE.
THE LAST HOPE OF WAKANDA NOW RESTS IN ITS MOST PERSISTENT FOE.
NO, T'CHALLA--
--HOPE FOR WAKANDA HAS NEVER RESTED IN ONE MAN, BUT IN WAKANDANS THEMSELVES.
WHEN DID YOU BECOME THE WISE ONE, SISTER?
WHEN THIS IS OVER, I PROMISE TO TELL YOU EVERYTHING.
MY KING, THE RESERVES ARE READY.
MANIFOLD AND I HAVE MOVED ALL NON-ESSENTIALS INTO SHELTERS.
SO WE ARE READY THEN. LET US GIVE THEM ALL WE HAVE.

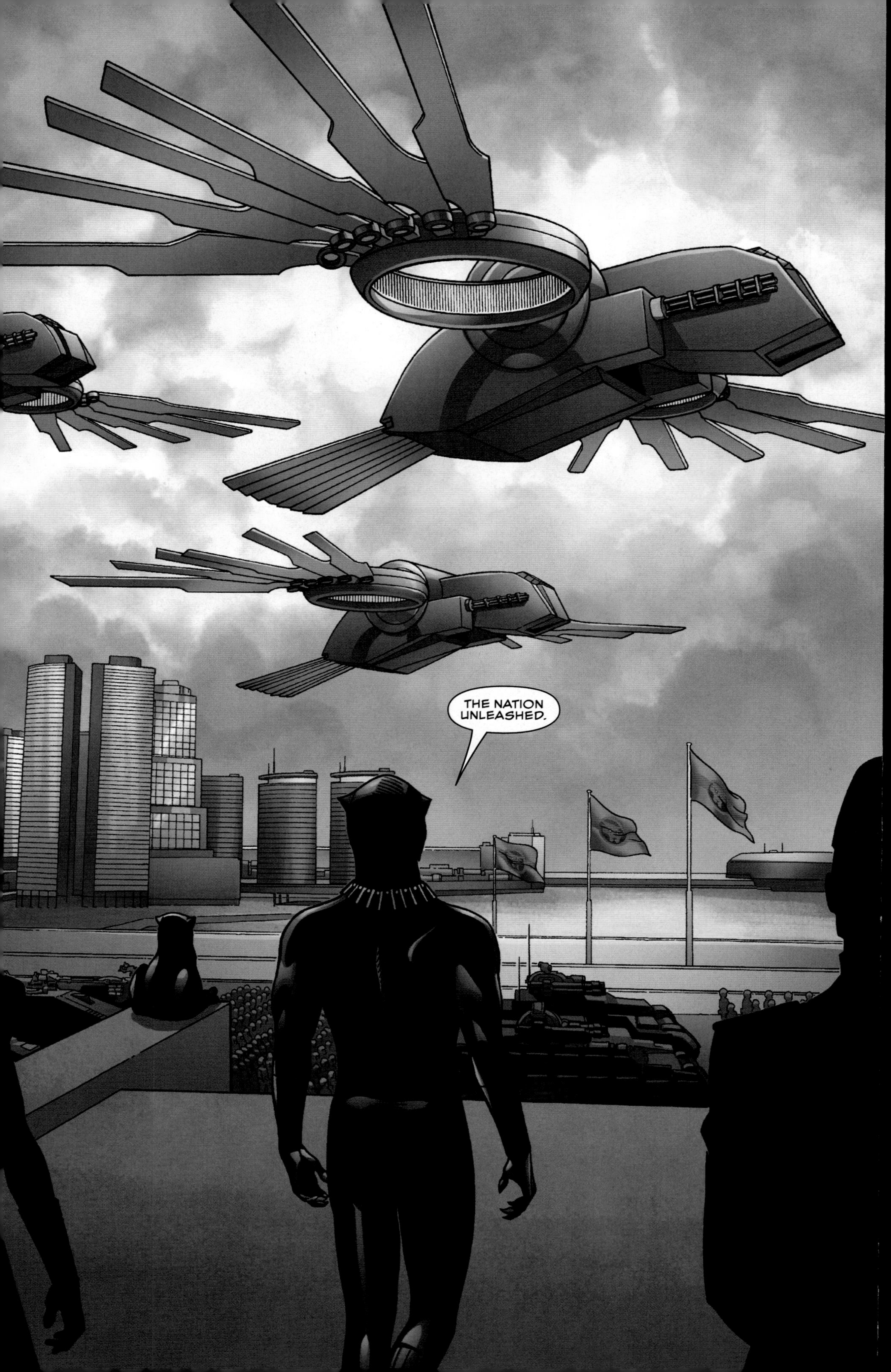
THE NATION UNLEASHED.

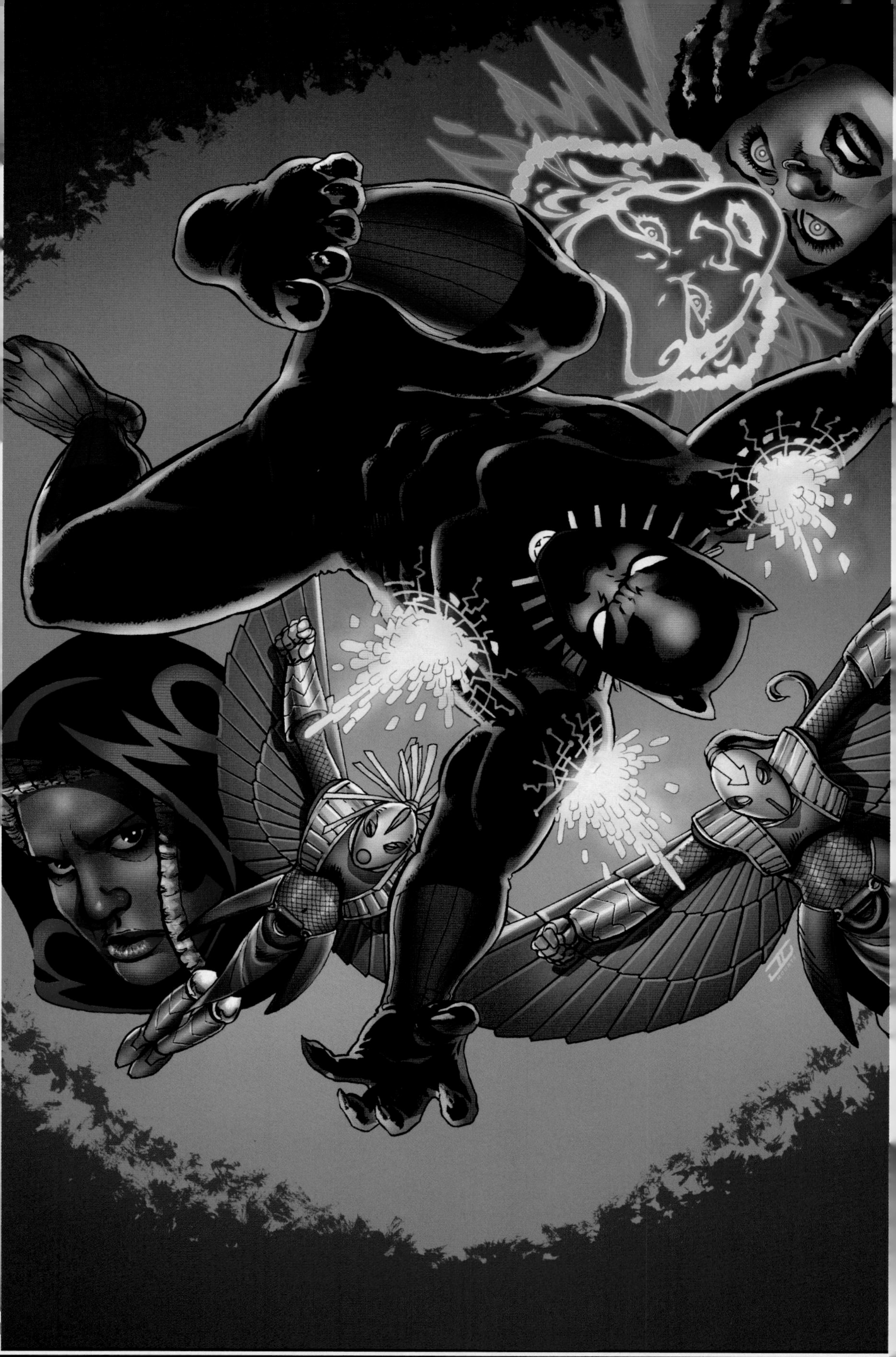

#5 STORY THUS FAR VARIANT BY **JOHN CASSADAY** & **PAUL MOUNTS**

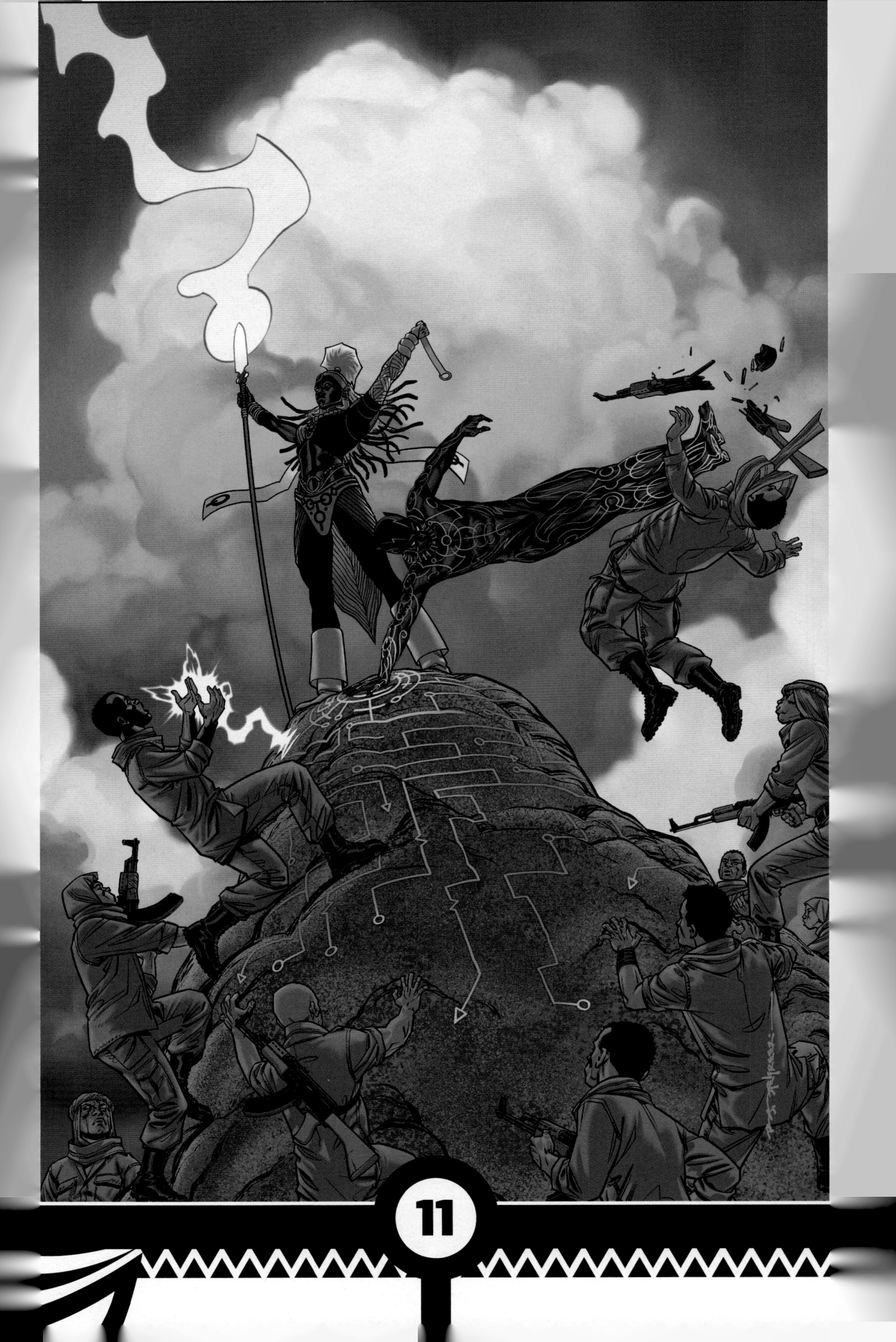

11

# NECROPOLIS, THE CITY OF THE DEAD

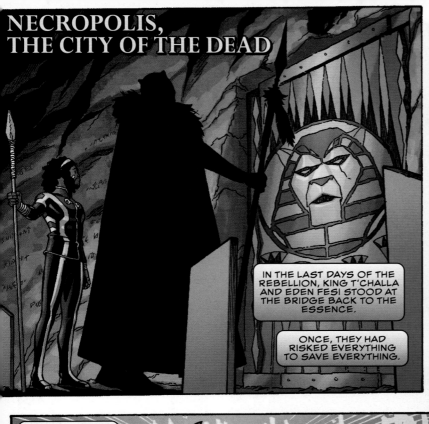

IN THE LAST DAYS OF THE REBELLION, KING T'CHALLA AND EDEN FESI STOOD AT THE BRIDGE BACK TO THE ESSENCE.

ONCE, THEY HAD RISKED EVERYTHING TO SAVE EVERYTHING.

NOW, TO SAVE THIS ONE THING, THEY RISKED IT ALL AGAIN.

EDEN PARTED THE GATE.

KING T'CHALLA SUMMONED THE LEGIONS.

AND THE DEAD RALLIED ONE LAST TIME...

...TO THEIR NOW AND FOREVER KING.

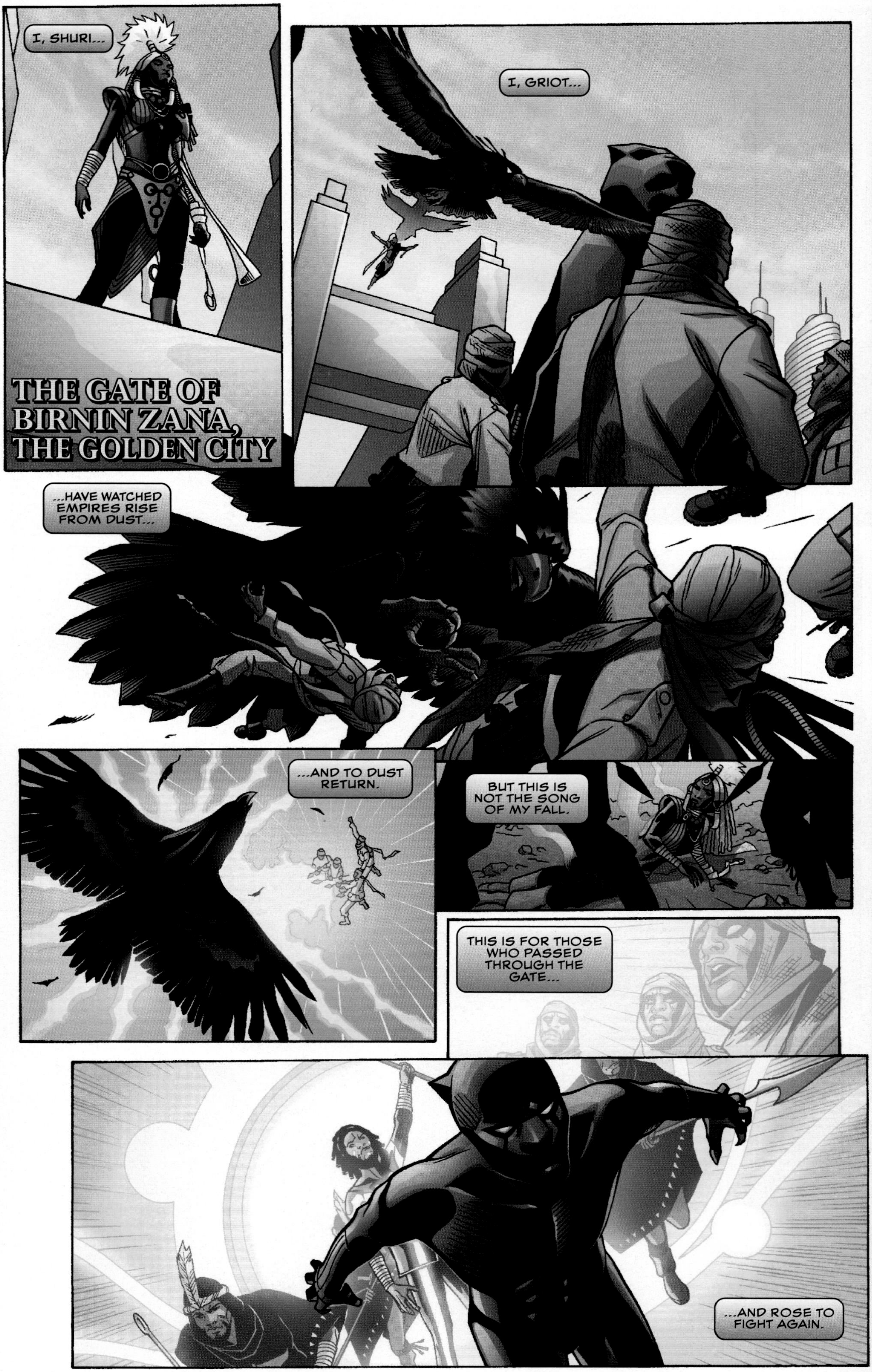
I, SHURI...
THE GATE OF BIRNIN ZANA, THE GOLDEN CITY
I, GRIOT...
...HAVE WATCHED EMPIRES RISE FROM DUST...
...AND TO DUST RETURN.
BUT THIS IS NOT THE SONG OF MY FALL.
THIS IS FOR THOSE WHO PASSED THROUGH THE GATE...
...AND ROSE TO FIGHT AGAIN.

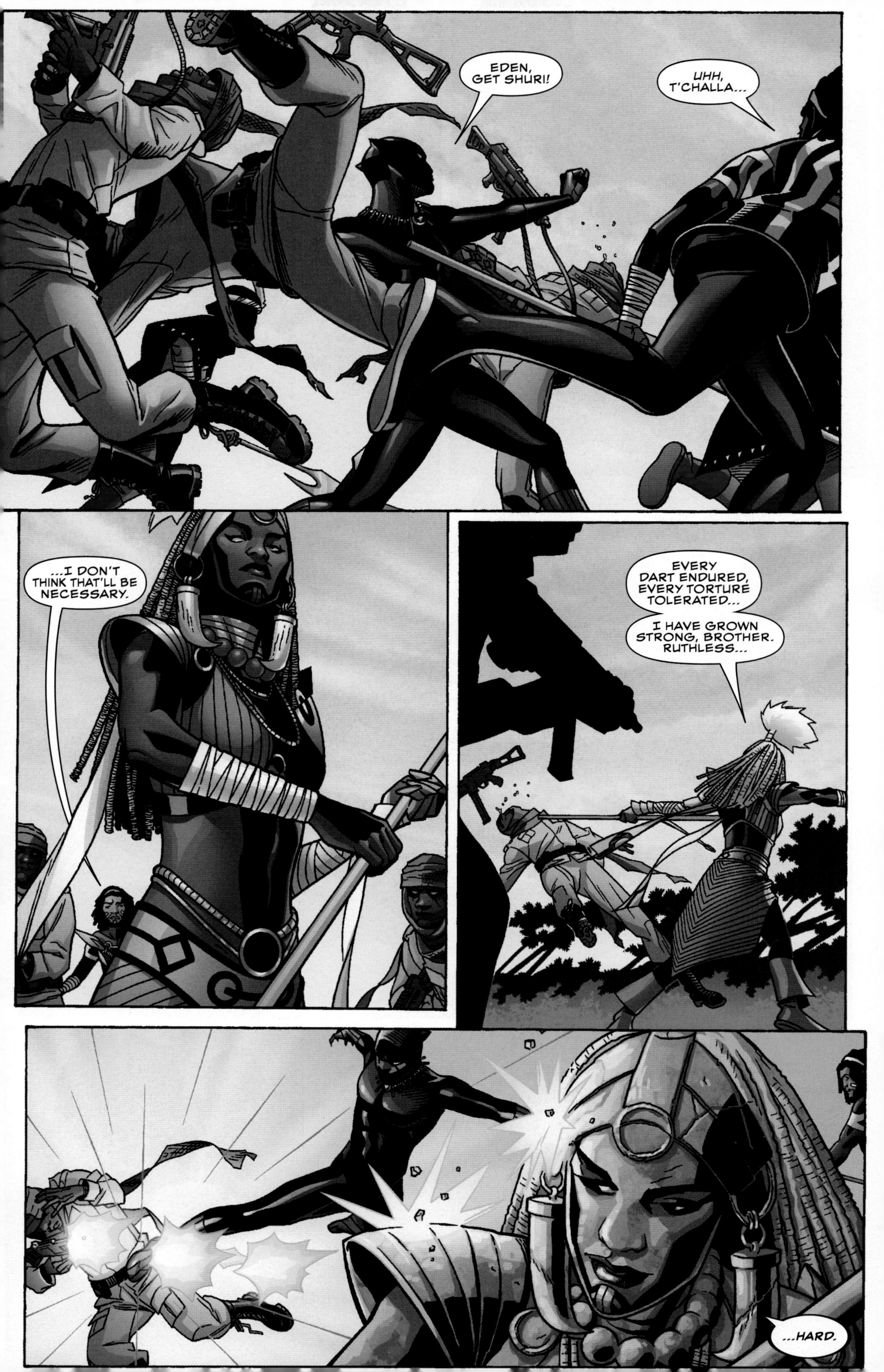
EDEN, GET SHURI!
UHH, T'CHALLA...
...I DON'T THINK THAT'LL BE NECESSARY.
EVERY DART ENDURED, EVERY TORTURE TOLERATED...
I HAVE GROWN STRONG, BROTHER. RUTHLESS...
...HARD.

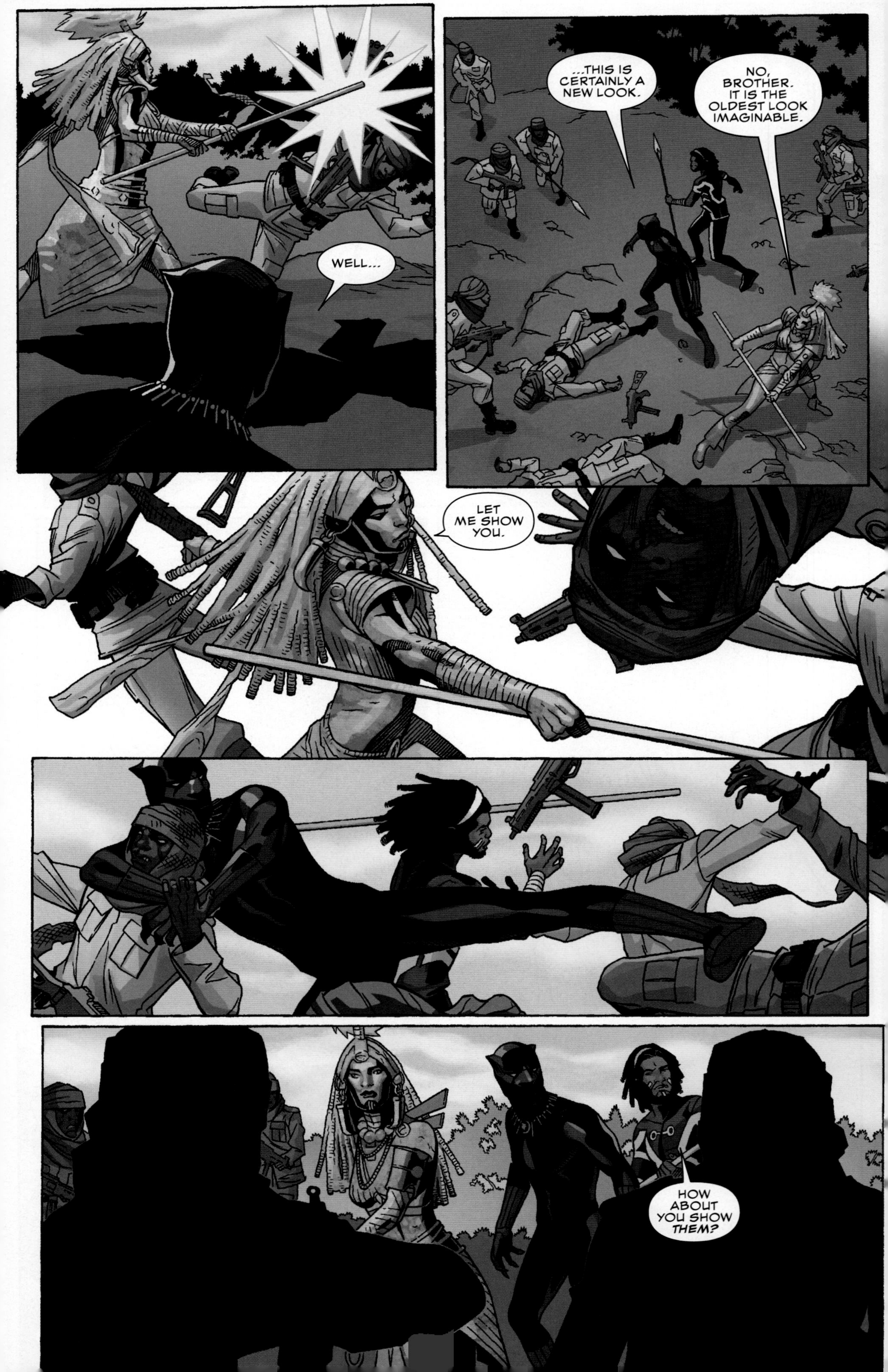
WELL...
...THIS IS CERTAINLY A NEW LOOK.
NO, BROTHER. IT IS THE OLDEST LOOK IMAGINABLE.
LET ME SHOW YOU.
HOW ABOUT YOU SHOW THEM?

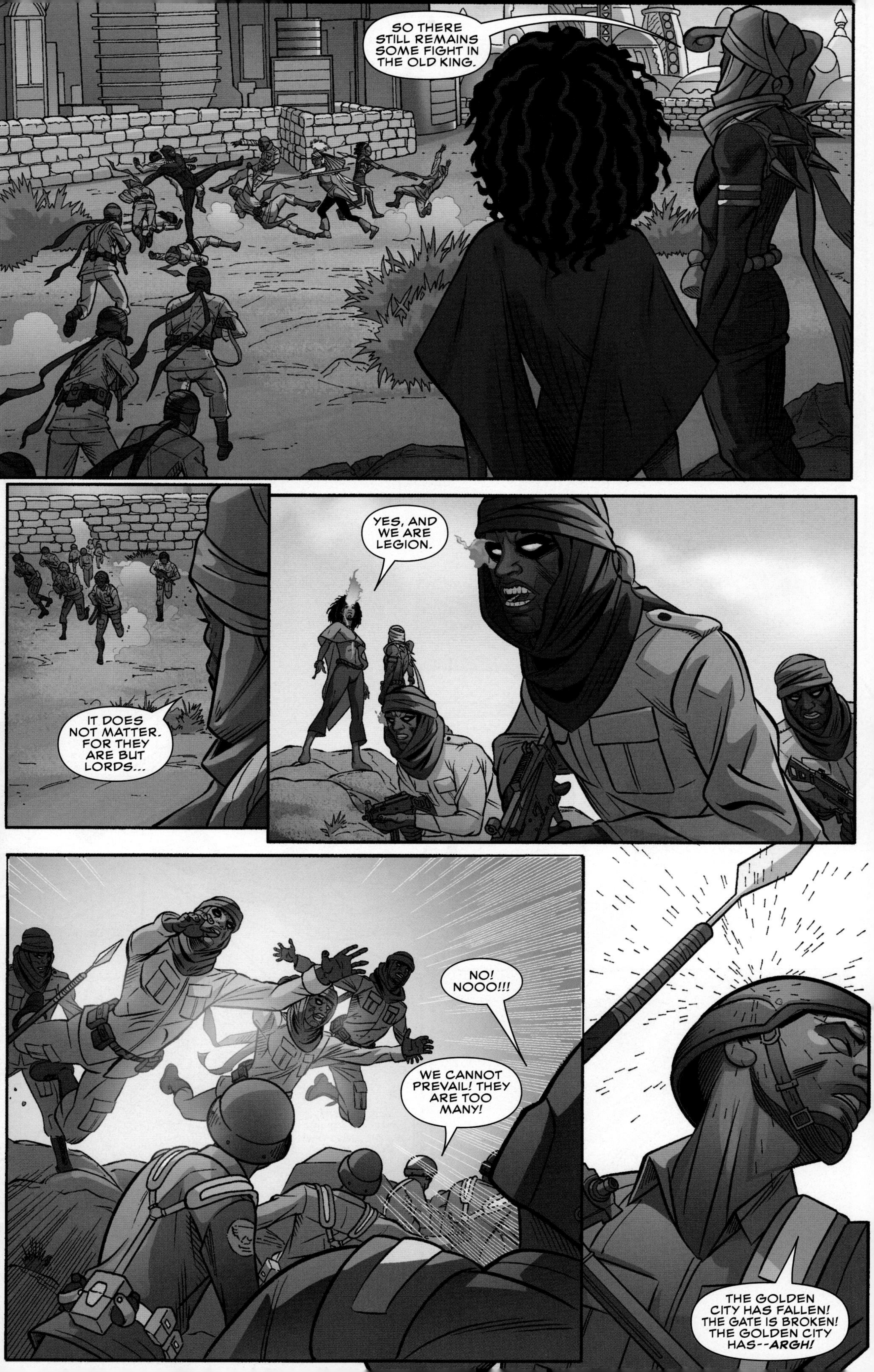
SO THERE STILL REMAINS SOME FIGHT IN THE OLD KING.
YES, AND WE ARE LEGION.
IT DOES NOT MATTER. FOR THEY ARE BUT LORDS...
NO! NOOO!!!
WE CANNOT PREVAIL! THEY ARE TOO MANY!
THE GOLDEN CITY HAS FALLEN! THE GATE IS BROKEN! THE GOLDEN CITY HAS--ARGH!

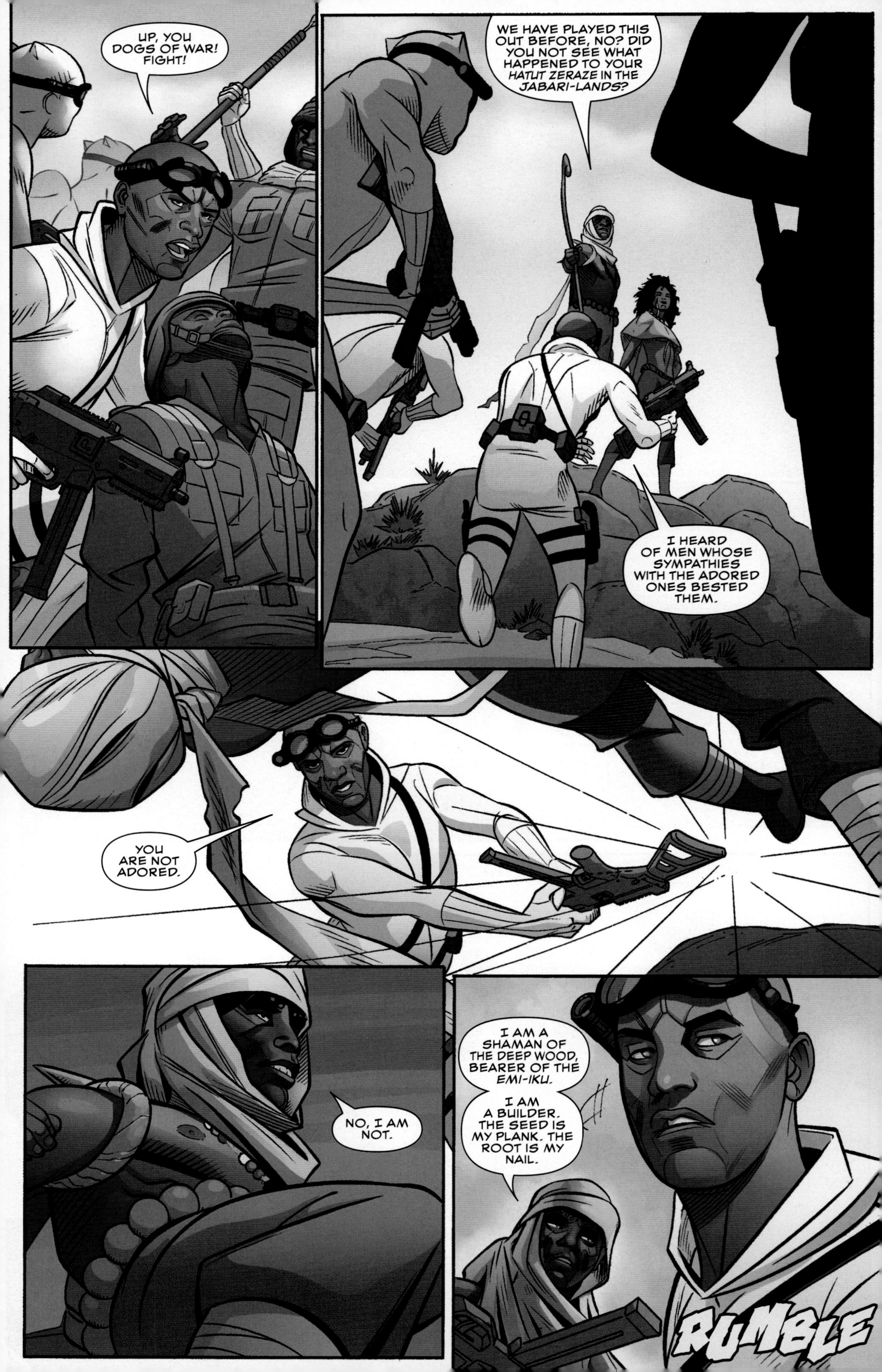
UP, YOU DOGS OF WAR! FIGHT!
WE HAVE PLAYED THIS OUT BEFORE, NO? DID YOU NOT SEE WHAT HAPPENED TO YOUR *HATUT ZERAZE* IN THE *JABARI-LANDS*?
I HEARD OF MEN WHOSE SYMPATHIES WITH THE ADORED ONES BESTED THEM.
YOU ARE NOT ADORED.
NO, I AM NOT.
I AM A SHAMAN OF THE DEEP WOOD, BEARER OF THE *EMI-IKU*.
I AM A BUILDER. THE SEED IS MY PLANK. THE ROOT IS MY NAIL.
RUMBLE

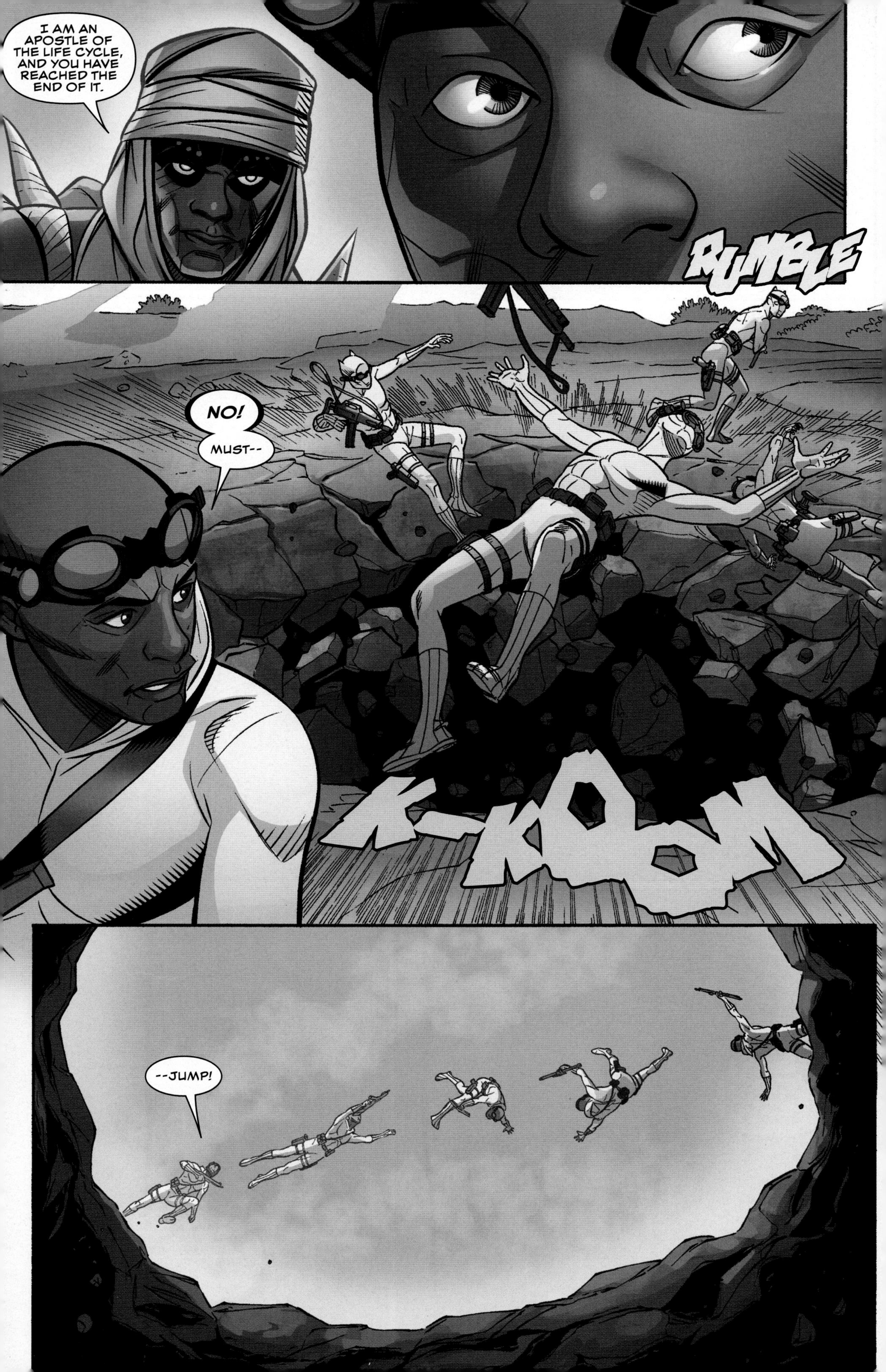
I AM AN APOSTLE OF THE LIFE CYCLE, AND YOU HAVE REACHED THE END OF IT.
RUMBLE
NO!
MUST--
K-KOOM
--JUMP!

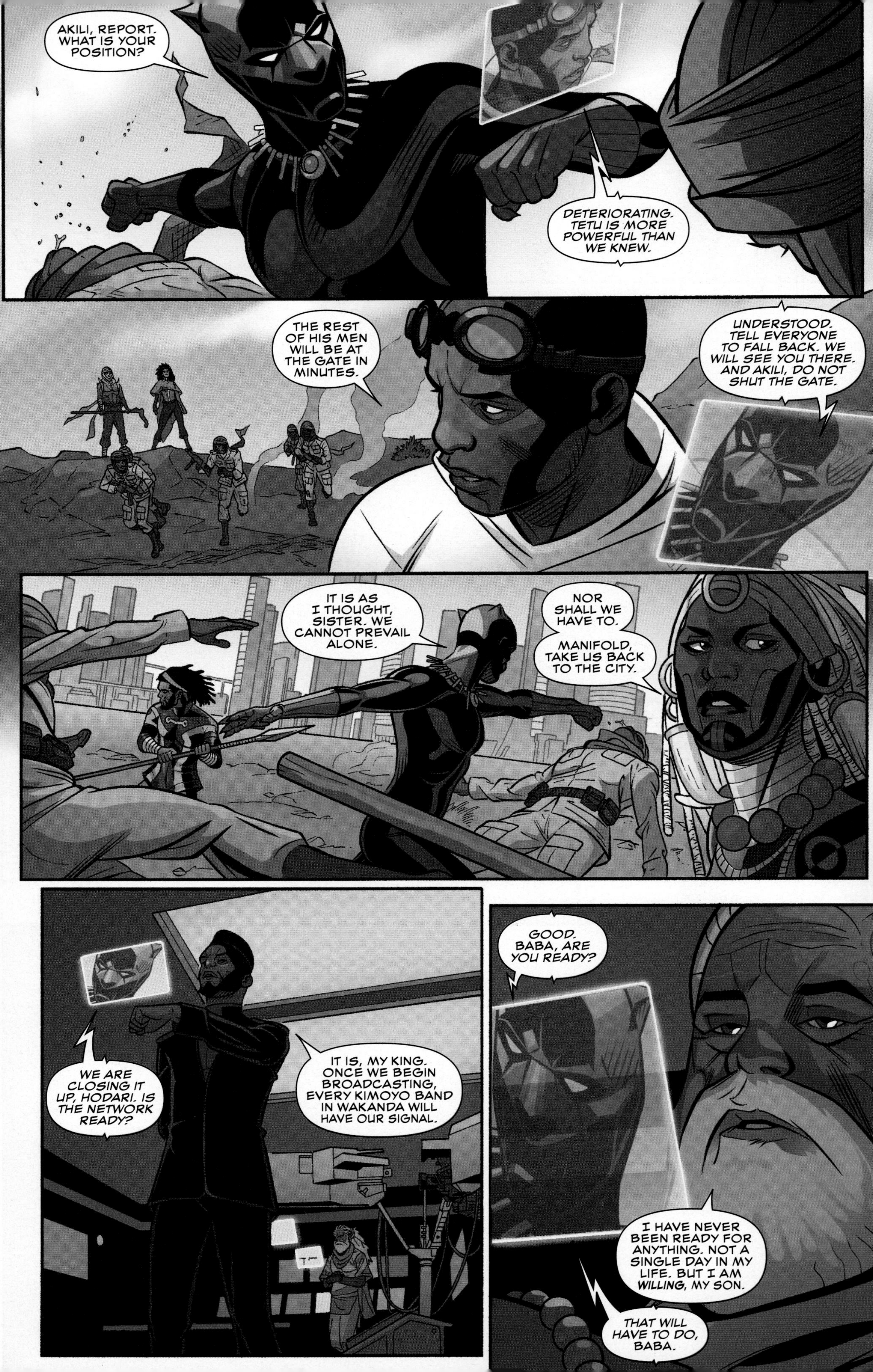
AKILI, REPORT. WHAT IS YOUR POSITION?
DETERIORATING. TETU IS MORE POWERFUL THAN WE KNEW.
THE REST OF HIS MEN WILL BE AT THE GATE IN MINUTES.
UNDERSTOOD. TELL EVERYONE TO FALL BACK. WE WILL SEE YOU THERE. AND AKILI, DO NOT SHUT THE GATE.
IT IS AS I THOUGHT, SISTER. WE CANNOT PREVAIL ALONE.
NOR SHALL WE HAVE TO.
MANIFOLD, TAKE US BACK TO THE CITY.
WE ARE CLOSING IT UP, HODARI. IS THE NETWORK READY?
IT IS, MY KING. ONCE WE BEGIN BROADCASTING, EVERY KIMOYO BAND IN WAKANDA WILL HAVE OUR SIGNAL.
GOOD. BABA, ARE YOU READY?
I HAVE NEVER BEEN READY FOR ANYTHING. NOT A SINGLE DAY IN MY LIFE. BUT I AM *WILLING*, MY SON.
THAT WILL HAVE TO DO, BABA.

AKILI, IT IS TIME.

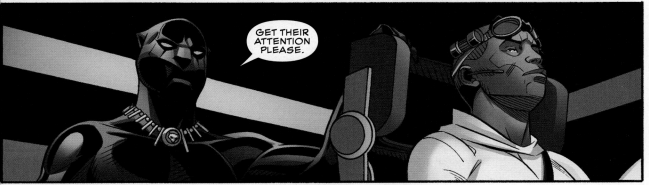

GET THEIR ATTENTION PLEASE.

KA-KOOM

"WE HAVE THEM, BABA. YOU HAVE TWO MINUTES AT MOST."

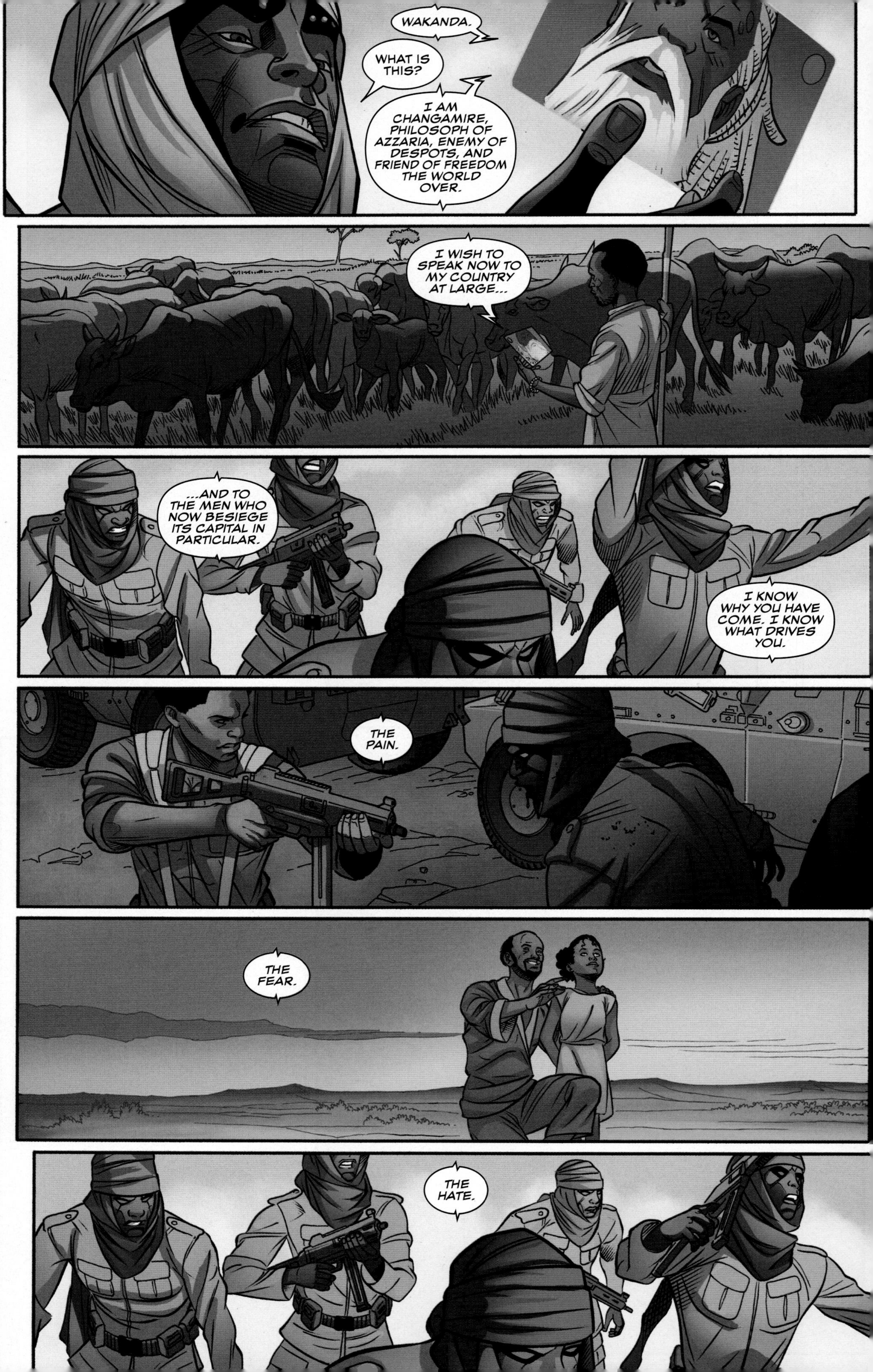
WAKANDA.
WHAT IS THIS?
I AM CHANGAMIRE, PHILOSOPH OF AZZARIA, ENEMY OF DESPOTS, AND FRIEND OF FREEDOM THE WORLD OVER.
I WISH TO SPEAK NOW TO MY COUNTRY AT LARGE...
...AND TO THE MEN WHO NOW BESIEGE ITS CAPITAL IN PARTICULAR.
I KNOW WHY YOU HAVE COME. I KNOW WHAT DRIVES YOU.
THE PAIN.
THE FEAR.
THE HATE.

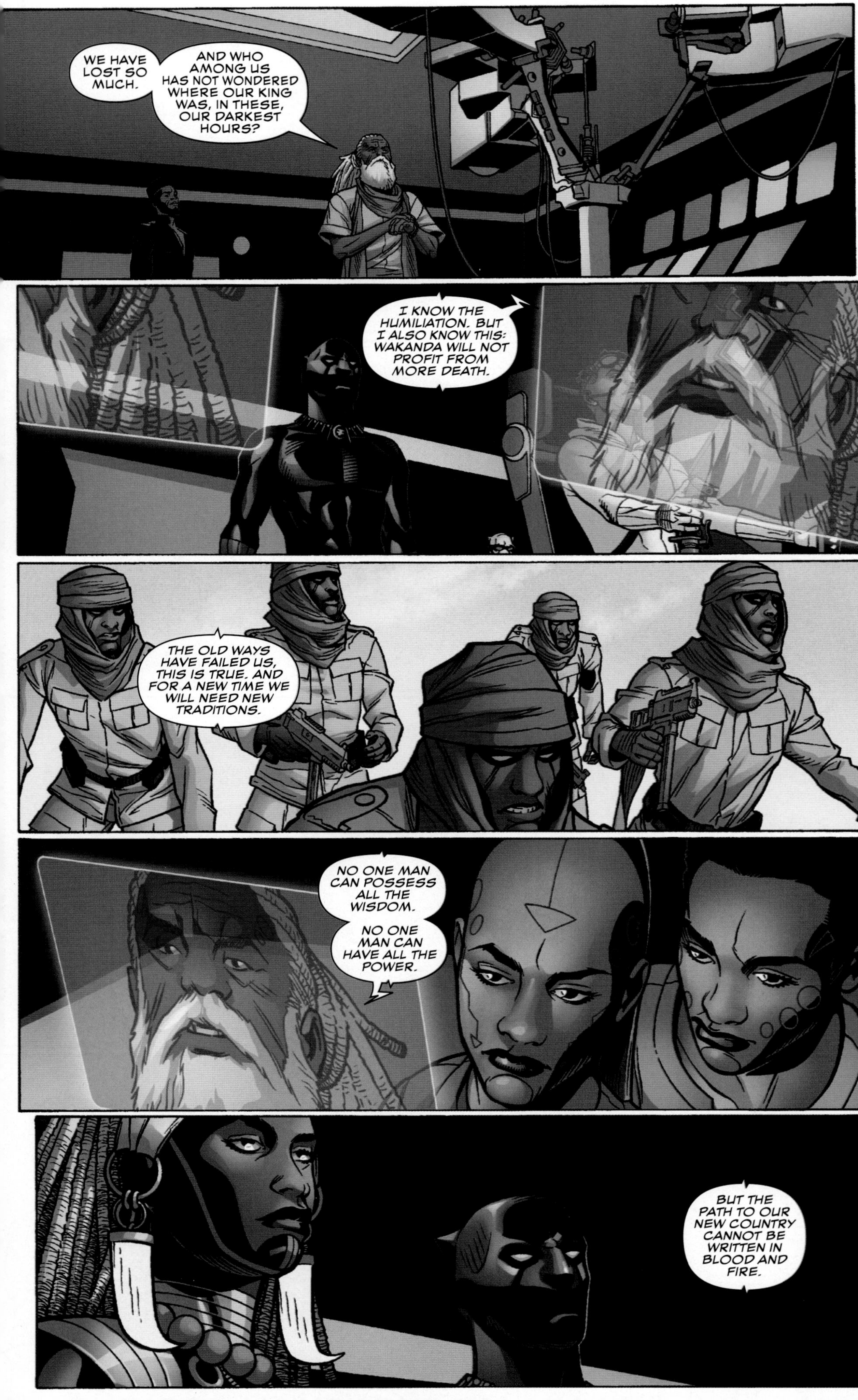
WE HAVE LOST SO MUCH.
AND WHO AMONG US HAS NOT WONDERED WHERE OUR KING WAS, IN THESE, OUR DARKEST HOURS?
I KNOW THE HUMILIATION. BUT I ALSO KNOW THIS: WAKANDA WILL NOT PROFIT FROM MORE DEATH.
THE OLD WAYS HAVE FAILED US, THIS IS TRUE. AND FOR A NEW TIME WE WILL NEED NEW TRADITIONS.
NO ONE MAN CAN POSSESS ALL THE WISDOM.
NO ONE MAN CAN HAVE ALL THE POWER.
BUT THE PATH TO OUR NEW COUNTRY CANNOT BE WRITTEN IN BLOOD AND FIRE.

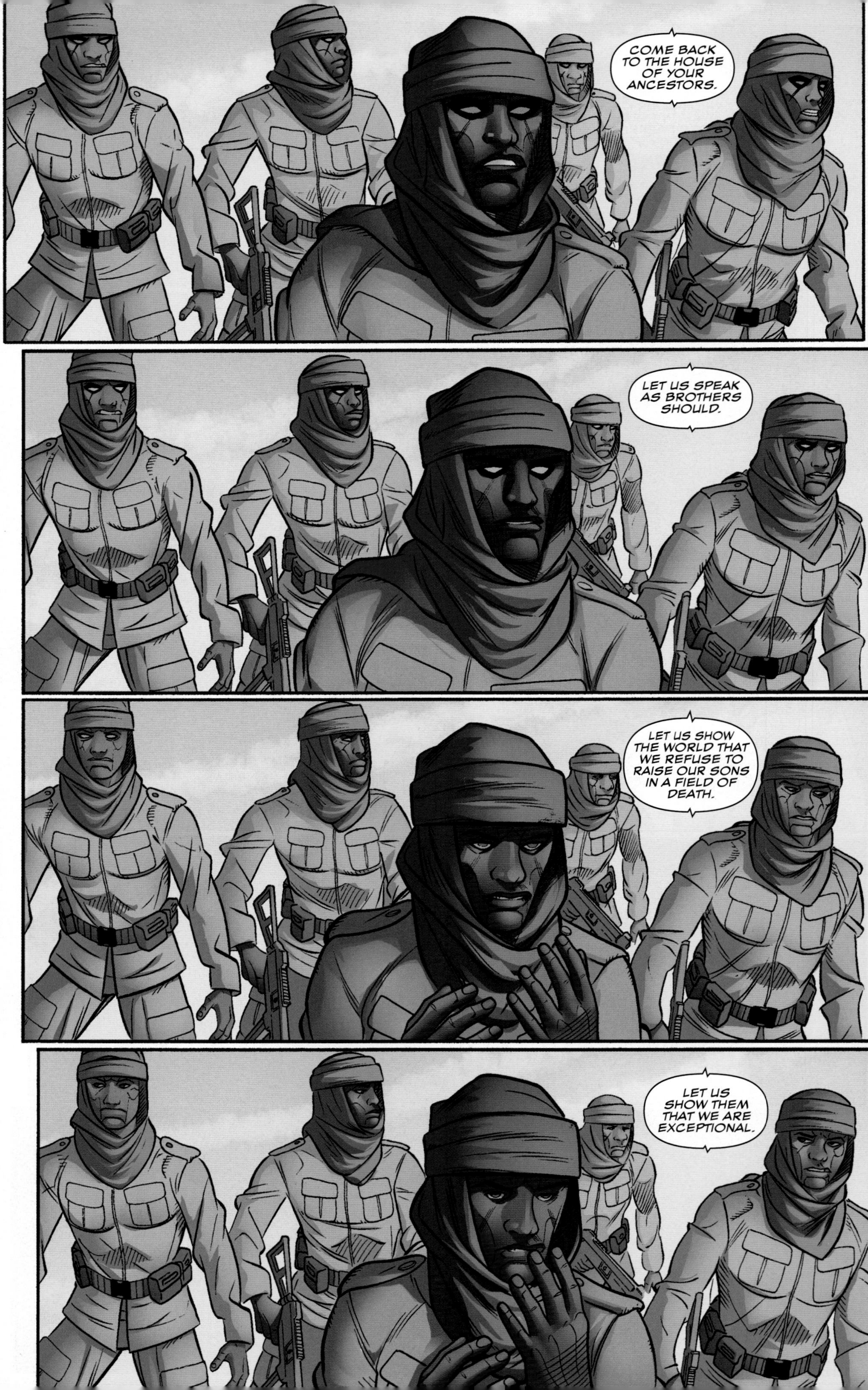
COME BACK TO THE HOUSE OF YOUR ANCESTORS.
LET US SPEAK AS BROTHERS SHOULD.
LET US SHOW THE WORLD THAT WE REFUSE TO RAISE OUR SONS IN A FIELD OF DEATH.
LET US SHOW THEM THAT WE ARE EXCEPTIONAL.

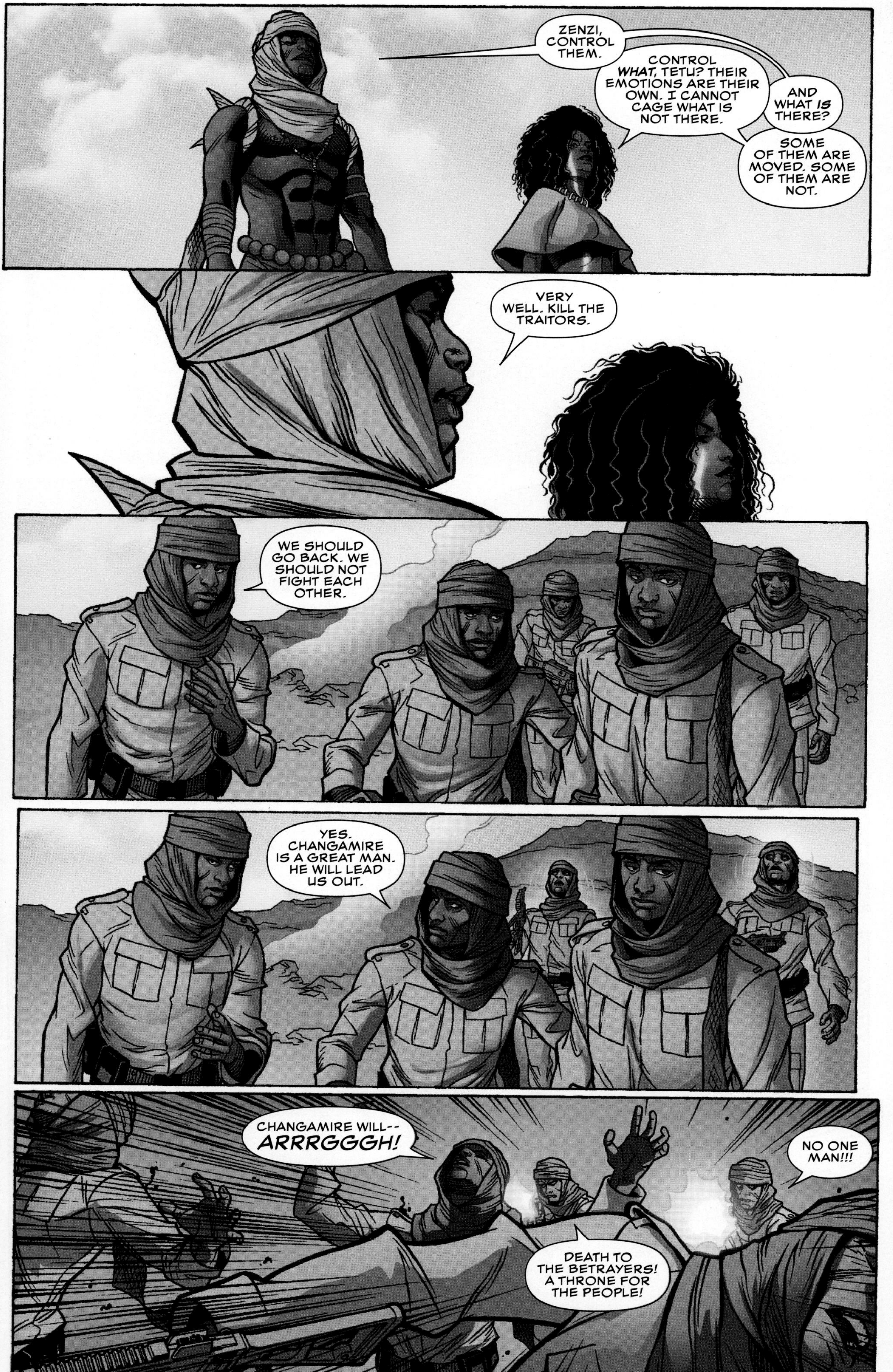
ZENZI, CONTROL THEM.
CONTROL *WHAT*, TETU? THEIR EMOTIONS ARE THEIR OWN. I CANNOT CAGE WHAT IS NOT THERE.
AND WHAT *IS* THERE?
SOME OF THEM ARE MOVED. SOME OF THEM ARE NOT.
VERY WELL. KILL THE TRAITORS.
WE SHOULD GO BACK. WE SHOULD NOT FIGHT EACH OTHER.
YES. CHANGAMIRE IS A GREAT MAN. HE WILL LEAD US OUT.
CHANGAMIRE WILL-- ARRRGGGH!
NO ONE MAN!!!
DEATH TO THE BETRAYERS! A THRONE FOR THE PEOPLE!

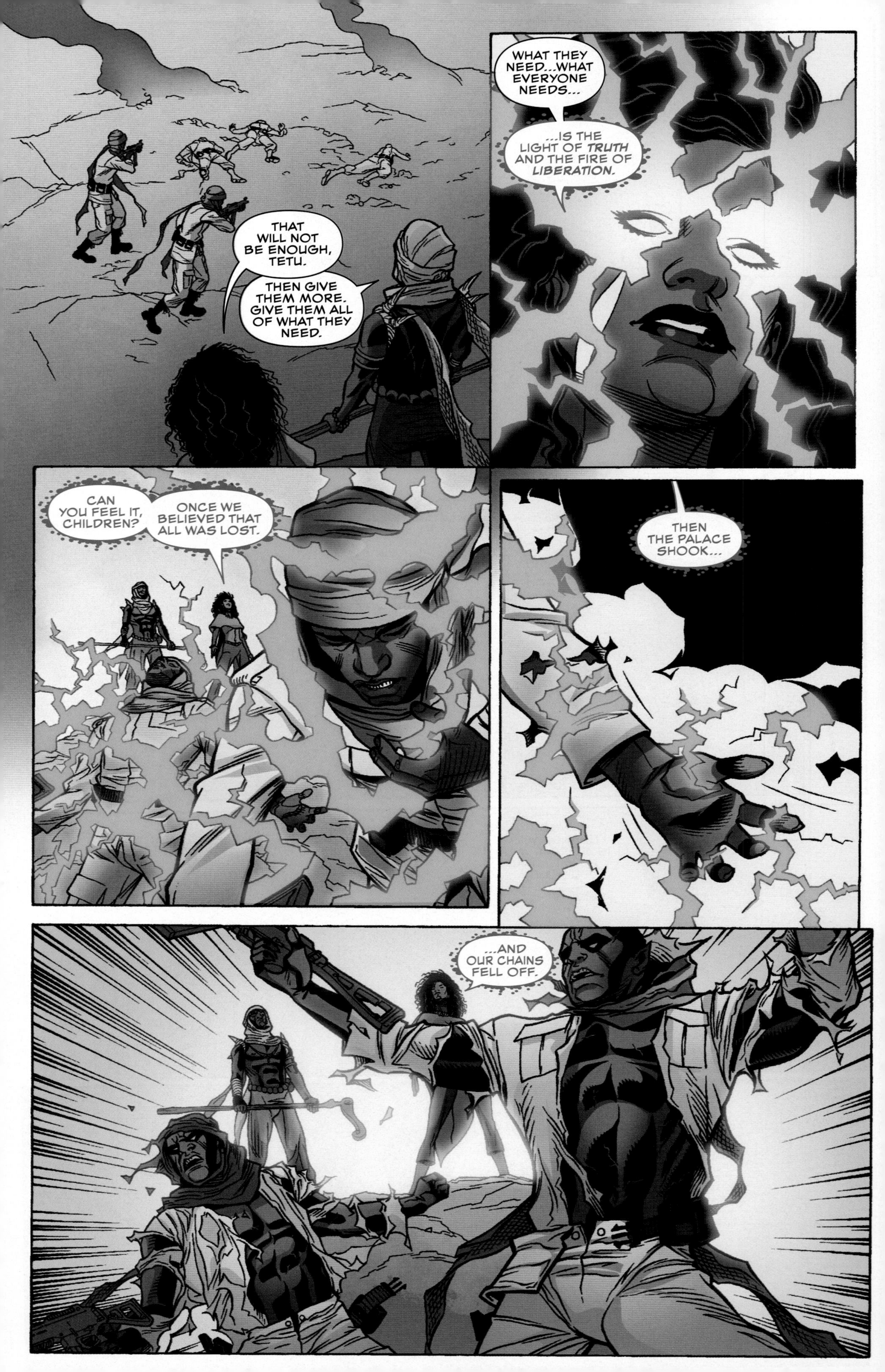
THAT WILL NOT BE ENOUGH, TETU.
THEN GIVE THEM MORE. GIVE THEM ALL OF WHAT THEY NEED.
WHAT THEY NEED...WHAT EVERYONE NEEDS...
...IS THE LIGHT OF TRUTH AND THE FIRE OF LIBERATION.
CAN YOU FEEL IT, CHILDREN?
ONCE WE BELIEVED THAT ALL WAS LOST.
THEN THE PALACE SHOOK...
...AND OUR CHAINS FELL OFF.

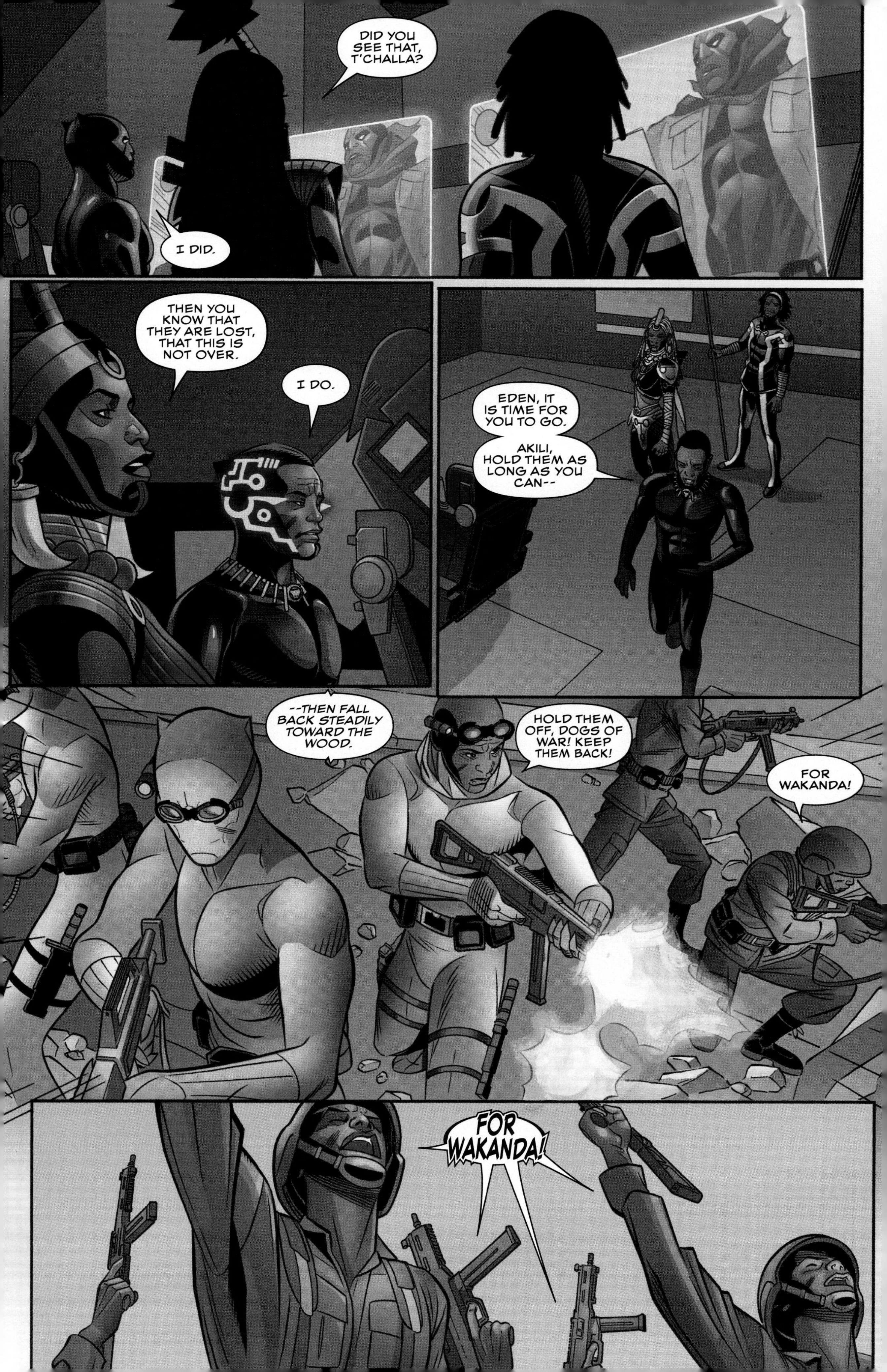
DID YOU SEE THAT, T'CHALLA?
I DID.
THEN YOU KNOW THAT THEY ARE LOST, THAT THIS IS NOT OVER.
I DO.
EDEN, IT IS TIME FOR YOU TO GO.
AKILI, HOLD THEM AS LONG AS YOU CAN--
--THEN FALL BACK STEADILY TOWARD THE WOOD.
HOLD THEM OFF, DOGS OF WAR! KEEP THEM BACK!
FOR WAKANDA!
FOR WAKANDA!

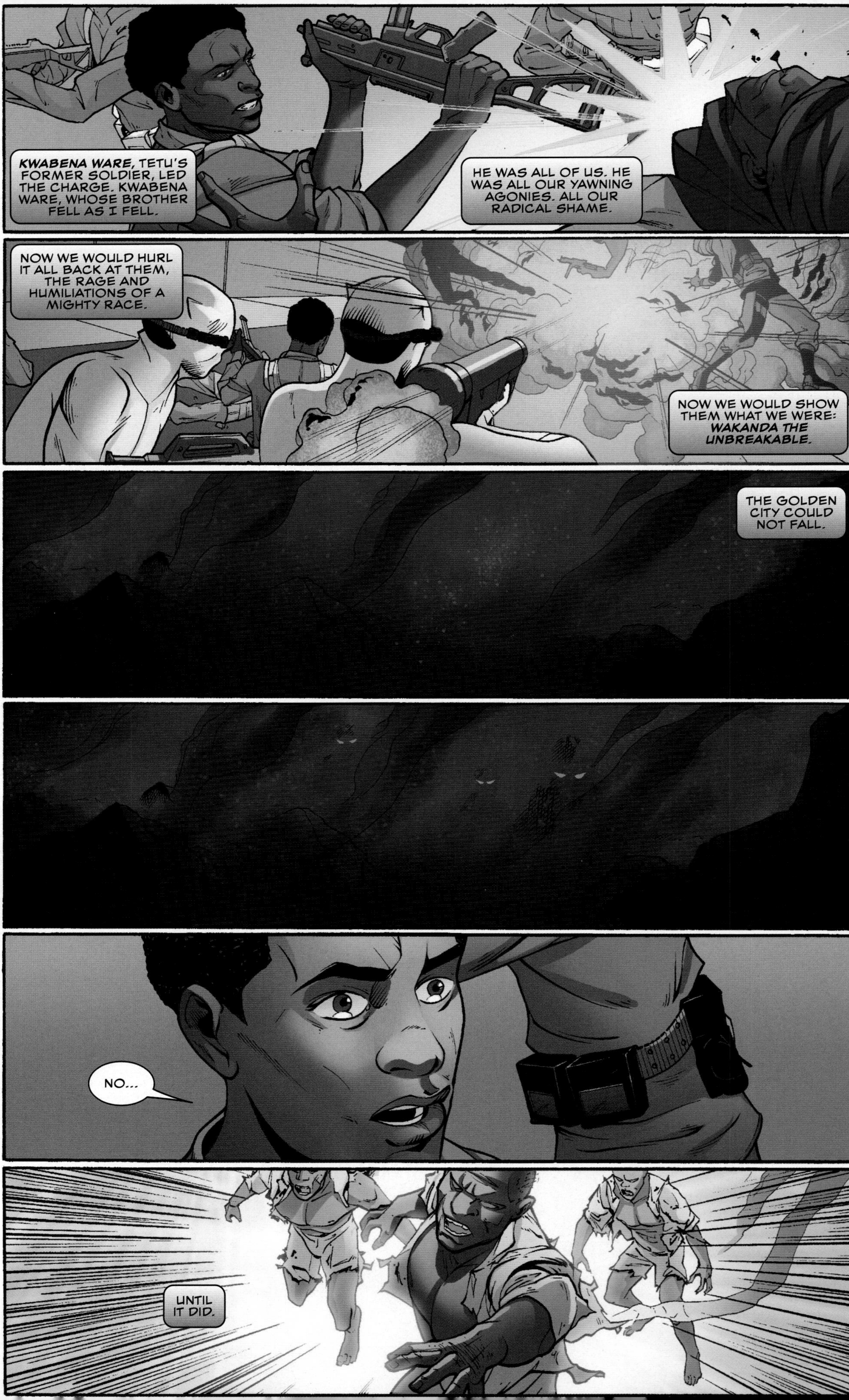
KWABENA WARE, TETU'S FORMER SOLDIER, LED THE CHARGE. KWABENA WARE, WHOSE BROTHER FELL AS I FELL.
HE WAS ALL OF US. HE WAS ALL OUR YAWNING AGONIES. ALL OUR RADICAL SHAME.
NOW WE WOULD HURL IT ALL BACK AT THEM, THE RAGE AND HUMILIATIONS OF A MIGHTY RACE.
NOW WE WOULD SHOW THEM WHAT WE WERE: WAKANDA THE UNBREAKABLE.
THE GOLDEN CITY COULD NOT FALL.
NO...
UNTIL IT DID.

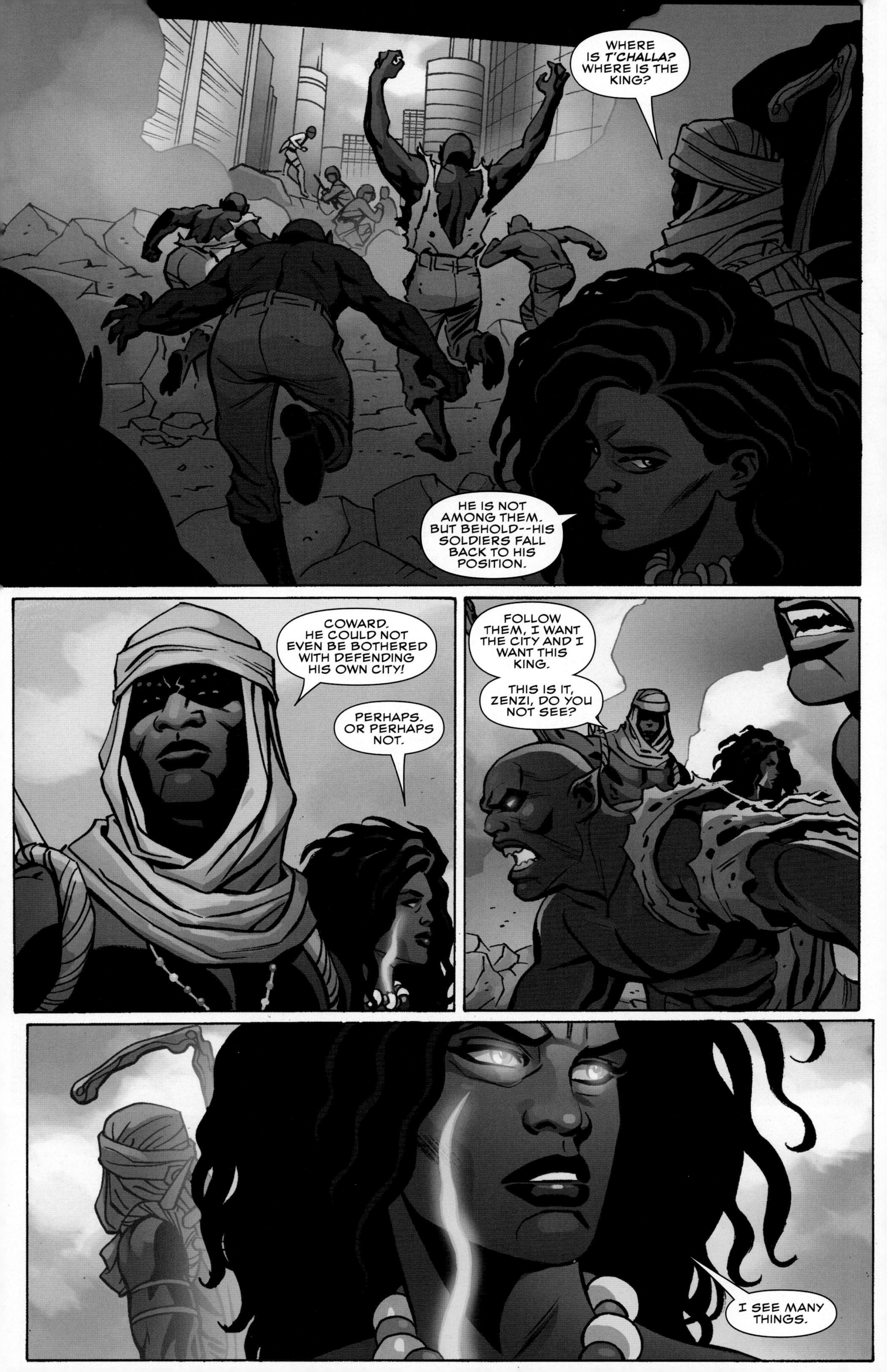
WHERE IS T'CHALLA? WHERE IS THE KING?
HE IS NOT AMONG THEM. BUT BEHOLD--HIS SOLDIERS FALL BACK TO HIS POSITION.
COWARD. HE COULD NOT EVEN BE BOTHERED WITH DEFENDING HIS OWN CITY!
PERHAPS. OR PERHAPS NOT.
FOLLOW THEM, I WANT THE CITY AND I WANT THIS KING.
THIS IS IT, ZENZI, DO YOU NOT SEE?
I SEE MANY THINGS.

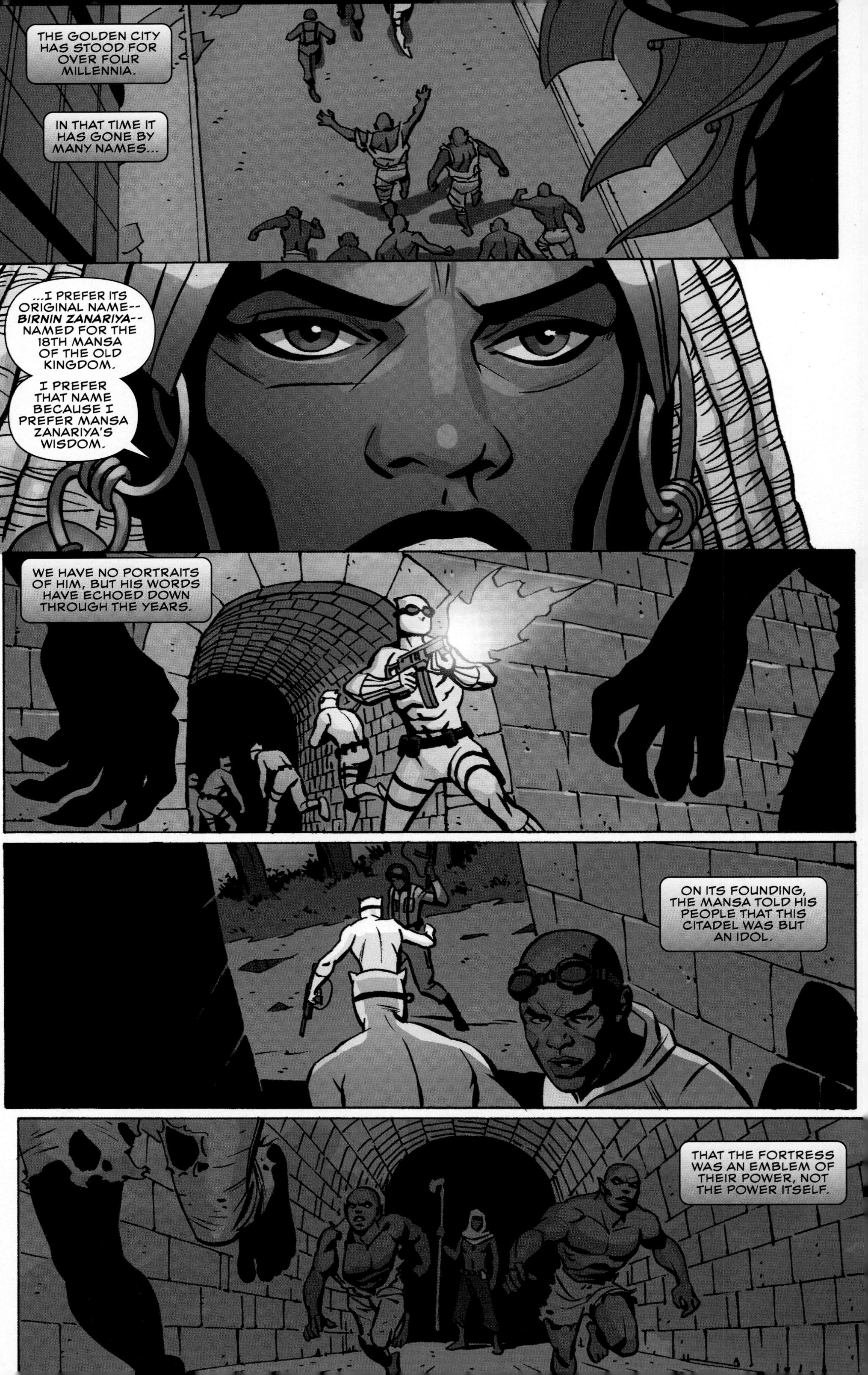
THE GOLDEN CITY HAS STOOD FOR OVER FOUR MILLENNIA.
IN THAT TIME IT HAS GONE BY MANY NAMES...
...I PREFER ITS ORIGINAL NAME-- BIRNIN ZANARIYA-- NAMED FOR THE 18TH MANSA OF THE OLD KINGDOM.
I PREFER THAT NAME BECAUSE I PREFER MANSA ZANARIYA'S WISDOM.
WE HAVE NO PORTRAITS OF HIM, BUT HIS WORDS HAVE ECHOED DOWN THROUGH THE YEARS.
ON ITS FOUNDING, THE MANSA TOLD HIS PEOPLE THAT THIS CITADEL WAS BUT AN IDOL.
THAT THE FORTRESS WAS AN EMBLEM OF THEIR POWER, NOT THE POWER ITSELF.

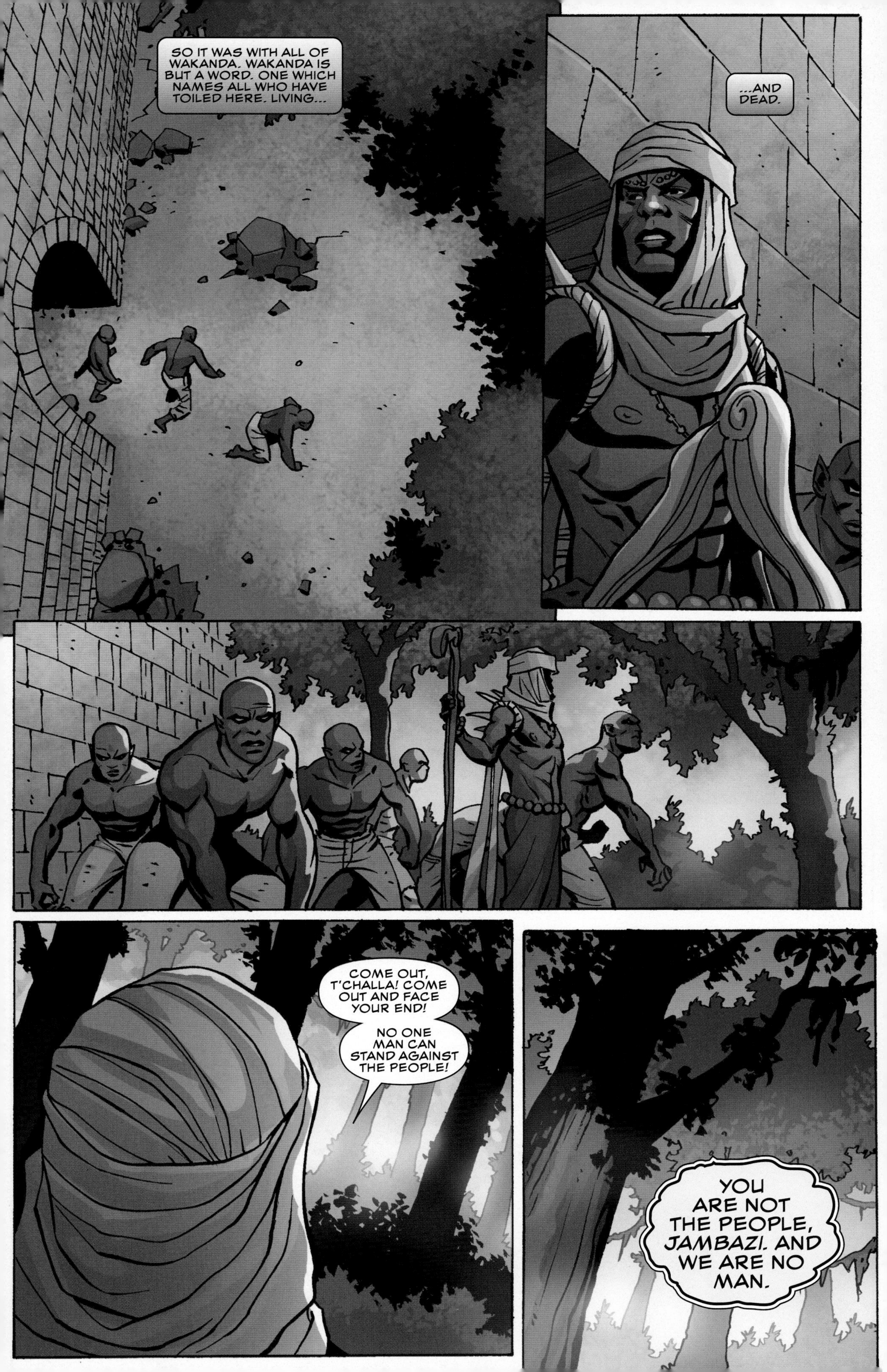
SO IT WAS WITH ALL OF WAKANDA. WAKANDA IS BUT A WORD. ONE WHICH NAMES ALL WHO HAVE TOILED HERE. LIVING...
...AND DEAD.
COME OUT, T'CHALLA! COME OUT AND FACE YOUR END!
NO ONE MAN CAN STAND AGAINST THE PEOPLE!
YOU ARE NOT THE PEOPLE, JAMBAZI. AND WE ARE NO MAN.

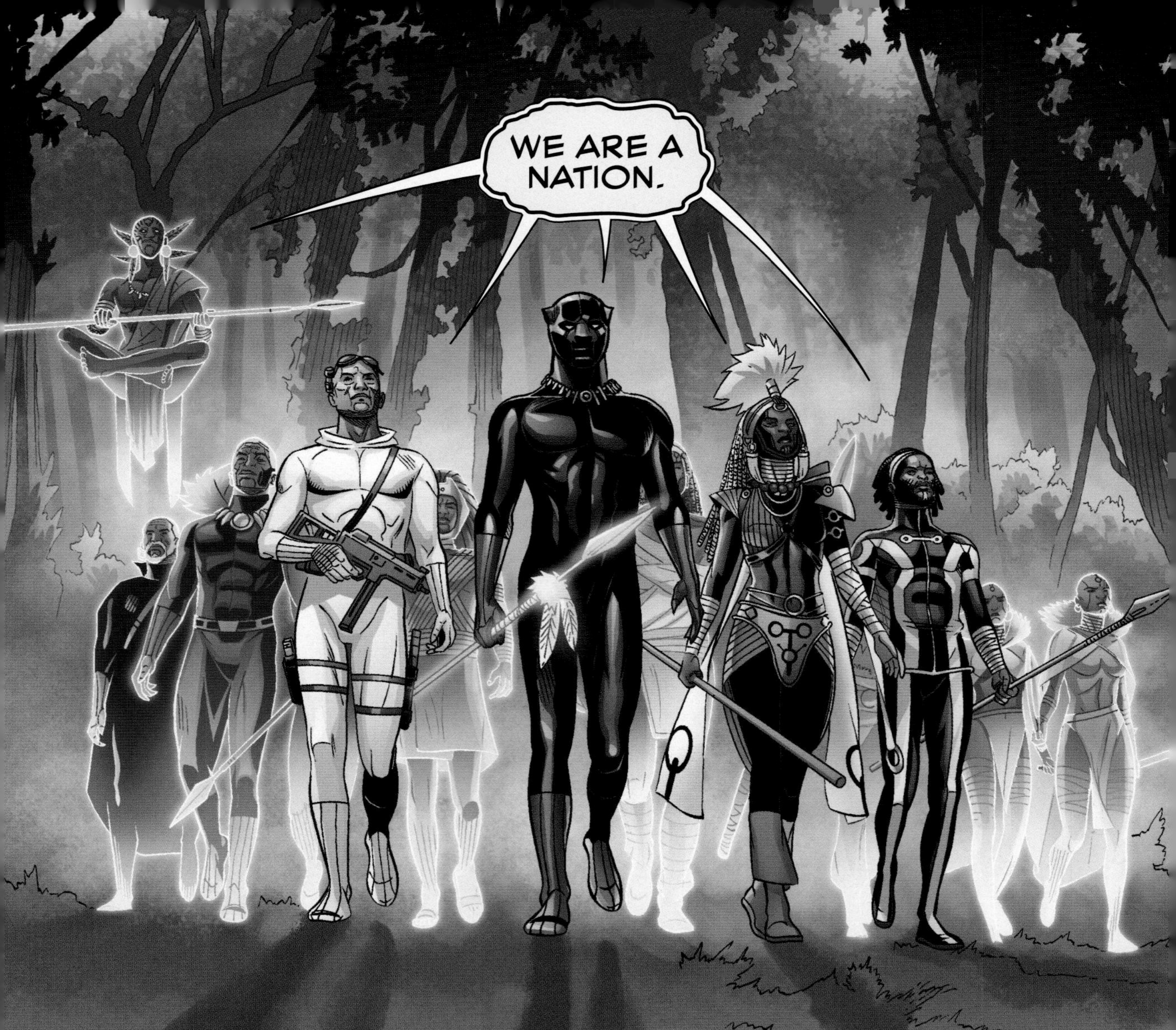
WE ARE A NATION.

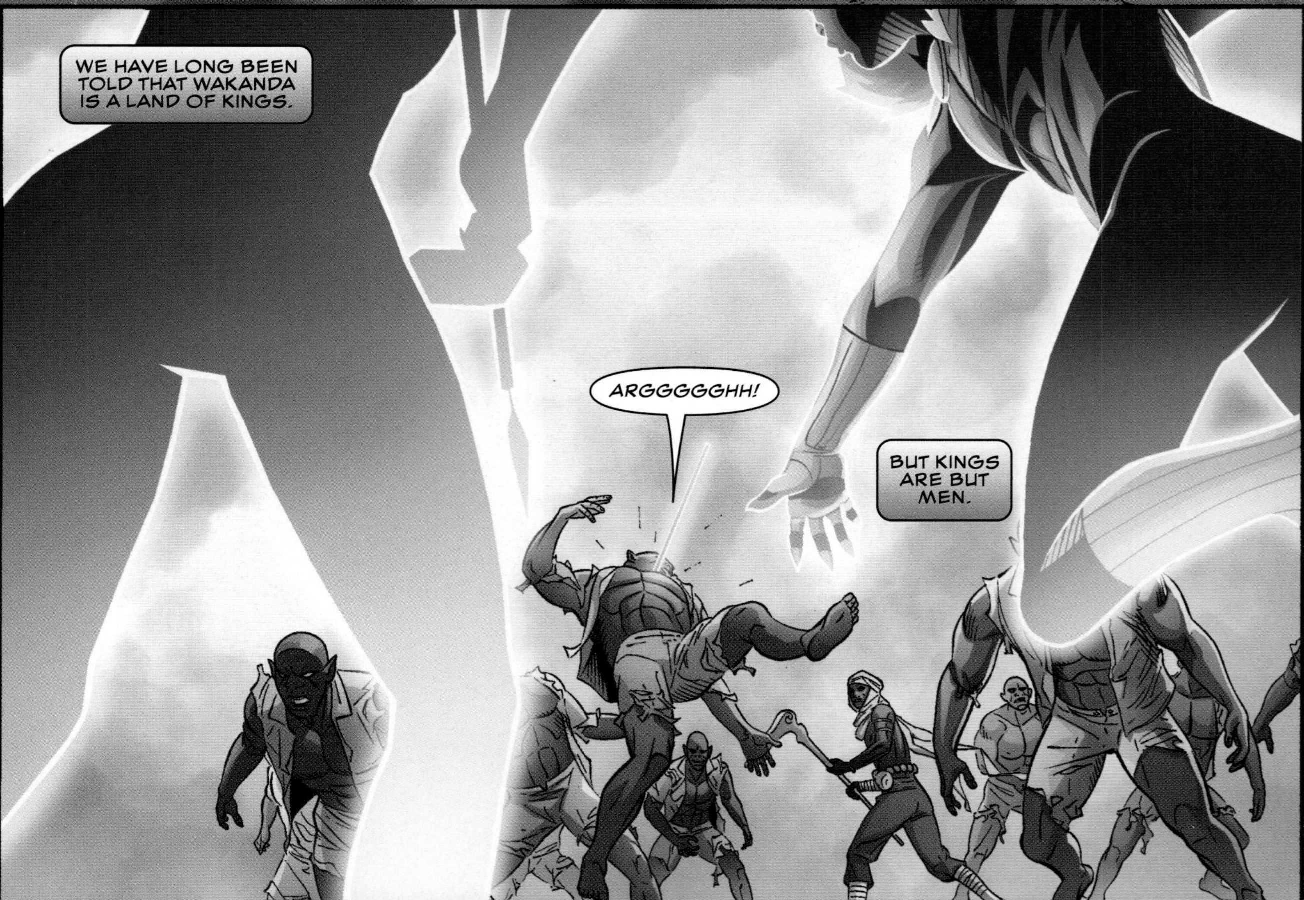
WE HAVE LONG BEEN TOLD THAT WAKANDA IS A LAND OF KINGS.
ARGGGGGHH!
BUT KINGS ARE BUT MEN.

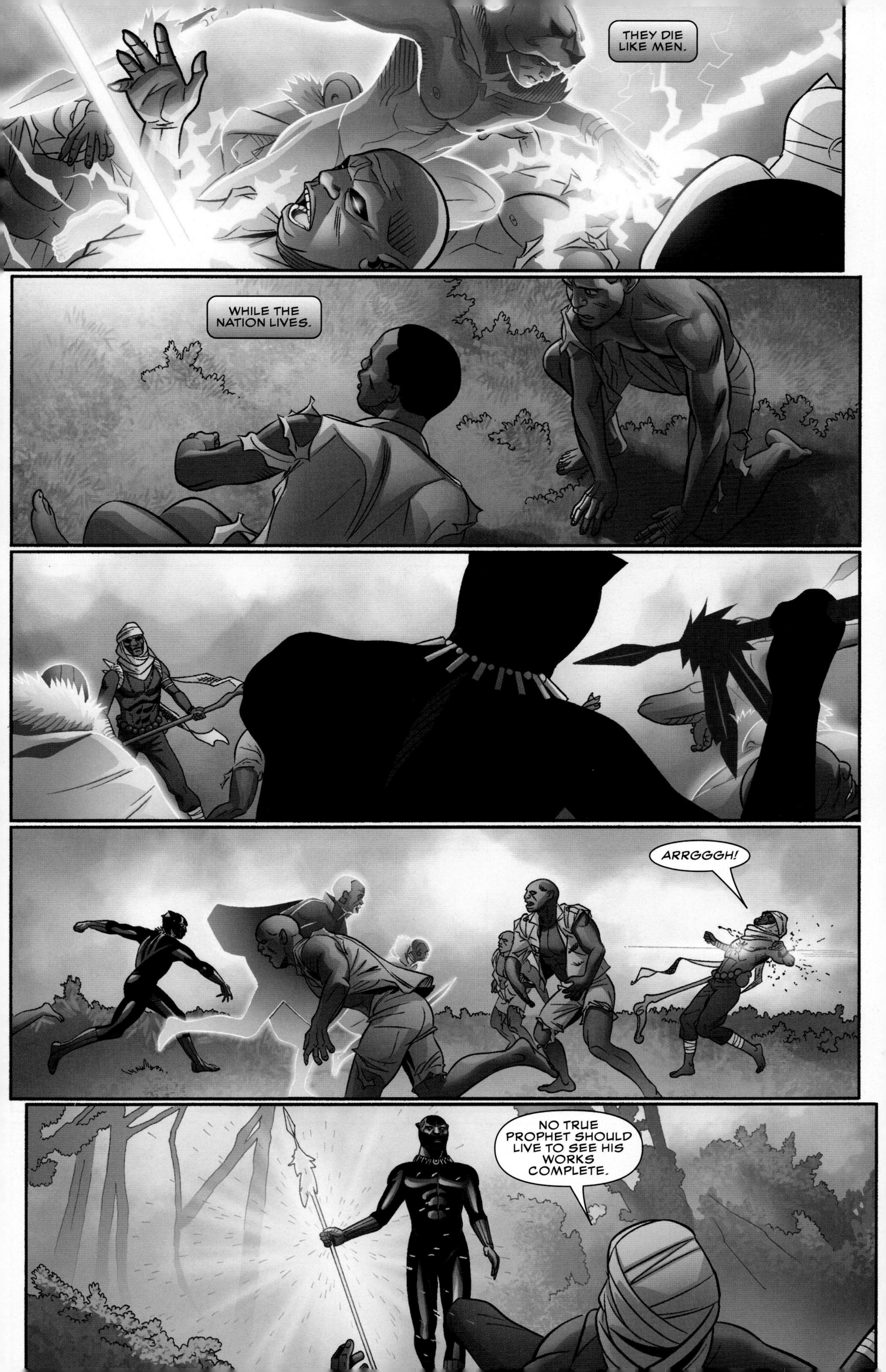
THEY DIE LIKE MEN.
WHILE THE NATION LIVES.
ARRGGGH!
NO TRUE PROPHET SHOULD LIVE TO SEE HIS WORKS COMPLETE.

IT DOES NOT MATTER.

I WILL DIE AND YOU WILL LIVE. BUT MY *COUNTRY* SHALL LIVE, WHILE *YOURS* CRUMBLES TO DUST.

THE DEAD WILL NOT HAVE YOU, TETU.

AND THE LIVING ARE NOT DONE WITH YOU YET.

NO, THIS IS NOT THE SONG OF MY FALL.

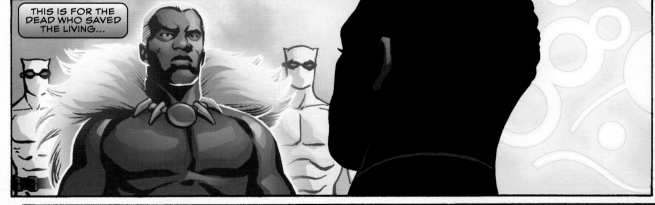

THIS IS FOR THE DEAD WHO SAVED THE LIVING...

FOR MY FATHER, WHO CROSSED THE BRIDGE...

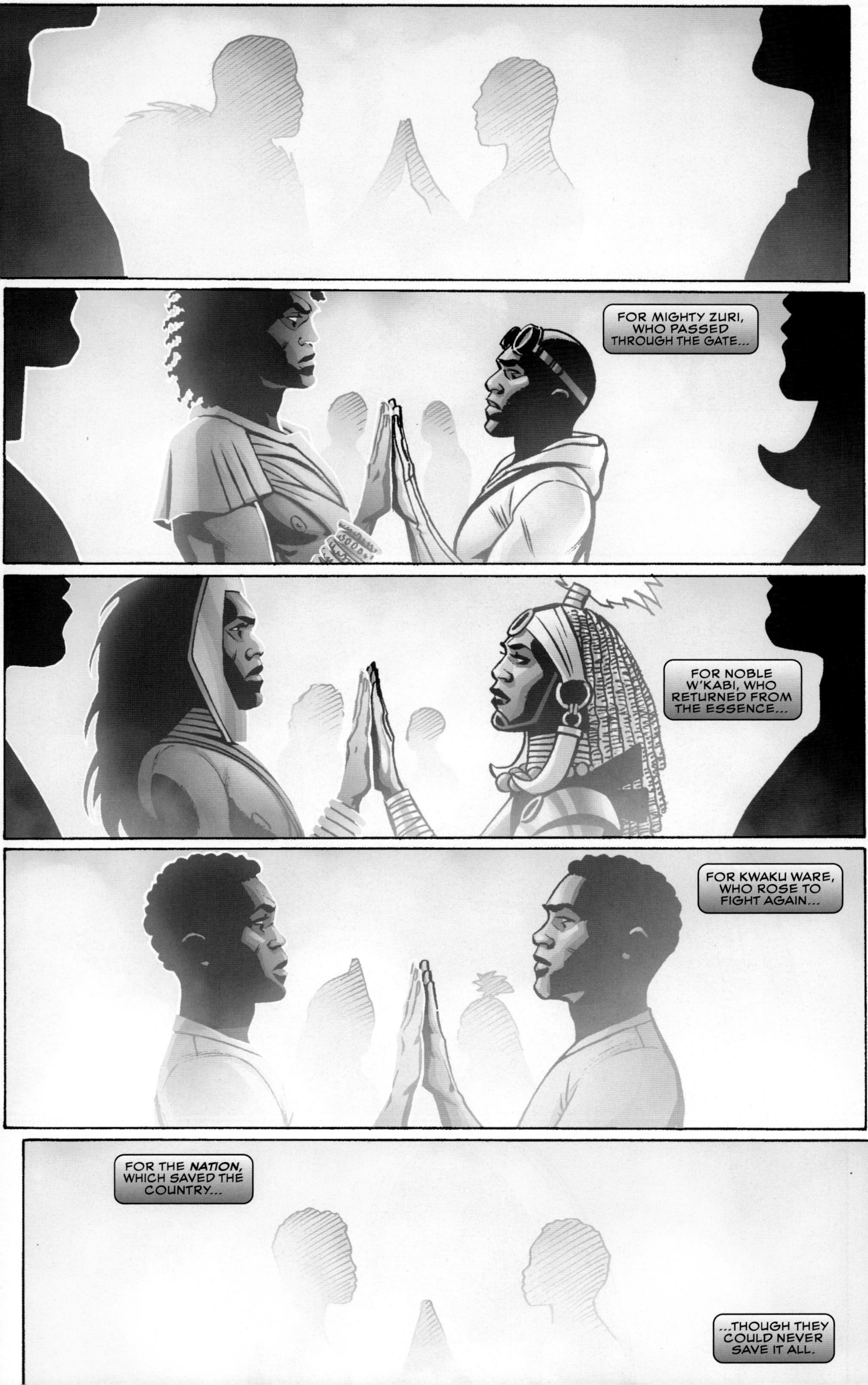
FOR MIGHTY ZURI, WHO PASSED THROUGH THE GATE...
FOR NOBLE W'KABI, WHO RETURNED FROM THE ESSENCE...
FOR KWAKU WARE, WHO ROSE TO FIGHT AGAIN...
FOR THE *NATION*, WHICH SAVED THE COUNTRY...
...THOUGH THEY COULD NEVER SAVE IT ALL.

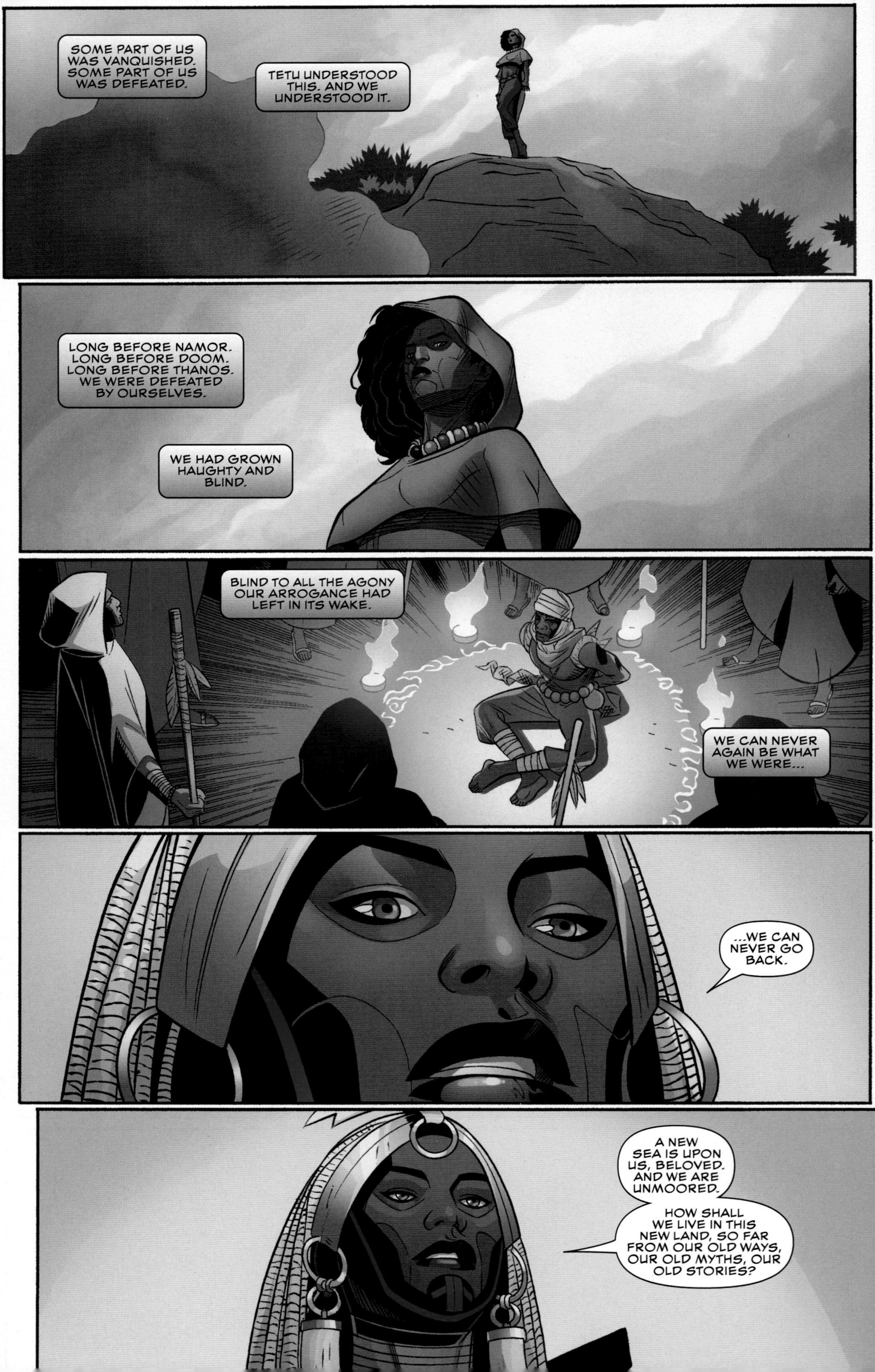

SOME PART OF US WAS VANQUISHED. SOME PART OF US WAS DEFEATED.
TETU UNDERSTOOD THIS. AND WE UNDERSTOOD IT.
LONG BEFORE NAMOR. LONG BEFORE DOOM. LONG BEFORE THANOS. WE WERE DEFEATED BY OURSELVES.
WE HAD GROWN HAUGHTY AND BLIND.
BLIND TO ALL THE AGONY OUR ARROGANCE HAD LEFT IN ITS WAKE.
WE CAN NEVER AGAIN BE WHAT WE WERE...
...WE CAN NEVER GO BACK.
A NEW SEA IS UPON US, BELOVED. AND WE ARE UNMOORED.
HOW SHALL WE LIVE IN THIS NEW LAND, SO FAR FROM OUR OLD WAYS, OUR OLD MYTHS, OUR OLD STORIES?

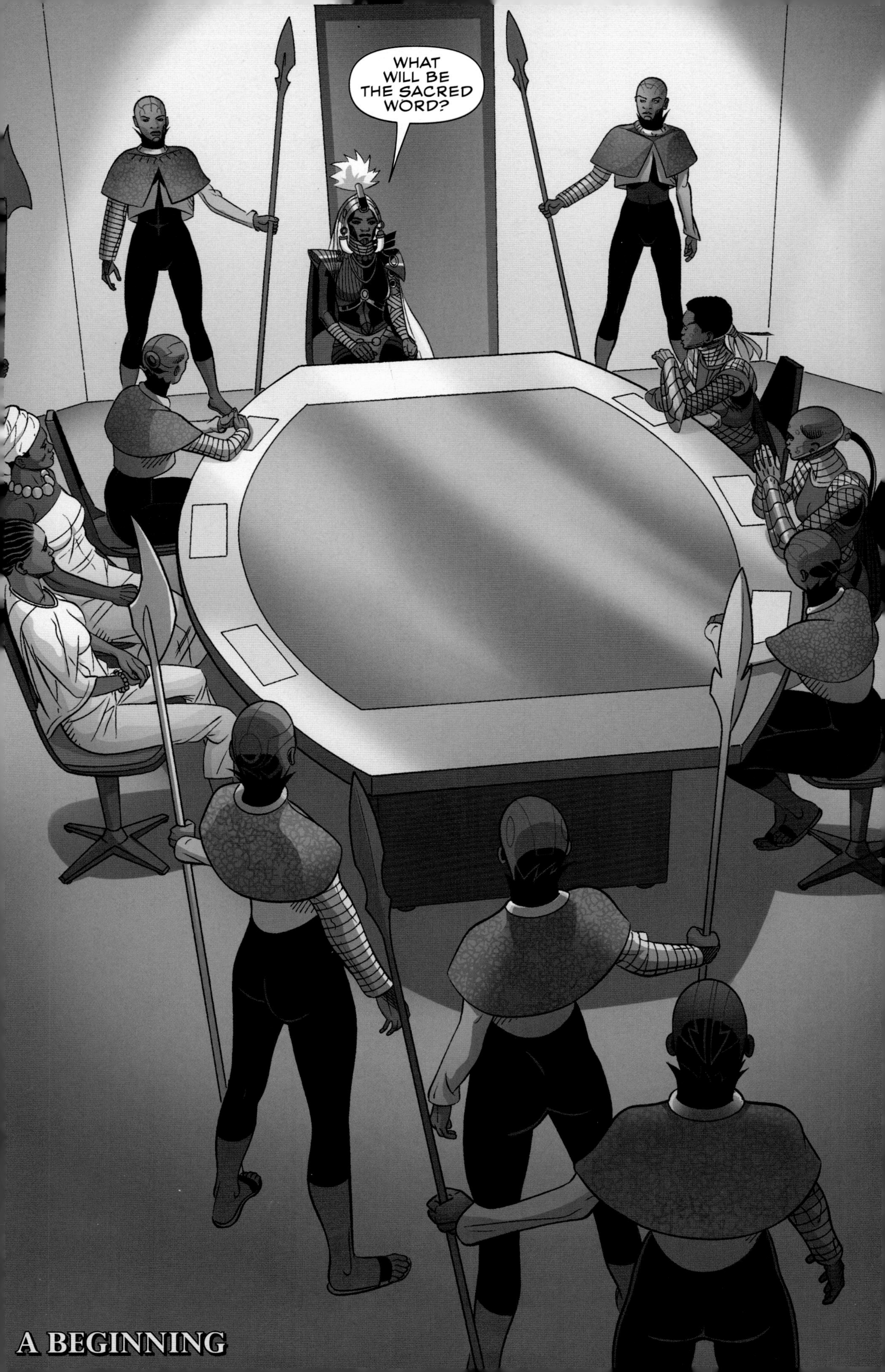
WHAT WILL BE THE SACRED WORD?

A BEGINNING

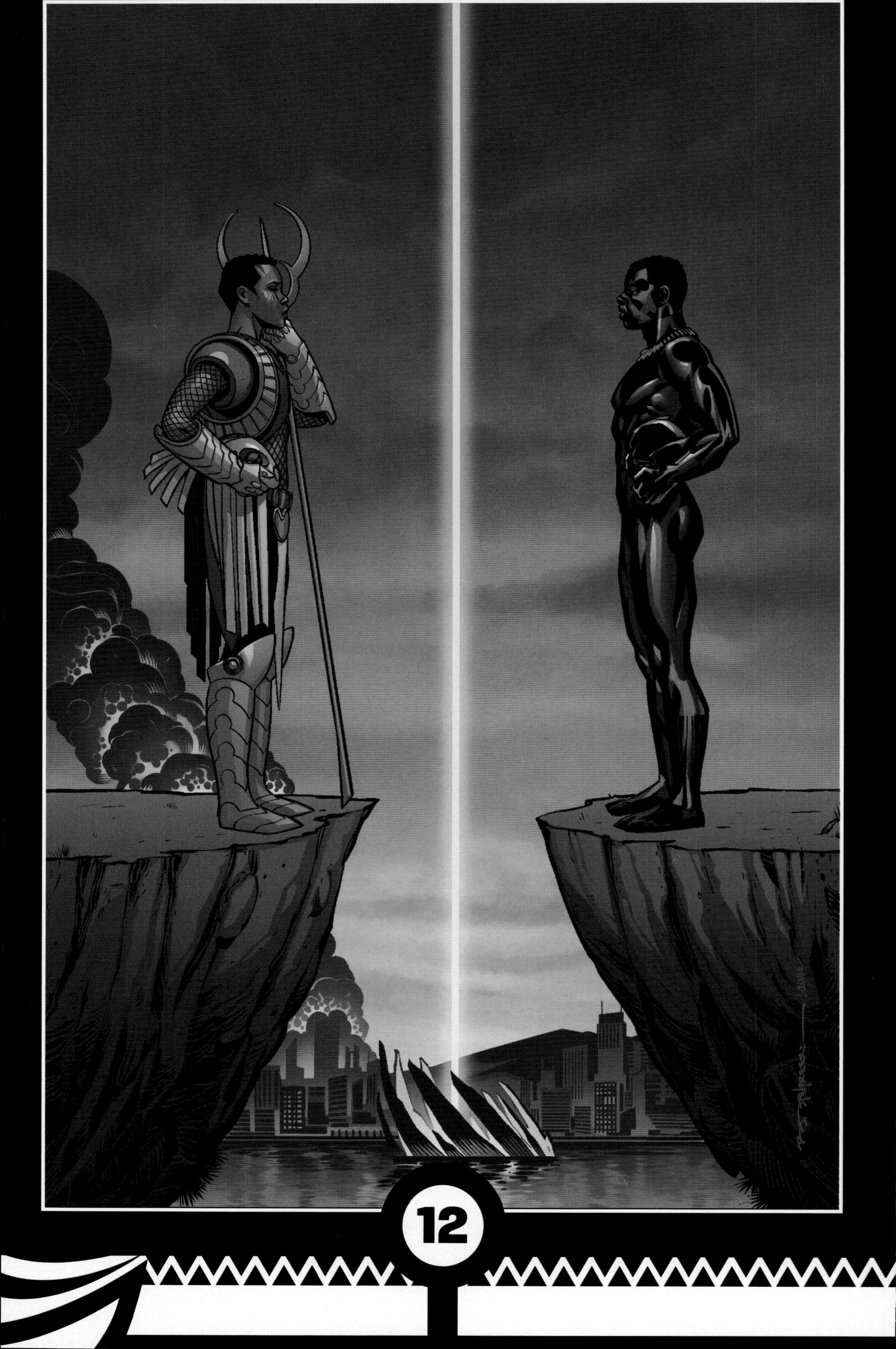
12

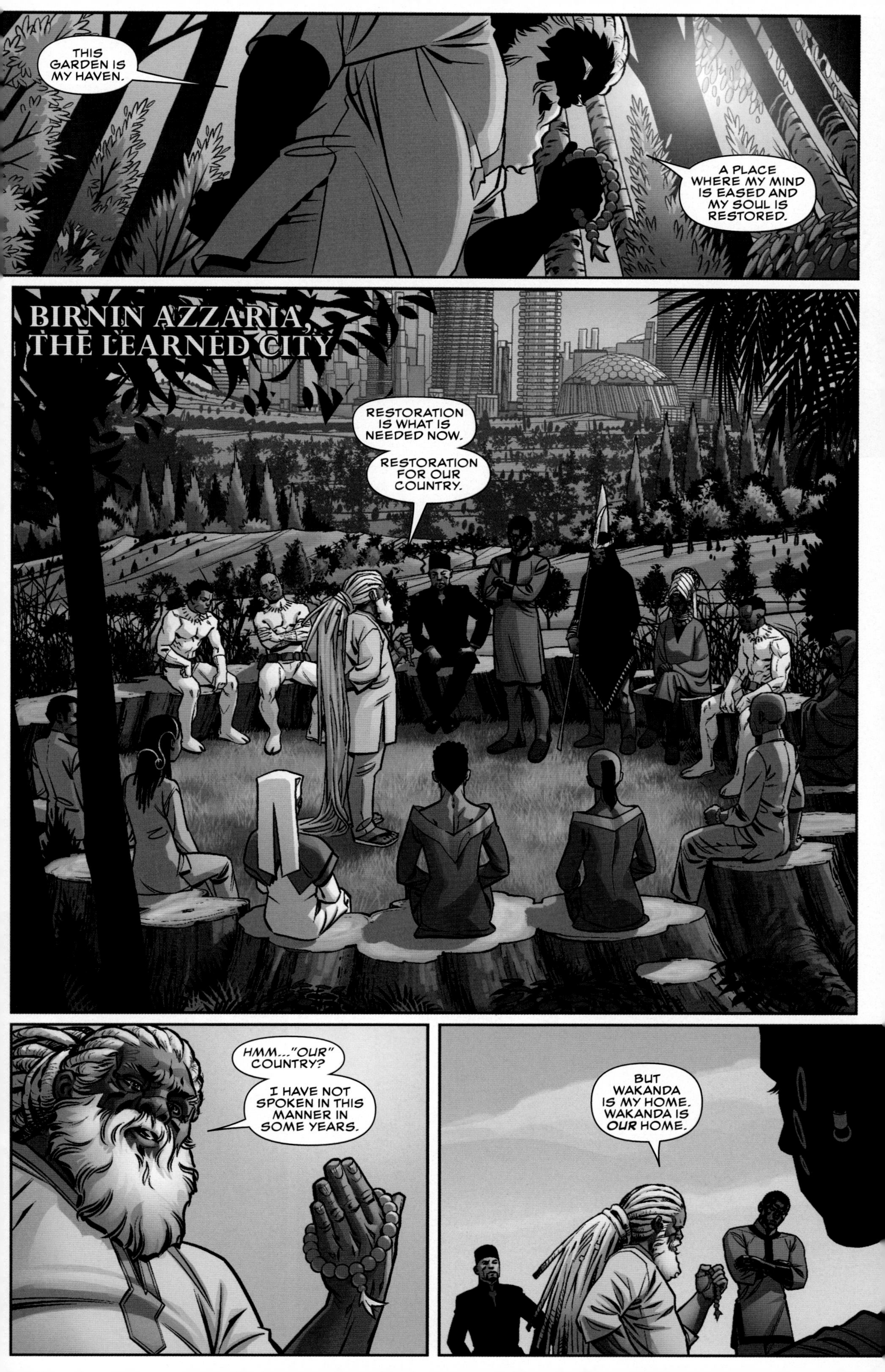
THIS GARDEN IS MY HAVEN.
A PLACE WHERE MY MIND IS EASED AND MY SOUL IS RESTORED.
BIRNIN AZZARIA, THE LEARNED CITY
RESTORATION IS WHAT IS NEEDED NOW.
RESTORATION FOR OUR COUNTRY.
HMM..."OUR" COUNTRY?
I HAVE NOT SPOKEN IN THIS MANNER IN SOME YEARS.
BUT WAKANDA IS MY HOME. WAKANDA IS *OUR* HOME.

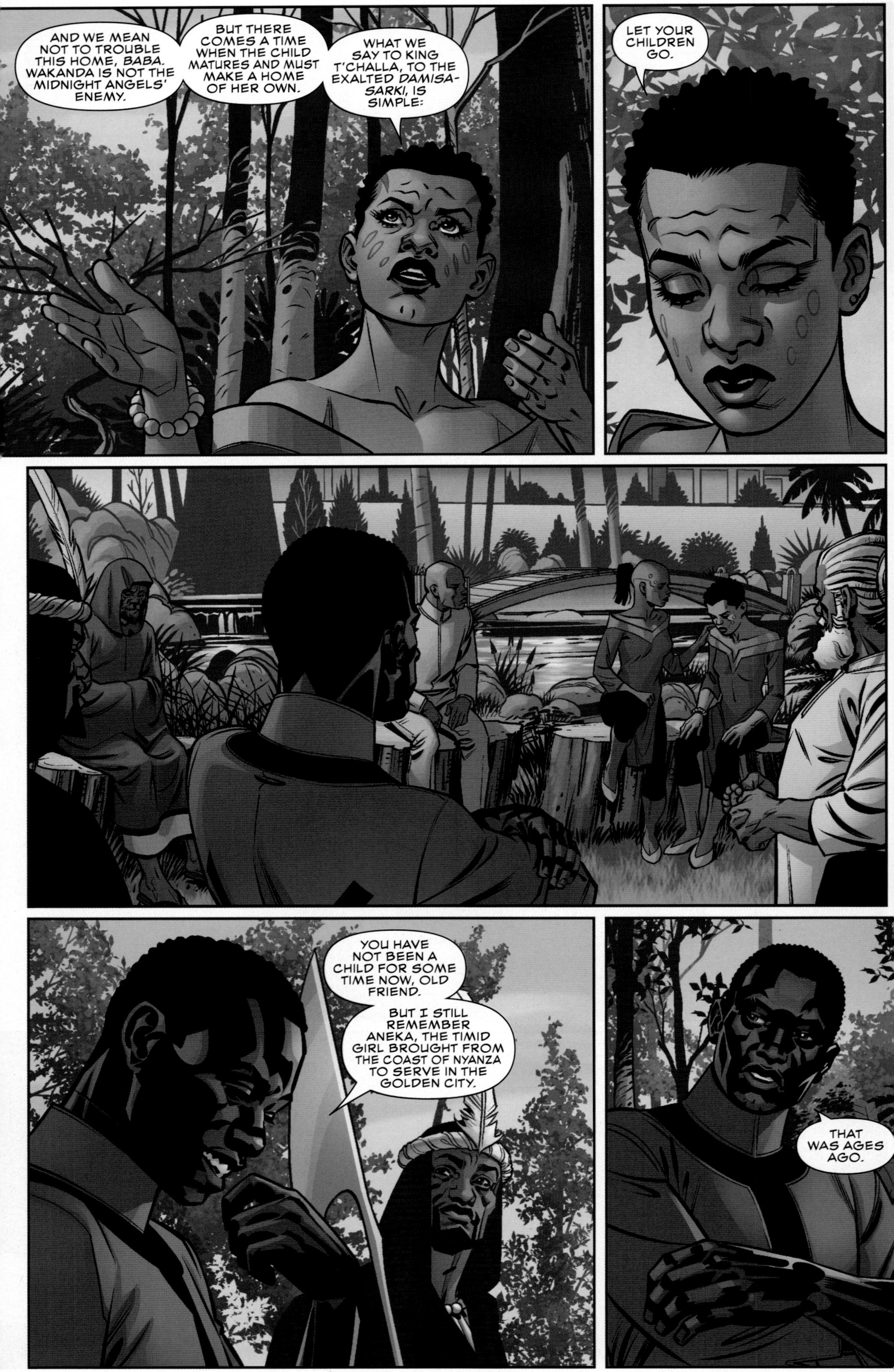
AND WE MEAN NOT TO TROUBLE THIS HOME, *BABA*. WAKANDA IS NOT THE MIDNIGHT ANGELS' ENEMY.
BUT THERE COMES A TIME WHEN THE CHILD MATURES AND MUST MAKE A HOME OF HER OWN.
WHAT WE SAY TO KING T'CHALLA, TO THE EXALTED *DAMISA-SARKI*, IS SIMPLE:
LET YOUR CHILDREN GO.
YOU HAVE NOT BEEN A CHILD FOR SOME TIME NOW, OLD FRIEND.
BUT I STILL REMEMBER ANEKA, THE TIMID GIRL BROUGHT FROM THE COAST OF NYANZA TO SERVE IN THE GOLDEN CITY.
THAT WAS AGES AGO.

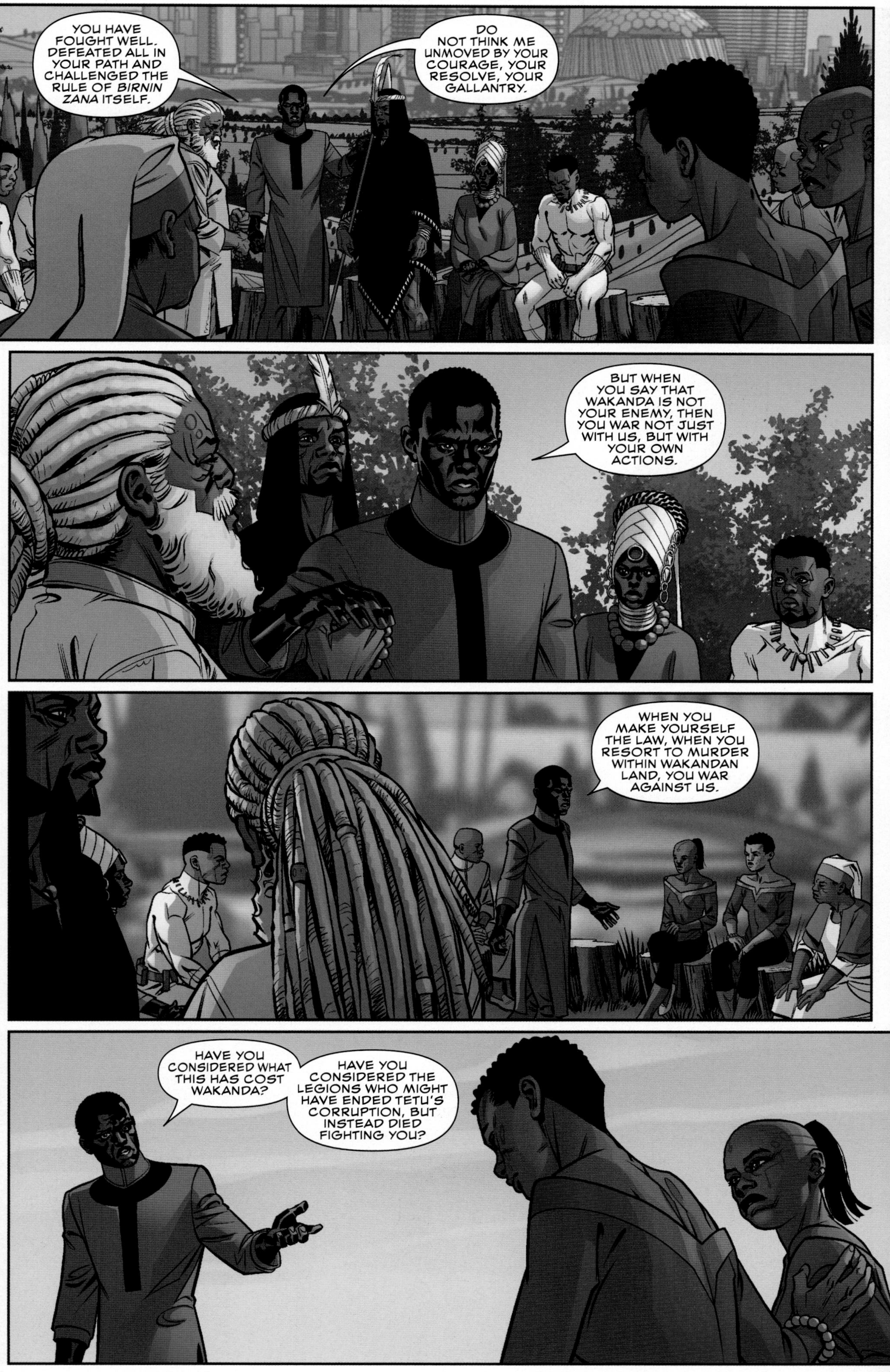
YOU HAVE FOUGHT WELL. DEFEATED ALL IN YOUR PATH AND CHALLENGED THE RULE OF *BIRNIN ZANA* ITSELF.
DO NOT THINK ME UNMOVED BY YOUR COURAGE, YOUR RESOLVE, YOUR GALLANTRY.
BUT WHEN YOU SAY THAT WAKANDA IS NOT YOUR ENEMY, THEN YOU WAR NOT JUST WITH US, BUT WITH YOUR OWN ACTIONS.
WHEN YOU MAKE YOURSELF THE LAW, WHEN YOU RESORT TO MURDER WITHIN WAKANDAN LAND, YOU WAR AGAINST US.
HAVE YOU CONSIDERED WHAT THIS HAS COST WAKANDA?
HAVE YOU CONSIDERED THE LEGIONS WHO MIGHT HAVE ENDED TETU'S CORRUPTION, BUT INSTEAD DIED FIGHTING YOU?

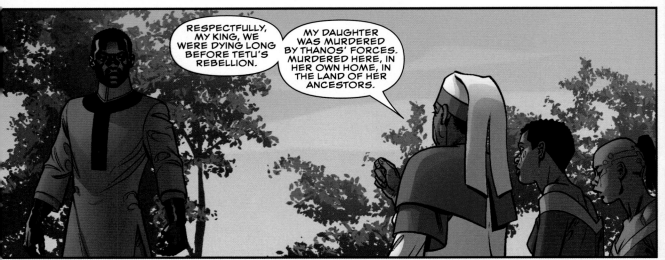

RESPECTFULLY, MY KING, WE WERE DYING LONG BEFORE TETU'S REBELLION.

MY DAUGHTER WAS MURDERED BY THANOS' FORCES. MURDERED HERE, IN HER OWN HOME, IN THE LAND OF HER ANCESTORS.

WE ESCAPED. BUT THE JAMBAZI FOUND US, SOLD MY GRANDDAUGHTER AND I. WHERE WAS DAMISA-SARKI, THEN?

I AM NOT AN IDEAL, MY LORD. AND MY DAUGHTER WAS NOT JUST A NOTION. WE ARE FLESH AND BONE.

AND THIS FLESH, MY FLESH, WOULD HAVE PERISHED IF NOT FOR THOSE WHOM YOU NOW UPBRAID.

WHAT WERE THEY SUPPOSED TO DO, MY LORD? LEAVE US TO BE RAPED AND KILLED?

YES, M'BALI. THAT IS EXACTLY WHAT THEY WERE SUPPOSED TO DO.

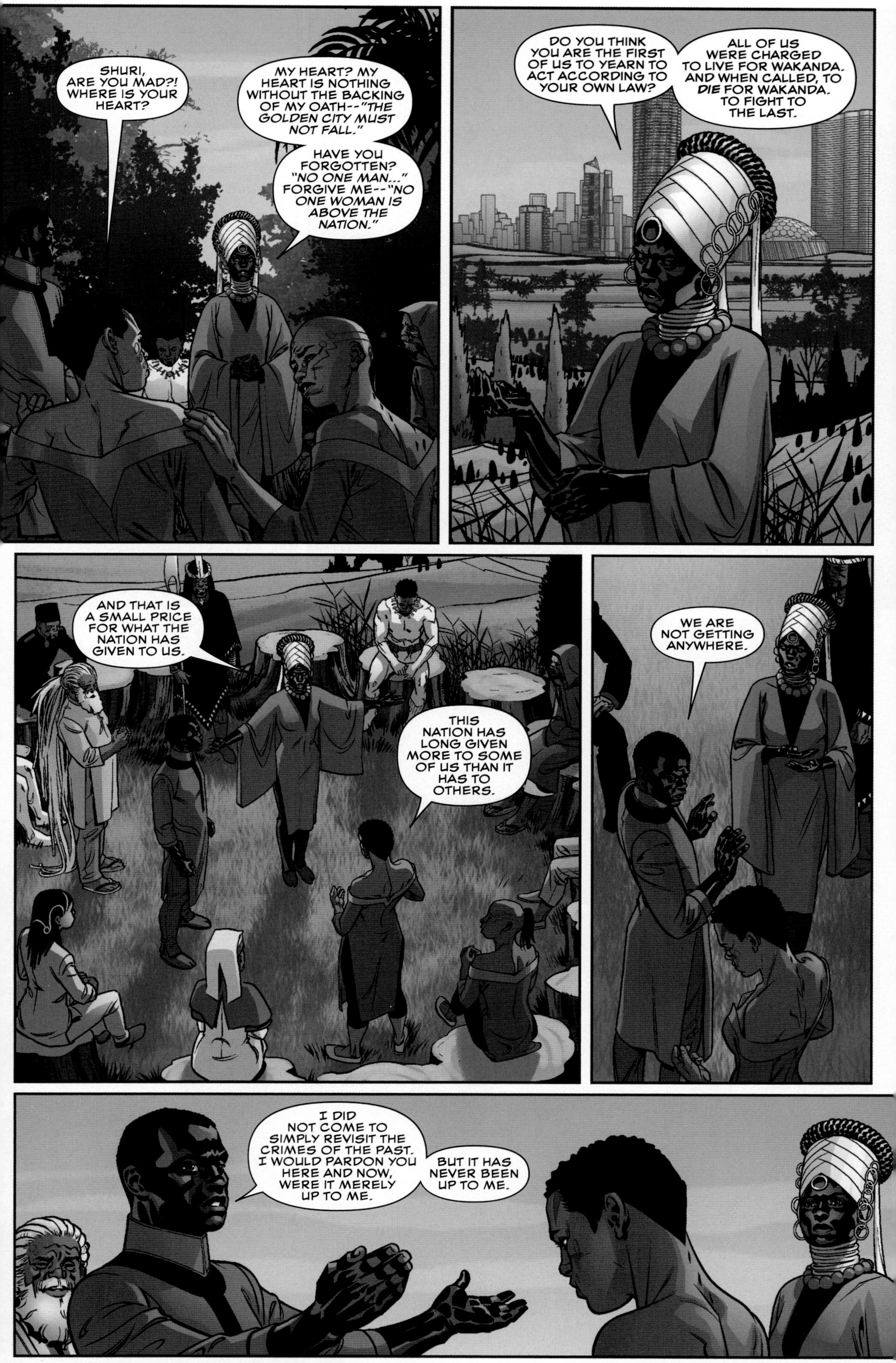
SHURI, ARE YOU MAD?! WHERE IS YOUR HEART?
MY HEART? MY HEART IS NOTHING WITHOUT THE BACKING OF MY OATH--"THE GOLDEN CITY MUST NOT FALL."
HAVE YOU FORGOTTEN? "NO ONE MAN..." FORGIVE ME--"NO ONE WOMAN IS ABOVE THE NATION."
DO YOU THINK YOU ARE THE FIRST OF US TO YEARN TO ACT ACCORDING TO YOUR OWN LAW?
ALL OF US WERE CHARGED TO LIVE FOR WAKANDA. AND WHEN CALLED, TO *DIE* FOR WAKANDA. TO FIGHT TO THE LAST.
AND THAT IS A SMALL PRICE FOR WHAT THE NATION HAS GIVEN TO US.
THIS NATION HAS LONG GIVEN MORE TO SOME OF US THAN IT HAS TO OTHERS.
WE ARE NOT GETTING ANYWHERE.
I DID NOT COME TO SIMPLY REVISIT THE CRIMES OF THE PAST. I WOULD PARDON YOU HERE AND NOW, WERE IT MERELY UP TO ME.
BUT IT HAS NEVER BEEN UP TO ME.

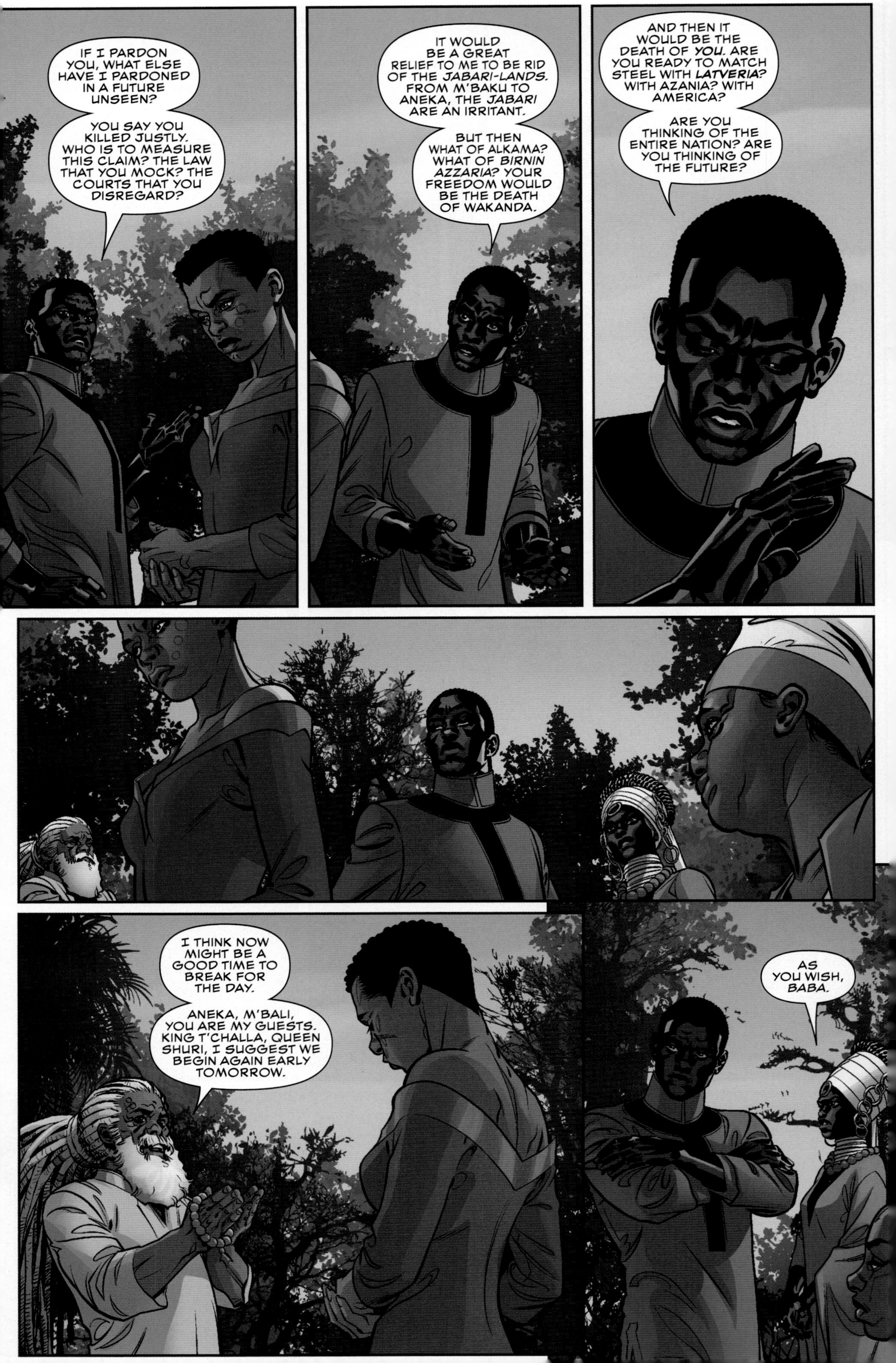
IF I PARDON YOU, WHAT ELSE HAVE I PARDONED IN A FUTURE UNSEEN?
YOU SAY YOU KILLED JUSTLY. WHO IS TO MEASURE THIS CLAIM? THE LAW THAT YOU MOCK? THE COURTS THAT YOU DISREGARD?
IT WOULD BE A GREAT RELIEF TO ME TO BE RID OF THE JABARI-LANDS. FROM M'BAKU TO ANEKA, THE JABARI ARE AN IRRITANT.
BUT THEN WHAT OF ALKAMA? WHAT OF BIRNIN AZZARIA? YOUR FREEDOM WOULD BE THE DEATH OF WAKANDA.
AND THEN IT WOULD BE THE DEATH OF YOU. ARE YOU READY TO MATCH STEEL WITH LATVERIA? WITH AZANIA? WITH AMERICA?
ARE YOU THINKING OF THE ENTIRE NATION? ARE YOU THINKING OF THE FUTURE?
I THINK NOW MIGHT BE A GOOD TIME TO BREAK FOR THE DAY.
ANEKA, M'BALI, YOU ARE MY GUESTS. KING T'CHALLA, QUEEN SHURI, I SUGGEST WE BEGIN AGAIN EARLY TOMORROW.
AS YOU WISH, BABA.

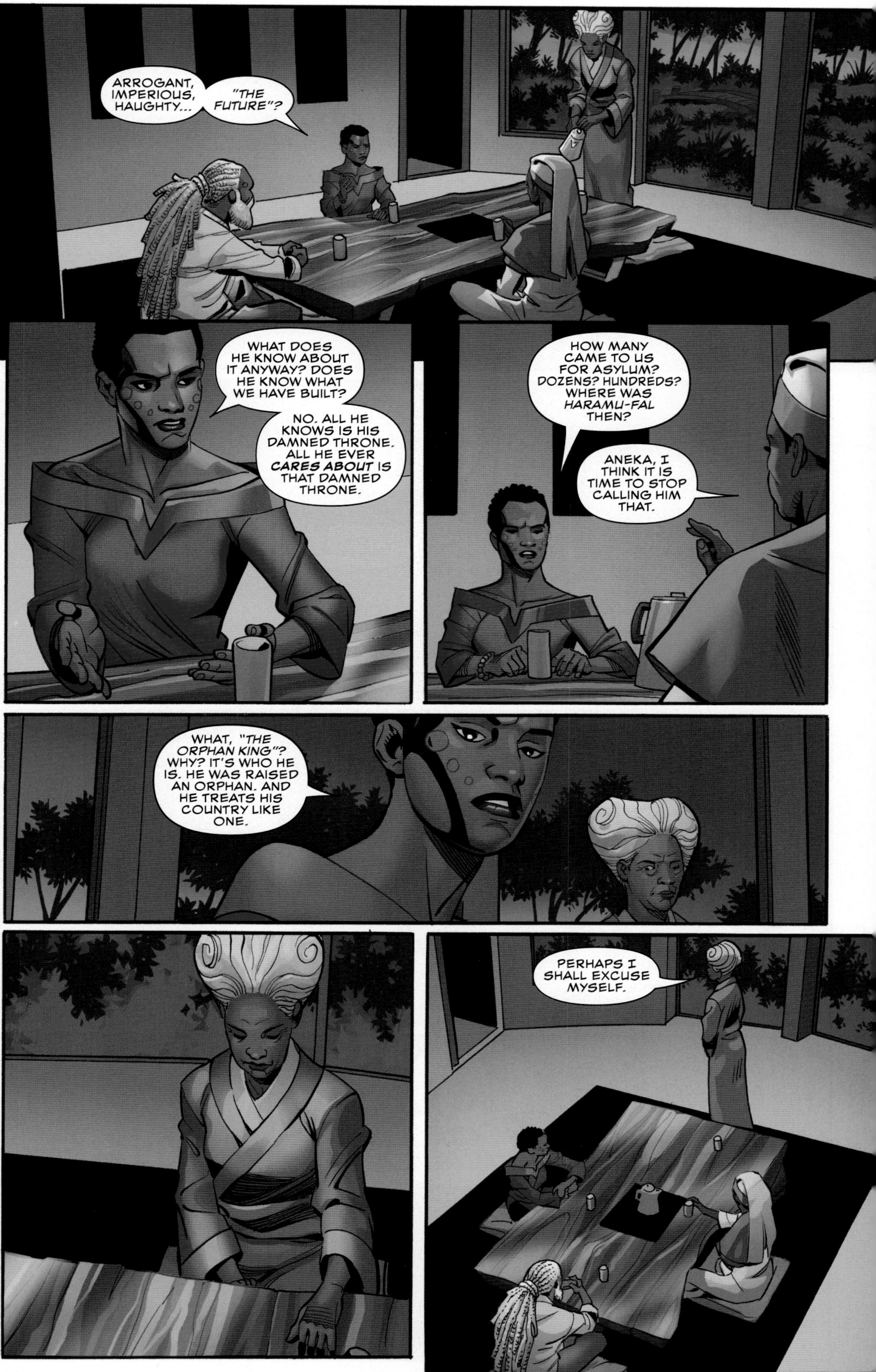
ARROGANT, IMPERIOUS, HAUGHTY...
"THE FUTURE"?
WHAT DOES HE KNOW ABOUT IT ANYWAY? DOES HE KNOW WHAT WE HAVE BUILT?
NO. ALL HE KNOWS IS HIS DAMNED THRONE. ALL HE EVER CARES ABOUT IS THAT DAMNED THRONE.
HOW MANY CAME TO US FOR ASYLUM? DOZENS? HUNDREDS? WHERE WAS HARAMU-FAL THEN?
ANEKA, I THINK IT IS TIME TO STOP CALLING HIM THAT.
WHAT, "THE ORPHAN KING"? WHY? IT'S WHO HE IS. HE WAS RAISED AN ORPHAN. AND HE TREATS HIS COUNTRY LIKE ONE.
PERHAPS I SHALL EXCUSE MYSELF.

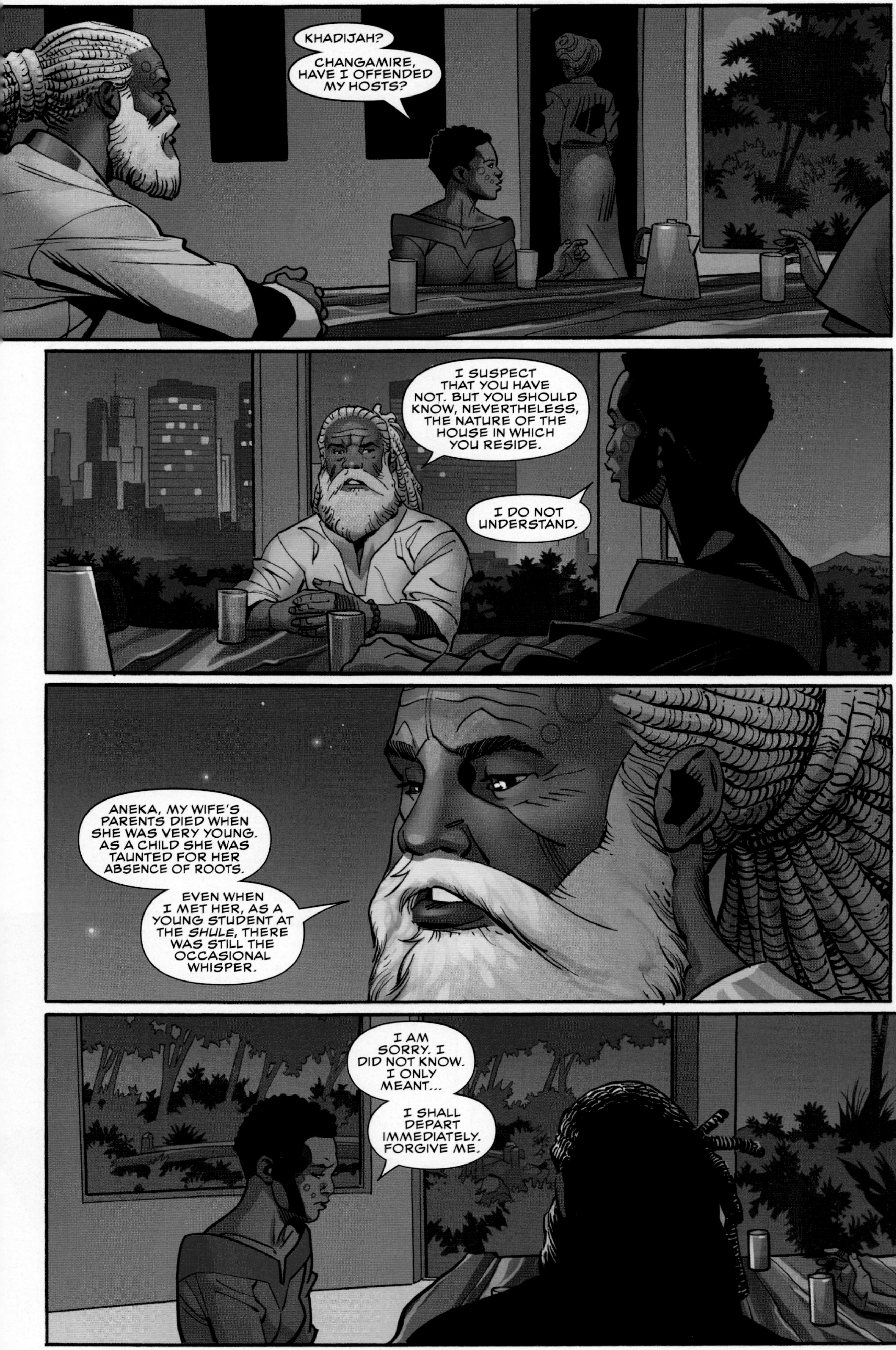
KHADIJAH?
CHANGAMIRE, HAVE I OFFENDED MY HOSTS?
I SUSPECT THAT YOU HAVE NOT. BUT YOU SHOULD KNOW, NEVERTHELESS, THE NATURE OF THE HOUSE IN WHICH YOU RESIDE.
I DO NOT UNDERSTAND.
ANEKA, MY WIFE'S PARENTS DIED WHEN SHE WAS VERY YOUNG. AS A CHILD SHE WAS TAUNTED FOR HER ABSENCE OF ROOTS.
EVEN WHEN I MET HER, AS A YOUNG STUDENT AT THE *SHULE*, THERE WAS STILL THE OCCASIONAL WHISPER.
I AM SORRY. I DID NOT KNOW. I ONLY MEANT...
I SHALL DEPART IMMEDIATELY. FORGIVE ME.

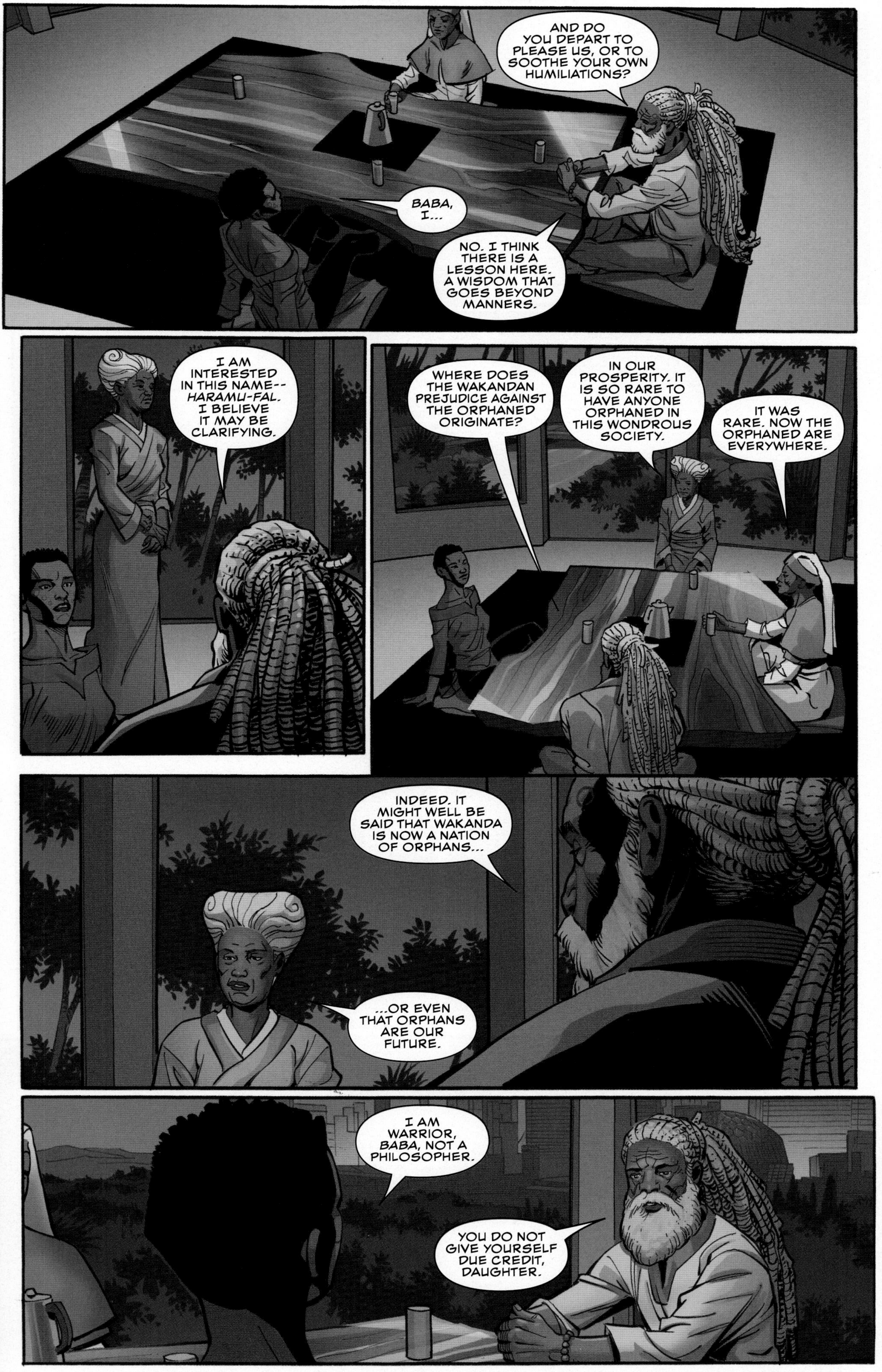

AND DO YOU DEPART TO PLEASE US, OR TO SOOTHE YOUR OWN HUMILIATIONS?
BABA, I...
NO. I THINK THERE IS A LESSON HERE. A WISDOM THAT GOES BEYOND MANNERS.
I AM INTERESTED IN THIS NAME-- HARAMU-FAL. I BELIEVE IT MAY BE CLARIFYING.
WHERE DOES THE WAKANDAN PREJUDICE AGAINST THE ORPHANED ORIGINATE?
IN OUR PROSPERITY. IT IS SO RARE TO HAVE ANYONE ORPHANED IN THIS WONDROUS SOCIETY.
IT WAS RARE. NOW THE ORPHANED ARE EVERYWHERE.
INDEED. IT MIGHT WELL BE SAID THAT WAKANDA IS NOW A NATION OF ORPHANS...
...OR EVEN THAT ORPHANS ARE OUR FUTURE.
I AM WARRIOR, BABA, NOT A PHILOSOPHER.
YOU DO NOT GIVE YOURSELF DUE CREDIT, DAUGHTER.

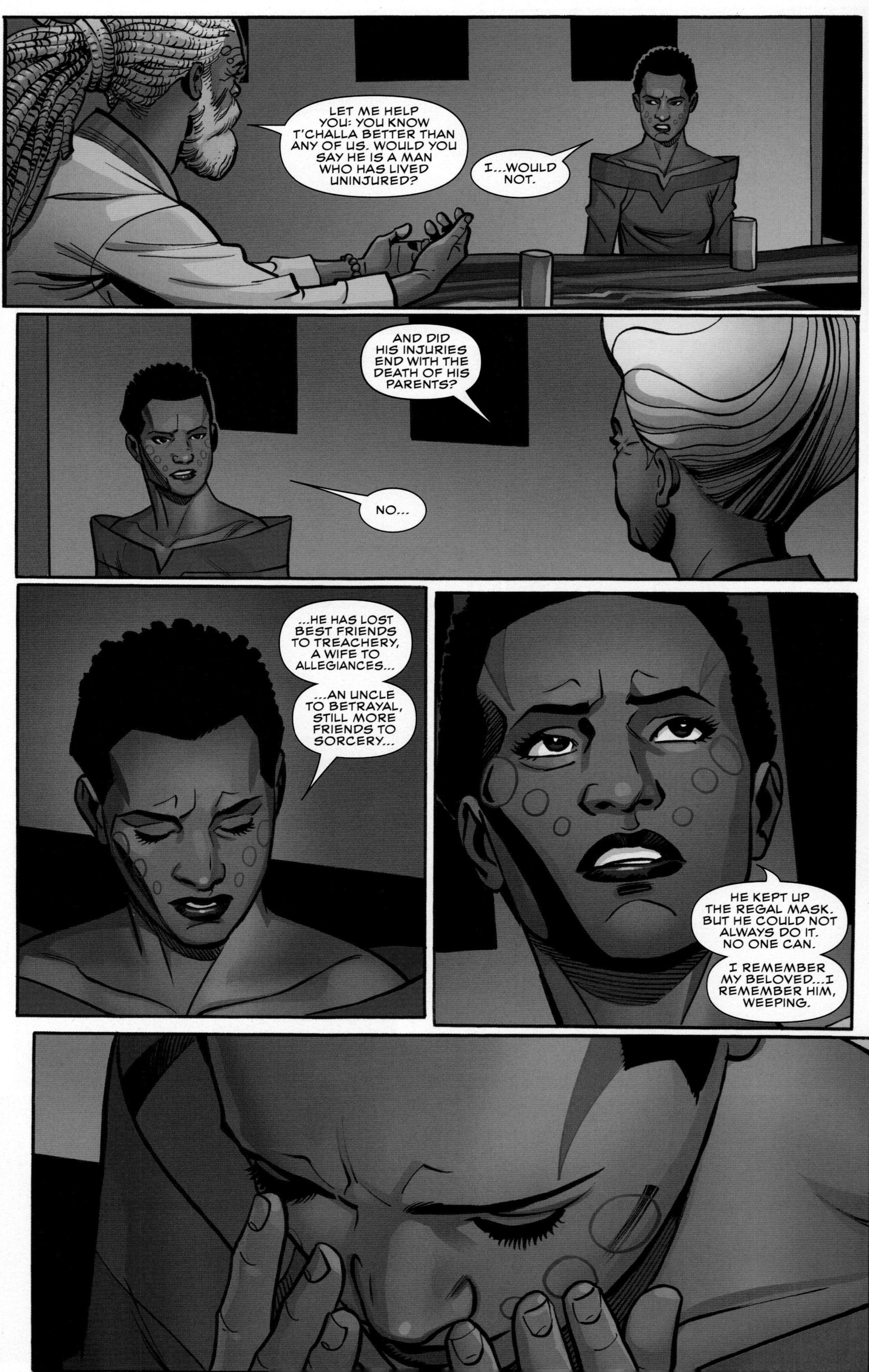
LET ME HELP YOU: YOU KNOW T'CHALLA BETTER THAN ANY OF US. WOULD YOU SAY HE IS A MAN WHO HAS LIVED UNINJURED?
I...WOULD NOT.
AND DID HIS INJURIES END WITH THE DEATH OF HIS PARENTS?
NO...
...HE HAS LOST BEST FRIENDS TO TREACHERY, A WIFE TO ALLEGIANCES...
...AN UNCLE TO BETRAYAL, STILL MORE FRIENDS TO SORCERY...
HE KEPT UP THE REGAL MASK. BUT HE COULD NOT ALWAYS DO IT. NO ONE CAN.
I REMEMBER MY BELOVED...I REMEMBER HIM, WEEPING.

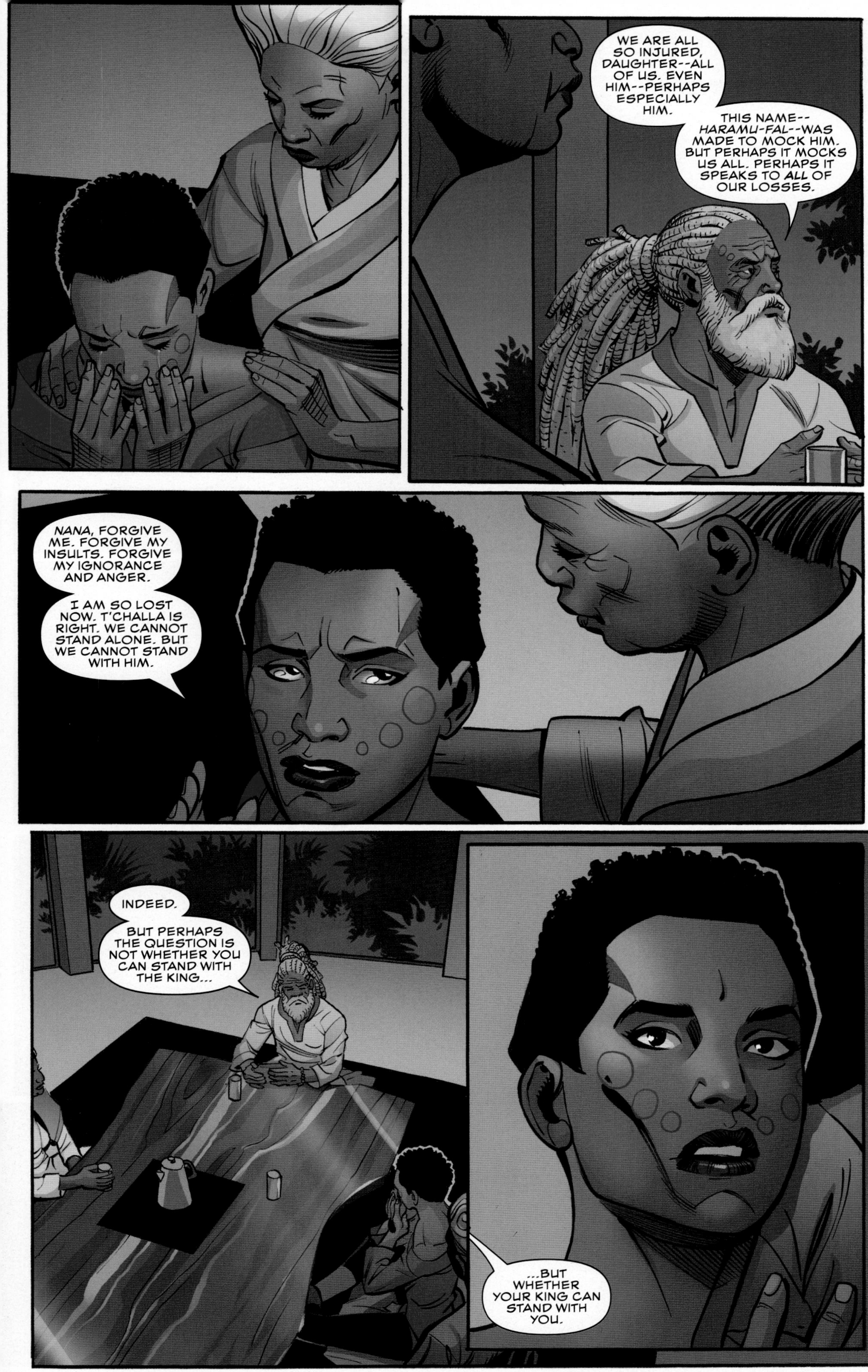
WE ARE ALL SO INJURED, DAUGHTER--ALL OF US. EVEN HIM--PERHAPS ESPECIALLY HIM.
THIS NAME--*HARAMU-FAL*--WAS MADE TO MOCK HIM. BUT PERHAPS IT MOCKS US ALL. PERHAPS IT SPEAKS TO ***ALL*** OF OUR LOSSES.
*NANA*, FORGIVE ME. FORGIVE MY INSULTS. FORGIVE MY IGNORANCE AND ANGER.
I AM SO LOST NOW. T'CHALLA IS RIGHT. WE CANNOT STAND ALONE. BUT WE CANNOT STAND WITH HIM.
INDEED.
BUT PERHAPS THE QUESTION IS NOT WHETHER YOU CAN STAND WITH THE KING...
...BUT WHETHER YOUR KING CAN STAND WITH YOU.

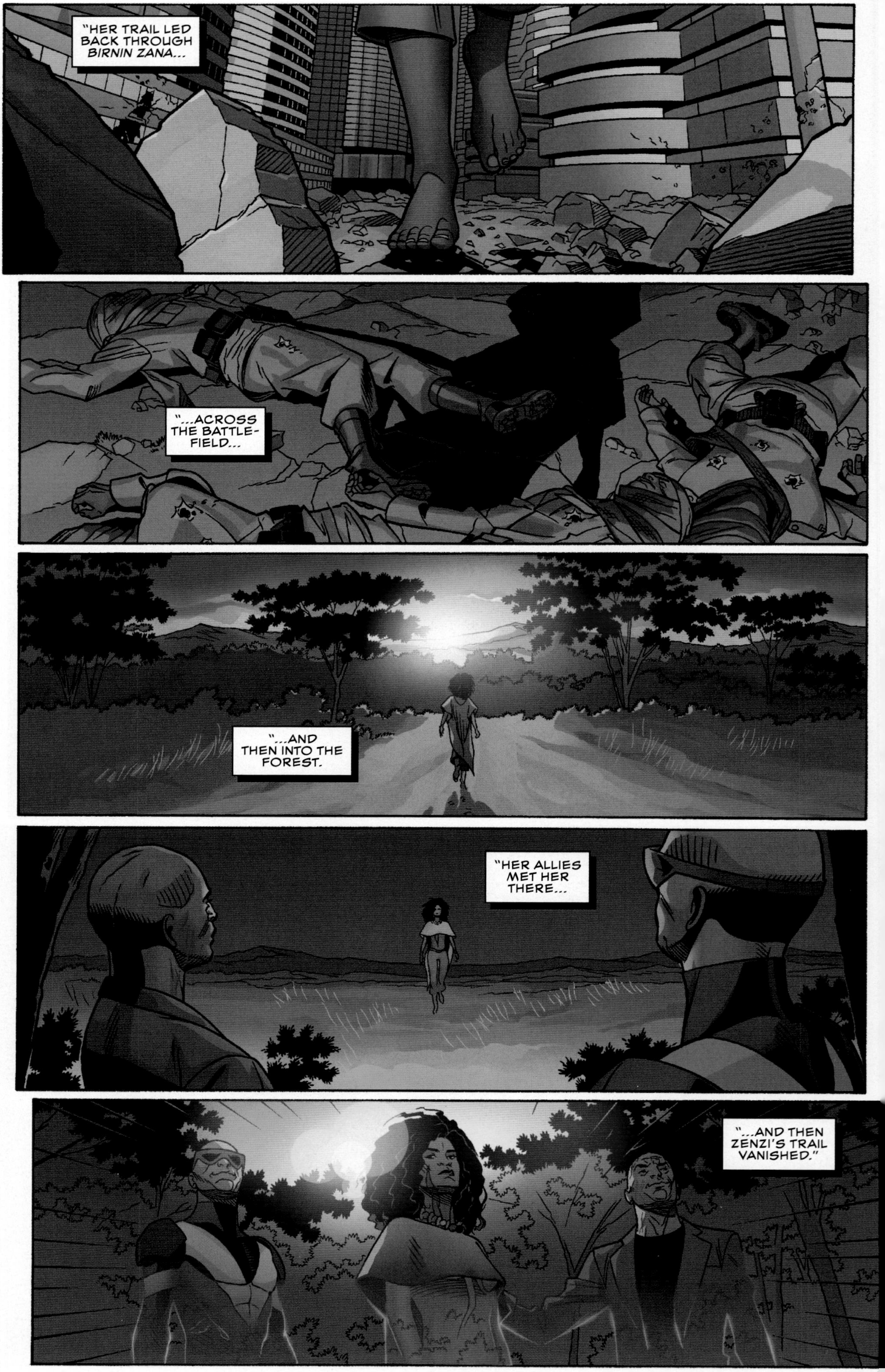
"HER TRAIL LED BACK THROUGH BIRNIN ZANA...
"...ACROSS THE BATTLE-FIELD...
"...AND THEN INTO THE FOREST.
"HER ALLIES MET HER THERE...
"...AND THEN ZENZI'S TRAIL VANISHED."

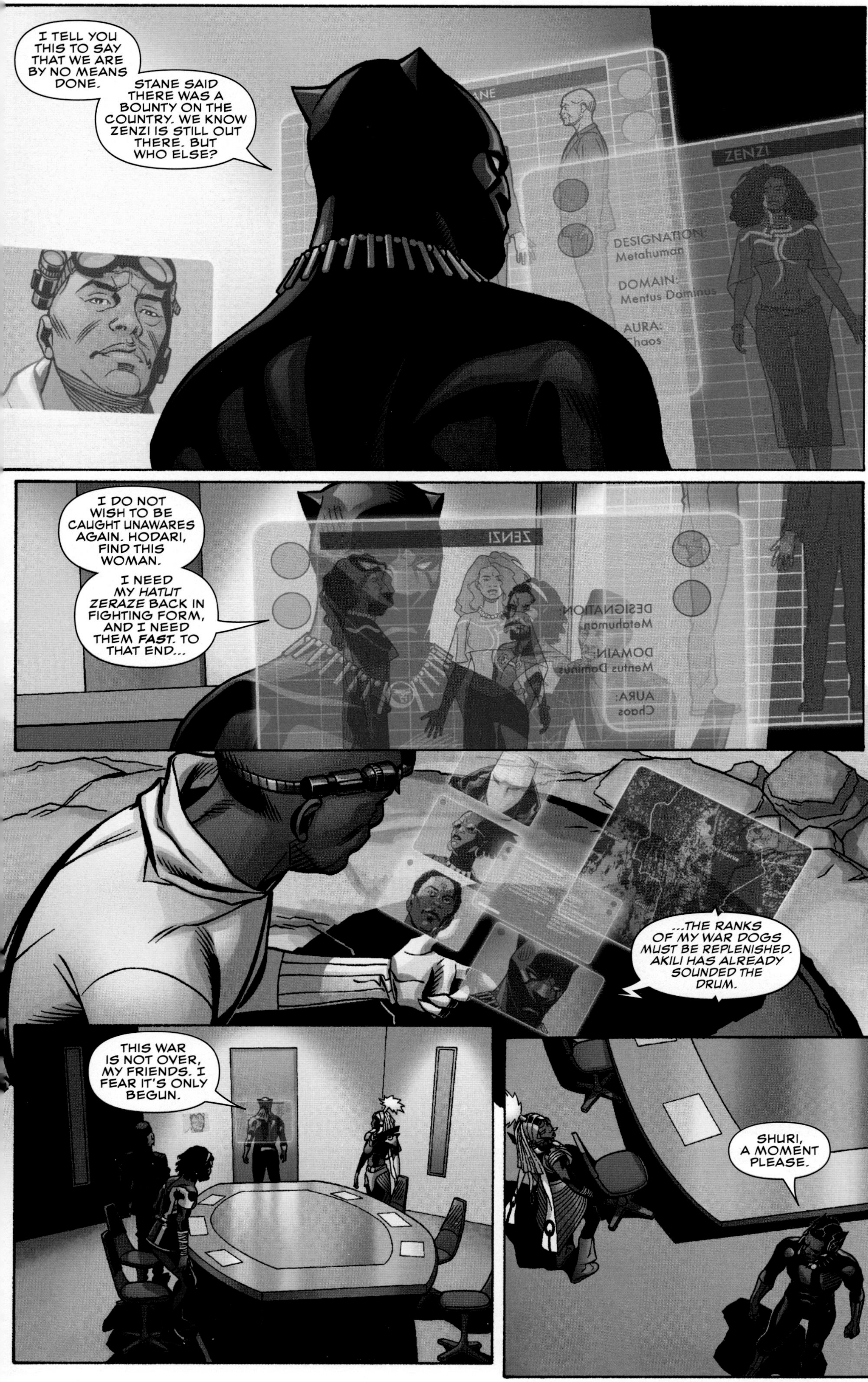

I TELL YOU THIS TO SAY THAT WE ARE BY NO MEANS DONE.
STANE SAID THERE WAS A BOUNTY ON THE COUNTRY. WE KNOW ZENZI IS STILL OUT THERE. BUT WHO ELSE?
ZENZI
DESIGNATION: Metahuman
DOMAIN: Mentus Dominus
AURA: Chaos
I DO NOT WISH TO BE CAUGHT UNAWARES AGAIN. HODARI, FIND THIS WOMAN.
I NEED MY *HATUT ZERAZE* BACK IN FIGHTING FORM, AND I NEED THEM *FAST*. TO THAT END...
...THE RANKS OF MY WAR DOGS MUST BE REPLENISHED. AKILI HAS ALREADY SOUNDED THE DRUM.
THIS WAR IS NOT OVER, MY FRIENDS. I FEAR IT'S ONLY BEGUN.
SHURI, A MOMENT PLEASE.

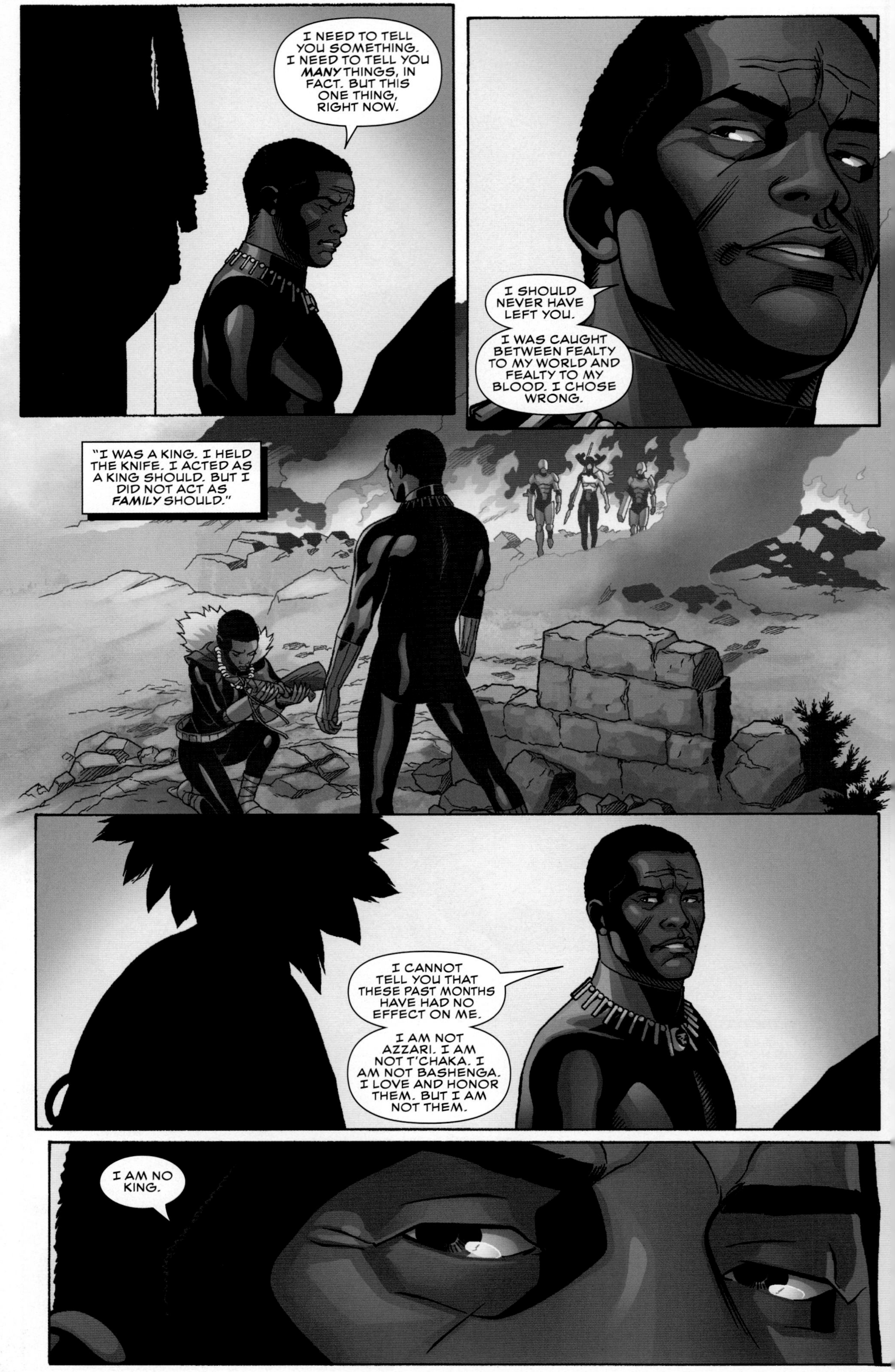
I NEED TO TELL YOU SOMETHING. I NEED TO TELL YOU *MANY* THINGS, IN FACT. BUT THIS ONE THING, RIGHT NOW.
I SHOULD NEVER HAVE LEFT YOU.
I WAS CAUGHT BETWEEN FEALTY TO MY WORLD AND FEALTY TO MY BLOOD. I CHOSE WRONG.
"I WAS A KING. I HELD THE KNIFE. I ACTED AS A KING SHOULD. BUT I DID NOT ACT AS *FAMILY* SHOULD."
I CANNOT TELL YOU THAT THESE PAST MONTHS HAVE HAD NO EFFECT ON ME.
I AM NOT AZZARI. I AM NOT T'CHAKA. I AM NOT BASHENGA. I LOVE AND HONOR THEM. BUT I AM NOT THEM.
I AM NO KING.

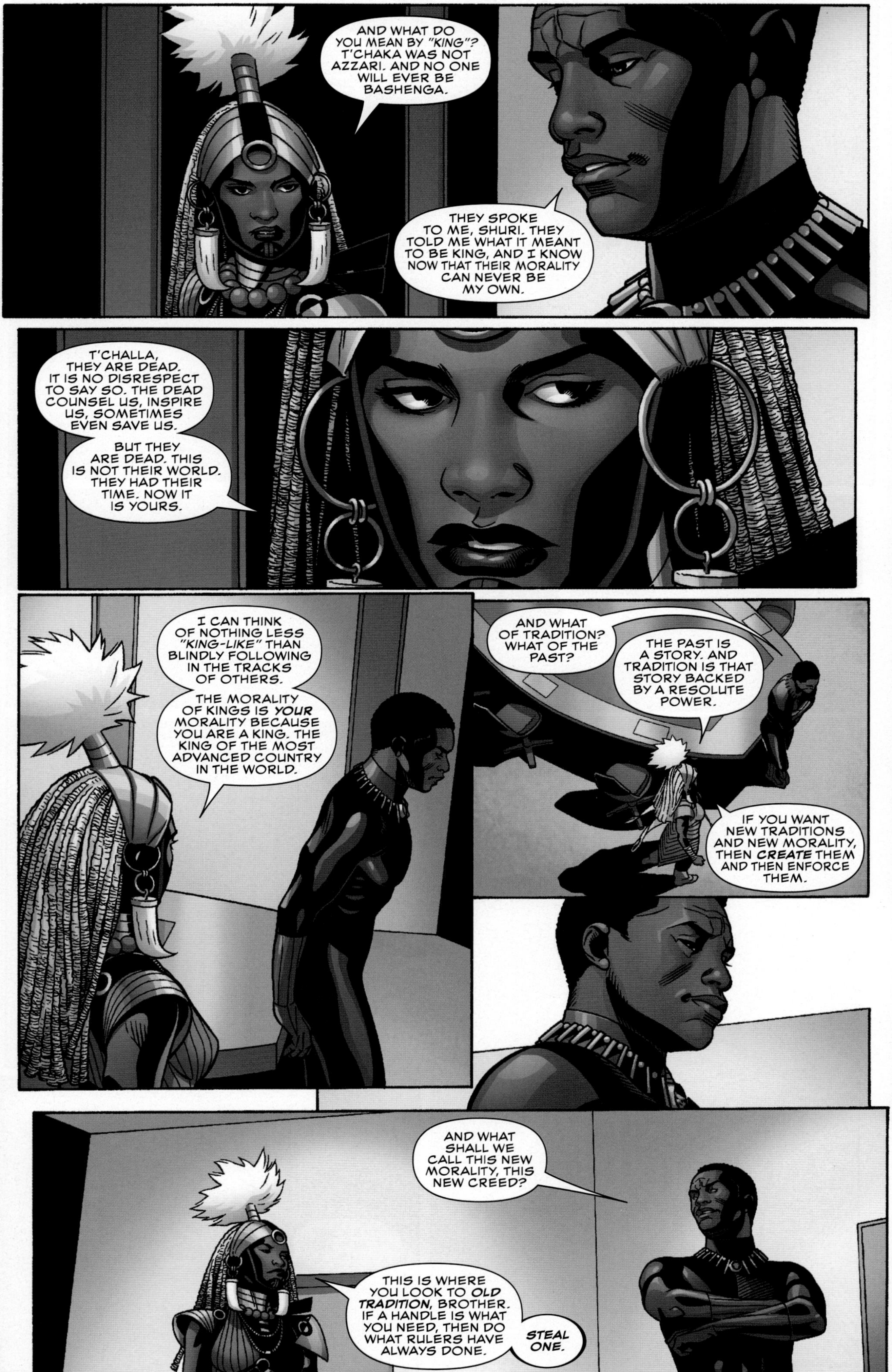
AND WHAT DO YOU MEAN BY "KING"? T'CHAKA WAS NOT AZZARI. AND NO ONE WILL EVER BE BASHENGA.
THEY SPOKE TO ME, SHURI. THEY TOLD ME WHAT IT MEANT TO BE KING, AND I KNOW NOW THAT THEIR MORALITY CAN NEVER BE MY OWN.
T'CHALLA, THEY ARE DEAD. IT IS NO DISRESPECT TO SAY SO. THE DEAD COUNSEL US, INSPIRE US, SOMETIMES EVEN SAVE US.
BUT THEY ARE DEAD. THIS IS NOT THEIR WORLD. THEY HAD THEIR TIME. NOW IT IS YOURS.
I CAN THINK OF NOTHING LESS "KING-LIKE" THAN BLINDLY FOLLOWING IN THE TRACKS OF OTHERS.
THE MORALITY OF KINGS IS YOUR MORALITY BECAUSE YOU ARE A KING. THE KING OF THE MOST ADVANCED COUNTRY IN THE WORLD.
AND WHAT OF TRADITION? WHAT OF THE PAST?
THE PAST IS A STORY. AND TRADITION IS THAT STORY BACKED BY A RESOLUTE POWER.
IF YOU WANT NEW TRADITIONS AND NEW MORALITY, THEN CREATE THEM AND THEN ENFORCE THEM.
AND WHAT SHALL WE CALL THIS NEW MORALITY, THIS NEW CREED?
THIS IS WHERE YOU LOOK TO OLD TRADITION, BROTHER. IF A HANDLE IS WHAT YOU NEED, THEN DO WHAT RULERS HAVE ALWAYS DONE.
STEAL ONE.

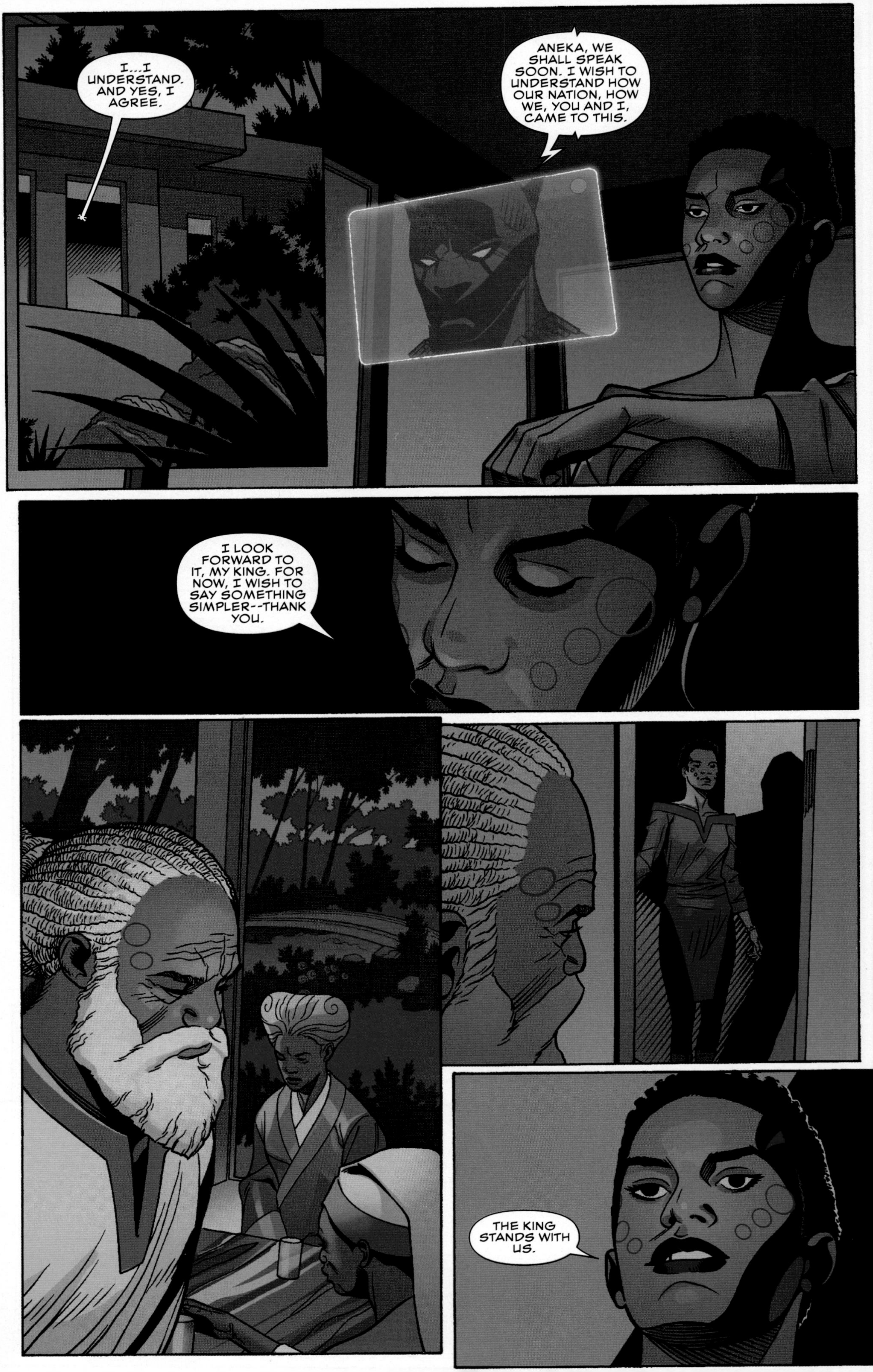
I...I UNDERSTAND. AND YES, I AGREE.
ANEKA, WE SHALL SPEAK SOON. I WISH TO UNDERSTAND HOW OUR NATION, HOW WE, YOU AND I, CAME TO THIS.
I LOOK FORWARD TO IT, MY KING. FOR NOW, I WISH TO SAY SOMETHING SIMPLER--THANK YOU.
THE KING STANDS WITH US.

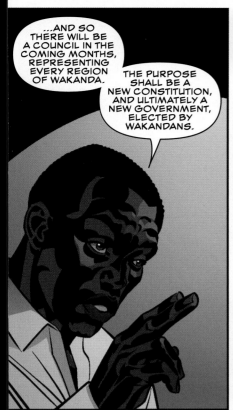

...AND SO THERE WILL BE A COUNCIL IN THE COMING MONTHS, REPRESENTING EVERY REGION OF WAKANDA.

THE PURPOSE SHALL BE A NEW CONSTITUTION, AND ULTIMATELY A NEW GOVERNMENT, ELECTED BY WAKANDANS.

THE CREED SHALL BE--NO ONE MAN.

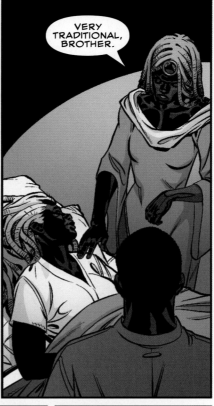

VERY TRADITIONAL, BROTHER.

YOU UNDERSTAND THIS DOES NOT REMOVE YOUR RESPONSIBILITY? YOU MUST REMAIN KING.

THE THRONE IS STILL THE GLUE OF WAKANDA, FOR THE THRONE IS THE WILL OF BAST HERSELF.

IT WILL STILL BE ONE MAN. AND YOU ARE HIM.

ONE MAN WHO REPRESENTS THE NATION, BUT NOT ONE WHO RULES THE PEOPLE.

I AM A KING, MOTHER. NOTHING CAN CHANGE THIS. BUT I WILL NOT BE A TYRANT.

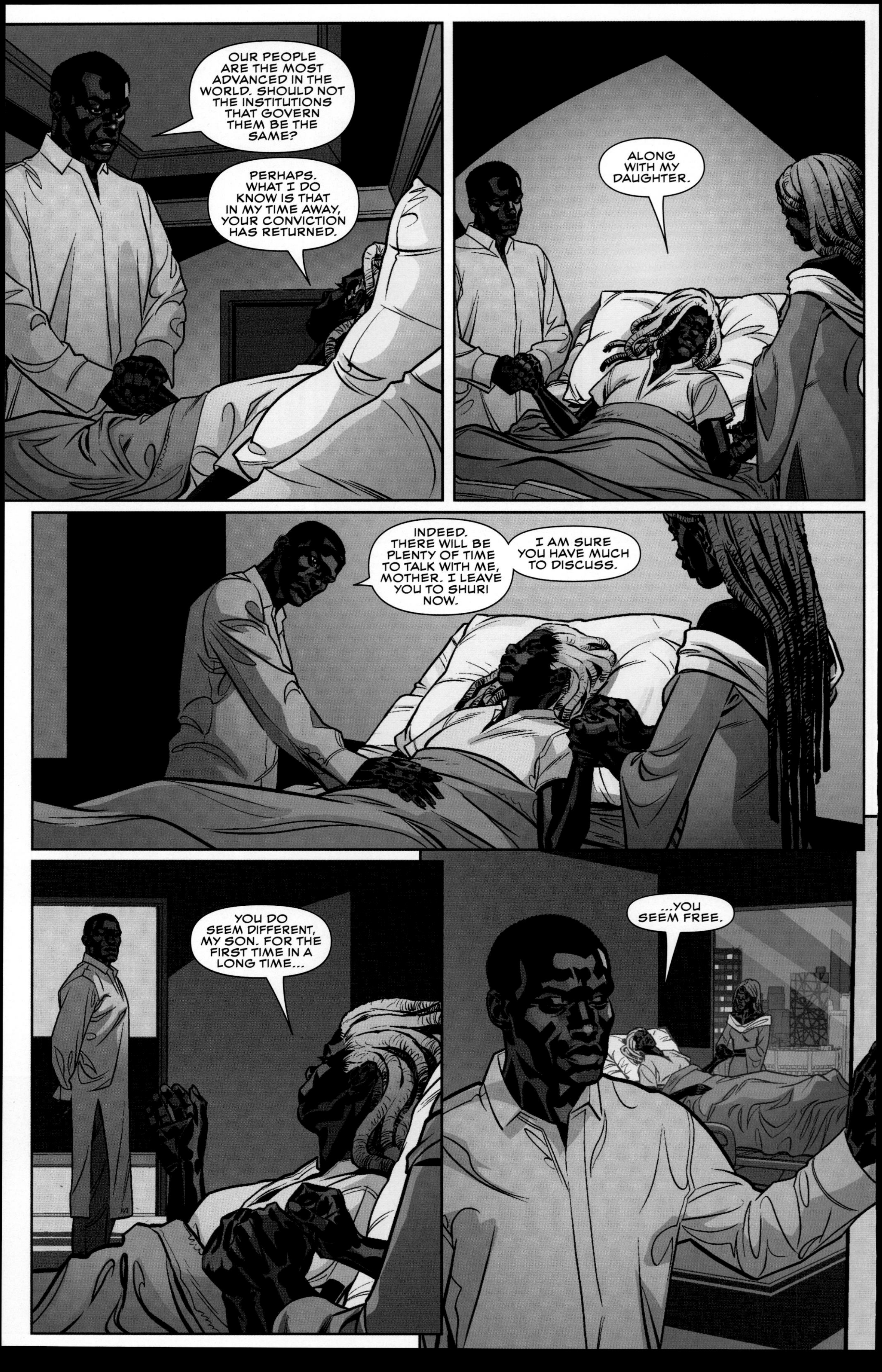

OUR PEOPLE ARE THE MOST ADVANCED IN THE WORLD. SHOULD NOT THE INSTITUTIONS THAT GOVERN THEM BE THE SAME?
PERHAPS. WHAT I DO KNOW IS THAT IN MY TIME AWAY, YOUR CONVICTION HAS RETURNED.
ALONG WITH MY DAUGHTER.
INDEED. THERE WILL BE PLENTY OF TIME TO TALK WITH ME, MOTHER. I LEAVE YOU TO SHURI NOW.
I AM SURE YOU HAVE MUCH TO DISCUSS.
YOU DO SEEM DIFFERENT, MY SON. FOR THE FIRST TIME IN A LONG TIME...
...YOU SEEM FREE.

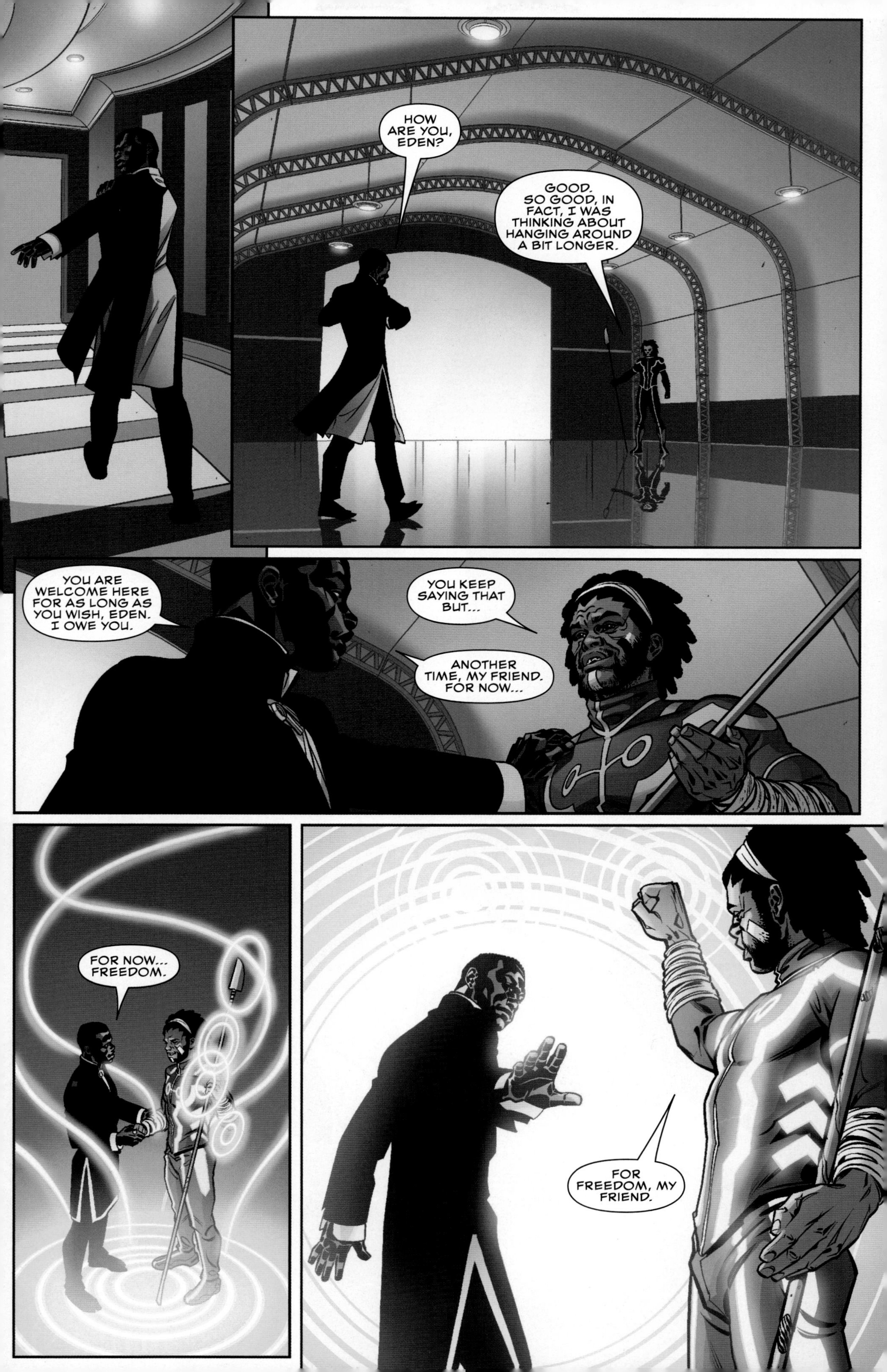
HOW ARE YOU, EDEN?
GOOD. SO GOOD, IN FACT, I WAS THINKING ABOUT HANGING AROUND A BIT LONGER.
YOU ARE WELCOME HERE FOR AS LONG AS YOU WISH, EDEN. I OWE YOU.
YOU KEEP SAYING THAT BUT...
ANOTHER TIME, MY FRIEND. FOR NOW...
FOR NOW... FREEDOM.
FOR FREEDOM, MY FRIEND.

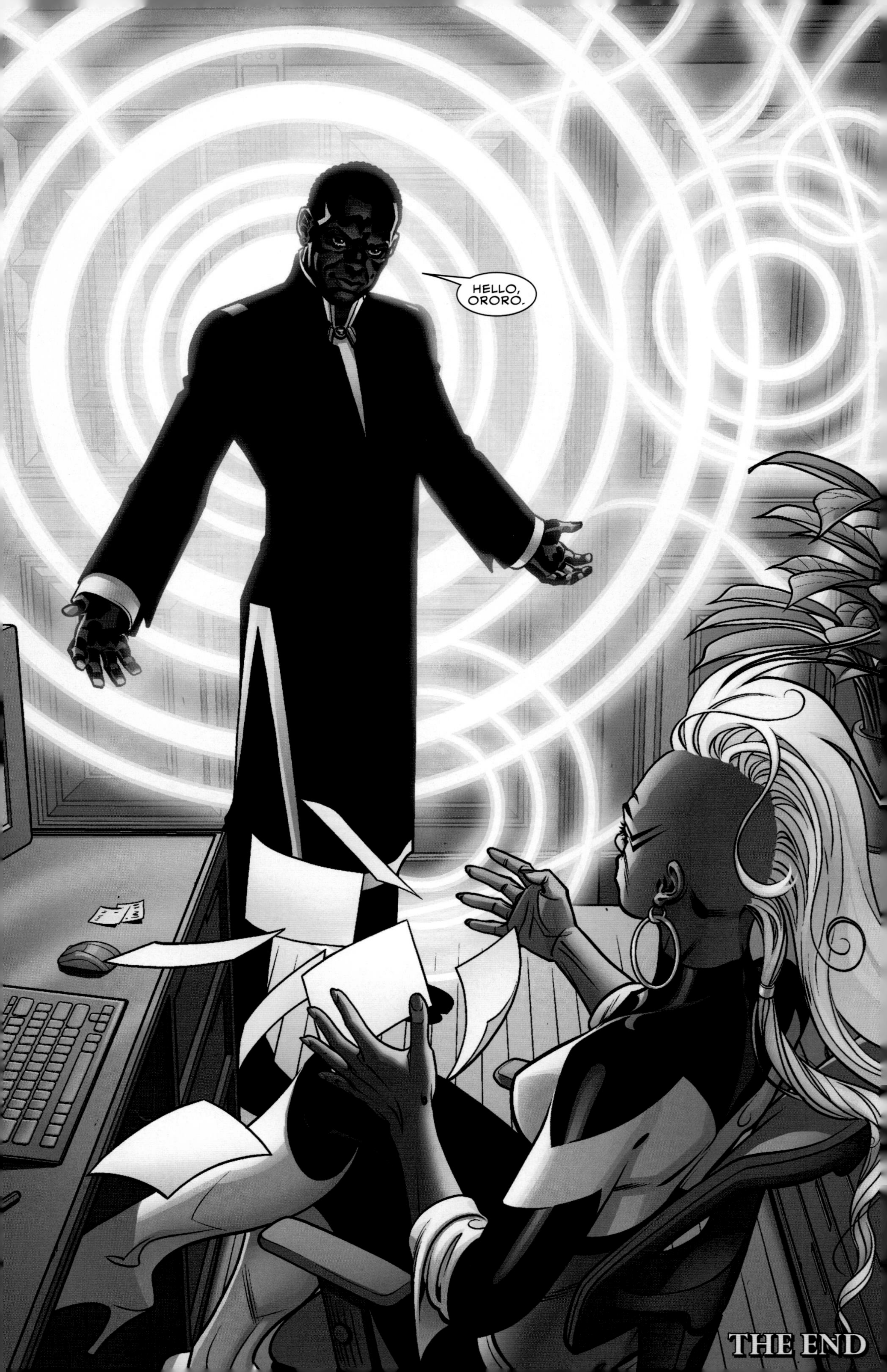
HELLO, ORORO.
THE END

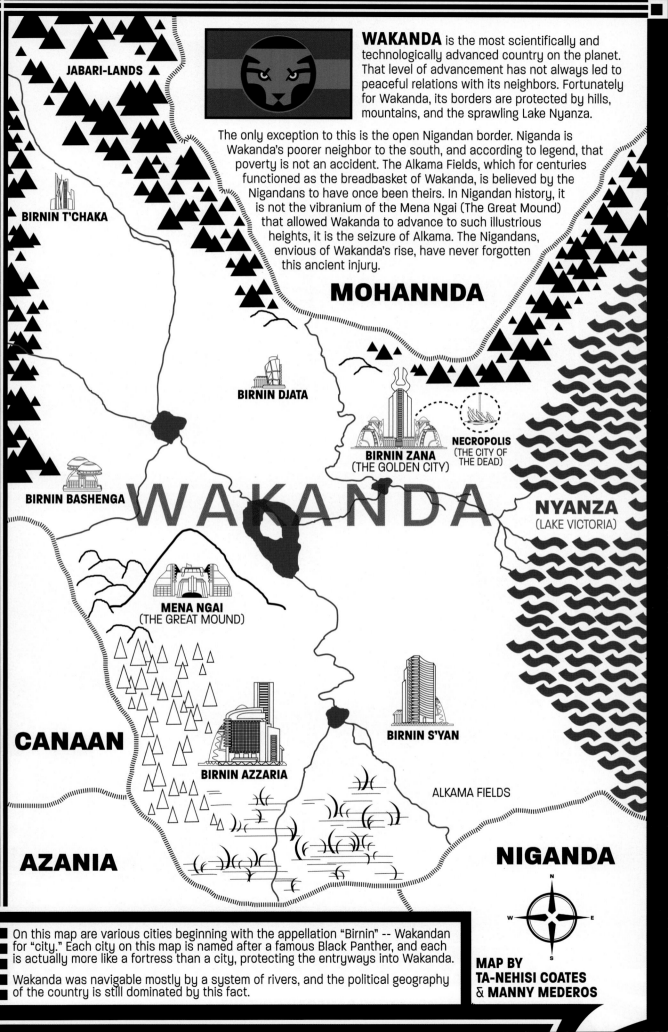

**WAKANDA** is the most scientifically and technologically advanced country on the planet. That level of advancement has not always led to peaceful relations with its neighbors. Fortunately for Wakanda, its borders are protected by hills, mountains, and the sprawling Lake Nyanza.

The only exception to this is the open Nigandan border. Niganda is Wakanda's poorer neighbor to the south, and according to legend, that poverty is not an accident. The Alkama Fields, which for centuries functioned as the breadbasket of Wakanda, is believed by the Nigandans to have once been theirs. In Nigandan history, it is not the vibranium of the Mena Ngai (The Great Mound) that allowed Wakanda to advance to such illustrious heights, it is the seizure of Alkama. The Nigandans, envious of Wakanda's rise, have never forgotten this ancient injury.

JABARI-LANDS

BIRNIN T'CHAKA

MOHANNDA

BIRNIN DJATA

BIRNIN ZANA
(THE GOLDEN CITY)

NECROPOLIS
(THE CITY OF
THE DEAD)

BIRNIN BASHENGA

WAKANDA

NYANZA
(LAKE VICTORIA)

MENA NGAI
(THE GREAT MOUND)

CANAAN

BIRNIN S'YAN

BIRNIN AZZARIA

ALKAMA FIELDS

AZANIA

NIGANDA

On this map are various cities beginning with the appellation "Birnin" -- Wakandan for "city." Each city on this map is named after a famous Black Panther, and each is actually more like a fortress than a city, protecting the entryways into Wakanda.

Wakanda was navigable mostly by a system of rivers, and the political geography of the country is still dominated by this fact.

**MAP BY
TA-NEHISI COATES
& MANNY MEDEROS**

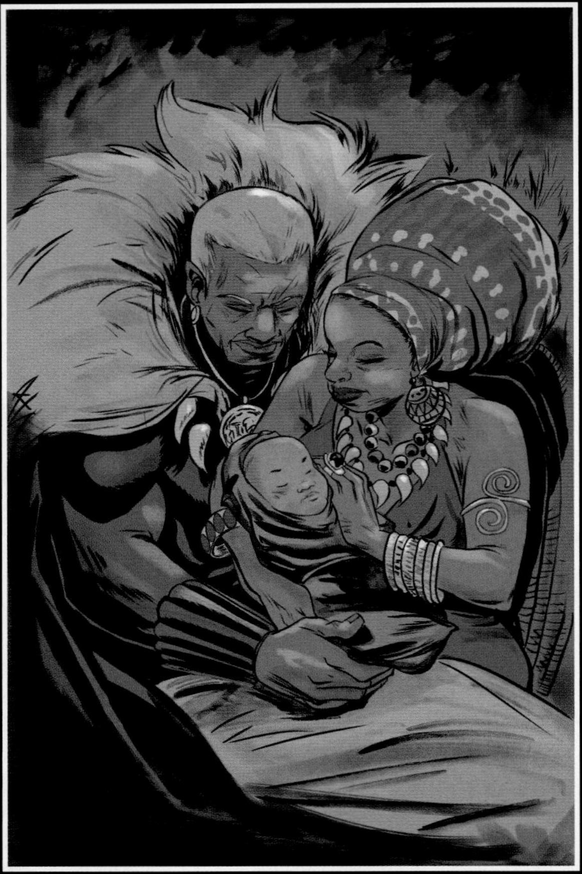

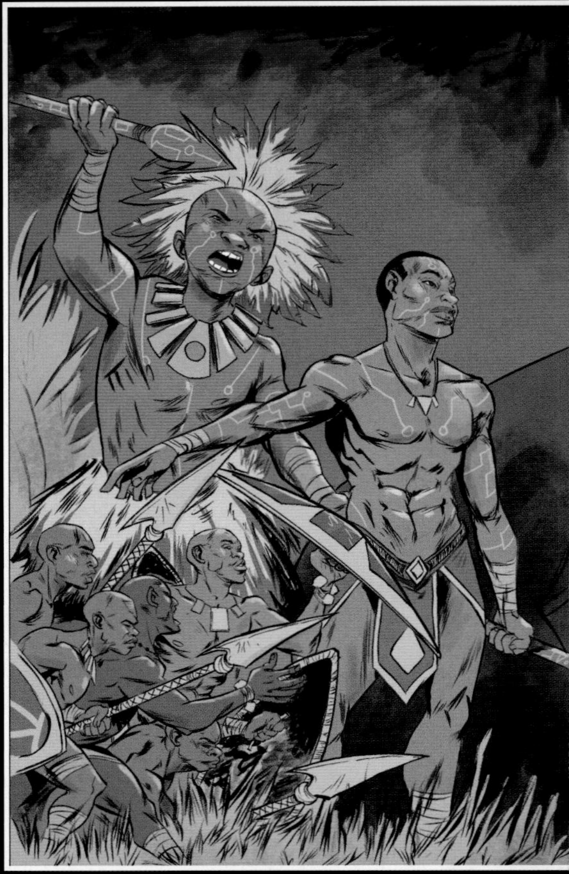

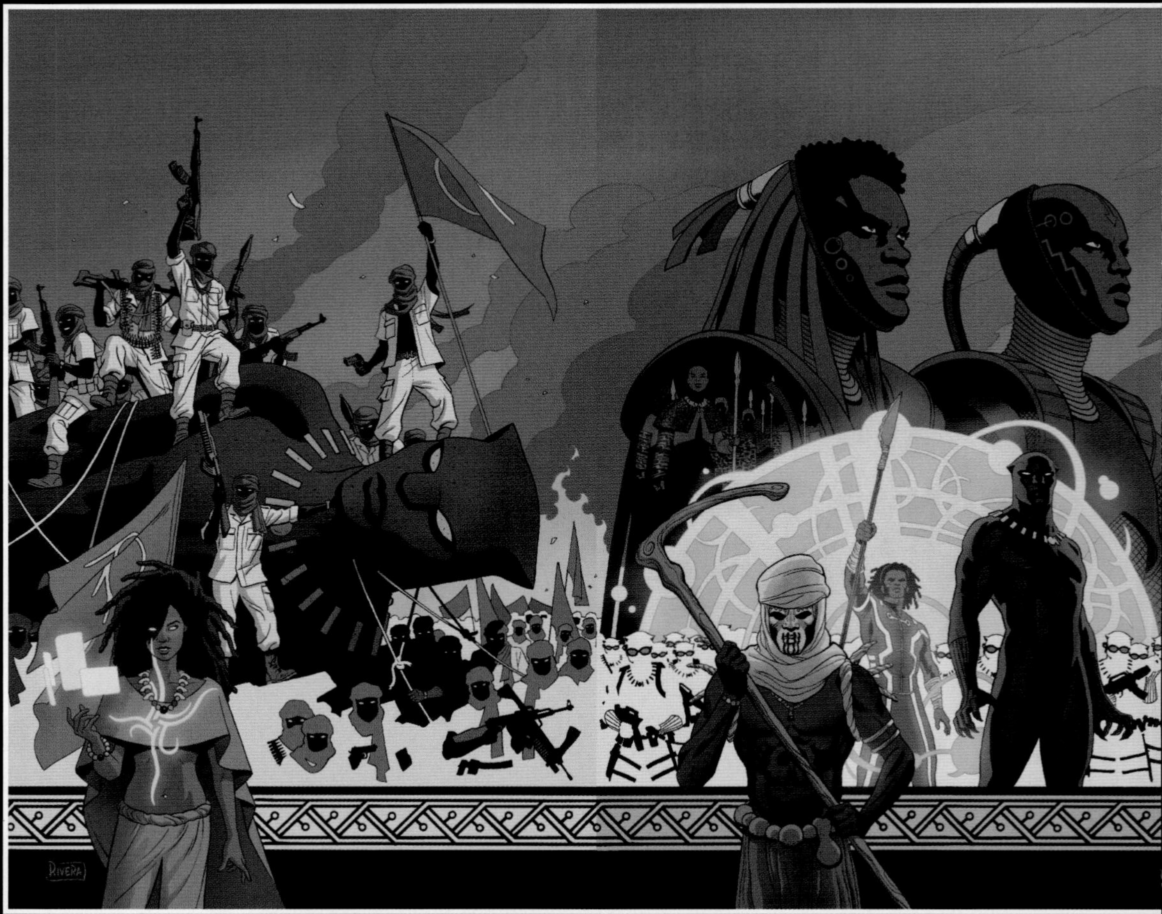
RIVERA

(TOP ROW) #1-4 VARIANTS BY **SANFORD GREENE**

(BOTTOM ROW) #9-12 COMBINED VARIANTS BY **PAOLO RIVERA** & **JOE RIVERA**

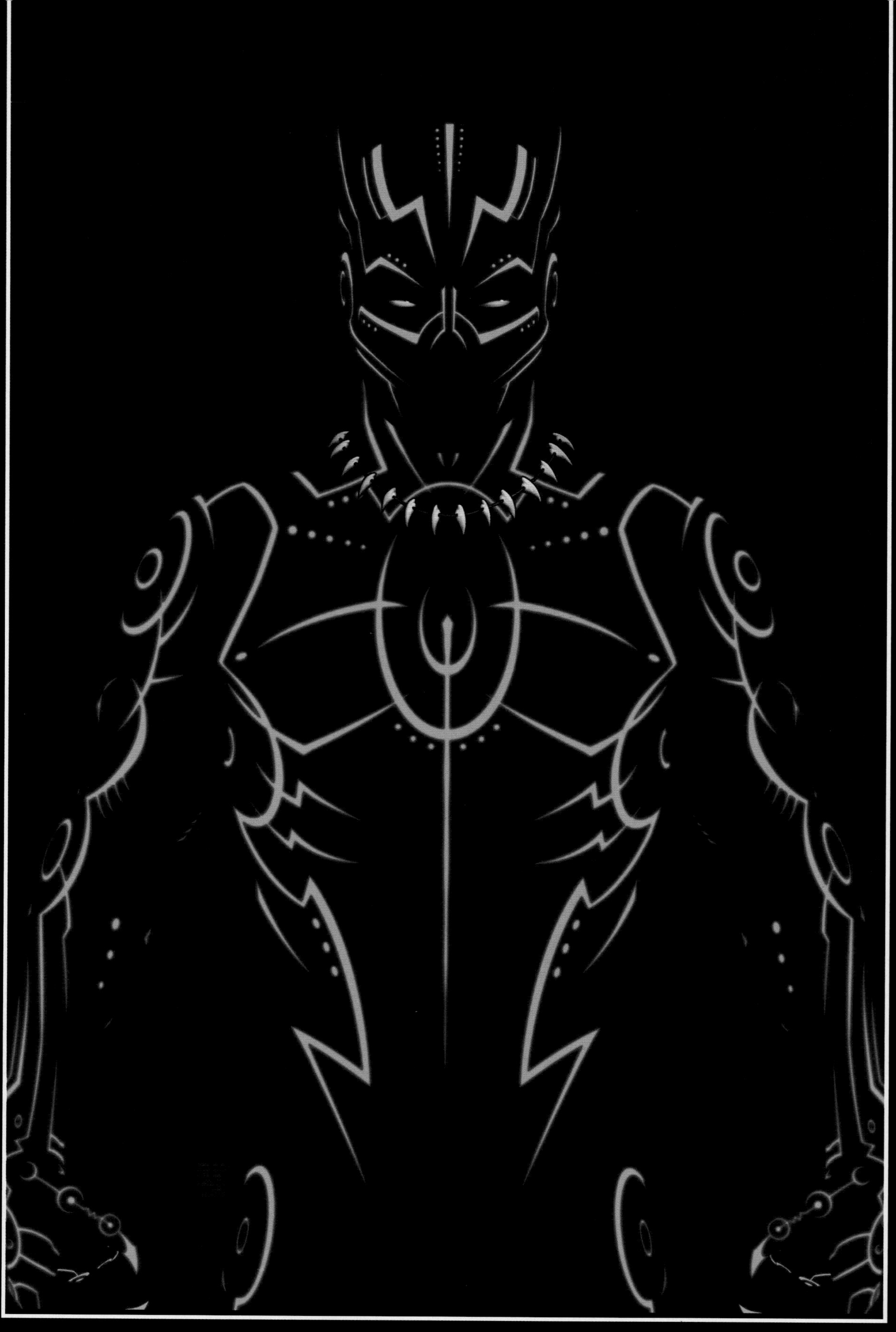

#1 VARIANT BY **JOHN TYLER CHRISTOPHER**

#6 VARIANT BY **UDON**

#7 TEASER VARIANT
BY **MIKE DEODATO JR.** & **FRANK MAR**

7 VARIANT BY **MARGUERITE SAUVAGE**

#11 CORNER BOX VARIANT
BY **JOE JUSKO**

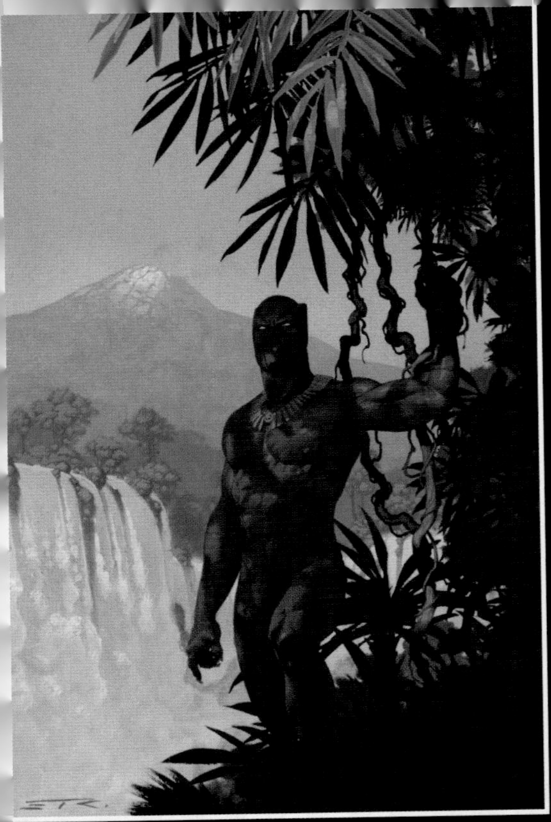

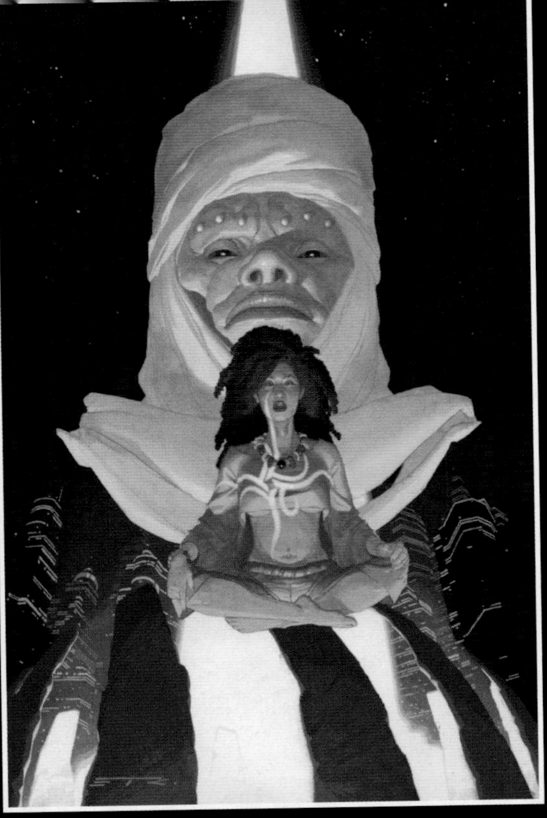

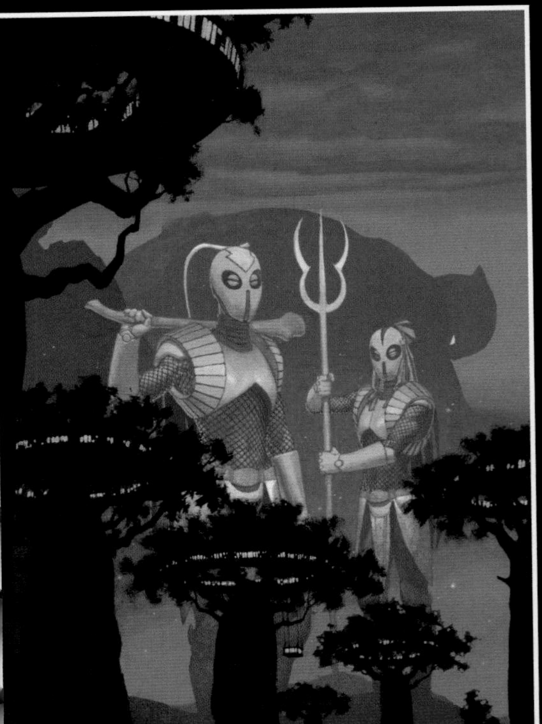

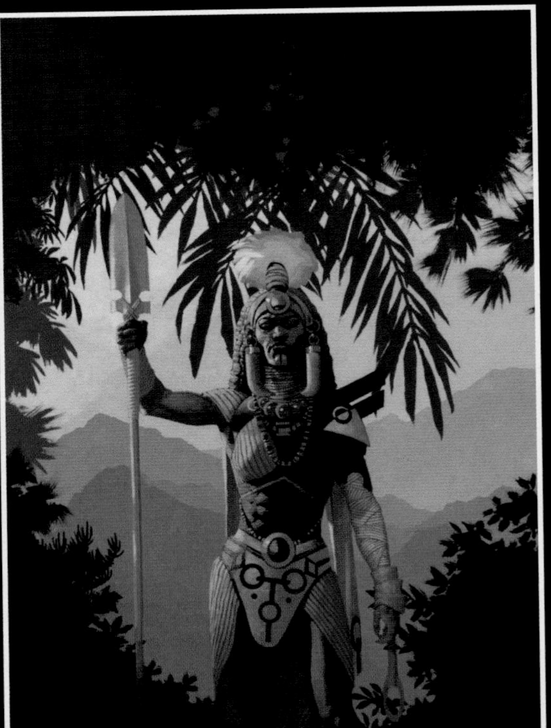

#5-8 VARIANTS BY **ESAD RIBIC**

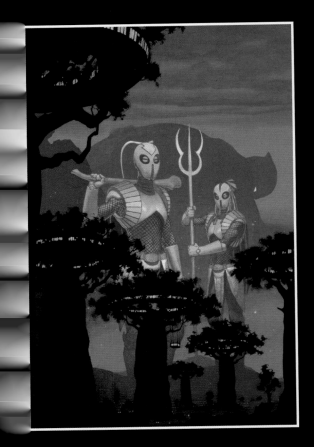

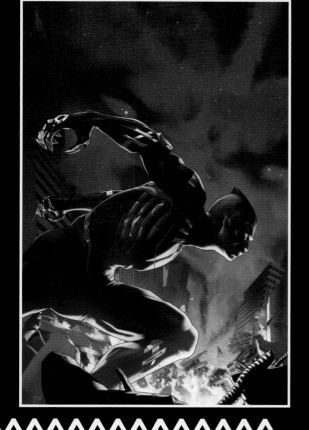

#2 AGE OF APOCALYPSE VARIANT
BY **JAMAL CAMPBELL**

#5 MARVEL TSUM TSUM TAKEOVER VARIANT
BY **SARA PICHELLI** & **JASON KEITH**

#12 VENOMIZED VARIANT
BY **ELIZABETH TORQUE**

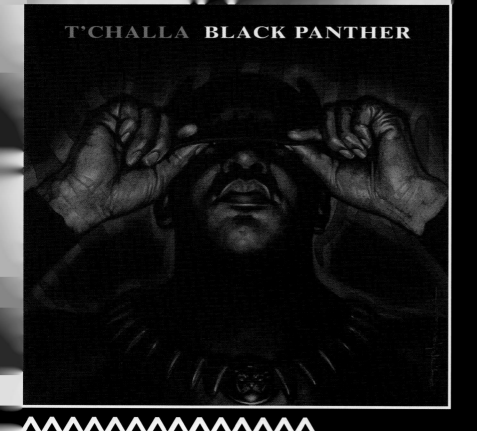

T'CHALLA **BLACK PANTHER**

#1 HIP-HOP VARIANT
BY **BRIAN STELFREEZE**

king t'challa long live wakanda

#7 HIP-HOP VARIANT BY
**BILL SIENKIEWICZ**

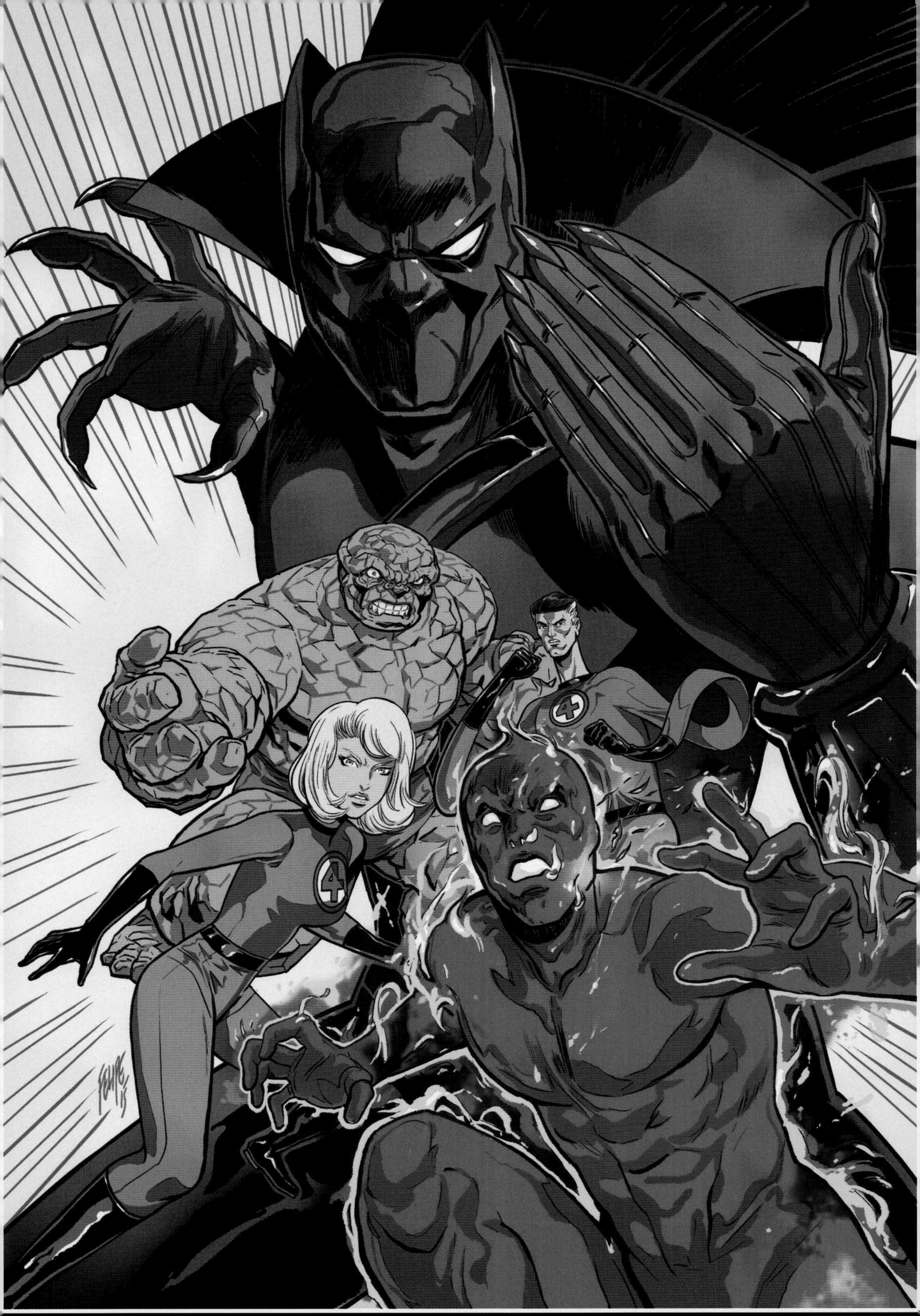

#1 BLACK PANTHER 50TH ANNIVERSARY VARIANT BY **FELIPE SMITH**

TOTALLY AWESOME HULK #10 BLACK PANTHER 50TH ANNIVERSARY VARIANT
BY **PHIL JIMENEZ** & **MARTE GRACIA**

# BLACK PANTHER and The Avengers

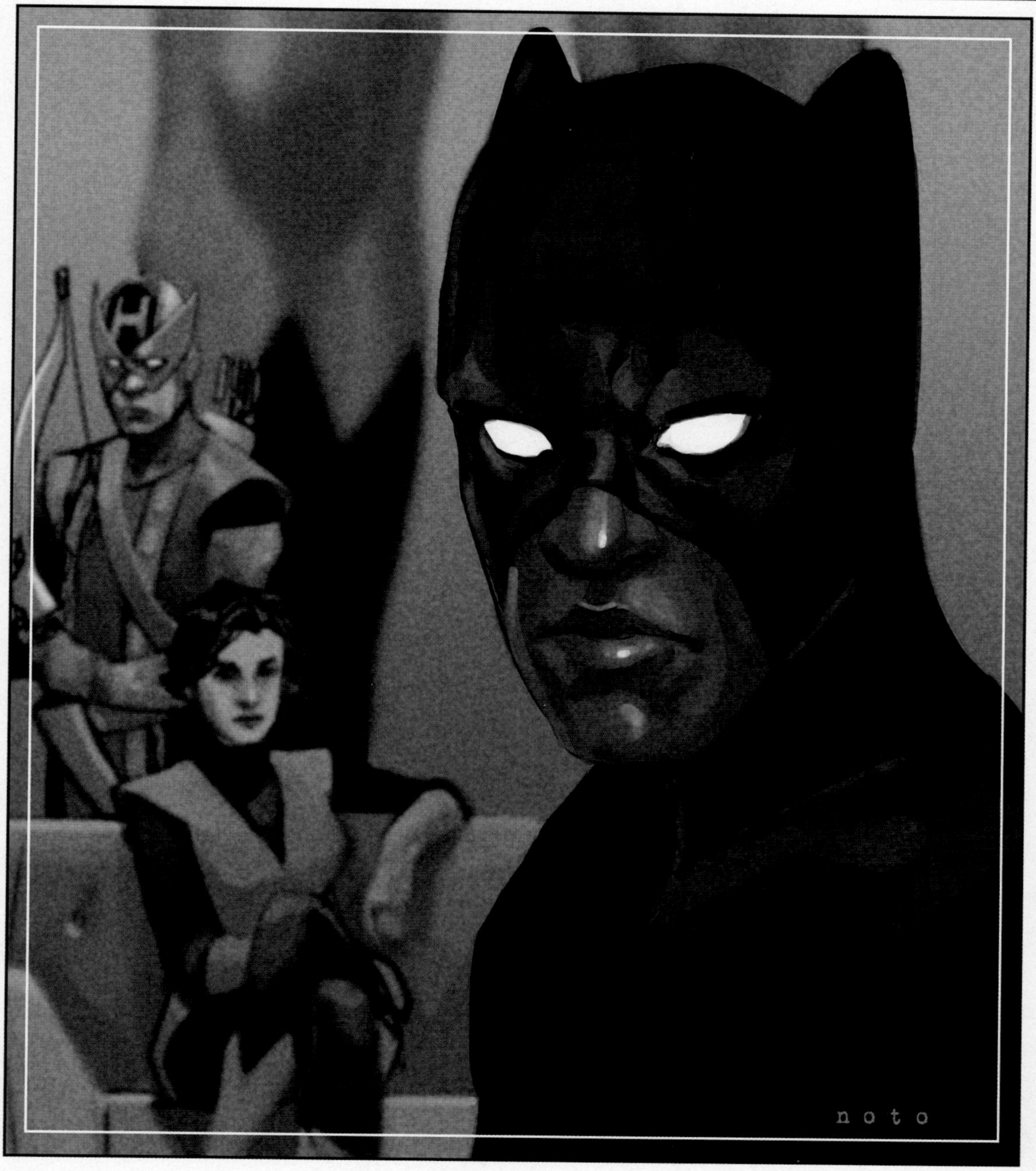
noto

PUNISHER #1 BLACK PANTHER 50TH ANNIVERSARY VARIANT
BY **PHIL NOTO**

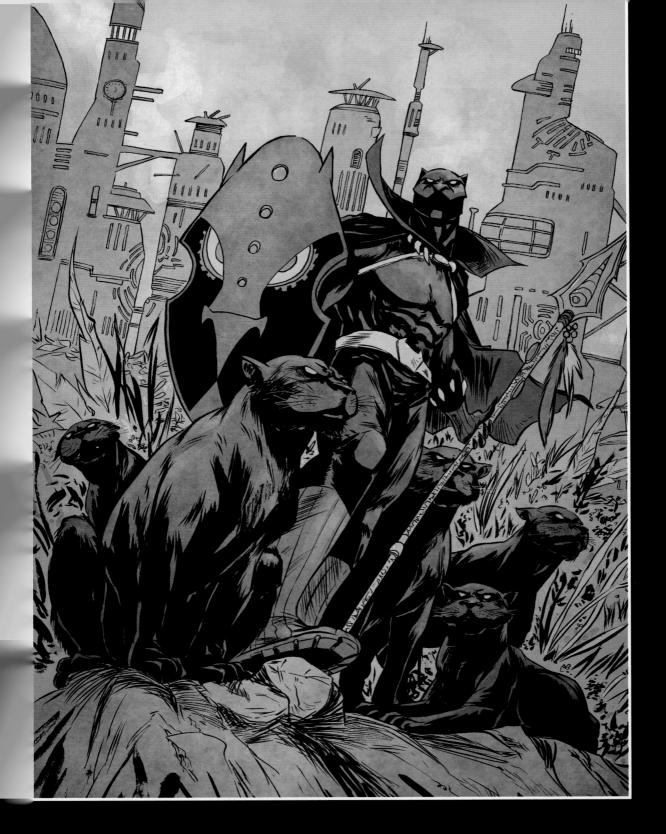

POWER MAN AND IRON FIST #1 BLACK PANTHER 50TH ANNIVERSARY VARIANT
BY **SANFORD GREENE**

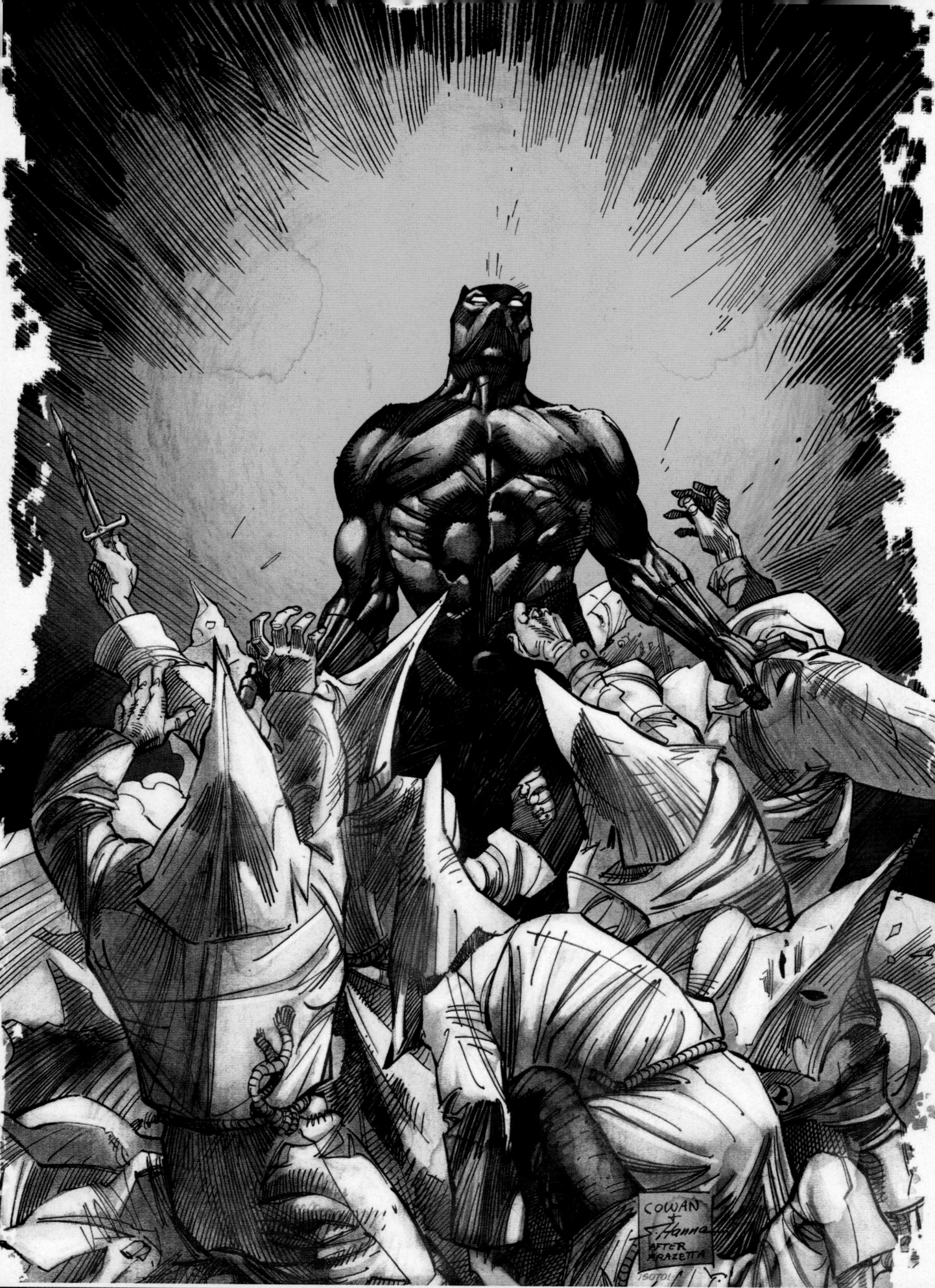
COWAN
S. Hanna
AFTER FRAZETTA

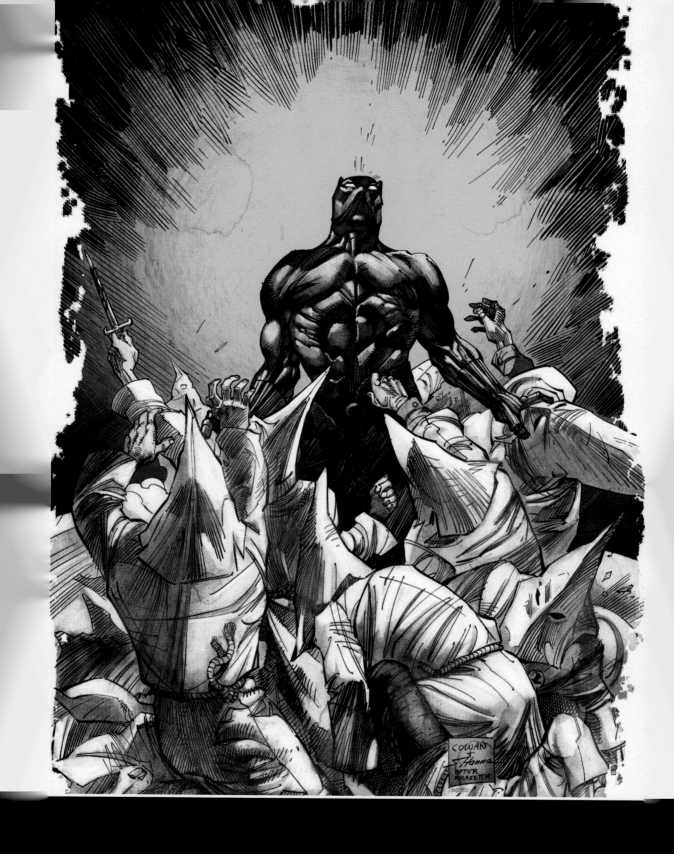

NEW AVENGERS #12 BLACK PANTHER 50TH ANNIVERSARY VARIANT
BY **DENYS COWAN**, **SCOTT HANNA** & **CHRIS SOTOMAYOR**

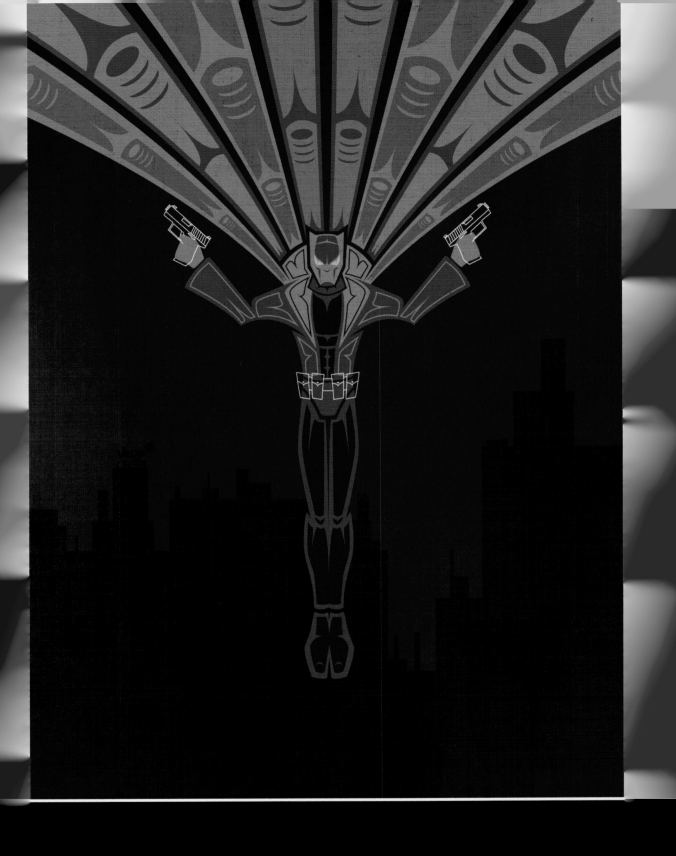

JESSICA JONES #1 BLACK PANTHER 50TH ANNIVERSARY VARIANT
BY **VEREGGE**

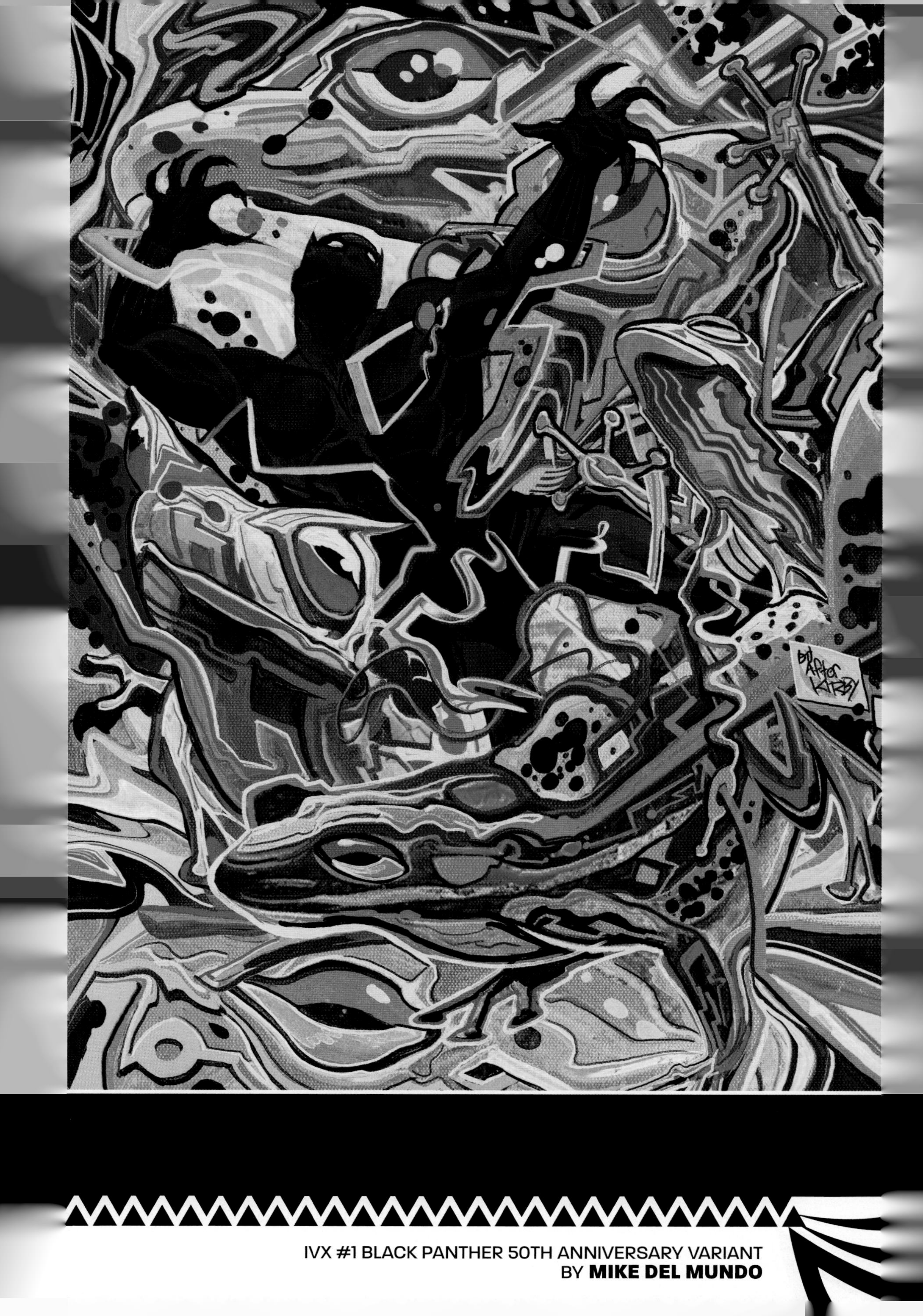

IVX #1 BLACK PANTHER 50TH ANNIVERSARY VARIANT
BY **MIKE DEL MUNDO**

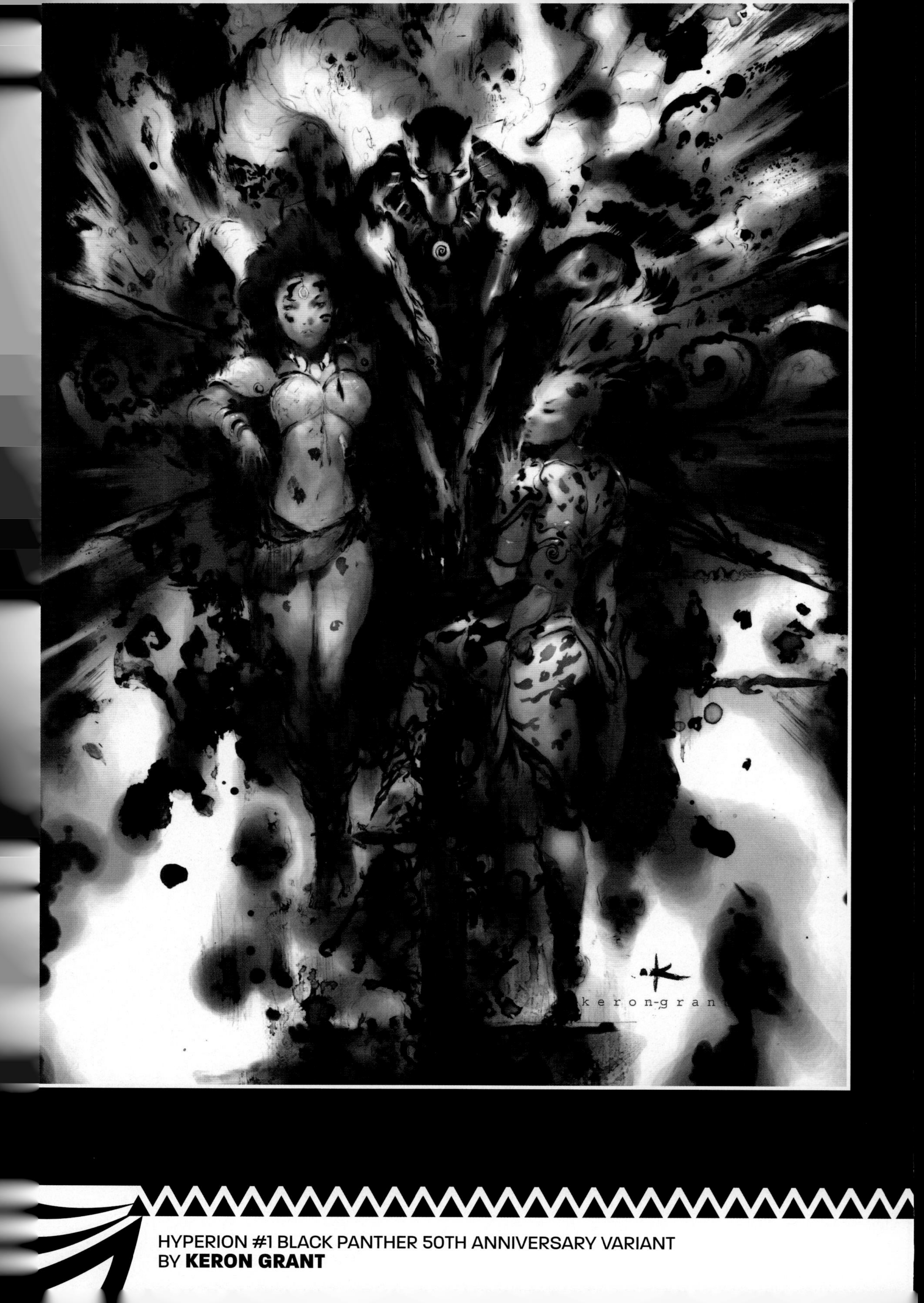
keron-gran

HYPERION #1 BLACK PANTHER 50TH ANNIVERSARY VARIANT
BY **KERON GRANT**

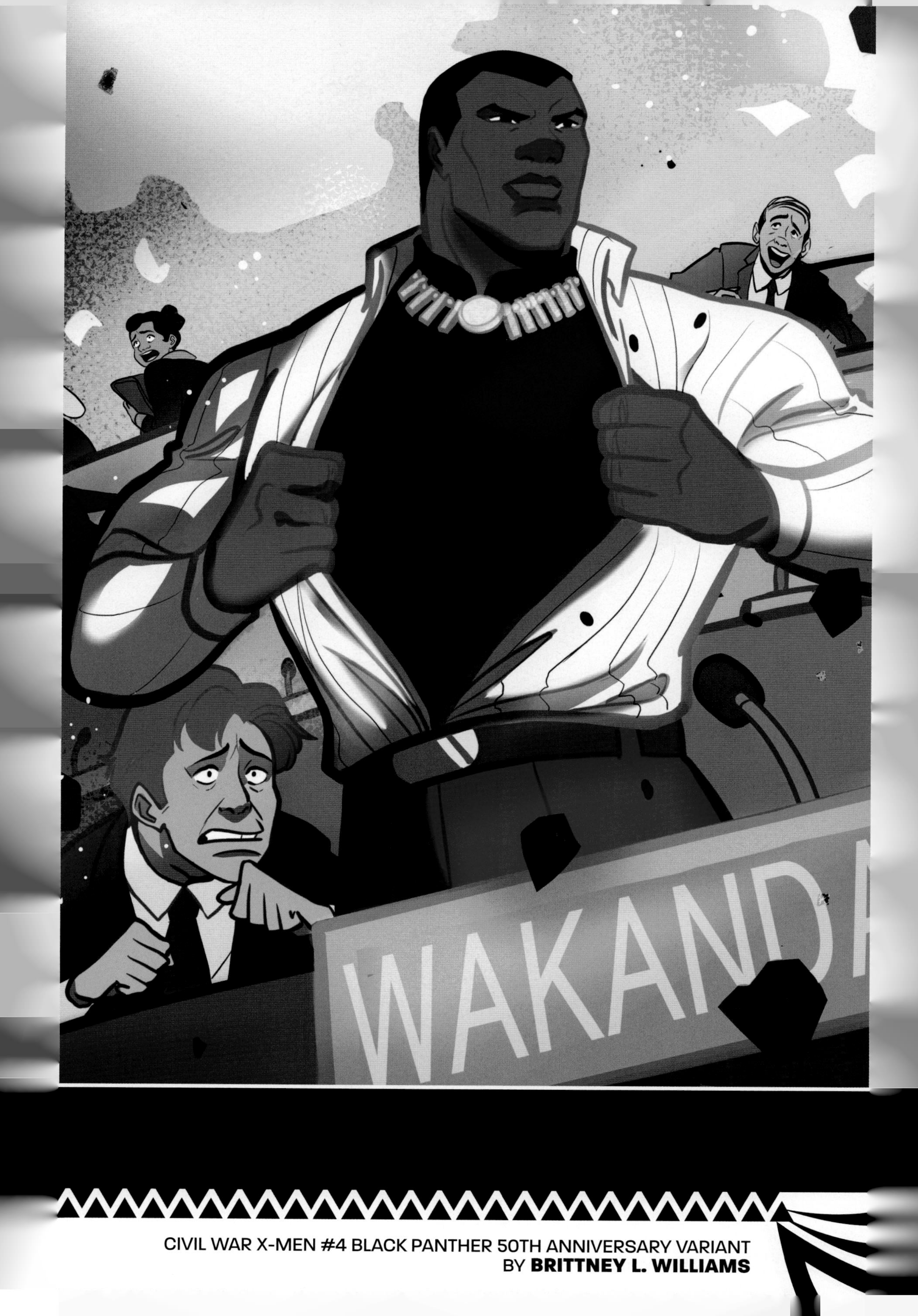
WAKAND

CIVIL WAR X-MEN #4 BLACK PANTHER 50TH ANNIVERSARY VARIANT
BY **BRITTNEY L. WILLIAMS**

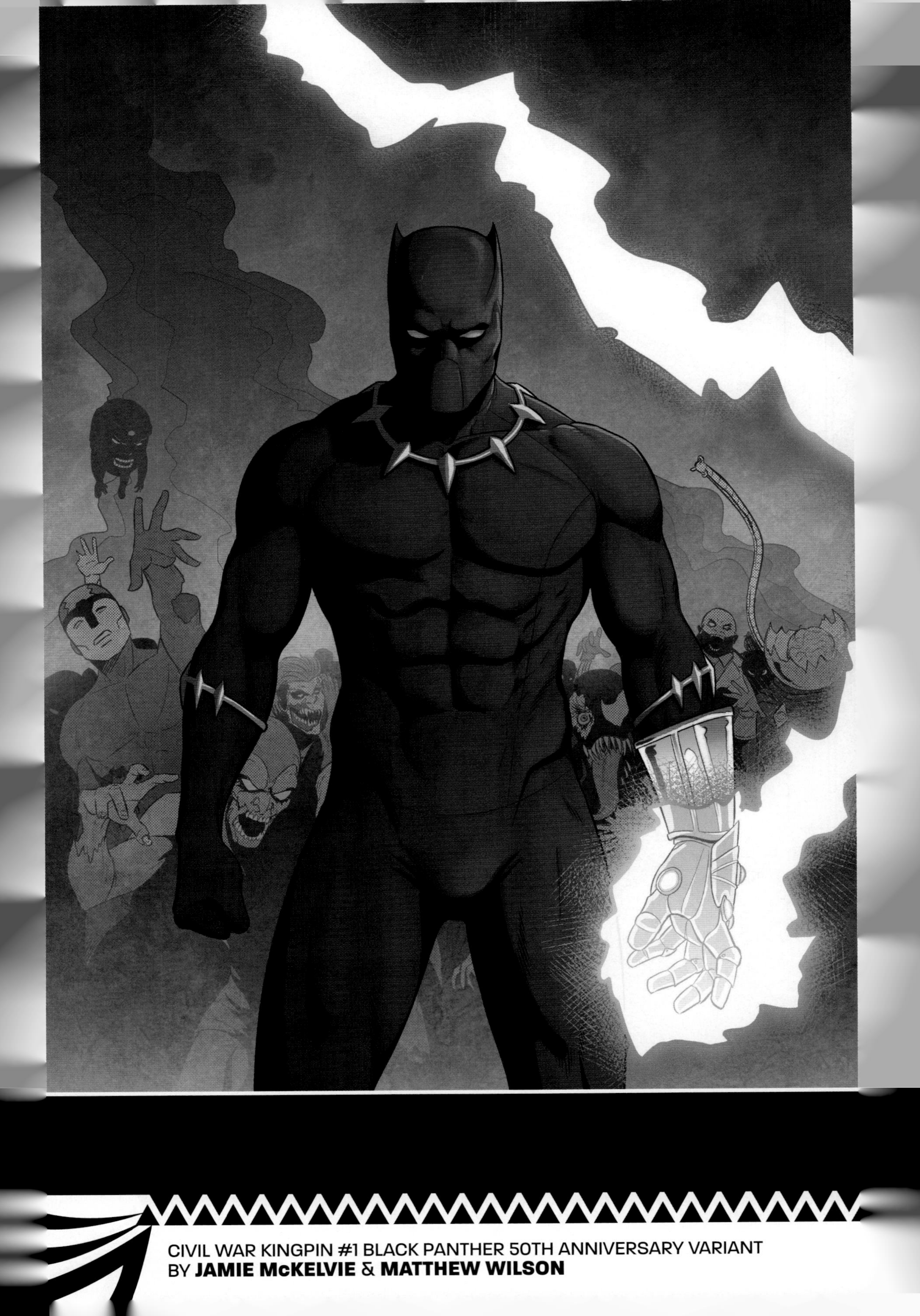

CIVIL WAR KINGPIN #1 BLACK PANTHER 50TH ANNIVERSARY VARIANT
BY **JAMIE McKELVIE** & **MATTHEW WILSON**

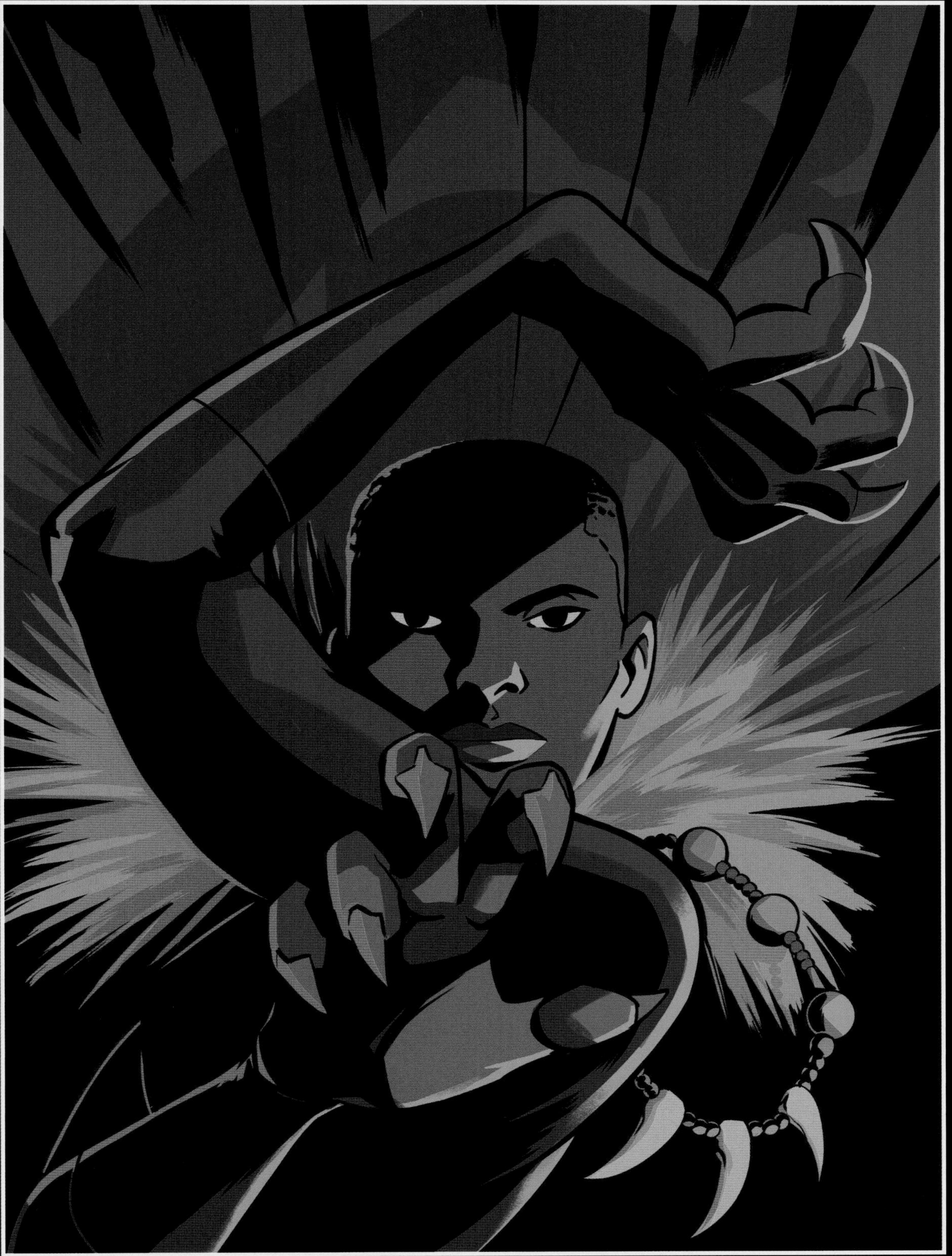

BLACK PANTHER WORLD OF WAKANDA #1 BLACK PANTHER 50TH ANNIVERSARY VARIANT BY **NATACHA BUSTOS**

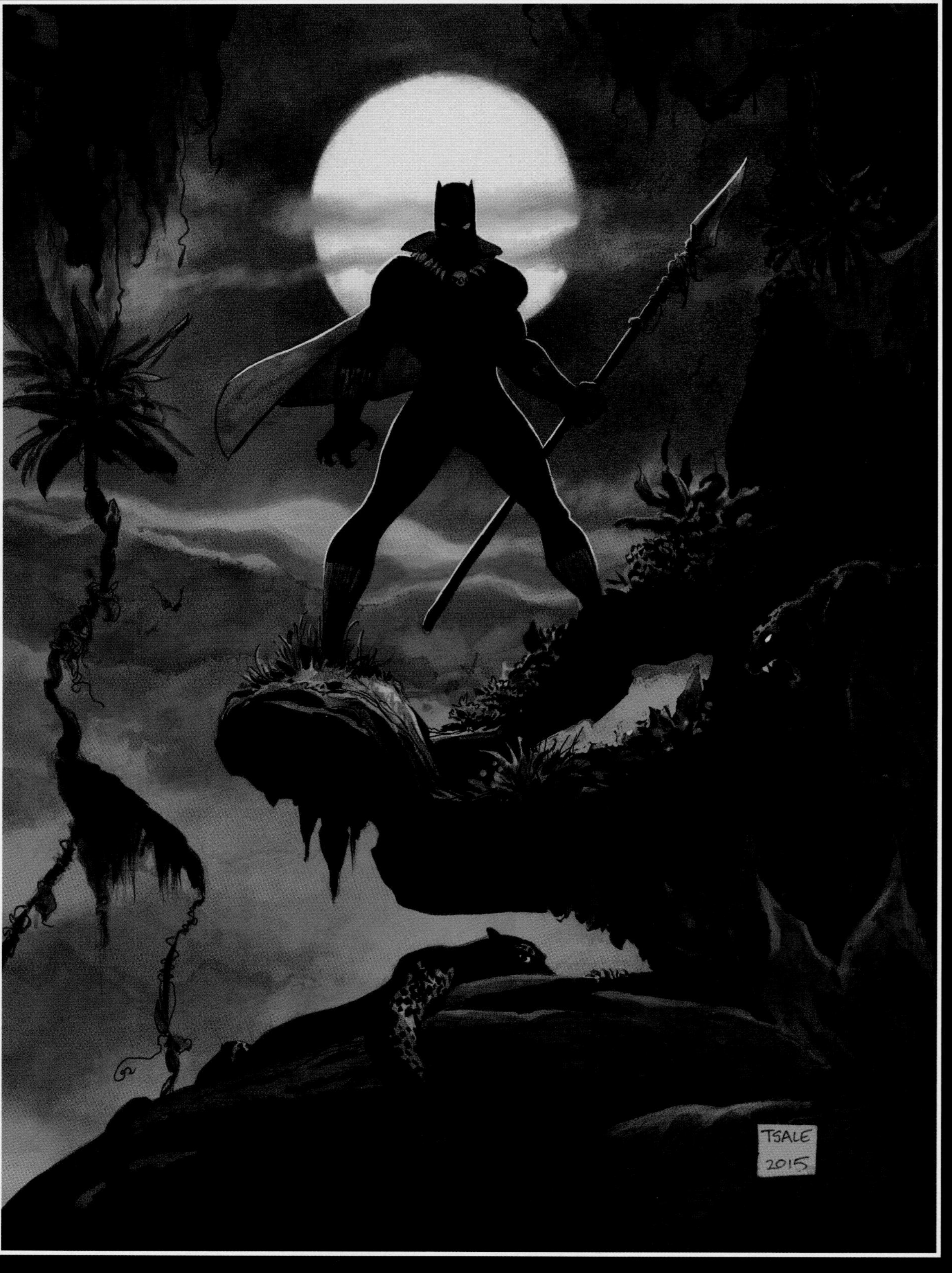
TSALE
2015

ULTIMATES #3 BLACK PANTHER 50TH ANNIVERSARY VARIANT
BY **TIM SALE** & **DAVE STEWART**

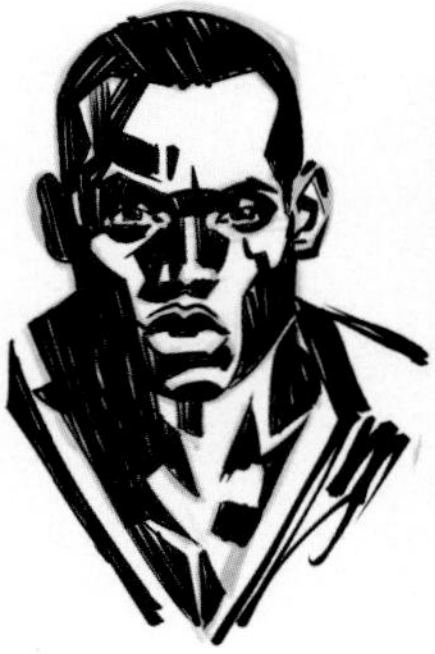

# BEHIND THE SCENES WITH BRIAN STELFREEZE

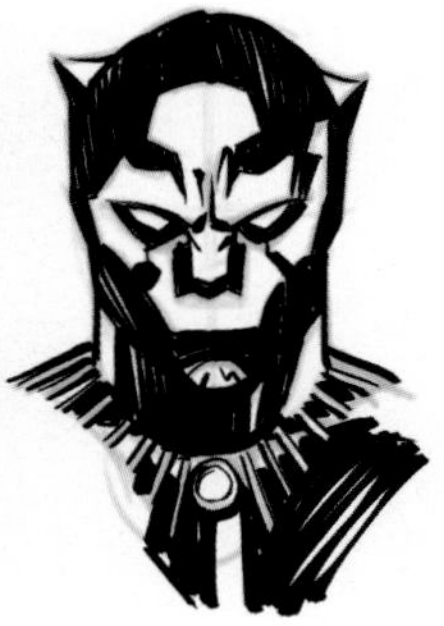

By TJ Dietsch for Marvel.com

**Marvel: Ta-Nehisi is an accomplished writer, but hasn't worked in comics before. How has collaborating with him been different than other writers you've worked with?**

**Brian Stelfreeze:** It's quite fascinating in a number of ways. Most established comic writers have a fixed style or methodology, so what you get on page one of the first issue is about the same for the last page of the series. Ta-Nehisi is still evolving as a comic book writer. It's really cool to see him not only learn the language of visual storytelling but also create new ways of doing it. I think Marvel brought me on to help him learn the ropes, but I find he's teaching me quite a bit as well.

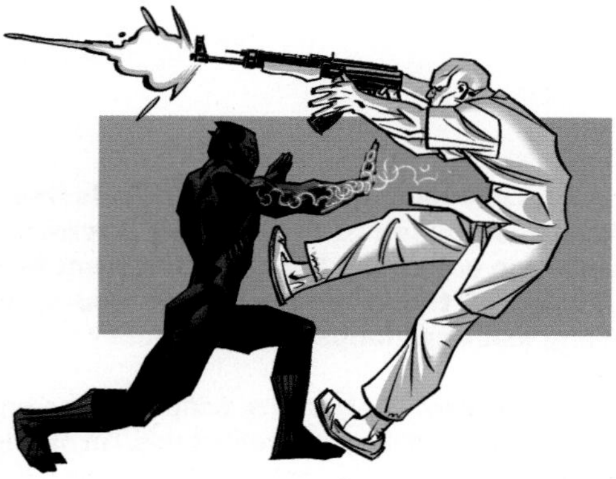

**Marvel: T'Challa's one of those classic characters whose costume has remained similar over the years but changed in small ways. What elements were you looking to update or change with your take?**

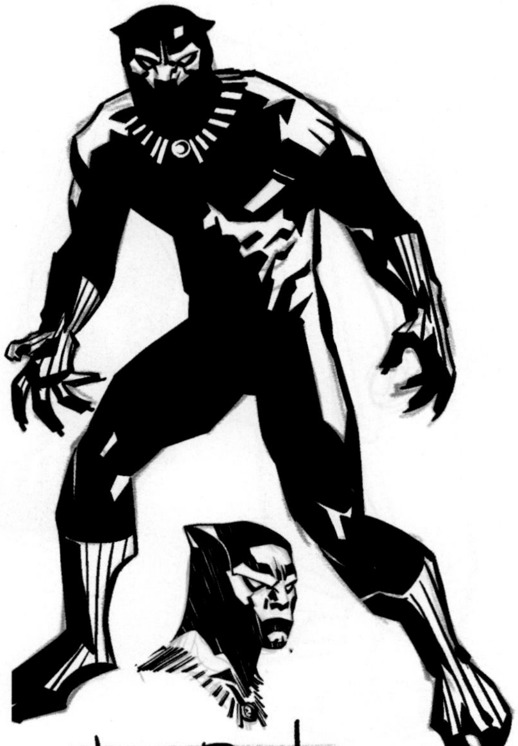
BLACK PANTHER

**Brian Stelfreeze:** I've always liked the simplicity of the Black Panther costume. I've never liked when people give him flashy capes and other adornments. Perhaps if he was called the "Black Lion" those accoutrements would make sense, but "Black Panther" suggests a sleek efficiency so I'm staying simple. I'm adding small touches to make him feel more aggressive and catlike, but just keeping it simple.

**Marvel: Black Panther also comes along with an amazing locale in Wakanda. What challenges does setting the book in that place offer you as an artist? Will it look different than we remember from previous incarnations?**

**Brian Stelfreeze:** Wakanda is one of the biggest characters in this new series so we've given that quite a bit of thought. I want the country to have a duality of old world and city of the future. Sometimes this juxtaposition should speak of a strong culture and heritage, but it should also hint at a growing schism. I've set the Golden City as a ring surrounding a giant crater lake to suggest that it's possibly the [result] of an ancient vibranium meteor strike.

**Marvel: As you alluded to, Wakanda finds itself invaded and pushed to the edge by a terrorist organization called the People. What went into the design of those members? Did you draw from any existing groups in the process?**

**Brian Stelfreeze:** Ta-Nehisi's script feels very African, so I wanted the art to reflect this. I'm pulling from cultures all over the continent to establish the look: Masai tribesmen, ancient Zulu warriors, and even modern Kalashnikov-wielding rebels will all influence the look of Wakanda.

**Marvel: Even though Wakanda prefers to keep to itself, will readers see any familiar faces from the rest of the Marvel Universe as the story progresses?**

**Brian Stelfreeze:** Not that it's a spoiler, but Namor shows up on page one. Wakanda is the Marvel world's most technologically advanced nation, and offensives there can have ramifications everywhere, so that leaves open great possibilities for cameos.

T'CHALLA

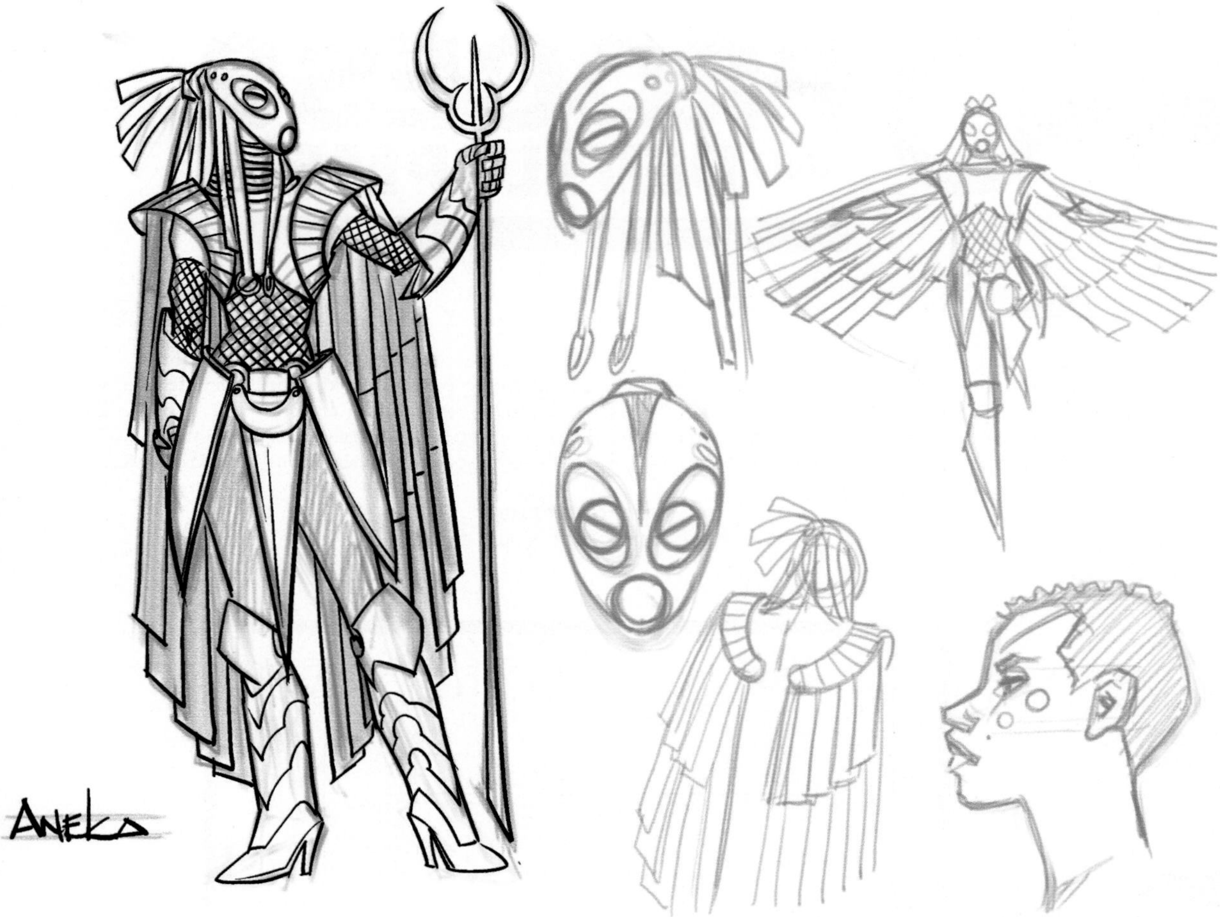
ANEKA

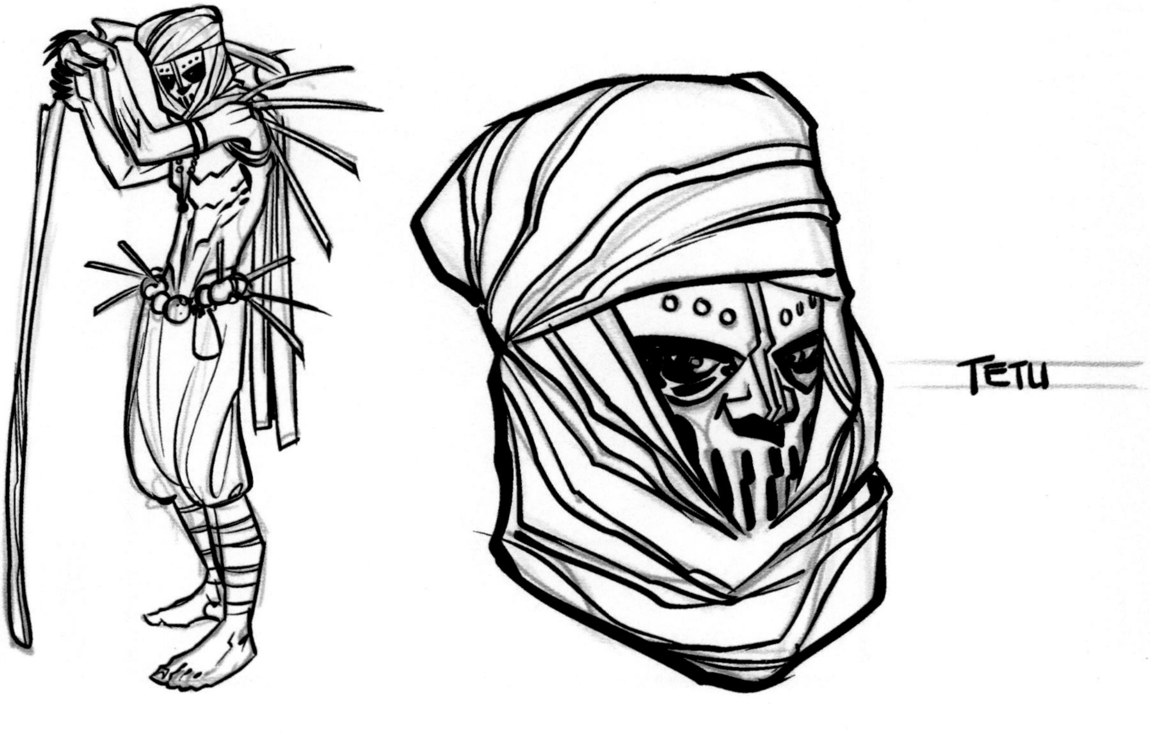
TETU

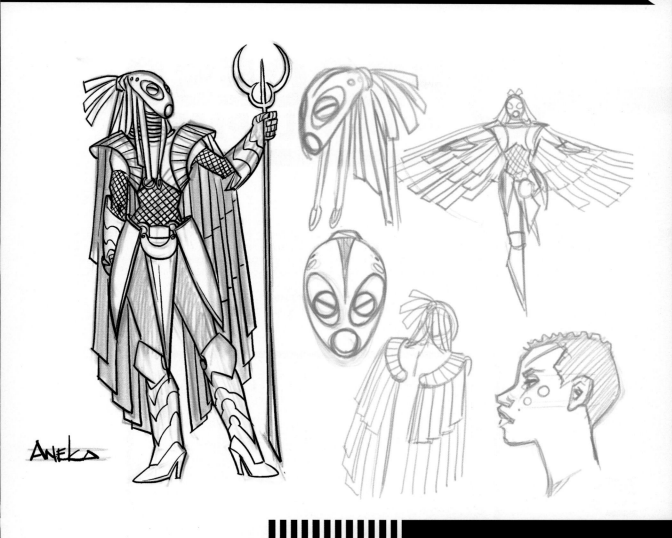

# PROCESS AND DEVELOPMENT

**PAGE 2**

PANEL 1
Big splash page. Zoom out and see several members of the Wakandan army firing wildly into a crowd of charging miners. T'CHALLA kneels, wounded, amidst the chaos. The sense should be that the soldiers have lost control of themselves. We want to allude to the Boston Massacre. This is the onset of a revolution--soldiers firing into a peaceful crowd.

**V/O CAPTION**
"You have lost your soul."

1

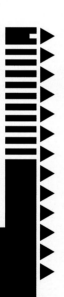

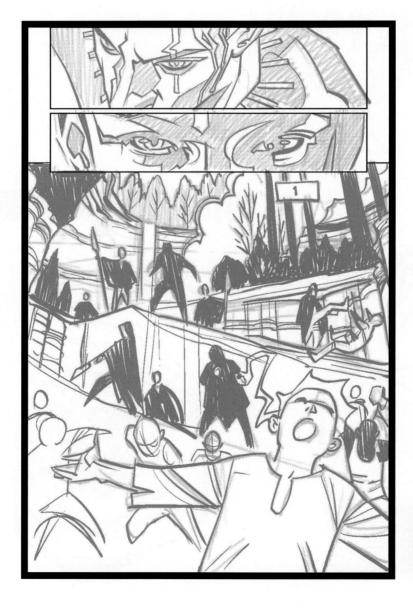

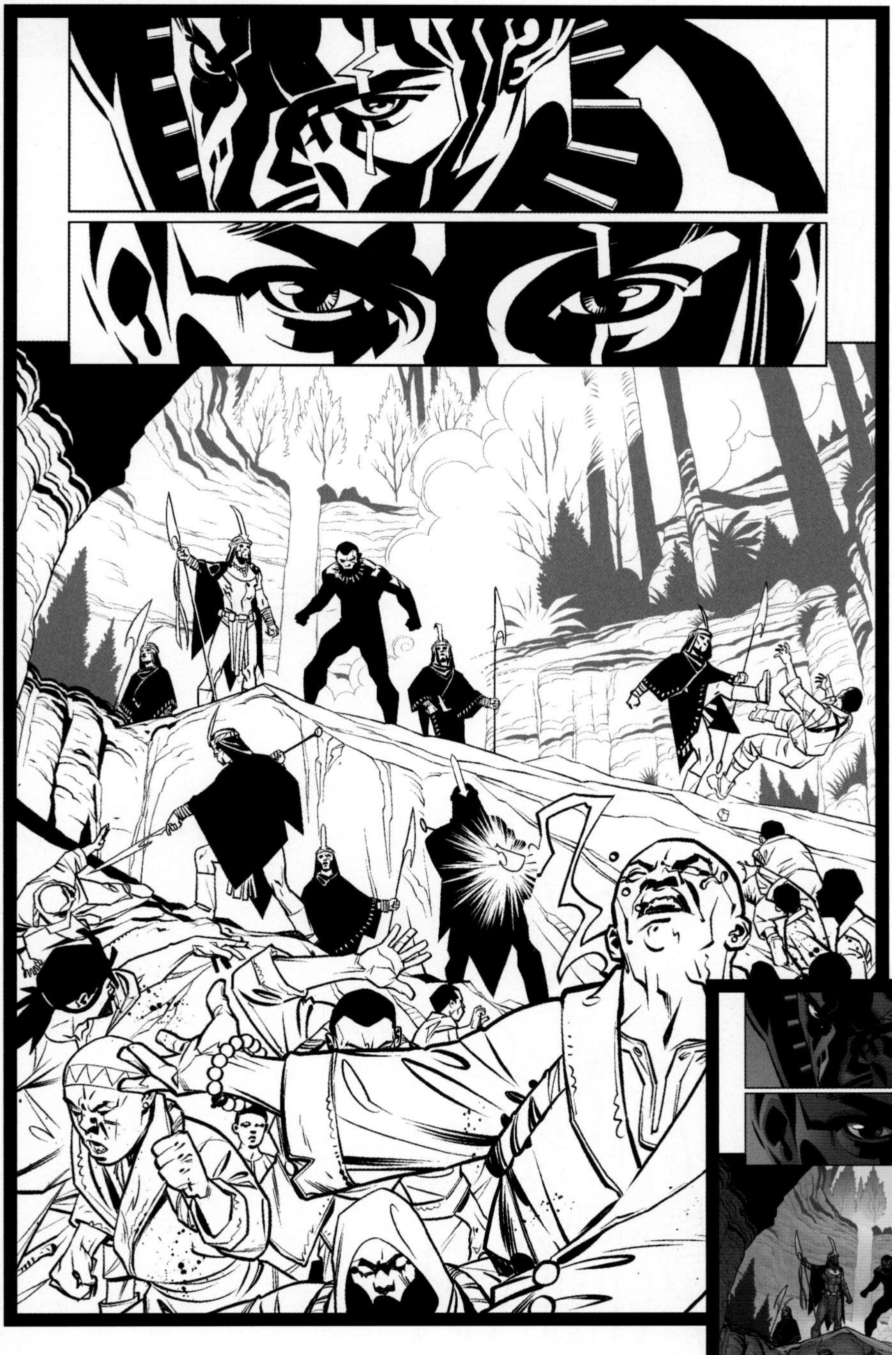
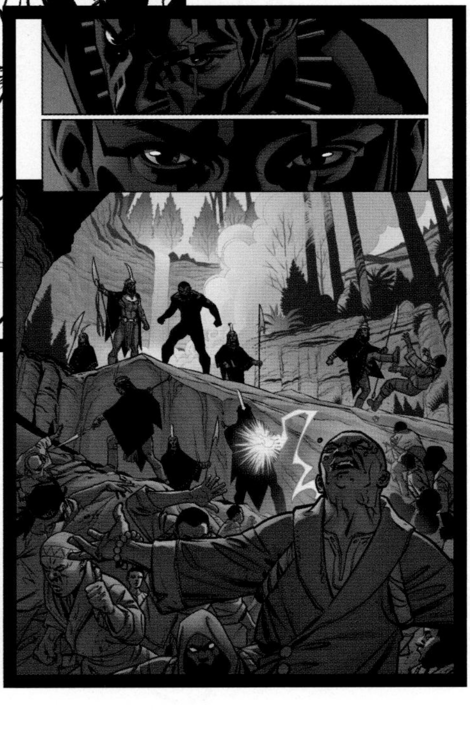

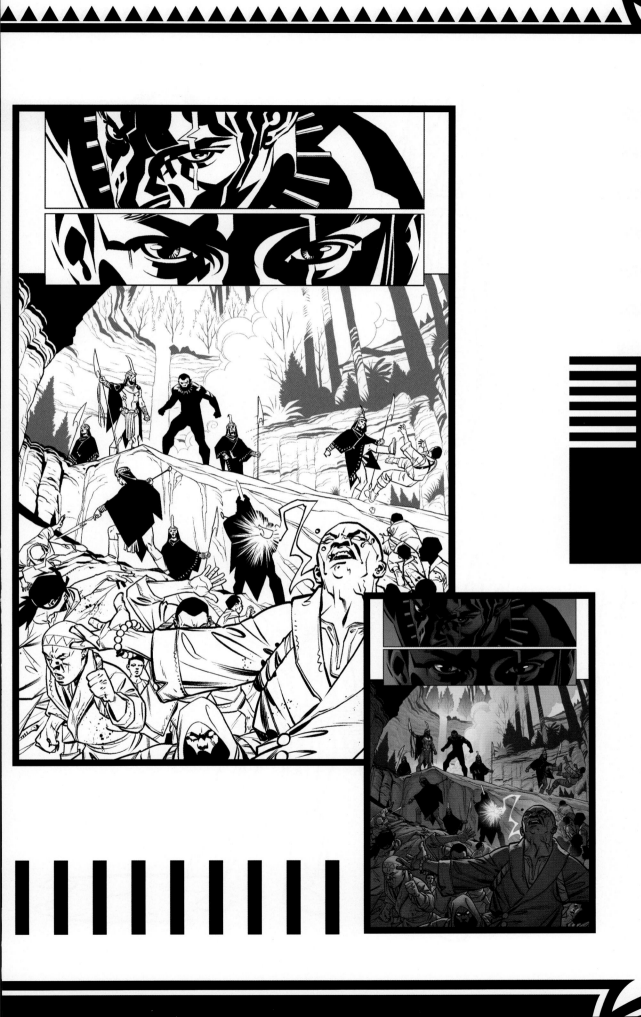

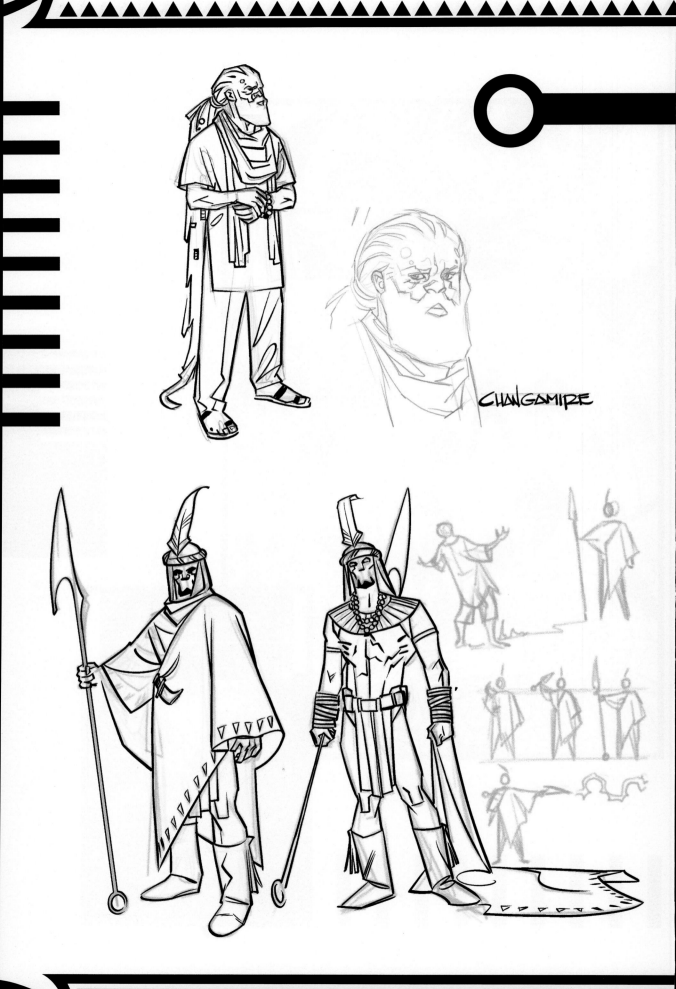

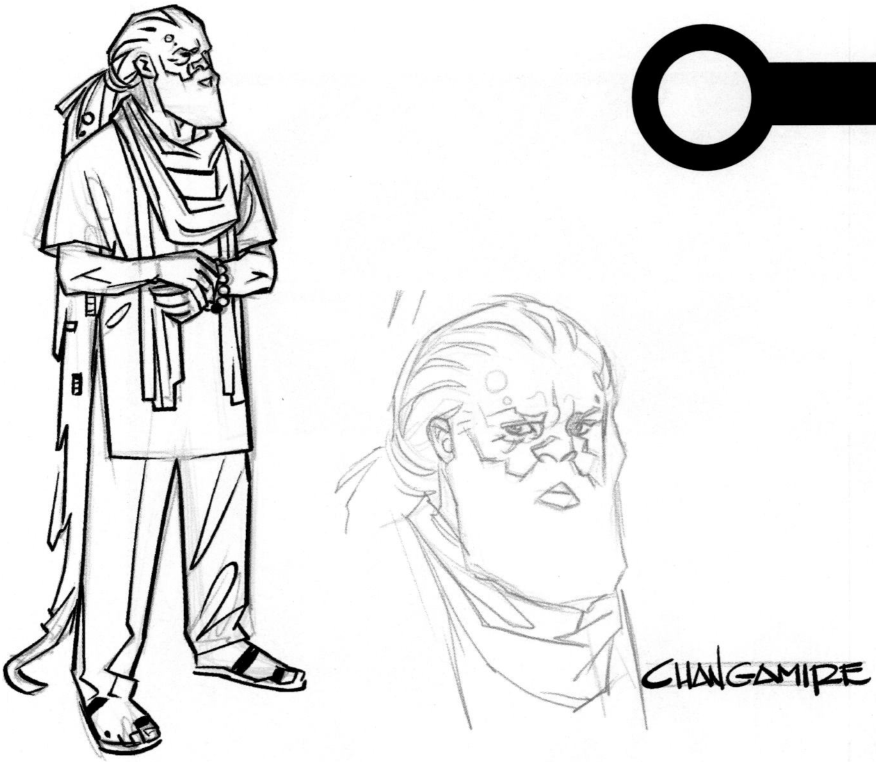
CHANGAMIRE
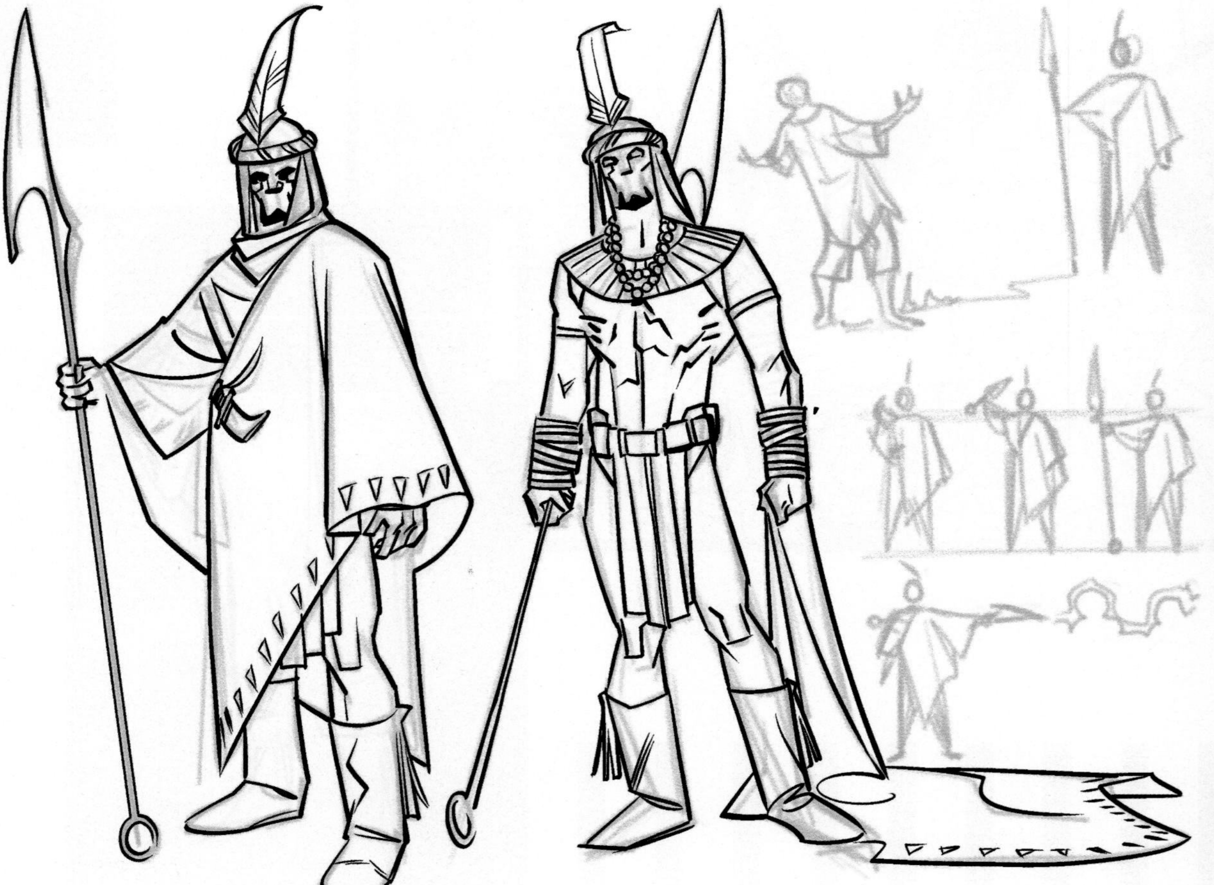

PRIME
BEAD

PRIME BEAD GIVEN AT BIRTH FOR
HEALTH CARE AND SUBSEQUENT
PAIRING FOR ADDITIONAL BEADS

— WAKANDA BEAD BRACELET—
WAKANDIANS ADD TECH BEADS
AS NEEDED IN OCCUPATION
OR LIFESTYLE

BEADS CAN BE ADDED
FOR ANY SITUATION INCLUDING:
CELL PHONE
HOME AND PERSONAL SECURITY
GEO TRACKING
WHAT EVER PERSONAL TECH WE NEED

# KIMOYO BAND

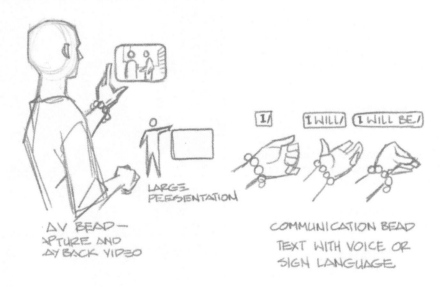

LARGE
PRESENTATION

AV BEAD—
CAPTURE AND
PLAY BACK VIDEO

COMMUNICATION BEAD
TEXT WITH VOICE OR
SIGN LANGUAGE

I / I WILL / I WILL BE /

"It's long been known that vibranium absorbs sound and kinetic energy, but that energy stays locked within the vibranium itself. Wakandan scientists can tap into this stored energy and use vibranium as a limitless power source, and this powers all Wakandan technology. All the military spears, and even the personal bracelets, network into this power source. This is why the extraordinary technology of Wakanda cannot be exported. It would be the equivalent of having the world's greatest laptop but with no battery. Perhaps this is a metaphor of the Wakandan people. They believe a part of their very soul exists within the country itself."

- Brian Stelfreeze

# PAGE 1

## PANEL 1

Open up with T'Challa. Mask off. Suit on. He's chained on the floor. ZEKE STANE is seated and over him. ANDREA and ANDREAS VON STRUCKER, VANISHER, and several SUN-TOUCHERS in the same room. It's a big room like a warehouse. The VON STRUCKERS are standing above, on a metal platform.

> **ZEKE STANE**
> I always thought I'd make a great king. I mean, I've got all the right attributes.

> **ZEKE STANE**
> Wise beyond my years.

> **ZEKE STANE**
> A regal mien.

## PANEL 2

ZEKE STANE kicks T'CHALLA. T'CHALLA looks pained.

> **ZEKE STANE**
> A love of wanton cruelty.

## PANEL 3

Pause here for a second. A shot of T'CHALLA. I want to pace this just right. It feels like there should be a beat here, before T'CHALLA turns the tables. T'CHALLA now looks like he might know something.

> **NO DIALOGUE**

## PANEL 4

T'CHALLA on the floor, looking up at ZEKE STANE. More confident now. Almost smiling perhaps--but sinisterly.

> **T'CHALLA**
> Ezekiel Stane...

> **T'CHALLA**
> ...You are no longer useful to me.

## PANEL 5

ZEKE STANE looking puzzled.

> **NO DIALOGUE**

## PANEL 6

ZEKE STANE now figuring it all out.

> **ZEKE STANE**
> Holy Hell...

## PAGE 2

### PANEL 1
Big splash panel. MANIFOLD opening a portal. We see STORM, LUKE CAGE, and MISTY KNIGHT bursting through. We see some of TETU's Sun-Touchers falling back under assault. ZEKE STANE and the SUN-TOUCHERS are falling back from the attack.

**ZEKE STANE**
Incoming!

## PAGE 3

### PANEL 1
Focus on MISTY KNIGHT side-kicking a SUN-TOUCHER. STORM flying overhead.

**MISTY KNIGHT**
What, no red, black and green? No Kwanzaa cake? I come back home, and this is reception I get?

### PANEL 2
STORM using wind to blow several of the SUN-TOUCHERS backwards. MISTY KNIGHT fighting below.

**STORM**
Still better than the the knife-wielding thugs I found in Harlem, Misty. You do remember, don't you?

**MISTY KNIGHT**
I resent the term "thug."

### PANEL 3
Now LUKE CAGE with like five dudes hanging on him.

**LUKE CAGE**
That's 'cause you a thug.

### PANEL 4
MISTY KNIGHT pummels some other dude.

**MISTY KNIGHT**
For life.

y **CHRIS SPROUSE** & **KARL STORY**

# SKETCHES
## BY BRIAN STELFREEZE

**TA-NEHISI** mentioned the idea of chainmail and I started riffing off of that. It led me to a cycle-style leather jacket reinforced with a single spun vibranium thread. The hood configuration gives them head protection when full-on battle time.

The necklace/sword is serpentine links that snap into place with a flick of the wrist, or it can work as a slashing whip. The shield also converts to a ridged body when it slides into its offensive position.

**-STELFREEZE**

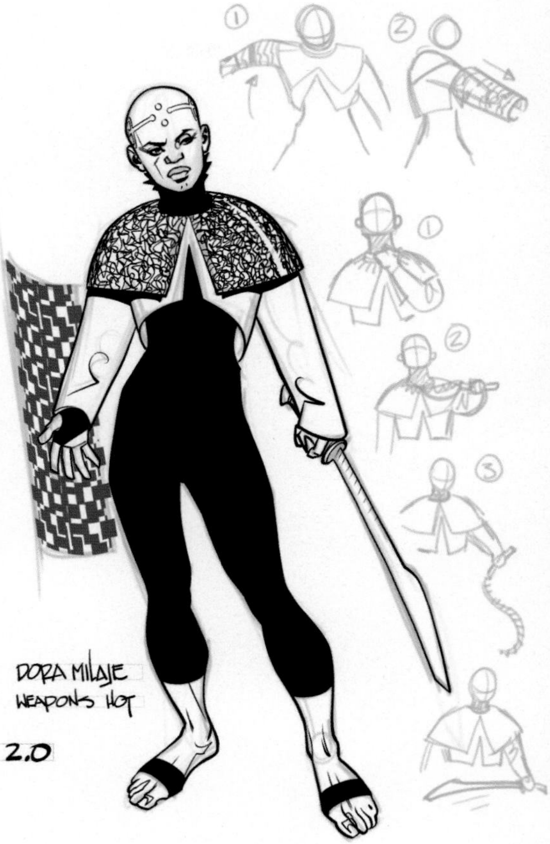
DORA MILAJE
WEAPONS HOT

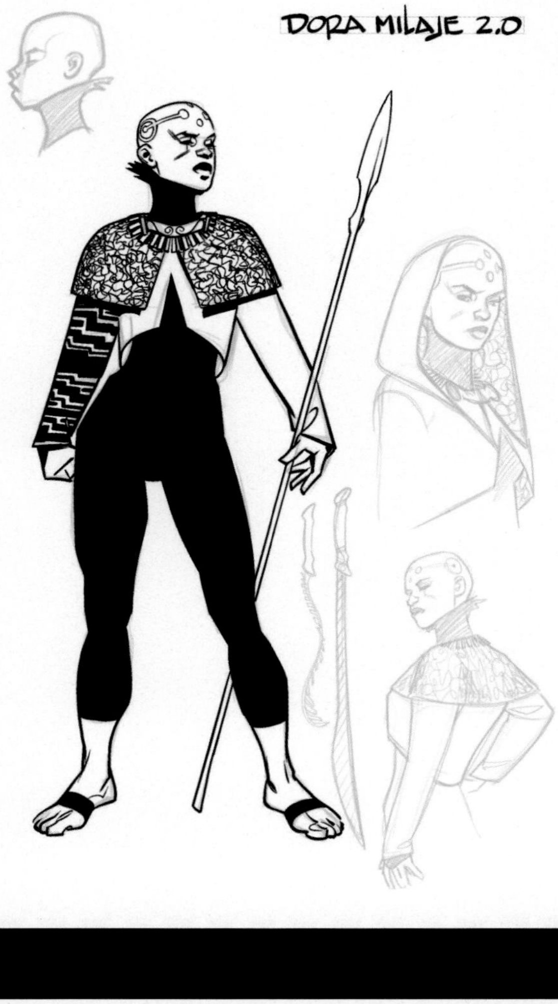
DORA MILAJE 2.0

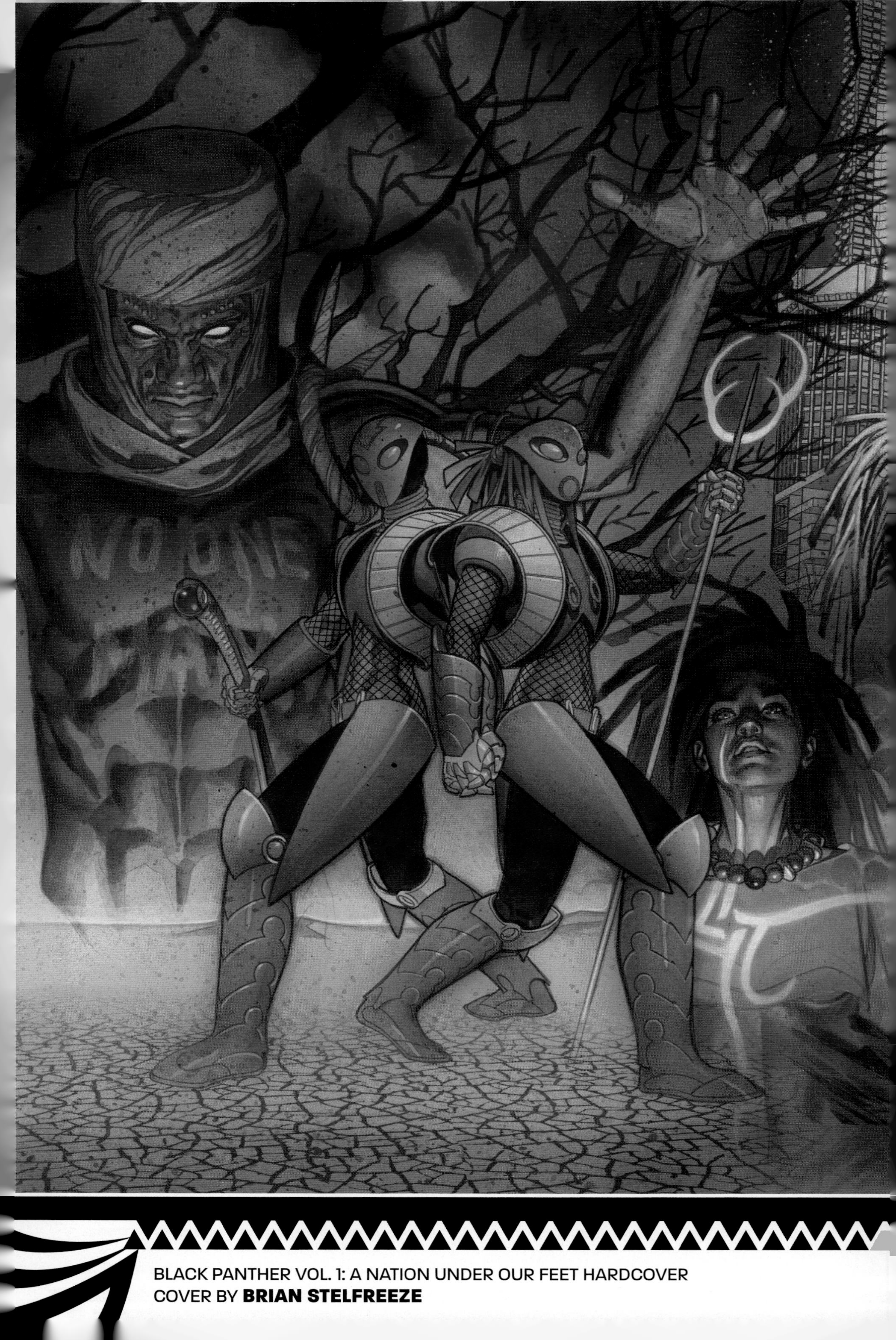
NO ONE

BLACK PANTHER VOL. 1: A NATION UNDER OUR FEET HARDCOVER
COVER BY **BRIAN STELFREEZE**

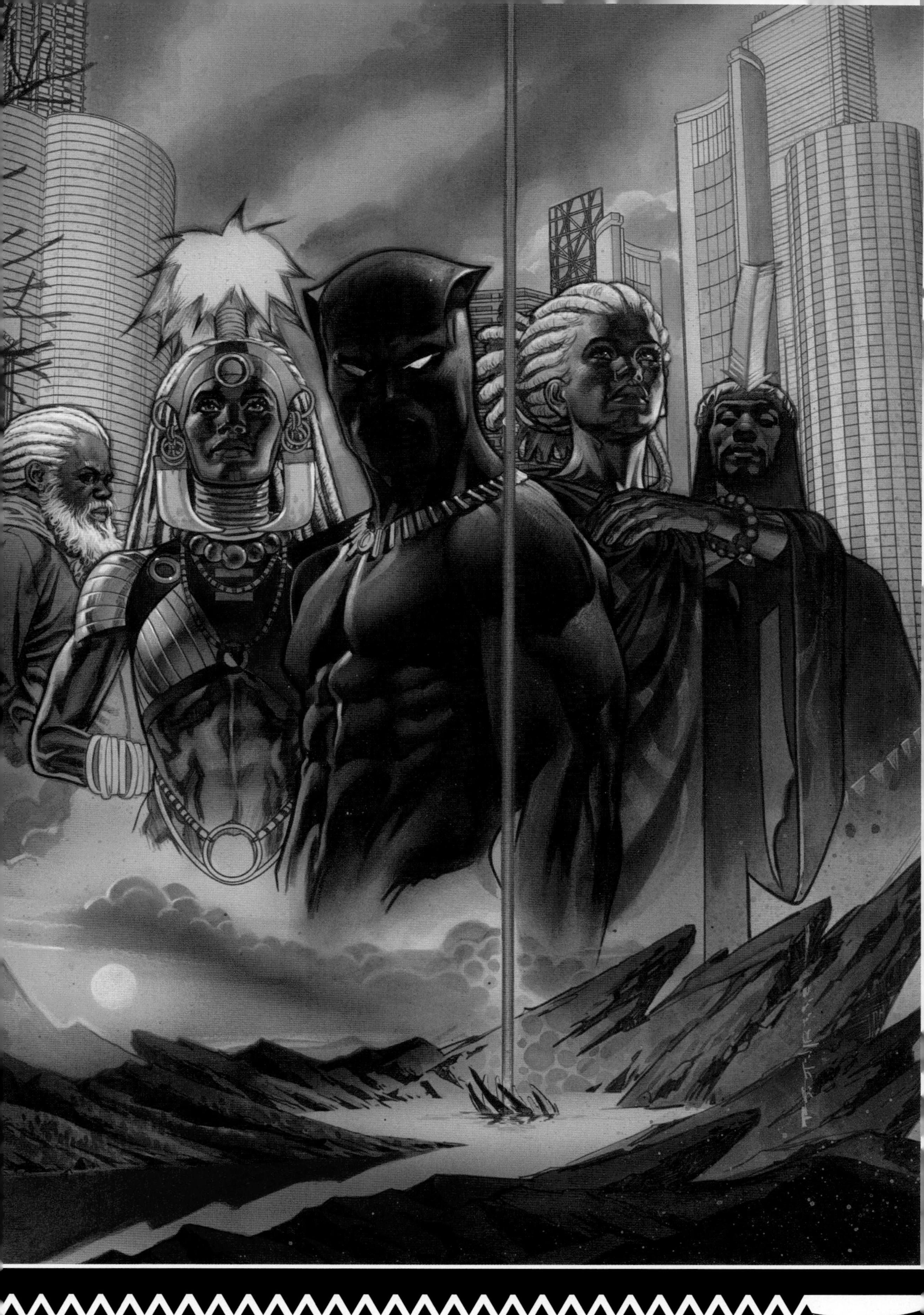

# BLACK PANTHER CHRONOLOGY

## "THE BLACK PANTHER!"

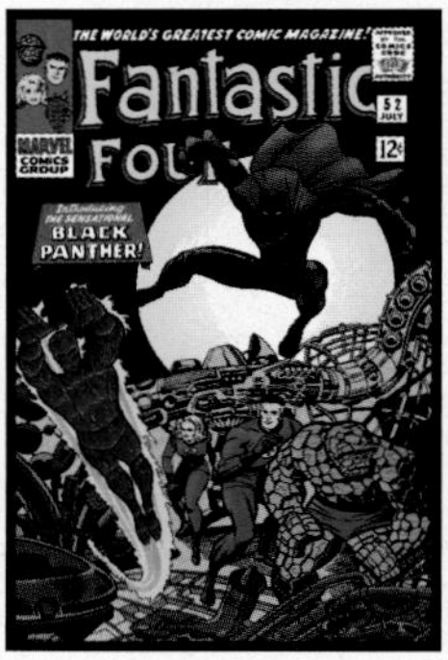

THE WORLD'S GREATEST COMIC MAGAZINE!
Fantastic Four
52
12¢
MARVEL COMICS GROUP
BLACK PANTHER!


In the Black Panther's first appearance, the King of Wakanda welcomes the Fabulous Foursome to his home country... only to attack the team upon their arrival! The FF must maneuver their way through the techno-logically advanced halls of Wakanda to discover the Panther's true agenda and learn his secret origin.

***FANTASTIC FOUR (1961) #52***

## "DEATH CALLS FOR THE ARCH-HEROES"

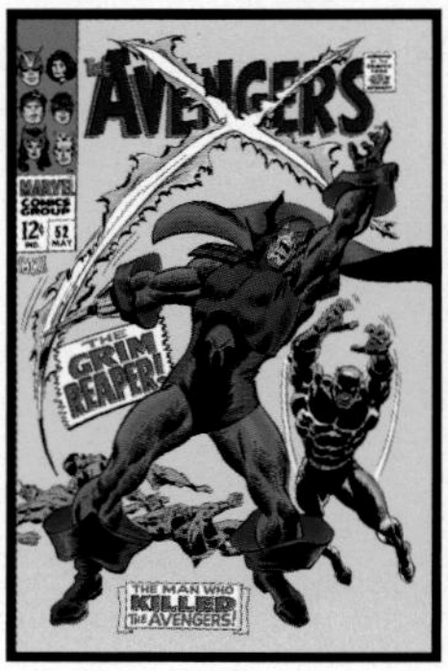

AVENGERS
MARVEL COMICS GROUP
12¢
52
THE GRIM REAPER!
THE MAN WHO KILLED THE AVENGERS!


Stumbling upon an eerily quiet Avengers Mansion, Panther winds up trying out for Earth's Mightiest Heroes in a rather unconventional manner... by breaking into their headquarters! T'Challa's suspicions prove warranted, however, as he finds the team seemingly dead on the floor once he makes it in. Solving that mystery is just the beginning of the Black Panther's first mission as an Avenger!

***AVENGERS (1963) #52***

## "PANTHER'S RAGE!"

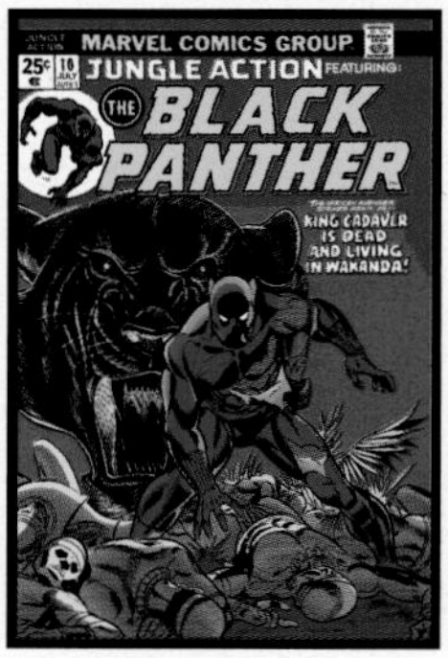

MARVEL COMICS GROUP
25¢
18
JUNGLE ACTION FEATURING:
THE BLACK PANTHER
KING CADAVER IS DEAD AND LIVING IN WAKANDA!


Writer Don McGregor and artists Rich Buckler, Billy Graham and others tell an epic adventure so huge it spanned across the savannah, into the deepest jungles and up snowcapped mountains. Over its course, McGregor would explore and expand the life and culture of Black Panther's Wakanda in compelling detail.

***JUNGLE ACTION (1972) #6 - 17***

## "KING SOLOMON'S FROG!"

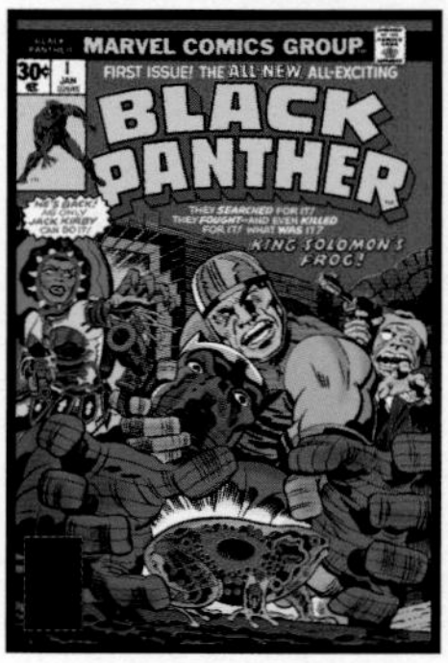

MARVEL COMICS GROUP
30¢
1
FIRST ISSUE! THE ALL-NEW ALL-EXCITING
BLACK PANTHER
KING SOLOMON'S FROG!


The Black Panther's co-creator, Jack Kirby, returned to write and draw new adventures for the hero in his first solo series! Kirby added a touch of the far-out to Panther's life beginning with this first adventure, in which the King of Wakanda chases after the mystically powered King Solomon's Frogs! Trust us—the Frog's true secret has to be seen to be believed.

***BLACK PANTHER (1977) #1***

## "THE CLIENT"

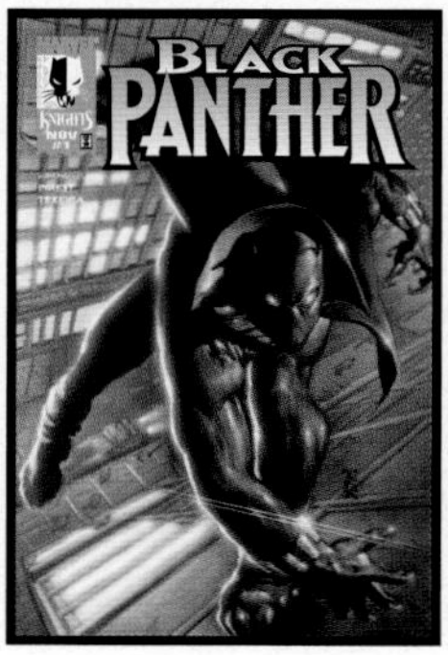

BLACK PANTHER


Writer Christopher Priest began his seminal Black Panther run with this story, introducing a new supporting cast for the Wakandan regent—including the pantsless Everett K. Ross—and infusing a healthy dose of humor and political intrigue to the Panther's adventures. This first arc alone features the devil, super hero action, geopolitics, and much more!

***BLACK PANTHER (1998) #1***

## "WHO IS THE BLACK PANTHER"

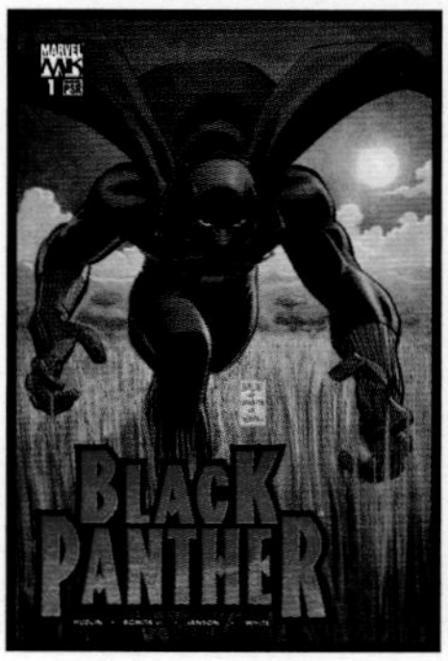

MARVEL
1
BLACK PANTHER


Writer Reginald Hudlin and artist John Romita Jr. return to the Panther's origins, updating T'Challa's early adventures to the modern day! Learn how our hero first donned the mantle of the Black Panther, and witness his early encounters with the larger Marvel Universe as he faces one of his greatest foes, the treacherous Klaw.

***BLACK PANTHER (2005) #1***